NOTES IN
THE CATALOG
RECORD

NOTES IN THE CATALOG RECORD

Based on AACR2 and LC Rule Interpretations

by
Jerry D. Saye
and
Sherry L. Vellucci

AMERICAN LIBRARY ASSOCIATION
Chicago and London 1989

Cover designed by Peter Broeksmit
Text designed by Charles Bozett

Composed by Impressions, Inc. in
  Times Roman and Helvetica
  on a Penta-driven Autologic APS-μ5
  phototypesetting system.

Printed on 50-pound Glatfelter B-16,
  a pH neutral stock, and bound in
  Kivar 9 by Braun-Brumfield, Inc.

The paper used in this publication meets the minimum requirements of
American National Standard for Information Sciences—Permanence of Paper for Printed Library Materials, ANSI Z39.48-1984.   ∞

Library of Congress Cataloging-in-Publication Data

Saye, Jerry D.
  Notes in the catalog record based on
AACR2 and LC rule interpretations.

  Bibliography: p.
  Includes indexes.
  1. Notes (Cataloging)   2. Anglo-American
cataloguing rules.   3. Descriptive cataloging
—Rules.   I. Vellucci, Sherry L.   II. Title.
Z693.3.N68S25 1988   025.3′2   88-950
ISBN 0-8389-3348-3

To Terri and Robin

Rule 284. Put into notes that information which is not given in the title but is required to be given by the plan of the catalog.

Charles A. Cutter
Rules for a Dictionary Catalog (1904)

Contents

Tables and Figures

Tables

Figures

Symbols

The following symbols are used with note examples to indicate the source of the note or to provide an explanation.

*   Used to indicate non-LC cataloging copy

\#   Used to identify the source of a cataloging example. The number that follows this symbol is the OCLC Control Number of the record from which the note was taken.

\+   Used to indicate that a non-AACR2 cataloging source has been changed to reflect AACR2 requirements.

Abbreviations

ALA 1908	*Catalog Rules: Author and Title Entries.* American ed.
AACCCM	Anglo-American Cataloguing Committee for Cartographic Materials
AACR1	*Anglo-American Cataloging Rules.* North American Text.
AACR1 Rev.	Used to indicate AACR1 revised chapters 6, 12, and 14.
AACR1 Rev. Ch. 6	*Anglo-American Cataloging Rules: Chapter 6, Separately Published Monographs.* North American Text.
AACR1 Rev. Ch. 12	*Anglo-American Cataloging Rules: Chapter 12, Revised, Audiovisual Media and Special Instructional Materials.* North American Text.
AACR1 Rev. Ch. 14	*Anglo-American Cataloging Rules: Chapter 14, Revised, Sound Recordings.* North American Text.
AACR2	*Anglo-American Cataloguing Rules.* 2nd ed.
AACR2 Rev.	*Anglo-American Cataloguing Rules.* 2nd ed., 1988 revision.
AACR2 Rev. 1982	*Anglo-American Cataloguing Rules. 2nd ed. Revisions.*
AACR2 Rev. 1983	*Anglo-American Cataloguing Rules. 2nd ed. Revisions 1983.*
AACR2 Rev. 1985	*Anglo-American Cataloguing Rules. 2nd ed. Revisions 1985.*

Complete citations to bibliographic works referred to here are in the Bibliography of this book.

AACR2 Ch. 9 Guidelines	*Guidelines for Using AACR2 Chapter 9 for Cataloging Microcomputer Software.*
AACR2 Rev. Ch. 9	*Anglo-American Cataloguing Rules. 2nd ed. Chapter 9, Computer Files.* Draft Revision.
ALA 1949	*A.L.A. Cataloging Rules for Author and Title Entries. 2nd ed.*
APPM	*Archives, Personal Papers, and Manuscripts: A Cataloging Manual for Archival Repositories, Historical Societies and Manuscript Libraries.*
BDRB	*Bibliographic Description of Rare Books: Rules Formulated under AACR2 and ISBD(A) for the Descriptive Cataloging of Rare Books and Other Special Printed Materials.*
Betz	*Graphic Materials: Rules for Describing Original Items and Historical Collections.*
CIP	Cataloging in Publication
CSB	Library of Congress. *Cataloging Service Bulletin.*
Cutter	*Rules for a Dictionary Catalog*
Dodd	*Cataloging Machine-Readable Data Files.*
IFLA	International Federation of Library Associations and Institutions
ISBD	International Standard Bibliographic Description
ISBD(G)	*International Standard Bibliographic Description (General).*
ISBD(M)	*International Standard Bibliographic Description (Monographs).*
JSCAACR	Joint Steering Committee for Revision of AACR
LC	Library of Congress
LC 1949	*Rules for Descriptive Cataloging in the Library of Congress.*
LCRI	Library of Congress rule interpretation
MCB	*Music Cataloging Bulletin.*
NUC	*National Union Catalog.*
OCLC	OCLC: Online Computer Library Center

Preface

In the cataloging process, notes are the one area of the bibliographic description principally left to the discretion of the cataloger. The provision in U.S. cataloging rules for the use of notes dates back to Charles A. Cutter's *Rules for a Dictionary Catalog*. In this work, he described notes as being used to provide information not given in the title of the work. He also identified more specific objectives for notes including:

1. To give any information about the author, the form of his name, his pseudonyms, etc., about the different editions or places of publication, or about the gaps in a set. . . .
2. To explain the title or correct any misapprehension to which it might lead. . . .
3. To direct the attention of persons not familiar with literature to the best books. . . .
4. To lay out courses of reading for that numerous class who are desirous of "improving their minds" . . . .
5. To state what is the practice of the catalog in the entry of the publications of Congress, Parliament, Academies, Societies, etc. [p. 105]

The 1908 cataloging rules issued by the American Library Association essentially provided a restatement, with slightly greater detail, of the notes objectives developed by Cutter. The *A.L.A. Cataloging Rules* issued in a preliminary edition in 1941, while retaining the objectives of Cutter, presented for the first time detailed instructions about specific types of notes to be made along with examples of some of the notes that could be generated from those rules. For the first time specific mention is made of notes to identify the source of the title proper, at head of title notes, bibliographical history notes, among others. These rules, with some revisions, later appeared in the *Rules for Descriptive Cataloging in the Library of Congress*, published in 1949, which was used in conjunction with the *A.L.A. Rules for Author and Title Entries* in the development of catalog records. The publication of AACR1 in 1967 and its later revisions provided further delineation of the types of notes that could or should be made.

These cataloging rules have generally provided few examples of notes for the cataloger to follow. Often the examples did not cover all situations addressed by a rule or were not exemplary of the most frequent or typical use of that type of note. To remedy some of these shortcomings, several books were published which were designed to provide catalogers with additional note examples. The most notable of these was *Notes Used on Catalog Cards* by Olive Swain, first published in 1940 and later issued in a second edition in 1963.

An important feature of the development of the second edition of AACR was the authors' attempt to provide overall uniformity of rule structure throughout the twelve chapters for description. Indeed, one main purpose, and a major perceived strength of these rules, is the use of International Standard Bibliographic Description (ISBD) for all material formats. Unfortunately, in order to achieve this standard it was often necessary to sacrifice the greater level of detail found in AACR1 to provide more generalized rule statements. The result was a code with fewer guidelines for the development and use of notes. Accompanying this standardization of the rules was the provision of relatively few examples for notes. In addition, the number of examples provided in AACR2 varies considerably from one material format and from one type of note to another. The publication of AACR2 1988 Revision, although adding a few more examples, did not significantly change the situation.

When AACR2 was adopted by the Library of Congress (LC), it became evident that LC was following practices in the formulation of notes that were not stated in AACR2 but were continued instead from AACR1. There was agreement at the outset by the members of the Joint Steering Committee that developed the code that the level of detail present in AACR1 could continue to be observed by individual institutions using AACR2 even though that detail was not delineated in the new code. This meant that procedures, wording, style, and so forth that were specifically required by AACR1 could continue to be used under AACR2 unless these practices were contrary to the existing rule. Since catalogers just entering the profession had not cataloged under the previous rules, it seemed unlikely that they would know the details of AACR1 and be able to use these rules as guidelines. We therefore felt it would be useful to provide more than just an improved selection of note examples over those found in the AACR2 text. In addition to examples, our text provides both an explanation of a note rule within its historical context and a statement of any relevant LC policy regarding the use of the note.

It is our hope that this collection and analysis of notes will assist in identifying standardized forms of notes. Use and knowledge of these note forms or templates has the potential of assisting in the retrieval of machine-readable catalog records in those situations where the note fields are searchable.

In quoting from AACR2 and AACR2, 1988 revision (AACR2 Rev.), the format of the source has sometimes been changed for emphasis or clarity. For example, items in an enumeration may be set separately instead of run in with the paragraph as in the source. Throughout, the subheads conform to the organization and typographical design of the book in hand. Throughout this text we use "AACR2" to refer to rules in both AACR2 and AACR2 Rev., e.g., AACR2 Rule 3.7B3 refers to that rule in either text. We differentiate in rule numbering between AACR2 and AACR2 Rev. when providing a direct quotation from either source and in those instances when a rule in AACR2 and AACR2 Rev. is so different that a clear differentiation between the two texts is essential for clarity.

Acknowledgments

This work is the result of the efforts of many individuals who assisted us in a variety of ways in its preparation. Thanks go to John B. Hall for his contributions to the genesis of this book. To all the graduate assistants at Drexel University and the University of North Carolina at Chapel Hill, especially Dr. Linda H. Bertland, Sue H. Jackson, Teresa S. Cho and Cathy Jacobs, who over the years searched, researched, typed, proofread and in other ways assisted in the development of this text, we express our sincere thanks. Thanks also go to members of the library staff of the Talbott Library of Westminster Choir College and to the faculties of the College of Information Studies, Drexel University and the School of Information and Library Science, University of North Carolina at Chapel Hill, for their patience and encouragement in this long project.

Gratitude is also expressed to those who assisted by providing us with cataloging copy of notes. In particular we wish to thank Sue A. Dodd, Steven L. Hensen, and Elizabeth W. Betz for allowing us to use examples from their texts, and the Library Corporation for providing us with several years of LC cataloging on microfiche during the early stages of our project. We also thank OCLC for allowing us to use notes taken from participant-contributed cataloging in the OCLC bibliographic database. Our appreciation also goes to Richard Smiraglia for his advice on the cataloging of music and sound recordings.

Finally, our special and most heartfelt thanks go to Terri O. Saye for her contributions to all stages of the development of this text and for putting up with us during this long process.

Introduction

Order of the Text

The basic organization of this text does not follow AACR2's arrangement, which is based on the physical medium of the item being cataloged. Instead, the chapters are organized according to the type of note, for example, source of title proper, audience, contents, and so forth, under consideration. This was done because of the belief that catalogers would be better served by having all the notes of one type grouped together rather than distributed throughout twelve chapters. There will be situations where the examples for a specific type of note in a particular chapter for description may not satisfactorily meet a cataloger's needs. The treatment accorded that same note in another chapter for description, however, might provide exactly the approach that cataloger needed. Therefore, the arrangement in this text is more problem oriented than material format oriented. All discussion to help resolve problems about the use of statements of responsibility notes appears subdivided by format rather than being scattered throughout twelve different chapters for description.

The consistent AACR2 rule numbering values have been used to identify the type of note being treated, that is, Chapter 1 contains notes for rule .7B*1* (Nature, Scope or Artistic Form of the Item) for each AACR2 chapter, for example, 2.7B*1*, 3.7B*1*, 4.7B*1* and so forth. Within each chapter there are subchapters arranged by the physical medium of the item using AACR2's chapter number order. Thus, the first subchapter deals with monographs; the second, cartographic materials, and so forth.

Each note example has an identifying number consisting of two elements:

> the final element of the note rule number
> the example number.

Figure 1 illustrates the structure of a typical example's numbering.

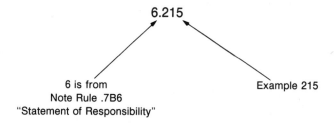

Figure 1. Example Numbering

AACR2 was designed to provide for uniform treatment of documents regardless of their physical format. The result was a general structure of twenty-two basic note types in AACR2, increased to twenty-three in AACR2 Rev. These basic note types are listed in Table 1.

Table 1. AACR2 Rev. General Note Rules (.7Bx)

1	Nature, Scope, or Artistic Form
2	Language of the Item and/or Translation or Adaptation
3	Source of Title Proper
4	Variations in Title
5	Parallel Titles and Other Title Information
6	Statements of Responsibility
7	Edition and History
8	Material (or Type of Publication) Specific Details
9	Publication, Distribution, etc.
10	Physical Description
11	Accompanying Material and Supplements
12	Series
13	Dissertations
14	Audience
15	Reference to Published Descriptions
16	Other Formats
17	Summary
18	Contents
19	Numbers Borne by the Item (Other Than Those Covered in Rule 1.8)
20	Copy Being Described, Library's Holdings, and Restrictions on Use
21	"With" Notes
22	Combined Notes Relating to the Original
23	Miscellaneous

It was not possible, however, to design a code that uniformly treated each physical format exactly the same. As a result, there are some notes which are present in most, but not all, chapters for description. In a few instances a particular note rule is present in only a single chapter. Table 2 provides a comparison of the general note types listed in Chapter 1 of AACR2 and the presence of these notes in each of its individual chapters for description.

Examples

In all cases cataloging copy in English was preferred over that in other languages. There were situations, however, when a particular type of note was not located in any record other than a non-English record. In those cases, the non-English note was provided in preference to not including the example at all. In no cases are notes written in a non-roman script included. Examples derived from pre-AACR2 codes have been limited to an absolute minimum. In the few cases where these have been included, they have been upgraded to AACR2 standards. These upgraded examples are preceded by a plus sign. In some other cases, note examples from records developed under AACR2 have been changed to reflect current Library of Congress practice. In most cases, these changes are in the punctuation of the note, for example, duration notes for music and sound recordings.

The selection of examples for this book was greatly influenced by the preference of catalogers in the United States for cataloging copy created by the Library of Congress. Catalogers nationwide utilize LC copy as a model for their own cataloging and thus tend to follow, either directly or indirectly, reluctantly or not, LC internal cataloging practices in addition to, or in place of, AACR2 itself. Accordingly, whenever possible, this preference was reflected in the selection of LC-devised examples to illustrate the note rules.

The *National Union Catalog* (NUC) was surveyed to gather examples of LC cataloging for books, music, sound recordings, audiovisual materials, and manuscripts. Due to the delayed publication of parts of the NUC, Cataloging In Publication (CIP) records were also used in addition to final LC catalog records. The exclusion or limited level of cataloging by LC of certain types of materials required us to use cataloging copy from sources other than the Library of Congress. In these cases, non-LC cataloging copy derived from cataloging agencies that report their cataloging nationally through the NUC or OCLC was preferred. Local library cataloging examples, not nationally reported, were used only in those cases in which cataloging copy was

Table 2. Comparison of Note Rules in Individual AACR2 Rev. Chapters

1 General Rules for Description	2 Books, Pamphlets and Printed Sheets	3 Cartographic Materials	4 Manuscripts	5 Music	6 Sound Recordings	7 Motion Pictures and Video-Recordings	8 Graphic Materials	9 Computer Files*	10 Three-Dimensional Artefacts and Realia	11 Microforms**	12 Serials
.7B1 Nature, Scope, or Artistic Form	•	Nature and Scope of the Item	Nature, Scope, or Form	Form of Composition and Medium of Performance	Nature or Artistic Form and Medium of Performance	Nature or Form	Nature or Artistic Form	Nature and Scope and System Requirements	Nature of the Item	Nature, Scope or Artistic or Other Form of an Item	Frequency
.7B2 Language of the Item and/or Translation or Adaptation	•	Language	Language	Language	Language	Language	Language	Language and Script	—	Language	Language
.7B3 Source of Title Proper	•	•	•	•	•	•	•	•	•	•	•
.7B4 Variations in Title	•	•	•	•	•	•	•	•	•	•	•
.7B5 Parallel Titles and Other Title Information	•	•	•	•	•	•	•	•	•	•	•
.7B6 Statements of Responsibility	•	•	•	•	•	•	•	•	•	•	•
.7B7 Edition and History	•	•	Donor, Source, etc., and Previous Owner(s)	•					•	•	Relationship with Other Serials
.7B8 Material (or Type of Publication) Specific Details	—	Mathematical and Other Cartographic Data	Place of Writing	Notation	—	—	[Rule Deleted]	File Characteristics	—	—	Numbering and Chronological Designation
.7B9 Publication, Distribution, etc.	•	•	Published Versions	•	•	Publication, Distribution, etc., and Date	•	•	•	•	•
.7B10 Physical Description	•	•	•	Duration of Performance and Physical Description	•	•	•	•	•	•	•
.7B11 Accompanying Material and Supplements	Accompanying Material	Accompanying Material	Accompanying Material	Accompanying Material	Accompanying Material	Accompanying Material	Accompanying Material	Accompanying Material	Accompanying Material	Accompanying Material	Accompanying Material

	C1	C2	C3	C4	C5	C6	C7	C8	C9
.7B12 Series	•	•	•	•	•	•	•	•	•
.7B13 Dissertations	•	•	—	•	•	•	—	•	—
.7B14 Audience	Access and Literary Rights	•	•	•	•	•	•	•	•
.7B15 Reference to Published Descriptions	•	—	—	—	—	—	—	—	—
.7B16 Other Formats	—	•	•	•	•	•	—	•	•
.7B17 Summary	•	—	—	•	•	•	•	•	
.7B18 Contents	•	•	•	•	•	•	•	•	Indexes
.7B19 Numbers Borne by the Item	Numbers	Publishers' Numbers and Plate Numbers	Publishers' Numbers	Numbers	Numbers	Numbers	Numbers	Numbers	Numbers
.7B20 Copy Being Described, Library's Holdings, and Restrictions on Use	•	•	•	•	•	•	•	•	•
.7B21 "With" Notes	•	•	•	•	•	•	•	•	"Issued With" Notes
.7B22 Combined Notes Relating to the Original	—	—	—	—	Note Relating to the Original	—	—	Note Relating to the Original	—
.7B23 Miscellaneous	Ancient, Medieval and Renaissance Manuscripts	—	—	—	—	—	—	—	Item Described

* AACR2 Rev. Ch. 9 (Computer Files).

** Not covered in this text.

• No changes from the title of the general rule.

— No rule in this chapter.

not available from other sources. Throughout this text, note examples which are not from the Library of Congress are preceded by an asterisk.

The note examples represent, as much as possible, Library of Congress cataloging practices current at the time of submission of this manuscript to the publisher. Selective editing of punctuation was made to some Library of Congress cataloging records when the previously selected examples were subsequently affected by a change in LC policy. Examples derived from CIP data were checked to ensure that the notes were still being used. However, when the Library of Congress issues final cataloging copy for these CIP works, changes are sometimes made to the note. Thus, in a few cases, a later version of the catalog record may actually have a note deleted. Similar editing changes to LC records occur less frequently for final catalog records.

Due to the predominance of monographic materials cataloged by the Library of Congress, this text frequently contains more monograph examples than those of other document formats. When there are few examples for other physical formats, the organization of the text by note type enables the cataloger to refer easily to the monographic examples for that type of note and to borrow this information for use in developing the note for the other document medium.

When selecting examples for the text, we frequently observed the practice of the Library of Congress of combining several types of notes into one note as recommended by AACR2 Rule 1.7A5. These combined note examples have been placed into the note type that seemed most useful for illustrative purposes. In some cases, it was difficult to identify the specific type of note being used, for example, nature, scope, or artistic form notes (.7B1) can frequently resemble informal contents notes (.7B18) and vice versa. In those cases when the order of the notes on the catalog record did not clarify the note type, the example was placed into what seemed the most appropriate category.

Frequency of Examples

The variety and number of note examples presented in the text reflect the uniqueness or relative frequency of use of that particular note type, that is, fewer examples indicate that the note is used less frequently. In AACR2, as the result of the standardization of the bibliographic description for all types of materials, most note rules are repeated in each chapter. This has resulted in providing note rules for situations that do not occur frequently, if at all, for some material formats. As the examples were collected and compiled it became obvious that certain notes provided for in the rules were not being used by the Library of Congress or other cataloging agencies. We did not attempt to create notes to fill these gaps, but preferred to allow this text to reflect current note usage. In many cases, the presence of few or no examples in a particular material format is offset by the presence of numerous examples of that note in use for a different format, for example, the absence of the use of a particular note for cartographic materials may be offset by the presence of many examples for books.

Formats Excluded

Included in this text are examples for materials covered in Chapters 2 through 12 of AACR2 except for Chapter 11 (Microforms). AACR2 introduced an approach to the descriptive cataloging of microforms different from that of previous codes. For microform reproductions of previously existing works, this new approach gave emphasis to the description of the reproduction rather than to the original document. The 1982 rule revisions by the Joint Steering Committee for the Revision of AACR (JSCAACR) resulted in combining all notes relating to the original document into a single note.

The Library of Congress, after considerable debate in the U.S. microform cataloging community, issued a rule interpretation that significantly changes the use of Chapter 11 when dealing with micro- and macroform reproductions. Essentially, the Library of Congress decision was to follow AACR2 only for the choice and form of headings for reproductions and to "emphasize in the bibliographic description data relating to the original item, giving data relating to the reproduction in a secondary position" (CSB 14). The Library of Congress does follow Chapter 11 for the cataloging of original microforms. As a result, a collection of LC note examples for microform reproductions would be highly repetitive of notes presented elsewhere in this text for other items in the same format as the original of the reproduction. The only difference between the records would be the inclusion of a single note dealing with the reproduction itself. The exceedingly small number of microform originals in existence, and thus the number of examples of cataloging for them, made note examples for this type of material virtually impossible to obtain. As a result, it was decided to exclude microforms from consideration in the major portion of this text. Appendix A provides the Library of Congress statement regarding microform notes along with examples of notes dealing with the reproduction aspect of a micro- or macroform reproduction. Also included is a selection of the rules for microform notes relating to original microform productions.

In addition to microforms, several other material types such as kits and other items made up of several kinds of materials have been excluded from coverage in this work. Also excluded are facsimiles, photocopies and other reproductions, and early printed monographs covered by the special note rules for this type of material (AACR2 Rule 2.18). We have, however, used some note examples for early printed monographs as examples of the cataloging of books when this was deemed useful and appropriate.

Order of Each Chapter

Each chapter of the text begins with a preliminary subchapter dealing with the note in general as presented in Chapter 1 (General Rules for Description) of AACR2. Figure 2 outlines the general structure of each of these preliminary subchapters.

Since Chapter 1 in AACR2 provides a title heading and several examples for each note type but does not provide a specific rule statement, a general description rule for each note type was developed. This general rule is, in most instances, our extrapolation of a rule from commonly occurring rule elements in this note in the chapters for the description of specific material formats. Unlike AACR2, AACR2 Rev. provides in a few instances a note rule in the General Rules for Description rather than just examples. In these cases we have quoted the rule and have changed the section heading from *Extrapolated General Rule* to *General Rule*. Also included in the preliminary subchapter are related rules from other parts of Chapter 1 when such exist. A related rule is considered to be any rule that, either directly or indirectly, refers a cataloger to the use of the specific note under consideration.

The statement of the general and related rules is followed by a statement of any Library of Congress rule interpretations (LCRIs) to the

```
Extrapolated General Rule
        Related AACR2 Rule
Library of Congress Policy
        Related Library of Congress Policy
Format
Chapter Applications
Exceptions and Additions
```

Figure 2. General Subchapter Format

general rule. When an LCRI has been issued to another rule that refers to the use of the note under consideration, or to the LCRI for the note rule, we have included them in a section titled *Related Library of Congress Policy*. These related LCRIs are similar in function to related rules mentioned previously. LC policy is quoted from the most current LCRI for that rule as published in the *Cataloging Service Bulletin* (CSB). These LCRI statements are complete through CSB number 39 (Winter 1988). The CSB source of the LCRI is indicated by the inclusion of the CSB issue number at the end of the statement. Some changes to the wording and the paragraph structure of some of the LCRIs have been made to facilitate clarity and transitions in the text. When changes in wording occur, the part of the text which was not changed is enclosed in quotation marks. Last, all of the LCRI examples have been excluded from this text.

A section on note format describes the LC policy if a general formatting structure is used for the note. Two final sections in each general subchapter provide an overview of the note's coverage and application in Chapters 2 through 12 (except for Chapter 11). These sections also indicate whether the provisions of the general rule are included in each chapter and whether the rule has been modified in an individual AACR2 chapter.

Order of Each Subchapter

The remaining subchapters for each note type follow the chapter order of AACR2. Each of these subchapters is organized in a manner similar to that of the General Rule subchapter. Figure 3 provides an outline of this subchapter organization.

The specific rule is quoted first. We have indicated those rules where the wording, whether major or minor, is different in AACR2 Rev. from

```
AACR2 Rule
        Related AACR2 Rule
    Library of Congress Policy
        Related Library of Congress Policy
            AACR2 Text Examples Revised to Reflect Library of
                Congress Policy
    Historical Background
    Note Examples
```

Figure 3. Specific Subchapter Format

that in AACR2. At times, the paragraph structure of the rule has been rearranged to clarify the meaning or add to the readability of the rule. The original AACR2 rules have been revised to reflect changes appearing in AACR2 Rev. This includes the extensive revisions in Chapter 9 (Computer Files). Rule statements are followed by any related rules when appropriate.

Each specific subchapter utilizes the same LC policy and related LC policy structure that is used in the general subchapter. When a general LCRI exists and no LCRI has been issued for an individual chapter, the general LCRI is not repeated in the individual chapter. If there is an individual LCRI for a specific subchapter, the individual LCRI is provided. This means that catalogers must consult the *Library of Congress Policy* area both within an individual subchapter and in the general subchapter.

The *Music Cataloging Bulletin* (MCB) was used in addition to the CSB as a source of rule interpretations and cataloging decisions for music and sound recordings. The MCB coverage is inclusive through volume 18, number 7 (July 1987). As with LCRIs, the source for the policy is indicated by citing the MCB number at the end of the policy statement.

For manuscripts, an additional source of Library of Congress practice and policy, *Archives, Personal Papers, and Manuscripts* (APPM) by Steven L. Hensen, has been used. The Library of Congress uses this manual to replace the rules in AACR2 Chapter 4. APPM provides an expansion of some AACR2 rules as well as additional rules. APPM rules have been treated as though they were LCRIs, with the APPM rule number following the rule statement. A list of APPM rule titles is given in Table 3.

A final part of both the *Library of Congress Policy* and *Related Library of Congress Policy* sections is an indication of any examples in the AACR2 text that would be altered if the LCRI were to be applied to them. The AACR2 text example is given first followed by the revised example. Whenever examples in AACR2 Rev. have been changed from the form in AACR2, we have used the AACR2 Rev. example. In some cases, the need for a revision to an AACR2 text example is not apparent without actually examining the source document, but the information supplied was not sufficient to identify the document from which an example was formulated. In these cases, there is no way to even suspect whether a change is appropriate or not. Therefore, only those examples that could be directly identified as needing revision have been changed. Whenever changes have been made, both the original AACR2 example and our revised text are included.

Table 3. *Archives, Personal Papers, and Manuscripts* Note Rules

4.7B1	Relationship Complexity
4.7B2	Copy/Repository
4.7B3	Biographical/Historical
4.7B4	Scope and Content/Abstract
4.7B5	Arrangement
4.7B6	Language(s)
4.7B7	Provenance
4.7B8	Source/Donor
4.7B9	Restrictions and Access
4.7B10	Literary Rights and Copyright
4.7B11	Finding Aids
4.7B12	Other Sources of Description
4.7B13	Published Versions
4.7B14	Physical Description/Condition
4.7B15	Title Transcription/Source
4.7B16	Variations in Title

Each rule is accompanied by a discussion of the historical background of the note emphasizing the most immediate pre-AACR2 practices, that is, AACR1 or its revisions. Differences in the application, structure, or use of a note from that of the previous code as well as gaps in coverage are indicated here. Older catalog codes, other than the most immediate, are mentioned only when their inclusion was considered necessary.

The final section of each subchapter is the listing of note examples. Frequently, the examples have been divided into categories that do not always reflect the division of the rule as it appears in the AACR2 text. This division follows the pattern of use of the note identified in our survey of cataloging records. When a note does not vary significantly among the various types of materials, we have given background information for the rule for each physical medium but have mainly provided monograph examples because of their wider availability and use.

Comments are interspersed throughout the text dealing with use of a note, formatting practices, changes in practice, and other observations.

Additional Sources of Note Rules and Guidelines

In addition to Library of Congress policy statements in the CSB, the MCB, and APPM, other sources are available to guide the cataloger in the development of notes for specific types of materials. The Library of Congress has replaced the Early Printed Monographs section in AACR2 Chapter 2 with the publication *Bibliographic Description of Rare Books* (BDRB). The exclusion of early printed monographs from consideration in this text means that no references are provided to the rules stated in BDRB. Table 4, however, provides a listing of BDRB rule titles.

The Library of Congress has also issued two auxiliary manuals to support and expand on the AACR2 Chapters 7 and 8:

> *Archival Moving Image Materials: A Cataloging Manual* compiled by Wendy White-Hensen
> *Graphic Materials: Rules for Describing Original Items and Historical Collections* compiled by Elisabeth W. Betz.

These two works present rules that supplement AACR2 Chapters 7 and 8 respectively rather than replace existing AACR2 rules as do

Table 4. *Bibliographic Description of Rare Books* Note Rules

7C1	Nature, Scope, or Artistic Form
7C2	Language of Publication, Translation, or Adaptation
7C3	Source of Title Proper
7C4	Variations in Title
7C5	Parallel Titles and Other Title Information
7C6	Statements of Responsibility
7C7	Edition and Bibliographic History
7C8	Publication
7C9	Signatures
7C10	Physical Description
7C11	Accompanying Material
7C12	Series
7C13	Dissertations
7C14	References to Published Descriptions
7C15	Summary
7C16	Contents
7C17	Numbers Borne by the Publication
7C18	Copy Being Described and Library's Holdings (Copy-Specific Notes)
7C19	"With" Notes

APPM and BDRB. References have been made to the existence of both sources in the appropriate subchapters but they have not been quoted as direct LC policy. Tables 5 and 6 provide a listing of the rule and subrule titles of these two reference sources.

All four of these LC publications use rule numbering that differs in varying degrees from that used in AACR2. Table 7 provides a comparison listing of the AACR2 rule numbers and titles and their LC counterparts in each of the four supplementary publications.

There are several non-LC publications that deal with the cataloging of specialized materials and can assist the cataloger in the formulation of notes. These works are:

Cartographic Materials: A Manual of Interpretation for AACR2, Hugo L. P. Stibbe, general editor; Vivien Cartmell and Velma Parker, editors

Cataloging Government Documents: A Manual of Interpretation for AACR2, Bernadine Abbott Hoduski, editor

Cataloging Machine-Readable Data Files: An Interpretive Manual, by Sue A. Dodd

Cataloging Microcomputer Files: A Manual of Interpretation for AACR2, by Sue A. Dodd and Ann M. Sandberg-Fox.

References have been made in this text to some statements in these publications. They have not, however, been treated as statements of LC policy and their rules have not been quoted. Only the cartographic materials manual contains significant changes and additions to the AACR2 rules for notes. Table 8 is a listing of the rule numbers and titles for these cartographic notes.

Indexes

Several indexes are provided to assist catalogers in the use of this text. The single most useful index is a subject arrangement by type of note. Reference is given to the example numbers that illustrate the particular aspect in question. This index has been made as specific as possible while keeping the number of entries under each term to a manageable size. Some index terms have been given secondary headings to aid in their use. Included in this subject index are entries under phrases which are used frequently to begin a particular type of note. The use of these phrases reflects specific AACR2 and/or LC policy. In other cases, the use of a phrase does not reflect a stated policy but does reflect actual LC practice.

In addition to the subject index, there is a control number index for notes appearing on catalog records that have been reported nationally. This index is provided to enable the librarian to consult the

Table 5. *Archival Moving Image Materials* Note Rules

7B1	Version with Minor Changes	
7B2	Copyright Registration Information	
	7B2a	Punctuation
	7B2b	Copyright and Country
	7B2c	Registration Notice
	7B2d	Copyright Owner (Claimant)
	7B2e	Unprotected Materials
	7B2f	Copyright Status Unknown
	7B2g	Subsequent Ownership/Versions with Minor Changes Copyright Information
7B3	Nature, Scope, or Artistic Form of the Item	
7B4	Language	
7B5	Source of Title Proper	
7B6	Variations in Title	
7B7	Parallel Titles and Other Title Information	
7B8	Statements of Responsibility	
	7B8a	Credits
	7B8b	Cast
7B9	History of Edition/Version	
7B10	Country of Production	
7B11	Publication, Distribution, etc.	
	7B11a	Place of Original Release
	7B11b	Trade Names
	7B11c	Television Sponsors.
	7B11d	Rerelease Information
	7B11e	Reissue Information
	7B11f	Version with Major Changes Distribution Information
	7B11g	Version with Minor Changes Distribution Information
7B12	Physical Description	
	7B12a	Incompleteness
	7B12b	Length or Duration

full cataloging record in those instances where a contextual reference would be helpful in understanding the use of a particular note. The control numbers used include the Library of Congress card numbers, the LC manuscript control numbers, and the OCLC control numbers. In cases where an example was derived from one of the guides mentioned previously, the source is cited giving the page number on which the example appears, for example, Dodd, p. 75. When an example is derived from a catalog record not reported nationally it is identified in the index by the term Local Record. Other indexes include an index

Table 5. (*Continued*)

	7B12c	Sound Characteristics
	7B12d	Color
	7B12e	Form of Copy
	7B12f	Variant Copies
	7B12g	Special Projection Requirements or Playback/Recording Mode
	7B12h	Other Physical Details Important for Use or Storage
	7B12j	Research Notes for Physical Description
7B13	Accompanying Material	
7B14	Series	
7B15	Dissertations	
7B16	Users/Intended Audience	
7B17	References to Published Reviews or Descriptions	
7B18	Other Formats Available	
7B19	Summary	
7B20	Contents	
7B21	Numbers Borne by the Item	
7B22	Copy Being Described and Archive's Holdings	
7B23	"With" Notes	
7B24	Genre	
7B25	Censorship	
7B26	Awards	
7B27	Other Rating Designations	
7B28	Collection	
7B29	Restrictions on Access	
7B30	Terms Governing Use	
7B31	Source of Acquisition	
7B32	Location of Related Materials	
7B33	Publications	

to pre-AACR2 rules cited in the text, an index to AACR2 rules cited other than the .7B rules for notes, and an index to the LCRIs cited.

As this book is going to press, word has been received of a possible change. The Library of Congress has indicated that among new and revised LCRIs it will issue to AACR2 Rev. will be one addressing Rule 2.7B18. This LCRI will limit all bibliography notes to the statement "Includes bibliographical references." Another interpretation to this rule will end the use of a note to indicate the presence of an index.

Table 6. *Graphic Materials* Note Rules

5B1	Source of Title Proper
5B2	Variations in Title
5B3	Parallel Titles and Other Title Information
5B4	Continuation of Title
5B5	Translation of Foreign Title
5B6	Picture Caption
5B7	Statements of Responsibility

5B7.1	Signatures and Inscriptions
5B7.2	Attributions and Conjectures
5B7.3	[No Subrule Title]

5B8	Publication, State, and Edition

5B8.1	[No Subrule Title]
5B8.2	[No Subrule Title]
5B8.3	[No Subrule Title]

5B9	Physical Description/Condition

5B9.1	[No Subrule Title]
5B9.2	[No Subrule Title]
5B9.3	[No Subrule Title]
5B9.4	[No Subrule Title]
5B9.5	Other Inscriptions
5B9.6	Markings and Stamps

5B10	Accompanying Material
5B11	Series
5B12	References to Published Descriptions
5B13	Characteristics of Original of Photographic Copy or Photomechanical Reproduction
5B14	Subject Description
5B15	Biographical/Historical Note
5B16	Arrangement
5B17	Contents
5B18	Finding Aids to Collections
5B19	Numbers or Letters Borne by the Material
5B20	Publication and Other Uses of the Material
5B21	Relationship Note
5B22	Addition Note
5B23	"With" Note
5B24	Terms of Access, Use, and Reproduction

5B24.1	[No Subrule Title]
5B24.2	Copyright

5B25	Provenance
5B26	Source

Table 7. Comparison of Note Rules in LC Auxiliary Support Manuals and AACR2 Rev.

AACR2	BDRB	APPM	WHITE-HENSEN	BETZ
.7B1 Nature, Scope, or Artistic Form	.C1 Nature, Scope, or Artistic Form	4.7B2 Copy/Repository 4.7B3 Biographical/Historical 4.7B4 Scope and Content/Abstract	7B3 Nature, Scope, or Artistic Form of the Item 7B24 Genre	5B14 Subject Description 5D15 Biographical/Historical
.7B2 Language of the Item and/or Translation or Adaptation	.C2 Language of Publication, Translation, or Adaptation	4.7B6 Language(s)	7B4 Language	—
.7B3 Source of Title Proper	.C3 Source of Title Proper	4.7B15 Title Transcription/Source	7B5 Source of Title Proper	5B1 Source of Title Proper
.7B4 Variations in Title	.C4 Variations in Title	4.7B16 Variations in Title	7B6 Variations in Title	5B2 Variations in Title
.7B5 Parallel Titles and Other Title Information	.C5 Parallel Titles and Other Title Information	—	7B7 Parallel Titles and Other Title Information	5B3 Parallel Titles and Other Title Information 5B4 Continuation of Title 5B5 Translation of Foreign Title
.7B6 Statements of Responsibility	.C6 Statements of Responsibility	—	7B8 Statements of Responsibility	5B7 Statements of Responsibility
.7B7 Edition and History	.C7 Edition and Bibliographic History	4.7B7 Provenance 4.7B8 Source/Donor	7B1 Version with Minor Changes 7B9 History of Edition/Version 7B31 Source of Acquisition	5B8 Publication, State, and Edition 5B25 Provenance 5B26 Source
.7B8 Material (or Type of Publication) Specific Details	—	—	—	—
.7B9 Publication, Distribution, etc.	.B8 Publication	4.7B13 Published Versions	7B10 Country of Production 7B11 Publication, Distribution, etc.	5B8 Publication, State and Edition
.7B10 Physical Description	.C9 Signatures .C10 Physical Description	4.7B14 Physical Description/Condition	7B12 Physical Description	5B9 Physical Description/Condition
.7B11 Accompanying Material and Supplements	.C11 Accompanying Material	4.7B11 Finding Aids	7B13 Accompanying Material	5B10 Accompanying Material 5B18 Finding Aids to Collections

— No Rule

cont.

Table 7. (*Continued*)

AACR2	BDRB	APPM	WHITE-HENSEN	BETZ
.7B12 Series	.C12 Series	—	7B14 Series	5B11 Series
.7B13 Dissertations	.C13 Dissertations	—	7B15 Dissertations	—
.7B14 Audience	—	4.7B9 Restrictions and Access 4.7B10 Literary Rights and Copyright 4.7B12 Other Sources of Description	7B2 Copyright Registration Information 7B16 Users/Intended Audience 7B27 Other Rating Designations 7B29 Restrictions on Access 7B30 Terms Governing Use	—
.7B15 Reference to Published Descriptions	.C14 References to Published Descriptions	—	7B17 References to Published Reviews or Descriptions 7B33 Publications	5B12 References to Published Descriptions
.7B16 Other Formats	—	—	7B18 Other Formats Available	—
.7B17 Summary	.C15 Summary	4.7B4 Scope and Content/ Abstract	7B19 Summary	—
.7B18 Contents	.C16 Contents	4.7B4 Scope and Content/ Abstract	7B20 Contents	5B17 Contents
.7B19 Numbers Borne by the Item (Other Than Those Covered in .8)	.C17 Numbers Borne by the Publication	—	7B21 Numbers Borne by the Item	5B19 Numbers or Letters Borne by the Material
.7B20 Copy Being Described, Library's Holdings, and Restrictions on Use	.C18 Copy Being Described and Library's Holdings (Copy-Specific Notes)	4.7B14 Physical Description/ Condition	7B22 Copy Being Described and Archive's Holdings	5B9 Physical Description/ Condition
.7B21 "With" Notes	.C19 "With" Notes	—	7B23 "With" Notes	5B23 "With" Notes
.7B22 Combined Notes Relating to the Original	—	—	—	5B13 Characteristics of Original of Photographic Copy or Photo-mechanical Reproduction
Others	—	4.7B1 Relationship Complexity 4.7B5 Arrangement	7B25 Censorship 7B26 Awards 7B28 Collection 7B32 Location of Related Materials	5B6 Picture Caption 5B16 Arrangement 5B21 Relationship 5B22 Addition

— No Rule

Table 8. *Cartographic Materials* Note Rules

7B1	[No Rule]	
	7B1a	Nature and Scope of the Item
	MANUSCRIPTS	
	7B1b	Nature, Scope, or Form of Manuscript(s)
	7B1c	[No Subrule Title]
	7B1d	[No Subrule Title]
	7B1e	[No Subrule Title]
	7B1f	[No Subrule Title]
	7B1g	[No Subrule Title]
7B2	Language	
7B3	Source of Title Proper	
7B4	Variations in Title	
7B5	Parallel Titles and Other Title Information	
7B6	Statements of Responsibility	
7B7	[No Rule]	
	7B7a	Edition and History
	7B7b	Donor, Source, etc., and Previous Owner(s)
	7B7c	Published Versions of Manuscript Cartographic Items
	7B7d	[No Subrule Title]
7B8	Mathematical and Other Cartographic Data	
7B9	Publication, Distribution, etc.	
7B10	[No Rule]	
	7B10a	Physical Description
	7B10b	Early Printed Cartographic Items, Signatures and Foliation
	7B10c	Reduction Ratio for Microforms
	7B10d	Reader
7B11	Accompanying Material	
7B12	Series	
7B13	Dissertations	
7B14	Audience	
7B15	Reference to Published Descriptions	
7B16	Other Formats Available	
7B18	[No Rule]	
	7B18a	Contents
	7B18b	[No Subrule Title]
7B19	Numbers	
7B20	[No Rule]	
	7B20a	Copy Being Described and Library's Holdings
	7B20b	[No Subrule Title]
	7B20c	Ancient, Medieval, and Renaissance Manuscripts
7B21	"With" Notes	

The Use of Notes in General

Notes are used to provide descriptive information not contained in other areas of the descriptive cataloging (Areas 1-6). The sections below provide an overview of the AACR2 approach to the creation of notes and how it has changed from that of previous codes. In addition to the general rules for notes (Rules 1.7A1 to 1.7A5), the Library of Congress has issued rule interpretations to these rules. These rule interpretations are given in their complete form in Appendix B of this text. Both AACR1 and its revised chapters devoted considerable attention to defining the role of notes in bibliographic description. AACR2 takes a more permissive or less prescriptive approach to the use of notes based on the assumption that catalogers know the role of notes in the descriptive cataloging process.

General Note Rules Applicable to All Material Formats

In both AACR1 and its revisions, the chapters for nonmonographic materials (serials, pictures, motion pictures, etc.) were supplementary, or in addition to the descriptive cataloging rules for monographs. The rules for monographs, including note rules, served as general rules for all types of materials even though they were not labeled as such. Thus, the rules for monographs applied equally to nonmonographic materials, except where inappropriate or where they were contravened by rules found in another chapter that were specific to the type of material being cataloged.

A somewhat similar approach is followed in AACR2 although the general rules are now derived from a general chapter for description rather than from the chapter for books. In some chapters of AACR2, there is no provision for a specific type of note. Chapter 10 (Three Dimensional Artefacts and Realia) has no provision for a language note .7B2. These notes may, however, be necessary for the description of a document covered by that chapter. In these cases, the cataloger may use the general rules in Chapter 1 as precedent for creating the note. Unfortunately, the notes area in Chapter 1 only provides a title heading for the note and some examples, but gives no textual explanation for the use, construction, or application of the note. A cataloger in these cases can, however, generalize from instructions for these notes from other chapters in which they are included.

Indispensable and Not Indispensable Notes

In guiding the cataloger regarding which notes to make, AACR1 and AACR1 Rev. distinguished between "indispensable" notes and notes that were important though "not indispensable." These two categories were delineated at length in the general rules for notes (AACR1 Rule 144B and Rev. Rule 143). AACR2, however, does not make this distinction between notes although, throughout the chapters for description, instructions are given stating that under particular conditions the cataloger should make specific notes. These required notes can be considered to be the equivalent of indispensable notes.

In other instances, AACR2 restricts the information given in Areas 1-6 and states that additional information related to these areas should be placed in a note. These notes can be considered to be important but not indispensable notes. In these latter cases, it is left to the discretion of the cataloger whether to make these notes.

Standards, Punctuation, and Style

AACR1 moved toward an international standardization of cataloging rules based largely on the "Statement of Principles" adopted by the International Conference on Cataloging Principles held in Paris in 1961. It was not until 1974, however, that the International Federation of Library Associations and Institutions (IFLA) adopted the first of a series of standards for bibliographic description that utilized a prescribed punctuation. These standards are collectively known as the International Standard Bibliographic Description (ISBD).

The first of these standards, ISBD(M), which applies only to monographs, prompted the revision of AACR1 Chapter 6 (the chapter for monographic materials) in that same year, 1974. The actual rules for description, other than changing punctuation, varied only slightly in this revision. Within the notes area, however, the conventions for prescribed punctuation were rather unevenly applied. In AACR1 Rev. Rule 143C, prescribed punctuation was called for only "in notes which include imprints given in conventional order." In all other cases, the cataloger could (not must) use prescribed punctuation when appropriate or use the previous conventional punctuation. Thus, while ISBD(M) succeeded in standardizing much of the bibliographic description for monographs, inconsistencies remained in the area of notes.

To complicate matters even further, AACR1 Chapter 12 (Motion Pictures and Filmstrips) was revised in 1975. Since there was still no official ISBD format for nonprint materials at that time, the revision was patterned after the ISBD(M) format as found in analogous parts of AACR1 Rev. Ch. 6. In 1976, Chapter 14 (Sound Recordings) was also revised but it did not use the pseudo-ISBD(M) structure. These revisions carried the inconsistencies in the application of prescribed punctuation for notes and other areas into the realm of nonprint materials. All other chapters for description in AACR1 continued to use the conventional style rather than ISBD(M) or pseudo-ISBD(M).

When AACR2 was being written, separate ISBD formats for materials such as serials, maps, and nonbook materials were still under development. In order to have a framework for achieving the fullest uniformity for standardization among all formats, IFLA adopted a General ISBD format, ISBD(G), in 1977. The ISBD(G) became the basis for the prescribed punctuation throughout the text of AACR2.

AACR2 Rule 1.7A3 calls for the use of prescribed punctuation when data in a note correspond to data found in Areas 1-6 of the bibliographical description except that a full stop is used in place of a full stop, space, dash, space. A further exception is made to this practice when information is given as a quotation. In that instance, the original punctuation is retained. What is implied, but unwritten in the text, is that if the note contains information that does *not* correspond to data found in Areas 1-6, but rather supplements or expands on that data, conventional punctuation is to be used. Until recently there appeared to be some confusion on this matter among catalogers at the Library of Congress. Their early AACR2 cataloging showed ISBD punctuation being used in almost all notes. Recent examples of LC cataloging indicate that the confusion is apparently being cleared up. ISBD punctuation is now only being used in notes that include data corresponding to data found in the bibliographic description area, while conventional punctuation is used for all other grammatical statements.

Format

AACR1 and its revised chapters did not address the issue of a general format for the notes area. AACR2 Rule 1.7A1, however, offers a choice of two formats. All notes may be presented either in one paragraph with the statements separated by a full stop, space, dash, space, or each note is to be started as a new paragraph. The Library of Congress has issued a rule interpretation to this rule (CSB 24) requiring that each note begin with a new paragraph and end with a full stop or other mark of final punctuation. LC further states that when a note statement ends with a closing bracket or parenthesis, a full stop must be added as the final mark of punctuation.

Formal and Informal Note Structure

AACR1 Rev. Rule 143C stated that fixed forms, that is, formal notes, were provided for by Rev. Rules 144-148. These rules covered notes for the following categories: "At head of title," "Bound with," Theses, and Contents. Notes giving other information were considered informal and could take the form of quotes, statements composed by the cataloger, or references to passages from the publication or other sources. Since fixed forms were not prescribed for these latter notes, AACR1 provided a lengthy listing of general principles for guidance in formulating these notes. AACR2 does not limit formal notes to the fixed forms prescribed by the rules, although many of the notes prescribed as formal in AACR1 are also given a formal structure in AACR2. AACR2 (Rule 1.7A3) defines formal notes as "employing an invariable introductory word or phrase or a standard form of words when uniformity of presentation assists in the recognition of the type of information being presented or when their use gives economy of space without loss of clarity." This definition implies that formal notes are not only notes prescribed by the rules, but are also notes devised by the cataloger using an "invariable" format. This definition provides for somewhat greater flexibility than did the AACR1.

In keeping with their general approaches, neither AACR1 nor AACR1 Rev. provided a general statement for the format and punctuation of formal notes. Both codes referred instead to those specific note rules that provided fixed forms. There was no general format to follow in cases not covered by a specific rule. AACR2 Rule 1.7A1 provides a general format guideline by requiring the introductory wording of a formal note to be separated from the main content of the note by a colon and a space. This instruction provides the cataloger with a fixed format that can be used to devise any type of formal note. To further clarify the formatting of formal notes, the Library of Congress has issued a rule interpretation to Rule 1.7A3 (CSB 22) informing catalogers that when introductory words such as "contents," "credits," or "summary" are used, they should be in upper and lowercase as illustrated in the AACR2 examples rather than in all uppercase. The need for this interpretation was apparently necessitated by some confusion caused by the fact that AACR1 Rev. and previous codes used all uppercase letters for these introductory words.

Sources of Information

In determining the sources of information for notes, AACR1 Rule 131 stated that there may be statements devised by the cataloger, statements quoted from the work itself or another bibliographic source, or a combination of the two. This implied that essentially any source could be used. AACR1 Rev. Rule 132A reiterated this statement. This rule then listed the principal sources of information for all areas of description except for notes. This omission further reinforced the idea that any source was acceptable. AACR2 (Rule 1.7A2) is now very specific in giving a prescribed source of information for each area of description in Chapters 2 through 12. The rule clearly states that information for notes may be taken from "any source." Square brackets are only to be used in notes where an interpolation is made within a quotation.

Order of Information

AACR1 did not address the order in which information was to be given in a note. AACR1 Rev. addressed only the order of imprint information within the context of prescribed punctuation. AACR2 (Rule 1.7A3), however, provides specific guidance for ordering information in the note area when that information corresponds to data found in Areas 1-6, that is, the information is to be given in the order in which the corresponding elements appear in Areas 1-6. No mention is made in any of the codes regarding the order of information when the data does not correspond to information found in the other descriptive areas of the cataloging record. In these cases, it is left to the discretion of the cataloger to provide a statement that is brief, lucid, and grammatically correct.

Romanization

The guidelines for romanizing in a note an author's name or the title of a work written in a nonroman script have changed considerably with the latest edition of the cataloging rules. AACR1 (Rule 144D) recorded the name of the author and the title of a work appearing in a nonroman alphabet in romanized form only when giving the source of information. In other cases, the nonromanized form was followed by the romanized form if it was needed for clarity or explanation. AACR1 Rev. (Rule 143C) called for providing this information in romanized form only for notes composed by the cataloger, for notes recording bibliographical relationships, or when citing the source of information. AACR2 (Rule 1.7A3) uses the original script in all notes whenever possible rather than the romanization of the name or title. The Library of Congress has issued a rule interpretation (CSB 22) that contradicts AACR2. It requires that all nonroman data (including quotations) recorded in the note area are to be given in romanized form in all cases. This is to be done even when the rest of the bibliographic description is given in nonroman script.

Spelling

AACR1 (Rule 144D) stated that *Webster's Third New International Dictionary of the English Language* was to be used as the authority for spelling words used in unquoted notes. AACR1 Rev. did not prescribe a spelling source but stated in a footnote to Rule 143C4 that the Library of Congress used the latest edition of *Webster's New International Dictionary* as the authority for its spelling in unquoted notes. AACR1 Rev. also stated that if alternative spellings were presented, the first spelling was preferred. AACR2 prescribes the use of *Webster's Third* as its spelling authority. However, in an effort to reconcile British and North American usage, where *Webster's Third* provides a British spelling as a permitted alternative, British spelling was adopted for use in the AACR2 text. This decision affects not only the spelling of words used in the rules themselves, it also affects the spelling of words used in examples, for example, Rule 6.7B11 uses the spelling "programme" for an example of an accompanying material note. It should be noted that catalogers are not obligated to follow the preference for British spelling in writing their notes. In a rule interpretation issued to Rule 1.7A3 (CSB 13), the Library of Congress has instructed its catalogers to follow American usage in *Webster's Third* when formulating notes.

Abbreviations

AACR1 (Rule 144D) and AACR1 Rev. (Rule 143C) both called for the use of abbreviations when citing sources of quoted information given in a note. Other instructions for the use of abbreviations were given in Appendix III of AACR1. These instructions explicitly stated that abbreviations could be used in notes except in those cases where a title was being recorded and in quoted notes. Although AACR2 has eliminated the statement regarding the use of abbreviations when citing the source of quoted notes, the text examples imply that abbreviations can still be used. The guidelines for the use of abbreviations in catalog records are given in an appendix. These guidelines allow for the use of abbreviations in all notes except in recording a title or statement of responsibility in a contents note and in recording a quoted note.

Quotations

Neither AACR1 (Rule 144D) nor AACR1 Rev. (Rule 143C) provided specific guidelines for the formatting and punctuation of quoted notes, although instructions were given for citing the source of the quote. Both codes called for recording the source following a dash after the quote. The author's name in direct form was given followed by the title of the work. Abbreviations were allowed for "commonly used and easily recognizable" words. When page references were recorded the cataloger was also instructed to record the edition (AACR1 Rule 144D and AACR1 Rev. Rule 143C). AACR2 (Rule 1.7A3) requires that quotations from the item itself or from other sources must be placed within quotation marks. The rule further requires that the source of the quotation must be given following the quotation. The rule does not, however, as did AACR1 and AACR1 Rev., give specifics about the formatting of the quotation source statement.

References

AACR1 (Rule 144D) and AACR1 Rev. (Rule 143C3) provided for the use of references to passages in the publication or in other sources in order to avoid the use of lengthy notes. While AACR2 (Rule 1.7A3) allows for the use of references for this purpose, it expands on their use to include the support of the cataloger's assertions.

> Authorship attributed to Gertrude Stein on p. 310.
> Authorship attributed to Adrian Bailey in the British national bibliography.
> Described in greater detail in: The compleat angler, 1653-1967 : a new bibliography / Bernard S. Horne.

Citations to Other Editions
of the Same Work or Other Works

AACR1 did not provide any instructions for the format or content of notes citing other editions of the same work or other works. AACR1 Rev. added a general statement on prescribed punctuation for notes that give imprint information in conventional order, but did not specifically discuss the information to be included in citing other editions or works. AACR2 (Rule 1.7A4) addresses the content of these citation notes and provides instructions for their format. AACR2 makes a distinction between notes that cite other editions of the same work, other works, and other manifestations of the same work.

In the case of other editions of the same work, the rule calls for providing only enough information to identify the edition cited (generally this includes only an edition statement and year of publication). The format and punctuation of this information would follow that prescribed under Rule 1.7A3, that is, ISBD style.

In cases where other works or other manifestations of the same work (other than different editions with the same title) are cited, Rule 1.7A4 instructs the cataloger to always give the title of the work and, when applicable, the statement of responsibility. The edition and date of publication may be added when necessary. Here the rule allows for a choice between two formats. The citation may be given in the form: Author, title proper; or Title proper / statement of responsibility. When necessary, the edition and/or the date of publication can be added to the citation.

Although it is not specifically called for in the rules, AACR2 examples consistently show a formal note structure for notes citing other editions and other works. This format consists of an introductory word or phrase followed by a colon and the citation information.

> Revision of: Boiler room questions and answers / Alex Higgins, Stephen Michael Elonka. 2nd ed.
> Sequel to: Christmas for Holly.
> Translation of : Du temps perdu au temps retrouvé.

AACR2 Rev. Rule 12.7A2 instructs that the name-title under which the serial is entered in the catalog should be used when referring to the serial in a note. If the serial is not in the catalog or if main entry is not used, the rule calls for use of the title and statement of responsibility.

The Library of Congress has issued rather detailed guidelines in CSB 22 for interpreting Rule 1.7A4. The LC policy concerns itself primarily with the provision of consistent linkage between the related records. This rule interpretation as well as the other rule interpretations to the general rule for notes are reproduced in their entirety in Appendix B. The paragraphs that follow highlight some of these interpretations.

For revised editions that are not revised translations, LC uses the AACR2 form of the title proper or uniform title to link AACR2 and non-AACR2 records. This is done, however, only if the revised edition has a different title or if there has been a change in choice of entry from that of the previous edition other than those changes caused by adoption of AACR2. If the heading change is caused by the adoption of AACR2, no note is made linking the records of either the earlier or later work.

When only the title has changed, LC uses a note only on the record for the later edition. The following format is suggested by LC:

[Name or Number] ed. of: [Title proper. Edition Statement. Date].

The Library of Congress also addressed the formatting of citations to other works. Except for serials, the citation to another work or another manifestation of the work employs the uniform title if one has been assigned. If no uniform title has been assigned, the title proper is recorded instead. If the work being cited is entered under a name heading different from that of the work being cataloged, "and the difference is not apparent from information given in the body of the entry," the name, in ISBD format, is added following the uniform title or title proper. The form of the name follows that of the source being used.

The publisher and place of publication were only to be included if needed for identification. LC cautions that the wording used in the introductory phrase will vary depending upon the information being reported.

When the choice of entry has changed, LC again makes a note only on the later record. The format used is:

[Name or Number] ed. of [Title Proper / First Statement of Responsibility.
Edition Statement. Date].

The title is recorded in the note even if it has not changed.

The Joint Steering Committee for the Revision of AACR2 added a third category under this rule to cover notes relating to items that are reproductions. This new rule calls for combining into one note all the notes relating to the original item. Here again, AACR2 states that the information should be given in the order of the areas of the bibliographic description to which they are related. AACR1 and AACR1 Rev. also provided for combining this information into one note, but did not give a specific order for the elements.

Order of Notes

AACR1 (Rule 144E) and AACR1 Rev. (Rule 143D) both included general statements on the order of notes that cautioned the cataloger against being too inflexible when following the order prescribed by the text. Indeed, the text itself offered options for positioning certain notes, for example, "At head of title" and "Bound with" notes, depending on individual circumstances involved. These general statements also directed the cataloger to combine notes when appropriate. In AACR2, the general statement regarding note order flexibility has been eliminated. Rule 1.7B presents the imperative to give the notes in the order listed in the rules. Options no longer exist for the positioning of notes in a different order based on individual circumstances. In one case, however, the Library of Congress has issued a rule interpretation moving a note to another position. The note for the manufacturer's number (Rule 6.7B19) for a sound recording is moved by LC from the last position to the first position (CSB 14).

While the note order varied somewhat between AACR1 and AACR1 Rev., analytical notes and notes referring to the original or later title took precedence over all other notes in the revised code, and the basic philosophy for note order was unchanged. The first category of notes included those that referred directly to elements in the formalized description, given in the same order as they appeared there, this is, title, subtitle, author, edition, imprint, collation, and physical description. The second category of notes included those that provided some bibliographical history or described the relationship of the item being cataloged to other works or other editions of the same work. Again, a basic order was followed with notes about titles given first, followed by authorship, edition, imprint, and physical description information. Generally the last notes given were contents and "bound with" notes, depending on the specific item.

AACR2 has, as first notes, information describing the general character of the work, that is, nature, scope, or artistic form, and language notes. It then follows the basic philosophy of giving notes in the order found in the formalized description Areas 1-6; however, notes that refer directly to elements in the main body of the description (Category 1 of AACR1) are now either combined or interspersed with notes providing bibliographical history (Category 2 of AACR1). This new struc-

Special Application

Record in a note the literary form of the book being cataloged if it contains one or more literary works by one author *and* it meets one of the following conditions:

1) the bibliographic record for the item bears one of the following symbols in conjunction with the LC control number: AM, ACN, HE, AJ, AK, NE, SA [These symbols refer to LC catalog records for works published in nonroman alphabets.];
2) the language of the item is indigenous to Africa and in a roman script;
3) the language of the item is indigenous to the Philippines.

Make the note whether or not the form is identified in the uniform title or in the body of the entry.

Literary Form Note

When giving the literary form note, base it on the following literary forms:
—drama;
—fiction;
—poetry;
—literature (used for an item containing works in more than one form).

The note should be worded according to the cataloger's approximation of the publication; the words chosen do not necessarily have to use one of the terms listed above (e.g., "Plays" instead of "Drama"). [CSB 35]

The Library of Congress frequently combines the elements of the Nature, Scope, or Artistic Form note and the language and/or translation elements of Rule 2.7B2.

RELATED LIBRARY OF CONGRESS POLICY

None issued.

AACR2 TEXT EXAMPLES REVISED TO REFLECT LIBRARY OF CONGRESS POLICY

None required.

HISTORICAL BACKGROUND

AACR2 places this note as the first note. AACR1 Rev. Ch. 6 placed it later in the note order.

AACR1 Rev. Rule 143B2c mentioned the use of a note to record the "nature and scope" or "literary form," if the title was misleading. It

3

also stated that literary form should not be indicated for a classic or for most fiction. The AACR2 rule does not specify these conditions, although the Library of Congress rule interpretation restates them.

AACR1 Rev. Rule 143D3b addressed the use of a note to record "other titles and title information" bearing on the "nature, scope, language, or literary form" of the work. This information is divided in AACR2 between this note and notes created under the provisions of AACR2 Rule 2.7B5 (Parallel Titles and Other Title Information).

AACR1 Rev. Rule 134B4a provided for an addition to the title if it needed explanation, and if the brief clarifying statement could be taken from the work itself. One example given under this rule included a literary form in brackets. AACR2 has retained the provision for additions to titles (cf. AACR2 Rule 1.1E6) and for the clarification of literary form.

These AACR1 Rev. Ch. 6 rules could also be used for works that were not separately published monographs unless the specific rules for the description of that format superseded or excluded their use.

NOTE EXAMPLES

In many cases, notes developed under this rule will combine elements from other notes (e.g., language, history, statement of responsibility) into one note.

Articles Previously Published

Many of the notes in this section could also fall under the provisions of the Edition and History note (Rule 2.7B7).

1.1 "All of these stories first appeared, some in somewhat different form, in the New Yorker"—Verso t.p.
1.2 Articles by the author published in Litigation from 1975-1981.
1.3 Articles from the author's column in The New Yorker.
1.4 Articles from various periodicals, covering period 1829-1863.
1.5 Articles previously published.
1.6 Articles previously published in Il tempo (Rome).
1.7 Chiefly articles from Library management bulletin, 1979-1980.
1.8 A collection of essays from the first 9 v. of the Journal of interdisciplinary history.
1.9 A collection of 39 essays published between 1975 and 1979.
1.10 Collection of newspaper articles.
1.11 Contains articles previously published in Jazz hot and Combat.
1.12 Contains essays previously published in various journals, chiefly translated from English, with 3 from French and one from Hebrew.
1.13 "The eight chapters . . . originally appeared as articles in the September 1981 issue of Scientific American"—T.p. verso.

4

1.14 "Nearly all of the text of this book appeared originally in the New Yorker"—Verso t.p.

1.15 Reprint of articles originally appearing in Judaism and Tradition.

1.16 A selection of articles from the first nine volumes of Sociological methods and research, and one from the American sociological review, vol. 40, Feb. 1975.

Artistic or Literary Form

1.17 "An annotated bibliography."

1.18 Autobiographical.

1.19 Cartoons.

1.20 Dance tunes, followed by directions for each dance.

1.21 Discography.

1.22 Discography of Broadway and Hollywood musicals.

1.23 Essays on materials at the Lyndon Baines Johnson Library presented at a conference held in the library in Jan. 1980.

1.24 Fiction.

1.25 "A fictional account set mostly during the period 1874-1890"—Half title.

1.26 Imaginary biographies.

1.27 Libretto.

1.28 Libretto of a musical comedy.

1.29 "A musical play for children"—p. 4.

1.30 Novel.

1.31 Previously unpublished novel of O.B. Mayer.

1.32 Opera libretto.

1.33 Opera libretto in Italian with word-for-word and line-by-line renderings in English and French (in the middle column) and English and French translations (in the outer columns); prefatory material and synopsis in English and French.

1.34 A paraphrase of parts of the Bible.

1.35 Play.

1.36 A play in 1 act. A version with 5 additional acts was published in 1930. Cf. A bibliog. and notes on the works of L. Abercrombie / J. Cooper.

1.37 Play in two acts.

1.38 A poem and a recipe for Christmas punch.

1.39 A poem, sent as Christmas greeting, 1955, by the author's family.

1.40 Poems.

1.41 Poems about Pope John Paul II.

1.42 Poems in Anglo-Saxon.

1.43 Short poem, beginning "Through North or South or East or West . . ." and signed "W.W.G.," printed as a holiday card for friends.

1.44 Quotations from Abraham Lincoln.

1.45 Short stories.

1.46 Short stories in Malay.

1.47 Songs, without musical notation.

1.48 Collection of speeches.
1.49 A spoof on the printing of Richard Bigus.
1.50 Verse and prose.
1.51 A verse from the Bible for each day of the year.
1.52 In verse.

Conversations and Interviews

1.53 Author's imagined interview with N. Boulanger.
1.54 "A conversation between Dr. Edward H. Stinnes and Andreas Kohl-schütter."
1.55 Edited conversations of Moshe Safdie and John Kettle concerning Safdie's Form & purpose.
1.56 Interviews conducted for French radio in 1952.
1.57 Interviews with women physicians.
1.58 Includes interviews with Robert Irwin and others taped between 1976 and 1979.
1.59 Part of text consists of selections from interviews with Picasso.

Exhibition Catalogs

1.60 Catalog.
1.61 "Katalog."
1.62 Catalog of an exhibition.
1.63 Exhibition catalog.
1.64 Catalogue of an exhibition at the Metropolitan Museum of Art.
1.65 Catalogue of an exhibition held April 26-June 21, 1981.
1.66 Catalog of an exhibition held at the Rijksmuseum, Amsterdam, Dec. 20, 1980-Mar. 15, 1981.
1.67 Catalog of an exhibition of the same title held at the Whitney Museum of American Art, Dec. 9, 1981-Feb. 7, 1982, and subsequently at the San Francisco Museum of Modern Art.
1.68 Catalogs of exhibitions of the annual salons of the Société des artistes indépendants, 1884-1891.
1.69 Catalogue of the touring exhibition.
1.70 Catalog of the manuscripts inherited by James A. de Rothschild from his father Baron Edmond de Rothschild, now the property of the National Trust for places of Historic Interest or Natural Beauty (of Great Britain).
1.71 The collection left by the author to the Institut für Musikwissenschaft, Salzburg, University.
1.72 Exhibition held at Fort Wayne Museum of Art, Feb. 6-Mar. 15, 1981, at Georgia Museum of Art, Athens, Ga., Mar. 28-Apr. 19, 1981, and at Mint Museum, Charlotte, N.C., May 24-July 19, 1981.
1.73 An exhibition held at the Aspen Center for the Visual Arts.
1.74 Facsim. reprints of exhibition catalogues of the Société des artistes indépendants.
1.75 Issued in conjunction with an exhibition at National Gallery of Art, Washington, D.C., June 28, 1981-May 2, 1982.

1.76 Selections from a traveling exhibit of the Children's Museum of Oak Ridge.

Festschriften

1.77 A collection of papers in honor of John Handin.
1.78 Commemoration volume for Sisir Gupta, former professor in diplomatic school, Jawaharlal Nehru University.
1.79 Festchrift in honor of Henry Nelson Wieman.
1.80 Published on the occasion of the author's 70th birthday, May 3, 1981.

Guides, Indexes, Inventories

1.81 "A complete guide to: New wave/punk records, small labels, distributors, record stores, fanzines, radio stations, clubs."—Cover.
1.82 Guide to accompany videotape of an edited version of a seminar held on April 16, 1982, in Atlanta, Ga., at the Annual Convention of the National School Boards Association.
1.83 A guide to the microfilm edition of the papers of W.E.B. Du Bois in the Library of the University of Massachusetts, Amherst.
1.84 A guide to the Microfilming Corporation of America's microfiche reproduction of the Natural Rehabilitation Information Center's rehabilitation research collection.
1.85 A guide to pts. 1-3 of the Corporation's ongoing Genealogy and local history program.
1.86 An index to American bibliography, a preliminary checklist, 1801 to 1819 / compiled by Ralph R. Shaw and Richard H. Shoemaker. New York : Scarecrow Press, 1958-1966.
1.87 Index to: Early American medical imprints / by Robert B. Austin.
1.88 Indexes photographs, paintings and sketches of more than 9,000 species of animals and plants found all over the world.
1.89 Indexes to marriages recorded in books <4> - <5> of the Probate Court.
1.90 Inventory of holdings in the Federal Archives Division of Public Archives Canada.

Lectures

1.91 Lecture notes.
1.92 Lectures given at a conference organized by the Center for Advanced International Studies, University of Miami, and held Feb. 1980.
1.93 "Lectures presented in the Great Hall of the Memorial Union at the University of Wisconsin, Madison"—Foreword.

Papers and Proceedings

1.94 Papers from the management workshops sponsored by the Special Libraries Association Library Management Division during the 70th annual conference of the Special Libraries Association held in Honolulu, Hawaii, June 7-14, 1979.
1.95 Papers from the Third International Symposium on Hypertension held in Mexico City, Feb. 12-14, 1979, sponsored by the Instituto Nacional de Cardiología and others.

1.96   "Papers . . . presented at a conference on American economic enter-
        prise, 1870-1914, held in October, 1980, at the Rockefeller Archive
        Center in Pocantico Hills, New York."—Introd.

1.97   Thirty-three papers presented at the 1980 annual meeting of the Amer-
        ican Council on Education in San Francisco.

1.98   Revision of papers from a symposium at the Universitat Trier, spon-
        sored by the Stiftung Volkswagenwerk, March 14-16, 1979.

1.99   Consists chiefly of rev. articles from an ABA national institute held in
        Chicago, Oct. 2-3, and in San Francisco, Oct. 17-18, 1980, sponsored
        by ABA Sections of Real Property, Probate and Trust Law, and Inter-
        national Law, in cooperation with the International Academy of Estate
        and Trust Law, and the American College of Probate Counsel.

1.100   Selected papers from the George Eliot Centennial Conference, held at
        the University of Puget Sound, Apr. 10-12, 1980.

1.101   Proceedings of a conference.

1.102   Proceedings of a conference organized by the Institute for Research in
        History held at Berkshire Place Hotel, New York, 18-19 October, 1979.

1.103   Proceedings of a national symposium.

1.104   "Proceedings of a satellite symposium . . . organized in conjunction with
        the XIth International Congress of Biochemistry, and held July 8-13,
        1979, in Toronto, Canada."—Verso of t.p.

1.105   Proceedings of the Third IUTAM Symposium in Structures.

1.106   Primarily speeches presented at various scientific sessions.

1.107   "The Conference on Women's Travel Issues . . . was held at the Na-
        tional Academy of Sciences in Washington, D.C., September 17-20,
        1978"—P. i.

1.108   "This book grew out of a conference which the Applied Sociology
        Program of the Department of Sociology at the University of Pittsburgh
        conducted in the Fall of 1977."

1.109   Outgrowth of an international meeting in 1981 sponsored by the Mus-
        cular Dystrophy Association.

Scope

1.110   Covers research done up to 1980 for subjects registered for research
        degrees since 1970.

1.111   "This book is a record of the society in the period 1955-1980, and
        differs from its more historically-oriented predecessor, Printing as an
        art, by Ray Nash (Cambridge, 1955)"—p. 1.

1.112   "This work covers developments which occurred on, or before June 1,
        1981. Subsequent developments will be covered in later supplements"—
        Introd.

Miscellaneous Nature

1.113   Albums containing facsims. of photos and letters collected by H.C.
        Andersen, accompanied by 2 v. with reprint of the text of the letters
        in the album (954 p. : ports ; 25 cm.).

1.114 A compilation of descriptive annotations of literature of the years 1954-1972.

1.115 Anthology of Latin inscriptions, with English introductory notes by the compiler, John Sparrow, who began the series in 1943.

1.116 An appeal for funds for the work of the press.

1.117 Art prints (4 wood engravings, 5 linocuts).

1.118 A collection of 3 Janus Press broadsides of various sizes and a theater poster (47 x 37 cm.) printed by Claire Van Vliet for the Bread and Puppet Theater.

1.119 A commentary on the Ley orgánica de la administración pública mexicana.

1.120 Posthumous compilation of commentaries previously issued separately or as parts of the author's collected works. Includes commentaries on epistles not covered by Hunnius: on the Epistle of James, those of Peter, and on Revelation by J. Winckelmann; on 2 Timothy, 2-3 John, and Jude by the editor.

1.121 A collection of discourses dictated by various Arisen Masters.

1.122 Facsim. of ms. (holograph?).

1.123 "102 programmable games designed for use with the Radio Shack TRS-80"—Cover.

1.124 Hearing held Sept. 22, 1980, in Los Angeles.

1.125 Keepsake for the 11th Congress of International Paper Historians, held at Arnhem, June 4-9, 1972.

1.126 Chiefly legislation.

1.127 "An annotated alphabetical listing of current and discontinued titles in the serials card file of the U.S. Superintendent of Documents' public documents library."

1.128 The award-winning titles from the annual competition sponsored by the Southeastern Library Association as published in Southern books competition.

1.129 Annotated list of materials in the reference collection of the Chicano Studies Research Library, UCLA.

1.130 List of records deposited in the Public Record Office and other English public archives.

1.131 Subject authority list for Index to current urban documents.

1.132 Consists largely of literary material drawn from General Grant's Personal memoirs.

1.133 Twenty-five hand-colored lithographs (incl. t.p.) of slightly varying sizes (approx. 38 x 28 cm.) mounted on paperboard.

1.134 Patterns from 2 exercise books at Flensborg Museum.

1.135 Consists chiefly of photos, from the collection of the Museum of London; text by Jasmin Cannon Bell.

1.136 Vol. 1, no. 1 consists of photoreproduction of pages from a 1901 pension book, Thomas Co., Ga.

1.137 Consists primarily of pictorial material from Artistic country-seats, edited by George William Sheldon.

1.138 Program.

1.139 "A self-contained program of instruction by which filers can learn the . . . ALA filing rules (1980)"—Pref.

1.140 Programs for 52 free concerts held at the John F. Kennedy Center for the Performing Arts Concert Hall, Washington, D.C.

1.141 Consists of recipes tested and approved by Better Homes and Gardens test kitchens.

1.142 Regulations adopted pursuant to the Maine Human Rights Act.

1.143 "Completion report for Project B-048-ORE, Office of Water Research and Technology, United States Department of the Interior."

1.144 Folded reproductions of 43 ink drawings with wash.

1.145 A collection of reproductions of pre-existing art work; with text added on interleaves.

1.146 "A compilation of the local rules of the Superior Courts for all 39 counties in the state"—Pref.

1.147 Salesman's sample. Special issue in 1 v. of portions of an edition published by subscription in 2 v.

1.148 Two scraps from unpublished journal notebooks cut up by Thoreau in producing his major works, now preserved as part of a collection of such scraps in the Huntington Library, San Marino, Calif.

1.149 Specimen book of J. Whatman handmade paper, incorporating the story of Whatman paper and of W. & R. Balston Ltd's Springfield Mills, where it is made today.

1.150 A solicitation for funds by the R.S.P.C.A. Fund for Sick and Wounded Horses.

1.151 Chiefly tables.

1.152 Statistical tables.

1.153 Statistical tables with text.

1.154 "Course text"—Cover.

1.155 A collection of the best ten years' worth of transcripts from the radio program, All things considered.

1.156 Type specimens.

Chapter 3 (Cartographic Materials)

AACR2 RULE

3.7B1 Nature and Scope of the Item [AACR2 Rev.]
    Make notes on the nature or scope of a cartographic item unless it is apparent from the rest of the description. Also make a note on unusual or unexpected features of the item.

RELATED AACR2 RULE

None.

LIBRARY OF CONGRESS POLICY

None issued.

RELATED LIBRARY OF CONGRESS POLICY

None issued.

AACR2 TEXT EXAMPLES REVISED TO REFLECT LIBRARY OF CONGRESS POLICY

None required.

HISTORICAL BACKGROUND

AACR1 Rule 212E6 provided for a note dealing with "scope and cultural features," in order "to clarify an indefinite or misleading title and to point out unusual features." AACR2 does not limit the clarification to ambiguity present only in the title, but expands it to include ambiguity not resolved by the rest of the description. AACR1 also provided for an explanation of "unusual features" as does AACR2.

The note order used in AACR1 varies somewhat from that of AACR2. AACR2 places this note as the first in order of priority while AACR1 had the "holdings of composite sets" note (Rule 212E1) first in priority and the "scope and cultural features" note later.

NOTE EXAMPLES

Although no formal structure is given to this note, many AACR2 text examples, as well as Library of Congress cataloging examples, begin this note with the term "Shows."

Nature and Scope

1.157 Also covers Passaic Township.
1.158 Covers boroughs of Freehold and Englishtown and townships of Freehold, Colts Neck, Marlboro, and Manalapan.
1.159 Covers selected region.
1.160 Covers Wheaton Central Business District.
1.161 Also shows mineral deposits.
1.162 Also shows state House of Representatives districts.
1.163 Does not show military positions, movements, or fortifications.
1.164 *Shows cross sections of selected counties of Mississippi, Alabama, and N.W. Florida.
1.165 Shows flood control dams, reservoirs, and benefited areas.

11

1.166 Shows international radio amateur prefixes by country.
1.167 *Shows land use.
1.168 Shows nature reserves in Israel.
1.169 Shows oil and gas fields, pipelines, industries, and mineral deposits.
1.170 Shows precinct boundaries.
1.171 Shows radial distances.
1.172 Shows roads, Kenning service stations, and repair centers.
1.173 Shows roads, railways, air routes, sea routes, magesterial districts, and Bantu homelands.
1.174 Shows touristic points of interest.
1.175 Ms. information shows: Rural system programs, Old highway system programs—state and federal aid funds, and N.R.A. programs.
1.176 "Natural gas pipelines, crude oil pipelines, petrochemical & product pipelines, industrial gas pipelines, related industry."
1.177 "100 wards within the jurisdiction of Calcutta Corporation"—Foreword.

Date of Situation or Data
1.178 "December 1980—January 1981."
1.179 "Compiled January 1981."
1.180 "Date of photography: August 1978."
1.181 "The information contained in this map is correct as of April 1978."
1.182 "About Australia's major urban areas . . . from the Census of Population and Housing of 30 June 1976"—V. 1, p. 1.
1.183 "Based on the latest Geological Survey quadrangles."
1.184 "Bulk of the data . . . pertain to the period 1976-1977"—P. 1.
1.185 Congressional and legislative reapportionments filed 1971.
1.186 "Information as of February 1981."
1.187 "Regent approved 3-9-79. Campus Planning Committee approved 1-3-79."
1.188 Shows land status in Alaska as of March 1974.
1.189 "State highways as of July 1, 1976."
1.190 "Starred information correct as at 1/3/73."

Relief
1.191 Depths shown by contours and soundings.
1.192 Relief shown by contours, shading, spot heights, and land form drawings. Depths shown by contours and soundings.
1.193 Relief shown by gradient tints.
1.194 Relief shown by gradient tints and spot heights. Depths shown by gradient tints.
1.195 Relief shown by hachures.
1.196 Relief shown by landform drawings.
1.197 Relief shown by land form drawings and spot highlights.
1.198 Relief shown pictorially.
1.199 Relief shown by shading, hypsometric tints, and spot heights. Depth shown by bathymetric tints.

1.200   Relief shown by spot heights.
1.201   Relief shown by spot heights on the political map. Relief shown by gradient tints and spot heights and depths shown by gradient tints on the physical map.

Miscellaneous

1.202   Aerial photographs of key entrances and anchorages, distance scales, harbor details, planning chart, course protractor, shore-to-shore coverage, launch ramps, includes all navigable rivers to Maryland and Virginia.
1.203   An atlas factice which forms part of the Gifford Pinchot Papers in the Manuscript Division.
1.204   Bird's-eye-view.
1.205   Partial cadastral map.
1.206   Facsimile.
1.207   "Gov't charts reproduced in book form"—P. 1 of cover.
1.208   *Ill. of vessels and native customs.
1.209   An introductory atlas taking the reader from the home to solar system.
1.210   *Navigational chart.
1.211   Photo map.
1.212   Photocopy maps show ms. information from ms. legends.
1.213   "A reference book using reproduced portions of Ocean Survey charts"—P. 1 of cover.
1.214   "This map has been compiled using satellite and conventional aerial photography with detailed information collected locally."
1.215   "A 'two-way' map publication—contemporary and traditional"—P. 1.

Chapter 4 (Manuscripts)

AACR2 RULE

4.7B1 Nature, Scope, or Form [AACR2 Rev.]

Nature

Make notes on the nature of a manuscript or a collection of manuscripts unless it is apparent from the rest of the description. Use one of the following terms, as appropriate:

holograph(s) (for manuscripts handwritten by the person(s) responsible for the work(s) contained there in)
ms. (for all other handwritten manuscripts)
mss. (for all other collections of handwritten manuscripts)
typescript(s) . . .

Signed Items

If the item is signed, add *signed.* . . .

Copies

If the item or collection being described is a copy or consists of copies, add

(carbon copy),
(photocopy), or
(transcript),

or the plural of one of these.

If a photocopy is negative, add *negative.*

Add

handwritten or *typewritten* to *transcript(s).* . . .

Collections with Variant Natures

If the items in a collection are not all of the same nature, word the qualification to indicate this. . . .

Location of Original

If the item is a copy, add the location of the original if this can be readily ascertained. . . .

Scope or Form

Indicate the scope or form of a manuscript item if it is not apparent from the rest of the description. . . .

Collections

In describing a collection of manuscripts,

name the types of papers, etc., constituting the collection and mention any other features that characterize it.

If the collection is of personal papers, give enough data to identify the person, either as a brief initial statement or as part of the summary of the nature of the collection.

If necessary, give the contents (see 4.7B18) as part of that summary.

RELATED AACR2 RULE

None.

LIBRARY OF CONGRESS POLICY

None issued. APPM, however, expands on the AACR2 text. It does not provide for an all-inclusive Nature, Scope, or Form of Manuscript note but instead creates separate rules for many of the subrules found within the AACR2 rule. APPM also provides additional rules that would fall within the broad concept of "nature, scope, or form" but are not specifically provided for in the AACR2 rule.

Relationship Complexity

If the manuscripts or records being cataloged are related by provenance, hierarchy, or function to a larger unit or other materials or are part of or an addition to an existing collection, group, or series, give the title for that unit as formulated under the principles outlined in 4.1A-4.1E [of APPM].

In addition indicate the relationship of the material being cataloged to the other unit using such phrases as

"Forms part of :,"
"In:,"
"Addition to:,"

and other introductory wording as appropriate. [APPM 4.7B1]

Copy/Repository

If the material being described is a copy of or is non-original, either entirely or in part, record its form and extent. Include the location of the originals, if known; if the location is unknown, give that information.

Record the presence or existence of microform or other copies of all or part of the material being described. If the originals have been destroyed after copying or are no longer extant, give this information.

Optionally, record the location of additional copies of the material. [APPM 4.7B2]

Biographical/Historical

Record any significant information on the creator/author of the manuscript(s) or records required to make the nature or scope of the materials clear. For persons this may include place of birth and domicile, occupations, information on original and maiden names or pseudonyms, significant accomplishments, place of death, etc. For corporate bodies, this may include information on the functions, purpose, and history of the body, its administrative hierarchy, and earlier, variant, or successor names. This information should be abstracted from the finding aids. [APPM 4.7B3]

Scope and Content/Abstract

For manuscript collections and archival records, give the types and forms and, if desirable, the arrangement of the materials being described; the dates within which the material bulks largest; the most significant topics, events, persons, places, etc., and, when appropriate, the most significant correspondents. Also note the presence of graphic or other non-textual materials such as illustrations, maps, charts, drawings, plans, photographs, sound recordings, or machine-readable files. If a substantial portion of the material is in a language other than English, or if translations are present, give this information. This note is drawn and abstracted from the finding aid.

For an individual manuscript, abstract the contents of the item, giving significant topics, persons, places, events, etc., mentioned. If it is not already in the title statement, give the form of the item and, for a letter, the recipient. In addition, if the date of delivery of a speech, sermon, etc., differs from the date of the manuscript as given in the title, record the date of delivery in this note, unless the date is already part of the title information. [APPM 4.7B4]

Arrangement

If the general arrangement of the materials is not given elsewhere, make a note on that arrangement specifying the internal structure and order. [APPM 4.7B5]

RELATED LIBRARY OF CONGRESS POLICY

None issued.

AACR2 TEXT EXAMPLES REVISED TO REFLECT LIBRARY OF CONGRESS POLICY

None required.

HISTORICAL BACKGROUND

Introductory notes to AACR1 Rule 201 for the description of single manuscripts called for a note indicating that the work was a manuscript. This is essentially the same as the provisions of Rule 4.7B1.

Signed Items

AACR1 Rule 202C provided for a note indicating that a manuscript letter was signed. AACR2 has expanded this to include any type of manuscript.

Copies

AACR1 Rule 207D provided for notes describing the form of manuscript if not original. This rule is equivalent to the AACR2 rule, although some of the terminology has been altered slightly.

Location of Original

Introductory notes to AACR1 Rule 201, as well as AACR1 Rule 207D, provided for a note on the location of the original if known. This is the same in AACR2.

Scope or Form

AACR1 did not provide for a note on the form of manuscript equivalent to the AACR2 rule. AACR1 Rule 207E did provide for a note on the scope of manuscripts, but combined this note with the contents note.

Collections

AACR1 Rule 207E is equivalent to the AACR2 rule. However, the AACR1 rule provided greater detail than does AACR2. In AACR1, guidelines were given for the kinds of information considered important for characterizing a collection. These included:

"dates for which the material bulks the largest"
"the phase most completely covered, or"
"particular segments of material included."

For personal papers this note also included:

"names which are significant for the collection."

The AACR1 rule also stated that biographical data, other than birth and death dates, be given to identify a person. This is not mentioned in AACR2 Rule 4.7B1.

Incorporation of Another Collection

AACR1 Rule 207E also provided for a situation not specifically covered by AACR2: "When the collection has incorporated another, earlier collection, such as the records of a predecessor body, this fact and the name of the earlier body or collector are noted."

NOTE EXAMPLES

For collections with variant formats, the Library of Congress follows a note construct implied in AACR1. The construct begins with the phrase "In part" followed by the term used to describe the manuscripts.

Nature
1.216   *Holographs.
1.217   *Holograph, addressee unknown.
1.218   Holograph sketches (photocopy) of the ballet.
1.219   *Holographs, typescripts (some carbon copies), printed matter.

1.220   In part, photocopies.
1.221   In part, photocopies (positive).
1.222   In part, photocopies of correspondence (ca. 200 items) between Phil-
        brick and Winfield Townley Scott.
1.223   In part, transcripts.
1.224   In part, transcripts (handwritten) of 18th century legal papers made by
        Parsons and his son.
1.225   In part, transcripts (typewritten), photocopies, and microfilm.
1.226   *Includes photocopy with original typescript.
1.227   *Mostly holographs; some leaves reproduced from holograph; some
        leaves blank.
1.228   *Ms.
1.229   *Printed matter, with ms. corrections.
1.230   *Promptbook.
1.231   *Reproduction of typescript.
1.232   *Typescript.
1.233   *Original typescript.
1.234   *Typescript (carbon copy).
1.235   Typescript (in part carbon copy).
1.236   *Typescript (photocopies).
1.237   *Typescript with ms. notations (negative photostat).

Nature—Signed

1.238   *Autograph letter signed.
1.239   *Autograph letter signed: Mounier; and addressed: Monsieur Beyle, R.
        Richelieu 71.
1.240   *Holograph signed.
1.241   *Holograph signed (initials).
1.242   *Holograph, signed; holographs; printed forms completed in ms; printed
        matter; printed matter (photocopy, negative).
1.243   *Holographs, signed; transcripts, signed.
1.244   *Holographs; signed; typescripts (some signed, some carbon copies);
        printed forms completed in ms.
1.245   *Ms. form with holograph inserts, signed.
1.246   *Ms. in clerical hand, signed.
1.247   *Ms. signed.
1.248   *Pencil sketches of Albert Einstein, signed, on the cover of the souvenir
        program.
1.249   *Printed form with ms. inserts, signed.
1.250   *Typed letter signed, document signed.
1.251   *Typed, signed.
1.252   *Typescript (photocopy) signed, Pat Nixon.

Nature—Location of Original

1.253   In part, copies and photocopies of originals in Library of Congress and
        Ohio Historical Center.

1.254 In part, photocopy of original owned by Mrs. David E. Claywood, Memphis, Tenn.

1.255 In part, transcripts (handwritten) of outgoing correspondence. Location of originals unknown.

1.256 *Ms. (photocopy reproduced from microfilm), original in the Öster-reichische Nationalbibliothek; "Photo M606, Cod 25456."

1.257 Photocopies made from originals in: British Public Record Office, London, England, compiled by Thomas J. Tobias.

1.258 *Photocopy of holograph. New York : Pierpont Morgan Library, 1976. 48, 66, 88 leaves of ms. music ; 28 cm.

Nature and Miscellaneous Notes

1.259 Holograph, in ink.

1.260 Holograph, in ink and pencil.

1.261 Holograph, in ink, with additions in blue pencil by the engraver.

1.262 Holograph, in ink, with additions in pencil and measure numbers stamped in ink.

1.263 Holograph, in ink, with emendations in red and blue pencil for the printer.

1.264 *Holograph (photocopy), original in the Pierpont Morgan Library, dated 1908 Dec. 25. 11 leaves containing only parts 2 and 3.

1.265 Holograph (rough copy) in ink.

1.266 *Holograph, signed; the salutation is explained in a letter of 1920 Nov. 16 (MS Frost 46).

1.267 Holograph signed (photocopy), formerly owned by Gisella Selden-Goth.

1.268 *Holograph signed, with envelope.

1.269 *Manuscript on paper. Title from opening words of the quotation.

Scope—Part of a Larger Collection

1.270 *Forms: Record Group 251, Records of the Illinois School for the Deaf.

1.271 Forms part of: Katherine S. Day collection.

1.272 Forms part of: Peter Force papers (Series 8D:31).

1.273 *Forms part of: Record Group 220, Records of Presidential Committees, Commissions and Boards.

Description

1.274 *Additional materials include deeds of sale for lands in Brookline and pews in the Church, wills of various family members, a 1792 description of Susannah Craft's innoculation for smallpox, a 1787 letter concerning a Shaysite mob, an 1846 copy of Thomas Handasyd Perkins' account of his visit to Mount Vernon, a series of letters of Capt. James J. Higginson, of the First Massachusetts Cavalry describing the Siege of Petersburg, and a neurological analysis of William Ellery Channing together with copies of two of his sermons.

1.275 *Among the papers are the reports on economic conditions in Germany—wages, prices, consumption, status of agriculture, analysis of imports, allocation of revenues, and credit and financial summaries. There are in addition weekly reports of the acting commercial attache, Douglas Miller, copies of miscellaneous speeches of the Secretary of the Treasury Andrew W. Mellon and the Undersecretary of the Treasury Ogden L. Mills, together with summaries and analysis of the German press.

1.276 *Census schedules of population of each county include information on households (numbers assigned to dwelling house and family in order of visitation, name of street and house number of families residing in cities, names of each individual residing therein); individuals (name, occupation, sex, color, number of months employed during year, nature of permanent or temporary illnesses or disabilities, whether attended school during year, reading and writing skills, birthplaces of individual and parents); enumeration (date of census, name and certification of enumerator, enumeration district number, recapitulation of totals).

1.277 Chiefly mss. of articles, lectures, and books by or about women in medicine. Includes unpublished autobiography of Rosina Wistein.

1.278 A composite collection consisting of small groups of papers or single items listed and described separately in the repository.

1.279 *Concerns financial expenditures, construction plans, employee salaries and resignations, and establishment of an Experimental School for the Instruction and Training of Idiots and Feeble-Minded Children. Also includes reports from the Committee on Building Plans and the Prudential Committee.

1.280 Contains bibliographical descriptions of the Arundel Society's publication, Fans of all countries (1871) and 3 publications by Charlotte Schreiber (1888, 1890, and 1892-1895).

1.281 *Contract with William E. Wood for the publication of a collection of poems, Shapes of clay (San Francisco, 1903), signed by Bierce and his attorney; letters on personal and business matters.

1.282 Correspondence and other papers (1779-1784) of Isaac Harleston (1745-1789), officer of 2d Regiment, South Carolina Line, Continental Establishment, during the Revolution; and letters (1860-1865) from Sabina Wells, of Charleston, S.C., and others, written to John Harleston, Confederate soldier and prisoner of war in New York. Isaac Harleston's correspondents include William DeBrahm, Benjamin Lincoln, Francis Marion, and C.C. Pinckney.

1.283 Correspondence, diaries, account books, genealogical data, and other family papers, beginning in 1796.

1.284 Correspondence, documents, and portraits of the 56 signers of the Declaration of Independence; correspondence and portraits of Charles Thomson, secretary to the Continental Congress, and of John Nixon who first read the declaration to the public; facsimiles of the signers' signatures; original letter (1912 Nov. 19) of donation from Morgan and reply from William Howard Taft.

1.285 *The correspondence is rich in the detail and routine of social and domestic life and, since most documents were generated by women, the collection provides a wealth of material on the education, activities, and attitudes of women in the nineteenth century.

1.286 Documents relating to shipping in Charleston and Georgetown, S.C., including ship entries and clearances, customs and cargo reports, and other records, with notes by Tobias.

1.287 *The Heath Family Papers consist of six generations of letters, diaries, copybooks, account books, and other miscellaneous financial and legal papers of the Heath family of Brookline, Massachusetts. The collection consists primarily of correspondence between and diaries kept by the children and grandchildren of John (1732-1804) and Susannah (Craft) Heath (1738-1808), especially Ebenezer Heath (1765-1845), Susan Heath (1795-1874), Anna Eliza Heath (b. 1797) and Mary Heath (1804-1824). Also included are letters and diaries of related Craft, Goddard, Howe, and White families.

1.288 *Includes minutes, agenda items, committee reports, and correspondence of the Arizona Medical Association.

1.289 *Includes ticket to the 1885 inaugural ball and pictorial commemorative of the 1885 inauguration, signed by Cleveland and T.A. Hendricks.

1.290 Index to Kemble's collection of prints depicting British actors and dramatists. Arranged alphabetically by subject's surname. Dated prints are from 1605 to 1791; the collection was sold at auction in 1821.

1.291 Journal kept by Hayne and others, containing birth, death, and marriage records (1764-1780); wills (18th and 19th centuries); abstracts from register of St. Philip's Church, Charleston, S.C.; St. Thomas and St. Denis Church records; and notes on the Huger family.

1.292 *Letter apparently accompanied some legal books which Goethe asked the recipient to put in her library. Goethe also enclosed additional copies of melodies for the muses almanac in the house, for Mrs. Loder, and Mrs. Paulus.

1.293 *A letter to his teacher in which he mentions his opera, Aida.

1.294 *One letter of Cleveland and 2 letters of Mrs. Cleveland, making arrangements for travel and special stops at Buzzards Bay on the Old Colony Railroad.

1.295 Letters by Mrs. Stowe to friends, relatives, and publishers during the course of her career while residing in Cincinnati, Ohio (1832-1850), Brunswick, Me. (1852), Andover, Mass. (1853-1864), Hartford, Conn. (1864-1896), and from her winter homes in Mandarin, Fla. (1868-1885); journal of travels in Italy (1860); brief biographical account of her childhood, describing the death of her mother Roxana (Foote) Beecher, wife of Lyman Beecher; draft for part of the novel, Agnes of Sorrento (1862); and mss. of articles, poems, and other writings.

1.296 *Letters to J.L. Sullivan and Benjamin Silliman (Sr.) regarding steam engines and steamboats; descriptions of his inventions; 10 original patents, signed by U.S. Presidents, Secretaries of State and Attorneys General; business papers relating to Orford, N.H. and Fairlee, Vt.

1.297   *Minutes of board meetings, 1839-1865; case files, 1902-1958; register of admission applications, 1877-1917; registers of pupils, 1845-1938; student health and travel records, financial records.

1.298   *Notes and key to characters, originally written in 1927, for Tropic of Capricorn, published in 1957.

1.299   *The papers of William E. Russell, 1846-1920, the thirty-third governor of Massachusetts consist of twenty-four archival boxes of loose manuscripts and 31 bound volumes of letterbooks and scrapbooks.

1.300   Poet and author noted for his Civil War poems. Chiefly mss. of articles and short stories; together with poems in ms., final draft, and printed form, verse translation of the Aeneid, and annotated scrapbook of clippings of Brownell's published works.

1.301   *Reply to Stendhal's letter of 9 February 1829, the autograph of which is in the Newberry Library, Chicago.

1.302   Scrapbooks containing programs, invitations, announcements, newspaper clippings, and photos, relating to church and school activities, with personal correspondence from contributors to the scrapbooks. Most of the material is from the 1940's and 1950's.

1.303   *Souvenir program of a banquet in honor of Albert Einstein.

1.304   *Speech delivered while Governor of New Jersey. Extract typed when President.

1.305   *Text of Chief Justice Marshall's opinion in an unidentified hand; extracts from the opinion in the hand of William Allen, President of Dartmouth University (1817-1819).

1.306   *Typewritten transcripts of tape-recorded interviews with early residents of State College, Pa., focusing on life in State College before 1920, including schools, churches, family and social life, businesses, transportation, notable families and events, residences, buildings and landmarks, life on the campus of Pennsylvania State College, and relations between students and townspeople. The interviews were conducted by Jo Hays, former Pennsylvania state legislator and mayor of State College, and C.O. Williams, dean of admissions emeritus, Pennsylvania State University.

1.307   Unpublished mss. on Washington state history, geography, counties, cities and towns, biography, cultural life, education, folklore, economic resources, religion, scenic attractions, and the part played by women in state development.

Identifying Information

1.308   *Anna Welty was an inmate of the California Insane Asylum in Stockton from 1873-1884.

1.309   *Antarctic explorer, zoologist, member of the U.S. Antarctic Service, and station scientific leader at Wilkes Station, 1957-1958.

1.310   Army officer and lawyer.

1.311   Author and reformer; b. Harriet Elizabeth Beecher, married (1836) Calvin Ellis Stowe (1802-1886).

1.312   Financier and collector.

1.313 *Hamilton was the son of James Alexander Hamilton and Irving's choice for Secretary to the legation at Madrid. The nomination presented some difficulties, due to Hamilton's political position.

1.314 *Historian, of Wilson, Raleigh, and Chapel Hill, N.C.; first archivist of the United States; secretary, North Carolina Historical Commission; professor at University of North Carolina; and author; full name: Robert Digges Wimberly Connor.

1.315 *Incorporated by Illinois General Assembly in 1839 as Illinois Asylum for the Education of the Deaf and Dumb, located in Jacksonville, Ill.; name changed to Illinois Institute for the Education of the Deaf and Dumb in 1903. Governed by board of directors until 1909 when administrative and executive control passed to newly created [Illinois] Board of Administration. Transferred to Department of Public Welfare, 1917; Department of Mental Health, 1961; and Department of Children and Family Services, 1963.

1.316 *Moses Kimball. Born Newburyport, Mass. owner and manager, Boston Museum. Massachusetts State Representative. 1895. Died Brookline, Mass.

1.317 News broadcaster; b. Chester Robert Huntley.

1.318 *Student, Yale University class of 1907.

Description and Identifying Information

1.319 *Army officer. Letterbook, 1838-1847; scrapbook of newspaper clippings; "Dade Massacre diary"; proceedings of court martial at West Point, 1835; correspondence, 1836-1849; undated correspondence, rosters of troops; military court proceedings, 1846-1847; correspondence with various military personnel including: Braxton Bragg, Leslie Chase, J.B. Crane, H.J. Hunt, Andrew Jackson, Roger Jones, Gideon J. Pillow, John Sanders, Winifred Scott, Martin Van Buren (signature cut away) and William J. Worth.

1.320 *Colonel, Colonial Army. Appointment as Major, 21 April 1780; appointment as Lt. Colonel 14 April 1787; letter, Paris 10 November 1790, from Rochefontaine to Bauman; letter New York, 30 May 1803, from Aaron Burr to Bauman; miscellaneous papers.

1.321 Law firm. — Legal and estate papers. Includes papers of the Seignious family, papers relating to Moultrie House Railroad Company (ca. 1854-ca. 1861) receipt book of South Carolina Commandery, No. 1, Knights Templar (1878-1883), and rolls of the Palmetto Guard (1865).

Description and Language

1.322 Ballerina. Correspondence, certificates, memorabilia, and photos, relating chiefly to Caccialanza's relationship with her teacher, Enrico Cecchetti (1850-1928). Includes letters from Cecchetti to Gisella, Maria, and Romeo Caccialanza, and material on the Cecchetti Society and Cecchetti Centennial (1950). Correspondents include Cyril W. Beaumont, Cia Fornarali, and Attilia Radice. In English and Italian.

1.323   Dance and movement theorist. Designs, crayon drawings, and india ink drawings of gestures and poses; 200 drawings for the poetics of gesture; notes for "the state of grace"; clippings and small scrapbooks; and commentaries on the exercises of Odic-Kintzel's system numbered in various sequences. In French.

1.324   Journal or day book (in Dutch) by an unknown person containing copies of correspondence, treaties, articles of agreement, declarations, admiralty lists, notes, commentary, poetry, and essays relating chiefly to the Fourth Anglo-Dutch War, 1780-1784, the fall of the Dutch Republic, and trade and diplomatic relations between the Netherlands and the emerging United States. Individuals represented in the journal include, in addition to various Dutch officials, military officers, members of the court and nobility, and poets, John Adams, Samuel Huntington, Henry Laurens, John de Neufville, Hyde Parker, and John Rutledge.

1.325   *Three letters written in French by Jules Massenet to unknown parties.

Chapter 5 (Music)

AACR2 RULE

5.7B1 Form of Composition and Medium of Performance [AACR2 Rev.]

Form of Composition

    If the musical form of a work is not apparent from the rest of the description, give the form in a word or brief phrase. . . .

Medium of Performance

    Name the medium of performance for which a musical work is intended unless it is named in the rest of the description in English or in foreign language terms that can be readily understood.

    Name voices before instruments.

    Name the voices and then the instruments in the order in which they are listed in the item being described.

    Name a voice or instrument in English unless there is no satisfactory English equivalent.

Instrument/Voice Identification

    If the work is for solo instruments, name them all if no more than eleven would be named.

    If the work is for an orchestra, band, etc., do not list the instruments involved.

    In describing ensemble vocal music, add to the appropriate term a parenthetical statement of the component voice parts, using

S (soprano),
Mz (mezzo-soprano),
A (alto),
T (tenor),
Bar (baritone), and
B (bass).
Repeat an abbreviation, if necessary, to indicate the number of parts. . . .

Supplementary Information

If the information relating to the medium of performance given in the rest of the description is ambiguous or insufficient, record supplementary information here.

RELATED AACR2 RULE

None.

LIBRARY OF CONGRESS POLICY

Do not name the medium of performance in a note if it is implied by the title or other title information (e.g. "Chorale prelude"; "Kaddish : symphony") or by the musical form stated in a note made under this rule (e.g., "Opera in two acts"; "Ballet").

If an item is described in the physical description area as "chorus score" or "vocal score" . . . give in a note the original medium of performance, and the instrument for which the accompaniment is arranged (or indicate that the accompaniment is omitted) if this information is not clear from the rest of the description. [MCB v.12, no. 6]

RELATED LIBRARY OF CONGRESS POLICY

None issued.

AACR2 TEXT EXAMPLES REVISED TO REFLECT LIBRARY OF CONGRESS POLICY

None required.

HISTORICAL BACKGROUND

AACR1, unlike AACR2, had separate note rules for "species" and "medium of performance."

AACR1 Rule 248A provided for a note to name the "species." The term species was changed to form of composition in AACR2, although the rule remains essentially the same.

25

AACR1 Rule 248B1-2 provided for notes on the medium of performance. This rule is equivalent to the AACR2 rule, although AACR1 gave more detailed guidelines.

It provided for a note on the original medium if the work in hand was an arrangement. This situation is not provided for in AACR2; however, the Library of Congress has allowed for the provision of this information in a cataloging decision (see *Library of Congress Policy*) and continues to make this note.

It provided for naming alternative instruments. AACR2 does not.

It clearly stated that instruments and voices were listed "in the order of the score." AACR2 uses the more general phrase "in the order of the item being described."

It stated that the key of wind instruments should not be given. AACR2 does not mention this.

It provided guidelines for naming instruments when the performing forces were the combination of an orchestra and a solo instrument (i.e., only the latter was to be named). AACR2 provides separate guidelines for solo instruments and orchestra, but does not provide guidelines for the combination of the two.

AACR1 Rule 248B3 provided for a note on supplementary information, as does AACR2. Again, however, AACR1 delineated the conditions for the use of the note in a much clearer way. It stated that "if the collation or uniform title description of the score and parts and statements appearing on the title page of the work present a discrepancy, or if they are otherwise inadequate" make the note. It also suggested combining this information with the medium of performance note.

AACR1 Rule 248B4 stated that for choral music before 1600, the voices were to be named in the language of the work being cataloged. AACR2 calls for the use of English in naming voices and instruments unless there is no satisfactory English term.

AACR1 Rule 248B5 addressed the issue of composite volumes or sets of music. It stated that "the note concerning medium of performance should be descriptive of the work as a whole." When the contents were of too miscellaneous a character, no note was to be made. AACR2 does not explicitly provide for this situation.

NOTE EXAMPLES

In addition to the constructs given in the rule, text examples, as well as Library of Congress cataloging examples, frequently introduce the medium of performance statement with the word "For."

Musical Form

1.326 Arrangements.
1.327 Arrangement of BWV 818, from book 1 of Das wohltemperierte Klavier.
1.328 Ballet.
1.329 Ballet excerpts.
1.330 Chance composition.
1.331 Chants and hymns.
1.332 Children's folksongs.
1.333 Children's opera.
1.334 "Compilation of instrumental music from Gluck's opera . . . put together for a recording"—Pref.
1.335 Excerpts from act 1 of the ballet.
1.336 Folk and patriotic music of Banat, Tara, Românească, and Moldavia.
1.337 Folk music.
1.338 Folksongs and ballads.
1.339 Fragments of incomplete works for horn and orchestra.
1.340 From the musical comedy.
1.341 Hymnal; chord symbols included.
1.342 Hymns, with music.
1.343 "Instrumental motet."
1.344 "Jazz song."
1.345 Motet.
1.346 Musical comedy excerpts.
1.347 Opera.
1.348 Opera excerpt.
1.349 Opera overture.
1.350 Original works and arrangements.
1.351 Prelude to the opera (1st version).
1.352 Secular part-songs.
1.353 Song cycle.
1.354 Songbook, without music.
1.355 Songs.
1.356 Suite.
1.357 Symphonic poem.
1.358 "This work is not a complete one; it is an index of musical elements, provided for following one another, in an order that the performer can settle . . . . "—Pref.
1.359 Traditional Catalan songs.
1.360 Trio sonata.
1.361 Unfinished opera.
1.362 Unused excerpt from the musical comedy.
1.363 The work consists of the feedback produced when the microphones swing over the loudspeakers.

Musical Form and Medium of Performance

1.364 Broad sheet songs; words set to traditional melodies (with chord symbols).

27

1.365 Cantata, for solo voices (SSAT), chorus (SSAT), and orchestra.
1.366 Chance composition for 4 voices, percussion (2 players), piano, pre-pared piano, 2 violins, 2 violoncellos, 2 optional male dancers, optional female dancer, and optional lighting panelist.
1.367 Chansons for 4 voices.
1.368 Chorale preludes for organ.
1.369 Folk ballad; for alto and chamber chorus.
1.370 Folk dance songs; unacc. melodies.
1.371 Instructions for using telephone recordings and recordings of bird calls to compile a chance composition; includes tables of numbers.
1.372 Intabulations of vocal and instrumental works.
1.373 March for band.
1.374 Principally masses, for 4-6 voices.
1.375 Opera; acc. arr. for piano.
1.376 Opera excerpts for orchestra.
1.377 Original works and arrangements; the last 2 works are guitar duets.
1.378 Passamezzos and saltarellos for lute.
1.379 Principally arrangements of movements from the composer's string quartets, op. 9, no. 1-2, 5, and op. 33, no. 3; final movements of 4th and 5th duets are from unknown sources.
1.380 "Satirical vignette . . . for actress, danseuse, or uninhibited female per-cussionist and pre-recorded tape."
1.381 School song-book; principally unacc. melodies or songs and choruses with or without piano.
1.382 "Simplified arrangements of songs from some of Gilbert and Sullivan's best loved light operas, for piano/vocal with guitar chord symbols."—Cover.
1.383 Song cycle; acc. arr. for guitar.
1.384 Suite for piano.
1.385 Suite for unspecified treble instrument and continuo.
1.386 Teaching pieces for 2 violins.
1.387 Toccatas and other works for harpsichord or organ.

Musical Form and Miscellaneous Notes

1.388 Dance music in letter notation.
1.389 Folk music; words in Serbo-Croatian (Roman).
1.390 Incidental music for the play by Ken Hill.
1.391 Javanese instrumental music in number notation.
1.392 National songs; unacc. melodies; Czech words.
1.393 Opera; Russian words.
1.394 Polish folk hymns in piano versions (with Polish words) and as unacc. melodies with chord symbols (with English words).
1.395 Songs to poems by Akesson; unacc. melodies, includes chord symbols.
1.396 Unacc. melodies; Eskimo songs from various Alaskan regions; words in the original languages with English translations.
1.397 Unacc. melodies, transcribed by Iliginio Anglés.

1.398　The 1st work is a free transcription of John Dunstable's motet.

Medium of Performance—Voice Alone

1.399　TTBB.

1.400　Chorus: SATB.

1.401　For SSAATTBB.

1.402　For cantus, quinta, altus, tenor, and bassus.

1.403　For chorus (SAATB, SSATB); Latin words.

1.404　For unacc. chorus (SATB).

1.405　For canto, alto, tenore, and basso.

1.406　For chorus or solo voices (SATB).

1.407　For medium voice.

1.408　For men's or children's chorus (2 parts).

1.409　For 1 or more voices.

1.410　For 2 groups each consisting of SSMzMzAATTBarBB, unaccompanied.

1.411　Melodies with chord symbols.

1.412　Sacred and secular choruses.

1.413　Unacc. melodies.

Medium of Performance—Voice and Accompaniment

1.414　Acc. for piano, violin, viola, and violoncello.

1.415　For acc. of consort of five instruments, keyboard instrument, or a combination.

1.416　For bass voice, chorus (SATB) and orchestra.

1.417　For SATB, 2 violins, 2 trumpets, and continuo realized for organ; Latin words.

1.418　In part for varying choruses and piano; in part for voice and piano; Ukrainian and Russian words.

1.419　For chorus (SATB), flute (piccolo), clarinet, bassoon, horn, trumpet, trombone, 2 violins, viola, violoncello, and double bass.

1.420　For congregation in unison (or baritone solo), chorus (SATB), flute, and string orchestra.

1.421　For either soprano, mezzo-soprano, contralto, tenor, baritone, or bass, with piano acc.

1.422　For medium voice and piano.

1.423　For men's chorus (TTBB), clarinet, contrabassoon, trombone, percussion, violoncello, and galets.

1.424　For mezzo-soprano and orchestra; acc. arr. for piano; Czech and German words..

1.425　For mezzo-soprano, clarinet, percussion (1 player), guitar, and harpsichord.

1.426　For mixed chorus and piano.

1.427　For mixed chorus, mezzo-soprano, speaker, and orchestra.

1.428　For narrator, oboe, mezzo-soprano, mixed chorus, and orchestra.

1.429　For solo voices, chorus (SATB), flute (piccolo), harp, piano, harmonica (ad lib.), and percussion (1 player).

1.430   For soprano, bass clarinet, and optional stereo tape recording.

1.431   For soprano, piccolo/flute/alto flute, oboe/English horn, bassoon, percussion, piano, harp, violin, viola, and violoncello.

1.432   For speaking chorus (SATB) and orchestra.

1.433   For 3-6 mixed voices and organ.

1.434   For unison voices, 3 recorders, percussion (3 players), guitar (optional), and piano.

1.435   For voice (S or Mz), percussion (1 performer playing inside the piano on strings with tape covered triangle beaters, 2 cowbells, 2 bowls balancing on piano strings, and using a superball mallet, flexatron and Jew's harp), piano, and flute.

1.436   For voice, violin, and piano.

1.437   For woman's voice, recorders (1 player, doubling crumhorn), violoncello (doubling viola da gamba), and harpsichord.

1.438   For wordless soprano and wind quintet.

1.439   In part for voice, flute, and string quartet; in part for voice alone; in part for voice and piano.

1.440   Principally for cantus, quintus, altus, tenor, and bassus.

1.441   Works 1-3 for chorus (SATB) and piano; works 4-11 for voice and piano.

Medium of Performance—Instrumental

1.442   Banjo music principally in tablature.

1.443   The chamber ensemble is made up of 4 groups: flute (piccolo), oboe, horn, bassoon; string quartet; trumpet, trombone, percussion; and piano, harp, percussion.

1.444   For bassoon and string orchestra with piano.

1.445   For clarinet/bass clarinet/saxophone, trumpet, violoncello, accordian, piano/electric organ, and percussion.

1.446   For dulcimer.

1.447   For electronically amplified panpipes (2), alto saxophones (2), pianos (4), bass guitars (2), and congas/marimbas (2).

1.448   For ensembles of Russian folk instruments in varying combinations.

1.449   For 5 viols and organ or 6 viols and organ.

1.450   For flute, oboe, clarinet, horn, bassoon, and string orchestra.

1.451   For flute/piccolo, clarinet, viola, violoncello, harpsichord, and percussion (1 player).

1.452   For 4 players, 3 tom toms each graduated in pitch.

1.453   For 4 trumpets, 4 horns, 4 trombones, baritone, 2 tubas, 2 percussion players, timpani, and harp.

1.454   For 4 unspecified instruments.

1.455   For harpsichord (piano) or organ.

1.456   For horn and piano.

1.457   For keyboard instrument.

1.458   For juvenile orchestra.

1.459   "For microphones, amplifiers, loudspeakers, and performers:" instructions for performance in English, German, and French.

1.460 For large tam-tam, microphones, filters, and potentiometers (6 performers).
1.461 For oboe (English horn), clarinet (bass clarinet), bassoon, horn, piano, percussion (1 player), violins (2), viola, violoncello, and double bass.
1.462 For piano, with interlinear words.
1.463 For 1 woodwind and 1 brass instrument.
1.464 For orchestra.
1.465 For orchestra and electronic tape.
1.466 For orchestra, tape, and visuals.
1.467 For percussion (6 players).
1.468 For piano, 4 hands, and orchestra.
1.469 For piano, left hand.
1.470 For recorder (SAT (one player)) and piano.
1.471 For "small orch."—New Grove dictionary.
1.472 For soprano, alto, tenor, and bass recorders.
1.473 For string quartet, string quintet (2 violins, viola, violoncello, double bass), or string orchestra.
1.474 "For treble and alto models of the African folk instrument (thumb piano) sold under various trademark names."
1.475 For 2 solo instruments (cornets?) and piano.
1.476 For 2 violins, viola, and violoncello.
1.477 For various combinations of 4 brass instruments: trumpets, cornets, horns, trombones, and/or baritones.
1.478 Instrumentation unspecified.
1.479 Keyboards: Piano/celesta.
1.480 The recorder player doubles on gongs, with tape recorder.
1.481 Scored for 2 violins, viola, and violoncello.
1.482 The 3rd movement is for harpsichord solo.
1.483 The 3 sets of concertos are for violin and string orchestra (oboes and horns ad lib.); the set of simphonies concertantes (without numbering) is for 2 violins and string orchestra.
1.484 The 6th work for trumpet and organ; includes part for optional treble voices (with German text) and trumpet on p. 56.
1.485 Unacc. melodies and dances for flute with acc. of castanets, drum, and sticks.
1.486 The violoncellist also speaks and sings (without words).

Medium of Performance—Original Only
1.487 Acc. originally for chamber orchestra.
1.488 Acc. originally for 6 violins, 2 violas, 2 violoncellos, and double bass.
1.489 Komm, Heiliger Geist and Gott, der Vater, originally for trumpet or oboe.
1.490 No. 3 originally for string quartet (Benton 321/li); the remainder originally for piano trio (Benton 431/i, 431/iii, 432/iii, 438/ii, 436/ii).
1.491 Originally for flute, or other soprano instrument.
1.492 Originally for 4 voices.

1.493   Originally for high voice and harp.
1.494   Originally for lute.
1.495   Originally for orchestra.
1.496   Originally for voice and ensemble.

Medium of Performance—Arrangements

1.497   Arr. for flute, oboe, bassoon, contrabassoon, horn, 2 trombones, hand-
        bells, and harp, from medieval motet.
1.498   Arr. for 4 or 5 guitars.
1.499   Arrangements for piano or organ, with chord symbols.

Medium of Performance—Including Original Medium of Performance

1.500   Acc. originally for flute, oboe, bassoon, trumpet, and harp; arr. for
        piano.
1.501   Arr. for 4 guitars; originally for chorus (TTBB).
1.502   Ed. for organ or harpsichord unacc.; originally for harpsichord or organ
        with or without string instruments.
1.503   For bassoon and piano; acc. originally for string orchestra.
1.504   For chimes, flute, violin "or almost any other instrument" and piano;
        probably originally for orchestra.
1.505   For tenor solo, chorus (SATB), and piano; acc. originally for chamber
        orchestra.
1.506   For 2 recorders (soprano and alto); pieces originally for harpsichord.
1.507   For voice and piano; includes chord symbols; originally for rock en-
        semble.
1.508   Harp part added to voices originally unacc.
1.509   Vocal and instrumental music, adapted principally for piano.

Medium of Performance—Accompaniment Arranged

1.510   Acc. arr. for piano.
1.511   For chorus and acc. arr. for keyboard.
1.512   For chorus (SATB) and orchestra; acc. arranged for piano.
1.513   For piano and orchestra; acc. arr. for 2nd piano.
1.514   For soloists (STB), chorus (SATB), baritone chorus, 3 guitars, and or-
        chestra; acc. arr. for piano.

Medium of Performance—Accompaniment Note

1.515   Chorus: SATB; without the acc.
1.516   For male soloist, mixed chorus and orchestra; without the acc.
1.517   For SSAAATTBBB; with piano reduction.
1.518   SSATB, with keyboard reduction.

Medium of Performance—Form/Key/Text

1.519   For Appalachian dulcimer, in part arrangements of folk music, in part
        songs with Appalachian dulcimer acc.

1.520 For piano; simplified arrangements.
1.521 For chamber orchestra; in D minor.
1.522 Originally composed in E major; now usually performed in E♭ major.
1.523 "Since descant recorders are rarely played today, the recorder part has here been notated at sounding pitch and also transposed down a step to make it suitable for a descant recorder in C . . . thus, the concerto was originally in A major but in the present edition is in G major."—Pref.
1.524 Transposed from original key of D major.

Figured/Unfigured Bass Realized

1.525 Figured bass realized for harpsichord.
1.526 Figured bass realized for harpsichord or organ and "can be reinforced by, say, a viola da gamba"—p. vi.
1.527 Figured bass realized for keyboard instrument.
1.528 Figured (1st movement only) and unfigured bass realized for harpsichord.
1.529 For soprano, double mixed chorus, 4 instruments (bassoons, trombones, or violin, 2 violas, and violoncello), and continuo; figured bass realized for organ.

Figured/Unfigured Bass Realized and Parts

1.530 Figured bass partially realized for keyboard or plucked instrument; includes part for bass instrument.
1.531 Figured bass realized for harpsichord; includes optional part for violoncello.
1.532 Figured bass realized for harpsichord, organ, theorbo, or guitar; includes part for bassoon or violoncello.
1.533 Figured bass realized for harpsichord by John Madden; includes part for violoncello, viola da gamba, or bassoon.
1.534 Figured bass realized for organ; "the continuo instrument should be the organ, though Castello suggests that harpsichord will serve."—Pref.
1.535 Parts for flutes (violins) and violoncello; figured bass realized for harpsichord.
1.536 Unfigured bass realized for piano; includes continuo part for violoncello.

Parts/Reduction Included

1.537 Includes alternative part for French horn.
1.538 Includes keyboard reduction.
1.539 Includes part for bassoon or violoncello to replace the pedal line if organ part is performed on harpsichord or piano.
1.540 Includes part for bass instrument.
1.541 Includes piano reduction for rehearsal only.
1.542 Includes piano reduction of the orchestral acc.
1.543 Includes reduction for bassoon and piano (47 p.) and solo part.

1.544 Includes 2 parts for tenor instrument, one in alto clef, the other in treble with subscript 8.

1.545 Instrumental interludes between each piece not included in vocal score.

1.546 Part for double bass only (with ensemble cues).

1.547 Parts for trumpet in D and Bb.

1.548 The score serves as part for 1st violin.

1.549 Score includes piano reduction of the orchestral parts.

1.550 The 2nd, 4th-5th works unacc.; keyboard reduction included for rehearsal only.

1.551 With keyboard reduction of the instrumental and vocal parts.

Performance Instructions

1.552 Can be performed with acc. of wind ensemble (original and optimum instrumentation) or band.

1.553 "Each solo belongs to one of four categories: 1) song; 2) song using electronics; 3) theatre; 4) theatre using electronics"—Pref. v. 1.

1.554 For left hand alone.

1.555 For 2 hands, with emphasis on left hand development.

1.556 "Instructions for the players' movements are in the parts and are designated by stand numbers . . . A separate solo part for individual practice only is included for stands 2, 3, & 4. Stand 1 can use the performance solo stand part for his individual practice."

1.557 May be realized as a scenic or concert performance.

1.558 May be staged.

1.559 "May be sung with or without other indeterminate music"—Pref., v. 1.

1.560 "The oboe part may be played by a 2nd clarinet, and the bassoon part by a cello"—p. iv.

1.561 "This duet arrangement can be played with the band accompaniment published by Chappell."—Caption.

1.562 A vocalist is optional in the 2nd pavan.

Chapter 6 (Sound Recordings)

AACR2 RULE

6.7B1 Nature or Artistic Form and Medium of Performance [AACR2 Rev.]

Form or Type

Make notes on the form of a literary work or the type of musical or other work unless it is apparent from the rest of the description. . . .

Medium of Performance

Name the medium of performance when necessary, as instructed in 5.7B1.

RELATED AACR2 RULE

None.

LIBRARY OF CONGRESS POLICY

None issued. Although no policy statement has been issued, the Library of Congress continues to make notes on the original medium of performance when the item in hand is an arrangement. AACR2 Rule 6.7B1 does not explicitly provide for this note, although it is included in the more general wording of this rule. AACR1 explicitly provided for this note. (See *Historical Background.*)

RELATED LIBRARY OF CONGRESS POLICY

None issued.

AACR2 TEXT EXAMPLES REVISED TO REFLECT LIBRARY OF CONGRESS POLICY

None required.

HISTORICAL BACKGROUND

AACR1 Rev. Rule 252F3 is essentially the same as a part of the AACR2 rule. AACR1, however, used the term "species." This term was changed to "artistic form" in this chapter of AACR2.

AACR1 Rev. Rule 252F4a combined the medium of performance note with the participant-performer note. AACR2 has separated them and combined the medium of performance with the form note.

AACR1 Rev. Rule 252F4b provided for an additional note on the original medium of performance if the item in hand was an arrangement. Although AACR2 does not explicitly address this situation, this note could be made under the general provisions of this rule.

The note order used in AACR1 Rev. Ch. 14 varies somewhat from that of AACR2. AACR2 places this note as the first in priority; AACR1 had it later.

NOTE EXAMPLES

Form

1.563   Ballets.

1.564   Band music; the last work originally for violoncello and piano, arr. by the composer.

1.565 Bluegrass music from the television series Austin city limits.

1.566 Cantatas.

1.567 Consort music.

1.568 Country music.

1.569 Excerpts from incidental music for an adaptation of A midsummer night's dream by Shakespeare.

1.570 The 1st work a theme and variations; the 3rd an excerpt from the suite Le tombeau de Couperin; the 4th a waltz.

1.571 The 1st work excerpts from a suite, originally for piano; the 2d work a suite.

1.572 The 1st work is for narrators, electronic music, and piano; words by the composer.

1.573 The 1st work, written as incidental music to Shakespeare's play, originally for mixed voices, harmonium, and orchestra; concert version for orchestra by the composer.

1.574 The 1st and 2nd works, taken from incidental music for the play by Alphonse Daudet, collected and arr. for large orchestra by the composer and E. Guiraud (respectively); 3rd work, originally for piano, 4 hands, orchestrated by the composer.

1.575 Folk dance music; arr. by the performers.

1.576 Folk music; vocal portions sung in Creole.

1.577 "Historical recordings of chants and songs from the Audio-recording collections, Department of Anthropology, Bernice Pauahi Bishop Museum"—Container.

1.578 Incidental music for Shakespeare's play, as adapted by John Dryden.

1.579 Instrumental ensembles and songs; Santana, guitars, percussion, and vocals; Herbie Hancock, keyboards and synthesizers; Wayne Shorter, saxophone; Ron Carter, bass, and others.

1.580 Instrumental improvisations.

1.581 Intermezzo.

1.582 Irish fiddle tunes.

1.583 Jazz.

1.584 Jazz; Call Tjader, vibes, and his sextet, in part with Mundell Lowe, guitar.

1.585 Jazz ensembles.

1.586 Jazz quintets (sides 1-2) and sextets (sides 3-4).

1.587 Jazz solos (in part overdubbed), duets, and trios.

1.588 Jazz trios; Ervin, saxophone; Richard Davis, double bass; Jaki Byard, piano; Alan Dawson, drums.

1.589 Jazz trios, quartets, and quintets.

1.590 K. 475 is a fantasia, published together with the Sonata, K. 457; K. 494 was composed originally as an independent rondo, later revised to form a sonata with the Allegro and andante, K. 533.

1.591 Marches.

1.592 Musical comedies.

1.593 Opera arias and songs.

1.594 Opera in 4 acts, sung in Italian.
1.595 Opera seria in 3 acts.
1.596 Piano trio and string quartet.
1.597 Principally musical numbers from the sound track of the picture starring the Marx Brothers.
1.598 Principally original banjo solos and songs.
1.599 Principally piano arrangements of opera excerpts intended to accompany ballet dance-class exercises.
1.600 Rock music.
1.601 The Sarabande and Polka are ballet excerpts.
1.602 Song cycles; words by Heine.
1.603 Songs.
1.604 Songs and instrumental music, principally arr. from traditional Celtic melodies by Stivell.
1.605 Songs from radio broadcasts aired originally in 1933-1934; Russ Columbo, with orchestra.
1.606 Symphonic poems.
1.607 Variations.
1.608 Venezuelan folksongs.

Nature

1.609 Comedy, starring and written by Graham Chapman, John Cleese, Terry Gilliam, Eric Idle, Terry Jones, and Michael Palin.
1.610 Comedy monologues.
1.611 Designed to be used with an annual report of a major company whose business involves manufacturing or commerce.
1.612 Dramatic readings performed by Sarah Bernhardt, Constant Coquelin, and Ernest Coquelin.
1.613 Excerpts from interviews.
1.614 Includes, together with paraliturgical elements, the Mass proper and selections from the liturgical office for the Feast of Circumcision (Jan. 1).
1.615 Interview, conducted by Hughes Desalle.
1.616 Lectures.
1.617 "Master class on singing presented by Luciano Pavarotti and Mirella Freni [at the Teatro Comunale de Modena in 1976] in live recording"—Bound-in transcription.
1.618 The 4 plays of St. Nicholas (12th century) found in the Fleury Playbook (part of Ms. 201 in the public library at Orleans).
1.619 Radio dramas.
1.620 Radio presentation; narrated by Stuart Finley.
1.621 Selections of American and English poets and writers.
1.622 Sermons, delivered from the pulpit of Marble Collegiate Church, New York City.
1.623 Two stories, read by the author.

Medium of Performance

1.624 The 1st work for flute, clarinet, soprano saxophone, violin, violoncello, and piano; 2nd-3rd works for flute, alto saxophone, and piano; 4th work for clarinet and alto/soprano saxophone.

1.625 The 1st work for soprano, flute, clarinet, bassoon, viola, and horn.

1.626 The 1st work for women's voices and instrumental ensemble; 2nd work for violin and electronic tape of 3 additional violin parts; 3rd work for piccolo, flute, 2 pianos, 2 violins, viola, and violoncello.

1.627 For 4 voices with instrumental doubling.

1.628 For harpsichord and string orchestra.

1.629 In part for string orchestra.

1.630 Principally for unspecified instruments.

1.631 String orchestra acc.

1.632 SWV 25 unacc., the remainder with instruments.

1.633 Unacc. 6-part choral works.

Medium of Performance and Form

1.634 Ballet excerpts for piano.

1.635 Band music, principally arrangements.

1.636 Carols, performed with organ, brasses, harp, or unacc.

1.637 First work for oboe and string orchestra; 2nd work a ballet suite.

1.638 Improvisations using various instruments and noise-making devices.

1.639 Jazz ensemble with orchestra.

1.640 Opera excerpts (1st work); the 2nd work, taken from orchestral suites collected and arr. by Bizet and E. Guiard, originally written as incidental music for the play by Alphonse Daudet.

1.641 Original works and an arrangement; the 4th work originally for piano duet.

1.642 The 6th work, originally for string orchestra, is an excerpt from a suite.

1.643 Suite for orchestra.

1.644 Traditional and original choruses without acc.

Medium of Performance—Original Only

1.645 Acc. in part, originally for piano.

1.646 The 1st work originally for violoncello and orchestra.

1.647 Originally an open score, without instrumental specification, but probably intended to be played on a keyboard instrument. Cf. Grove, 5th ed.

1.648 Originally for piano solo (1st work) or piano 4 hands (2nd-3rd works).

1.649 Originally for various instrumental combinations.

1.650 Originally notated in open score, probably for keyboard instrument.

1.651 The 2nd work originally for piano.

Medium of Performance—Including Original Medium of Performance

1.652 For piano; the 2d work originally for glass harmonica, the 3rd originally for orchestra, the 5th originally for mechanical organ.

1.653 String orchestra arrangements of principally violin and piano music.
1.654 With string orchestra acc.; 3rd work originally acc. by string orchestra and 2 horns.

Chapter 7 (Motion Pictures and Videorecordings)

AACR2 RULE

7.7B1 Nature or Form
Make notes on the nature or form of a motion picture or videorecording unless it is apparent from the rest of the description.

RELATED AACR2 RULE

None.

LIBRARY OF CONGRESS POLICY

None issued. For archival moving image materials, the Library of Congress supplements AACR2 Chapter 7 with the guidelines in *Archival Moving Image Materials* by White-Hensen.

RELATED LIBRARY OF CONGRESS POLICY

None issued.

AACR2 TEXT EXAMPLES REVISED TO REFLECT LIBRARY OF CONGRESS POLICY

None required.

HISTORICAL BACKGROUND

Although AACR1 Rev. Ch. 12 and previous codes had no rule equivalent to AACR2 Rule 7.7B1, the nature, scope, and form note provisions for separately published monographs in these earlier codes could be used for motion pictures and videorecordings. (See *Historical Background* under Rule 2.7B1.)

NOTE EXAMPLES

The use of this note is somewhat limited due to the frequent inclusion of nature and/or form indication as part of the summary note (AACR2 Rule 7.7B17).

1.655 An AMCEE videotape conference, recorded live at the 1979 National Conference on Energy Auditing and Conservation.

1.656 An animated film focusing on the movement of a fly.

1.657 A dramatization of Shakespeare's play The taming of the shrew.

1.658 Parody of the motion picture: Close encounters of the third kind.

Chapter 8 (Graphic Materials)

AACR2 RULE

8.7B1 Nature or Artistic Form

Make notes on the nature or artistic form of a graphic item unless it is apparent from the rest of the description.

RELATED AACR2 RULE

None.

LIBRARY OF CONGRESS POLICY

None issued. For original items and historical collections, the Library of Congress supplements AACR2 Chapter 8 with the guidelines in *Graphic Materials* by Betz.

RELATED LIBRARY OF CONGRESS POLICY

None issued.

AACR2 TEXT EXAMPLES REVISED TO REFLECT LIBRARY OF CONGRESS POLICY

None required.

HISTORICAL BACKGROUND

Although AACR1 Rev. Ch. 12, AACR1 Ch. 15, and previous codes had no rule equivalent to AACR2 Rule 8.7B1, the nature, scope, and form note provisions for separately published monographs in these earlier codes could be used for graphic materials. (See *Historical Background* under Rule 2.7B1.)

NOTE EXAMPLES

The use of this note for projection materials is very limited, particularly for projection graphic materials. The nature or artistic forms of these materials are generally covered as part of a summary note (AACR2 Rule 8.7B17).

Nonprojection Graphic Materials

1.659 *Idealized chart of a typical weather system, with slide-out insert simulating its passage over two stations. Explanation on back of chart. Designed to teach short-range weather prediction.

1.660 A collection of prints executed by Robert N. Essick.

1.661 Separate copy of an illustration for the poem, L'art d'aimer, as published in: Oeuvres de P.J. Bernard / ornées de gravures d'après les dessins de Prud'hon . . . A Paris : De l'impr. de P. Didot l'aîné, 1797.

1.662 *Literary selections designed for appreciation and as topics for composition.

1.663 Sixty original drawings, in pen-and-ink and blue wash, made for the Limited Editions Club edition, published in New York, 1935. The drawings are on 53 boards, which have been matted. Eleven of the boards are accompanied by proofs printed in black and olive.

1.664 The plates are illustrations detached from the 19th and early 20th century books named, and presented as examples of the processes described.

1.665 Portfolio contains 8 sheets with text (incl. t.p.) and 20 art prints.

1.666 Relief-etched facsimile prints based on electrotypes in Gilchrist's Life of Blake (title page, The lamb, The divine image, and The school boy). Executed by John W. Wright; see his articles in Blake newsletter 26 (1973) and 36 (1976).

1.667 *"175 sets printed . . . from the original wood blocks . . . Each set consists of twenty-nine prints . . . 160 for sale numbered 1 to 160, 15 out of series I to XV"—Front paste-down endpaper of portfolio.

1.668 Sketches for a proposed monument on Greenwich Hill. Flaxman included a design for the monument (engr. by William Blake) as a frontispiece to his A letter to the committee for raising the naval pillar, or monument . . . London, 1799.

1.669 Seventeen hand-colored woodcuts taken from printed books (mostly 15th- and 16th-century) and mounted on 13 leaves of a scrapbook.

Chapter 9 (Computer Files)

AACR2 RULE

9.7B1 Nature and Scope and System Requirements [AACR2 Rev.]

a) *Nature and scope*

Make notes on the nature or scope of the file unless it is apparent from the rest of the description. . . .

b) *System requirements*

Make a note on the system requirements of the file if the information is readily available.

Begin the note with *System requirements:*. Give the following characteristics in the order in which they are listed below. Precede each characteristic, other than the first, by a semicolon.

the make and model of the computer(s) on which the file is designed to run

the amount of memory required

the name of the operating system

the software requirements (including the programming language)

the kind and characteristics of any required or recommended peripherals. . . .

c) *Mode of access*

If a file is available only by remote access, always specify the mode of access.

RELATED AACR2 RULE

9.5 Physical Description Area [AACR2 Rev.]
3. Do not give a physical description for a computer file that is available only by remote access. See 9.7B1c and 9.7B10.

9.5B1 Extent of Item (Including Specific Material Designation) [AACR2 Rev.]
Record the number of physical units of the carrier by giving the number of them in arabic numerals and one of the following terms as appropriate:

computer cartridge
computer cassette
computer disk
computer reel . . .

When new physical carriers are developed for which none of these terms is appropriate, give the specific name of the physical carrier as concisely as possible, preferably qualified by *computer*. . . .

If the information is readily available and if desired, indicate the specific type of physical medium. . . .

Optionally, if general material designations are used (see 1.1C1), omit *computer* from the specific material designation.

Give a trade name or other similar specification in a note (see 9.7B1b).
[emphasis added]

9.5C1 Other Physical Details [AACR2 Rev.]

If the file is encoded to produce sound, give *sd.* If the file is encoded to display in two or more colours, give *col.* ...

Give details of the requirements for the production of sound or the display of colour in a note (see 9.7B1b). [emphasis added]

9.7B2 Language and Script [AACR2 Rev.]

Give the language(s) and/or script(s) of the spoken or written content of a file unless this is apparent from the rest of the description. ...

Record the programming language as part of the system requirements note (see 9.7B1b). [emphasis added]

LIBRARY OF CONGRESS POLICY

None issued for AACR2 Rev. Ch. 9.

RELATED LIBRARY OF CONGRESS POLICY

None issued for AACR2 Rev. Ch. 9.

AACR2 TEXT EXAMPLES REVISED TO REFLECT LIBRARY OF CONGRESS POLICY

None required for AACR2 Rev. Ch. 9.

HISTORICAL BACKGROUND

Computer files were not covered by AACR1 or previous codes. The original AACR2 Chapter 9 limited its coverage to notes dealing with the nature or scope of the computer file. AACR2 Rev. Ch. 9 adds the system requirements and mode of use aspects of this note. Previously, a form of the mode of use note was covered by AACR2 Rule 9.7B15. This same rule, as modified in the AACR2 Ch. 9 *Guidelines,* also included a listing of the system requirements, although the elements to be recorded differed somewhat from those in the current note.

NOTE EXAMPLES

Nature and Scope

1.670 *Biomedical measurements taken from underwater laboratory experiments lasting 1,440 hours.

1.671 *Computer transcription of Greek author Thucydides, coding for: diacritics, punctuation, capitals, and Greek symbols.

1.672 *Database management program.

1.673   *Digitized pictures.

1.674   *Game.

1.675   *Input text for a concordance to the novel, edited by Noel Polk and Kenneth L. Privatsky.

1.676   *Interactive program written in standard BASIC for maximum likelihood estimation of parameters of unrestricted latent class models.

1.677   *Learning package designed to be used in American Government classes.

1.678   *PARSENT system file, formatted and coded for: part-of-speech label, pronunciation, etymology, definitions, verbal illustrations, usage notes, synonymy paragraphs, etc.

1.679   *Part of a series of summary statistic files each containing detailed characteristics of the U.S. population by geographic area based on the 1970 census population questionnaire.

1.680   *"First pre-election study: Sept. 23, 1972-Oct. 11, 1972; second pre-election study, Oct. 20, 1972-Nov. 6, 1972; post-election study: Dec. 9, 1972-Dec. 30, 1972."

1.681   *Program designed as utility program for geographic base file manipulation.

1.682   *Quantification of historical conflict behavior.

1.683   *Records cover the science and technology of textiles, plus relevant patent literature in the United Kingdom and United States from 1970 to the present.

1.684   *A set of FORTRAN subroutines allowing users to find maximum likelihood estimates of supplied parameter values and compute the estimate of their variance-covariance matrix.

1.685   *Simulation model of the U.S. economy structured after the Wharton Econometric Model.

1.686   *Tape summary/analysis, plus multi-file copying program.

1.687   *This program is a combined time series analysis and graph plotting system.

System Requirements

1.688   *System requirements: Apple II, II Plus, or IIe; 48K RAM; 1 disk drive.

1.689   *System requirements: Commodore 64; 64K RAM; 1 disk drive; color monitor.

1.690   *System requirements: IBM PC/XT or AT; 256K RAM; PC DOS 2.0 or higher; monitor (color preferable); printer (optional).

1.691   *System requirements: IBM PC/XT, AT or compatible; 256K RAM; PC DOS or MS DOS 2.0 or higher; word processing program or text editor capable of generating and editing ASCII text files; monochrome adapter for 80 column display; 2 360K or 1.2M disk drives or 1 disk drive and 1 hard disk.

1.692   *System requirements: Macintosh; 512K RAM; 1 external disk drive; Apple Personal Modem 1200 or Hayes Smartmodem (optional); Imagewriter printer (optional).

Mode of Use

1.693 *Available only through the University's Computation Center using dial access.

1.694 *Available online through DIALOG.

1.695 *Available through dedicated terminals or online through dial access.

1.696 *Mode of access: Dedicated terminal system, available only through PLATO.

Chapter 10 (Three-Dimensional Artefacts and Realia)

AACR2 RULE

10.7B1 Nature of the item

Give the nature of the item unless it is apparent from the rest of the description.

RELATED AACR2 RULE

None.

LIBRARY OF CONGRESS POLICY

None issued.

RELATED LIBRARY OF CONGRESS POLICY

None issued.

AACR2 TEXT EXAMPLES REVISED TO REFLECT LIBRARY OF CONGRESS POLICY

None required.

HISTORICAL BACKGROUND

Although AACR1 Rev. Ch. 12 and previous codes had no rule equivalent to AACR2 Rule 10.7B1, the nature, scope, and form note provisions for separately published monographs in these earlier codes could be used for three-dimensional artifacts and realia. (See *Historical Background* under Rule 2.7B1.)

NOTE EXAMPLES

Frequently, "nature of the item" aspects will be included as part of a summary note (AACR2 Rule 10.7B17).

1.697 *Designed to increase children's awareness of verbal and non-verbal signals used in the communication process. Teaches and reinforces positive communication skills.

1.698 *Each puzzle board has 10 empty spaces for insertion of word pieces corresponding to the name of the picture shown.

1.699 *A farewell gift to Sir William Wanless.

1.700 *Sections of human livers, showing the effects of cirrhosis due to hepatitis, alcoholism, or glue sniffing. With explanatory information below the specimens.

1.701 *Simulation game of the Allied campaign to capture Sicily in the summer of 1943.

1.702 *System consists of a random access projector, a rear screen projector, slides and a guide.

Chapter 12 (Serials)

AACR2 RULE

12.7B1 Frequency [AACR2 Rev.]

Make notes on the frequency of the serial unless it is apparent from the content of the title and statement of responsibility area or is unknown. Also make notes on changes in frequency. (The examples given here [i.e., in the AACR2 text] do not constitute an exhaustive list.)

RELATED AACR2 RULE

12.2B2 Edition Statement [AACR2 Rev.]

Give statements indicating volume numbering or designation, or chronological coverage (e.g., *1st ed., 1916 ed.)* in the numeric and/or alphabetic, chronological, or other designation area (see 12.3). Give statements indicating regular revision (e.g., *Rev. ed. issued every 6 months*) in the note area. [emphasis added]

LIBRARY OF CONGRESS POLICY

Always make a note on the known frequency of a serial even if the frequency is apparent from the rest of the description. [CSB 21]

RELATED LIBRARY OF CONGRESS POLICY

None issued.

AACR2 TEXT EXAMPLES REVISED TO REFLECT LIBRARY OF CONGRESS POLICY

None required.

HISTORICAL BACKGROUND

AACR1 Rule 167B essentially provided for the same frequency notes as does the AACR2 rule. AACR1, however, allowed this information to be placed in the collation if it was only a brief statement. AACR2 places all frequency statements in the note area, regardless of length. In addition, AACR1 stated the Library of Congress policy establishing when the frequency varies note was to be used, that is, "3 or more variations in frequency." No such policy statement is given in AACR2.

NOTE EXAMPLES

1.703   Issued at least once a year.
1.704   Two no. a year.
1.705   Three no. a year (orientation, fall and spring).
1.706   Four no. from Oct.-May.
1.707   Four no. a year (irregular).
1.708   Five times a school year.
1.709   Ten monthly issues with two semiannual cumulations.
1.710   Daily.
1.711   Biweekly.
1.712   Monthly (during the school year).
1.713   Monthly (except Aug. and Sept.).
1.714   Monthly (except combined Dec.-Jan. issue).
1.715   Bimonthly (with additional summer issue).
1.716   Monthly, with semi-annual cumulations.
1.717   Quarterly (irregular).
1.718   Quarterly, with the last issue being cumulative for the year.
1.719   Every two years.
1.720   Triennial.
1.721   Frequency varies.
1.722   Irregular.

Frequency—Current and Former

1.723   Three no. a year (Sept.-Dec. 1973-May-Aug. 1974), Annual (Jan.-Dec. 1975-<Jan.-Dec. 1976>).
1.724   Six issues yearly (1978-1979), Four issues yearly (spring 1980-<summer 1980>).
1.725   Bimonthly (June 1978-Oct. 1979), Monthly, (Nov. 1979-   ).
1.726   Bimonthly (<Jan./Mar. 1976-June 1976), Semiannual (July 1976-<Dec. 1979>).

1.727 Bimonthly (fall 1976-Apr./May 1980), Quarterly (winter-summer, 1976), Quarterly (summer 1980-   ).

1.728 Monthly (except July and Aug.) (<Sept. 1968>-Jan. 1977), Monthly (except bimonthly June/July and Aug./Sept.) (Feb. 1977-   ).

1.729 Quarterly, 3 issues yearly (<fall-winter 1977-   >).

1.730 Weekly (Oct. 13, 1969-June 22, 1975), Biweekly (June 23, 1975-   ).

1.731 Indexes the tables, graphs, and formatted data presented in the statistical publications of the EIA.

1.7B2. Language of the Item and/or Translation or Adaptation

EXTRAPOLATED GENERAL RULE

Give the language(s) of the item unless it is apparent from the rest of the description.

RELATED AACR2 RULE

Information regarding the language of the title on the title page or its equivalent is covered under the provisions of note .7B5 under each of the chapters for description.

GENERAL LIBRARY OF CONGRESS POLICY

Generally restrict the making of language and script notes to the situations covered in this directive.

(*Note:* In this statement "language" and "language of the item" mean the language or languages of the content of the item (e.g., for books the language of the text); "title data" means title proper and other title information.)

If the language of the item is not clear from the transcription of the title data, make a note naming the language whether or not the language is named after a uniform title.

Use "and" in all cases to link two languages (or the final two when more than two are named). If more than one language is named, give the predominant language first if readily apparent; name the other languages in alphabetical order. If a predominant language is not apparent, name the languages in alphabetical order. For the form of the name of the language, follow *Library of Congress Subject Headings.*

(*Exception:* Use "Greek" for classical Greek and modern Greek. If, however, the item is a translation from classical Greek into modern Greek, use "Modern Greek" in the note. If the item includes text in both, use "Classical Greek" and "Modern Greek" in the note.)

For some "dialects" that cannot be established as subject headings, a specific language will be used in the note area only. (See LCRI 25.5D for the use of language names in uniform titles.) . . .

In addition, record in a note the language of the item being cataloged (whether or not the language is identified in the uniform title or in the body of the entry) in the following cases:

49

1) When the bibliographic record for the item bears one or more of the following symbols in conjunction with the LC control number: AM, HE, NE, SA. (*Exception:* Do not make the note for an item in Arabic, Armenian, Hebrew, Indonesian, modern Turkish, or Vietnamese unless the language is being recorded for another reason.)
2) When the language of the item is indigenous to Africa and is in a roman script.
3) When the language of the item is indigenous to the Philippines.
4) When the language of the item is not primarily written in one script. Name both the language and the script in language notes. (*Note:* Do not add "script" to the name of the script unless the name is also the name of a language.)
4, [i.e., 5]) When the language of the item is written in a script other than the primary one for the language. Name both the language and the script in the language notes. . . .
5, [i.e., 6]) More information may be added to language and script notes whenever the case warrants it. [CSB 35]

There is an unstated policy followed by the Library of Congress that is employed when a record in a nonroman script has been romanized. When the romanization has been done, a note to this effect is provided. This note is worded:

Romanized record.

Only Chapter 2 (Books, etc.) expands the coverage of the language note to include statements about translations and adaptations. There are instances, however, when the Library of Congress appears to use this note to record the existence of the work in another language although that work is not the one being cataloged. This practice by LC does not fall under the provision of Rule .7B16 (Other Formats Available) that limits itself to other "medium or media" differences rather than language or content differences.]

RELATED LIBRARY OF CONGRESS POLICY

None issued.

FORMAT

No instructions for the formatting of language notes have been provided with any of the specific chapters for description nor are there any general instructions that apply to all chapters.

CHAPTER APPLICATION

This note is not present in Chapter 10 (Three-Dimensional Artefacts and Realia).

EXCEPTIONS AND ADDITIONS

Chapter 2 (Books, Pamphlets, and Printed Sheets) expands the use of this rule to include translations or adaptations of a work.

Chapter 4 (Manuscripts) also expands the coverage of this rule to include translations and adaptations.

Chapter 5 (Music) also uses this note to indicate vocal texts published with part of the music.

Chapter 6 (Sound Recordings) uses this note to comment on the language used in the audio format.

Chapter 7 (Motion Pictures and Videorecordings) employs this note to comment on languages used on either an audio or textual format.

Chapter 8 (Graphic Materials) employs this note to comment on languages used on either audio or textual format.

Chapter 9 (Computer Files, AACR2 Rev.) expands the coverage of this note to include an indication of the script used.

Chapter 2 (Books, Pamphlets, and Printed Sheets)

AACR2 RULE

2.7B2 Language of Item and/or Translation or Adaptation [AACR2 Rev.]

Make notes on the languages of the item, or on the fact that it is a translation or adaptation, unless this is apparent from the rest of the description.

In this chapter, the coverage of the note is expanded to include the indication that the work is a translation or adaptation. Although the rule deals with "adaptations," this term is not directly defined anywhere in AACR2. A definition is provided for "adaptation (music)" but this definition is not germane to Chapter 2. A form of definition is provided in AACR2 Rule 21.10 where the provisions for the access points for adaptations are provided. This rule refers to a "paraphrase, rewriting, adaptation for children, or version in a different literary form (e.g., novelization, dramatization)." It is for these types of works that examples for adaptations have been provided.

51

RELATED AACR2 RULE

None.

LIBRARY OF CONGRESS POLICY

None issued.

RELATED LIBRARY OF CONGRESS POLICY

The Library of Congress Rule Interpretation for AACR2 Rule 2.7B18 [CSB 25] indicates that a contents note is given when a publication contains items of importance that require stressing. In giving a listing of some of these situations, summaries in languages other than that of the text are included. Thus, this type of note could be considered an informal contents note rather than as a language of the item note.]

AACR2 TEXT EXAMPLES REVISED TO REFLECT LIBRARY OF CONGRESS POLICY

None required.

HISTORICAL BACKGROUND

AACR1 Rev. Rule 143D3b required a language note if the language was not "unmistakably indicated by the wording of the title page."

AACR1 Rev. Rule 143D2a provided for a note to record the original title of a translated work unless it had been given in the title and statement of responsibility area or had been given in a uniform title preceding the title page title.

AACR1 Rev. had no rule that specifically addressed adaptations, although AACR1 Rev. Rule 143D4a provided for a note identifying the author or editor of later editions if there was a change in responsibility.

These AACR1 Rev. Ch. 6 rules could be used for works that were not separately published monographs unless specific rules for the description of a format superseded or excluded their use.

The note order used in AACR1 Rev. varied somewhat from that of AACR2. AACR2 uses this note as the second in order of priority while AACR1 Rev. had the original title note (Rev. Rule 143D2a) second in priority and the language note later. AACR2 currently places all this information in one note.

NOTE EXAMPLES

Language(s)

2.1 In Church Slavic.
2.2 In German of ca. 1400.
2.3 In Hindi.
2.4 In Santali (01).
2.5 In Serbo-Croatian (Cyrillic).
2.6 In Serbo Croatian (Roman).
2.7 In Macedonian, Serbo-Croatian (Cyrillic), Serbo-Croatian (Roman) or Slovenian.
2.8 Aztec and Spanish.
2.9 Dutch and Papiamento.
2.10 French and Senufo.
2.11 South American Indian languages and Spanish.
2.12 English, French, and Sango.
2.13 Danish, Dutch, English, French, German, and Italian.
2.14 "Original espanol."
2.15 "English-French, French-English."
2.16 Text in Chinese.
2.17 Text in English and Spanish.
2.18 Includes text in French.
2.19 Part of text in English.
2.20 Text in German, Latin, and Romansh.
2.21 French with some English and Italian.
2.22 English and/or Norwegian.
2.23 Dutch, English, and/or Spanish.
2.24 Afrikaans or Dutch.
2.25 Latin or Swedish.
2.26 Middle High German or Latin.
2.27 Bulgarian, English, French, German, Russian, or Spanish.
2.28 Text also in English and French.
2.29 Text partly in English and German.
2.30 Includes text in Italian and Latin.
2.31 An author-title catalog, in 2 main sections: Western works (mostly English) listed in the language of the work; Japanese, Chinese and Korean works, listed in Japanese.
2.32 The introductory vol., in Catalan and Spanish, includes a transcription and a Spanish translation of the ms. text. The introduction proper includes bibliographical references.
2.33 Polyglot.
2.34 In various languages.
2.35 In various languages with annotations in Czech.
2.36 Texts by various authors in English, French, German, or Italian.
2.37 German text, parallel English translation.
2.38 Lepcha text, parallel Hindi translation.
2.39 Parallel Latin text and English translation.

2.40   English text and German translation on facing pages.
2.41   Text in Greek and English on opposite pages; commentary in English.
2.42   Romanian text with Latin and Cyrillic alphabet on opposite pages.

Language of a Part

2.43   Bâton's Mémoire is in English translation.
2.44   Abstracts in English.
2.45   One article in Kalmyk.
2.46   Includes articles in English and French.
2.47   Caption titles in English, French, Russian, and Spanish.
2.48   Captions in English, French, and German.
2.49   Captions translated into English.
2.50   Includes citations in Greek.
2.51   Includes citations in French and Italian.
2.52   Commentary volume, by Hermann Knaus, in German; includes bibliographical references.
2.53   Contributions chiefly in German, with 3 in French and 1 in Italian.
2.54   Four contributions in English.
2.55   Documents (p. 441-524) chiefly in Italian and Latin.
2.56   Documents in English, German, and Hebrew.
2.57   Includes documents in Catalan, Latin, and Spanish.
2.58   Includes excerpts from related legislation in French, and in Danish, Dutch, English, and Italian with German translation.
2.59   Foreword also in Esperanto.
2.60   Glossary in English, Finnish, and Russian.
2.61   Introduction and annotations of documents in Serbo-Croatian (Cyrillic); documents in Italian or Latin.
2.62   Introduction in English and Russian.
2.63   Introd. and commentary in English, text in English and Italian.
2.64   Introd. and summaries also in English and French.
2.65   Introductory material in English.
2.66   Introductory material in English and French.
2.67   Legends also in English.
2.68   Legends to photos. in Dutch, English, and French.
2.69   Includes German translation of libretto.
2.70   List of illustrations in English and Russian.
2.71   List of illustrations also in English, French, and German.
2.72   Mss. in English, German, and Latin.
2.73   Includes 2 papers in French.
2.74   Poem in English.
2.75   Poems in Calabrian dialect and Italian.
2.76   Includes poems in Sinhalese.
2.77   Pref. in English.
2.78   Pref. in English, German, and Hebrew.
2.79   Pref. also in Hebrew.

2.80   Preface in English; introd. and text in German.
2.81   Prefatory matter in English and French; text in English.
2.82   Song texts in Arabic with English translations: p. 74-84.
2.83   Includes song texts in English and German translations of Greek and Chilean folksongs.
2.84   Table of contents in Romanian, English, and Russian.
2.85   Table of contents also in Russian.
2.86   Tables of contents, figures, and tables also in English; summaries in English.
2.87   Text of the Constitution also in Basque, Catalan, Gallegan.
2.88   Vol. 3: English and Portuguese.

Language of the Work and a Part

2.89   Text of the convention in English, French, Russian, and Spanish; other text in English, French, German, and Italian.
2.90   English or French with some materials in both languages.
2.91   In Sanskrit; critical apparatus in English.
2.92   Text in German with examples in Bulgarian and various other languages.
2.93   Basic text in Khanty with German and Hungarian translation; introd. and commentaries in German and Hungarian.
2.94   English, French, and German with introduction in Italian, Dutch, and Spanish.
2.95   English and Syriac; introductory matter in English.
2.96   Text in Latin, introd. and notes in English.
2.97   Text in English, notes in Hebrew.
2.98   Latin and Italian; includes passages in Greek.
2.99   In Gujarati; includes quotations in English, Bengali (Gujarati script), and Hindi (Gujarati script).
2.100   Text in English, notes and responsa supplement in Hebrew.
2.101   Text in Korean with summary in English.
2.102   Original Arabic, Persian, and Turkish texts with translation and commentary in French.
2.103   In Kawi (Roman); translation and critical apparatus in English.
2.104   Some text and captions also in English and French.

Translation

2.105   "Authorized translation."
2.106   Translated from the manuscript.
2.107   Translated sections from various sources.

Translation—Language of the Original

2.108   Translated from the author's manuscript in French.
2.109   Translated from the French.
2.110   Translated from the original Greek.
2.111   Translated in part from German, Russian and Slovak.

2.112   A translation, probably from the Latin.
2.113   Translation made from Corderius' Greek text.
2.114   Parts of text translated from the Dutch.
2.115   Preface translated from the Russian.
2.116   "Translated from Latin, French, and the various dialects of Middle English"—Pref.
2.117   Letters translated from their original English, with the exception of those addressed to Nicolás T. Bernal, Mexico.

Translation—Title of the Original

2.118   Translation of: Abingdon Bible handbook.
2.119   Translation of: La marine dans l'Antiquité.
2.120   Translation of: Saints and survival.
2.121   Translation of: Briefe. Bd. 1. Karl Barth-Rudolf Bultmann Briefwechsel, 1922-1966.
2.122   Translation of: Beiträge zur Ethik, pt. 1 of Ethik und Ekkesiologie.
2.123   Translation of Summa theologica, pars 1, quaestio 75-88.
2.124   Translation of: Die Weltkirche im 20. Jahrhundert.
2.125   Translation of: Chung-kuo tai cheng chih te shih. Rev. ed. 1955.
2.126   Translation of: Saint Jean de la Croix. 1979.
2.127   "Originally published in Germany in a translation under the title, Das waren die Klaars"—T.p. verso.
2.128   First essay, translation of: Du contrat social. Second essay, translation of: Discours sur l'economie politique. Second essay preceded by the pref. to: Discours sur l'origine et les fondements de l'inégalité parmi les hommes.
2.129   Translation of the poem Skilmálarnir from the Icelandic text published in: Icelandic lyrics : originals and translations / Richard Beck. Reykjavik, 1956.
2.130   Translation of two works: Die christliche Lehre nach dem Heidelberger Katechismus and Einführung in den Heidelberger Katechismus.
2.131   Translation of: Guillaume Apollinaires fantastiska liv, perhaps from an unpublished version. The Swedish version published in 1971 by Wahlströom & Widstrand, Stockholm, differs substantially from this translation.

Translation—Modified Texts

2.132   Abridged translation of v. 1 of: Englische Geschichte im achtzehnten Jahrhundert.
2.133   Abridgement and translation of Political imprisonment in the People's Republic of China.
2.134   Expanded translation of: Mies van der Rohe, Lehre und Schule.
2.135   Revised translation of: Atlas de histología normal.
2.136   Revised translation of: Bussei; part 1. rev. 2nd ed.
2.137   Revised and updated translation of: Geochemie uhlí.
2.138   Updated translation of: Die roten Handelsflotten.

Adaptations

2.139 Adapted from: Avventure di Pinocchio.

2.140 Adapted from: Ants and their world / by Satoshi Kuribayashi, originally published under title: Ari no sekai.

2.141 Adapted from Vision '80s published in The journal of typographic information.

2.142 Adapted from the author's Monkey face.

2.143 An adaptation of Snow White and the seven dwarfs.

2.144 Adaptation of: The French lieutenant's woman / by John Fowles.

2.145 Adaptation of: The wind in the willows / Kenneth Grahame.

2.146 Based on a translation of Vergleichende Verhaltensforschung, with revisions.

2.147 Based on: La Tosca / Victorien Sardou.

2.148 Based on the novel by L. Frank Baum.

2.149 Based on a program of the same name in the television series The world of survival.

2.150 "Based on a story by Steven McGraw and a screenplay by Steven McGraw and Janet Ward"—Verso t.p.

2.151 Based on a television program named Världen i fokus.

2.152 Based on the Brooksfilms/Twentieth Century Fox motion picture of the same title.

2.153 An imitation of: The tour of Doctor Syntax in search of the picturesque / William Combe ; aquatints by Thomas Rowlandson.

2.154 "The dictionary here offered is a translation into English and complete re-arrangement of R. van Eck's Eerste proeve van enn Balineesch-Hollandsch Woordenboek (Utrecht, 1876), supplemented from other sources"—Pref.

Chapter 3 (Cartographic Materials)

AACR2 RULE

3.7B2 Language [AACR2 Rev.]

Give the language(s) of captions, etc., and text unless this is apparent from the rest of the description.

RELATED AACR2 RULE

None.

LIBRARY OF CONGRESS POLICY

None issued.

RELATED LIBRARY OF CONGRESS POLICY

None issued.

AACR2 TEXT EXAMPLES REVISED TO REFLECT LIBRARY OF CONGRESS POLICY

2nd Example

AACR2 TEXT
Includes text in Finnish, Swedish, English, and German

AACR2 TEXT REVISED
Includes text in English, Finnish, German, and Swedish

4th Example

AACR2 TEXT
Legend in English and Afrikaans

AACR2 TEXT REVISED
Legend in Afrikaans and English

The language order has been changed to reflect alphabetical order assuming that no predominant language was apparent.

HISTORICAL BACKGROUND

AACR1 Rule 212E6 did not specifically address the issue of language of the text, but instead provided for a note to "clarify an indefinite or misleading title and to point out unusual features of the map." However, examples provided with this rule in AACR1 illustrate its use to indicate the language of the work.

NOTE EXAMPLES

2.155   English and Afrikaans.
2.156   French and Polish.
2.157   English, French, German, Portuguese, and Spanish.

Captions, etc.

2.158   Cover title and legend in Italian, English, French, and German.
2.159   Index place names in English, Finnish, German, Russian, and Swedish.
2.160   Legend in English and Arabic.
2.161   Legends in English, French, and German.

2.162   Notes in French, English, German, Italian, and Spanish.
2.163   Panel title and legend in German, Russian, English, and French.
2.164   Place names on maps in Finnish and Swedish.
2.165   Includes pronunciation table in German, French, and English.
2.166   Publication statement in English and Welsh.

Text

2.167   Text in English, Spanish, and Hebrew.
2.168   Text in Italian, French, English, and German, street index, directory of points of interest, and map of Tuscany on verso.
2.169   Place names in English and romanized Korean. Text in English.
2.170   Title and text in English. Place names in romanized Korean and English.
2.171   Legend and glossary in English, German, French, and Italian. Text and motoring information in German, French, and English.
2.172   Legend in Spanish, French, German, and English. Headings and text in German, French, and Spanish.

Chapter 4 (Manuscripts)

AACR2 RULE

4.7B2 Language [AACR2 Rev.]

Make notes on the language(s) of the item, or on the fact that it is a translation or adaptation, unless this is apparent from the rest of the description.

RELATED AACR2 RULE

None.

LIBRARY OF CONGRESS POLICY

None issued. APPM, however, expands on the AACR2 text.

Language(s)

Give the language or languages of the material being described, unless they are noted elsewhere or are apparent from other elements of the description.

Also note any distinctive alphabets or symbol systems employed. [APPM 4.7B6]

RELATED LIBRARY OF CONGRESS POLICY

None issued.

AACR2 TEXT EXAMPLES REVISED TO REFLECT LIBRARY OF CONGRESS POLICY

None required.

HISTORICAL BACKGROUND

AACR1 Rule 201B2 for ancient, medieval and Renaissance manuscripts, recorded, following the title, the language of the text "when not indicated by the title." AACR2 has moved this information to the note area. AACR2 Rev. added the instruction to note translations or adaptations. AACR1 did not provide for this.

For manuscripts other than ancient, medieval and Renaissance, AACR1 and previous codes applied the language note provisions for separately published monographs. (See *Historical Background* under Rule 2.7B2.)

NOTE EXAMPLES

Language(s)

2.173 *In German.
2.174 In German or English.
2.175 *Written in German.

Language(s) Qualified

2.176 *In cursive Spanish.
2.177 *In Russian longhand.
2.178 *Note by H.G. Wells in English; Letter by Vincent d'Indy in French.
2.179 *Portions of some letters are in French.
2.180 *Text in incorrect German and phonetically spelled English.

Chapter 5 (Music)

AACR2 RULE

5.7B2 Language [AACR2 Rev.]

Language of the Text
    Give the language(s) of the textual content of the work unless this is apparent from the rest of the description.

Text with Partial Music
    Indicate vocal texts published with part of the music.

In Chapter 5, "text" refers only to the words set to music and any translation of those words. Textual matter such as prefaces, performance instructions, historical notes, etc., are considered material accompanying the score, and therefore should be described in a note under AACR2 Rule 5.7B11 as accompanying material.

RELATED AACR2 RULE

None.

LIBRARY OF CONGRESS POLICY

None issued.

RELATED LIBRARY OF CONGRESS POLICY

None issued.

AACR2 TEXT EXAMPLES REVISED TO REFLECT LIBRARY OF CONGRESS POLICY

None required.

HISTORICAL BACKGROUND

AACR1 Rule 248C provided for notes on the text, language, etc., of music scores.

AACR1 Rule 248C1 allowed the cataloger to combine this note with the medium of performance note if so desired. The AACR2 rule does not specifically state this; however, AACR2 Rule 1.7A5 allows for notes to be combined when appropriate.

AACR1 Rule 248C1 also stated that the language of the text should be given if it differs from that on the title page. AACR2 has changed this wording, but the intent of the rule is essentially the same.

AACR1 Rule 248C1 further stated that the languages should be given "in the order in which they appear in the work." No order for recording multiple languages is specified in AACR2 although LC has done so.

AACR1 Rule 248C2 stated that, if the text was printed on preliminary pages as well as with the music, this should not be mentioned unless "the edition is one that might be used for the sake of the text." The AACR1 text examples indicate that this rule did not refer to translations of the text, but rather to texts printed in the same language as the underlaid text. AACR2 does not address this issue explicitly, but AACR2 text examples imply that this practice is still applicable.

AACR1 Rule 248C3 called for the use of a note when vocal works were published without a text, when the text was published with only part of the music, or when arbitrary syllables were used as text. Although AACR2 seems to have narrowed the scope of this rule, the AACR2 text examples, as well as Library of Congress cataloging, indicate that all of these earlier applications are still being used.

AACR1 Rule 248C4 provided for a note naming the author or source of the text. AACR2 has moved this information to AACR2 Rule 5.7B6, the statement of responsibility note.

The note order used for these AACR1 notes varied somewhat from that which is used in AACR2. AACR2 places this note second in order or priority while AACR1 had the species note (Rule 248A) second in priority and the language note later.

NOTE EXAMPLES

Language of Texts

2.181   Includes words.
2.182   With the words.
2.183   English words.
2.184   Catalan or Latin words.
2.185   English and Latin words.
2.186   The 5th and 6th songs include Welsh words.
2.187   Includes French words spoken by the ensemble.
2.188   In Hindi (Bengali script), with explanatory notes in Bengali.
2.189   In part with Latin, French, Italian, or Spanish words.
2.190   Principally Catalan or Spanish words.
2.191   Principally German words, with sections in Hebrew (romanized) and Latin.
2.192   Settings of the Magnificat in Hebrew (1st movement) and Greek (last movement).
2.193   Sung on vowel sound ah.
2.194   Text of liturgy in church Slavic.
2.195   Transliterated Hebrew words.
2.196   Romanized words underlaid; also printed in Hebrew alphabet as texts with English translations, p. 2-18.
2.197   Words are in late Ancient Greek written in the style of Anakreon; English words printed as text on p. 1.
2.198   Words in English, German, French, and other languages.
2.199   Words in various languages.
2.200   English words; without the dialogue.
2.201   First line of text: Painters all of ev'ry station.
2.202   In part French words; in part wordless.
2.203   "Sung in French and recited in English (in retrograde motion)."

Words as Text

2.204   Words printed as text (p. 6-7).
2.205   Words printed as text on p. [2].
2.206   Words also printed as text on p. vi-x.
2.207   English words printed as text: p. [2-3].
2.208   German words, also printed as text: p. [70]-[71].
2.209   Words printed as text on 3rd prelim. page.

Original Text

2.210   English words, most include original German texts.
2.211   Text originally in Lithuanian.

Translations

2.212   Italian words; English translation: p. 2.
2.213   Italian words; words also printed as text with English translation on p. [3].
2.214   Latin words, also printed as text with German translation: p. [4].
2.215   English translations printed at end of each work.
2.216   English translations of the Latin text: p. vii-viii.
2.217   English translation of the French words printed as text on p. [2].
2.218   Italian words with non-singing English translation underlaid.
2.219   *Words, by various authors, in English, French, Latin, Polish, or Spanish; partially printed as text with Polish translations (p. [4-5]).
2.220   Words printed as romanized texts with English translation ([2] p.).

Chapter 6 (Sound Recordings)

AACR2 RULE

6.7B2 Language [AACR2 Rev.]
Give the language(s) of the spoken or sung content of a recording unless this is apparent from the rest of the description.

This rule does not specifically include any requirement to record the language of any textual material accompanying the sound recording. Language notes for these materials are covered under the provisions for notes dealing with accompanying material (AACR2 Rule 6.7B11).

It should be cautioned that for all items covered by this chapter the cataloger may actually have to listen to the item in order to detect the use of different languages that are not evident from the language of the title or other written documentation.

RELATED AACR2 RULE

None.

LIBRARY OF CONGRESS POLICY

None issued.

RELATED LIBRARY OF CONGRESS POLICY

None issued.

AACR2 TEXT EXAMPLES REVISED TO REFLECT LIBRARY OF CONGRESS POLICY

None required.

HISTORICAL BACKGROUND

AACR1 Rev. Rule 252F5 provided for a note identifying the language of the performance if it was not apparent from the uniform or transcribed titles. The AACR2 rule both broadens and narrows the sources from which a language can be apparent. It instructs that this note not be made if the language is apparent from the rest of the description, rather than limiting its use to languages apparent only in the transcribed titles. In most cases, though, titles are the source that would indicate language so the rules are essentially the same in practice. AACR2, unlike AACR1, does not allow the language to be apparent from the uniform title. AACR2 also provides some additional clarity by specifically including content that is either spoken or sung.

The AACR1 rule also provided for notes naming the author of the text if necessary. AACR2 has moved this information to AACR2 Rule 6.7B6, the statement of responsibility note.

The note order used for these AACR1 Rev. notes varied somewhat from that used in AACR2. AACR2 places this note as the second in order of priority while AACR1 Rev. had the source of title note (252F2) second in priority and the language note later.

NOTE EXAMPLES

2.221   In French.
2.222   Sung in Breton.
2.223   Sung in Italian, French, or English.
2.224   Sung in the original languages.
2.225   Sung principally in Latin; several sections sung in medieval French and German.
2.226   The 4th work sung in Basque.

2.227   Read in Middle English by Prunella Scales and Richard Bebb ; directed by Derek Brewer.

Chapter 7 (Motion Pictures and Videorecordings)

AACR2 RULE

7.7B2 Language [AACR2 Rev.]
Give the language(s) of the spoken, sung, or written content of a motion picture or videorecording unless this is apparent from the rest of the description.

Virtually all formats in which language can be presented with motion pictures and videorecordings are covered by this note. There are, however, some 8 mm. film loops that have their sound on accompanying material. While Chapter 8 (Graphic Materials) contains specific recommendations to record the language of accompanying recorded sound in a language note, the language note in this chapter does not include a similar recommendation.

It is not clear from this rule whether the written content referred to in the note deals only with written content on the medium itself, that is, subtitles or captions, or also written content associated with accompanying material.

It should be cautioned that for all items covered by this chapter, a cataloger may have to view and/or listen to the item or its accompanying material in order to detect the use of languages on the audio/video portion that are not evident from the language of the title or other written documentation.

RELATED AACR2 RULE

None.

LIBRARY OF CONGRESS POLICY

If the videorecording incorporates closed-captioning for the hearing impaired, make the following note:

Closed-captioned for the hearing impaired.   [CSB 32]

For archival moving image materials, the Library of Congress supplements AACR2 Chapter 7 with the guidelines in *Archival Moving Image Materials* by White-Hensen.

RELATED LIBRARY OF CONGRESS POLICY

None issued.

AACR2 TEXT EXAMPLES REVISED TO REFLECT
LIBRARY OF CONGRESS POLICY

None required.

HISTORICAL BACKGROUND

Although AACR1 Rev. Ch. 12 and previous codes had no rule equivalent to AACR2 Rule 7.7B2, the language note provisions for separately published monographs in these earlier codes could be used for motion pictures and videorecordings. (See *Historical Background* under Rule 2.7B2.)

NOTE EXAMPLES

Spoken
2.228   In English and Spanish.
2.229   English version of the film of the same title.

Spoken and Written
2.230   In Hungarian with English subtitles.
2.231   Spanish dialogue, English subtitles.

Chapter 8 (Graphic Materials)

AACR2 RULE

8.7B2 Language [AACR2 Rev.]
> Give the language(s) of the spoken or written content of a graphic item and its accompanying sound unless this is apparent from the rest of the description.

The distinction between the spoken language and the language of the accompanying sound is based on whether the sound is considered to be integral, that is, located on the graphic medium. In most cases, materials covered by Chapter 8 do not have sound that is integral. Therefore, most notes developed from this chapter that address the language of the audio component are referring to the sound on the accompanying material. Although this note deals with the accompanying material, it is considered a language note, not an accompanying material note (AACR2 Rule 8.7B11).

For items such as filmstrips and slides, the language of written material usually refers to accompanying written material, although it can also apply to captions on the graphic item.

It should be cautioned that for all items covered by this chapter, a cataloger may have to view and/or listen to the item or its accompanying material in order to detect the use of languages on the audio/video portion that are not evident from the language of the title or other written documentation.

RELATED AACR2 RULE

None.

LIBRARY OF CONGRESS POLICY

None issued. For original items and historical collections, the Library of Congress supplements AACR2 Chapter 8 with the guidelines in *Graphic Materials* by Betz.

RELATED LIBRARY OF CONGRESS POLICY

None issued.

AACR2 TEXT EXAMPLES REVISED TO REFLECT LIBRARY OF CONGRESS POLICY

2nd Example

AACR2 TEXT
Sound tape in Spanish and English

AACR2 TEXT REVISED
Sound tape in English and Spanish

The language order has been changed to reflect alphabetical order assuming that no predominant language was apparent.

HISTORICAL BACKGROUND

Although AACR1 Rev. Ch. 12, AACR1 Ch. 15, and previous codes had no rule equivalent to AACR2 Rule 8.7B2, the language note provisions for separately published monographs in these earlier codes could be used for graphic materials. (See *Historical Background* under Rule 2.7B2.)

NOTE EXAMPLES

Projection and Nonprojection Graphic Materials

SPOKEN CONTENT (INCLUDING ACCOMPANYING SOUND)
2.232   Narration in German.
2.233   In English and French.

WRITTEN CONTENT
2.234   Booklet in English, French, German, Russian, and Spanish.
2.235   Booklets in English, French, and Serbo-Croatian (Cyrillic).
2.236   With script in English and French.
2.237   With script in English and Spanish.
2.238   With teacher's manual in French and English.
2.239   The introductory sheet has identical information in English on one side and in Hebrew on the other.
2.240   Texts of the prints are in various languages, by various authors.

Chapter 9 (Computer Files)

AACR2 RULE

9.7B2 Language and Script [AACR2 Rev.]

Give the language(s) and/or script(s) of the spoken or written content of a file unless this is apparent from the rest of the description. . . .

Record the programming language as part of the system requirements note (see 9.7B1b).

RELATED AACR2 RULE

9.7B1 Nature and Scope and System Requirements [AACR2 Rev.]

b) *System requirements*

Make a note on the system requirements of the file if the information is readily available.

Begin the note with *System requirements:*. Give the following characteristics in the order in which they are listed below. Precede each characteristic, other than the first, by a semicolon.

the make and model of the computer(s) on which the file is designed to run
the amount of memory required
the name of the operating system
the software requirements (including the programming language)
the kind and characteristics of any required or recommended peripherals. [emphasis added]

68

LIBRARY OF CONGRESS POLICY

None issued for AACR2 Rev. Ch. 9.

RELATED LIBRARY OF CONGRESS POLICY

None issued for AACR2 Rev. Ch. 9.

AACR2 TEXT EXAMPLES REVISED TO REFLECT LIBRARY OF CONGRESS POLICY

None required for AACR2 Rev. Ch. 9.

HISTORICAL BACKGROUND

Computer files were not covered by AACR1 or previous codes. The original AACR2 Chapter 9 covered the elements present in this revised rule and also provided for recording the type of characters used if they were not apparent from the rest of the description. No specific statement was made in the original rule to exclude recording the programming language as is done in the revised rule.

NOTE EXAMPLES

Language(s)
2.241   *In Castilian.
2.242   *In French.

Script(s)
2.243   *Faithful transcription in Waterloo Script.
2.244   *Semi-paleographic transcription of original 13th cent. ms. (MS h. I. 15) housed in Biblioteca de El Escorial.

Chapter 12 (Serials)

AACR2 RULE

12.7B2 Language [AACR2 Rev.]
Make notes on the language(s) of the serial unless this is apparent from the rest of the description.

RELATED AACR2 RULE

None.

LIBRARY OF CONGRESS POLICY

None issued.

RELATED LIBRARY OF CONGRESS POLICY

None issued.

AACR2 TEXT EXAMPLES REVISED TO REFLECT LIBRARY OF CONGRESS POLICY

1st example

AACR2 TEXT
Text in French and English

AACR2 TEXT REVISED
Text in English and French

The language order has been revised to reflect alphabetical order assuming that no predominant language was apparent.

HISTORICAL BACKGROUND

Although AACR1 and previous codes had no rule equivalent to AACR2 Rule 12.7B2, the language note provisions for separately published monographs in these earlier codes could be used for serials. (See *Historical Background* under Rule 2.7B2.)

NOTE EXAMPLES

2.245   In Italian.
2.246   Chinese and English.
2.247   English and Russian.
2.248   English, French, and Spanish.
2.249   Danish, Dutch, English, French, German, and Italian.
2.250   English or Hebrew.
2.251   In English, French, and German.
2.252   Chiefly English; some Kannada.
2.253   Multilingual, with English translations.
2.254   Text in English and Portuguese.

Part or Section in Other Language(s)

2.255   Added title page in Latin.
2.256   Summaries in English.

2.257 Summaries in French, German, and Italian.

2.258 In French with summaries in Serbo-Croatian.

2.259 In English with summaries in French, German, Portuguese, and Spanish.

2.260 Catalan, summaries in English and Spanish.

2.261 Italian with English summaries.

2.262 Text in German; added article titles and some summaries in English.

2.263 Text in Swedish; English summaries.

2.264 Text in English, French, Spanish and Portuguese. Abstracts in English and Spanish.

2.265 Text in English or French; summaries in both languages.

1.7B3. Source of Title Proper

EXTRAPOLATED GENERAL RULE

Make notes on the source of the title proper if it is other than the chief source of information.

RELATED AACR2 RULE

1.0A2 Items Lacking a Chief Source of Information [AACR2 Rev.]

If no part of the item supplies data that can be used as the basis of the description, take the necessary information from any available source, whether this be a reference work or the content of the item itself. This technique may be necessary for printed works, the title pages of which are lost; collections of pamphlets or other minor material assembled by the library or by a previous owner and that are to be catalogued as a single item; nonprocessed sound recordings, etc. In all such cases give in a note the reason for and/or source of the supplied data. [emphasis added]

1.1B1 Title Proper [AACR2 Rev.]

Due to its length this rule has been abridged to include only the part related to the use of notes.

If the title proper is not taken from the chief source of information, give the source of the title in a note (see 1.7B3). [emphasis added]

GENERAL LIBRARY OF CONGRESS POLICY

None issued. See the separate sections that follow for any Library of Congress policies that apply to individual AACR2 chapters for description.

RELATED LIBRARY OF CONGRESS POLICY

1.1G2 Items without a Collective Title

Due to its length, this LC policy statement has been abridged to include only the part related to the use of notes.

Multiple Sources

If there is no single chief source of information for a single part item and it is not possible to say which work is first, second, etc., transcribe them in English alphabetical order.

For materials such as books that normally confine the source for the title and statement of responsibility area to one location within the item, make a note to explain the situation when there is no single chief source for the single part item (e.g., "No collective t.p. Titles transcribed from individual title pages."). [emphasis added] [CSB 25]

FORMAT

None prescribed. Although no particular format is prescribed for this note, the Library of Congress uses one of several constructs:

1. A statement indicating the title used, e.g.,

   Cover title.
   Running title.

2. A "title from" statement, identifying the location of the title from within the work, e.g.,

   Title from . . .

3. A statement that the title or all the cataloging was derived from a source not a part of the item. This statement generally follows the "title from" format or uses a more detailed sentence structure. This note is especially common for certain audiovisual materials that have been cataloged from data sheets.
4. A combination of this note with other notes. When this dual note practice is used the source of title information is frequently given last.

CHAPTER APPLICATION

This note is present in all chapters for description. Although present in all chapters, its use is more common for print formats (i.e., books, maps, atlases, manuscripts, serials) than it is for audiovisual materials. These latter items are seldom issued without a title unless they are locally prepared single copies, or naturally occurring objects or manufactured realia not designed for communication and have more broadly defined chief sources of information.

EXCEPTIONS AND ADDITIONS

Chapter 9 (Computer Files, AACR2 Rev.) prescribes the use of this note for all catalog records regardless of whether the title was derived from a prescribed source of information for Area 1.

Chapter 2 (Books, Pamphlets, and Printed Sheets)

AACR2 RULE

2.7B3 Source of Title Proper
> Make notes on the source of the title proper if it is other than the chief source of information.

RELATED AACR2 RULE

2.1B1 Title Proper [AACR2 Rev.]
> Transcribe the title proper as instructed in 1.1B. . . .
> If the title proper is not taken from the title page, give the source of the title in a note (see 2.7B3). [emphasis added]

LIBRARY OF CONGRESS POLICY

None issued.

RELATED LIBRARY OF CONGRESS POLICY

None issued.

AACR2 TEXT EXAMPLES REVISED TO REFLECT LIBRARY OF CONGRESS POLICY

None required.

HISTORICAL BACKGROUND

AACR1 Rev. Rule 143D3a, while not specifically addressing the issue of the source of the title proper, did specify an order to the notes that refer to elements of the formalized description. The first of these elements, for "Title proper," gave an example of a note indicating the source of a title.

This AACR1 Rev. Ch. 6 rule could be used for works that were not separately published monographs unless specific rules for the description of a format superseded or excluded its use.

NOTE EXAMPLES

3.1   Cataloged from t.p. of catalog.
3.2   Caption title.

3.3   Title from case.
3.4   Title from colophon of the facsim. volume.
3.5   Title from the commentary volume.
3.6   Cover title.
3.7   Title, etc., from inside of lower cover.
3.8   Title from p. [2] of cover.
3.9   Title from covering leaf in ms.
3.10   Title from graphic representation of "fs" on cover.
3.11   Title from introductory volume.
3.12   Title, etc., from label on recto of lower cover.
3.13   Title from portfolio.
3.14   Title, etc., from publisher's label pasted to the inside of lower cover.
3.15   Title from first line of poem.
3.16   Title extracted from statement on p. [1]: John C. Tarr wrote the following poem for Beatrice Warde upon her departure from England for the United States in 1942. Mrs. Warde returned to England in March 1944.
3.17   Title from Sotheby sale cat. (Mar. 2-9, 1937) of the library of W.E. Moss, lot 267.

Combined with Other Notes
3.18   Title from inside of lower cover; on spine: Wenzelsbibel 2, Leviticus, Numeri.
3.19   Title from v. 2, which reads: Samuel Palmer's sketch-book, 1824 : an introduction and commentary / by Martin Butlin ; with a preface by Geoffrey Keynes.
3.20   Almanacs for Mexico City and Puebla, published in one or the other of those cities by various publishers. Title supplied by LC.

Chapter 3 (Cartographic Materials)

AACR2 RULE

3.7B3 Source of Title Proper
    Make notes on the source of the title proper if it is other than the chief source of information.

RELATED AACR2 RULE

3.1B1 Title Proper [AACR2 Rev.]
    Transcribe the title proper as instructed in 1.1B. . . .
    If the title proper is not taken from the chief source of information, give the source of the title in a note (see 3.7B3). [emphasis added]

LIBRARY OF CONGRESS POLICY

None issued.

RELATED LIBRARY OF CONGRESS POLICY

None issued.

AACR2 TEXT EXAMPLES REVISED TO REFLECT LIBRARY OF CONGRESS POLICY

None required.

HISTORICAL BACKGROUND

AACR1 Rule 212E2 provided for the indication of the source of the title and variant titles as the second possible note.

NOTE EXAMPLES

3.21   Cover title.
3.22   Ms. cover title.
3.23   Title from cover, p. 2.
3.24   Title from cover of 1980 ed.
3.25   Title from index cover.
3.26   Title from label on cover.
3.27   Title from leaf 1.
3.28   Title from maps.
3.29   Panel title.
3.30   Title from portfolio cover.
3.31   *Title from producer's catalog: Decorative map of Spain.
3.32   Title derived from publisher's catalog.
3.33   Running title.
3.34   Title from sheet no. 1.
3.35   Title from slip case.

Chapter 4 (Manuscripts)

AACR2 RULE

4.7B3 Source of Title Proper

Make notes on the source of the title proper if it is other than the chief source of information.

RELATED AACR2 RULE

4.1B Title Proper [AACR2 Rev.]

4.1B1 Transcribe the title proper as instructed in 1.1B. . . .

If the title proper is not taken from the chief source of information, give the source of the title in a note (see 4.7B3). [emphasis added]

4.1B2 If a manuscript or manuscript collection lacks a title, supply one as instructed below. Give the source of a supplied title (other than one composed by the cataloguer) in the note area (see 4.7B3). [emphasis added]

LIBRARY OF CONGRESS POLICY

None issued. APPM, however, expands on the AACR2 text.

Title Transcription/Source

Make a note if the title has been transcribed rather than supplied. Give the source of the title if desired. (APPM 4.7B15)

RELATED LIBRARY OF CONGRESS POLICY

None issued.

AACR2 TEXT EXAMPLES REVISED TO REFLECT LIBRARY OF CONGRESS POLICY

None required.

HISTORICAL BACKGROUND

AACR1 Rule 202C required the use of a note to indicate the source of bracketed information in the body of the entry if this information came from a source other than the endorsement or a published description named in another note. The use of this note would apply to the source of bracketed titles. The intent of the AACR2 rule is essentially the same.

NOTE EXAMPLES

3.36 *Cover title.
3.37 Title from cover.
3.38 Title from: Vier Gesange, op. 43. 1868.
3.39 *Title transcribed.
3.40 *Title transcribed from title page; spine title: Práctica de la globos, celeste, y terrestre.
3.41 *Title supplied by cataloger.
3.42 Without title. Begins: Gijž Babilon welmi klesa . . .

Chapter 5 (Music)

AACR2 RULE

5.7B3 Source of Title Proper
> Make notes on the source of the title proper if it is other than the
> chief source of information.

Since music scores often lack a title page, the chief source of information is frequently the cover title or caption title. In order to accommodate music better, this note is usually made whenever the chief source of information is other than the title page.

RELATED AACR2 RULE

5.1B1 Title Proper [AACR2 Rev.]
> Transcribe the title proper as instructed in 1.1B. If a title consists
> of the name(s) of one or more type(s) of composition, or one or more
> type(s) of composition and one or more of the following:

> > medium of performance
> > key
> > date of composition
> > number

> treat type of composition, medium of performance, etc., as the title
> proper. . . .
> In all other cases, if one or more statements of medium of performance, key, date of composition, and/or number are found in the
> source of information, treat those elements as other title information
> (see 5.1E). . . .
> In case of doubt, treat statements of medium of performance, key,
> date of composition, and number as part of the title proper.
> If the title proper is not taken from the chief source of information,
> give the source of the title in a note (see 5.7B3). [emphasis added]

LIBRARY OF CONGRESS POLICY

None issued.

RELATED LIBRARY OF CONGRESS POLICY

None issued.

AACR2 TEXT EXAMPLES REVISED TO REFLECT
LIBRARY OF CONGRESS POLICY

None required.

HISTORICAL BACKGROUND

Although AACR1 and previous codes had no rule equivalent to AACR2 Rule 5.7B3, the source of title note provisions for separately published monographs in these earlier codes could be used for music. (See *Historical Background* under Rule 2.7B3.) AACR1 Rule 248, however, did make the general statement that notes referring to the title area should be given first.

NOTE EXAMPLES

3.43   Title from accompanying material.
3.44   Caption title.
3.45   Title from caption.
3.46   Title from penciled caption.
3.47   Title from colophon.
3.48   Cover title.
3.49   Title from cover of Overture.
3.50   Title from portfolio.
3.51   Caption title; cover title: Sonata, D XII 6, for 2 trumpets [sic], strings and basso continuo.

Chapter 6 (Sound Recordings)

AACR2 RULE

6.7B3 Source of Title Proper [AACR2 Rev.]
Make notes on the source of the title proper if it is other than the chief source of information or if it is a container or accompanying textual material (see 6.0B1).

RELATED AACR2 RULE

6.0B1 Chief Source of Information [AACR2 Rev.]
Due to the length of this rule, it has been abridged to include only the part related to the use of notes.

Treat accompanying textual material or a container as the chief source of information if it furnishes a collective title and the parts themselves and their labels do not. In this case, make a note (see 6.7B3) indicating the source of information. [emphasis added]

6.1B1 Title Proper [AACR2 Rev.]
Transcribe the title proper as instructed in 1.1B. For data to be included in titles proper for musical items, see 5.1B. . . .

If the title proper is not taken from the chief source of information or if it is taken from a container that is a unifying element, give the source of the title in a note (see 6.7B3). [emphasis added]

LIBRARY OF CONGRESS POLICY

None issued.

RELATED LIBRARY OF CONGRESS POLICY

None issued.

AACR2 TEXT EXAMPLES REVISED TO REFLECT LIBRARY OF CONGRESS POLICY

None required.

HISTORICAL BACKGROUND

AACR1 Rev. Rule 252F2 provided for a note indicating the source of the title if the information was taken from a source other than the recording itself. This is equivalent to the AACR2 rule.

The note order used in the AACR1 Rev. Ch. 14 varied somewhat from that used in AACR2. AACR2 places this note third in order of priority while AACR1 Rev. Ch. 14 placed the species note third in priority and the source of title note earlier in priority.

NOTE EXAMPLES

3.52   Title from container.
3.53   Titles from containers.
3.54   Title from container spine.
3.55   Title from spine of container.
3.56   Title from syllabus.

Chapter 7 (Motion Pictures and Videorecordings)

AACR2 RULE

7.7B3 Source of Title Proper
      Make notes on the source of the title proper if it is other than the chief source of information.

RELATED AACR2 RULE

7.1B1 Title Proper [AACR2 Rev.]
      Transcribe the title proper as instructed in 1.1B. . . .
      If the title proper is not taken from the chief source of information, give the source of the title in a note (see 7.7B3). [emphasis added]

LIBRARY OF CONGRESS POLICY

None issued. For archival moving image materials, the Library of Congress supplements AACR2 Chapter 7 with the guidelines in *Archival Moving Image Materials* by White-Hensen.

RELATED LIBRARY OF CONGRESS POLICY

None issued.

AACR2 TEXT EXAMPLES REVISED TO REFLECT LIBRARY OF CONGRESS POLICY

None required.

HISTORICAL BACKGROUND

AACR1 Rev. Rule 229.2B required a note to record the source of the title for motion pictures and videorecordings if the title did not come from the work or its accompanying material. AACR2 requires this note even when the title is taken from the accompanying material.

NOTE EXAMPLES

The use of this note is relatively rare for motion pictures and videorecordings because these materials are seldom issued without a title indication on the item itself. The Library of Congress, however, frequently makes use of the note to record the fact that it has cataloged the item from a data sheet rather than from the item in hand.

3.57   Title from data sheet.

Chapter 8 (Graphic Materials)

AACR2 RULE

8.7B3 Source of Title Proper [AACR2 Rev.]
Make notes on the source of the title proper if it is a container or if it is other than the chief source of information (see 8.0B1).

RELATED AACR2 RULE

8.0B1 Chief Source of Information [AACR2 Rev.]
The chief source of information for graphic materials is the item itself including any labels, etc., that are permanently affixed to the item or a container that is an integral part of the item. If the item being

described consists of two or more separate physical parts (e.g., slide set), treat a container that is the unifying element as the chief source of information if it furnishes a collective title and the items themselves and their labels do not. In this case, make a note (see 8.7B3) indicating the source of information. [emphasis added] If information is not available from the chief source, take it from the following sources (in this order of preference):

container (e.g., box, frame)
accompanying textual material (e.g., manuals, leaflets)
other sources

In describing a collection of graphic materials as a unit, treat the whole collection as the chief source.

8.1B1 Title Proper [AACR2 Rev.]

Transcribe the title proper as instructed in 1.1B. . . .

If the title proper is taken from a container that is a unifying element, or if it is not taken from the chief source of information, give the source of the title in a note (see 8.7B3). [emphasis added]

LIBRARY OF CONGRESS POLICY

None issued. For original items and historical collections, the Library of Congress supplements AACR2 Chapter 8 with the guidelines in *Graphic Materials* by Betz.

RELATED LIBRARY OF CONGRESS POLICY

None issued.

AACR2 TEXT EXAMPLES REVISED TO REFLECT LIBRARY OF CONGRESS POLICY

None required.

HISTORICAL BACKGROUND

AACR1 Rev. Rule 229.2B required a note to record the source of the title for graphic materials if the title did not come from the work or its accompanying material. AACR2 requires this note even when the title is taken from the accompanying material.

NOTE EXAMPLES

The use of this note for projection-oriented graphic materials (filmstrips, slides, etc.) is relatively rare because these materials are seldom issued without a title indication on the item itself. This is not the case with other forms of graphic materials where the title is often not from the chief source of information. For locally prepared materials and original items the cataloger often has to supply the title.

The Library of Congress makes frequent use of this note when cataloging filmstrips, slides, and transparencies to record the fact that it has cataloged the item from a data sheet rather than from the item itself.

Projection Graphic Materials
3.58 Title from container.
3.59 *Title from teacher's guide.
3.60 Title from data sheet.

Nonprojection Graphic Materials
3.61 *Title from adhesive label.
3.62 Title from cover of booklet.
3.63 *Title from frame inscription.
3.64 *Title from handwritten notation below image.
3.65 Title from inscription on mat.
3.66 Title from the introductory sheet containing, in addition, an essay by F. Schiff.
3.67 *Title from printed label affixed to verso of Library's copy.
3.68 Title from portfolio labels.
3.69 *Title from loose printed page (from original album?).
3.70 *Date and identification from pencil inscription inside back cover.
3.71 Issued without t.p.? Title taken from Appleton.

Chapter 9 (Computer Files)

AACR2 RULE

9.7B3 Source of Title Proper [AACR2 Rev.]
Always give the source of the title proper.

Unlike the source of title proper rule in other chapters for description, this rule requires the indication of the source of title in all cases, not just when the chief source of information is not used as the source.

RELATED AACR2 RULE

9.1B2 Title Proper [AACR2 Rev.]
Always give the source of the title proper in a note (see 9.7B3). If the title has been supplied (see 1.1B7), give the source of the supplied title in a note (see 9.7B3). [emphasis added]

LIBRARY OF CONGRESS POLICY

None issued for AACR2 Rev. Ch. 9.

RELATED LIBRARY OF CONGRESS POLICY

None issued for AACR2 Rev. Ch. 9.

AACR2 TEXT EXAMPLES REVISED TO REFLECT LIBRARY OF CONGRESS POLICY

None required for AACR2 Rev. Ch. 9.

HISTORICAL BACKGROUND

Computer files were not covered by AACR1 or previous codes. The original AACR2 Chapter 9 specifically called for recording the source of title proper if it was taken from any source other than the computer file itself. The current version of this rule calls for recording the source in all cases.

NOTE EXAMPLES

3.72 *Title from "catalogue record" provided by producer.
3.73 *Title from codebook.
3.74 *Title from data abstract supplied by author.
3.75 *Title from data abstract supplied by contact person.
3.76 *Title from data abstract supplied by creator of file.
3.77 *Title from disk label.
3.78 *Title from documentation.
3.79 *Title from "Get Info" window.
3.80 *Title from menu screen.
3.81 *Title from printed source.
3.82 *Title from related publication.
3.83 *Title from tape layout.
3.84 *Title from technical memo.
3.85 *Title from title screen.
3.86 *Title from user's guide.
3.87 *Title from: Directory of Data Files, prepared by the Bureau of the Census.
3.88 *Title from ICPSR Guide to resources and services. 1976-1977.
3.89 *Title supplied by cataloger.
3.90 *Title supplied by cataloger and in correspondence with creator of file.

Chapter 10 (Three-Dimensional Artefacts and Realia)

AACR2 RULE

10.7B3 Source of Title Proper
　　　Make notes on the source of the title proper if it is other than the chief source of information.

RELATED AACR2 RULE

10.1B1 Title Proper [AACR2 Rev.]
Transcribe the title proper as instructed in 1.1B. . . .
If the title proper is not taken from the chief source of information,
give the source of the title in a note (see 10.7B3). [emphasis added]

LIBRARY OF CONGRESS POLICY

None issued.

RELATED LIBRARY OF CONGRESS POLICY

None issued.

AACR2 TEXT EXAMPLES REVISED TO REFLECT
LIBRARY OF CONGRESS POLICY

None required.

HISTORICAL BACKGROUND

AACR1 Rev. Rule 229.2B required a note to record the source of a
title for three-dimensional artifacts and realia if the title did not come
from the work or its accompanying material. AACR2 is in accord with
this earlier rule.

NOTE EXAMPLES

This note is frequently used to record the fact that the cataloger
provided the title. This is particularly true for realia and other noncom-
mercially prepared items covered by Chapter 10. The wording of this
particular type of note does not vary greatly in structure.

3.91   *Title from advertisement.
3.92   *Title from entry in Educator's guide to free filmstrips.
3.93   *Title supplied by cataloger.

Chapter 12 (Serials)

AACR2 RULE

12.7B3 Source of Title Proper [AACR2 Rev.]
Make notes on the source of the title proper if it is other than the
chief source of information or if it is the title page substitute of a printed
serial.

RELATED AACR2 RULE

12.0B1 Printed Serials [AACR2 Rev.]
Due to the length of this rule it has been abridged to include only
the part related to the use of notes.

Chief Source of Information
The chief source of information for printed serials is the title page
... (whether published with the issues or published later) or the title
page substitute of the first issue of the serial. Failing this, the chief
source of information is the title page of the first available issue. The
title page substitute for an item lacking a title page is (in this order of
preference) the analytical title page, cover, caption, masthead, editorial
pages, colophon, other pages. Specify the source used as the title page
substitute in a note (see 12.7B3). [emphasis added] If information traditionally given on the title page is given on facing pages, with or
without repetition, treat the two pages as the title page.

12.1B1 Title Proper [AACR2 Rev.]
Transcribe the title proper as instructed in 1.1B. . . .
If the title proper is not taken from the chief source of information
or if, in a printed serial, it is taken from a title page substitute (see
12.0B1), give the source in a note (see 12.7B3). [emphasis added]

LIBRARY OF CONGRESS POLICY

None issued.

RELATED LIBRARY OF CONGRESS POLICY

See *Reprints of Serials*, page 110.

AACR2 TEXT EXAMPLES REVISED TO REFLECT
LIBRARY OF CONGRESS POLICY

No examples were given in AACR2 or AACR2 Rev.

HISTORICAL BACKGROUND

Although AACR1 and previous codes had no rule equivalent to
AACR2 Rule 12.7B3, the source of title note provisions for separately
published monographs in these earlier codes could be used for serials.
(See Historical Background under Rule 2.7B3.)

NOTE EXAMPLES

3.94   Caption title.
3.95   Title from caption.
3.96   Cover title.
3.97   Title from cover.
3.98   Masthead title.
3.99   Title from masthead.
3.100 Title from spine.

Combined with Other Notes

3.101 Description based on: 5th (1981); title from cover.
3.102 Description based on: Vol. 3, no. 1 (Oct. 31-Nov. 5, 1980 season); title from cover.

1.7B4. Variations in Title

EXTRAPOLATED GENERAL RULE

Variant Title
Make notes on titles borne by the item other than the title proper.

Romanization
Optionally, give a romanization of the title proper.

RELATED AACR2 RULE

1.1B1 Title Proper [AACR2 Rev.]

Transcribe the title proper exactly as to wording, order, and spelling, but not necessarily as to punctuation and capitalization. Give accentuation and other diacritical marks that are present in the chief source of information (see also 1.0G). Capitalize according to appendix A. . . .

An alternative title is part of the title proper (see Glossary, appendix D). Precede and follow the word *or* (or its equivalent in another language) introducing an alternative title by a comma. Capitalize the first word of the alternative title. . . .

If the title proper as given in the chief source of information includes the punctuation marks . . . or [ ], replace them by — and ( ), respectively. . . .

If the title proper as given in the chief source of information includes symbols that cannot be reproduced by the facilities available, replace them with a cataloguer's description in square brackets. <u>Make an explanatory note if necessary.</u> . . . [emphasis added]

GENERAL LIBRARY OF CONGRESS POLICY

Variant Titles
A note may be essential to show a variation from the chief source title appearing elsewhere in the item. Although the source may contain more than one title, record in a note only the needed variant title, not titles already given in the description. (Always include in the note the source of the variant.)

Nonroman Records
For languages that have bibliographic cards that are not romanized, the Library of Congress observes the practices detailed below.

1) *Entries filed, or subfiled, under publication title.* On bibliographic cards for which no uniform title is appropriate, entries under a name heading show the romanized title proper printed within parentheses under the heading; the "Title romanized" note is omitted. For items

entered under title proper, the romanized title proper is enclosed within parentheses and printed in boldface as a hanging indention; the nonroman item title appears under this as another hanging indention beginning on a separate line. *Exception for writing systems that read from right to left:* For title entries the romanized title begins at the left margin, i.e., where each nonroman line in the body of the entry ends; the nonroman item title appears as a hanging indention beginning at the right margin.

2) *Entries filed, or subfiled, under uniform title.* For the benefit of other libraries, cards that have a uniform title also bear a romanization of the title proper within parentheses under the uniform title. The title is traced as "Title"-period if an added entry for it is being made (cf. 21.30J). (A romanization of the title proper is made even if it is identical to the uniform title.)

Note: If the title being romanized begins with an article, omit it from the romanized title.

3) *Length of title romanized.* When romanizing a title proper, generally romanize the whole title proper (including an alternative title). However, 1.1B4 does provide for a shortening technique, necessary in cases of "long" titles. A "long" title should be understood as a title that is "too long," with a more precise understanding of this extreme length left to the judgment of the cataloger. Keep in mind that a general shortening is not what the rule suggests. Normally, as already stated, romanize the entire title proper. The rule provides a technique for use after the cataloger has felt a need for it. Note that in applying the technique, words omitted must always be at the end, never before the sixth word nor somewhere in the middle, and the part preceding the omission must be a phrase that will stand alone. Abridge the title romanization and the transcription of the nonroman title proper to the same extent. Indicate the omission by the mark of omission in the title and statement of responsibility area but not in the title romanization.

4) *Items without a collective title.* If the item lacks a collective title, romanize all the titles up to the first recorded parallel title, other title information, or statement of responsibility, whichever occurs first (cf. LCRI 21.30J). (These provisions are applicable even if no added entry is being made for the title of the item and without regard to the uniform title that may be assigned to the record.)

5) *Corrected titles (cf. 1.0F)*

a) *Titles corrected by "[i.e. . . .]" or "[sic]."* If the nonroman title being romanized has been corrected in the nonroman transcription by the "[i.e. . . .]" or "[sic]" technique, romanize the title in this form, i.e., romanize the title that appears on the item and include "[i.e. . . .]" or "[sic]." (If an added entry is needed, make one added entry for the romanized form of the title with the "[i.e. . . .]" or "[sic]" and another added entry for the romanized form of the title as if it had appeared correctly. Trace the titles explicitly except trace as "Title"-

period the title containing "[i.e. . . . .]" or "[sic]" when it appears within parentheses according to 2) above.)

b) *Titles corrected by bracketing missing letters.* If the nonroman title being romanized has been corrected in the nonroman transcription by supplying in brackets a missing letter or letters, romanize the title in this form, i.e., romanize the title with brackets and the supplied letter or letters. (If an added entry is needed, make one added entry for the title romanized with the brackets and the supplied letter or letters and another added entry for the romanized form of the title as it appears on the item. Trace the titles explicitly except trace as "Title"-period the title containing the brackets and the supplied letter or letters when it appears within parentheses according to 2) above.) [CSB 39]

RELATED LIBRARY OF CONGRESS POLICY

1.0E Language and Script of the Description

Due to its length, this LC policy statement has been abridged to include only the parts related to the use of notes.

Matter Than Cannot Be Reproduced by the Typographical Facilities Available

The rule, in effect, requires as much fidelity to the source as the capacity for printing, typewriting, database-inputting, etc., within the cataloging agency will allow. It recommends a "cataloguer's description in square brackets" for any "matter that cannot be reproduced by the typographical facilities available." Generally, this is a practicable solution, but here are special instances in which doing other than describing the matter is appropriate. The main purposes of these instructions are to categorize all the methods to be employed, including a "cataloguer's description" and to give specific directions for each in terms of the particular character set phenomenon encountered.

In the context of machine-readable catalog records note that as used in 1.0E and in the preceding paragraph, "typographical facilities available" means the totality of characters that can be represented in machine-readable form and displayed/printed (known as the "MARC character set"; referred to hereafter as "the character set"). Conventions appropriate to particular character set situations have been developed as follows:

Super/subscript characters
Greek letters
Special marks of contraction (e.g., older printed Latin)
Special letters, diacritical marks, punctuation marks
Signs and symbols

Apply the appropriate conventions described in the following sections. As judged appropriate, use notes to explain and added entries to provide additional access. In the special provisions that follow, notes are suggested as possible models for form, not to require the use of the note. [emphasis added]

Super/Subscript Characters

[Examples are provided in this section with suggested notes to explain the access point.]

Signs and Symbols

The objective in treating signs and symbols not represented in the character set is to render or convey the intention without undue time and effort and with a minimum of interpolation, using one of the techniques described in this section . Note that a minimum of interpolation is wanted because those searching the machine catalog cannot very often be expected to "second-guess" the cataloger in this respect, i.e., users will normally formulate search keys that necessarily do not take interpolations into account. As judged appropriate, use notes to explain and added entries to provide additional access [emphasis added] . . .

1) If the symbol is judged not to be an integral or essential part of the title, use an explanatory note instead of interventions in the description. [emphasis added] Note this is ordinarily the case with symbols of trademark, patent, copyright, etc.

2) Use existing characters when this can be done without serious distortion or loss of intelligibility.

[Examples are provided with suggested notes to explain the access point.]

3) Use the double underscore convention (cf. the [earlier] section [in this LCRI] on *Special Letter, Diacritical Marks and Punctuation Marks*.)

4) Substitute in the language of the context the word, phrase, etc., that is the obvious spoken/written equivalent (if unknown in the language of the context, use English); bracket the interpolated equivalent. If the element in the source is not preceded or followed by a space, in general precede or follow the bracketed interpolation by a space unless the preceding or following character in the source is itself also a separator or unless the use of a space would create an unintended result for searching.

[Examples are provided with suggested notes to explain the access point.]

Exception 1: Do not transcribe characters that indicate birth (e.g., an asterisk) or death (e.g., a dagger) even if such characters are in the

91

character set. <u>Do not use a mark of omission; instead, explain the omission in a note.</u> [emphasis added] . . .

Exception 2: Ignore the superscript and subscript "R" enclosed in a circle indicating the registered trademark symbol, although the symbol is in the character set. <u>Do not explain its presence in a note.</u> [emphasis added] (Ignore the symbol also when it appears with elements used in headings.)

If the spoken/written equivalent is not obvious or if there is doubt that it is obvious or if it is unknown, give an explanation and a description in the language of the context (if unknown in the language of the context, use English).

[Examples are provided with suggested notes to explain the access point.]

If a title consists solely of a sign or symbol, provide an equivalent in all cases, even if the particular symbol is itself in the character set.

[Examples are provided with suggested notes to explain the access point.]

[CSB 38]

1.1F6 Statements of Responsibility

If subordinate titles (e.g., appendices or other subsidiary texts) appear after a statement(s) of responsibility, record them as subsequent statements of responsibility whether or not they actually name a person or body. <u>If they are very lengthy, record them in a note.</u> [emphasis added] (If such titles appear before a statement(s) of responsibility, record them as other title information (1.1E). If such titles are given equal prominence with the first work in the item, apply 1.1G.) [CSB 17]

FORMAT

In addition to the formatting instructions in LC's policy, a formalized construct appears repeatedly in examples in various AACR2 chapters for description. This construct is:

[Introductory phrase]: [variant title.]

The introductory phrase generally gives the source of the variant title, e.g., cover title, title on container, etc. However, it is not confined to use with variant titles exclusively. It can also be used to introduce a romanized title, an original title, or any other type of title variation.

CHAPTER APPLICATION

This note is present in all chapters for description. All the provisions of the Extrapolated General Rule and its terminology are present.

EXCEPTIONS AND ADDITIONS

Chapter 12 (Serials), in addition to the requirements of the Extrapolated General Rule, specifically calls for a note to record the presence of special titles for individual issues of a serial.

Chapter 2 (Books, Pamphlets, and Printed Sheets)

AACR2 RULE

2.7B4 Variations in Title [AACR2 Rev.]

Variant Title
> Make notes on titles borne by the item other than the title proper.

Romanization
> *Optionally*, give a romanization of the title proper.

RELATED AACR2 RULE

None.

LIBRARY OF CONGRESS POLICY

Source of Variant Title
> If the variant title being recorded in a note appears in a source that meets the criteria for an added title page, record the note as

>> "Title on added t.p."

> followed by a colon-space and the title.
> If the variant title appears in another source, specify its location (e.g., "Title on p. [4] of cover:").
> There is no situation for which the notes "Added title." or "Added title:" or "Added t.p.:" are appropriate.
> If a title in another language appears prominently on the publication, record the title in a note and make an added entry for it. (It does not matter if the source is an added title page or if there is text in the language of the title.)

Binder['s] Titles
> If a binder's title varies significantly from the title proper of the item (cf. 21.2A), record it in a note and make an added entry for it.
> If a monograph has been bound only for LC's collections (i.e., it was not bound by the publisher or it was not one of the multiple copies that were bound subsequent to publication as part of a cooperative

acquisitions program), give only the note and not the added entry. In such a case, make the note a copy-specific one (LCRI 1.7B20), e.g.,

"LC copy has binder's title ..."

In case of doubt, do not assume that the item was bound only for LC. [CSB 27]

RELATED LIBRARY OF CONGRESS POLICY

None issued.

AACR2 TEXT EXAMPLES REVISED TO REFLECT LIBRARY OF CONGRESS POLICY

None required.

HISTORICAL BACKGROUND

AACR1 Rev. Rule 143B1a considered notes giving variant title information to be indispensable. Such notes included "variation from the title page title appearing elsewhere in the work, . . . variations in the title in a work of several volumes, . . . or . . . variant or supplemental information appearing on an added title page." This rule provided greater detail than does the AACR2 rule.

AACR1 Rev. Rule 143D2 provided notes for original titles "when the title of the edition or translation of the work being cataloged varies from the title of the original edition . . . ." No distinction was made between parallel and variant titles. AACR1 Rev. Rule 143D2a allowed for recording both types of titles while AACR1 Rev. Rules 143D2b-e applied only to variant titles. Great detail was given in AACR1 Rev. Rule 143D2 regarding translations, reissues, uniform titles, and later editions. AACR2 does not delineate any of these situations, although text examples and LC cataloging examples indicate that these types of notes are still being made.

AACR1 (Rev. Rule 143D3a) provided for notes on the title proper in addition to notes for original titles (AACR1 Rev. Rule 143D2). Although no further guidelines were given, AACR1 Rev. text examples indicated that this rule included variant titles (e.g., cover title) as well as notes about the source of title proper. AACR2 has made the source of title a separate note (see Rule 2.7B3).

AACR1 Rev. Rule 150 provided for a Title romanized note. This note was to be given as the last note, following the International Standard Book Number. The rule clearly stated that the note should be made "unless the romanization has been given preceding the transcription of the title, or unless a uniform title has been used." This rule also discussed the length of the title, as well as romanization procedures for numerals and abbreviations. The AACR1 Rev. rule also provided a strict construct for a title romanized note, i.e., "Title romanized: . . . ." AACR2 Rule 2.7B4 calls for a romanization note but does not provide any detailed guidelines for its use. It does not call for the use of the AACR1 construct or any other specific construct nor does it offer text examples of such a note. The Library of Congress has issued a rule interpretation that has restated most of the AACR1 guidelines (see *General Library of Congress Policy* under Extrapolated General Rule 1.7B4).

These AACR1 Rev. Ch. 6 rules could be used for works that were not separately published monographs unless specific rules for the description of a format superseded or excluded its use.

NOTE EXAMPLES

At Head of Title
4.1 At head of title: Catalogs of the Far Eastern Library, University of Chicago, Chicago, Illinois.
4.2 At head of title: Consumer guide.
4.3 At head of title: How to prepare for College Board achievement tests.
4.4 At head of title: Radio broadcasts, 1924-1941.
4.5 At head of title: West's California codes.

Caption Titles
4.6 Caption title: Classicists and friends of the classics in New England.
4.7 Caption title: Free from poetry.
4.8 Caption title: List of microfilms of Maine town records and Maine census records.
4.9 Caption title: They toiled in love.

Colophon Titles
4.10 Colophon reads: Thesaurum apostolicum imprimebat Witebergae Christianus Gerdesius . . .
4.11 Colophon reads: Witebergae, Christianus Gerdesius . . . typographus . . .
4.12 Title in colophon: Còdigo civil de la República y leyes que lo modifican y complementan.
4.13 Title in colophon: Rozhdenie zhenshchiny.
4.14 Title in colophon, v. 1-2: Collection "Études de gestion."

Cover Titles
4.15 "World Population Year"—Cover.
4.16 Cover: Ochman.

4.17 Cover title: Collecting debts with small claims actions in Oregon.
4.18 Cover title: Marriage records, 1821-1879, Clark County, Arkansas.
4.19 Cover title: P.R. Stephensen, bibliography.
4.20 Cover title: Sango-English dictionary, 1980.
4.21 Cover title: St. Vital Parish, 1877-1977, Battleford, Sask.
4.22 Cover title and title of v. 3: Agricultural census of Tanzania, 1971/72.
4.23 Cover title in Japanese: Mishigan Daigaku Nihon kenkyu ronshu.
4.24 On cover: 1974-1981.
4.25 On cover: A pocket guide to Chicago.
4.26 On cover: I. Respiratory care   II. Hypertension.
4.27 On cover: Walt Disney Productions, The fox and the hound.
4.28 On cover and spine: DCA commemorative keepsake, 1980.
4.29 Title on cover: Record albums price guide.
4.30 Title on cover and spine: The Odes of Solomon.
4.31 Title handwritten on cover: The Smith-Schmitt chronicle.

Half Titles
4.32 Half title: Decorative needlework for the home.
4.33 Half title: An essay on the art of etching upon copper.
4.34 Half title: The Life-Guards.
4.35 Half title: The pictures in the collection of Her Majesty the Queen: the Dutch pictures.
4.36 Half title: Poems.
4.37 Half title, v. 3-6: Collection "Études de gestion comptable."

Running Titles
4.38 Running title: Alfred Hitchcock's anthology.
4.39 Running title: Gibson authoritative guide to strings.
4.40 Running title: Photoconservation bibliography.
4.41 Running title: Tozzer Library index to anthropological subject headings.

Spine Titles
4.42 Individual titles listed on spine.
4.43 Label on spine: Bakery products industry.
4.44 On spine: Coastal ecosystems of the Southeastern United States.
4.45 On spine: EEC competition law reporter.
4.46 On spine: New York State tax law, 1980.
4.47 Spine title: The listener's guide to jazz.
4.48 Spine title: The Soviet war machine.
4.49 Spine title: 1976-1977-1978 NEC rail passenger statistics.
4.50 Spine title: v. 1: Oklahoma criminal benchbook.
4.51 Title from spine: Passages.
4.52 Title on spine: Crisler genealogy.
4.53 Title on spine: Sams VCR service data.
4.54 Issued in a case with spine title: Liber fundatorum Zwetlensis Monasterii, Hs. 2/1, "Bärenhaut."

Title on [Source]

4.55 Title on added t.p.: Collected works.

4.56 Titles on added t.p.: Italian violin makers. Mâitres luthiers italiens.

4.57 Title on added t.p.: Russian gold and silver filigree.

4.58 Title on boards: Khro chu Dug gdoṅ nag po' i sgrub skor.

4.59 Title on box: Un atlas des étoiles Be.

4.60 Title on leaf preceding t.p.: Opisanie Warszawy.

4.61 Title on p. [1] of cover: Sizemore family of Pickens, S.C.

4.62 Title on p. [17]: Eden anto, or, The fate of a copy of a rare edition of Ariosto's Orlando furioso.

4.63 Title in Japanese on added t.p.: Eiburahamu Rinkan korekushon.

4.64 Titles on page facing t.p.: Zhivopis' Belorussii XII-XVIII vekov; Byelorussian painting of XII-XVIII centuries.

4.65 Title on verso of t.p.: The Ukrainian question and Russia.

4.66 Title on verso of t.p., v. 1-   : The Dramas.

Volume Title

4.67 Vol. 2 has title: Early Christian and early Byzantine architecture in Palestine (including Jordan).

4.68 Vol. 2 has title: The works of Meister Eckhart.

4.69 Vol. 3 has title: Explosives, their history, manufacture, properties, and tests.

4.70 Vol. 3 has title: Mining Court and Mining Commissioners' cases, Ontario.

4.71 Vol. 2 has title: The Victoria history of the County of Middlesex; v. 5-6 have title: A history of Middlesex.

4.72 Vols. 1-10 have title: The colonial records of North Carolina collected and edited by William L. Saunders.

4.73 Vol. 1 also has special title: National defense.

4.74 Vol. 8 also issued separately under title: Oil and gas terms.

4.75 Vol. 1 lacks general title.

Titles—Miscellaneous

4.76 Title varies.

4.77 T.p. titles vary slightly.

4.78 Binder's title. Preceding same title: Collection de général Read.

4.79 British ed. Originally published as: Electronic testing and fault diagnosis. 1980.

4.80 Includes unnumbered vols. entitled: Rules of practice ; Federal rules of evidence ; Finding aids.

4.81 Original title statement on verso of t.p. is erroneous.

4.82 Poem commonly known by 1st line: Buffalo Bill's.

4.83 Main work has special title: Text.

4.84 Revised French translation has title: La partie générale du droit des obligations.

4.85 Some pieces have added title: Technical reports on occupational safety and health; one piece has added title: Statistical report, 1970-1975.

Chapter 3 (Cartographic Materials)

AACR2 RULE

3.7B4 Variations in Title [AACR2 Rev.]

Variant Title
> Make notes on titles borne by the item other than the title proper.

Romanization
> *Optionally*, give a romanization of the title proper.

RELATED AACR2 RULE

None.

LIBRARY OF CONGRESS POLICY

None issued.

RELATED LIBRARY OF CONGRESS POLICY

None issued.

AACR2 TEXT EXAMPLES REVISED TO REFLECT LIBRARY OF CONGRESS POLICY

None required.

HISTORICAL BACKGROUND

AACR1 Rule 212E2 provided for notes on the "source of title and variant titles." AACR2 provides for a "source of title" note under a separate rule (AACR2 Rule 3.7B3).

Although AACR1 and previous codes had no romanization of title rule equivalent to AACR2 Rule 3.7B4, the romanization note provisions for separately published monographs in these earlier codes could be used for cartographic materials. (See *Historical Background* under Rule 2.7B4.)

NOTE EXAMPLES

4.86   On each map: Texaco touring map of . . .
4.87   Alternative title: U.B.D. Adelaide street directory.

98

4.88   Alternate cover title: Roma globale : con raccordo anulare e linee della metropolitana, nuova pianta = Nouveau plan = New map = Neuer Stadtplan.

4.89   Alternate cover title: Stream evaluation map-1980, State of Montana.

4.90   At head of title: Visual encyclopedia.

4.91   Head of title: Voyage de Humboldt et Bonpland. Première partie, relation historique.

4.92   Caption title: Road & rail atlas of New South Wales.

4.93   Caption title: World atlas and gazetteer.

4.94   Cover title: Atlas of diesel fuel stations.

4.95   Cover title: Calabria, carta stradale = Road map = Carte routìre = Strassenkarte.

4.96   Cover title: Guide map of India : with detailed tourist information.

4.97   On cover: Peugeot.

4.98   Half title: Atlas géographique et physique.

4.99   Legend title: How to read your map of Delaware, Maryland, Virginia, W. Virginia.

4.100   Panel title: Colorado : with mini-maps of Boulder, Colorado Springs, Pikes Peak region, Denver, Denver mountain area, Mesa Verde National Park, Pueblo, United States Air Force Academy.

4.101   Panel title: France, départments-régions: tableaux des distances = France, départments-regions : distance charts.

4.102   Panel title: La Porte : 1979 street map & guide.

4.103   Panel title: Street map of Holland-Zeeland area.
Variant panel title: Holland, Michigan 1981-1982.

4.104   Running title: Report for development of water resources in Appalachia.

4.105   Running title: Sketch showing city streets on the state highway system in the city of . . . , . . . County, Pa.

4.106   Spine title: Whico Gulf coast atlas.

4.107   Title in preface: Scott Foresman world atlas.

4.108   Title on container: Bett's patent portable globe.

4.109   Title p. 1: Gubia CAMPSA 1979.

4.110   Title at bottom of legend and at lower margin: JRO Strassenkarte Dänemark 1:400 000 50 20 20/6'.

4.111   Title at upper margin: Brick Town, Ocean County, N.J.

4.112   Title in margin: Vittel 88800.

4.113   Title in margin on verso: Troyes 1000, bouchon-de-Champagne.

4.114   Title in right upper margin: Sheffield.

4.115   Title in upper and lower right margins: Idaho.

4.116   Title near upper margin: Malta.

4.117   Title in lower left corner: Roma : scala 1:20.000.

4.118   Vol. 1 and 2 issued as: Carte géologique du Territoire français des Afars et des Issas / Université de Bordeaux III — Territoire français des Afars et des Issas, Centre d'études géologiques et de développement, 1974-1975.

Chapter 4 (Manuscripts)

AACR2 RULE

4.7B4 Variations in Title [AACR2 Rev.]

Variant Title
> Make notes on titles borne by the item other than the title proper.

Romanization
> *Optionally*, give a romanization of the title proper.

RELATED AACR2 RULE

None.

LIBRARY OF CONGRESS POLICY

None issued. APPM, however, expands on the AACR2 text.

Variations in Title
> Make a note on other titles associated with the material or item; these may include traditional titles or other titles on the item in addition to the title proper. [APPM 4.7B16]

RELATED LIBRARY OF CONGRESS POLICY

None issued.

AACR2 TEXT EXAMPLES REVISED TO REFLECT LIBRARY OF CONGRESS POLICY

None required.

HISTORICAL BACKGROUND

Although AACR1 and previous codes had no rule equivalent to AACR2 Rule 4.7B4, the variant title and romanization of title note provisions for separately published monographs in these earlier codes could be used for manuscripts. (See *Historical Background* under Rule 2.7B4.)

NOTE EXAMPLES

4.119   Also known as: Anglo Dutch war collection.

4.120   A Latin version by the author has title: De sex erroribus.
4.121   Title on cover: Grand prelude & fugue in B minor for organ.

Chapter 5 (Music)

AACR2 RULE

5.7B4 Variations in Title [AACR2 Rev.]

Variant Title
Make notes on titles borne by the item other than the title proper.

Romanization
Optionally, give a romanization of the title proper.

RELATED AACR2 RULE

None.

LIBRARY OF CONGRESS POLICY

None issued.

RELATED LIBRARY OF CONGRESS POLICY

None issued.

AACR2 TEXT EXAMPLES REVISED TO REFLECT LIBRARY OF CONGRESS POLICY

None required.

HISTORICAL BACKGROUND

AACR1 Rule 248 stated in its introductory paragraph that "notes referring to the title are given first." This general statement is the only reference to title notes for music (other than contents notes) in AACR1. AACR2 changed the note order of title notes, moving them to the 3rd, 4th, and 5th note positions.

AACR1 Rule 235B3a provided for romanization of a title if the original language was in a nonroman alphabet. While this rule did not specify that this information was to be given in a note, the example in the text uses the traditional "Title romanized: . . ." note form.

NOTE EXAMPLES

4.122 Added caption title: A great dark sleep.

4.123 Caption title: Heures de loisir.

4.124 Caption title: She's as sweet as honey (and gives me metallic brainfever).

4.125 Caption title: Sinfonia no. 10, pour 2 trompettes et orchestra à cordes: (1685).

4.126 Title in caption of piano part: Poème antique : d'après Virgile.

4.127 Cover title: En blasekvintett.

4.128 Cover title: Sonata in F major for two violins (with cello and piano ad libitum).

4.129 Title on cover: Klavierunterricht mit Felix Mendelssohn Bartholdy.

4.130 Title on p. [4] of cover: Shevil he-halav.

4.131 On verso of t.p.: A gift of song.

Chapter 6 (Sound Recordings)

AACR2 RULE

6.7B4 Variations in Title [AACR2 Rev.]

Variant Title
> Make notes on titles borne by the item other than the title proper.

Romanization
> *Optionally*, give a romanization of the title proper.

RELATED AACR2 RULE

None.

LIBRARY OF CONGRESS POLICY

None issued.

RELATED LIBRARY OF CONGRESS POLICY

None issued.

AACR2 TEXT EXAMPLES REVISED TO REFLECT LIBRARY OF CONGRESS POLICY

None required.

HISTORICAL BACKGROUND

AACR1 Rev. Rule 253D2 stated that additional data such as "variants of well-known titles," or in the case of translations "better-known or original titles," may be mentioned in a note. This rule was limited to nonprocessed sound recordings. Unlike AACR2, however, it was not limited in its application to "titles borne by the item."

Although AACR1 Rev. Ch. 14 and previous codes had no romanization of title rule equivalent to AACR2 Rule 6.7B4, the romanization note provisions for separately published monographs in these earlier codes could be used for processed sound recordings. (See *Historical Background* under Rule 2.7B4.)

NOTE EXAMPLES

4.132 Vol. 2 has title: From ragtime to ballroom.
4.133 Title on container: Arch Oboler's Plays—Lights out, everybody.
4.134 Title on container: Hawkland on secured transactions.
4.135 Title on container: Werke für Violoncello und Klavier.
4.136 Titles on container: Fantasy op. 17 / Schumann. Sonata in B minor / Liszt.
4.137 Added title on container: The unicorn, or, The triumph of chastity.
4.138 "Monty Python's American diary" on container.
4.139 Title on notes in container: Musical boxes at the Victoria & Albert Museum.

Chapter 7 (Motion Pictures and Videorecordings)

AACR2 RULE

7.7B4 Variations in Title [AACR2 Rev.]

Variant Title
Make notes on titles borne by the item other than the title proper.

Romanization
Optionally, give a romanization of the title proper.

RELATED AACR2 RULE

None.

LIBRARY OF CONGRESS POLICY

When considering 7.7B4 and 8.7B4 for a variation in title, decide first whether an added title entry is needed under the variant title. Decide this primary issue by consulting 21.2.

If the variation in title is as great as the differences in title described in 21.2, make the added entry and justify the added entry by means of a note formulated under 7.7B4 or 8.7B4. Otherwise, do not apply 7.7B4 or 8.7B4. [CSB 13]

For archival moving image materials, the Library of Congress supplements AACR2 Chapter 7 with the guidelines in *Archival Moving Image Materials* by White-Hensen.

RELATED LIBRARY OF CONGRESS POLICY

None issued.

AACR2 TEXT EXAMPLES REVISED TO REFLECT LIBRARY OF CONGRESS POLICY

None required.

HISTORICAL BACKGROUND

AACR1 Rev. Rule 229.2C provided for notes on "variations in title, etc., within the work." This rule is equivalent to AACR2 Rule 7.7B4.

In addition, the AACR1 Rev. rule provided for the use of variant title notes for "separately issued parts of a work cataloged as a set," unless the information was given as a contents note. AACR2 does not specifically address this situation.

Although AACR1 Rev. Ch. 12 and previous codes had no romanization of title rule equivalent to AACR2 Rule 7.7B4, the romanization note provisions for separately published monographs in these earlier codes could be used for motion pictures and videorecordings. (See *Historical Background* under Rule 2.7B4.)

NOTE EXAMPLES

4.140   At head of title: Designs in energy.
4.141   Title on booklet: The Rules of soccer, simplified.

Chapter 8 (Graphic Materials)

AACR2 RULE

8.7B4 Variations in Title [AACR2 Rev.]

Variant Title
Make notes on titles borne by the item other than the title proper.

Romanization
> *Optionally*, give a romanization of the title proper.

RELATED AACR2 RULE

None.

LIBRARY OF CONGRESS POLICY

> When considering 7.7B4 and 8.7B4 for a variation in title, decide first whether an added title entry is needed under the variant title. Decide this primary issue by consulting 21.2.
>
> If the variation in title is as great as the differences in titles described in 21.2, make the added entry and justify the added entry by means of a note formulated under 7.7B4 or 8.7B4. Otherwise, do not apply 7.7B4 or 8.7B4. [CSB 13]

For original items and historical collections, the Library of Congress supplements AACR2 Chapter 8 with the guidelines in *Graphic Materials* by Betz.

RELATED LIBRARY OF CONGRESS POLICY

None issued.

AACR2 TEXT EXAMPLES REVISED TO REFLECT LIBRARY OF CONGRESS POLICY

None required.

HISTORICAL BACKGROUND

AACR1 Rev. Rule 229.2C provided for notes on "variations in title, etc., within the work." This rule is equivalent to AACR2 Rule 8.7B4.

In addition, the AACR1 Rev. rule provided for the use of variant title notes for "separately issued parts of a work cataloged as a set," unless the information was given as a contents note. AACR2 does not specifically address this situation.

AACR1 Rule 272C2 provided for variant title notes for a picture if it was "commonly known by a title other than the one on the work in hand." This rule goes beyond the AACR2 stipulation that the variant title be "borne by the item."

AACR1 Rule 265A4 provided for the use of a caption note "if the pictorial element of the work has a distinctive caption independent of the chosen title." AACR2 does not specifically provide for this although such a note could be made.

Although AACR1 Rev. Ch. 12, AACR1 Ch. 15, and previous codes had no romanization of title rule equivalent to AACR2 Rule 8.7B4, the romanization note provisions for separately published monographs in these earlier codes could be used for graphic materials. (See *Historical Background* under Rule 2.7B4.)

NOTE EXAMPLES

Projection Graphic Materials

4.142   Title on booklet: Choosing toys for children.

4.143   Titles on booklet: Yugoslavia's Adriatic coast, etc.

4.144   Title on cover: Quick & easy sewing; Quick & easy techniques.

4.145   Title on guide: Un Voyage a travers la Normandie.

4.146   Title on instructor's guide: Energy—crisis, conservation, sources.

4.147   Title on slides: Srednjovekovne freske i arhitektura.

4.148   "PsychINFO."

Nonprojection Graphic Materials

4.149   *At head of title: Why does the elephant eat mothballs?

4.150   Binders title.

4.151   *Caption card: Eight-year old Jack taking care of the colt . . . 3972 Western Mass., Aug. 1915. See Hine Report, Rural Child Labor, August 1915.

4.152   *Picture caption: No, Ma'am, no! I am not a damaged article.

4.153   The prints have cover with title: Shaped poetry, the suite of thirty prints.

4.154   The editorial matter (35 p.), incl. the t.p., has paper cover with title: Shaped poetry, the companion volume.

4.155   *Explanatory title in English and German: The hair = Die Haut . . .

4.156   *Manuscript title on verso: Mrs. Humphrey's garden.

4.157   Ms. title on spine.

4.158   *Same image published with other titles: Bird's-eye view of Cincinnati; Cincinnati, 1878.

4.159   On portfolio: Mosheh Tamir [in Hebrew characters] / Moshe Tamir.

4.160   *In slipcase; title on slipcase: Bender's anatomy charts for courtroom use.

4.161   *"The Chief's Daughter"—in ink on verso; possibly inscribed by Imogen Cunningham.

4.162   *Title inscribed by artist: Romany Marye's.

4.163   Title page reads: Adolph Hitler. Aquarelle . . .

4.164   *Title varies on no. 2 and 6: Illustration from the Siberian War.

Chapter 9 (Computer Files)

AACR2 RULE

9.7B4 Variations in Title [AACR2 Rev.]

Variant Title
Make notes on titles borne by the item other than the title proper.

Romanization
Optionally, give a romanization of the title proper. . . .

File or Data Set Name
Optionally, transcribe a file name or data set name if it differs from the title proper. For a locally assigned file name or data set name, see 9.7B20.

RELATED AACR2 RULE

9.1B Title Proper [AACR2 Rev.]
9.1B3. Do not record a file name or a data set name as the title proper unless it is the only name given in the chief source. If desired, give a file name or data set name not used as the title proper in a note (see 9.7B4). [emphasis added]

LIBRARY OF CONGRESS POLICY

None issued for AACR2 Rev. Ch. 9.

RELATED LIBRARY OF CONGRESS POLICY

None issued for AACR2 Rev. Ch. 9.

AACR2 TEXT EXAMPLES REVISED TO REFLECT LIBRARY OF CONGRESS POLICY

None required for AACR2 Rev. Ch. 9.

HISTORICAL BACKGROUND

Computer files were not covered by AACR1 or previous codes. The original AACR2 Chapter 9 specifically called for recording variant titles on the file, its accompanying material, or other descriptions of the file. The current revision of the rule, more general in its wording, does not specify the location from which variant titles can be derived.

NOTE EXAMPLES

4.165   *Also called Historical census data for the United States, 1790-1970.

4.166   *Called also: Federal employees' attitudes toward political activity.

4.167   *Called also: German embassy study.

4.168   *Also known as: 1970 Census Fourth Count Population File (A, B, or C) Summary Tapes.

4.169   *Also known as: Volksfiler information management system.

4.170   *Labels on each disc: "Apple PILOT: author" and "Apple PILOT: lesson."

4.171   *Manual titles: "Apple PILOT: editors manual" and "Apple PILOT: language reference manual."

4.172   *Title on container: Drawing conclusions, chief of detectives.

4.173   *Title on disk label and documentation: Word volcano.

4.174   *Title on instruction booklet and container: Context clues.

Chapter 10 (Three-Dimensional Artefacts and Realia)

AACR2 RULE

10.7B4 Variations in Title [AACR2 Rev.]

Variant Title

Make notes on titles borne by the item other than the title proper.

Romanization

Optionally, give a romanization of the title proper.

RELATED AACR2 RULE

None.

LIBRARY OF CONGRESS POLICY

None issued.

RELATED LIBRARY OF CONGRESS POLICY

None issued.

AACR2 TEXT EXAMPLES REVISED TO REFLECT LIBRARY OF CONGRESS POLICY

None required.

HISTORICAL BACKGROUND

AACR1 Rev. Rule 229.2C provided for notes on "variations in title, etc., within the work." This rule is equivalent to AACR2 Rule 10.7B4.

In addition, the AACR1 Rev. rule provided for the use of variant title notes for "separately issued parts of a work cataloged as a set," unless the information was given as a contents note. AACR2 does not specifically address this situation.

Although AACR1 Rev. Ch. 12 and previous codes had no romanization of title rule equivalent to AACR2 Rule 10.7B4, the romanization note provisions for separately published monographs in these earlier codes could be used for three-dimensional artifacts and realia. (See *Historical Background* under Rule 2.7B4.)

NOTE EXAMPLES

4.175 *Title on box: "Hi! Open this box and discover why they call me the transformer."

4.176 *Legend: Francis Makemie — Father of American Presbyterianism.

Chapter 12 (Serials)

AACR2 RULE

12.7B4 Variations in Title [AACR2 Rev.]

Variant Title
> Make notes on titles borne by the serial other than the title proper.

Romanization
> *Optionally*, give a romanization of the title proper. . . .

Special Titles for Individual Issues
> If individual issues of a serial (other than a monographic series) have special titles, give the individual titles if they are considered important.

RELATED AACR2 RULE

None.

LIBRARY OF CONGRESS POLICY

None issued.

RELATED LIBRARY OF CONGRESS POLICY

12.0B1 Sources of Information. Printed Serials

Due to its length, this LC policy statement has been abridged to include only the parts related to the use of notes.

Serials

The basis for the description is the first issue of the serial. In determining which issue is first, disregard the date of publication, etc., and use the designation on the issues. For serials that carry numeric or alphabetic designations, the first issue is the one with the lowest or earliest (in the alphabet) designation. For serials that do not carry numeric or alphabetic designations, the first issue is the one with the earliest chronological designation. (If the actual first issue is not available, use these same guidelines to determine which issue should be used as the basis for the description.)

Since the title page (or title page substitute) of the first issue is the chief source of information for a printed serial, a title page that is published later to cover one or more issues cannot be used as the chief source. (However, data from such a title page may be put into the note area when necessary.) [emphasis added]

If the description has been formulated from the first issue of a serial, the body of the entry remains unchanged throughout the life of the serial. If issues after the first have data different from those recorded in the body of the entry, record the different data in the note area as necessary. [emphasis added] However, if the differences are in the title proper, create a separate record when appropriate (21.2C). (For changes in the main entry heading, see 21.3B.) . . .

Reprints of Serials

In order that the description of the reprint resemble and file with the description of the original, the earliest *issue* reprinted is used as the chief source for the first three areas of the description. Data for these areas may be taken from any place on the reprinted issue without the use of brackets. If it is known that the description of the original would include data that are not on the reprinted issue, the data may be supplied in brackets.

In area four the place of publication, publisher, and date of the reprint are recorded, using brackets if the data do not come from a prescribed source on the reprint.

The physical description area gives the physical description of the reprint, not the original.

A series is recorded if the reprint appears in a series.

Usually a single note (see 12.7B7g) gives important details about the original while other notes give necessary information about the reprint. Notes giving the source of the title or the issue on which the description is based are not given. [emphasis added] [CSB 38]

12.1B6 Title Proper

If a date or numbering occurs at the end of the title proper, do not transcribe it as part of the title proper. However, use the mark of omission to indicate this in the following two cases only:

1) there is a linking word between the designation and the preceding part of the title proper. . . .
2) case endings of one or more words in the chronological designation link these words with antecedents within the preceding part of the title proper. . . .

Omit from a title proper, using a mark of omission, any name or number that can be expected to vary. Since these omissions will not be items that are part of the numeric or chronological designation of the serial, they may be explained in notes if it is considered important to do so. [emphasis added] [CSB 28]

AACR2 TEXT EXAMPLES REVISED TO REFLECT LIBRARY OF CONGRESS POLICY

5th Example

AACR2 TEXT
Added t.p. in Uzbek

AACR2 TEXT REVISED
Title on added t.p. in Uzbek.

See *Library of Congress Policy* for Rule 2.7B4 for an explanation of this change. The fourth example in AACR2 that would have required a revision was rewritten in AACR2 Rev.

HISTORICAL BACKGROUND

AACR1 Rule 167K provided greater detail in the use of notes for variant titles than does AACR2 Rule 12.7B4. For minor variations that did not affect filing, the phrases "Title varies slightly" or "Subtitle varies" were used in AACR1. This wording is not specifically provided for in AACR2, although it could be used.

AACR1 Rule 167K also provided for notes for "varying forms of the title used on different parts of the publication" if they contributed to the identification of the publication. Variants such as running title, cover title, and binder's title fell into this category. The current rule provides for such notes, but does not have the level of detail prescribed in AACR1.

The general rule for notes (AACR1 Rule 167A2) instructed that when "describing bibliographical change in a serial publication, reference is generally made to the date of the volume or issue showing the change . . . ." Although that rule did not specifically state that dates should be given for volumes that included variant titles, every example given under AACR1 Rule 167K included the date (either open-ended or closed). AACR1 Rule 167K did provide an exception to the general date policy when "varying forms of the title appear on all volumes of a work that has ceased publication." In these situations, it was not necessary to record the inclusive dates in the note. AACR2 does not call for the inclusion of dates for variant titles nor do any of the text examples provide them.

AACR1 Rule 167L provided for notes on special titles of individual issues in much the same way as does AACR2 Rule 12.7B4. However, AACR1 stated that this note should be the last note if the serial is still in progress. AACR2 does not specify this order.

NOTE EXAMPLES

4.177   Caption title: Annual report.
4.178   Caption title: Report on the working of the minimum wages act, 1948, the year . . . in the state of Tamil Nadu.
4.179   Cover title: Annual report of the National Committee on Discrimination in Employment and Occupation,   -1974-75.
4.180   Cover title: Annual report to the Secretary of Labor under the Federal Mine Safety and Health Act of 1977.
4.181   Cover title: Assessed valuations. Volume b.
4.182   Cover title: ASCE combined index.
4.183   Cover title: CDE stock ownership directory. Fortune 500.
4.184   Cover title: Fodor's India & Nepal.
4.185   Cover title: Official NBA register.
4.186   Cover title: S.O.S. 8th ed.
4.187   Distinctive title: Farm organization and performance in the 1970's.
4.188   Distinctive title: Speakers.
4.189   Other title: Annual program plan for adult education programs under Adult Education Act.
4.190   Other title: Kentucky Philological Association Bulletin, 1974-
4.191   Other title: MLC.
4.192   Other title: Pennsylvania media directory.
4.193   Other title: PIB/LNA analysis of . . . magazine advertising.
4.194   Other title: Proceedings of the Royal Society of Edinburgh. Section A.
4.195   Other title: Twilight zone magazine.
4.196   Running title: Annual livestock slaughter.
4.197   Running title: Arthur Frommer's Rome.
4.198   Running title: Broadcasting yearbook, 1980.
4.199   Running title: F.I.L.E.
4.200   *Running title: Legislative journal — House.
        Running title: Legislative journal — Senate.

4.201   Running title: TRGA . . . annual directory.
4.202   Spine title: AIPG . . . membership directory.
4.203   Spine title: Condition of education. Volume 2, Town profiles.
4.204   Spine title: DCRT annual report FY. . . .
4.205   Spine title: IBRS.
4.206   Spine title: Let's go. Greece, Israel and Egypt.
4.207   Spine title: Publications catalog.
4.208   Spine title: Stock ownership directory. Fortune 500.
4.209   Each issue has a distinctive title.
4.210   Includes a separately numbered title: Monthly statement.
4.211   Some issues have distinctive titles.
4.212   Some vols. also have distinctive titles.
4.213   Some issues have title: In-fisherman.

1.7B5. Parallel Titles and Other Title Information

EXTRAPOLATED GENERAL RULE

Give the title in another language and other title information not recorded in the title and statement of responsibility area if they are considered to be important.

This rule does not limit the source of this information to "titles borne by the item." It would appear logical to limit other title information to information on the item itself; however, original title information in a language different from the title proper, which falls into the category of parallel titles, can be given in a note even if it does not appear on the item in hand.

RELATED AACR2 RULE

1.1D Parallel Titles [AACR2 Rev.]
    1.1D3. Transcribe an original title in a language different from that of the title proper appearing in the chief source of information as a parallel title if the item contains all or some of the text in the original language, or if the original title appears before the title proper in the chief source of information. Transcribe as other title information an original title in the same language as the title proper (see 1.1E). In all other cases give the original title in a note. [emphasis added]
    1.1D4. Give parallel titles appearing outside the chief source of information in a note (see 1.7B5). [emphasis added]

1.1E3 Lengthy Other Title Information
    If the other title information is lengthy, either give it in a note (see 1.7B5) or abridge it. [emphasis added]
    Abridge other title information only if this can be done without loss of essential information. Never omit any of the first five words of the other title information. Indicate omissions by the mark of omission.

GENERAL LIBRARY OF CONGRESS POLICY

None issued. See the separate sections that follow for any LC policies or interpretations that apply to individual AACR2 chapters for descriptions.

114

RELATED LIBRARY OF CONGRESS POLICY

1.1D4 Parallel Titles

Record in a note parallel titles appearing outside the chief source of information only if they are considered to be important. [emphasis added] [CSB 11]

1.1G2 Items without a Collective Title

Due to its length, this LC policy statement has been abridged to include only the part related to the use of notes.

Other Title Information

If a single statement of other title information applies to all the titles listed, record it after all the titles if all the titles are by the same person(s) or body (bodies). Precede the statement by a space-colon-space. Otherwise, record it in a note. [emphasis added] [CSB 25]

1.7 Note Area [at Head of Title]

There is no mention of an "at head of title" note apart from an example under 2.7B6. According to 1.1A2, 1.1F3, etc., other title information and statements of responsibility appearing at head of title are transposed to their proper position. Occasionally, however, a phrase or name that is clearly not other title information or a statement of responsibility appears at head of title. Use an "at head of title" note for these and any other indeterminate cases. [emphasis added] [CSB 11]

FORMAT

No general instructions for formatting have been provided. However, a formalized construct for subtitle notes does appear repeatedly in the AACR2 text examples in many chapters for description. This construct is:

Subtitle: . . .

CHAPTER APPLICATION

This note is present in all chapters for description. In all chapters, the provisions of the Extrapolated General Rule are present and the terminology is consistent.

EXCEPTIONS AND ADDITIONS

Chapter 12 (Serials), in addition to the Extrapolated General Rule, specifically provides for notes on variations in parallel titles and other title information.

Chapter 2 (Books, Pamphlets, and Printed Sheets)

AACR2 RULE

2.7B5 Parallel Titles and Other Title Information [AACR2 Rev.]
Give the title in another language and other title information not recorded in the title and statement of responsibility area if they are considered to be important.

RELATED AACR2 RULE

None.

LIBRARY OF CONGRESS POLICY

Apply 2.7B5 only to parallel titles and other title information not already covered by specific rules. For example, lengthy other title information appearing in the chief source must be either abridged or given in a note regardless of its importance (cf. 1.1E3). [CSB 11]

The Library of Congress appears to be stressing that the cataloger should apply the descriptive rules for parallel titles (AACR2 Rule 1.1D2) and other title information (AACR2 Rule 1.1E) first. If the item in hand contains a parallel title and/or other title information that cannot be dealt with adequately by either of these rules but is still considered important, a note would be made under the provisions of AACR2 Rule 2.7B5.

RELATED LIBRARY OF CONGRESS POLICY

None issued.

AACR2 TEXT EXAMPLES REVISED TO REFLECT LIBRARY OF CONGRESS POLICY

None required.

HISTORICAL BACKGROUND

The term parallel title was never used in relation to notes in AACR1 Rev. Ch. 6 because parallel titles were always recorded in Area 1.

By definition in AACR2, other title information includes original titles as well as subtitles, etc. AACR1 Rev. Rule 143D2 indicated that original title notes should be recorded as the second note following analytical notes. Subrules to this rule identified situations in which these notes would and would not be made.

AACR1 Rev. Rule 143D3b instructed that notes related to other titles should be recorded between notes related to the title proper and those related to statements of authorship. AACR2 docs not call for separate notes for original titles and other forms of other title information. Instead, all of these titles are recorded in AACR2 Rule 2.7B5. In AACR2, these types of notes are placed between variant title notes and statement of responsibility notes.

These AACR1 Rev. Ch. 6 rules could be used for works that were not separately published monographs unless specific rules for the description of a format superseded or excluded their use.

NOTE EXAMPLES

5.1 Title on added t.p.: Directives régissant la conservation préventive.
5.2 Added t.p. in English, French, and German; English title: Russian tapestry; French title: Tapisserie russe; German title: Russische Bildteppiche.
5.3 French title on added t.p.: Catalogue de l'incomparable et la seule complette collection des estampes de Rembrant ...
5.4 On verso of t.p.: Dissidents and Jews—who has torn the Iron Curtain?
5.5 Title on verso of t.p.: Le livre de la grande émigration en Grande-Pologne (1831-1862).
5.6 Titles on p. facing t.p.: Istoriografikila v Chekhoslovakii 1970-1980. Historiography in Czechoslovakia 1970-1980.
5.7 Title on p. 3: Boris Pasternak in den zwanziger Jahren.

At Head of Title
5.8 At head of title: Preamble compilation.
5.9 At head of title: Joint committee print.
5.10 At head of title: The complete study guide for scoring high.
5.11 At head of title: An information report.

Original Title
5.12 Original title: The friendly instructor, or, A companion for young ladies and young gentlemen. Cf. Evans 5600.
5.13 Original title in Spanish: Asi se compone un cuadro.

Other Title Information
5.14 "1818-1978"—Cover.
5.15 "A compendium of schedules and services, May 1, 1971-May 1, 1981"—Cover.
5.16 "Naval Education and Training Command rate training manual"—Cover.

5.17 "Project no. 99-R099, Final report."
5.18 "A report submitted to the U.S. Department of Agriculture and U.S. A.I.D. under contract numbers 12-53-319R-8-15 and 53-319R-8-11."
5.19 "Research study report"—Cover.
5.20 "Summary report."
5.21 Title page shows titles preceded by "Book I" and "Book II."
5.22 Vol. 2: 1920-1950.
5.23 On cover: 1974-1981.
5.24 On cover: Containing a designation table for Parts 800-899.
5.25 On cover of v. 1: 666-1600.
5.26 On cover: A practical music technique for musicians, singers, and songwriters who play by ear.
5.27 Subtitle: 1868-1874.
5.28 Subtitle: Abbreviations, acronyms, anonyms, appellations, computer terminology, contractions, criminalistic and data-processing terms, eponyms, geographical equivalents, government agencies, historical, musical, and mythological characters, initialisms, medical and military terms, nations of the world, nicknames, ports of the world, short forms, shortcuts, signs and symbols, slang, superlatives, winds of the world, zip coding, zodiacal signs.
5.29 Subtitle: A compilation of hundreds of tracker bar, key frame, and note layouts for automatic music machines, together with historical and technical information and a collector's portfolio of outstanding mechanical musical instruments.
5.30 Subtitle: A newspaper design manual including the design concept, the design revolution, one newspaper's redesign, American newspaper design, 1980, and principles of design and layout rules of the Minneapolis Tribune.
5.31 Subtitle: The proceedings of a conference sponsored by Division of Behavioral Science Research, Tuskegee Institute, Tuskegee Institute, Alabama, held in Tuskegee Institute in September 1980.
5.32 Subtitle: Proceedings of the 1980 Argentine Endocrine Foundation meetings, Buenos Aires, Argentina: Physiopathology of thyroid diseases, September 29-October 4; Physiopathology of hypothalamic-hypophysial disorders, October 27-31; Mechanisms of hormone action, October 27-31.
5.33 Cover has subtitle: Il romanzo di Francesco d'Assisi.
5.34 Subtitle on cover: Tradition with innovation.
5.35 Subtitle on v. 1 cover: Dalle origini alla dominazione normanna.
5.36 Vol. 2 has subtitle: Scelta iconografica a cura de Carlo Sisi.

Language of Parallel Title
5.37 Added t.p. in English.
5.38 Added t.p. in English and Russian; English title: Problems of the modelling and measurement of economic process in the People's Republic of Bulgaria; Russian title: Problemy modelirovanikiia i izmerenikīa ekonomicheskikh protsessov v NR Bolgarii.

5.39 Parallel title in Chinese characters.
5.40 Parallel title in Chinese characters: Chung-kuo ta hsüen yü chuan k'o chi kan mu lu.
5.41 Parallel title in English, French, and German.
5.42 Parallel title in non-roman script.
5.43 Title also in Japanese: Tessaku no uchi.
5.44 Title also in Chinese on p. vi: Ssu shih t'ien yüan tsa hsing.

Chapter 3 (Cartographic Materials)

AACR2 RULE

3.7B5 Parallel Titles and Other Title Information [AACR2 Rev.]
Give the title in another language and other title information not recorded in the title and statement of responsibility area if they are considered to be important.

RELATED AACR2 RULE

None.

LIBRARY OF CONGRESS POLICY

None issued.

RELATED LIBRARY OF CONGRESS POLICY

None issued.

AACR2 TEXT EXAMPLES REVISED TO REFLECT LIBRARY OF CONGRESS POLICY

None required.

HISTORICAL BACKGROUND

Although AACR1 and previous codes had no rule equivalent to AACR2 Rule 3.7B5, the other title note provisions for separately published monographs in these earlier codes could be used for cartographic materials. (See *Historical Background* under Rule 2.7B5.)

NOTE EXAMPLES

5.45 Title in French, Arabic, Spanish, and English.
5.46 Vol. 2 has subtitle: Entidad municipal metropolitana y otros municipios.

5.47 Parallel title on cover: Helsinki : virastokartta = Helsingfors : äm-
betsverkskarta.

5.48 "Existing water development (1980) and future plan elements [over-
lay]"—Subtitle on each map pair.

Chapter 4 (Manuscripts)

AACR2 RULE

4.7B5 Parallel Titles and Other Title Information [AACR2 Rev.]

Give the title in another language and other title information not
recorded in the title and statement of responsibility area if they are
considered to be important.

RELATED AACR2 RULE

4.4B2 Date of the Manuscript [AACR2 Rev.]

If the date of delivery of a speech, sermon, etc., differs from the
date of the manuscript, give the date of delivery in a note unless this
date is part of the title information. [emphasis added]

LIBRARY OF CONGRESS POLICY

None issued. APPM does not provide a guideline for this note.

RELATED LIBRARY OF CONGRESS POLICY

None issued.

AACR2 TEXT EXAMPLES REVISED TO REFLECT
LIBRARY OF CONGRESS POLICY

No examples were given in AACR2 or AACR2 Rev.

HISTORICAL BACKGROUND

Although AACR1 and previous codes had no rule equivalent to
AACR2 Rule 4.7B5, the other title note provisions for separately pub-
lished monographs in these earlier codes could be used for manuscripts.
(See *Historical Background* under Rule 2.7B5.)

NOTE EXAMPLES

5.49 Subtitle on leaf 27: El fuego nuevo.

Chapter 5 (Music)

AACR2 RULE

5.7B5 Parallel Titles and Other Title Information [AACR2 Rev.]
Give the title in another language and other title information not recorded in the title and statement of responsibility area if they are considered to be important.

RELATED AACR2 RULE

None.

LIBRARY OF CONGRESS POLICY

None issued.

RELATED LIBRARY OF CONGRESS POLICY

None issued.

AACR2 TEXT EXAMPLES REVISED TO REFLECT LIBRARY OF CONGRESS POLICY

No examples were given in AACR2 or AACR2 Rev.

HISTORICAL BACKGROUND

AACR1 did not provide specific rules for notes on parallel titles or other title information for music. The introductory paragraph to AACR1 Rule 248 made the general statement that "notes referring to the title are given first, followed by those describing the music." It did not define "title notes." AACR2 has changed this note order, moving notes referring to the title to the 3rd, 4th, and 5th note positions.

AACR1 Rule 248F4 provided for the inclusion in a contents note of a second title in parentheses if the titles in a song collection appeared in two languages. This was the only reference made to a parallel title in a note rule for music; however, it applied only to contents notes.

NOTE EXAMPLES

5.50 "Op. 51, no. 1"—Caption.
5.51 Parallel titles in captions: Skizzen = Esquisses ; Spiele = Jeux.

5.52   Subtitle on cover: A collection of favorite songs and singing games for children.

Chapter 6 (Sound Recordings)

AACR2 RULE

6.7B5 Parallel Titles and Other Title Information [AACR2 Rev.]
Give the title in another language and other title information not recorded in the title and statement of responsibility area if they are considered to be important.

RELATED AACR2 RULE

None.

LIBRARY OF CONGRESS POLICY

None issued.

RELATED LIBRARY OF CONGRESS POLICY

None issued.

AACR2 TEXT EXAMPLES REVISED TO REFLECT
LIBRARY OF CONGRESS POLICY

None required.

HISTORICAL BACKGROUND

AACR1 Rev. Rule 253D2 allowed for a note identifying the "original title" of a translation. This would be one form of a parallel title. The rule applied only to nonprocessed sound recordings however, and gave no further detail.

Although AACR1 Rev. Ch. 14 and previous codes had no rule equivalent to AACR2 Rule 6.7B5, the other title information note provisions for separately published monographs in these earlier codes could be used for processed sound recordings. (See *Historical Background* under Rule 2.7B5.)

NOTE EXAMPLES

LC cataloging examples seem to indicate a common format for subtitle notes using the introductory phrase: Subtitle on container:

5.53 Additional titles on container: La reine indienne = Die indianische Königin.

5.54 Parallel title: La Virtuosité à l'orgue.

5.55 Parallel titles on container: Songs of the Synagogue of Florence = Manginot Bet ha-keneset ha-gadol shel Firentsi = Chants de la Synagogue de Florence = Canticos de la Sinagoga de Florencia.

5.56 Subtitle on container: A sacred and secular eighteenth-century organ recital.

5.57 Subtitle on container: 31 variations for piano.

5.58 Subtitles on container: In celebration of the winter solstice : traditional and ritual carols, dances, and processionals.

5.59 Title on container: Klavierkonzert No. 1 = Piano concerto no. 1.

Chapter 7 (Motion Pictures and Videorecordings)

AACR2 RULE

7.7B5 Parallel Titles and Other Title Information [AACR2 Rev.]

Give the title in another language and other title information not recorded in the title and statement of responsibility area if they are considered to be important.

RELATED AACR2 RULE

None.

LIBRARY OF CONGRESS POLICY

None issued. For archival moving image materials, the Library of Congress supplements AACR2 Chapter 7 with the guidelines in *Archival Moving Image Materials* by White-Hensen.

RELATED LIBRARY OF CONGRESS POLICY

None issued.

AACR2 TEXT EXAMPLES REVISED TO REFLECT LIBRARY OF CONGRESS POLICY

None required.

HISTORICAL BACKGROUND

AACR1 Rev. Rule 229.2A provided for "earlier title" notes, including original titles, when the titles were different from those in the edition in hand. No mention was made, however, of this title being in a different language. Therefore, it cannot be concluded that this rule covered parallel titles, but probably referred only to variant titles of previous editions.

NOTE EXAMPLES

5.60 French version entitled: Mer mere.
5.61 Subtitle: Themes on perception.

Chapter 8 (Graphic Materials)

AACR2 RULE

8.7B5 Parallel Titles and Other Title Information [AACR2 Rev.]
Give the title in another language and other title information not recorded in the title and statement of responsibility area if they are considered to be important.

RELATED AACR2 RULE

None.

LIBRARY OF CONGRESS POLICY

None issued. For original items and historical collections, the Library of Congress supplements AACR2 Chapter 8 with the guidelines in *Graphic Materials* by Betz.

RELATED LIBRARY OF CONGRESS POLICY

None issued.

AACR2 TEXT EXAMPLES REVISED TO REFLECT LIBRARY OF CONGRESS POLICY

None required.

HISTORICAL BACKGROUND

AACR1 Rev. Rule 229.2A provided for "earlier title" notes, including original titles, when the titles were different from those in the edition in hand. No mention was made, however, of this title being in a different language. Therefore, it cannot be concluded that this rule covered parallel titles, but probably referred only to variant titles of previous editions.

NOTE EXAMPLES

Projection Graphic Materials
5.62   Title on notes: Schuman-Casey at the bat.

Nonprojection Graphic Materials
5.63   *Title continues: . . . height 6 ft. 1 1/2 inch, fighting weight from 180 to 185 lbs.
5.64   *Title continues: . . . knows a little about science and is more than a little crazy, likes to preform [sic] innocent little experiments on his fellow humans.
5.65   *Below title: There hath not been the like of them, neither shall there be any more after them, even to the years of many generations.
5.66   Hebrew title romanized: Mosheh Tamir, demuyot me'ofefot.

Chapter 9 (Computer Files)

AACR2 RULE

9.7B5 Parallel Titles and Other Title Information [AACR2 Rev.]
Give the title in another language and other title information not recorded in the title and statement of responsibility area if they are considered to be important.

RELATED AACR2 RULE

None.

LIBRARY OF CONGRESS POLICY

None issued for AACR2 Rev. Ch. 9.

RELATED LIBRARY OF CONGRESS POLICY

None issued for AACR2 Rev. Ch. 9.

AACR2 TEXT EXAMPLES REVISED TO REFLECT LIBRARY OF CONGRESS POLICY

No examples were given in AACR2 Rev. Ch. 9.

HISTORICAL BACKGROUND

Computer files were not covered by AACR1 or previous codes. The original AACR2 Chapter 9 was exactly the same as this rule in AACR2 Rev. except that the term "parallel titles" is not used.

NOTE EXAMPLES

Many commercially produced computer files have statements that may be subtitles defining the nature of the file. These subtitle statements may be recorded in this note or as part of a nature and scope note. The following examples are such statements.

5.67 *Subtitle on disk label: A bibliographic program.
5.68 *Subtitle on disk label, guide and container: The typing instruction game.

Chapter 10 (Three-Dimensional Artefacts and Realia)

AACR2 RULE

10.7B5 Parallel Titles and Other Title Information [AACR2 Rev.]

Give the title in another language and other title information not recorded in the title and statement of responsibility area if they are considered to be important.

RELATED AACR2 RULE

None.

LIBRARY OF CONGRESS POLICY

None issued.

RELATED LIBRARY OF CONGRESS POLICY

None issued.

AACR2 TEXT EXAMPLES REVISED TO REFLECT LIBRARY OF CONGRESS POLICY

None required.

HISTORICAL BACKGROUND

AACR1 Rev. Rule 229.2A provided for "earlier title" notes, including original titles, when the titles were different from those in the edition in hand. No mention was made, however, of this title being in a different language. Therefore, it cannot be concluded that this rule covered parallel titles, but probably referred only to variant titles of previous editions.

NOTE EXAMPLES

No examples identified.

Chapter 12 (Serials)

AACR2 RULE

12.7B5 Parallel Titles and Other Title Information [AACR2 Rev.]

Give the title in another language and other title information not recorded in the title and statement of responsibility area if they are considered to be important. Make notes on variations in parallel titles and other title information.

The wording of this rule is slightly different from that of equivalent rules in all other chapters on description. It does not require recording the actual parallel title or other title information, but rather calls for notes *about* these titles. It was probably thought best to be more general in wording due to the continuing nature of serials and, therefore, the increased possibility of changes in title information.

The wording of the second sentence of this rule is also different from this rule in other chapters. AACR2 Rule 12.7B4 covers only variations in the title proper, and does not include variations in parallel titles or other title information. This rule (AACR2 Rule 12.7B5) covers these latter title variations.

RELATED AACR2 RULE

None.

LIBRARY OF CONGRESS POLICY

The following parallel title situations may occur when the same title proper appears on the chief source of both issues involved:

127

1) The chief source of another issue has a parallel title that did not appear on the chief source of the issue on which the description was based;*
2) The chief source of another issue does not have a parallel title that appeared on the chief source of the issue on which the description was based;
3) The chief source of another issue has a variation of the parallel title that appeared on the chief source of the issue on which the description was based.

If this information is considered to be important, record it in a note. Include in the note the name of the language of the title being referred to. Do not use the term "parallel title" in notes. [CSB 26]

RELATED LIBRARY OF CONGRESS POLICY

12.0B1 Sources of Information. Printed Serials.

Due to its length, this LC policy statement has been abridged to include only the parts related to the use of notes.

Serials

The basis for the description is the first issue of the serial. In determining which issue is first, disregard the date of publication, etc., and use the designation on the issues. For serials that carry numeric or alphabetic designations, the first issue is the one with the lowest or earliest (in the alphabet) designation. For serials that do not carry numeric or alphabetic designations, the first issue is the one with the earliest chronological designation. (If the actual first issue is not available, use these same guidelines to determine which issue should be used as the basis for the description.)

Since the title page (or title page substitute) of the first issue is the chief source of information for a printed serial, a title page that is published later to cover one or more issues cannot be used as the chief source. (However, data from such a title page may be put into the note area when necessary.) [emphasis added]

If the description has been formulated from the first issue of a serial, the body of the entry remains unchanged throughout the life of the serial. If issues after the first have data different from those recorded in the body of the entry, record the different data in the note area as necessary. [emphasis added] However, if the differences are in the title

---

*Do not consider the title proper to have changed although the addition of the title in another language or script would affect the choice of title proper if the description were based on the other issue (LCRI 21.2A).

proper, create a separate record when appropriate (21.2C). (For changes in the main entry heading, see 21.3B.) . . .

Reprints of Serials

In order that the description of the reprint resemble and file with the description of the original, the earliest *issue* reprinted is used as the chief source for the first three areas of the description. Data for these areas may be taken from any place on the reprinted issue without the use of brackets. If it is known that the description of the original would include data that are not on the reprinted issue, the data may be supplied in brackets.

In area four the place of publication, publisher, and date of the reprint are recorded, using brackets if the data do not come from a prescribed source on the reprint.

The physical description area gives the physical description of the reprint, not the original.

A series is recorded if the reprint appears in a series.

Usually a single note (see 12.7B7g) gives important details about the original while other notes give necessary information about the reprint. Notes giving the source of the title or the issue on which the description is based are not given. [emphasis added] [CSB 38]

AACR2 TEXT EXAMPLES REVISED TO REFLECT LIBRARY OF CONGRESS POLICY

None required.

HISTORICAL BACKGROUND

AACR1 gave a general introduction to cataloging serials describing how that process varied from monographic cataloging. AACR1 Rule 160C stated that a "subtitle is frequently presented in a supplementary note." AACR1 Rule 162A expanded on this by indicating that long subtitles should be given in a note instead of in the body of the entry. This is identical to the AACR2 general rule for description, Rule 1.1E3.

AACR1 Rule 167K provided an "umbrella" instruction for variations in titles that covered both subtitles and titles proper. AACR2 provides separate rules for variations in parallel titles and other title information (Rule 12.7B5) and variations in the title proper (Rule 12.7B4).

NOTE EXAMPLES

The Library of Congress frequently places the subtitle in the notes area rather than in the Title and Statement of Responsibility Area. The subtitle for a serial frequently identifies the audience for whom the serial is intended. Examples of this type of subtitle note appear under AACR2 Rule 12.7B14 in this text.

5.69   Directory of feminist library workers.
5.70   Some numbers have sub-title: Midwest edition.
5.71   Vols. for <1970/76-> have parallel title: Prix du gaz.
5.72   Vols. for 1962/64-   lack English title.

1.7B6. Statements of Responsibility

EXTRAPOLATED GENERAL RULE

Variant Names

Note variant names of persons or bodies named in statements of responsibility if they are considered to be important for identification.

Additional Statements of Responsibility

Note statements of responsibility not recorded in the title and statement of responsibility area. Note persons or bodies connected with a work not already named in the description.

Previous Editions

Note persons or bodies connected with previous editions and not already named in the description.

A note used to refer to a previous edition of a work that includes a statement of responsibility relating to the previous edition is considered to be a statement of responsibility note and is covered by the provisions of this rule in the individual chapters for description. When a note referring to a previous edition of a work does not include a statement of responsibility element, it is treated as an edition and history note (.7B7).

RELATED AACR2 RULE

1.1F Statements of Responsibility [AACR2 Rev.]

1.1F2. If no statement of responsibility appears prominently in the item, neither construct one nor extract one from the content of the item. Give the relevant information in a note (see 1.7B6). [emphasis added]

Do not include in the title and statement of responsibility area statements of responsibility that do not appear prominently in the item. If such a statement is necessary, give it in a note. [emphasis added]

1.1F9. Replace symbols or other matter that cannot be reproduced by the facilities available with the cataloguer's description in square brackets. Make an explanatory note if necessary. [emphasis added]

GENERAL LIBRARY OF CONGRESS POLICY

In general, when recording a name in a statement of responsibility note, give the name in the form it appears in whatever source is at hand. If there is no such source, or if the form in the source is unsatisfactory for any reason, approximate the form required by 22.1-22.3 (for personal names) or 24.1-24.3 (for corporate names).

Do not routinely record in a note the name of the person or body chosen as the main entry heading if the name does not appear in the body of the entry or the note area for another reason. [CSB 14]

RELATED LIBRARY OF CONGRESS POLICY

1.1F Statements of Responsibility

The rule assumes that the cataloger will recognize a statement of responsibility as such and then directs the cataloger to record the statement in the title and statement of responsibility area—provided it appears prominently in the item. ("Prominent" sources are defined in 0.8 as those prescribed for the title and statement of responsibility area and the edition area.) Statements that do not appear prominently should be ignored unless they seem important in relation to the remainder of the description or they provide needed justification for an added entry. If a non-prominent statement must be given for any reason, record it in the note area. [emphasis added] If no statement of responsibility is recognized in the item, do not formulate one. (It frequently happens that there is no statement of responsibility in the title and statement of responsibility area.)

If the corporate body named at the head of title is responsible for the content of the material contained in the item, give it as a statement of responsibility. [CSB 12]

1.1F6 Statements of Responsibility

If subordinate titles (e.g., appendices or other subsidiary texts) appear after a statement(s) of responsibility, record them as subsequent statements of responsibility whether or not they actually name a person or body. If they are very lengthy, record them in a note. [emphasis added] (If such titles appear before a statement(s) of responsibility, record them as other title information (1.1E). If such titles are given equal prominence with the first work in the item, apply 1.1G.) [CSB 17]

1.7 Note Area [At Head of Title]

There is no mention of an "at head of title" note apart from an example under 2.7B6. According to 1.1A2, 1.1F3, etc., other title information and statements of responsibility appearing at head of title are transposed to their proper position. Occasionally, however, a phrase or name that is clearly not other title information or a statement of responsibility appears at head of title. Use an "at head of title" note for these and any other indeterminate cases. [emphasis added] [CSB 11]

FORMAT

No general format structures exist that are applicable to all chapters for description. Examples in some AACR2 Rev. chapters indicate a change in punctuation practice from that originally used in AACR2. AACR2 placed a space, semicolon, space between the names of persons performing on different instruments, etc., as well as between the names of persons performing different functions. AACR2 Rev. examples now use only a semicolon, space. The examples in the sections that follow reflect the punctuation followed (AACR2) when the note was written.

CHAPTER APPLICATION

This note is present in variant forms in all chapters for description. Some of these chapters do not specifically include all the provisions of the Extrapolated General Rule.

EXCEPTIONS AND ADDITIONS

Chapter 4 (Manuscripts) excludes the provision for recording persons or bodies from previous editions.

Chapter 6 (Sound Recordings) uses this note to record performers and their medium of performance. This chapter excludes a note for variant names and one for the names of persons or bodies from previous editions.

Chapter 7 (Motion Pictures and Videorecordings) uses this note to record the names of the cast and credits for persons who have made artistic and/or technical contributions to the work.

Chapter 8 (Graphic Materials), in addition to the Extrapolated General Rule, provides a note for the donor or source of the item and information on the previous owner.

Chapter 12 (Serials), in addition to providing for statements of responsibility that did not appear in Area 1, also provides for expansions of names that have appeared in abbreviated form elsewhere in the description. This note is also used to record the name of an editor considered to be "an important means of identifying the serial."

Chapter 2 (Books, Pamphlets, and Printed Sheets)

AACR2 RULE

2.7B6 Statements of Responsibility [AACR2 Rev.]

Variant Names

Make notes on variant names of persons or bodies named in statements of responsibility if these are considered to be important for identification.

Additional Statements of Responsibility

Give statements of responsibility not recorded in the title and statement of responsibility area. Make notes on persons or bodies connected with a work, or

Previous Editions

significant persons or bodies connected with previous editions and not already named in the description.

RELATED AACR2 RULE

None.

LIBRARY OF CONGRESS POLICY

None issued.

RELATED LIBRARY OF CONGRESS POLICY

None issued.

AACR2 TEXT EXAMPLES REVISED TO REFLECT LIBRARY OF CONGRESS POLICY

None required.

HISTORICAL BACKGROUND

AACR1 Rev. Rule 143D3c referred to a note to record statements of authorship. AACR2 uses the more general phrase "statements of responsibility."

AACR1 Rev. Rule 143D4a provided that a note be made to record the name of an author or editor of "earlier or subsequent editions" if there had been "a change of author heading." AACR2 still provides for such a note although under AACR2 it would be a statement of responsibility note rather than a bibliographic history note.

AACR1 Rev. Rule 144 provided for the use of an "at head of title" note when the author's name in the heading varied from that at the head of title (Rev. Rule 144A) and when a corporate body was not chosen as the author heading but was named at the head of title (Rev. Rule 144B). It also provided for a note for initials, seals, and other insignia appearing at the head of title for which an added access point was desired (Rev. Rule 144C). When recording the wording that appeared at the head of title, AACR1 Rev. Rule 144 prescribed the use of the introductory phrase, "At head of title." AACR2 does not actually use or index the phrase "At head of title" although examples in various chapters use the traditional "At head of title" phrase. Essentially the "At head of title" rules that existed in the past are still being employed but without any specific instructions from AACR2. The Library of Congress is also continuing to use the "At head of title" construct. This is provided for by the Library of Congress Rule Interpretation to AACR2 Rule 1.7.

These AACR1 Rev. Ch. 6 rules could be used for works that were not separately published monographs unless specific rules for the description of a format superseded or excluded their use.

NOTE EXAMPLES[1]

Statements of Responsibility—Personal

6.1 Author's name written on t.p.
6.2 Michael J. Fogg, principal author.
6.3 Authors: Tacy A. Arledge, Laura Frankhauser, Virginia C. Stout.
6.4 "By Robert Pokras, Edmund J. Graves, and Charles F. Dennison."—Introd.
6.5 "Atlas de Louvain [par] F. Deputdt, H. van der Haegen."
6.6 Catalog designed and edited by T. Kempas.
6.7 "Celia Hunter and Ginny Wood . . . contributed the text for this issue"—P.3.
6.8 Commentary volume, by K.H. Staub, P. Ulveling, and F. Unterkircher, includes bibliographical references.
6.9 Composer not named.
6.10 Edited by Sandra Rosenbloom.
6.11 Edited by Kai Hermann and Horst Rieck from the taped transcripts.
6.12 Essay by Gene Baro.
6.13 Festschrift dedicated by Dr. Wolfgang Wetzel.
6.14 Final two chapters completed after the author's death by his wife, Roberta R. Jackson.

---

1. See comment under *Format* on page 133.

6.15 "Illustrations by Gary Hebley"—T.p. verso.

6.16 Three of the illustrations are by Henry Tresham. Cf. Pref.

6.17 "Indexed by Ronald L. Nelson"—Cover.

6.18 Introduction by: P.M. Bardi, director.

6.19 Label mounted on t.p.: Herman H. Henkle.

6.20 Three lectures by Bo Schembechler, H. Roy Kaplan, and Ray Meyer.

6.21 Letters of Jenny Marx Longuet, Laura Marx Lafargue, and Eleanor Marx Aveling.

6.22 Libretto, by H. Meilhac and L. Halévy after the novel by P. Mérimée.

6.23 Most of the photos. reproduced are the work of J.E. Thompson and are from the McClung Historical Collection, Knoxville-Knox County Public Library.

6.24 Music by Stefan Kisiclewski.

6.25 On cover, spine: Jean Mathieux, Gerard Vincent.

6.26 On spine: R.C. Perés.

6.27 "Original manuscript . . . prepared by Anne C. Lewis"—Acknowledgments.

6.28 Originated by Harry E. Figgie, Jr.

6.29 Papers by Karen K. Christofferson, Mary Catherine Pedersen, and Kitty Smith.

6.30 Papers written by various individuals who were invited to offer recommendations which in their opinion might assist the Task Force in preparing its final report.

6.31 Photographs (36 mounted woodbury-types) by J. Thomson; text by A. Smith.

6.32 Includes photographs by A. Terziev, N. Rakhmanov, and R. Papik'ïan.

6.33 "Rewritten, revised and expanded from the first edition by Rita Claire Dorner, O.P."—p. [ii].

6.34 Screenplay by Howard J. Green, Brown Holmes, and Sheridan Gibney, based on the book by Robert Elliott Burns.

6.35 Text by A. Grimm; photographs by M. Du Camp and F. Frith.

6.36 Translated by: Edita Lausanne.

6.37 Translated by Alexander Nesbitt, with a new introd. by Andrew Hoyem.

6.38 Translated from Estonian by Gustav Liiv.

6.39 The U.S. Geographical Surveys West of the 100th Meridian were under the direction of George M. Wheeler.

6.40 "Updated by Patrick Moore"—Jacket.

6.41 "Written by Cynthia Cavenaugh Jones"—Cover.

6.42 Written by M. Leanne Lachman and Lewis Bolan (Real Estate Research Corporation).

Statements of Responsibility—Corporate

6.43 "Arthur D. Little, Inc."—Cover.

6.44 "Lyndon B. Johnson Space Center."

6.45 "National Institute on Drug Abuse."

6.46 "Army Research Office."—T.p. verso.
     "Dept. of Meteorology, Texas A&M University"—T.p. verso.

"Atmospheric Sciences Division, Space Sciences Laboratory, NASA, Marshall Space Flight Center"—T.p. verso.

6.47 An activity of the National Information Center for Special Education Materials.

6.48 Compiled by Arthur Young & Company and the ABA Section of Economics of Law Practice.

6.49 Co-sponsored by NSF Grant PFR 77-07301 and the College of Agricultural and Environmental Sciences, University of California, Davis.

6.50 "Funded by: Freeport Minerals Company, New York and Reno; National Endowment for the Arts, a Federal agency."

6.51 Initiated by the Committee for the Study of War Documents of the American Historical Association and continued in July 1963 by the National Archives and Record Service.

6.52 Inventory commissioned by Institut für Denkmalpflege.

6.53 "Issued under the auspices of the Institute of Southeast Asian Studies, Singapore, and the International Academy of Indian Culture, New Delhi."

6.54 On cover: Dept. of the Environment.

6.55 On leaf preceding t.p.: Akademiĭa nauk Gruzinskoĭ SSR. Institut istorii gruzinskogo iskusstva im. G. Chubinashvili.

6.56 On p. facing t.p.: Polska Akademia Nauk. Instytut Rozwoju Wsi i Rolnictwa.

6.57 On t.p.: Brigham Young University, Provo, Utah, U.S.A. Language and Intercultural Research Center, New World Languages Research Division.

6.58 Outgrowth of three international symposia held from 1973-1979 under the auspices of Brown, Boston, and Harvard universities.

6.59 Papers from 5 symposia sponsored by the Tort and Insurance Practice Section of the American Bar Association.

6.60 Participating museums: National Gallery of Art, Washington, D.C., et al.

6.61 "Prepared by the Federal Aviation Agency, Flight Standards Service, Maintenance Division"—Pref.

6.62 Prepared for the Directorate of Sanitary Engineering.

6.63 "Prepared for the Congressional Research Service by Lewin and Associates, Inc."—P. ix.

6.64 A project of the Smithsonian Tropical Research Institute.

6.65 "Promulgated and amended by the United States Supreme Court"—p. iii.

6.66 A publication of the Oklahoma Image Project which is jointly sponsored by the Oklahoma Dept. of Libraries and the Oklahoma Library Association.

6.67 Research conducted by System Design Concepts, Inc.

6.68 "A special report of the Virginia colonial records project."

6.69 Sponsored by the Marin Cultural Center.

6.70 A study sponsored by the National Conference of Catholic Bishops' Committee on Evangelization.

6.71 "Validated by the International Fire Service Training Association."

6.72 Written by the editors and staff of Runner's world magazine.

Statements of Responsibility—At Head of Title

6.73 At head of title: The Chicago Historical Society.

6.74 At head of title: Conference organized in the jubilee year of the 60th anniversary of the Association of Polish Electrical Engineers.

6.75 At head of title: 96th Congress, 2d session. Committee print.

6.76 At head of title: Joel Whitburn's Record Research.

6.77 At head of title: Reorganized Church of Jesus Christ of Latter Day Saints.

6.78 At head of title: State of Michigan.

Statements of Responsibility—Clarification

6.79 Anonymous. By Elinor Wylie.

6.80 Issued anonymously. An expansion, by T. FitzRoy Fenwick, of the descriptions of the Meerman manuscripts published by Sir Thomas Phillipps, their late owner, in only the briefest form (Catalogus liborum manuscriptorum in bibliotheca d. Thomae Phillipps, bart., A.D. 1837. p. 17-22). Cf. Munby.

6.81 Published anonymously. The author revealed her identity in a later ed. (New York : Harper & Row, 1972).

6.82 Published anonymously. By James Christie. Cf. Dict. nat. biog.

6.83 The artist who made the sketches is identified as Charles Ellery Stedman in the 1950 reprint. The lithographic work has been attributed to Winslow Homer. Cf. Antiques, Nov. 1974, p. 844-[851]; The Civil War sketchbook of Charles Ellery Stedman / Jim Dan Hill. 1976. p. 23-28.

6.84 Attributed to Sextus Pythagoreus; also attributed to Sixtus II—Encycl. Brit. and Cath. encycl.

6.85 Author identified in BN and in A bibl. of printing / E.C. Bigmore.

6.86 Authorship is traditionally ascribed to Shih Nai-on or Lo Kuan-chung or to both in collaboration.

6.87 Copyright by Pamela Bruce.

6.88 Curtius Soredd is a character invented by R.O.B. (Roland Orvil Baughman) the real author.

6.89 Edited by L. Valentine? Cf. Shakespeare bibliography / W. Jaggard.

6.90 First ed. (1932) and copyright application of author/claimant Paul Johnston give his pseudonym as J.H.B., Jr.

6.91 Generally attributed to Adam Ferguson.

6.92 Signed at end: A Questionist.

6.93 Signed at end: Young Durham. Sabin (70540) lists an issue signed Terry Durham and incorrectly dates it 181-?

6.94 Foreword signed: Roger Bogus.

6.95 Introd. signed: M.K. Vaughan.

6.96 Preface signed: H.P.K.

6.97 Written by the author under various aliases.

Statements of Responsibility—Multiple Volumes

6.98 Beginning with v. 5, issued by Mining and Lands Commissioner and published by Ontario Ministry of Natural Resources.

6.99 Issue no. 7 prepared by the Special Projects and Policy Research Branch of the Alberta Municipal Administrative Services Division.

6.100 Part B- : edited by Laszlo Lorand.

6.101 Vol. 2, editor: John A. Scanlan.

6.102 Vol. 2: Centennial edition. Compiled and written by the Joshua Historical Book Committee.

6.103 Vol. 3: Trial techniques / by Charles Kramer.

6.104 Vol. 3, containing indexes, was prepared in collaboration with W. Peeters.

6.105 Vol. 4 compiled by the staff of the United States Historical Documents Institute.

6.106 Vols. 7- : James L. Mooney, editor, in association with Richard T. Speer.

6.107 Vol. 2 edited by William Page; v. 3 edited by Susan Reynolds; v. 4 edited by J.S. Cockburn and T.F.T. Baker; v. 5-8 edited by T.F.T. Baker.

Previous Editions

6.108 Authors' names in reverse order in 1st ed. 1972.

6.109 Authors' names in reverse order in 2nd ed.

6.110 Apparently based on work of the same title by Ramón D. Perés.

6.111 Based on: La Tosca / Victorien Sardou.

6.112 Based on: Life on the Mississippi / Mark Twain.

6.113 Edition for 1978 entered under Kalton C. Lahue.

6.114 Edition for 1976 by H.A. Linde and G. Bunn.

6.115 Expansion and revision of 2 works by William Matthews: American diaries and American diaries in manuscript, 1580-1954.

6.116 Fifth ed.: Botany / T. Elliot Weier, C. Ralph Stocking, Michael G. Barbour.

6.117 First ed. (1972) by Farrel A. Branson, Gerald F. Gifford, and J. Robert Owen.

6.118 First ed.: Computers and the UDC / prepared by Malcolm Rigby.

6.119 First ed.: Synopsis of gynecology / Harry Sturgeon Crossen. 1932.

6.120 First published in 1959 as: Educational administration / Edgar L. Morphet, Roe L. Johns, Theodore L. Reller.

6.121 Later ed. of: Travel research bibliography / Travel Reference Center. 1976.

6.122 Originally edited by Stanley Rubel.

6.123 Previous ed. (1977) edited by A.S. Burack.

6.124 Previous ed.: Douglas Ehninger, Alan H. Monroe, Bruce E. Grombeck. 8th ed. c1978.

6.125 Previous eds. by Virginia State Chamber of Commerce.

6.126   Previous ed. (1965) entered under: Markowski, Benedict.

6.127   Previous ed. by Special Libraries Association, Illinois Chapter.

6.128   Previous editions entered under: Lange, Heinrich, 1900-1977.

6.129   Second ed. (c1980), without Florida supplement, by L. Atbetman, E. McMahon, and E.L. O'Brien.

Chapter 3 (Cartographic Materials)

AACR2 RULE

3.7B6 Statements of Responsibility [AACR2 Rev.]

Variant Names

Make notes on variant names of persons or bodies named in statements of responsibility if these are considered to be important for identification.

Additional Statements of Responsibility

Give statements of responsibility not recorded in the title and statement of responsibility area. Make notes on persons or bodies connected with a work, or

Previous Editions

significant persons or bodies connected with previous editions and not already named in the description.

RELATED AACR2 RULE

None.

LIBRARY OF CONGRESS POLICY

None issued.

RELATED LIBRARY OF CONGRESS POLICY

None issued.

AACR2 TEXT EXAMPLES REVISED TO REFLECT LIBRARY OF CONGRESS POLICY

None required.

HISTORICAL BACKGROUND

AACR1 Rule 212E7 prescribed a note for "every person having a hand in or direct responsibility for an early map" if they had not been named in the body of the entry. AACR2 does not require this note for "every person," nor does it restrict its use to early maps.

NOTE EXAMPLES[2]

Additional Statements of Responsibility

6.130 "Gifford Pinchot"—Cover.

6.131 "Stahlnecker, Secretary to the governor"—Cover.

6.132 At head of title: Department of the Capital Territory.

6.133 At head of title: Foreign Scouting Service.

6.134 At head of title: M.O. Collins.

6.135 At head of title: Oxford/Philip.

6.136 At head of title: Presented by Time.

6.137 At head of title: United States Air Force Academy.

6.138 "Atlas designed by Mal. M. Petty."

6.139 "The Bahamian section was compiled for and in conjunction with the Ministry of Education and Culture."

6.140 *Base map prepared by the Arkansas State Highway Dept., Division of Planning and Research, in cooperation with the U.S. Dept. of Commerce, Bureau of Public Roads.

6.141 "Compiled . . . from information obtained by the Survey, Commonwealth Bureau of Mineral Resources, Geology Department of the University of Western Australia, and oil and mineral exploration companies."

6.142 "Copyright Collins-Longman Atlases"—Cover and most plates.

6.143 On all maps: Copyright Murray Book Distributors Pty. Limited.

6.144 Fire insurance information by Renié Admap Co.; maps and index map by Thomas Bros. Maps.

6.145 Foreword by Clifford Lee Lord.

6.146 "Issued by Automobile Club of Southern California and California State Automobile Association."

6.147 A joint project with the Dept. of Regional Economic Expansion.

6.148 Map 38 signed by Barriere and Dien as sculpsit and other maps are signed by E. Dussy as engraver.

6.149 Maps are engr. by Augustine Ryther, Remigius Hogenberg, Leonard Terwoort, Nicholas Reynolds, Cornelius Hogius, and Francis Scatter.

6.150 "Maps are supplied by the Property and Insurance Office . . . updated and revised by the City Engineering Department"—Verso t.p.

6.151 On cover: Lineas Aereas Internacionales de Espana IBERIA.

---

2. See comment under *Format* on page 133.

6.152 On most maps: "The Edinburgh Geographical Institute. Copyright John Bartholomew & Son, Ltd."
6.153 On cover: Presented by Fortune.
6.154 On all maps: Munger service.
6.155 On each map: Prepared by Geographic Mapping Division, RTSD.
6.156 "Published with the approval of the Bolton Corporation."
6.157 Real Estate Data reproduced both volumes which are compiled by Dept. of Real Estate Assessment of Alexandria, Va.
6.158 "Sponsored by the Center for Great Plains Studies, University of Nebraska-Lincoln, and the American Philosophical Society, Philadelphia."
6.159 Stamped on: Chamber of Commerce Cumming-Forsyth County.
6.160 Street index "Compiled by the Clayton County Planning Section of the Public Works Department. Corrected July 1, 1981."
6.161 *Survey and map preparation: George F. Metzler.

Chapter 4 (Manuscripts)

AACR2 RULE

4.7B6 Statements of Responsibility [AACR2 Rev.]

Variant Names

Make notes on variant names of persons or bodies named in statements of responsibility if these are considered to be important for identification.

Additional Statements of Responsibility

Give statements of responsibility not recorded in the title and statement of responsibility area. Make notes on persons or bodies connected with a work or the manuscript and not already named in the description.

As one would expect for manuscripts, no provision is made for recording the names of persons or bodies from previous editions.

RELATED AACR2 RULE

None.

LIBRARY OF CONGRESS POLICY

None issued. APPM has no rule equivalent to AACR2 Rule 4.7B6.

RELATED LIBRARY OF CONGRESS POLICY

None issued.

AACR2 TEXT EXAMPLES REVISED TO REFLECT
LIBRARY OF CONGRESS POLICY

None required.

HISTORICAL BACKGROUND

AACR1 Rule 204C provided for a note to record "signatures or marks of officials and witnesses" on legal papers.

AACR1 Rule 207E provided for a note to record "names which are significant to" a manuscript collection.

Although these AACR1 notes are not specifically called for by AACR2, they could be made under the more general wording of the current rule.

NOTE EXAMPLES[3]

6.162   *Leighton, M.D., 1833 on verso.
6.163   At end: Daniel Ingalis.
6.164   *Autograph albums of: James C. Weston, J.B. Barrows, A.T. Akerman.
6.165   Collection originally begun by David McNeely Stauffer and completed by Mr. Morgan.
6.166   Commissioned by the Elizabeth Sprague Coolidge Foundation in the Library of Congress, Washington, D.C.
6.167   *Countersigned by John D. Long, Secretary of the Navy.
6.168   *Engraving by D. Orme.
6.169   *Money order made out to Col. Tench Tilghman, signed by Franklin.
6.170   *"Okayed by Clarence Brown. From: Ben Maddow. 12-8-48. Run: 12-16-48."
6.171   *"Prepared for the Eighth World Congress of Sociology, Toronto, August 18-24, 1974."
6.172   *Registered no. 3; signed by Wm. M. Smith, reg.
6.173   Scenario, by Nuitter ; choreography by St. Léon.
6.174   *Signature on cover: Best wishes to H. Bauer from John D. Marshall, Mayor of Cleveland, October 8th, 1931.
6.175   *Signature on cover: Sincerely, John Marshall.

Chapter 5 (Music)

AACR2 RULE

5.7B6 Statements of Responsibility [AACR2 Rev.]

Variant Names

Make notes on variant names of persons or bodies named in statements of responsibility if these are considered to be important for identification.

---

3. See comment under *Format* on page 133.

Additional Statements of Responsibility
> Give statements of responsibility not recorded in the title and statement of responsibility area. Make notes on persons or bodies connected with a work, or

Previous Editions
> significant persons or bodies connected with previous editions and not already named in the description.

It is also appropriate to record statements of responsibility for things other than persons or bodies, e.g., for music, the textual source is frequently given under this rule. (See *Historical Background*.)

RELATED AACR2 RULE

None.

LIBRARY OF CONGRESS POLICY

None issued.

RELATED LIBRARY OF CONGRESS POLICY

None issued.

AACR2 TEXT EXAMPLES REVISED TO REFLECT LIBRARY OF CONGRESS POLICY

None required.

HISTORICAL BACKGROUND

AACR1 Rule 248C4 had a narrower focus than does the AACR2 rule but was delineated in greater detail. This earlier rule specifically provided for recording the:

name of the author of the text of an extended vocal work
name of the author and title of a work on which a text may be based
identification of Biblical or liturgical texts
names of translators.

The rule also specified that this information was to be recorded for "lesser works," and Biblical and liturgical texts only when it was stated in the copy in hand. A similar restriction applied to statements about translators. AACR2 expands the coverage of the AACR1 rule to include all possible situations involving responsibility for a work (not just text). In so doing, AACR2 loses some of the useful details delineated in the earlier rules.

NOTE EXAMPLES[4]

Additional Statements of Responsibility

6.176 Arranged by the composer from his vaudeville-opera The Eatonswill election.

6.177 "Ascribed to Ockeghem by Guillaume Cretius"—Pref.

6.178 At head of title: Istituto internazionale L. Cherubini.

6.179 At head of title: Mel Bay presents.

6.180 "The authenticity of the work has been questioned by Georg Kinsky in his Das Werk Beethoven[s], but has been certified by Wilhelm Altman as an arrangement by Beethoven of the First string trio, opus 3"— p. [4].

6.181 "Commissioned by the AGO Midwinter Conclave, 1973, St. Petersburg, Florida."

6.182 Compilation and introd. by Mejia Sanchez.

6.183 Compiled by Gerald S. Doyle.

6.184 Composed in part by L. Beaulieu and J. Salmon. Cf. Fétis. Biog. univ. des musiciens. 2. éd., p. 232.

6.185 "Created by Joybug Teaching Aids, inc."

6.186 "Edited by Henri Temianka of the Paganini Quartet"—caption.

6.187 Edited by R.P. Block.

6.188 English translations by Ian Howard and Paul Willenbrock.

6.189 Freely adapted by Henze (music) and Di Leva (libretto) from the original, music by Paisiello, libretto by Lorenzi, after the novel by Cervantes ; German translation by Karlheinz Guthelm.

6.190 "Guitar fingerings by Alan Rinehart."

6.191 Libretto by the composer?

6.192 Orchestral instrumentation reduced by the composer.

6.193 Original French libretto by E. Cormon and H. Crémieux based on the novel by Daniel Defoe.

6.194 Original piano solo version by Schubert ; arr. for piano and orchestra by Liszt.

6.195 The piano part edited by Donald F. Tovey ; the violoncello part edited by Paul Such.

6.196 Piano reduction by Joseph Vieland.

6.197 Piano reduction by the composer.

6.198 Prepared by "une commission spéciale composée de MM. Goossec, Roze, Ozi et Rogat"—Pref.

6.199 Text adaptation by the composer.

---

4. See comment under *Format* on page 133.

6.200   Theme by Rossini.
6.201   Unfigured bass realized by Robert Paul Block.
6.202   Vol.   edited by Maurice Cauchie and Kenneth Gilbert ; v.   edited by André Schaeffner and Kenneth Gilbert.
6.203   Words and/or music in part in collaboration with others.

Additional Statements of Responsibility—Text

6.204   Poems taken from Joyce's Pomes penyeach (1927).
6.205   Text by Wilhelm Müller.
6.206   Text from Alice's adventures in Wonderland (prefatory poem) by Lewis Carroll.
6.207   Text from Nicolas de Flue.
6.208   Text from the author's Lavorare stanca.
6.209   Text from the earliest English poems, translated by Michael Alexander.
6.210   "The verbal text is a 'found poem,' assembled by the composer from various municipal and provincial traffic signs of south-central Ontario."—Pref.
6.211   Words by A.E. Housman.
6.212   Words by John Milton (Paradise lost XI 799-805) and Wm. Shakespeare (Ulysses' speech, Troilus and Cressida, Act 1, Scene 3).
6.213   Words by Rainer Maria Rilke, Nr. XXI from Sonette an Orpheus, Teil 2.
6.214   Words by various poets.
6.215   Words compiled by the composer.
6.216   Words by V. Soloukhin originally in Russian.
6.217   Words from the Bible.
6.218   Words from the Bible, printed as text on prelim. pages.
6.219   Words taken from Ingelow's High tide on the coast of Lincolnshire; printed also as text on p. 63-64.

Previous Editions

6.220   "After Czerny studies."—New Grove.
6.221   Based on a romance from Nicolo Isouard's opera Joconde.
6.222   Based on Ancelot's Elisabeth d'Angleterre.
6.223   Based on Corneille's play Polyeucte.
6.224   Based on Marcha Zacatecas, by G. Codina, Vals Club Verde, by R. Campondonico, and the folksong La Adelita.
6.225   Based on a theme from the hymn by Thomas Hastings.
6.226   Based on the story, Le avventure di Pinocchio by Carlo Lorenzini.
6.227   Based on themes from: I puritani / Bellini.
6.228   Based on themes from the song by Louis Lambert (P.S. Gilmore).
6.229   The 1st movement based on pastoral melody from William Tell overture; 2nd movement based on theme from Italian in Algiers (Pappataci, che mai sento).
6.230   Music based on holograph in Central Music Library of Kirov Opera and Ballet Theatre, Leningrad ; libretto based on version published in St. Petersburg in 1792 under supervision of librettist.

6.231   Words based on chorale text by Paul Gerhardt.

Chapter 6 (Sound Recordings)

AACR2 RULE

6.7B6 Statements of Responsibility [AACR2 Rev.]

Variant Names
> Make notes on variant names of persons or bodies named in state-
> ments of responsibility if these are considered to be important for
> identification.

Additional Statements of Responsibility
> Give the names of performers and the medium in which they per-
> form if they have not been named in the statements of responsibility
> and if they are judged necessary. Make notes relating to any other
> persons or bodies connected with a work that are not named in the
> statements of responsibility. . . .

*Combination of Statements of Responsibility into the Contents
Note*
> Incorporate the names of performers into the contents note if
> appropriate (see 6.7B18).

Although not specified in the rules, information besides the names
of persons or bodies can be included in the statement of responsibility
note for sound recordings when that information is considered important. Examples of the following types of information have been found
in Library of Congress cataloging copy:

> Source of the music, i.e., author and or/title of a work on which the
> music is based
> Source of the text, i.e., author, librettist, Biblical source, title of work,
> etc.
> Information about the specific instrument(s) being performed on, i.e.,
> location of organ, builder or manufacturer of keyboard instrument,
> original instruments, etc.
> Qualifiers to relate performers to a specific work on a recording, i.e.,
> work number, side number, thematic index number, etc.

RELATED AACR2 RULE

6.1F Statements of Responsibility
> **6.1F1 [AACR2 Rev.]** Transcribe statements of responsibility relating
> to writers of spoken words, composers of performed music, and col-
> lectors of field material for sound recordings as instructed in 1.1F.

If the participation of the person(s) or body (bodies) named in a statement found in the chief source of information goes beyond that of performance, execution, or interpretation of a work (as is commonly the case with "popular," rock, and jazz music), give such a statement as a statement of responsibility.

If, however, the participation is confined to performance, execution, or interpretation (as commonly the case with "serious" or classical music and recorded speech), give the statement in the note area (see 6.7B6). [emphasis added]

6.1F2 If the members of a group, ensemble, company, etc., are named in the chief source of information as well as the name of the group, etc., give them in the note area (see 6.7B6) if they are considered important. [emphasis added] Otherwise omit them.

LIBRARY OF CONGRESS POLICY

In giving the names of players in nonmusic sound recordings, caption the note "Cast." Add the roles or parts of players if deemed appropriate, in parentheses after the name (cf. 7.7B6). [CSB 13]

This results in the following construct:

Cast: [Name (role)]

For medium of performance and performer notes, when only one instrument and one performer are given, the Library of Congress frequently uses the following note constructs:

[Instrument: Performer]
[Performer, instrument]

RELATED LIBRARY OF CONGRESS POLICY

1.7A3 Forms of Notes

When nonroman data (including quotations) are being recorded in the note area, give them in romanized form in all cases, including those cards that contain nonromanized elements in the body of the entry.

When a note begins with a formal introductory term such as "contents," "credits," or "summary," do not use all caps in any case; instead, use upper and lower case as illustrated in AACR 2. [emphasis added] [CSB 22]

AACR2 TEXT EXAMPLES REVISED TO REFLECT LIBRARY OF CONGRESS POLICY

None required.

HISTORICAL BACKGROUND

AACR1 Rev. Rule 252F4a provided for a note to record the names of participants, performers, and performing groups as well as information about the medium of performance. Detailed instructions were given on the formulation of these notes, including their punctuation and the use of definite articles.

AACR1 Rev. Rule 252F5 provided for a note recording information about the language of the performance and, if necessary, the authorship of the text.

AACR1 Rev. Rule 252F11, while not specifically addressing the issue of statements of responsibility, did provide examples in which performers were given as a part of the summary note. AACR2 does not give any instructions to follow this practice.

AACR1 Rev. Rule 252F12 provided for the combination of performer note with the contents note if this was deemed necessary for relating performers to a specific work (e.g., a collection of works by several performers). AACR2 instructs that these statements be combined in the statement of responsibility note.

NOTE EXAMPLES[5]

Musical Works

PERFORMERS (SPECIFIED)

6.232 Allegri String Quartet ; with Moray Welsh, violoncello.

6.233 Amadeus-Quartett.

6.234 Art Blakey, drums ; Jazz Messengers (Ronnie Matthews, piano ; Larry Evans, bass ; Bill Hardman, trumpet ; Julian Priester, trombone ; Billy Harper, tenor saxophone).

6.235 Barbara Hendricks, Linda Zoghby, sopranos ; Della Jones, mezzo-soprano ; Philip Langridge, tenor ; Benjamin Luxon, baritone ; Brighton Festival Chorus ; Royal Philharmonic Orchestra ; Antal Dorati, conductor.

6.236 Beverly Sills, soprano, with various additional vocal soloists, orchestras, and conductors.

6.237 Boston Camerata ; Joel Cohen, director.

6.238 Bournemouth Symphony Orchestra ; the composer conducting.

---

5. Examples in AACR2 Rev. Chapter 6 indicate a change in punctuation practice from that originally used in AACR2. AACR2 placed a space, semicolon, space between the names of performers on different instruments, of different vocal parts, etc. AACR2 Rev. examples now use only a semicolon, space. The examples above reflect the punctuation followed (AACR2) when the note was written.

6.239   Brendan Mulvihill, fiddle, principally with Mick Moloney, guitar, mandolin, or bouzouki.

6.240   Bryan Bowers, autoharp and vocals, with ensemble.

6.241   Chicago Symphony Orchestra ; Sir Georg Solti, conductor.

6.242   Cleo Laine, singer ; James Galway, flute ; ensemble conducted by John Dankworth.

6.243   Count Basie, piano, and orchestra.

6.244   Ensemble vocal et instrumental "Les Arts florissants" ; William Christie, director.

6.245   John Adams, director.

6.246   Gerald Gifford, organ-conductor ; Northern Sinfonia Orchestra.

6.247   Harry "Sweets" Edison, trumpet ; Eddie "Lockjaw" Davis, tenor sax ; Dolo Coker, piano ; Harvey Newmark, bass ; Jimmie Smith, drums.

6.248   C. Burris, vocals, harmonica, and bones.

6.249   Janet Baker, mezzo-soprano ; Helen Watts, alto ; Robert Tear, tenor ; John Shirley-Quirk, baritone ; Benjamin Luxon, bass-baritone . . . et al. ; London Voices ; English Chamber Orchestra ; Raymond Leppard, conductor.

6.250   Jean-Pierre Rampal, flute ; English Chamber Orchestra ; Claudio Scimone, conductor.

6.251   Jerry Rasmussen, vocals and guitar, with assisting instrumentalists

6.252   Judy Holliday, Sydney Chaplin (Bells are ringing) ; Ethel Merman, Jack Klugman (Gypsy) ; Barbra Streisand, Sydney Chaplin (Funny girl).

6.253   Lennie Tristano, piano, with ensemble or alone.

6.254   Lieder Quartet (SATB) with 2nd unidentified tenor ; Marie-Claude Arbaretaz, piano ; Jean-Noel Crocq, Alain Damien, basset horns/clarinets ; Jean-Marc Volta, basset horns.

6.255   Lily Pons, Noel Coward, Cathleen Nesbitt, Richard Burton, and others, with orchestra ; Lehman Engel, conductor.

6.256   Luciano Pavarotti, tenor, with other soloists, and various choruses, orchestras, and conductors.

6.257   Mike Moloney playing the banjo, mandolin, guitar, and bouzouki in over-dubbed recordings.

6.258   Saint Louis Symphony Orchestra ; Walter Susskind, Leonard Slatkin, conductors.

6.259   Slide Hampton . . . et al., trombone, with Albert Dailey, piano, Ray Drummond, bass, and Leroy Williams, drums.

6.260   Statman, mandolin, with ensemble.

6.261   Sung by the composer and others as specified below.

6.262   Various ensembles ; Mingus, double bass and director.

6.263   Various ensembles under the auspices of Revels, Inc. ; John Langstaff, director.

6.264   Various performers, featuring Fats Waller, vocals, piano, and organ.

6.265   Various soloists ; Wiener Philharmoniker ; Karl Böhm, conductor.

6.266   Vladimir Ashkenazy, piano and conductor ; Philharmonia Orchestra.

6.267 William Christie, Arthur Haas, harpsichords.

6.268 With: Members of the Concerto Soloists of Philadelphia ; Daniel Beckwith, organ ; Joseph Flummerfelt, conductor.

PERFORMERS (UNSPECIFIED)

6.269 Ensemble of musicians of various tribes.

6.270 Different tenors, with orchestra.

6.271 Various bands.

6.272 Various male gospel quartets from Birmingham and surrounding Jefferson Co., Ala.

6.273 Various performers.

6.274 Various vocalists and groups.

PERFORMER AND INSTRUMENT INFORMATION

6.275 Brigitte Haudebourg, harpsichord (Wittmayer, copy of I. Ruckers, 1640) ; Pro Arte Orchestra ; Kurt Redel, conductor.

6.276 Edward Tarr, trumpet ; Elisabeth Westenholz playing the organ of the Vangede Church, Copenhagen.

6.277 English concert (on period instruments) ; Trevor Pinnock, conductor and harpsichord.

6.278 Esterhazy Baryton Trio (baryton, viola, and violoncello).

6.279 J.S. Darling, playing the organ at Bruton Parish Church, Williamsburg.

6.280 Piano (Steinway): Yasuo Watanabe.

6.281 Quartett Collegium Aureum ; performed on original instruments.

PERFORMERS (SPECIFIC PIECES)

6.282 Donald Byrd, trumpet (2nd-4th, 6th-9th works) ; Lee Morgan, trumpet (1st, 5th works) ; Hank Mobley, tenor saxophone ; Ronnie Ball, piano (2nd-3rd, 6th, 9th works) ; Barry Harris, piano (4th, 7th-8th works) ; Hank Jones, piano (1st, 5th works) ; Doug Watkins, bass ; Kenny Clarke, drums (2nd-4th, 6th-9th works) ; Art Taylor, drums (1st, 5th works).

6.283 Gérard Jarry, violin, or (in op. 7, no. 3) Christian Lardé, flute ; Jean-François Paillard Chamber Orchestra ; Jean-François Paillard, conductor.

6.284 Ian Reynolds, flute (3d work) ; unidentified orchestra ; Graham Nash, conductor.

6.285 Jim French, saxophones, recorder, pibcorn, and panpipe (side 1) and in improvisations with Henry Kaiser, guitar and Diamánda Galás, voice (side 2).

6.286 Light Music Society Orchestra ; Sir Vivian Dunn, conductor ; with David Parkhouse, piano (4th work).

6.287 Marcel Moÿse, flute ; Adolf Busch, violin (2d work) ; Rudolf Serkin, piano (2d work) ; Adolf Busch Chamber Orchestra ; Adolf Busch, conductor.

6.288 Milt Jackson, vibes ; Ray Brown, bass ; Cedar Walton, piano ; John Collins, guitar (2nd work) ; Vaughn Andre, guitar (7th work) ;

Billy Higgins, drums (1st, 3rd, 6th, and 8th works) ; Frank Severino, drums (2nd work).

6.289 Strauss-Quartett ; Eduard Brunner, clarinet, Irma Zucca-Sehlbach, piano (in the 2nd work).

6.290 Ulf Hoelscher, violin ; North German Radio Symphony Orchestra ; Klaus Tennstedt, conductor ; cadenza by Kreisler (in the 1st movement).

6.291 1st work: Czech Philharmonic Orchestra ; Jiří Bělohlávek, conductor. 2d work: Plzeň Radio Orchestra ; Mario Klemens, conductor.

6.292 1st work: Royal Philharmonic Orchestra ; Per Dreier, conductor. 2nd work: Clas Pehrsson, recorders ; Solveig Faringer, soprano (wordless) ; Cecilia Peijel, guitar ; Carl-Axel Dominique, piano. 3rd work: Gunilla von Bahr, flute ; Diego Blanco, guitar ; Stockholm Chamber Ensemble ; the composer conducting.

6.293 In the 1st work: Members of the St. Paul Chamber Orchestra ; William McGlaughlin, conductor. In the 2nd: St. Paul Chamber Orchestra ; Dennis Russell Davies, conductor. In the 3rd: Cynthia Stokes, flute and piccolo.

6.294 Vienna Philharmonic Orchestra ; Berlin State Opera Orchestra (last work) ; Franz Schalk, conductor.

6.295 Julian Lloyd Webber, violoncello (3d work) ; London Philharmonic Orchestra ; Nicholas Braithwaite, conductor.

PERSONS OTHER THAN PERFORMERS

6.296 Cadenzas and completion of K. 371 (originally a fragment) by the soloist.

6.297 Cadenzas for K. 491 by Ashkenazy.

6.298 Completed by Deryck Cooke, final version.

6.299 Edited by Paul Kresh ; presented by Arthur Luce Klein.

6.300 The 1st, 3rd, and 7th songs by Nancy Lou Johnson, the remainder traditional.

6.301 "Reconstruction by Frederick Renz"—Program booklet.

6.302 Recorded in association with the British Council.

6.303 The 2nd, 6th-8th works composed by Milt Jackson.

6.304 "Translated by Leonard J. Kent and Elizabeth C. Knight"— Container.

6.305 Written and produced by the Firesign Theatre: Philip Austin, Peter Bergman, David Ossman, Philip Proctor.

SPURIOUS OR QUESTIONABLE STATEMENTS

6.306 Authenticity of the 1st work doubtful.

6.307 "Sonatas BWV 1020, 1031, and 1033 are strongly suspected of inauthenticity"—Program notes.

TEXT

6.308 Libretto by John Dryden and Sir Robert Howard.

6.309 "Text by F. Romani"—Annals of opera, 1597-1910 / Alfred Loewenberg.

6.310 "The text is taken from the New Testament Book of Revelation, but punctuated by modern hymn-like poems by Hjalmar Gullberg"—Container.

6.311 Text of op. 71 by Karl Busse.

6.312 Text of the 1st work adapted from the Bible (Deuteronomy 32 and Matthew) ; text of the 2d, Psalm 112.

6.313 Words of 1st work by Heinrich Heine.

Nonmusical Works

6.314 Cast: Freeman F. Gosden, Charles J. Correll.

6.315 David McCallum, Carole Shelley, readers.

6.316 Narrator: Stuart Finley.

6.317 Read by James Mason.

6.318 Read by E.G. Marshall ; introductory commentary read by Louis Nizer.

6.319 Read by Maureen Stapleton ; directed by Paul Kresh.

Chapter 7 (Motion Pictures and Videorecordings)

AACR2 RULE

7.7B6 Statements of Responsibility [AACR2 Rev.]

Cast

List featured players, performers, narrators, and/or presenters. . . .

Combination of Cast and Contents Notes

Incorporate names of the cast into the contents note if appropriate (see 7.7B18).

Credits

List persons (other than the cast) who have contributed to the artistic and/or technical production of a motion picture or videorecording and who are not named in the statements of responsibility (see 7.1F). Do not include the names of assistants, associates, etc., or any other persons making only a minor contribution. Preface each name or group of names with a statement of function.

RELATED AACR2 RULE

7.1F1 Statements of Responsibility [AACR2 Rev.]

Transcribe statements of responsibility relating to those persons or bodies credited in the chief source of information with participation in the production of a film (e.g., as producer, director, animator) that are considered to be of major importance. <u>Give all other statements of responsibility (including those relating to performance) in notes.</u> [emphasis added]

LIBRARY OF CONGRESS POLICY

For audiovisual items, generally list persons (other than producers, directors, and writers) or corporate bodies who have contributed to the artistic and technical production of a work in a credits note (see LCRI 7.1F1).

Give the following persons or bodies in the order in which they are listed below. Preface each name or group of names with the appropriate term(s) of function.

photographer(s); camera; cameraman/men; cinematographer
animator(s)
artist(s); illustrator(s); graphics
film editor(s); photo editor(s); editor(s)
narrator(s); voice(s)
music
consultant(s); adviser(s)

Do not include the following persons or bodies performing these functions:

assistants or associates
production supervisors or coordinators
project or executive editors
technical advisors or consultants
audio or sound engineers
writers of discussion, program, or teacher's guides
other persons making only a minor or purely technical contribution
[CSB 22]

For archival moving image materials, the Library of Congress supplements AACR2 Chapter 7 with the guidelines in *Archival Moving Image Materials* by White-Hensen.

RELATED LIBRARY OF CONGRESS POLICY

1.7A3 Forms of Notes

When nonroman data (including quotations) are being recorded in the note area, give them in romanized form in all cases, including those cards that contain nonromanized elements in the body of the entry.

When a note begins with a formal introductory term such as "contents," "credits," or "summary," do not use all caps in any case; instead, use upper and lower case as illustrated in AACR 2. [emphasis added] [CSB 22]

7.1F1 Statements of Responsibility

When deciding whether to give names in the statement of responsibility (7.1F1, 8.1F1) or in a note, generally give the names in the statement of responsibility when the person or body has some degree of overall responsibility; use the note area for others who are responsible for only one segment or one aspect of the work. [emphasis added] Be liberal about making exceptions to the general policy when the person's or body's responsibility is important in relation to the content of the work, i.e., give such important people and bodies in the statement of responsibility even though they may have only partial responsibility. . . .

Normally the Library of Congress considers producers, directors, and writers (or, in the case of slides and transparencies, authors, editors, and compilers) as having some degree of overall responsibility and gives them in the statement of responsibility. [CSB 36]

AACR2 TEXT EXAMPLES REVISED TO REFLECT LIBRARY OF CONGRESS POLICY

Credits—1st Example

AACR2 REV. TEXT
Credits: Screenplay, Harold Pinter; music, John Dankworth; camera, Gerry Fisher; editor, Reginald Beck.

AACR2 REV. TEXT REVISED
Credits: Camera, Gerry Fisher; editor, Reginald Beck; music, John Dankworth.

Credits—2nd Example

AACR2 REV. TEXT
Credits: Script, John Taylor; calligraphy and design, Alan Haigh; commentator, Derek G. Holroyde.

AACR2 TEXT REVISED
Credits: Calligraphy and design, Alan Haigh; commentator, Derek G. Holroyde.

Revised examples reflect LC's prescribed order and function priorities. LC would place the writers given in the two examples in the statement of responsibility area rather than in a note. The examples in AACR2 used space, semicolon, space between statements of function.

HISTORICAL BACKGROUND

Cast
AACR1 Rev. Rule 229.2J instructed that a cast note was to begin with the term "CAST" followed by a list of the featured players. AACR2 uses "Cast:".

Persons whose voice was their only representation in the work could be named in either the cast or credits notes. AACR2 is essentially similar to the AACR1 Rev. rule except that the statement regarding vocal only representation is absent.

There was no rule in AACR1 Rev. equivalent to that portion of the current rule that instructs the cataloger to combine the cast note and contents note "when appropriate." The nearest AACR1 Rev. comes to this type of statement is the instruction (AACR1 Rev. Rule 229.2J) to record the names of actors and other persons photographed on a filmstrip in notes other than the cast note. A summary note is suggested as one type of note in which these names could appear.

Credits

AACR1 Rev. Rule 229.2K provided for a note that began with the term "CREDITS:" for persons involved in the artistic and technical production of the work whose "contribution is of special significance." AACR2 also provides for the use of this term but records it as "Credits:".

An optional listing of likely significant participants was provided. This list is similar to that given in the LC Rule Interpretation to the AACR2 rule. However, AACR1 would have placed producers, directors, and writers in a note, while LC places them in the statement of responsibility area.

NOTE EXAMPLES[6]

Cast

6.320   Cast: Host: Bill Moyers.
6.321   Cast: Lloyd Bridges, Britt Ekland, Cathy Rigby.
6.322   Cast: Paul Benjamin, Diahann Carroll, Ruby Dee, Roger Mosley, Esther Rolle, Madge Sinclair, Sonny Jim Gaines, Art Evans, Constance Good, John M. Driver.
6.323   Cast: Elizabeth Ashley (Erica), Richard Crenna (Brian).
6.324   Cast: Ike Eisenmann (Jason), Julie Dolan (Sue), Sal Ponti (Detective Butoni), Pamela Nelson (Eve).

Credits

6.325   *Credits: Camera, Richard Beymer ; editors, Daniel Kutt, Gregory Bennett, Gregory William Schmidt ; music, Robert Ragland, and Michael Bernard ; executive producer, Ellwood Kieser.
6.326   Credits: Cameraman, Julius Potocsny ; editor, Harry Howard.
6.327   Credits: Commentary, Nelson Max, Stephen Smale, Charles Pugh, Judith Bregman.

---

6. See comment under *Format* on page 133.

6.328 Credits: Consultants, Robert Shusta, James Davis, James Edison, Ted Kozak, Michael Rolan.

6.329 Credits: Medical consultant, Eric Fine.

6.330 Credits: Photographer and editor, Lynn Hirst Turner.

6.331 Credits: Photographers, Tom McDonough . . . [et al.] ; editors, David Peoples, Ralph Wikke ; narrator, Paul Frees ; music, Martin Bresnick.

6.332 Credits: Voices, Don Knotts, Don Messick, Ronnie Burkett, Janet L. Swenson, Corey Sprague, Dorothy L. Behling.

Additional Statements of Responsibility

6.333 American version prepared by International Film Bureau in consultation with the Erikson Institute for Early Education.

6.334 American version, with new sound track prepared by International Film Bureau.

6.335 Developed at the University of Kansas.

6.336 Developed by a consortium of U.S. and Canadian education agencies as part of the Secondary School Television Project.

6.337 Funded by Texas Education Agency, Texas Dept. of Human Resources, and Texas Dept. of Community Affairs.

6.338 Funded by the U.S. Office of Education and developed by Sharon Gadberry.

6.339 Produced in cooperation with Canadian International Development Agency and Vision Habitat.

6.340 Produced in cooperation with John's Hopkins University Applied Physics Laboratory.

6.341 Produced in cooperation with the International Association of Fire Chiefs, U.S. Consumer Product Safety Commission, Fire Dept. of New York, Miami Fire Dept. and State University of New York.

6.342 "Produced under the direction of the Chemistry ETV Committee: Charles F. Wilcox, James Burlitch, and Stanley T. Marcus"—Booklet.

6.343 "Produced with the cooperation of the Suicide Prevention and Crisis Center of San Mateo Country" [sic]—Guide.

6.344 Researched and developed by Drs. Dorothy G. and Jerome L. Singer.

6.345 A segment of CBS reports, hosted by Harry Reasoner.

6.346 Sponsored by the National Swedish Board of Education under the auspices of the Council of Europe.

Previous Editions

6.347 Rev. version of: Run to live / Black College Fund. 1976.

6.348 Rev. version of the 1973 motion picture entitled: Boys aware / Sid Davis Productions.

Chapter 8 (Graphic Materials)

AACR2 RULE

8.7B6 Statements of Responsibility [AACR2 Rev.]

Variant Names

Make notes on variant names of persons or bodies named in statements of responsibility if these are considered to be important for identification.

Additional Statements of Responsibility

Give statements of responsibility not recorded in the title and statement of responsibility area. Make notes on persons or bodies connected with a work, or

Previous Editions

significant persons or bodies connected with previous editions and not already named in the description.

Donor, Source, etc., and Previous Owner(s)

Make notes on the donor or source of an original graphic item and on previous owners if they can be easily ascertained. Add the year or years of accession to the name of the donor or source, and the year or years of ownership to the name of a previous owner.

RELATED AACR2 RULE

None.

LIBRARY OF CONGRESS POLICY

For audiovisual items, generally list persons (other than producers, directors, and writers) or corporate bodies who have contributed to the artistic and technical production of a work in a credits note (see LCRI 7.1F1).

Give the following persons or bodies in the order in which they are listed below. Preface each name or group of names with the appropriate term(s) of function.

photographer(s); camera; cameraman/men; cinematographer
animator(s)
artist(s); illustrator(s); graphics
film editor(s); photo editor(s); editor(s)
narrator(s); voice(s)
music
consultant(s); adviser(s)

Do not include the following persons or bodies performing these functions:

assistants or associates
production supervisors or coordinators
project or executive editors
technical advisors or consultants
audio or sound engineers
writers of discussion, program, or teacher's guides
other persons making only a minor or purely technical contribution
[CSB 22]

For original items and historical collections, the Library of Congress supplements AACR2 Chapter 8 with the guidelines in *Graphic Materials* by Betz.

RELATED LIBRARY OF CONGRESS POLICY

1.7A3 Forms of Notes

When nonroman data (including quotations) are being recorded in the note area, give them in romanized form in all cases, including those cards that contain nonromanized elements in the body of the entry.

When a note begins with a formal introductory term such as "contents," "credits," or "summary," do not use all caps in any case; instead, use upper and lower case as illustrated in AACR 2. [emphasis added] [CSB 22]

8.1F1 Statements of Responsibility

When deciding whether to give names in the statement of responsibility (7.1F1, 8.1F1) or in a note, generally give the names in the statement of responsibility when the person or body has some degree of overall responsibility; use the note area for others who are responsible for only one segment or one aspect of the work. [emphasis added] Be liberal about making exceptions to the general policy when the person's or body's responsibility is important in relation to the content of the work, i.e., give such important people and bodies in the statement of responsibility even though they may have only partial responsibility. . . .

Normally the Library of Congress considers producers, directors, and writers (or, in the case of slides and transparencies, authors, editors, and compilers) as having some degree of overall responsibility and gives them in the statement of responsibility. [CSB 36]

AACR2 TEXT EXAMPLES REVISED TO REFLECT LIBRARY OF CONGRESS POLICY

None required.

159

HISTORICAL BACKGROUND

Cast

AACR1 Rev. Rule 229.2J instructed that a cast note was to begin with the term "CAST:" followed by a list of the featured players. AACR2 uses "Cast:".

This AACR1 Rev. rule further instructed that the names of actors and other persons photographed for a filmstrip presentation were to be placed in other notes. A summary note was suggested as one place where this type of statement could appear. AACR2 does not provide such an instruction.

The same AACR1 Rev. rule also stated that persons whose only representation on a filmstrip was their voice were allowed to appear in either the cast or credits note. AACR2 does not have a similar instruction.

Credits

AACR1 Rev. Rule 229.2K provided for a note that began with the term "CREDITS" for persons involved in the artistic and technical production of the work or whose "contribution is of special significance." AACR2 also provides for the use of this term but records it as "Credits:".

An optional listing of likely significant participants was provided. This list is similar to that given in the LC Rule Interpretation to the AACR2 rule. However, AACR1 would have placed producers, directors, and writers in a note, while LC places them in the statement of responsibility area.

Pictures

AACR1 Rule 272C1 provided for the use of a note to "show the signature if not used in the body of the entry and to describe marks, monograms, etc.," that could not be recorded in the body of the entry.

A note was also provided to record "artists, engravers, draftsmen, etc.," who were "significant" in the production of the picture and also to record artists after whose original work a picture had been made.

Additionally, a note was also made for attributions of authorship in cases of doubtful authorship.

AACR2 allows for the use of notes for all of these situations but is not nearly as detailed in its guidelines as was its predecessor. The examples used in the AACR2 text, in fact, specifically illustrate the use of some of the AACR1 notes provisions.

NOTE EXAMPLES[7]

Projection Graphic Materials

CREDITS

6.349 Credits: Art, Judy Almendariz ; editor, Sheryl Niemann ; consultants, Ronald E. Reed, Paul Bloomquist.

6.350 Credits: Art director, Gordon D. Hayduk ; supervising editor, Susan Watkins.

6.351 Credits: Consultants, Anne E. Nesbit, Donna L. Osness.

6.352 Credits: Illustrator, Ann Rankin ; narrator, Michael King.

6.353 Credits: Photographers, Ron Tunison, Kathleen Talbot, Dewitt Neild, Jr., Alan Hershowitz ; graphics, David Prebenna ; narrator, Jenna Whidden.

6.354 Credits: Photo editor, Carol Deegan.

6.355 Credits: Photography, Lynda Medwell ; graphics, S.A. Murryweather-Budd, Sue Hasted ; narration, Derek Benfield, Rowena Cooper.

6.356 Credits: Photography and graphics, Charles G. Casey.

ADDITIONAL STATEMENTS OF RESPONSIBILITY

6.357 Created by Gregory Talley.

6.358 Created under the guidance of the U.S. Sewing Products Division of the Singer Company.

6.359 Filmed in cooperation with Hillcrest Kidney Disease Treatment Center, Tulsa, Okla.

6.360 "Funded by Iowa State University Research Foundation."

6.361 "This program has been reviewed and revised in consultation with the Prenatal/Neonatal Subcommittee of the American Group Practice Association's Patient Education Advisory Committee."

PREVIOUS EDITIONS

6.362 Expanded and rev. version of the filmstrip issued in 1976 by the U.S. Dept. of Agriculture, Forest Service, entitled: A forest is also— nuts, berries, and leaves.

6.363 Revised version of the 1961 filmstrip: American in Paris by George Gershwin.

Nonprojection Graphic Materials

6.364 *Attribution made by donor Mrs. Maude Hunt Patterson, daughter of Leavitt Hunt.

6.365 *Attribution made on the basis of the relationship of this print to Baillie's "Miss Mary Taylor & Mr. F.S. Chanfrau in the new piece called 'A glance at New York,' " for which Magee is delineator.

---

7. See comment under *Format* on page 133.

6.366   The engravings are by Paul Revere, from the obverse and reverse of the original copperplate mentioned in: Paul Revere's engravings / C.S. Brigham. Rev. ed. 1969. p. 196. They were printed Mar. 1973 and signed: E. O'Brien.

6.367   "The etchings were printed by Emiliano Sorini."

6.368   Illustrations for James Fenimore Cooper's novels, engr. by various artists after F.O.C. Darley.

6.369   On portfolio: Aubrey Schwartz.

6.370   *Photographed, at least in part, by William H. Pennington.

6.371   *Photographers include G.V. Buck, Clinedinst, Edmonston, and Harris & Ewing.

6.372   *Possibly photographed by Edward Sheriff Curtis.

6.373   Preface signed: Harmann Nasse.

6.374   Prefatory text signed: Lawrence Barrett.

6.375   *Printed and signed by Cole Weston, son of the photographer.

6.376   Text by Stanley Morison. Cf. Appleton.

6.377   "This portfolio was commissioned by the Wisconsin Arts Council. Every print was executed, pulled, and signed by the individual printmakers in an edition limited to forty copies"—T.p.

6.378   *Variously attributed to Mathew B. Brady and Timothy O'Sullivan.

6.379   The woodcuts are by unidentified 15th-century artists. Each is one of 25 copies printed Oct. 1968 and signed: Hoehn.

Donor

6.380   *Bequest of Erwin Swann, 1974 (DLC/PP-1977:215).

6.381   *Exchange with the U.S. Army Signal Corps Museum, Fort Monmouth, N.J., 1960.

6.382   *From the collection of L. McGarry, 1948-1957.

6.383   From the library of H.C. Levis. Some of the woodcuts were transferred by Levis from scrapbooks in the library of Frederick Hendriks, sold at Sotheby's, Nov. 11-12, 1909 (item 227).

6.384   *In Lot 11696.

6.385   *International exchange, 1948.

6.386   *Most copyright deposit of E.H. Harriman, 1899; source of remainder unknown.

6.387   The original copperplate and blocks were given by Mr. Rosenwald to the National Gallery of Art, Washington.

6.388   *Original in the collection of Joseph H. Hirshhorn.

6.389   *Originally collected by Paul Jones and maintained by his nephew, John Smith, after Jones' death. Purchased in 1878 by Henry Green, who added prints and drawings purchased at auctions in New York and Paris, 1878-1893.

6.390   *Provenance: Roger Marx (Lugt 2215b).

6.391   "This collection of the original drawings . . . is presented to Lynwood Giacomini"—Artist's inscription, dated Nov. 1942, inside 1st portfolio.

6.392   *Transfer from the Manuscript Division (Josephus Daniels papers), 1948.

Chapter 9 (Computer Files)

AACR2 RULE

9.7B6 Statements of Responsibility [AACR2 Rev.]

Variant Names
> Make notes on variant names of persons or bodies named in statements of responsibility if they are considered to be important for identification.

Additional Statements of Responsibility
> Give statements of responsibility not recorded in the title and statement of responsibility area. Make notes on persons or bodies connected with a work, or

Previous Editions
> significant persons or bodies connected with previous editions and not already named in the description.

RELATED AACR2 RULE

9.1F1 Statements of Responsibility [AACR2 Rev.]
> Transcribe statements relating to those persons or bodies responsible for the content of the file as instructed in 1.1F. . . .
> Give statements relating to sponsors, etc., or to persons or bodies who have prepared or contributed to the production of the file, in a note (see 9.7B6). [emphasis added]

LIBRARY OF CONGRESS POLICY

None issued for AACR2 Rev. Ch. 9.

RELATED LIBRARY OF CONGRESS POLICY

None issued for AACR2 Rev. Ch. 9.

AACR2 TEXT EXAMPLES REVISED TO REFLECT
LIBRARY OF CONGRESS POLICY

None required for AACR2 Rev. Ch. 9.

HISTORICAL BACKGROUND

Computer files were not covered by AACR1 or previous codes. The original AACR2 Chapter 9 covered the elements present in this revised rule.

NOTE EXAMPLES[8]

6.393   *Additional contributors to program: Eric Rosenfeld and Debra Spencer.
6.394   *Computer adaptation: Methods & Solutions, Inc.
6.395   *Consultant: Deborah K. Adcock.
6.396   *Data collected by World Data Analysis Program, Yale University.
6.397   *Data collected in collaboration with Christiane Klapisch, Ecole Pratique des Hautes Etudes, Paris, France.
6.398   *Data prepared in collaboration with the U.S. Bureau of the Census under contract with the Employment and Training Administration, U.S. Dept. of Labor.
6.399   *Developed by Don Ross.
6.400   *Developed for Apple Computer, Inc. by Business & Professional Software, Inc.
6.401   *"The fieldwork was carried out by DIVO Institute [sic], Frankfurt, DIVO project no. 298."
6.402   *File creator, Donald C. Spinelli.
6.403   *Guide by Marley W. Watkins, Larry Johnson, Linda Bloom.
6.404   *Notes and guide by John Harris.
6.405   *Original program by Gene Kusmiak.
6.406   *Prepared at the Institute for Research in Social Science, University of North Carolina.
6.407   *Principal investigators: G. Baumert, E. Scheuch, R. Wildenmann.
6.408   *"Produced by Microsoft, Inc."
6.409   *Produced under contract with Bureau of Labor Statistics.
6.410   *Project director, Herbert S. Parnes.

Chapter 10 (Three-Dimensional Artefacts and Realia)

AACR2 RULE

10.7B6 Statements of Responsibility [AACR2 Rev.]

Variant Names

Make notes on variant names of persons or bodies named in statements of responsibility if these are considered to be important for identification.

Additional Statements of Responsibility

Give statements of responsibility not recorded in the title and statement of responsibility area. Make notes on persons or bodies connected with a work, or

---

8. See comment under *Format* on page 133.

Previous Editions
>   significant persons or bodies connected with previous editions and not already named in the description.

RELATED AACR2 RULE

None.

LIBRARY OF CONGRESS POLICY

None issued.

RELATED LIBRARY OF CONGRESS POLICY

None issued.

AACR2 TEXT EXAMPLES REVISED TO REFLECT LIBRARY OF CONGRESS POLICY

None required.

HISTORICAL BACKGROUND

Although AACR1 Rev. Ch. 12 and previous codes had no rule equivalent to Rule 10.7B6 for three-dimensional artifacts and realia, the statement of responsibility note provisions for separately published monographs in these codes could be used for these materials. (See *Historical Background* under Rule 2.7B6.)

NOTE EXAMPLES[9]

6.411   *Assembled by Vocational Industries of Somerset Area.
6.412   *By Richard and Florence May.
6.413   *Conceived and designed by Bob Whitehead.
6.414   *Created by Dr. John Pescosolido, Central Connecticut State College.
6.415   *Deposited for the Presbyterian Church of the Evangel by Philadelphia Presbytery.
6.416   *Design: drawing of Francis Makemie based on a painting by Harry A. Ogden and showing the old Presbyterian Church in Ramelton, Co. Donegal.
6.417   *Inscribed: "Presented by / the Old Students & Xns / from S.M.C. in Poona 1928."

---

9. See comment under *Format* on page 133.

Chapter 12 (Serials)

AACR2 RULE

12.7B6 Statements of Responsibility [AACR2 Rev.]

Additional Statements of Responsibility

Make notes or statements of responsibility that do not appear in the title and statement of responsibility area. . . .

Expansion of Names

Give a fuller form of the name of a person or body that appears only in abbreviated form in the rest of the description if the fuller form is considered to be necessary. . . .

Editors

Give the name of any editor considered to be an important means of identifying the serial (e.g., if a particular person edited the serial for all or most of its existence; if the person's name is likely to be better known than the title of the serial).

RELATED AACR2 RULE

12.1F3 Statements of Responsibility [AACR2 Rev.]

Do not record as statements of responsibility statements relating to persons that are editors of serials. If a statement relating to an editor is considered necessary by the cataloguing agency, give it in a note (see 12.7B6). [emphasis added]

LIBRARY OF CONGRESS POLICY

None issued.

RELATED LIBRARY OF CONGRESS POLICY

12.0B1 Sources of Information. Printed Serials

Due to its length, this LC policy statement has been abridged to include only the parts related to the use of notes.

Serials

The basis for the description is the first issue of the serial. In determining which issue is first, disregard the date of publication, etc., and use the designation on the issues. For serials that carry numeric or alphabetic designations, the first issue is the one with the lowest or earliest (in the alphabet) designation. For serials that do not carry numeric or alphabetic designations, the first issue is the one with the earliest chronological designation. (If the actual first issue is not available, use these same guidelines to determine which issue should be used as the basis for the description.)

Since the title page (or title page substitute) of the first issue is the chief source of information for a printed serial, a title page that is published later to cover one or more issues cannot be used as the chief source. (However, data from such a title page may be put into the note area when necessary.) [emphasis added]

If the description has been formulated from the first issue of a serial, the body of the entry remains unchanged throughout the life of the serial. If issues after the first have data different from those recorded in the body of the entry, record the different data in the note area as necessary. [emphasis added] However, if the differences are in the title proper, create a separate record when appropriate (21.2C). (For changes in the main entry heading, see 21.3B.) . . .

Reprints of Serials

In order that the description of the reprint resemble and file with the description of the original, the earliest *issue* reprinted is used as the chief source for the first three areas of the description. Data for these areas may be taken from any place on the reprinted issue without the use of brackets. If it is known that the description of the original would include data that are not on the reprinted issue, the data may be supplied in brackets.

In area four the place of publication, publisher, and date of the reprint are recorded, using brackets if the data do not come from a prescribed source on the reprint.

The physical description area gives the physical description of the reprint, not the original.

A series is recorded if the reprint appears in a series.

Usually a single note (see 12.7B7g) gives important details about the original while other notes give necessary information about the reprint. Notes giving the source of the title or the issue on which the description is based are not given. [emphasis added] [CSB 38]

AACR2 TEXT EXAMPLES REVISED TO REFLECT LIBRARY OF CONGRESS POLICY

None required.

HISTORICAL BACKGROUND

AACR1 Rule 160D specified that no "author statement" was placed in the body of the entry. If such a statement was needed, it was placed in the note area. AACR2 allows the placement of a statement of responsibility in either Area 1 or in a note. The location is dependent on whether the statement of responsibility is stated "prominently" in the serial.

AACR1 Rule 160J required that a note be made to record the fact that a serial served as the organ of a "society or other body." AACR1 Rule 167J stated that the use of this note was dependent on the statement being presented in terms used by the publication or the English equivalents. This note can still be made under the general provisions of AACR2. The Library of Congress is frequently recording this "organ relationship" information by the use of AACR2 Rule 12.7B5 (Parallel titles and other title information). Often, the subtitle defines the relationship of a serial to a society or other body and thus imparts this information.

AACR1 Rule 167M provided guidance for recording the name of issuing or sponsoring bodies in a note if: (1) another body was the publisher, or (2) the name of the issuing body changed and the serial was entered under the title, or (3) there was more than one successive issuing body for a serial that was entered under title. The Library of Congress also provided an issuing body note if the name of the issuing body changed and the serial was entered under the issuing body. AACR1 Rule 167M also provided for the use of a note to record minor variations in the name of an issuing body. This issuing body note is covered by the general intent of the AACR2 rule. The Library of Congress continues to make this note as it did under AACR1.

AACR1 Rule 160E specifically excluded editors from the body of the entry. AACR1 Rule 167N provided for the use of a note for persons who were better known than the exact title of the serial and for persons who had been associated with the serial throughout its lifetime or for a "notably long period." An informal note was used for works that had ceased publication and had the same editor(s) for their lifetime. An informal note was also used in place of the conventional note when it was "more satisfactory for other reasons." In other cases, a conventional note was used to record information about editors. This note used the construct:

Editor or Compiler: [Inclusive dates of contribution, Name.]

AACR2 is in agreement about the location of editor information and provides for a similar note for editors. However, AACR2 lacks any of the fine provisions for use or the prescriptive elements of the earlier code. No formal note structure is required. The Library of Congress is using a style very much like that provided for by AACR1.

NOTE EXAMPLES[10]

Additional Statements of Responsibility

6.418   Cumulative supplement by Justine T. Antopol.

6.419   "Approved by the World Food and Agricultural Outlook and Situation Board." P. 3.

6.420   At head of title: CHE.

6.421   At head of title: Commission of the European Communities.

6.422   At head of title: Zimbabwe Rhodesia.

6.423   Authors: Flora Crater, Elizabeth Vantrease, Meg Williams, 1979-.

6.424   " . . . compiled from the . . . survey conducted by the Statistics & Demographic Section of Ministry of Finance & Economic Planning . . ."— Introd.

6.425   Conferences sponsored by: Departmento de Economia Rural, Universidade Estadual Paulista "Júlio de Mesquita Filho".

6.426   Connecticut State Dept. of Education, Division of Administrative Services, Bureau of Research, Planning and Evaluation, Research and Planning Unit.

6.427   Each vol. is a report of a different Kerala Department or Committee.

6.428   Founded by: Eugene Fodor.

6.429   " . . . from the working files of Berger & Associates Cost Consultants."— Introd.

6.430   Jointly presented by the: ABA Section of Taxation and ALI-ABA.

6.431   Patton G. Wheeler, COSG executive director, was responsible for the preparation of the 1977 summary.

6.432   Prepared by: Arthur W. Rovine, 1973-1974; Eleanor C. McDowell, 1975-1976; John A. Boyd, 1977; Marian L. Nash, 1978-

6.433   Prepared by: Kansas State Dept. of Education, Division of Financial Services, 1975-

6.434   Prepared by the Bureau of Registration and Health Statistics.

6.435   Published on behalf of: Institute of Mathematics and Its Applications.

6.436   "A service of Johnson & Johnson Products, Inc.", June 1980-<Sept. 1980>.

6.437   Sponsored by: American Association for Partial Hospitalization, 1979-

6.438   Sponsored by: National Guard Association of Texas, 1971-   ; the Association and McAdams Foundation, vol. 13, no. 1-

6.439   "Submitted by Department of Elementary & Secondary Education."

6.440   Vols. for 1981-1982-   by I. Keown.

6.441   Vols. for <-1982> prepared by the Economic Research Service, U.S. Dept. of Agriculture for the Committee on Agriculture, Nutrition, and Forestry, United States Senate.

6.442   Vols. for <1979-80> sponsored by the State Bar of Texas, Professional Development Program.

---

10. See comment under *Format* on page 133.

Editors

6.443   Compiled and edited by: R. Pooley.

6.444   Compiled by the research staff of SM/Databank.

6.445   Compilers: 1981-82 ed.-   S. Haggart and D. Porter.

6.446   Editor: 1981-   Randall L. Schultz.

6.447   Editor: J.F. McPartland, 1979-

6.448   Editor: Marietta Chicorel.

6.449   Published with the editorial cooperation of Associated Industries of Massachusetts.

Issuing Body

6.450   Formerly issued by the Division under its earlier name: Pakistan. Central Statistical Office.

6.451   Issued by: University of California, San Francisco. Continuing Education in Health Sciences.

6.452   Issued by: the Swedish Society Oikos, 1978-   ; by the Nordic Society Oikos, ⟨Nov. 1980⟩.

6.453   Issued by: Connecticut State Dept. of Education, Division of Administrative Services, Bureau of Research, Planning and Evaluation, 1977-78; by the bureau's Research and Planning Unit, 1978-79.

6.454   Issued by: National Association of Career Education, spring 1976; National Association for Career Education, winter 1977-

6.455   Issued by: Small Business Division, 7th ed.; issued by Office of Small Business, 8th-   ed.

6.456   Issued by the Institution under its later name: Institution of Mechanical and General Technician Engineers, 1979-⟨1980⟩.

6.457   Issued jointly by: the University of Oklahoma School of Geology and Geophysics and: Stovall Museum of Science and History, 1981-8   ; by: the Society of Vertebrate Paleontology and the Florida State Museum, ⟨1984-   ⟩

6.458   Issued with the collaboration of the Société historique polonaise, Commission d'histoire médiévale.

6.459   Vols. for 19   issued by the United States Civil Service Commission, Office of Labor-Management Relations; ⟨July 1979⟩-July 1982 by the United States Office of Personnel Management, Office of Labor-Management Relations.

Organ

6.460   "An Annual technical publication of the Metallurgy Society of the Department of Metallurgical Engineering, Institute of Technology, Banaras Hindu University"—Editorial p.

6.461   Journal of: the Liturgical Conference.

6.462   Journal of the I.R.E.P.

6.463   Official bulletin of the Italian Neurological Society.

6.464   Official journal of: Group Health Association.

6.465   Official publication of the Armed Forces Staff College.

6.466   Organ of the Pasadena Symphony Orchestra.

1.7B7. Edition and History

Make notes relating to the edition being described or the bibliographic history of the work.

RELATED AACR2 RULE

None.

GENERAL LIBRARY OF CONGRESS POLICY

No general rule interpretations have been issued by the Library of Congress to directly modify, or amplify on, AACR2 Rule 1.7B7. See the sections that follow for any LC policies and interpretations that apply to specific formats.

RELATED LIBRARY OF CONGRESS POLICY

1.2B1 Edition Statement

Due to its length, this LC policy statement has been abridged to include only the part related to the use of notes.

> Whenever a publication bears a statement that calls attention to changes from a previous issue, the statement must be a formal one to qualify as an edition statement. (The normal characteristic of a non-formal statement is that it is found in a sentence of text, no matter whether this sentence appears prominently or not.) Non-formal statements may be quoted in a note when considered important. [emphasis added]
>
> Formal statements of printing, manufacture, etc., also qualify as edition statements when they contain an indication of change. . . . (In such cases, the date of printing, manufacture, etc., is the date of *publication* for the item being cataloged.)
>
> Large print editions present a special case. Although rule 2.5B4 for books requires the addition of "(large print)" to the extent statement, nevertheless, also transcribe the phrase as an edition statement if it appears as a formal statement in the item.
>
>   *N.B.* 1) "First edition" statements must be recorded as edition statements, although there is no earlier issue from which changes could have been made.
>
>   *N.B.* 2) See also LCRI 1.2B4 for special situations in which the cataloger may extrapolate information from the publication and create an edition statement. [CSB 33]

1.11C Facsimiles, Photocopies, and Other Reproductions

When the date, etc., of the original publication appears after the title on the chief source of a later edition, do not transcribe these data in the title area. Instead, incorporate the information into the note area. [emphasis added] [CSB 17]

FORMAT

No general instructions on the formatting of this note exist. However, when information is related to data associated with the Edition Area, the Publication, Distribution, etc., Area, or the Series Area, the note should be structured using ISBD style whenever possible (cf. AACR2 Rule 1.7A3). A full stop is used to end each area within the note rather than a full stop, space, dash, space.

CHAPTER APPLICATION

This note is present in variant forms in all chapters for description, although in some instances, the rule is quite different from the provisions of the Extrapolated General Rule.

EXCEPTIONS AND ADDITIONS

Chapter 4 (Manuscripts) uses this note to record the name of the donor of a manuscript or manuscript collection and the year of accession. It also is used to record the names of the previous owners and the years of ownership.

Chapter 9 (Computer Files, AACR2 Rev.) in addition to the provisions of the Extrapolated General Rule, uses this note to indicate the source of the edition statement if different from the source of the title proper. This note is also used to record minor changes in the work and identify works on which the content of the computer file is dependent. Additionally, dates relating to data in the file and dates for accompanying material are given in this note.

Chapter 10 (Three-Dimensional Artefacts and Realia), in addition to the provisions of the Extrapolated General Rule, uses this note to cite works on which the item is dependent for its content.

Chapter 12 (Serials) uses this note to detail the relationship between the serial being described and preceding, succeeding, or simultaneously published serials.

Chapter 2 (Books, Pamphlets, and Printed Sheets)

AACR2 RULE

2.7B7 Edition and History

Make notes relating to the edition being described or to the bibliographic history of the work.

RELATED AACR2 RULE

None.

LIBRARY OF CONGRESS POLICY

Due to its length, this LC policy statement has been abridged to include only the parts related to the use of notes.

Reprint Editions

This interpretation is for new editions that are merely photographic reprints by a different publisher; generally it does not apply to belles lettres or to reissues of classics. For items within scope, make notes of the types shown below to give information about the original publication. Take the information from the reprint being cataloged. If the reprint being cataloged lacks the information about the original, give simply "Reprint" in a note.

Exception: If an existing bibliographic record for the original needs to be examined for another reason, then more complete information about the original is given in the note. Do not search solely to discover information about the original publication. When recording information about the original, always give the date of the original edition even if it is the same as the copyright date recorded in the publication, distribution, etc., area. For non-Gregorian dates, give only Gregorian equivalents in the note. However, if the non-Gregorian date cannot be converted to a single Gregorian date, give both non-Gregorian and Gregorian dates. . . .

If there is any question about whether a new edition is a reprint or not (make a quick decision in all cases), treat it as such for the purpose of making these notes. In this case, however, omit the introductory word "Reprint" and begin the note instead with the next phrase "Originally published:"

If the reprint edition combines two or three formerly independent publications, make a note for each work contained. If there are more than three, make a single note, generalizing the information; however, specifically mention the span of publication dates. . . .

173

The purpose of this note is 1) to date the writing of the text approximately and 2) to give a more bibliographically significant imprint than that shown in the publication, distribution, etc., area. Thus an earlier imprint that is itself a reprint is of no significance and should be ignored. Situations will arise, however, when the cataloger, after excluding any earlier reprints, will not feel comfortable in using the phrase "Originally published"; e.g., there may be a still earlier imprint that was not discovered (and no special searching may be done). In these situations, use "Previously published" rather than "Originally published."

CIP Cataloging

When the front matter and data sheet supplied do not make it clear whether a photographic reprint is involved, but one sees it as a reasonable possibility, make the note anyway. Note that regardless of appearances do not consider as "photographic reprints" cases of *approximately* simultaneous publication as

1) the re-publication is one in paper and the original is a hardback;
2) the re-publication is an American edition of a British edition or vice-versa.

Limited Editions

Give limited edition statements, preferably in quoted form, for editions of 500 copies or less. If the statement cannot be quoted, phrase it so that the number does not come first (to avoid spelling out the number; cf. Appendix C.3). . . .

When the statement of limitation includes the unique number of the copy being cataloged, give only the statement of limitation here. Give the copy number (introduced by the phrase "LC has copy") as a copy-specific note (cf. LCRI 1.7B20). . . .

Photoreproduction

"Photoreproduction" is a generic term that is no longer used, since the inception of AACR2, to indicate a particular kind of reproduction. If a macroreproduction is one that is "on demand," i.e., the result of the reproduction process comprises only a single copy, the applicable term is "photocopy"; use the guidelines in LCRI 11.0A to catalog such an item. If a macroreproduction process comprises copies that represent an edition, use a general statement in a note to indicate the fact of reproduction, as appropriate, but do not use the term "photoreproduction." [CSB 34]

RELATED LIBRARY OF CONGRESS POLICY

2.2 Edition Area

If one volume of a multivolume monograph is in one edition and another volume is in another edition, create a separate bibliographic record for each edition that is to be cataloged as a unit. However, in

174

very exceptional cases (e.g., if the publisher supplies more than one volume of a work at the same time and these volumes bear different edition statements; or, for legal materials, there is explicit evidence that each volume is to be continuously revised), create one bibliographic record for the work. In such exceptional cases, record the edition statement of the first volume in the body of the entry. Give the edition statements of the volumes that vary in the note area, only if all the volumes are unanalyzable. If one bibliographic record has been created and other editions of already cataloged volumes are received subsequently, add the note "Includes other editions of some volumes." (Apply this both to sets having analyzable parts and those that do not.) Do not adjust the edition statements in the note area to reflect the latest edition of each volume. [emphasis added] (This information is available in the [LC] shelflist.) [CSB 13]

AACR2 TEXT EXAMPLES REVISED TO REFLECT LIBRARY OF CONGRESS POLICY

None required.

HISTORICAL BACKGROUND

AACR1 Rev. Rule 143D3d indicated that the edition note was to be located between the statements of authorship note and notes related to the imprint. This order remains the same in AACR2.

AACR1 Rev. Rule 143D4 provided for notes to indicate the relationship between the work in hand and other editions of that work or other works. AACR2 allows for a similar note.

AACR1 Rev. Rule 143D4b provided for a note to indicate works that the work in hand continues and/or works that continue it. For works of imagination, the term "sequel" was prescribed. For works not of the imagination, the terms "continues," "continued by," or the phrase "suggested by the work itself" were used. Under AACR2, this note can continue to be made, although no prescription exists for the use of the word "sequel" or other terms. Nothing, however, prohibits their use and one example in the AACR2 text employs the term "sequel."

AACR1 Rev. Rule 143D4c provided for a note to record information about the original publication of a work being cataloged as a reprint edition. This information included the publisher, publication date, and series. The date of publication was omitted if the copyright date given in the description of the reprint was the same as the date of publication of the original. AACR1 Rev. Rule 136D presented rules for imprint statements for photographically reproduced reprint and facsimile editions. These notes can still be made under the provisions of AACR2,

175

although the descriptive elements in the note now include edition statements, place of publication, and new materials added to the text and appear in ISBD order. The copyright date restriction in AACR1 Rev. is not present in AACR2 and is also not applied by the Library of Congress.

AACR1 Rev. Rule 143D4d allowed for the use of a note to record information about the original publication of a work of which the work in hand was a part. This note was given only if the reference to the publication could be stated in a form that could lead to the earlier work. AACR2, although not specifically addressing this type of note, allows for its use.

These AACR1 Rev. Ch. 6 rules could be used for works that were not separately published monographs unless specific rules for the description of a format superseded or excluded their use.

NOTE EXAMPLES

Notes that incorporate statements of responsibility along with edition and bibliographic history information also appear as examples of statement of responsibility notes. See AACR2 Rule 2.7B6.

Abridgments
7.1   Abridged.
7.2   "Abridged — revision of a longer volume by the authors entitled Promoting innovation and change in organizations and communities."—Introd.
7.3   Abridged translation of: Inflaation, syyt ja torjunta. 1980.
7.4   Abridged version, with new introductory material and modernized spelling, of Human nature displayed in the history of Myddle.
7.5   Abridgement of: Fundamentals of legal research. 1977.
7.6   Shortened version of: Guide to reference materials (v.1, 4th cd., 1979; v. 2-3, 3rd ed., 1975-77).

Expansions, Revisions, Updates, etc.
7.7   Enl. ed. of: Geology and engineering. 2nd ed. 1962.
7.8   Expanded and updated ed. of: The opening doors. 1954.
7.9   On cover: Rev. ed., Oct. 1979.
7.10 Rev. ed. of: Automobile electrical equipment.
7.11 Rev. ed. of: The Jupiter effect. 1976.
7.12 Rev. ed. of: The wages of war, 1816-1965 / J. David Singer, Melvin Small. 1972.
7.13 Rev. ed. of: Index to subject headings / Library of the Peabody Museum of Archaeology and Ethnology, Harvard University.
7.14 Rev. ed. of: Medical resident's manual / William J. Grace, Richard J. Kennedy, Frank B. Flood. 3rd ed. 1971.

7.15 Rev. ed. of: Writer's guide and index to English. 6th ed. c1978.

7.16 Rev. ed. of: Area handbook for the People's Republic of China / Donald P. Whitaker, Rinn-Sup Shinn . . . [et al.]. 2nd ed. 1972.

7.17 Rev. and expanded ed. of: Catalogue of census returns on microfilm, 1825-1871 / Public Archives of Canada. 1978.

7.18 Rev. English text of: Vom Korn zum Brot.

7.19 Rev. and enl. ed. published as: Politics and script. 1972.

7.20 Rev. and updated ed. of the author's Song and dance man.

7.21 Revised and updated from the German edition: Rosen, Rosen, Rosen.

7.22 "Revised and expanded edition"—Verso t.p.
Originally published in 1975 as: The economic modernisation of France.

7.23 Rev. and enl. ed. of the author's original German ms. which was first published in English in 1963.

7.24 Rev., updated ed. of: The first hundred years. 1954 ; and, After the first hundred years. 1961.

7.25 Label on cover: Revision, October 1, 1980.

7.26 Revision of: 1976 ed.

7.27 Revision of: Barnett, West's California code forms with practice commentaries. 1972.

7.28 Revision of: Area handbook for Ethiopia / Irving Kaplan, et al. 1971.

7.29 Revision of: Subject index to the U.S. Bureau of the Census' current population survey reports, 1970-current / [compiled by Admina Mishkoff].

7.30 Revision of: London ; New York : Hamlyn, 1972.

7.31 Revision of: Report on claims and misleading descriptions. London : H.M.S.O., 1966.

7.32 Revision of: 2nd ed. / Arthur A. Frost, Ralph G. Pearson. 1961.

7.33 Third revision of: British South Africa Company. Rev. ed. 1973.

7.34 "Now revised and updated."—Cover.

7.35 Second ed. of: The wired society. c1978.

7.36 Update of a 1977 report.

7.37 An update, covering the years 1970-1975, of the 2nd ed. of A.E. Mourant's text published in 1976.

7.38 "Updated edition."

7.39 Updated ed. of: Linda Craig and the ghost town treasure. 1st ed. [1964].

7.40 Updated ed. published as: Type specimen book. 1940.

7.41 Updated, greatly expanded version of: Libraries and information centers in the Chicago metropolitan area. 2nd ed., rev. and enl. 1976.

7.42 Updated, rev., and expanded ed. of: Glad rags. c1979.

7.43 Updates: Bibliography of taro and edible aroids / by Peter P. Rotar, Donald L. Plucknett, and Barbara K. Bird. 1978.

7.44 "Updates a 1976 staff study"—P. iii.

7.45 Updates a 1977 report entitled: The hearing examiner in the State of Washington.

7.46 Updates the 1977 study.

7.47 Updates the Missouri population estimates, 1971-1978, MCHS no. 8.4.

7.48 Updates the 4th ed. of The heart, arteries, and veins, edited by J. W. Hurst.

7.49 An updating of: Minerals of California : centennial volume, 1866-1966 / by Joseph Murdoch and Robert Wallace Webb.

7.50 "Compiled to again update, enlarge upon and correct this author's previous volumes published in 1972 and 1977"—Pref.

Previously Published—Title of Work

7.51 According to Cahill, this anonymous pamphlet reprints the text of broadcast first printed in the Listener for Nov. 27, 1929. It was later issued in the trade as: World conflict / H. Belloc. 1951.

7.52 Also published, in 1928, in A conversation with an angel and other essays / H. Belloc. Cf. The English first editions of Hilaire Belloc / P. Cahill. 1953. p. 39.

7.53 Articles by an anonymous contributor reprinted from the Albany evening journal, issues of December 1848.

7.54 Articles published in the Glass industry magazine since 1920.

7.55 Articles reprinted from the New journalist.

7.56 Collected from the author's Musical events column in the New Yorker.

7.57 A collection of articles from the periodical Voluntary action leadership, 1975-1979.

7.58 Columns originally published in the Charlotte observer.

7.59 Contains 25 contributions selected from: Leben in Schlesien. 1962, and Meine schlesischen Jahre. 1964.

7.60 The contents of this book were originally published in the author's three-volume work entitled Building Services and Equipment (1976 and 1979).

7.61 The contents of this text have been taken from the 7th ed. of Accident prevention manual for industrial operations.

7.62 An earlier version of the second poem was published in the Georgia review.

7.63 Essays originally published in Southern quarterly, v. 18, no. 4, summer 1980.

7.64 Essays reprinted from the author's previous works: The intellectuals and the powers, and other essays, Center and periphery, and The calling of sociology and other essays on the pursuit of learning.

7.65 Excerpts from Tour guide to old Western forts.

7.66 Extracts from Education for students with learning disabilities: a guideline for development of programs and services, and from, French-speaking exceptional students' programs and needs.

7.67 First part also published independently as: Writer's guide. 7th ed. c1982.

7.68 "First published in Philosophical transactions of the Royal Society of London, series B, volume 290 (no. 1040), pages 277-430."

7.69 "Five chapters of this book originally appeared in a slightly different form, as articles in Harvard magazine"—Verso t.p.

7.70 The ill. were originally published in: In fairyland : a series of pictures from the elf-world / by Richard Doyle ; with a poem by William Allingham. 1870.

7.71 "This material combines the first 40 reports in the series Country Labor profiles, published as individual pamphlets during 1979 and 1980 by the Bureau of International Affairs, U.S. Department of Labor"—verso t.p.

7.72 Material previously published by DIAL.

7.73 Offprint of the Royal Society of Literature's Katja Reissner lecture for 1969 from Essays by divers hands, v. 36.

7.74 "The original manuscript . . . was made available for publication in the Whitman College quarterly (XVI, no. 2, 1913)"—Introd.

7.75 Originally an article in the New Yorker, the essay is published here with the footnotes added in 1965 on its inclusion in the author's Assorted prose.

7.76 Originally contributed as part of a series of six unsigned articles to the Nation in the early 1870's; these two were omitted when the others were reprinted in Portraits of places / H. James. 1885.

7.77 Originally published as: Teachers College record. Vol. 81, no. 2 (winter 1979).

7.78 Plates 1-22 were published in 1901 under title: The Library of Congress, Washington, D.C. : its principal architectural and decorative features in the colors of the originals.

7.79 A poem, originally published in the author's Drift and other poems. 1866.

7.80 "Portions of this book were published under the title Introduction to sociology, 2d ed."—Verso t.p.

7.81 "Previously published as part of 30 classic Mexican menus in Spanish and English"—Verso t.p.

7.82 Published in the Humanist (London), June 1926.

7.83 Represents the rhetoric and composition portion of The complete writer's guide and index to English, 7th ed.

7.84 Reprinted from: The seer ; or, Common-places refreshed / by Leigh Hunt. 1840. Cf. p. [29].

7.85 "Reprinted from the Department of State Bulletin of January, 1981"—P. 1.

7.86 Reprints the 5 plays contained in v. 1 of the two-volume Viking Press ed. (1957-1981) of Arthur Miller's collected plays.

7.87 Reproduction, with minor changes and corrections of: What I can remember. (Staff paper — Montana State University (Bozeman). Dept. of Agricultural Economics and Economics ; 79-4).

7.88 Selections from Milbank Memorial Fund quarterly.

7.89 Selected from the author's column The Cook's nook, published in the Houston home journal, Perry, Ga.

7.90 Selections from the writings of Henry David Thoreau originally published: Boston : Houghton Mifflin, 1906. 20 v.

7.91 "Some of this material has been published in abridged form in The mighty micro, Victor Gollancz Ltd., 1979."

7.92 Speeches previously published in L'Osservatore romano, English ed.

7.93   "The story The Umpire (here, p. [14]-[15]) first appeared in Some magazine during the spring of 1976"—p. [3].

7.94   "Text originally appeared in Derriere le miroir, no. 224-May 1977"—Copyright p.

7.95   "Text reprinted from Oregon revised statutes."

7.96   The text was issued separately in 1897 as: Verses written for Nicholson's "Almanac of sports for 1898." Cf. Livingston 144.

7.97   "This volume is a compilation of 9 chapters from our larger volume (Constitutional law cases and materials—sixth edition)"—Pref.

Previously Published—Statement of Responsibility

7.98   Previous ed.: Being a nursing aide / Hospital Research and Educational Trust. 2nd ed. c1978.

7.99   Previous ed. issued in 1968 as: Standardized jury instructions for the District of Columbia / Junior Bar Section, Bar Association of the District of Columbia.

7.100 Previously published as: Perspectives de France / by Arthur Bieler, Oscar A. Haac, and Monique Leon. 1972.

Previously Published—Publishing, Distribution, etc., Information

7.101 First ed. published in 2 v. with special titles.

7.102 Originally published under the auspices of the California State Vinicultural Association: San Francisco : E. Bosqui, 1877.

7.103 Originally published: 1775.

7.104 Originally published: c1972.

7.105 Originally published: London, 1854.

7.106 Originally published: West Hartford, Conn. : Witkower Press, c1978.

7.107 Originally published: Barre, Mass. : Barre Publishers, 1969-1971.

7.108 Originally published: New York : Harcourt, Brace & World, 1962? (Harbrace modern classics).

7.109 Originally published: New York : Schuman, 1950. (Publication / Historical Library, Yale University School of Medicine ; no. 24) (The Life of science library ; 13).

7.110 Originally published: Genuine memoirs of the celebrated Miss Maria Brown. London : Printed for I. Allcock, 1766.

7.111 Originally published: Ball four / edited by Leonard Schector. New York : World Book Pub. Co., 1970. New section: Ball five—ten years later.

7.112 Originally published in Geneva in 1872, this collection is set to modern Russian orthography with some of the stories translated into English.

Reprints

7.113 Reprint: 1971 ed.

7.114 Reprint. Originally published: [Atlanta] Atlanta Town Committee of the National Society Colonial Dames of America in the State of Georgia for the Dept. of Archives and History in the Office of Secretary of State, State of Georgia. 1962.

7.115   Reprint. Originally published: Boston : G.M. Smith, 1887.
7.116   Reprint. Originally published: New Haven : Ticknor & Fields, 1981.

Reprints—Title and Statement of Responsibility Area

7.117   Reprint. Originally published: Catalogue of the books, maps, and charts belonging to the library established in the Capitol at the City of Washington for the two houses of Congress, to which are annexed the statutes and bye-laws relating to that institution. Washington City : printed by R.C. Weightman, 1812.
7.118   +Reprint. Originally published: The English-American, his travail by sea and land or, A new survey of the West-India's, 1648. New ed. published Norman : University of Oklahoma Press, 1958.
7.119   Reprint. Originally published: The Heidelberg Catechism for today. Richmond : John Knox Press, c1964.
7.120   Reprint. Originally published: My early travels and adventures in America and Asia. Volume 1. London : S. Low, Marston, 1895.
7.121   Reprint. Originally published: Piano study : application & technique. New York : MCA music, 1969.
7.122   Pages 1-309: Reprint. Originally published: Advance, a history of Southern Baptist foreign missions / Baker J. Cauthen, and others. Nashville : Broadman Press, [1970].

Reprints—Edition Area

7.123   Reprint. Originally published: 1st ed. Norman : University of Oklahoma Press, 1949.
7.124   Reprint. Originally published: Rev. ed. New York : Meridian Books, 1959. (Greenwich editions).
7.125   Reprint. Originally published: 2nd ed. entirely rewritten. London : Routledge and Kegan ; New York : E.P. Dutton, 1951.
7.126   Reprint. Originally published: 5th American, from the 4th London ed. Philadelphia : T. & J.W. Johnson, 1872.
7.127   Reprint. Originally published: Baptism in its mode and subjects. 5th American ed. Philadelphia : American Baptist Publication Society, 1853.

Reprints—Publication, Distribution, etc., Area

7.128   Reprint. Originally published: Berkeley : University of California Press, 1964 printing.
7.129   Reprint. Originally published: Dearborn, Mich. : Dearborn Pub. Co., 1920-1922.
7.130   Reprint. Originally published: Lathrop, Calif. : Printed for the author by Pacific Press Pub. Co., 1901.
7.131   Reprint. Originally published: London : J.M. Watkins, 1956 (v. 1). 1952 (v. 2).
7.132   Reprint. Originally published: London : Macmillan ; New York : St. Martin's Press, 1966.

7.133   Reprint. Originally published: London ; New York : issued under the auspices of the Royal Institute of International Affairs by the Oxford University Press.

7.134   Reprint. Originally published: London ; New York : Oxford University Press, 1961.

7.135   Reprint. Originally published: Manchester (Greater Manchester) ; published on behalf of the Institute for Social Research, University of Zambia, by Manchester University Press, 1968.

7.136   Reprint. Originally published: New York : Published for the author, 1874.

7.137   Reprint. Originally published: New York : Random House, [1962].

7.138   Reprint. Originally published: New York : Ronald Press, [1971?] c1943.

7.139   Reprint. Originally published: Washington : National Bureau of Standards, U.S. Dept. of Commerce : for sale by the Supt. of Docs., U.S. G.P.O., 1977. (NBS monograph ; 155).

Reprints—Series Area

7.140   Reprint. Originally published: Cambridge, Mass. : Harvard University Press, 1920. (Harvard historical studies ; v. 25).

7.141   Reprint. Originally published: Columbus, Ohio : Merrill, 1973. (Merrill political science series).

7.142   Reprint. Originally published: Boston : Little Brown, 1972. (A Documentary history of modern Europe / Thomas G. Barnes, Gerald D. Feldman ; v. 4).

7.143   Reprint. Originally published: Durham, N.C. : Duke University Press, 1957. (Publication / Duke University Commonwealth-Studies Center ; no. 4).

7.144   Reprint. Originally published: 1st ed. New York : Viking Press, 1980. (Einstein Anderson, science sleuth ; 2).

7.145   Reprint. Originally published: London : Sight and sound, 1948. (Special supplement to Sight and sound. Index series ; no. 15).

7.146   Reprint. Originally published: New Haven : Yale University Press, 1966. (Yale historical publications. Miscellany ; 83).

7.147   Reprint. Originally published: New York : Macmillan, 1954. (Murder revisited mystery novel ; no. 7) (Cock Robin mystery).

Reprints—Changes from the Original Publication

7.148   Reprint. Originally published: Englewood Cliffs, N.J. : Prentice-Hall, 1968. With an addendum to the original bibliography.

7.149   Reprint. Originally published: History of a branch of the Morrison family whose progenitor emigrated to America. Charleston, W. Va. : Jarrett Print. Co., 1928? With new index.

7.150   Reprint. Originally published: Jean Piaget, the man and his ideas. New York : Dutton, 1973. With a new introd.

7.151   Reprint. Originally published: New York : Arno Press, 1978, c1934. (Mythology) With new foreword.

7.152   Reprint. Originally published: New York : Bantam Books, 1966. With new afterword.

7.153   Reprint. Originally published: New York : D. Appleton, 1891. With a new foreword by Jeffrey Paul and a new index.

7.154   Reprint. Originally published: 2nd ed. London : G. Allen & Unwin, 1947. With new appendix.

7.155   Reprint. Originally published: 2nd ed. London ; New York : Longman, 1957. (African handbook of birds. Series 1). With addenda and corrigenda.

Reprint—Multiple Works

7.156   Reprint of 2 works. Originally published: West Brookfield, Mass. : Power Press of O.S. Cooke, 1849.

7.157   Reprint (1st work). Originally published: London : Wynkyn de Worde, [1525?]
Reprint (2nd work). Originally published: London : T. Berthelet, 1545.
Reprint (3rd work). Originally published: London : Printed by T.R. and M.D. and sold by Henry Million, 1670.

7.158   Reprint (1st work). Originally published: 5th ed. Dallas, Tex. : Allison Non-profit Press, 1972.
Reprint (2nd work). Originally published: Dallas, Tex. : Allison Press, c1958.

7.159   Reprint (main work). Originally published: Seaton, Ill. : N.L. Flack, 1918.
Reprint (supplement). Originally published: The Faris family supplement. Seaton, Ill. : N. Flack, 1946.

7.160   Reprint (Studies in Hume's ethics). Originally published: Uppsala : Almqvist Wiksells, 1937.
Reprint (David Hume, a symposium). Originally published: London : Macmillan, 1963.

Edition

7.161   On spine: 1981 edition.

7.162   "First edition"—Kirkpatrick.

7.163   "lst edition, 1965."

7.164   First ed., 2nd issue. Cf. Eckert.

7.165   First ed., 2nd or later impression. Cf. Gilcher.

7.166   "Second printing, revised."

7.167   American ed. of pt. 1 of: A day at a time.

7.168   "A dual media edition of the U.S. Superintendent of Documents' public documents library shelflists with accompanying indexes."

7.169   Large print ed.

7.170   "Paper cover edition . . . incorporating minor changes"—p. [ii].

7.171   "Preliminary."

7.172   Prepublication issues of 1st American ed.

7.173   "This edition is a pre-publication printing"—T.p. verso.

7.174   Ed. statement on v. 2.: Deuxième édition, 1980-1981.

7.175   Vol. 2.: 3rd ed., rev. spelling.
7.176   Vols. 4-6 lack ed. statement.
7.177   Vol. 6 omits edition statement.
7.178   Edition statement stamped on cover and half title.

Based On

7.179   "Based on Acme's proof of a prima facie defense, by Steven Corwin, originally published in 1968 by Acme Law Book Co., Inc. at Amityville, New York"—Pref.
7.180   Based on author's Handbook for evaluation of academic programs.
7.181   Based on the CRREL (U.S. Army Cold Regions Research and Engineering Lab.) Special report 79-5 entitled Physical and thermal disturbances and protection of permafrost, by J. Brown and N.A. Grave.
7.182   Based on entries for "Mark" in the Elenchus bibliographicus Biblicus, 1954 to 1977-1978; New Testament abstracts, 1956-1980; and Ephemerides theologicae Lovanienses, 1978-1980.
7.183   Based on: Finite mathematics, a modeling approach / J. Conrad Crown, Marvin L. Bittinger. 2nd ed. c1981 and Calculus, a modeling approach / Marvin L. Bittinger. 2nd ed. 1980.
7.184   Based on the 1789 ed.
7.185   Based on the dissertation lists published in the Professional geographer from 1969 through 1979 and the Guide to graduate departments of geography of the United States and Canada after 1979.
7.186   Pt. 1 based on the diary of A.H. Biogenesse.
7.187   Mildred Lawson is based in part on An art student, which appeared in the Spring 1895 no. of Today. John Norton is rev. and condensed from A mere accident. Cf. Gilcher.

Companion Works

7.188   Companion to: Greece in the 1940's : a nation in crisis.
7.189   A companion volume of commentary by Joachim Rössl was published in 1981.
7.190   "A companion volume to John W. Thompson's Index to illustrations of the natural world (North America)."
7.191   Companion vol. to the author's St. Thomas Aquinas on the existence of God.
7.192   Companion volume: Victor Hammer, artist and craftsman / John Rothenstein. 1978.
7.193   "Intended to complement . . . the editor's Choosing an automated library system"—Pref.
7.194   "Keyed to specific pages of . . . Textbook of medical physiology, by Arthur C. Guyton, 6th edition, 1981"—Pref.
7.195   Study guide to the film The life and times of Rosie the Riveter.
7.196   To accompany: Selections from Agricola / Tacitus ; [edited by] D.E. Soulsby. 1973.
7.197   Two companion volumes published in French under collective title: Géologie des pays européens.

7.198 "Volume I, a companion to Fundamentals of genealogical research."
"Volume II, a companion to Genealogical records of Utah."

Continuations
7.199 Continues: Index to AMA resources of the seventies : 1970-1976. c1977.
7.200 Continues: Modern microeconomics.
7.201 Continues: Paint additives / G.B. Rothenberg. 1978.
7.202 Continues: Traditional medicine / Ira E. Harrison and Sheila Cosminsky. 1976.
7.203 Continues the bibliography prepared by T.G. Melone and L.W. Weis; incorporates the bibliography prepared by J.F. Splettstoesser and S.A. Sloan.
7.204 Continues the 8 chapters of: John Henry Nash : the biography of a career / Robert D. Harlan. 1970.
7.205 Continuation of: La mainlevée d'opposition, 1940.
7.206 Continuation of: Papers relating to the late disturbances in Barbados.

Indexes
7.207 Index to: Early American medical imprints / by Robert B. Austin.
7.208 Indexes the 1981 bibliography of cases, issued as v. 7.

Limited Editions
7.209 "Sixty-five copies"—p. [28].
7.210 "Two hundred fifty copies . . . have been printed."
7.211 "First printing 250 copies"—Verso t.p.
7.212 "Edición de 500 ejemplares"—T.p. verso.
7.213 "Limited edition."
7.214 Limited ed. of 8 copies.
7.215 "Ltd. edition of 100 copies"—Label on p. 279.
7.216 Limited ed. of 100 numbered copies, signed by the editor.
7.217 Limited ed. of 150 copies. Cf. New Cambridge bibl. of Eng. lit. v. 4, column 239.
7.218 Limited ed. of about 200 copies, according to information received with the book from the Newberry Library.
7.219 Limited ed. of 300 copies (200 copies bound).
7.220 "Limited to ninety copies numbered 1-90/90. Ten additional copies, I-X/X, were printed for the author and the publisher. Copies numbered 1-15/90 and I-V/X were bound in parchment"—Colophon.
7.221 Two hundred copies on paper. Cf. Sparling.
7.222 "Five hundred copies have been printed, of which copies numbered 1 to 480 are for sale; copies i-xx are reserved for the publisher"—P. [144].
7.223 "Special" issue limited to 230 numbered copies.

Sequels
7.224 Sequel to: Boston's North Shore.
7.225 Sequel to: The episode of the thermometer.
The story is not concluded here, but the title of the sequel is unknown.

7.226 "Sequel to [author's] Money and the real world"—Pref.
7.227 "Sequel to the author's first text, Applied kinesiology—the advanced approach in chiropractic (1976)"—Pref.
7.228 Sequel to the poem by William Roscoe.

Supersedes

7.229 Supersedes DA pam. 500-28.
7.230 "Supersedes first edition."
7.231 "Supersedes Miscellaneous no. 10 (1969) Cmnd. 3958."
7.232 "Successor volume to Re, Cases and materials on equity and equitable remedies."
7.233 "This edition . . . supersedes the six previous editions . . . "—P. iv.

Supplements

7.234 Addenda to the author's article published in: Mountains and lowlands / edited by Louis D. Levine and T. Cuyler Young, Jr. 1977.
7.235 "Intended to supplement the information given in South Africa and South African bibliography"—p. ix.
7.236 "Issued as a supplement to the South Carolina historical magazine, volume 83, number 3"—Verso t.p.
7.237 Kept up to date with cumulative supplements.
7.238 *Kept up-to-date by West's general digest, 6th series.
7.239 Supplement 1 to NBS special publication 505: Bibliography on atomic transition probabilities.
7.240 "Supplement to America's democracy."
7.241 Supplement to: A bibliographical guide to the history of Indian-white relations in the United States / Francis Paul Prucha. Chicago : University of Chicago Press, 1977.
7.242 "A supplement to . . . Conservation of library materials"—Vol. 2, introd.
7.243 Supplement to: International law of the sea / N. Papadakis.
7.244 "Supplement no. 3 to Arthur E. Gropp's A bibliography of Latin American bibliographies."
7.245 Supplements: Medical radiation physics. 2nd ed. 1979.
7.246 Supplements: Russia, the USSR, and Eastern Europe : a bibliographic guide to English language publications, 1964-1974 / Stephen M. Horak. 1978.
7.247 Supplements the 1975 work by Unesco published under title: Planned buildings and facilities for higher education.
7.248 Supplements the 1979 ed.
7.249 Supplements the Pacific digest, covering v. 101-366 Pacific reporter, 2nd ser., 1940-1962, the Pacific digest, covering v. 1-100 Pacific reporter, 2nd ser., 1931-1940, and the Pacific digest, covering v. 1-300 Pacific reporter and the pre-reporter decisions, 1850-1931.
7.250 Supplements and updates: Judgment by confession in Pennsylvania / Richard Henry Klein, 1929, and: Handbook on the use of judgment notes in Pennsylvania / Philip Shuchman, 1961.

Chapter 3 (Cartographic Materials)

AACR2 RULE

3.7B7 Edition and History

Make notes relating to the edition being described or to the history of the cartographic item.

RELATED AACR2 RULE

None.

LIBRARY OF CONGRESS POLICY

None issued.

RELATED LIBRARY OF CONGRESS POLICY

None issued.

AACR2 TEXT EXAMPLES REVISED TO REFLECT LIBRARY OF CONGRESS POLICY

None required.

HISTORICAL BACKGROUND

AACR1 Rule 212E8 provided greater detail in describing the use of this note than does the corresponding rule in AACR2.

For maps based on a single source, AACR1 Rule 212E8a provided for the indication of that source. AACR2 Rule 3.7B7 does not specifically mention "single source" maps but does refer to the "history" of the item. Examples for this note in the AACR2 text are the same as those used to indicate a single source.

AACR1 Rule 212E8b distinguished different editions of a map. AACR1 stressed the importance of date changes while AACR2 simply refers to notes "relating to the edition." The intent of the two rules is, however, the same. The AACR1 rule does comment on the nature of early engraved maps, while AACR2 makes no mention of this.

NOTE EXAMPLES

7.251   Awarded blue ribbon in 1979 American Congress on Surveying and Mapping Map Design Competition.

7.252 Includes various issues of some sheets.
7.253 Limited ed. of 490 copies.

Base Maps

7.254 "Base compiled from 1:500,000 U.S.G.S. state base map ..."
7.255 "The base map, at a scale of 1:25,000,000, has been obtained by photographical reduction of the 1:5,000,000 scale map of the world of the American Geographical Society of New York, and by a contraction of ocean areas. For the Americas, the bipolar oblique conformal projection has been used; elsewhere, the Miller stereographic projection, modified in three conformal zones and adopted for the FAO/Unesco Soil map of the world in 16 sheets, has been utilized."
7.256 Base map title: State of New York.
7.257 Base map United States Geological Survey: Compiled in 1964. Edition of 1967. Highways corrected to l966.
7.258 "Base géographique : Carte échelle 1:5,000,000 de L'Amérique du Sud (projection conique oblique bipolar) 1953."
7.259 "Mapá base: I.G.M."

Earlier Editions

7.260 Originally published as: Modern school atlas of comparative geography. 1906.
7.261 Previous ed.: 1977.
7.262 Previous ed.: Turner Map Co.
7.263 Previously published as: Atlas of the Borough of Manhattan, city of New York. New York : G.W. Bromley Co., 1916.
7.264 Reprint. Original published: London : S. Harding, 1733.
7.265 Eighth ed. published as: U.B.D. complete street directory of Adelaide city & suburbs.

Related Works

7.266 Compiled to accompany the Report "Guidelines for the control of oil spills," Task T04, Publication number 211.
7.267 Principal maps also published separately in the "Australia l:5,000,000 map series"—Preface.
7.268 "Produced for the topic 'Soils' of the Atlas of Australian resources, 3rd series."
7.269 "Special bonus of 'Biblical Archeologist', 43:4, Fall 1980."
7.270 Supplement to: Atlas de Kinshasa, 1975.
7.271 Supp. to: First landowners of Ogemaw County, Michigan / Althea Cascadden Phillips and Donald J. de Zeeuw. Lansing, Mich. : Michigan Genealogical Council, Michigan State Library, Michigan Unit, 1980.
7.272 "Supplement to Pinetown Municipal brochure."
7.273 "Supplement to the National Geographic, December l980, page 704A, vol. 158 no. 6-Mexico and Central America."

7.274   To accompany: Informe final del estudio de aquas subterráneas en el valle de la Cuidad de Guatemala. 1978.

7.275   To accompany: Relation historique, 1814-1834 which constitutes pt. 1 of: Voyage de Humboldt . . . 1805-1834.

Revision, Update, etc.

7.276   Rev. ed. of: Atlas of Australian resources, 2nd series. 1962.

7.277   Rev. ed. of: Chart-kit, Block Island, R.I. to Portsmouth, N.H. 1977. Rev. ed. published as: Chart-kit BBA, Block Island, R.I., to the Canadian border. 1980.

7.278   Rev. ed. of: General highway and transportation map[s] / prepared by the Iowa State Highway Commission . . . 1952.

7.279   Rev. ed. of: Hamlyn's Sydney street directory. 27th ed. 1976?

7.280   Rev. ed. of: Hampton & Newport News street map. 1977. Rev. ed. published as: Virginia peninsular street map. 1981.

7.281   Rev. ed. of: Metro-Atlanta area, Ga. street map. c1979.

7.282   Rev. ed. of: Texaco road maps for 1942.

7.283   Revision of: The 1978 atlas of Boone County, Iowa.

7.284   Revision of: The 1972 [atlas] of Fillmore County, Nebraska.

Source of Data

7.285   Appears in W.Va. Dept. of Natural Resources' Comprehensive study of the Potomac River basin.

7.286   Based on: General highway map . . . County, Texas.

7.287   "Based on Student Map Manual, section 14."

7.288   Based on: The Atlas of congressional roll calls / prepared by the Historical Records Survey in New York City, 1938-39 and New Jersey, 1940-42.

7.289   "Basic information obtained from general highway maps made by Mississippi State Highway Department in cooperation with the Federal Highway Administration."

7.290   "Compiled from 1:250,000 USGS map sheets."

7.291   From Handbook for monitoring stations.

7.292   "Information from official maps reproduced under Government Printer's copyright authority no. 3250 of 18/11/63."

7.293   Maps are reduced from official assessment maps.

7.294   "Reproduced from an engraving in the collection of Historic Urban Plans, Ithaca, New York."

7.295   Reproduced from Speed's 1611 atlas: The theatre of the Empire of Great Britaine.

7.296   "Source: Maine State Planning Office interpretation of Soils and Slope Coastal Inventory Maps . . . "

7.297   "Source: USGS base map and official highway map of South Dakota watershed information from field technicians."

7.298   "Source data: U.S. Dept. of the Interior—Geological Survey topographic maps, U.S. Dept. of the Army—Corps of Engineers topographic maps."

7.299 "These maps were developed from data available as of January 1980 from numerous agencies, institutions, and individual countries, in consultation with independent experts, and with support of the U.S. Agency for International Development."

7.300 "This map has been compiled from 1:250,000 sheets and other material as available."

Chapter 4 (Manuscripts)

AACR2 RULE

4.7B7 Donor, Source, etc., and Previous Owner(s) [AACR2 Rev.]
Make notes on the donor or source of a manuscript or manuscript collection, and on previous owners if readily ascertainable. Add the year or years of accession to the name of the donor or source, and add the years of ownership to the name of a previous owner.

RELATED AACR2 RULE

None.

LIBRARY OF CONGRESS POLICY

None issued. APPM, however, expands on the AACR2 text.

Provenance
Make a note on the history of the custody of the materials being cataloged. Include information on successive transfers of ownership and custody of the materials and the dates thereof. If the provenance and source (see [APPM] 4.7B8) are the same, do not make this note, but record the information in the source note. [APPM 4.7B7]

Source/Donor
Make a note on the donor or source (i.e., the immediate prior custodian) of the material being cataloged. Indicate the status (i.e., gift, purchase, deposit, transfer, etc.) of the acquisition, the date of the acquisition, whether any additions are anticipated, and, if desired, any accession numbers associated with the material. In addition, the donor's relationship to the materials may be indicated. Omit any confidential information. If the source is unknown, record that information. [APPM 4.7B8]

RELATED LIBRARY OF CONGRESS POLICY

None issued.

AACR2 TEXT EXAMPLES REVISED TO REFLECT
LIBRARY OF CONGRESS POLICY

None required.

HISTORICAL BACKGROUND

In AACR1, the "Introductory Notes" to the rules for the description of single manuscripts (preceding AACR1 Rule 201) state that a note was provided for the name of the donor, other acquisition sources, year of acquisition and provenance when this information was readily available.

AACR1 Rule 201B3 called for a note to record "significant provenance" for ancient, medieval, and Renaissance manuscripts.

AACR1 Rule 207K addressed the use of a note to record the provenance of a manuscript collection. This note recorded the donor or other source, the year(s) of accession and, when available, an identification of previous owners. The donor or source information was excluded when the information was confidential.

AACR1 Rule 207E provided for a note for the name of a collector whose collection had been incorporated into another collection.

These AACR1 notes are in general agreement with the AACR2 rule except that AACR2 adds the years of ownership to the names of the previous owners. AACR2 does not address the issue of confidentiality and does not provide any special instructions for identifying the provenance of ancient, medieval, or Renaissance manuscripts. AACR2 does, however, cover them in the general provisions of this rule.

NOTE EXAMPLES

Acquisition Mode
7.301   Acquired as part of the N. & W.W. Billings records, 1914.
7.302   Acquired from the estate of Elizabeth D. Williams.
7.303   Acquired from the heirs of Dorothea (Miller) Post, the last family member who lived in Macculloch Hall, 1949.
7.304   *The association annually donates its non-current records to the collection.
7.305   Portions of the papers were formerly part of the repository's National Broadcasting Company records.
7.306   *Source unknown.
7.307   *Source unknown; acquired, 19th century.

Acquisition Mode—Deposit
7.308   Deposited by Riley W. Gunther, Memphis, Tenn., 1971.
7.309   Deposited by Rutherford P. Lilley, 1973.
7.310   *Deposited by the Naval Historical Foundation, 1964.

7.311   Deposited by the owner.
7.312   Permanent deposit, 1976.
7.313   Permanent deposit by Botany Dept., Iowa State University, 1973.

Acquisition Mode—Gifts

7.314   Anonymous gift.
7.315   *Bequest of Mr. Smith, 1922.
7.316   Chiefly gift of Caroline McDouglas Neilson, Washington, D.C., 1967.
7.317   Chiefly gift of Imagineering Enterprises, owners of the former N.P. Bowsher buildings, 1977.
7.318   Chiefly gift of Julian Magarey Barclay after the death of Mrs. Barclay, 1951.
7.319   *Deposit, converted to gift, 1976.
7.320   Gift.
7.321   *Gift of composer.
7.322   Gift of Donald P. Drain and Jessie L. Bowen, last owners of the yard, 1975.
7.323   Gift of Doris C. Morse, widow of Carleton D. Morse, the original compiler of the collection, and their daughter, Elizabeth, 1958.
7.324   Gift of Elizabeth Sprague Coolidge, 1944.
7.325   *Gift of George Matthew Adams, Harold G. Rugg, and Friends of the Library.
7.326   *Gift of Herbert B. Wilcox, Frederick Chase, and by purchase.
7.327   Gift of Gisella Selden-Goth, Dec. 30, 1968.
7.328   *Gift of John McLane and from the Rugg autograph collection.
7.329   *Gift of Leo Allen Whitehill and Sarah Ruth Whitehill in honor of Mr. Whitehill's father Samuel Weiselberg, 1977. San Angelo, Tex.
7.330   *Gift of Marion Page Bunger, March 1971. Gift of General Charles T. Menoher.
7.331   Gift of Mr. Barnett's widow, Etta Moten Barnett, 1977.
7.332   Gift of the association through Anita Terauds, secretary, 1975.
7.333   Gift of the author.
7.334   Gift of the club.
7.335   Gift, probably from a descendant of the Billings family, 1914.
7.336   Gifts, 1892-1979.
7.337   Gifts from various sources.
7.338   Gifts of Mr. Huntley, John Ellsworth, and the National Broadcasting Company, 1962-1974.

Acquisition Mode—Purchase

7.339   Acquired through Dance Committee Purchase Fund.
7.340   *Purchased, May 1978.
7.341   Purchased and gifts, 1977-1981.
7.342   Purchased prior to 1976.
7.343   *Purchased from B. Altman & Co., 1982.
7.344   *Purchased from Christie's, New York, "Wagner sale", 1978 October 27, Lot No. 60/C36.

7.345   Purchased from In Our Time, Cambridge, Mass., upon recommen-
        dation of Dr. Roger Esson, Memphis State University Dept. of English,
        1977.
7.346   *Purchased from Walter R. Benjamin, Inc., Hunter, N.Y., 1980.

Previous Owners
7.347   Bookplate of: Howard C. Levis.
7.348   Bookplates of: Henry B.H. Beaufoy; Howard C. Levis.
7.349   *From the Harold Goddard Rugg autograph collection.
7.350   Gift of Gisella Selden-Goth, 1966 ; formerly owned by Ignaz Mos-
        cheles.
7.351   Gift of Macie Conrad, Great Falls, Mont., 1955. Formerly part of the
        Helena Banking Group collection.
7.352   *Provenance unknown.

Chapter 5 (Music)

AACR2 RULE

5.7B7 Edition and History

Make notes relating to the edition being described or to the bibliographic history of the work.

RELATED AACR2 RULE

5.7B19 Publishers' Numbers and Plate Numbers [AACR2 Rev.]

Give publishers' numbers and/or plate numbers that appear on the
item. Precede the numbers by *Publisher's no.:* or *Pl. no.:*, as appropriate.
If a number is preceded by an abbreviation, word, or phrase designating
a publisher, give that abbreviation, word, or phrase as part of the number.

In describing an item in several volumes, give inclusive numbers if
the numbering is consecutive; otherwise give individual numbers or,
if there are more than three of these, the first number and the last
number separated by a diagonal slash. Give letters preceding a number
before the first number, letters following a number after the last number,
but letters preceding and following numbers in conjunction with each
number. . . .

In describing a reprint, give the plate or publisher's number(s) together with the statement that the item is a reprint (see 5.7B7). [em-
phasis added]

LIBRARY OF CONGRESS POLICY

None issued.

RELATED LIBRARY OF CONGRESS POLICY

None issued.

AACR2 TEXT EXAMPLES REVISED TO REFLECT LIBRARY OF CONGRESS POLICY

1st Example

AACR2 TEXT
Reprinted from the 1712 ed.

AACR2 TEXT REVISED
Reprint. Originally published: 1712.

2nd Example

AACR2 REV. TEXT
Reprint in reduced format of the full score: Berlin : Harmonie, 1910.

AACR2 REV. TEXT REVISED
Reprint in reduced format of the full score. Originally published: Berlin : Harmonie, 1910.

The wording of the second example was slightly different in AACR2. The third example in AACR2, which would have required a revision, was rewritten in AACR2 Rev. and no longer requires a revision.

HISTORICAL BACKGROUND

Although AACR1 and previous codes had no rule equivalent to AACR2 Rule 5.7B7, the edition and history note provisions for separately published monographs in these earlier codes could be used for music. (See *Historical Background* under Rule 2.7B7.)

NOTE EXAMPLES

Source

7.353 Based on autograph score in collection Renzo Giorgano, opere sacre v. 3, at Biblioteca Nazionale, Turin.

7.354 Edited from 1649 ed. in British Museum.

7.355 Edited from a copy of the 1644 reprint of the original ed. in the Bodleian Library (Ms. Mus. Sch. c155a-e).

7.356   Edited from a copy of the 1st ed. in the Royal College of Music, London (Amsterdam : E. Roger, ca. 1702).

7.357   Edited from a ms. copy in the Conservatory of Music, Brussels.

7.358   Edited from a ms. in the British Library (Add. 5336).

7.359   Edited from a private ms. (not holograph) and "attentive hearing of the tape of Toscanini's performance"—P. 2.

7.360   Edited from a set of ms. part-books in the British Library (Royal app. 59-62).

7.361   Edited from a tablature in the Musikhistorisk Museum, Copenhagen.

7.362   Edited from copyist's ms., Add. MS 49599 in the British Library.

7.363   Edited from: Holograph, Bayer. Staatsbibliothek (Mus. Mss. 5789).

7.364   Edited from: Ms. parts in the Carolino Augusteum Museum, Salzburg (Sign. Hs 579).

7.365   Edited from ms. parts in the hand of Leopold Mozart in the Bavarian State Library, Munich.

7.366   Edited from mss. in the Kongelige Bibliotek, Copenhagen (Mu 6806.1399). Universitetsbiblioteket, Lund, Sweden (Samling Wenster Litt. G. 29), and the Universitetsbibliotek, Uppsala, Sweden (Ihre 285 ; Instrumentalmusik i handskrift 410).

7.367   Edited from original edition.

7.368   Edited from set of parts from original ed. published by Peters, Leipzig.

7.369   Edited from the 1st ed. copy bound into the composer's set of 1st eds. of his works in the Robert-Schumann-Haus, Zwickau.

7.370   Edited from the 1st ed. published: Leipzig : H.A. Probst, ca. 1831.

7.371   Edited from the holograph in the British Library (R.M. 20.f.1.).

7.372   Edited principally from the holograph score in the Hessische Landes- und Hochschubibliothek, Darmstadt, Mus. ms. 1447.

7.373   Source: Early Scottish keyboard music / edited by Kenneth Elliot. London : Stainer & Bell, 1967.

7.374   "The source of this edition . . . is Raccolta Renzo Giordano, Opera sacre, tome V. ff 89-113 in the Biblioteca nazionale in Turin"—T. p. verso.

7.375   Transcription of: Second livre contenant xxxi. chansons musicales (Paris : Pierre Attaingnant, 1536). RISM 1536/3.

Publication History

7.376   Advance publication from the Neue Mozart Ausgabe, Serie IV, Werk- gruppe 11, Band 1-2.

7.377   From: Motetti C. Venice : O. Petrucci, 1504.

7.378   "From the Breitkopf & Härtel complete works edition."

7.379   Originally published in the 9th and 10th lesson of Der getreue Musik- meister.

7.380   Previous ed. published in 1532 as: Musica teusch. Cf. New Grove.

7.381   The 2nd and only remaining movement of the composer's Trumpet concerto, which was performed in Strasbourg in 1933.

7.382   "This edition contains four previously unpublished organ works."— Pref.

7.383 "Unabridged republication of all nineteen Concerti grossi from volumes 21 and 30 of Georg Friedrich Händel's Werke as originally published in 1865 and 1869 by the Deutsche Handelgesellschaft in Leipzig"—Cover.

Reprints
7.384 Reprint. Originally published: State Historical Society of Missouri, 1946-50.
7.385 Reprint. Originally published: Frankfurt, West Germany : IM Insel-Verlag, 1962. With new English translation of the Nachwort.
7.386 Reprint of the ed. published: Paris : Au Magasin de musique du Conservatoire imper. 1, [1814]. Pl. no.: 212.
7.387 Reprint of works originally published 1800-1826.
7.388 Reprinted from various 19th century eds.
7.389 Reprinted from the composer's Werke, originally published: Leipzig : Breitkopf & Härtel, 1880-1887.
7.390 Reprints of works originally published by Bailleux or Sieber, Paris.

Reproductions
7.391 Reproduction of a ms. choirbook copied by the workshop of Petrus Alamire between 1526 and 1534 and originally the property of Pompejus Occo.
7.392 Songs are reproduced directly from editions of the sheet music.

Revised and Limited Editions
7.393 "Revised 1979"—Caption.
7.394 Rev. version, 1901, with Prologue and Epilogue added.
7.395 "Limited composer's edition."

Composition History
7.396 "Composed between 19th May and 20th July, 1977 . . ."
7.397 Overture composed for the Milan premiere of Aïda but rejected by the composer.
7.398 "This work was written between 14 March and 1 May, 1979"—verso t.p.
7.399 Works composed on the occasion of the 3rd centennial of the death of Camõe in 1880.

Chapter 6 (Sound Recordings)

AACR2 RULE

6.7B7 Edition and History [AACR2 Rev.]
Make notes relating to the edition being described, to the edition of the work performed, or to the history of the recording. . . .

This category of note includes information on when and where the recording was made, as well as its bibliographic history including previous releases and label name. Also included here, although not clearly stated in the rule, is information about the edition being recorded (i.e., the edition of the score used for the performance).

> For a nonprocessed sound recording, give the available details of the event.

RELATED AACR2 RULE

6.4F2 Date of Publication, Distribution, etc. [AACR2 Rev.]
If the date of recording appears on a published sound recording, give it in a note (see 6.7B7). [emphasis added]

LIBRARY OF CONGRESS POLICY

None issued.

RELATED LIBRARY OF CONGRESS POLICY

None issued.

AACR2 TEXT EXAMPLES REVISED TO REFLECT LIBRARY OF CONGRESS POLICY

None required.

HISTORICAL BACKGROUND

AACR1 Rev. Rule 252F6 provided for a note on the edition of the original work used for the recording (i.e., the score). AACR2 provides for this, but does not provide the detail of the earlier rule.

AACR1 Rev. Rule 252F7 provided for notes on "details concerning the event," including the place, date, and other significant recording information. While the AACR2 rule does provide for recording this information, the rule is not as specific as in the AACR1.

AACR1 Rev. Rule 252F9 provided for notes on abridgments, if the information is known without a special search. The general wording of the AACR2 rule allows these notes to be made, and the text examples include such a note; however, there is no specific mention of abridgments in AACR2 as there was in AACR1.

NOTE EXAMPLES

Edition and History—Miscellaneous
7.400 Abridged.
7.401 An abridgement of the translation by Lowell Bair, published: New York : Bantam Books, c1972.
7.402 "Complete version"—Container.

7.403 Conference proceedings (10 sound cassettes) also issued under same title.

7.404 First recited at St. James's Palace, London, in Nov. 1978.

7.405 The 1st work, written in 1978, was extensively revised in 1979.

7.406 From films of 1943, 1944, and 1945.

7.407 "An original BBC record."

7.408 "An original recording of Discos Columbia, S. A./Spain."

7.409 Pre-conference tapes (2 sound cassettes) also issued under same title.

7.410 "Substantial portions of this album are contained in the soundtrack of the motion picture, The Secret life of plants"—Container.

Recording History—Place

7.411 The 1st work recorded in St. Paul, Minn., the 2nd-3rd at the Church of the Holy Trinity, New York.

7.412 Recorded at A & R Studio, New York City, by Sound Stream Digital Recorders.

7.413 "Recorded at Soundmixers, New York, N.Y."—Container.

7.414 Recorded at the Eastman School of Music (Downey and Johnston works) and at the Gasparo studios, Nashville (Seeger).

7.415 Recorded at the Mulvihill home, Bronx, N.Y. and at Golden East Recording Studio, New Canaan, Conn.

7.416 "Tracks 1 and 5 . . . were recorded live at a concert of improvised music in London"—Container.

Recording History—Date

7.417 The 1st work recorded Oct. 1936; the 2nd Oct. 1935.

7.418 Recorded in the later 1950's.

7.419 Recorded June 3-7, 1980.

7.420 Recorded June 28, 1960 (quintets) and June 27, 1961 (sextets).

7.421 Recorded 1900-1930 (Records 1-3); 1930-1955 (Records 4-5); 1955-1980 (Record 6).

7.422 Recorded principally 3 Dec. 1963 and 2 Oct. 1964.

7.423 Recorded 30 Jan.-2 Feb. 1978 (1st work), and 24-26 Nov. 1975 (2nd work).

Recording History—Place and Date

7.424 The 1st work recorded Jan. 9, 1975, from a broadcast on the Hessischen Rundfunks. The 2nd and 3rd works recorded Dec. 1976 in Paris.

7.425 The 1st-2nd works recorded May 26, 1980, Universalist Church, New York ; the 3rd Sept. 25, 1979, Abraham Gordon House, New York.

7.426 The 1st work recorded during a performance at the Teatro Municipal do Rio de Janeiro on Oct. 24, 1961; the remainder are from a broadcast of Oct. 24, 1961.

7.427 Recorded Aug. 1979 in Hertz Hall, University of Calif., Berkeley (1st work) and in Hellman Hall, San Francisco Conservatory of Music (2nd work).

7.428 Recorded Aug. 13, 1963, at the Van Gelder Studio, Englewood Cliffs, N.J.; released here for the first time.

7.429 Recorded during the 1975 and 1976 Tucson Meet Yourself festivals.

7.430 "Recorded, edited and remixed at Olympic Sound Studios, London, March 1978"—Container notes.

7.431 Recorded from a live performance by children's voices, Notre Dame de Paris, Jan. 1978.

7.432 Recorded from remote broadcasts from the Meadowbrook in Cedar Grove, N.J. (Nov. 10, 1944) the Chatterbox in Mountainside, N.J. (June 30, 1940) and the Meadowbrook in Culver-City, Calif. (Feb. 14, 1946).

7.433 Recorded in concert, June 1979, in Willisau, Switzerland.

7.434 Recorded May 13, 1978, at the Premises, Norwich, and June 22, 1978, at the London Musicians Collective.

7.435 Recorded principally at the 6th Annual Telluride Bluegrass and Country Music Festival, June 22-24, 1979.

7.436 Recorded principally in New York or Camden, 1922-1943.

Recording History—Miscellaneous

7.437 Live recording.

7.438 Observations recorded from original radio appearances of 1933-1935.

7.439 Recorded by the O. R. T. F.

7.440 Recorded from Capitol nickelodeon rolls 2169, 2254, 2301, and 2310, originally recorded in Chicago in the 1920's.

7.441 Recorded from live performances in 1964, 1965, and 1967.

7.442 Recorded from the Television Española production.

7.443 Recorded from twelve episodes of the program of the same title, Feb.-May,1945.

7.444 Recorded under severe weather conditions.

7.445 "The actual broadcast by the Mercury Theatre on the air as heard over the Columbia Broadcasting System October 30, 1938."

Edition Recorded

7.446 Ed. recorded: Frankfurt ; New York : Peters, 1975-1976.

7.447 Edition recorded: Kassel : Bärenreiter, 1967 (Neue Bach-Gesamtausgabe VII, 1).

7.448 Ed. recorded: New York : Doubleday, cl980.

7.449 Ed. recorded: Oceana Music ; except East wind blues: Garden Street Music.

7.450 Edition recorded: Presser.

7.451 Ed. recorded: on realization by Jean-Pierre Dautel based on original ms. in the Bibliothèque nationale.

7.452 Ed. recorded: [S.l.] : Editions Ricordi-Amphion.

7.453 Editions recorded: Hinshaw Music (3rd work) and American Composers Editions (remainder).

7.454 Eds. recorded: Neue Schubert Ausg., Bärenreiter (1st work) ; Edition Eulenberg (2nd work).

7.455 Eds. recorded: New York : Ballantine Books, cl964 ; New York : Ballantine Books, cl960.

7.456   Editions recorded: Peters (1st, 2nd, and 5th works) ; Kalmus (3rd and 4th works).

7.457   Editions recorded: Seesaw Music, Edizioni Suvini Zerbone, Éditions A. Luduc, Ars Viva.

7.458   The 3rd-5th works were originally published together as: Three elegies upon the much lamented death of our late Queen Mary.

7.459   "Sources: M.A. Charpentier, Meslanges, Bibliothèque nationale, Paris, rés."

History of the Recording—Licensing

7.460   "Licensed by Erato Records of France."

7.461   "Licensed from Arion 38462."

History of the Recording—Previous Releases

7.462   1st and 3rd works originally issued on Savoy 12131 and 12136.

7.463   The 1st-7th works originally issued with title Here's Jaki (New Jazz 8256) ; the 8th work originally issued on Out front! (Prestige 7397) ; the 9th-16th works originally issued with title IIi fly (New Jazz 8273).

7.464   "The 148th release."

7.465   "All selections previously released."

7.466   In part previously issued on Savoy 12025 and 12040.

7.467   "Originally issued as CL897 on October 8, 1956 and titled The Jazz Messengers . . . reissued as 32 16 0216 on August 26, 1968 and re-titled Art Blakey with the original Jazz Messengers"—Container.

7.468   Originally issued in France on Isabel Records.

7.469   Originally issued on Columbia (Bells are ringing, Gypsy) and Capitol (Funny girl) labels.

7.470   "Originally released as part of CRL5-1415"—Container.

7.471   "Originally released in 1959"—Container.

7.472   Previously issued by University of Illinois Campus Folksong Club Records, CFC 301.

7.473   Previously released.

7.474   Previously released on Atlantic 1224 and 1357.

7.475   Quintets originally issued with title Looking ahead (New Jazz 8247) ; sextets originally issued with title The quest (New Jazz 8269), and have been previously issued by Prestige (Prestige 7579).

7.476   Recorded 1903-1918 ; originally issued on wax cylinders by Gramophone and Typewriter Co., Zon-o-phone, Edison Wax Cylinder, and Aeolian Vocalion.

7.477   Recorded Apr. 13, 1958, and Feb. 13, 1959. Previously issued as Ramblin' with Mose (Prestige 7215) and Autumn song (Prestige 7189).

7.478   Recorded Feb. 1979 at Évangélique Allemande Church, Paris; previously released as Erato 71277.

7.479   Recorded Nov. 15 and Dec. 13, 1957, and Mar. 16, 1961, at Van Gelder Studios in Hackensack and Englewood Cliffs, N.J. In part previously issued on Prestige 7209, 7229, and 7307.

7.480   "Re-issued from the original Dawn Recordings"—Container.

7.481 Reissue of: Deutsche Grammophon 138 974 (1st work) ; Deutsche Grammophon 139 016 (2nd work).

7.482 Reissue of: EMI/HMV Concerto Classics, SXLP 20043.

7.483 Report by Dr. Goodman previously issued on cassette with Improving body implants / F. Horowitz.

7.484 Selections from The London Virtuosi, v. 1-2, Abbey PHB 722-PHB 723.

7.485 Smetana pieces originally released in 1957 ; other works recorded in 1977.

7.486 "Yellow bird was originally released in 1973 as part of Avant Records AV1009"—Container.

Chapter 7 (Motion Pictures and Videorecordings)

AACR2 RULE

7.7B7 Edition and History

Make notes relating to the edition being described or to the history of the motion picture or videorecording.

RELATED AACR2 RULE

None.

LIBRARY OF CONGRESS POLICY

When an item is known to have an original master in a different medium and the production or release date of the master is more than two years earlier than that of the item being cataloged, give an edition/history note. . . .

Make a similar note when an item is known to have been previously produced or issued (more than two years earlier) if in a different medium, but the original medium is unknown. . . .

If the date of production or release of an original master or an earlier medium is unknown or if the difference between its production or release date and the production or release date of the item being cataloged is two years or less, indicate the availability of the other medium or media in a note according to 7.7B16 and 8.7B16. [CSB 15]

For archival moving image materials, the Library of Congress supplements AACR2 Chapter 7 with the guidelines in *Archival Moving Image Materials* by White-Hensen.

RELATED LIBRARY OF CONGRESS POLICY

None issued.

AACR2 TEXT EXAMPLES REVISED TO REFLECT LIBRARY OF CONGRESS POLICY

None required.

HISTORICAL BACKGROUND

AACR1 Rev. Rule 229.2A provided for a note for an earlier title of a work now issued under a different title. This same type of note could also be made under the provisions of AACR2, although no specific mention is made of it.

AACR1 Rev. Rule 229.2F provided for a note to record other works on which the item being cataloged depended for its "intellectual or artistic content." This note was also used to indicate the existence of other versions of the work. AACR2 provides for essentially the same note.

NOTE EXAMPLES

Adaptations
7.487 Adapted from the filmmaker's book of the same name.
7.488 Adapted from the book: Sam and his cart / Arthur Honeyman.
7.489 An adaptation of the story of the same title by Saki.

Based On
7.490 Based on: A Design guide for home safety.
7.491 Based on: Ballet shoes / Noel Streatfeild.
7.492 Based on: What Katy did / Susan Coolidge. What Katy did at school / Susan Coolidge.
7.493 Based on the book of the same name by Colin Thiele.
7.494 Based on the book: The Hoffnung music festival / Gerard Hoffnung. London : Dobson, [1956].
7.495 Based on the cartoons of Gerard Hoffnung.
7.496 Based on the fairy tale: Pinocchio.
7.497 Based on the fairy tale: The Wonderful Wizard of Oz / by L. Frank Baum.
7.498 Based on the novel by James Joyce.
7.499 Based on the play: The Front page / Ben Hecht and Charles Mac-Arthur.
7.500 Based on the short story of the same title by Roch Carrier.

Edited Versions

7.501 Edited from: For parents only. 1980.

7.502 Edited from the 90-min. televised feature film of the same name.

7.503 Edited from the longer version (50 min.) of the same title.

7.504 First 10 minutes of the motion picture entitled: Champions never quit.

7.505 Issued in 1978 in longer version (49 min.).

7.506 A segment from the television program: 60 minutes.

7.507 Selections reissued from the series entitled: Special delivery.

Original Format, Release Date, etc.

7.508 Originally broadcast on HBO.

7.509 Originally broadcast on the BBC television network.

7.510 Originally issued as filmstrip in 1975.

7.511 Originally issued as filmstrip and as slide set in 1977.

7.512 Originally issued as filmstrip in 1967 and as motion picture in 1968.

7.513 Originally released in 1969.

7.514 Originally released in Canada in 1975.

7.515 Originally shown in Canada on the television program entitled: Portraits of power.

7.516 Originally shown on the ABC News television program 20/20.

7.517 Previously broadcast on PBS.

7.518 Previously issued as motion picture in 1942.

7.519 Previously issued as motion picture and filmstrip in 1945.

7.520 Previously released in 1974.

Other Versions

7.521 American version produced by International Film Bureau.

7.522 First released in Spain under title: Goya en su tiempo.

7.523 French version entitled: Mer mère.

7.524 Issued also in German.

7.525 Originally released in England under title: The life cycle of a flowering plant.

Related Works

7.526 Book, based on the series, published as: The body in question / Jonathan Miller. New York : Random House, c1978.

7.527 Correlated with: A guide to physical examination / Barbara Bates.

7.528 Companion film: The wood shell / Peter John Lodge.

7.529 Companion videorecording: The right-on roofer safework series.

7.530 Sequel: There's always a risk.

7.531 Sequel to: A Boy and a boa. 1975.

Revision, Updates, etc.

7.532 Previous version issued in 1955 entitled: Reading maps.

7.533 Previous version, issued as motion picture in 1963, has title: Laws of heredity.

7.534 Revised version.

7.535 Rev. version of: From mountains to microns. 1959.

7.536 Rev. version of 1978 videorecording of the same title.

7.537 Rev. version of the motion picture of the same title issued in 1969.

7.538 Rev. version of the videorecording of the same title: Berkeley, Calif. : University of California Extension Media Center, 1962. (Automobile safety series).

7.539 Rev. version of the 1973 motion picture entitled: Boys aware / Sid Davis Productions.

7.540 Second ed. of the motion picture of the same title issued in 1965.

7.541 Updated version of the 1972 motion picture of the same name issued by Films/West.

7.542 Updated version of the 1975 motion picture entitled: Up with teachers.

Chapter 8 (Graphic Materials)

AACR2 RULE

8.7B7 Edition and History
Make notes relating to the edition being described or to the history of the item.

RELATED AACR2 RULE

None.

LIBRARY OF CONGRESS POLICY

When an item is known to have an original master in a different medium and the production or release date of the master is more than two years earlier than that of the item being cataloged, give an edition/history note. . . .

Make a similar note when an item is known to have been previously produced or issued (more than two years earlier) if in a different medium, but the original medium is unknown. . . .

If the date of production or release of an original master or an earlier medium is unknown or if the difference between its production or release date and the production or release date of the item being cataloged is two years or less, indicate the availability of the other medium or media in a note according to 7.7B16 and 8.7B16. [CSB 15]

For original items and historical collections, the Library of Congress supplements AACR2 Chapter 8 with the guidelines in *Graphic Materials* by Betz.

RELATED LIBRARY OF CONGRESS POLICY

None issued.

AACR2 TEXT EXAMPLES REVISED TO REFLECT LIBRARY OF CONGRESS POLICY

None required.

HISTORICAL BACKGROUND

AACR1 Rev. Rule 229.2A provided for a note for an earlier title of a work now issued under a different title. This same type of note could also be made under the provisions of AACR2, although no specific mention is made of it.

AACR1 Rev. Rule 229.2F provided for a note to record other works on which the item being cataloged depended for its "intellectual or artistic content." This note was also used to indicate the existence of other versions of the work. AACR2 provides for essentially the same note.

AACR1 Rule 268B called for a note to record the date of execution of a picture if that date differed "significantly" from its publication date. AACR2 does not specifically address this note, although it could be made under the provisions of the AACR2 rule.

AACR1 Rule 272C4 provided for a note to record the existence of works related to the pictures being cataloged. This rule applied to accompanying textual materials, other forms in which the material had been published, or the identification of a text the pictures were intended to illustrate. AACR2 does not provide any specific guidelines for pictures under AACR2 Rule 8.7B7. The notes made under AACR1 could still be made under AACR2, although, when the items accompany the work, the information becomes part of an accompanying materials statement (AACR2 Rule 8.5E) or an accompanying material note (AACR2 Rule 8.7B11).

AACR1 Rule 272C5 provided for a provenance note for pictures if the information was known and considered useful to the identification of the work. The existence of previous collectors' marks was also noted under this rule.

AACR1 Rule 272C6 provided for an indication of the location of the original work if the picture being cataloged was a reproduction.

AACR1 Rule 272C8 provided information on the source of the picture. The accession number of the item could be included as part of this note. This source note was to be the last note in the description.

The last three AACR1 notes mentioned above are not specifically provided for in AACR2, although they are similar to the type of note AACR2 provides for manuscripts under AACR2 Rule 4.7B7. There is, however, nothing in AACR2 Rule 8.7B7 that would prohibit their continued use. Many of the aspects of these AACR1 rules are incorporated into the Betz guidelines being used by the Library of Congress.

NOTE EXAMPLES

Projection Graphic Materials

7.543 Correlated with the textbook: The Social sciences, concepts and values.

7.544 First issued as: Obesity—what your doctor wants you to know. 1975.

7.545 First issued in 1974.

7.546 French version of: Stop and shop.

7.547 Issued as filmstrip in 1979 by Sunburst Communications.

7.548 Issued in 1970 under title: Common trees I.

7.549 Originally issued as filmstrip set by Human Relations Media.

7.550 Sequel to the filmstrip: The Snacking Mouse.

7.551 Spanish version of: Stop and shop.

ADAPTATIONS

7.552 Adapted from episode 3 of the PBS television series: Life on earth. Based on: Life on earth / David Attenborough.

7.553 Adapted from the 1962 Universal Pictures motion picture: Freud—the secret passion, starring Montgomery Clift and Susannah York.

7.554 Adapted from: The adventures of Tom Sawyer / Mark Twain.

7.555 Adapted from the animated Chinese film: Havoc in heaven.

7.556 Adapted from the book: Anatomy of an illness as perceived by the patient / by Norman Cousins.

7.557 Adapted from the book of the same name by James Marshall.

7.558 Adapted from the motion picture of the same name issued by Universal Pictures in 1975.

7.559 Adapted from the NBC televised white paper of the same name.

7.560 Derived from the motion picture of the same title.

7.561 Taken from Dr. Carl Sagan's television series of the same name.

BASED ON

7.562 Based on: A golden thread / by Ken Butti and John Perlin.

7.563 Based on: Solar gain : winners of the passive solar design competition / California Energy Commission [and] Governor's Office of Appropriate Technology.

7.564 Based on the book by Carol Nicklaus.

7.565 Based on the books of the same titles by John Barrett.

7.566 Based on the stories of the same titles by Mark Twain, O. Henry, and Nathaniel Hawthorne.

7.567 Based on two chapters of the book: Ishi, last of his tribe / Theodora Kroeber.

7.568 Based on two episodes from the book: Henry Huggins / Beverly Cleary. New York : Morrow, 1950.

REVISIONS, UPDATES, ETC.

7.569 Rev. ed. of the filmstrips issued separately under title: Drug information series. 1970.

7.570 Rev. version of the 1973 slide set of the same title.

7.571 Revised version of the filmstrip issued in 1975 by Human Relations Media under the same name.

7.572 Rev. version of the filmstrips issued in 1971-72.

7.573 Rev. version of the transparency issued in 1972.

7.574 Revised version of a filmstrip issued in 1977 in a set entitled: What's your message?

7.575 Rev. version of: Hospital fire safety series. 1977, c1969.

7.576 Revised version of the 1971 filmstrip: American decades—1970's : decade of challenge, issued by Filmstrip House.

7.577 Updated and rev. version of: Values, goals, decisions. New York : Butterick Publishing, 1976. (Lifestyles—options for living).

7.578 Updated from: Laboratory parasitology. Part 1, Intestinal parasites. 1973 ; Laboratory parasitology. Part 2, Blood and tissue parasites and arthropods. 1973.

7.579 Updated version of the 1977 filmstrip entitled: Satisfaction guaranteed; previously issued as part of the set entitled: The Butterick consumer education series.

7.580 Updated version of the 1977 filmstrip of the same name.

7.581 Updated version of the slide set of the same title issued in 1972.

7.582 Second ed. of: Full circle. 1979.

Nonprojection Graphic Materials

7.583 *2d state.

7.584 Cartoons from Le Charivari and La Caricature, 1837-1864.

7.585 "Edition of 40 proofs: I-XL"—Hardie.

7.586 *Edition of 50.

7.587 The edition was suppressed and only a few copies were distributed. Cf. Recollections of a collector / L.J. Rosenwald. 1976. p. 45; and Lessing J. Rosenwald : tribute to a collector / R.E. Fine. 1982. p. 88.

7.588 "Issued in one hundred and fifty copies signed and numbered 1-150, and ten more sets of artist's proofs."

7.589 *Plate from: Reise in das innere Nord-America in den Jahren 1832 bis 1834 / Maximilian Alexander Philipp, Prinz von Wied-Neuwied. Coblenz : J. Hölscher,1839-1841. — Hand col. plate in French edition: Voyage dans l'intérieure de l'Amérique du Nord. Paris : Arthus Bertrand, 1840-1843.

7.590 *Trial proof, with pencil corrections.

Chapter 9 (Computer Files)

AACR2 RULE

9.7B7 Edition and History [AACR2 Rev.]

Give the source of the edition statement if it is different from that of the title proper. . . .

Make notes relating to the edition being described or to the history of the item. . . .

Give details of minor changes such as those listed in 9.2B4 if they are considered to be important. . . .

Cite other works upon which the item depends for its content. . . .

Give the following dates and details about them if they are considered to be important to the understanding of the content, use, or nature of the file:

> the date(s) covered by the content of a file
> the date(s) when data were collected
> the date(s) of accompanying material not described separately if they differ from those of the file being described.

RELATED AACR2 RULE

9.2B Edition Statement [AACR2 Rev.]

9.2B1. Transcribe a statement relating to an edition of a computer file that contains differences from other editions of that file, or to a named reissue of a file, as instructed in 1.2B. . . .

Give the source of the edition statement in a note (see 9.7B7) if it is different from the source of the title proper. [emphasis added]

9.2B4. Do not treat an issue of a file that incorporates minor changes as a new edition. Such minor changes include corrections of misspellings of data, changes in the arrangement of the contents, changes in the output format or the display medium, and changes in the physical characteristics (e.g., blocking factors, recording density). If desired, give the details of such changes in a note (see 9.7B7). [emphasis added]

9.2C1 Statements of Responsibility Relating to the Edition [AACR2 Rev.]

Transcribe a statement of responsibility relating to one or more editions, but not to all editions, of a file as instructed in 1.2C and 9.1F. If desired, transcribe other statements of responsibility relating to the edition in a note (see 9.7B7). [emphasis added]

9.4F3 Date of Publication, Distribution, etc. [AACR2 Rev.]

Give any other useful dates (e.g., dates of collection of data) in a note (see 9.7B7 and 9.7B9). [emphasis added]

LIBRARY OF CONGRESS POLICY

None issued for AACR2 Rev. Ch. 9.

RELATED LIBRARY OF CONGRESS POLICY

None issued for AACR2 Rev. Ch. 9.

AACR2 TEXT EXAMPLES REVISED TO REFLECT LIBRARY OF CONGRESS POLICY

None required for AACR2 Rev. Ch. 9.

HISTORICAL BACKGROUND

Computer files were not covered by AACR1 or previous codes. The original AACR2 Chapter 9 covered the elements present in the revised rule except that, when recording dates, the original Chapter 9 specifically called for recording the date when data were copied from an outside source. AACR2 Rev. Ch. 9 does not mention this situation. AACR2 Rev. Ch. 9 adds two additional elements to the rule. It calls for recording the source of the edition statement whenever its source is different from that used to derive the title. The original Chapter 9 makes no mention of this. AACR2 Rev. Ch. 9 also calls for recording the minor types of changes to a computer file listed in AACR2 Rule 9.2B4 when those details are considered important. The original Chapter 9 (Rule 9.7B7) did not specifically call for recording this information, although the original AACR2 Rule 9.2B4 did call for the use of a note in this situation.

NOTE EXAMPLES

7.591   *Edition statement from disk label.
7.592   *On disk: Version 4.03M, generic MS-DOS Ver. 1.2 DS.
7.593   *Revision of MacLightning.

Works Upon Which Content Is Dependent
7.594   *Accompanies Perception (v. 14, no. 2, 1985).
7.595   *Adapted from: Pinball.
7.596   *Adapted from: Word attack / by Richard Eckert and Janice Davidson.
7.597   *Based on: A sentimental journey through France and Italy by Mr. Yorick / Laurence Sterne ; edited by Gardner D. Stout. Berkeley, Calif. : University of California Press, 1967.
7.598   *Based on printed title: Historiae / edited by H.S. Jones and J.E. Powell ; repr. of 1942 ed. Oxford : Clarendon Press, 1967-1970, 2 vols.

7.599 *Correlated to Ginn '82 Basal series.
7.600 *Data taken from the Fall omnibus survey conducted by the Economic Behavior Program, Survey Research Center.
7.601 *Module taken from data file entitled: Participation in American study, principal investigators, Sidney Verba and Norman Nie.
7.602 *Source of data: Clinical Observations, Johns Hopkins University Hospital, Aug.-Dec., 1978.
7.603 *Source of data: Parliamentary papers, Great Britain Foreign Press Office, 1845.
7.604 *Transcribed from: The sound and the fury / William Faulkner. New York : Modern Library, 1967.

Dates
7.605 *Machine transcription originally produced by Princeton University Computer Service, 1975.
7.606 *Migration patterns from 1930-1960.
7.607 *New England sermons from 1790-1900.
7.608 *Project begun in 1967 by C. Wrigley: 1st-20th sessions issued in 1971.
7.609 *Time period: 1809-1949.

Chapter 10 (Three-Dimensional Artefacts and Realia)

AACR2 RULE

10.7B7 Edition and History
Make notes relating to the edition being described or to the history of the item.

Cite other works upon which the item depends for its intellectual or artistic content.

RELATED AACR2 RULE

None.

LIBRARY OF CONGRESS POLICY

None issued.

RELATED LIBRARY OF CONGRESS POLICY

None issued.

AACR2 TEXT EXAMPLES REVISED TO REFLECT LIBRARY OF CONGRESS POLICY

None required.

HISTORICAL BACKGROUND

AACR1 Rev. Rule 229.2A provided for a note for an earlier title of a work now issued under a different title. This same type of note could also be made under the provisions of AACR2, although no specific mention is made of it.

AACR1 Rev. Rule 229.2F provided for a note to record other works on which the item being cataloged depended for its "intellectual or artistic content." This note was also used to indicate the existence of other versions of the work. AACR2 provides for essentially the same note.

NOTE EXAMPLES

No examples were located.

Chapter 12 (Serials)

AACR2 RULE

12.7B7 Relationships with Other Serials [AACR2 Rev.]

Make notes on the relationship between the serial being described and any immediately preceding, immediately succeeding, or simultaneously published serial.

a) *Translation*

If a serial is a translation of a previously published serial (as opposed to a different language edition of a serial, for which see 12.2B1), give the name of the original. . . .

b) *Continuation*

If a serial continues a previously published serial, whether the numbering continues or is different, give the name of the preceding serial. (See also 21.2C and 21.3B.) . . .

c) *Continued By*

If a serial is continued by a subsequently published serial, whether the numbering continues or is different, give the name of the succeeding serial, and, *optionally* the date of the change. (See also 21.2C, 21.3B.) . . .

d) *Merger*

If a serial is the result of the merger of two or more other serials, give the names of the serials that were merged. . . .

If a serial is merged with one or more other serials to form a serial with a new title, give the title(s) of the serial(s) with which it has merged and the title of the new serial. . . .

e) *Split*

If a serial is the result of the split of a previous serial into two or more parts, give the name of the serial that has been split, and *optionally* the name(s) of the other serial(s) resulting from the split. . . .

If a serial splits into two or more parts, give the names of the serials resulting from the split. . . .

If a serial has separated from another serial, give the name of the serial of which it was once a part. . . .

f) *Absorption*

If a serial absorbs another serial, give the name of the serial absorbed and *optionally* the date of absorption. . . .

If a serial is absorbed by another serial, give the name of the absorbing serial. . . .

g) *Edition [formerly AACR2 Rule 12.7B7h]*

If a serial is a subsidiary edition differing from the main edition in partial content and/or in language, give the name of the main edition. . . .

If the title of the main edition is not readily available, make a general note.

h) *Numerous Editions [formerly AACR2 Rule 12.7B7j]*

If a serial is published in numerous editions, give

Numerous editions

j) *Supplements [formerly AACR2 Rule 12.7B7k]*

If a serial is a supplement to another serial, give the name of the main serial. . . .

If a serial has supplement(s) that are described separately, make notes identifying the supplement(s). . . .

Make brief general notes on irregular, informal, numerous, or unimportant supplements that are not described separately.

RELATED AACR2 RULE

12.1B6 Title Proper [AACR2 Rev.; formerly AACR2 Rule 12.1B5]

If the title of a section or supplement is presented in the chief source of information without the title that is common to all sections, give the title of the section or supplement as the title proper. In the case of a section, give the title that is common to all sections as the title proper of the series (see 12.6B). In the case of a supplement, give the title of the main serial in a note (see 12.7B7j). [emphasis added]

12.2B Edition Statement [AACR2 Rev.]

12.2B2 Give statements indicating volume numbering or designation, or chronological coverage (e.g., *1st ed., 1916 ed.*) in the numeric and/or alphabetic, chronological, or other designation area (see 12.3).

Give statements indicating regular revision (e.g., *Rev. ed. issued every 6 months*) in the note area. [emphasis added]

12.2B4 For serials published in numerous editions, see 12.7B7h. [emphasis added]

LIBRARY OF CONGRESS POLICY

a) *Translated Editions*

If a serial has been translated, give the title of the translation in a note on the bibliographic record for the original. (This is in addition to the data about the original that appear on the bibliographic record for the translation.) If the title is not known, give a general note. [CSB 28]

c) *Continued by*

Apply [the option] whenever the information is readily available. [CSB 8]

e) *Split*

Do not apply [the option]. [CSB 8]

f) *Absorption*

Apply both options whenever the information is readily available. [The second option was deleted in AACR2 Rev.] [CSB 8]

[g, formerly] h) *Editions*

If a serial has another edition differing in partial content and/or in language, give the title of the other edition on the bibliographic record for the edition being cataloged. If the title of the other edition is not known, or is the same as the edition being cataloged, give a general note. [CSB 28]

[j, formerly] k) *Supplements*

Serial Supplements to Other Serials

Note serial supplements on the bibliographic records for the related serial even if the supplements are represented by their own bibliographic records (cf. LCRI 21.28B). Also, on those separate bibliographic records created for some serial supplements, give linking notes to the related serials. . . . [CSB 33]

RELATED LIBRARY OF CONGRESS POLICY

12.0B1 Sources of Information. Printed Serials.

Due to its length, this LC policy statement has been abridged to include only the parts related to the use of notes.

Serials

The basis for the description is the first issue of the serial. In determining which issue is first, disregard the date of publication, etc., and use the designation on the issues. For serials that carry numeric or alphabetic designations, the first issue is the one with the lowest or earliest (in the alphabet) designation. For serials that do not carry numeric or alphabetic designations, the first issue is the one with the earliest chronological designation. (If the actual first issue is not available, use these same guidelines to determine which issue should be used as the basis for the description.)

Since the title page (or title page substitute) of the first issue is the chief source of information for a printed serial, a title page that is published later to cover one or more issues cannot be used as the chief source. (However, data from such a title page may be put into the note area when necessary.) [emphasis added]

If the description has been formulated from the first issue of a serial, the body of the entry remains unchanged throughout the life of the serial. If issues after the first have data different from those recorded in the body of the entry, record the different data in the note area as necessary. [emphasis added] However, if the differences are in the title proper, create a separate record when appropriate (21.2C). (For changes in the main entry heading, see 21.3B.) . . .

Reprints of Serials

In order that the description of the reprint resemble and file with the description of the original, the earliest *issue* reprinted is used as the chief source for the first three areas of the description. Data for these areas may be taken from any place on the reprinted issue without the use of brackets. If it is known that the description of the original would include data that are not on the reprinted issue, the data may be supplied in brackets.

In area four the place of publication, publisher, and date of the reprint are recorded, using brackets if the data do not come from a prescribed source on the reprint.

The physical description area gives the physical description of the reprint, not the original.

A series is recorded if the reprint appears in a series.

Usually a single note (see 12.7B7g) gives important details about the original while other notes give necessary information about the reprint. Notes giving the source of the title or the issue on which the description is based are not given. [emphasis added] [CSB 38]

1.5E1 Accompanying Material

Due to its length, this LC policy statement has been abridged to include only the part related to the use of notes.

Supplements

Catalog separately all supplements, etc., to serials except for indexes that may be noted (according to 12.7B7 and 12.7B17) or supplements, etc., that may be noted informally accorded to method c.

Exception: Describe in a note supplements that are usable only in conjunction with the main work. [CSB 29]

AACR2 TEXT EXAMPLES REVISED TO REFLECT LIBRARY OF CONGRESS POLICY

None required.

HISTORICAL BACKGROUND

a) *Translation*

Although AACR1 and previous codes had no equivalent to AACR2 Rule 12.7B7a, the translation of original title note provisions for separately published monographs in these earlier codes could be used for serials. (See *Historical Background* under Rule 2.7B7.)

b) *Continuation*

AACR1 Rule 167G provided a note for a serial that continued another serial. When the numbering was continued, the term "continued" was used in the note. If the numbering was not continued, the term "supersedes" was used. AACR2 does not draw this distinction between "continues" and "supersedes." Instead, AACR2 uses "continues" for both numbering situations.

c) *Continued By*

AACR1 Rule 167Q provided a note for serials "continued, superseded, or absorbed by, or merged with" another serial. This note also called for recording the "date of the action" when the holdings of the library were incomplete, or when the action did not immediately follow the publication of the final issue. AACR2 covers these situations, although this rule covers only works "continued by" another serial. Superseded, continued, absorbed, and merged serials are covered under AACR2 rules 12.7B7b, 12.7B7d, and 12.7B7f respectively.

d) *Merger*

See the discussion under 12.7B7c (Continued By).

e) *Split*

This note could fall under the provisions of AACR1 Rule 167Q discussed above for Continued By notes, although no specific mention is made in AACR1 of serials splitting or separating.

f) *Absorption*

AACR1 Rule 167H provided a note to record the title of a serial absorbed by another. The date of absorption was supplied whenever possible. AACR2 agrees with this rule except that AACR2 also addresses the situation of absorbing another serial rather than just being absorbed by another serial. (See also the discussion under 12.7B7c (Continued By) for recording the title of a serial absorbing another.)

g) *Reproduction*
This rule was deleted in AACR2 Rev.
g) *Edition*
This rule had no equivalent in AACR1. This rule was numbered 12.7B7h in AACR2. In AACR2 Rev. it is changed to 12.7B7g.
h) *Numerous Editions*
This rule had no equivalent in AACR1. This rule was numbered 12.7B7j in AACR2. In AACR2 Rev. it is changed to 12.7B7h.
j) *Supplements*
AACR1 Rule 160K mentioned that serials frequently have special issues that need to be described. This rule was numbered 12.7B7k in AACR2. In AACR2 Rev. it is changed to 12.7B7j.

AACR1 Rule 168 specifically addressed the treatment of supplements. AACR1 Rule 168A provided a "dashed" entry for supplements that were themselves serials. Supplements that were monographic were treated under the rule for monograph supplements (AACR1 Rev. Rule 155) generally using a dashed entry. AACR2 would provide for the use of separate bibliographic entries for both types of supplements.

AACR1 Rule 168B provided for an informal note for "irregular and unnumbered" and "unimportant" supplements. This note could still be made under AACR2, although AACR2 Rule 12.7B7j makes no specific mention of these minor supplements.

NOTE EXAMPLES

Translation
No examples were located.

Continuation
7.610 Continues: Abstracts of Bulgarian scientific literature. Biology and biochemistry.
7.611 Continues: American Association of Sex Educators and Counselors. National register of certified sex educators, certified sex therapists, ISSN 0145-9805.
7.612 Continues: Broadcasting cablecasting yearbook, ISSN 0732-7196.
7.613 Continues: Bulletin (Moravian Music Foundation).
7.614 Continues: Condition of public elementary and secondary education in Connecticut. Volume 2, Digest of education statistics.
7.615 Continues: Ellis, Iris. Save on shopping.
7.616 Continues: Fats and oils situation (United States. Dept. of Agriculture. Economics, Statistics, and Cooperatives Service), ISSN 0014-8865.
7.617 Continues: Harvard University. Class of 1960. Harvard 1960 class directory, ISSN 0361-2082.
7.618 Continues: Illustrator (Minneapolis, Minn. : 1942).

7.619 Continues: Ireland. Forest and Wildlife Service. Report of the Minister for Lands on the Forest and Wildlife Service.

7.620 Continues: Journal (Institution of General Technician Engineers).

7.621 Continues: Massachusetts Turnpike Authority. Quarterly report, initial turnpike, including semi-annual audit as of . . . of the Massachusetts Turnpike Authority to thc First National Bank of Boston as trustee.

7.622 Continues: Proceedings of the Royal Society of Edinburgh. Section A, Mathematical and physical science.

7.623 Continues: Texas State Library. Archives Division. Texas state documents, ISSN 0363-4736.

Continued By

7.624 Continued by: Aviation travel and times, ISSN 0273-7191.

7.625 Continued by: Dallas Opera magazine, Vol. 4, no. 1.

7.626 Continued by: Ireland. Forest and Wildlife Service. Report of the Minister for Fisheries and Forestry on the Forest and Wildlife Service.

7.627 Continued by: Jacobsen's . . . painting and bronze price guide.

7.628 Continued by: Tamil Nadu (India). Report on the working of the Minimum Wages Act, 1948 for the year . . .

7.629 Continued by: U.S. Nuclear Regulatory Commission. Division of Technical Information and Document Control. Nuclear Regulatory Commission issuance (1981).

7.630 Continued in 1974 by: Proceedings. Section B, Natural environment.

7.631 Continued in 1981 by: Territory digest.

7.632 Continued in July 1979 by: Newsletter of the Knarr-Knerr-Knorr Family.

Merger

7.633 Formed by the merger of: Draft counselors newsletter, and: Newsletter on military law and counseling.

7.634 Merger of: Advances in ophthalmology, ISSN 0065-3004; Bibliotheca ophthalmologica; and: Modern problems in ophthalmology, ISSN 0077-0078.

7.635 Merger of: Broadcasting yearbook; and, Broadcasting, cable sourcebook.

7.636 Merger of: Gulfstream (Silver Spring, Md.); and: Fishing information.

7.637 Merger of: Moody's commercial paper record. Monthly statistical supplement and, Moody's commercial paper record. Quarterly reference edition.

7.638 Merged with: Latin America political report to form: Latin America weekly report.

7.639 Previously issued in three parts: Friendly societies, industrial assurance companies and general; Building societies; Industrial and provident societies.

Split

7.640 Continues in part: American motorist, ISSN 0199-0268.

7.641 Continues in part: Annual reports on the progress of chemistry. Section A, Physical and inorganic chemistry.

7.642   Continues in part: Arkansas health manpower statistics, ISSN 0197-6478.
7.643   Continues in part: Proceedings. Section A, Mathematical and physical sciences.
7.644   Continues in part: Sheet music magazine. Standard/easy organ.
7.645   Continued in part by: United States. Congress. Senate. Committee on Interior and Insular Affairs. Legislative calendar.
7.646   Separated from: Journal of the Society of Cosmetic Chemists, 1979.
7.647   Split into: Proceedings. Section A, Mathematics; and, Communications. Physical sciences.

Absorption
7.648   Absorbed: Focus, technical cooperation.
7.649   Absorbed: Great Britain. Registry of Friendly Societies. Report of the Industrial Assurance Commissioner.
7.650   Absorbed by: Videoscope.

Reproduction
7.651   Reprint. Originally published: City of Washington : sn., (Printed at the Globe Office, by F.P. Blair).
7.652   Reprint. Originally published monthly: London : Dawbarn & Ward.

Edition
7.653   Also available in Danish, Dutch, French, German, and Italian editions.
7.654   Also published in Spanish with the same title.
7.655   English ed. of: Proceso de integración en América Latina.
7.656   French ed. of: An Index to Government of Canada programs and services available to the public in Canada, ISSN 0707-9583.
7.657   Issued also in French.
7.658   Issued also in English under title: The . . . Per Jacobsson lecture; and in French under title: Fondation Per Jacobsson de . . .
7.659   Other editions available: Trends in the hotel industry in the Pacific Northwest.
7.660   Other editions available: United States. Congress. Congressional record. Daily record.

Numerous Editions
7.661   *Numerous editions.

Supplemented By
7.662   Supplement: Almanac of Virginia politics. Supplement
7.663   Supplement: América Latina book news.
        Supplement: Latin America Newsletter Ltd. book news.
7.664   Supplements accompany some numbers.
7.665   Supplements (music) accompany each no.
7.666   A supplementary cumulative serials list was issued for 1975, and subsequent cumulations are planned.

7.667 Has supplement: Accessions list. Brazil. Annual list of serials.

7.668 Has supplement: Trends in the hotel industry. International edition.

7.669 Some numbers issued with supplements.

Supplements To

7.670 Supplement to: Indiana state rail plan, final phase 2.

7.671 Supplement to: International trade reporter's U.S. import weekly, ISSN 0195-7589.

7.672 Supplement to: Rio Grande do Sul (Brasil). Diároio oficial.

7.673 Supplement to: Top rhythm & Blues records, 1949-1971.

7.674 An introductory number called v.1, no. 0 issued as a supplement to Latin America. Cf. New serial titles.

7.675 Issued as a special number of Bulletin de l'Afrique noire.

7.676 Issued as a supplement to: Soviet gramophone records catalogue.

1.7B8. Material (or Type of Publication) Specific Details

Make notes giving details that are specific to the material format being described.

None.

None issued. See the sections that follow for any LC policies or interpretations that apply to individual AACR2 chapters for description.

None issued.

None prescribed.

This note is present in five of the eleven chapters for description. It is used to provide information unique to each specific material format and, therefore, its application varies from chapter to chapter. Although only five chapters use a material specific note at present, the existence of AACR2 Rule 1.7B8 as a general note would allow for its use in other chapters in the future.

Chapter 3 (Cartographic Materials) uses this note to describe "mathematical and other cartographic data," such as the magnitude of celestial charts, data for remote-sensing imagery, and scale variation.

Chapter 4 (Manuscripts) uses this note to describe the "place of writing" of a manuscript.

Chapter 5 (Music) uses this note to describe the musical "notation" if it is considered unusual.

Chapter 8 (Graphic Materials) previously used this rule to describe the "characteristics of an original art reproduction, poster, postcard, etc." This rule has been deleted and replaced by AACR2 Rev. Rule 8.7B22.

Chapter 9 (Computer Files, AACR2 Rev.) uses this note to describe characteristics of a file. It can also be used to record the number of records, statements, etc., in the parts of a file.

Chapter 12 (Serials) uses this note to describe the "numbering and chronological designation of a serial." This includes complex or irregular numbering, identifying the period covered by a volume if other than a calendar year, and information about suspension and resumption of publication.

EXCEPTIONS AND ADDITIONS

Since the specific nature of this note makes the Extrapolated General Rule so indefinite, there are no exceptions or additions.

Chapter 3 (Cartographic Materials)

AACR2 RULE

3.7B8 Mathematical and Other Cartographic Data [AACR2 Rev.]

Celestial Charts

Make notes on the magnitude of celestial charts, give the magnitude. . . .

Remote-Sensing Imagery

Give mathematical data not already included in the mathematical data area for remote-sensing images. . . .

Additional Information

Give other mathematical and cartographic data additional to, or elaborating on, that given in the mathematical data area. . . .

Scale Variation

If the scales vary (see 3.3B5) and if one or more of the scales is readily discernible and can be expressed concisely, give the scale(s).

RELATED AACR2 RULE

3.3D1 Statement of Coordinates and Equinox [AACR2 Rev.]

For terrestrial maps, etc., give the coordinates in the following order:

westernmost extent of area covered by item (longitude)
easternmost extent of area covered by item (longitude)

221

northernmost extent of area covered by item (latitude)
southernmost extent of area covered by item (latitude)

Express the coordinates in degrees (°), minutes ('), and seconds (")
of the sexagesimal system (360° circle) taken from the Greenwich prime
meridian. Precede each coordinate by W, E, N, or S, as appropriate.
Separate the two sets of latitude and longitude by a diagonal slash
neither preceded nor followed by a space. Separate each longitude or
latitude from its counterpart by a dash. . . .

Optionally, give other meridians found on the item in the note area
(see 3.7B8). [emphasis added]

LIBRARY OF CONGRESS POLICY

None issued.

RELATED LIBRARY OF CONGRESS POLICY

None issued.

AACR2 TEXT EXAMPLES REVISED TO REFLECT LIBRARY OF CONGRESS POLICY

None required.

HISTORICAL BACKGROUND

AACR1 Rule 212E5 limited the information in this note to the name
of the map projection and the prime meridian, if other than Greenwich.
AACR2 has expanded the coverage of this rule to provide for all other
types of mathematical or cartographic data deemed important. AACR2
Rev. expanded the rule coverage to include scale variations.

NOTE EXAMPLES

8.1 Irish grid.
8.2 National grid.
8.3 U.T.M. grid.
8.4 "U.T.M. grid zone 36. Grid lines at 2000 metres."
8.5 "The Universal transverse Mercator (UTM) grid overlay is based on the Everest geodetic system."
8.6 "The grids, datums, and spheroids shown on this index are for use in the production of new and revised topographic maps, joint operation graphics, and certain large scale coastal nautical charts."
8.7 Oriented with north to right.

8.8   Oriented with north toward the lower right.

8.9   Some maps oriented with north to the left.

8.10   "This map contains a 20% vertical distortion due to computer line-printer format."

8.11   On some maps: Longitude du Meridien de Paris.

8.12   Prime meridian: Ferro.

8.13   Principal maps at scale 1:316,800 or 5 miles to 1 inch.

8.14   Principal maps 1:5,000,000; supplementary maps at various scales.

8.15   Atlanta vicinity maps scale ca. 1:41,000 or $1'' = 3,331'$.

Chapter 4 (Manuscripts)

AACR2 RULE

4.7B8 Place of Writing [AACR2 Rev.]

Give the name of the place in which a manuscript was written if it is found in the item and is not given elsewhere in the description.

Give the source of the information.

RELATED AACR2 RULE

None.

LIBRARY OF CONGRESS POLICY

None issued. APPM has no rule equivalent to AACR2 Rule 4.7B8.

RELATED LIBRARY OF CONGRESS POLICY

None issued.

AACR2 TEXT EXAMPLES REVISED TO REFLECT
LIBRARY OF CONGRESS POLICY

None required.

HISTORICAL BACKGROUND

AACR1 had three separate provisions for the use of a note to record the place of writing for manuscripts. AACR1 Rule 201A addressed modern manuscripts, AACR1 Rule 201B3 covered ancient, medieval, and Renaissance manuscripts, and AACR1 Rule 204C handled legal papers. These rules are essentially the same as the AACR2 rule that applies to all types of manuscripts.

223

NOTE EXAMPLES

While no specific format is prescribed, many notes made by the Library of Congress and others utilize the construct:

[Source of information]: [Place of writing.]

8.16 At end: Paris ce 28 Avril 1846, Rue Labrugère 15. Souvenir à mon ami Julius Stern.
8.17 At end: Wien, 27 April 859.
8.18 In caption: Nvr. 1818, Zeliz.
8.19 *On t.p.: Wien.
8.20 Written probably in (eastern?) Bohemia.

Chapter 5 (Music)

AACR2 RULE

5.7B8 Notation
Give the notation used in an item if it is not the notation normally found in that type of item.

RELATED AACR2 RULE

None.

LIBRARY OF CONGRESS POLICY

None issued.

RELATED LIBRARY OF CONGRESS POLICY

None issued.

AACR2 TEXT EXAMPLES REVISED TO REFLECT
LIBRARY OF CONGRESS POLICY

None required.

HISTORICAL BACKGROUND

AACR1 Rule 248D called for a note to record variations in the "normal" notation of a type of work. The AACR2 rule is the same as this earlier rule.

NOTE EXAMPLES

8.21 Dulcimer tablature.
8.22 "French tablature"—New Grove dictionary.
8.23 Guitar tablature.
8.24 Vol. 1 includes lute tablature.
8.25 "Lute tablature and keyboard notation"—Cover.
8.26 Tablature and staff notation.
8.27 Staff and tablature notation; includes chord symbols.
8.28 Staff notation and tablature vertically aligned.
8.29 Eleven pieces for three lyra viols in tablature as well as in modern notation.
8.30 Tablature notation; in part with words.
8.31 Includes music in letter notation.

Chapter 8 (Graphic Materials)

AACR2 RULE

8.7B8 Characteristics of Original of Art Reproduction, Poster, Postcard, etc.

Give the location (if known) of, and other information about, the original of a reproduced art work.

This rule has been deleted in AACR2 Rev. A new AACR2 rule, 8.7B22, serves the function of the deleted rule.

Chapter 9 (Computer Files)

AACR2 RULE

9.7B8 File Characteristics [AACR2 Rev.]

Give important file characteristics that are not included in the file characteristics area. . . .

If a file consists of numerous parts the numbering of which cannot be given succinctly in the file characteristics area, and if the information is considered to be important, give the number or approximate number of records, statements, etc., in each part.

RELATED AACR2 RULE

9.3B2 Number of Records, Statements, etc. [AACR2 Rev.]

If a file designation is given and if the information is readily available, give the number or approximate number of files that make up the content (use *file* or *files* preceded by an arabic numeral) and/or these other details:

a) *Data*. Give the number or approximate number of records and/ or bytes. . . .

b) *Programs*. Give the number or approximate number of statements and/or bytes. . . .

c) *Multipart files*. Give the number or approximate number of records and/or bytes, or statements and/or bytes, in each part. . . .

If such numbering cannot be given succinctly, omit the information from this area. If desired, give it in a note (see 9.7B8). [emphasis added]

LIBRARY OF CONGRESS POLICY

None issued for AACR2 Rev. Ch. 9.

RELATED LIBRARY OF CONGRESS POLICY

None issued for AACR2 Rev. Ch. 9.

AACR2 TEXT EXAMPLES REVISED TO REFLECT LIBRARY OF CONGRESS POLICY

None required for AACR2 Rev. Ch. 9.

HISTORICAL BACKGROUND

Computer files were not covered by AACR1 or previous codes. The original AACR2 Chapter 9 used this note to record a program's version or level. In AACR2 Rev. Ch. 9, this information is usually recorded in the Edition Area (AACR2 Rev. Rule 9.2) or in an edition and history note (AACR2 Rev. Rule 9.7B7). Information on file characteristics and file size was given under Rule 9.7B10 in the original Chapter 9.

NOTE EXAMPLES

8.32   *HFS file structure.
8.33   *File size varies.
8.34   *Files contain up to 36,487 records that can have 32 fields of up to 254 characters with a maximum of 1000 characters per record.
8.35   *File size not verified, consists of 130 printed pages.
8.36   *File size not verified, received as 18 disks.
8.37   *Size of file not verified, ca. 436 variables.
8.38   *File size: 84, 153, 178, 45 records.

Chapter 12 (Serials)

AACR2 RULE

12.7B8 Numbering and Chronological Designation [AACR2 Rev.]

Numbering

Make notes on complex or irregular numbering, etc., not already specified in the numeric and/or alphabetic, chronological, or other designation area. Make notes on peculiarities in the numbering, etc. . . .

Coverage Period

If the period covered by a volume, issue, etc., of an annual or less frequent serial is other than a calendar year, give the period covered. . . .

Suspension of Publication

If a serial suspends publication with the intention of resuming at a later date, give this fact. If publication is resumed, give the dates or designation of the period of suspension.

RELATED AACR2 RULE

None.

LIBRARY OF CONGRESS POLICY

If the duration of publication is known, it is stated in a note unless it is shown in the numeric and/or alphabetic, chronological, or other designation area or the publication, distribution, etc., area. [CSB 32]

RELATED LIBRARY OF CONGRESS POLICY

12.0B1 Sources of Information. Printed Serials.

Due to its length, this LC policy statement has been abridged to include only the parts related to the use of notes.

Serials

The basis for the description is the first issue of the serial. In determining which issue is first, disregard the date of publication, etc., and use the designation on the issues. For serials that carry numeric or alphabetic designations, the first issue is the one with the lowest or earliest (in the alphabet) designation. For serials that do not carry numeric or alphabetic designations, the first issue is the one with the earliest chronological designation. (If the actual first issue is not available, use these same guidelines to determine which issue should be used as the basis for the description.)

Since the title page (or title page substitute) of the first issue is the chief source of information for a printed serial, a title page that is published later to cover one or more issues cannot be used as the chief source. (However, data from such a title page may be put into the note area when necessary.) [emphasis added]

If the description has been formulated from the first issue of a serial, the body of the entry remains unchanged throughout the life of the serial. If issues after the first have data different from those recorded in the body of the entry, record the different data in the note area as necessary. [emphasis added] However, if the differences are in the title proper, create a separate record when appropriate (21.2C). (For changes in the main entry heading, see 21.3B.) . . .

Reprints of Serials

In order that the description of the reprint resemble and file with the description of the original, the earliest *issue* reprinted is used as the chief source for the first three areas of the description. Data for these areas may be taken from any place on the reprinted issue without the use of brackets. If it is known that the description of the original would include data that are not on the reprinted issue, the data may be supplied in brackets.

In area four the place of publication, publisher, and date of the reprint are recorded, using brackets if the data do not come from a prescribed source on the reprint.

The physical description area gives the physical description of the reprint, not the original.

A series is recorded if the reprint appears in a series.

Usually a single note (see 12.7B7g) gives important details about the original while other notes give necessary information about the reprint. Notes giving the source of the title or the issue on which the description is based are not given. [emphasis added] [CSB 38]

12.3B1 Numeric and/or Alphabetic Designation

The numeric and/or alphabetic designation of the first issue of a serial being recorded in this area should be an identifying designation, i.e., one that is unique to the particular issue of the serial. A numeric and/or alphabetic designation that is exactly the same for more than one issue of the serial is not recorded in this area. It may be given in a note (cf. 12.7B8). [emphasis added]

Record the numeric and/or alphabetic designation according to the way it appears on the chief source. If it does not appear on the chief source, then in the way it appears on one of the other preliminaries or on the colophon (if it does not appear on the preliminaries). If it does not appear on any of these, record it (in brackets) according to the way it appears anywhere in a formal statement. All elements of the numeric and/or alphabetic designation must be taken from the same source, i.e., the designation cannot be pieced together from different sources. Generally consider that when volume numbering appears on the same source with consecutive numbering of issues, the serial has one system of numeric designation rather than two. [CSB 23]

12.3E More Than One System of Designation

Record a second or third system of numeric and/or alphabetic designation with the first system if the second or third system appears on the same source used in recording the first system and if it, too, identifies the piece (cf. 12.3B1). Since it is not always possible to determine the order of the systems as presented on the source, prefer to record as the first a system that uses the form of volume number and internal number. If more than one numeric system is recorded, generally record the chronological system with the first numeric system (cf. 12.3C4).

Give in a note information about a second or third system of numeric/alphabetic designation that either does not identify the item or does not appear on the same source with the first system (cf. 12.7B8) whenever the second or third system appears prominently enough on the publication for one to assume that the serial may be asked for or identified by that system. [emphasis added] [CSB 23]

12.3G Successive Designations

Due to its length, this LC policy statement has been abridged to include only the part related to the use of notes.

New Designation Systems

Do not consider that a serial has adopted a new designation system when there is just a change in numeric or chronological designation, e.g., as when a serial begins by having both a numeric and a chronological designation and the numeric designation is dropped, or a serial begins with a chronological designation only and a numeric designation is added later. Explain such changes in notes (see 12.7B8). [emphasis added] [CSB 26]

AACR2 TEXT EXAMPLES REVISED TO REFLECT LIBRARY OF CONGRESS POLICY

None required.

HISTORICAL BACKGROUND

AACR1 Rule 160H indicated the need in serials cataloging for the use of a note to record the suspension and resumption of publication.

AACR1 Rule 167C provided for a note to record the report year of an annual publication if it was other than the calendar year. This information was also recorded, when possible, for reports other than annuals. The AACR2 rule is virtually identical to its AACR1 predecessor.

AACR1 Rule 167E called for a note to record the date or volume designation of a serial that had ceased publication but with the intention of resuming publication at a later date. Inclusive dates of suspension were to be given if publication was resumed. The AACR2 rule calls for recording the same information.

AACR1 Rule 167F was used to record "irregularities and peculiarities" in serial numbering. This rule delineated the following types of irregularities: double numbering; combined issues or volumes; confusion in the use of series numbering or whole numbers; publication of preliminary editions not included in the regular series numbering; numbering that does not begin with volume one, etc. AACR2 agrees in general with this AACR1 rule, except that it does not provide a listing of specific types of irregularities.

NOTE EXAMPLES

Also Called
8.39 First issue called also Vol. 1.
8.40 Introductory no., called summer 1970.
8.41 Introductory no. called no. 000, issued Apr. 1978.
8.42 Issue for Jan. 1976 called promotional issue, Feb. 1976 called premiere issue.
8.43 Issues for 1979-<80> called only no. 3 & 4-<6>.
8.44 No. for Dec. 1980 called also: Premiere issue.
8.45 No. 1 called inaugural number.
8.46 Vol. 1, no. 1 also called "inaugural issue."
8.47 Vol. 1, no. 3 (winter 1973) called Special issue.
8.48 Vol. 17, no. 2/3- called also "Nova serija," v. 1, no. 1/2-
8.49 "Has also been published as Science and technology libraries, volume 3, number 3, Spring 1983"—T.p. verso.
8.50 Vol. for 1982 issued as Vol. 32, no. 13 of Printing impressions.

Began/Ceased Publication
8.51 Began in 1943.
8.52 Began in 1976. Cf. New serial titles.
8.53 Began in 1964? Cf. New serial titles.
8.54 Began with ER EEI 81-00 (Jan. 1981).
8.55 Began with July 24, 1980 issue.
8.56 Began with issue for 1968 through 1970.
8.57 Began with report for 1971.
8.58 Began with v. 56, no. 3, Sept. 1970.
8.59 Ceased publication in 1981.
8.60 *Ceased publication, 1975?

8.61 Ceased with summer 1980. Cf. letter from publisher.

Chronological Numbering

8.62 Beginning with no. 3 vol. numbering was dropped.
8.63 Month designation dropped año 1, no. 2-año 2, no. 7.
8.64 With April 1979 dropped vol. numbering and began whole numbering, e.g., no. 5 (April 1977).
8.65 Carries the vol. numbering of an earlier related publication, 1979-
8.66 Double annual issue, 1977/78.
8.67 Each vol. has 6 no., numbering within vols. begins in Mar. and Sept.
8.68 Issued in two or more vols. a year.
8.69 Issues are cumulative for each Congress.
8.70 Journals for 1946 combined in one issue.
8.71 Numbering begins each year with no. 1.
8.72 Resumes the numbering of Rudder (vol. 93, no. 4-97, no. 10 not published).
8.73 Some vols. issued in combined form.
8.74 Some vols. issued in parts.
8.75 Vol. and numbering irregular.
8.76 Vols. for 1976-<1980> published in 3 pts.
8.77 Vol. designations correspond to years, issues are numbered consecutively without regard to vol.
8.78 Vol. 4, no. 1 has stamp which reads: "The special double issue contains vol. 4, nos. 1 & 2".

Irregularities

8.79 Vol. 1 has only 2 issues.
8.80 Vol. 5 omitted in numbering.
8.81 Vol. 16, no. 5 also called v. 16, no. 4 in error.
8.82 Some issues lack chronological designation.
8.83 Vol. 1, no. 1 issued without chronological designation; v. 1, no. 2-called Jan. 1982-
8.84 First issue published, Mar. 1977, erroneously called no. 2.
8.85 Issue for Aug. 1979 contains note to correct vol. numbering of Apr. 1979 issue from v. 3, no. 1 to v. 1, no. 1.
8.86 Issues for summer 1976-<fall/winter 1977> carry whole numbering only.
8.87 Issues for fall and spring carry vol. designation and date, but orientation issues carry date designation only.

Report Year or Coverage

8.88 Data included for the following year.
8.89 Each issue covers: July 1-June 30.
8.90 First issue covers publications Oct. 1977-Sept. 1980.
8.91 Publication covers school years.
8.92 Report covers fiscal year.
8.93 Report covers heating year, Apr.-Mar.
8.94 Report for 1978 covers period Mar. 29, 1978-Dec. 31, 1978.

8.95 Report year ends June 30.
8.96 Report year irregular.
8.97 Vol. for 1978 covers the period 1971-78.
8.98 Vol. numbering covers six months.
8.99 1968 used as base year.

Suspended Publications

8.100 None published, 1968.
8.101 Suspended 1944-1947.
8.102 Suspended winter 1979-fall 1980.

1.7B9. Publication, Distribution, Etc.

EXTRAPOLATED GENERAL RULE

Make notes on publication, distribution, etc., details not already included in the publication, distribution, etc., area and not considered to be important.

RELATED AACR2 RULE

1.4B5 Publication, Distribution, etc., Area. General Rule [AACR2 Rev.; formerly AACR2 Rule 1.4B6]

If the original publication details are covered by a label containing publication details relating to a reproduction, reissue, etc., give the publication details of the later publication in this area. Give the publication details of the original in a note (see 1.7B9) if they can be ascertained readily. [emphasis added]

1.4F2 Date of Publication, Distribution, etc. [AACR2 Rev.]

Give the date as found in the item even if it is known to be incorrect. If a date is known to be incorrect, add the correct date.... If necessary, explain any discrepancy in a note. [emphasis added]

GENERAL LIBRARY OF CONGRESS POLICY

None issued.

RELATED LIBRARY OF CONGRESS POLICY

1.4B6 Publication, Distribution, etc. General Rules.

If any element of the publication, etc., area is transcribed from a stamp or a label, apply bracketing conventions as if the information were printed in the item (see 1.4A2). Make a note to convey that such information is stamped or expressed on a label. [emphasis added] [CSB 12]

1.4D1 Name of Publisher, Distributor, etc.

Due to its length, this LC policy statement has been abridged to include only the part related to the use of notes.

Privately Printed Works

For cataloging purposes, treat privately printed works as published works even if they have been distributed only to a very limited group (e.g., a keepsake for dinner guests or a Christmas greeting for friends).

Treat the person or body issuing the item, whether a commercial publisher, a private press, or a person or group for whom it may have been printed, as the publisher. If it is stated in the item that it has been privately printed, this fact may be expressed in a note, usually quoted. [emphasis added] (*Note*: Private presses should be considered publishers of the items they print if there is no evidence to the contrary in the item or in reference sources consulted.) [CSB 25]

1.4D5 Name of Publisher, Distributor, etc.

Due to its length, this LC policy statement has been abridged to include only the part related to the use of notes.

Recording Multiple Entities, etc.

If the names of two or more entities appear in separate statements on the item, do not routinely give in the publication, distribution, etc., area the entities that are not involved with the publication, distribution, etc., of the item. Generally give them in a quoted note instead. [emphasis added] [CSB 33]

FORMAT

No instructions for format exist that apply to all the chapters for description. However, AACR2 Rule 1.7A3 specifies that data recorded in a note related to data normally found in Areas 1 through 6 (title and statement of responsibility through series) should be recorded in the order prescribed for that area using the punctuation appropriate for that area (except that a full stop is used in place of a full stop, space, dash, space). Thus publication, distribution, etc., notes should use the following construct and its expansions for distributor, printer, etc., whenever possible:

[Place] : [Publisher,] [date].

CHAPTER APPLICATION

This note is present, in variant forms, in all chapters for description.

EXCEPTIONS AND ADDITIONS

Chapter 4 (Manuscripts) does not contain the provisions of the Extrapolated General Rule. Instead, this note is used to record publication details of a manuscript or a manuscript collection that has been, or is being, published.

Chapter 7 (Motion Pictures and Videorecordings) contains the provisions of the Extrapolated General Rule, but expands the use of the note to provide the date of original production. This note is also used to record the country of original release.

Chapter 12 (Serials) follows the spirit of the Extrapolated General Rule, but specifically emphasizes its use in recording "variations, peculiarities, irregularities, etc.," of the publication.

Chapter 2 (Books, Pamphlets, and Printed Sheets)

AACR2 RULE

2.7B9 Publication, Distribution, etc. [AACR2 Rev.]

Make notes on publication, distribution, etc., details that are not included in the publication, distribution, etc., area and are considered to be important.

RELATED AACR2 RULE

None.

LIBRARY OF CONGRESS POLICY

None issued.

RELATED LIBRARY OF CONGRESS POLICY

2.7B Notes. General Rule.

When a publication has a date of release or transmittal in a prominent position, include it in the bibliographic description. Typically these special dates consist of month or month and day as well as year and appear on the title page or cover. If the date is in a phrase that is being recorded as an edition statement, so record it. If an edition statement is not appropriate quote the date in a note, including with it any associated words. [emphasis added] . . .

Note that a date of release or transmittal is not a publication date. If the publication lacks a copyright date or a date of manufacture (cf. LCRI 1.4F6), the publication date *may* be inferred from the date of release or transmittal. Then, give the inference in brackets in the publication, etc., area and follow the above instructions for the date of release or transmittal. In case of doubt as to the character of a date, treat it as a date of release or transmittal. [CSB 17]

AACR2 TEXT EXAMPLES REVISED TO REFLECT LIBRARY OF CONGRESS POLICY

None required.

HISTORICAL BACKGROUND

AACR1 Rev. Rule 143D3e, while not providing any detail about the use of notes to record publication, etc., information, did give the order for notes dealing with the "imprint" area. The examples provided gave some indication of the type of note that could be made. These notes are similar to those that can be developed under the provisions of AACR2.

This AACR1 Rev. Ch. 6 rules could be used for works that were not separately published monographs unless specific rules for the description of a format superseded or excluded their use.

NOTE EXAMPLES

Publication, Distribution

9.1 Imprint from label.
9.2 Part of imprint from label in colophon.
9.3 U.S. place of publication from label on fly leaf.
9.4 Imprint from label on p. [2] of cover.
9.5 Place of publication from label on p. [4] of cover.
9.6 Publisher from label on t.p.
9.7 Second publisher from label on jacket.
9.8 Printing data on t.p. Publication data from engraved series t.p.
9.9 U.S. place of publication stamped on t.p.
9.10 Publisher statement from spine. Imprint on t.p. reads: London : Henry and Co.
9.11 Publisher and date at foot of first page of text.
9.12 Fictitious imprint. Cf. Pedrell.
9.13 Published anonymously. By John Macgowan.
9.14 Wingate imprint on t.p.
9.15 On t.p. in imprint position: Los Angeles, 1979.
9.16 Place of publication appears on t.p. as "Minor Confluence, Wisconsin."
9.17 Blind stamp on t.p.: NdA.
9.18 Imprint under label reads: HM+M Publishers.
9.19 Imprint on cover covered by label: Paris, Librarie centrale des sciences . . . J. Michelet.
9.20 Imprint of v. 1 covered by label: New York, Humanities Press.
9.21 Colophon reads: The Hart Press, December 1940.
9.22 Published: Detroit : Information Coordinators, 1973.
9.23 "Original limited edition (Rockmaster, 1978) and revised, expanded edition (Rock record, 1979) published and produced in the United Kingdom by Terry Hounsome. This edition published in the United Kingdom in 1981 by Blandford Books Ltd., as New rock record."—p. [iv].
9.24 Vol. 2 published: San Diego : A.S. Barnes ; London : Tantivy Press.
9.25 Vol. 4 published by Ontario Dept. of Mines and Northern Affairs.
9.26 Vols. 7-   issued by: Naval Historical Center, Dept. of the Navy.

9.27 Beginning in 1970, published by West Pub. Co., St. Paul, Minn.

9.28 Imprint varies: v. 14-18 : Wien : Hölder-Pichler-Tempsky; v. 20-21: Wien : in Kommission bei R.M. Rohrer; v. 22-25: Wien : H. Böhlaus Nachf.; v. 26-28, 30 : Wien : Verlag der Österreichischen Akademie der Wissenschaften.

9.29 Imprint varies: vol. 8- has imprint: London , New York . Academic Press ; vol. 9- : Amsterdam ; Princeton : Excerpta Medica ; New York : Sole distributors for the USA and Canada, Elsevier North-Holland.

9.30 "Published for the Company of Biologists Limited."

9.31 "Published . . . for the William Blake Trust, London"—Leaf [1] at end.

9.32 Published in association with the Australian Heritage Commission.

9.33 "Published in cooperation with the Institute for the Study of Contemporary Social Problems."

9.34 Published in cooperation with Work in America Institute.

9.35 Published simultaneously in Canada by George J. McLeod.

Distribution

9.36 Distributor from label inserted.

9.37 Distributor statement from label on verso of t.p.

9.38 Distributor from label on t.p.

9.39 Distributor from label on p. [4] of cover.

9.40 Vol. 1: Distributor from label on verso of t.p.

9.41 Distributor from stamp on t.p.

9.42 Distributor: New English Library, London.

9.43 "The hardcover edition of this catalogue is being distributed as a New York Graphic Society book by Little, Brown and Co., Boston"—T.p. verso.

9.44 Pt. 1 for sale by Supt. of Docs., U.S. G.P.O. ; pt. 4, G.P.O. sales statement incorrect in publication.

Printing

9.45 "Privately printed."

9.46 "Privately printed and published."

9.47 "Printed by Sam Hartz"—Colophon.

9.48 "Privately printed exclusively for members of the First Edition Society" —Prelim. p.

9.49 "Eighty-five copies have been printed at Bob Middleton's Cherryburn Press by David Woodward"—p. [31].

9.50 "Two hundred and fifty copies have been printed . . . by . . . Henry Morris. Copies I-XXV are for distribution by Mr. Rosenwald, copies 1-160 for other members of the Club, and copies 161-225 have been made available to their fellow collectors"—Colophon.

9.51 "Printed at Frank Wiggins Trade School, Los Angeles"—The Ward Ritchie Press and Anderson, Ritchie & Simon / Ward Ritchie. 1961. p. 127.

9.52 Imprint on t.p. reads: Dublin : Printed by W. Huband. 1810. Twelve copies re-printed, with additions, by A. O'Neill . . . 1823.

237

9.53 On 30th leaf of plates: Manufactured by Chisholm Bros., Portland, Me., for the American Souvenir Co. of Chicago, Ill.

9.54 Vol. 4, 6 printed by the Times Pub. Co.

Dates

9.55 Copyright from label on verso of t.p.

9.56 Imprint date from label on verso t.p.

9.57 "August 1980"—Cover.

9.58 "Issued September 1981."

9.59 "Produced 1981"—Verso t.p.

9.60 "Date published: November 1980."

9.61 At head of title: 1981.

9.62 Dated Syracuse, Feb. 9, 1846, and signed: John Wilkinson, Pres't, V.W. Smith, secretary.

9.63 Some of the lithographs are dated 1826.

9.64 The "log" is dated at end: Sept. 29, 1969.

9.65 Pref. dated 1972.

9.66 Prefatory note dated "Christmas 1951."

9.67 Stamped on cover: Jul 1981.

9.68 Imprint date in ms.

9.69 "Copyright, 1920, by George H. Doran Company."

9.70 Deposited for copyright Sept. 12, 1907.

9.71 Stories copyrighted 1947-1959.

9.72 Colophons in v. 1 and 3 give printing dates 1952 and 1966.

9.73 Vol. 2: 2nd printing, 1979.

9.74 Pt. 1: "February 27, 1981."
Pt. 2: "July 10, 1981."

9.75 Pt. 1: "Washington, D.C., November 21, 1980."
Pt. 2: "Washington, D.C., December 2, 1980."
Pt. 3: "Washington, D.C., December 3, 1980."
Pt. 4: "Washington, D.C., December 4, 1980."

Chapter 3 (Cartographic Materials)

AACR2 RULE

3.7B9 Publication, Distribution, etc.

Make notes on publication, distribution, etc., details that are not included in the publication, distribution, etc., area and are considered to be important.

Notes dealing with the date of situation are covered by the provisions of AACR2 Rule 3.7B1.

RELATED AACR2 RULE

None.

LIBRARY OF CONGRESS POLICY

None issued.

RELATED LIBRARY OF CONGRESS POLICY

None issued.

AACR2 TEXT EXAMPLES REVISED TO REFLECT LIBRARY OF CONGRESS POLICY

None required.

HISTORICAL BACKGROUND

Although AACR1 and previous codes had no rule equivalent to AACR2 Rule 3.7B9, the imprint note provisions for separately published monographs in these earlier codes could be used for cartographic materials. (See *Historical Background* under Rule 2.7B9.)

NOTE EXAMPLES

Publication, Distribution, Printing

9.76 "Published by Arnold D. Baldwin."
9.77 "Designet [sic]: State Cartographical Publishing House, Warzawa"—Portfolio.
9.78 Stamped on: Vassar Chamber of Commerce . . .
9.79 "The Upper Keys Edition of Who's Where is published three times a year by Who's Where Publishing Company, Inc . . . ."
9.80 Published by GEO projects in association with Oxford University Press.
9.81 "Published by the Ipswich Chamber of Commerce in co-operation with Essex County Tourist Council."
9.82 "Published by the Metropolitan Fort Myers Chamber of Commerce through its Fort Myers Lee County News Bureau."
9.83 "Published by Wales Gas by kind permission of The National Museum of Wales."
9.84 Trade edition simultaneously published by Prentice-Hall as: Prentice-Hall's Great international atlas.
9.85 "De l'imprimerie de Smith"—Verso of special t.p.
9.86 Maps engraved and printed by U.S. Geological Survey.
9.87 Printed and bound in the Republic of South Africa by Cape & Transvaal Printers Ltd.
9.88 Printed and bound in Scotland by Wm. Collins Sons & Co. Ltd.
9.89 "Sold by the proprietors S. Harding . . . St. Martins Lane, and W.H. Toms . . . in Union Court near Hatton Garden Holbord"—leaf [3].

Dates

Chapter 4 (Manuscripts)

AACR2 RULE

4.7B9 Published Versions [AACR2 Rev.]

If the work contained in a manuscript or the content of a collection of manuscripts has been, or is being, published, give the publication details.

RELATED AACR2 RULE

None.

LIBRARY OF CONGRESS POLICY

None issued. APPM, however, provides the following guidelines:

Published Versions

If the work contained in a manuscript or the content of a manuscript collection or archival record has been, or is being published (including microform publication), give the publication details. [APPM 4.7B13]

These guidelines expand the AACR2 definition of "published" to include microform publications.

240

RELATED LIBRARY OF CONGRESS POLICY

None issued.

AACR2 TEXT EXAMPLES REVISED TO REFLECT LIBRARY OF CONGRESS POLICY

None required.

HISTORICAL BACKGROUND

AACR1 Rule 207F provided for a note to record publication of a "substantial or significant portion" of a manuscript when that information was readily available. The "*introductory notes*" to the description of manuscripts (preceding AACR1 Rule 201) also stated this. Essentially the AACR2 rule is the same as that in AACR1 except for the "readily available" statement.

NOTE EXAMPLES

9.109   Published: Berlin : E. Bote & G. Bock ; New York : Associated Music Publishers, 1930.

9.110   Published: Leipzig : J. Rieter-Biedermann, 1868.

9.111   *"Published in 1921 by New Jersey Music Publishing Company."—T.p.

9.112   Williams' journal was published by the repository as: The New Zealand Journal, 1842-1844, of John B. Williams, of Salem, Massachusetts . . . edited by Robert W. Kenny (1956).

9.113   *The present letter is published in: Correspondence / Stendhal, édition établie et annotée par Henri Martineau et V. Del Litto (Paris : 1967), v.2, p. 838 (no. 179) This publication (from a secondary source) shows no major deviations from the autograph.

9.114   Isaac Harleston's papers published in: Records of the 2nd Regiment, South Carolina Line, Continental Establishment, South Carolina Historical and Genealogical Magazines, vols. 5-9 (1904-1909).

9.115   *Published in Selected Letters of Robert Frost, 1964, as no. 317.

9.116   In part, published in: South Carolina Historical and Genealogical Magazine, v. 10-12 (1911-1913).

9.117   Portions of the collection have been published in: The Robert R. Churches of Memphis / by Annette E. Church and Roberta Church. Memphis, Tenn., 1974.

9.118   Parts of the collection are published in: The Letter Book of Esek Hopkins, Commander-in-Chief of the United States Navy, 1775-1777 (1932) and The Correspondence of Esek Hopkins, Commander-in-Chief of the United States Navy (1944), both published by the repository.

9.119   In part, published in: "The Antebellum Rice Planter as Revealed in the Letter Book of Charles Manigault, 1846-1848" / by James M. Clifton: South Carolina Historical Magazine, v. 74, nos. 3 & 4 (July-Oct. 1973).

9.120   *Published as: Chapter 8, Antheil, Joyce, and Pound; Chapter 35, A distaste for music, in Virgil Thomson. New York : Knopf, 1966.

9.121   A microfilm (38 reels) of the papers has been published by the Center for Western Studies, Augustana College, Sioux Falls, S.D., with an accompanying guide entitled: Guide to the Microfilm Edition of the Richard F. Pettigrew Papers at the Pettigrew Museum, Sioux Falls, South Dakota / edited by Gary D. Olson (1978).

Chapter 5 (Music)

AACR2 RULE

5.7B9 Publication, Distribution, etc. [AACR2 Rev.]

Make notes on publication, distribution, etc., details that are not included in the publication, distribution, etc., area and are considered to be important.

RELATED AACR2 RULE

None.

LIBRARY OF CONGRESS POLICY

None issued.

RELATED LIBRARY OF CONGRESS POLICY

None issued.

AACR2 TEXT EXAMPLES REVISED TO REFLECT
LIBRARY OF CONGRESS POLICY

None required.

HISTORICAL BACKGROUND

Although AACR1 and previous codes had no rule equivalent to AACR2 Rule 5.7B9, the imprint note provisions for separately published monographs in these earlier codes could be used for music. (See *Historical Background* under Rule 2.7B9.)

242

NOTE EXAMPLES

9.122 Additional imprint on label mounted on t.p.: Frankfurt ; New York : C.F. Peters.

9.123 Available from Stanton's Music, Columbus, Ohio, and the Worthington Historical Society.

9.124 Distributor from label mounted on cover.

9.125 Distributor from label on t.p.

9.126 Imprint from label mounted on cover; stamp on various pages: New York, N.Y. : Boosey & Hawkes, Rental Dept.

9.127 Distributor on t.p.: New York : Leeds Music Corp.

9.128 Imprint from label on p. [2] of cover.

9.129 Imprint on label: Frankfurt ; New York : C. F. Peters.

9.130 Imprint under label reads: Wellington: A.H. & A.W. Reed.

9.131 Label on t.p.: Frankfurt, New York : C.F. Peters.

9.132 Original imprint (covered by label): Mount Tahoma Music Publishers.

9.133 Publishers from label on t.p. Publication date and ISBN from label on verso t.p.

9.134 Date from stamp on p. 1.

Chapter 6 (Sound Recordings)

AACR2 RULE

6.7B9 Publication, Distribution, etc. [AACR2 Rev.]
Make notes on publication, distribution, etc., details that are not included in the publication, distribution, etc., area and are considered to be important.

RELATED AACR2 RULE

None.

LIBRARY OF CONGRESS POLICY

None issued.

RELATED LIBRARY OF CONGRESS POLICY

None issued.

AACR2 TEXT EXAMPLES REVISED TO REFLECT LIBRARY OF CONGRESS POLICY

None required.

HISTORICAL BACKGROUND

Although AACR1 Rev. Ch. 14 and previous codes had no rule equivalent to AACR2 Rule 6.7B9, the imprint note provisions for separately published monographs in these earlier codes could be used for processed sound recordings. (See *Historical Background* under Rule 2.7B9.)

NOTE EXAMPLES

9.135 "Co-Produktion mit Polydor International, G.m.b.H., Hamburg."
9.136 Distributor from label on container.
9.137 Distributor from label mounted on container.
9.138 Distributed in the U.S. by: Palo Alto, Calif. : Pendragon House Inc.
9.139 Imprint from superimposed label.
9.140 Imprint on container covered by label: Odeon.
9.141 Imprint under label reads: EMI Voz de su Amo.
9.142 "Marketed in the U.S.A. by Euroclass Record Distributors' Ltd."—
Label on container.

Chapter 7 (Motion Pictures and Videorecordings)

AACR2 RULE

7.7B9 Publication, Distribution, etc., and Date [AACR2 Rev.]

Make notes on publication, distribution, etc., details that are not included in the publication, distribution, etc., area and are considered to be important. . . .

Give a date of original production differing from the date of publication, distribution, etc. . . .

Give the country of original release if it is not stated or implied elsewhere in the description.

RELATED AACR2 RULE

7.4F2 Date of Publication, Distribution, etc. [AACR2 Rev.]

Optionally, give a date of original production differing from the date of publication, distribution, etc., of a published item in the note area (see 7.7B9). [emphasis added]

LIBRARY OF CONGRESS POLICY

When a foreign firm, etc., is given in the source as emanator or originator, do not assume that the item was either made or released in that country if not so stated.

Provide a note using the following construct:

A foreign [media type] ([Country])

> For a U.S. emanator and foreign producer or a foreign emanator and a U.S. producer, do not make the note. [CSB 13]

For archival moving image materials, the Library of Congress supplements AACR2 Chapter 7 with the guidelines in *Archival Moving Image Materials* by White-Hensen.

RELATED LIBRARY OF CONGRESS POLICY

7.4F2 Date of Publication, Distribution, etc.
Give a date of original production differing from the dates of publication/distribution or copyright, etc., in the note area (see 7.7B9 and 8.7B9). [emphasis added] Apply the provision if the difference is greater than two years. . . .
(When dealing with different media, see 7.7B7 and 8.7B7.) [CSB 33]

AACR2 TEXT EXAMPLES REVISED TO REFLECT LIBRARY OF CONGRESS POLICY

None required.

HISTORICAL BACKGROUND

AACR1 Rev. Rule 227D provided that for "motion pictures and similar works," when a year of production differed from the year of release, both dates were recorded in the Release/Publication Area. The date of production was preceded by the word "made" or its foreign equivalent. AACR2 places the date of production in a note rather than in the Publication, Distribution, etc., Area.

AACR1 Rev. Rule 229.2G provided for a note for motion pictures and filmstrips to record the country of release that was not implied in the description. Although this rule specifically mentioned only motion pictures, it could also be applied to videorecordings. Except for this difference, this aspect of the AACR1 and AACR2 rules is the same.

For the remaining aspects of AACR2 Rule 7.7B9, AACR1 Rev. had no equivalent rule. However, the imprint note provisions for separately published monographs could be used to record this remaining information. (See *Historical Background* under Rule 2.7B9.)

NOTE EXAMPLES

9.143   A foreign film (Argentina).
9.144   A foreign videorecording (England).

9.145   First released in Canada.
9.146   First released in Costa Rica under title: La Guerra de los filibusteros.
9.147   Originally released in England.
9.148   Simultaneously released in Canada.
9.149   Motion picture distributed by: Canyon Cinema.
9.150   First released in 1977.
9.151   Made in 1978.

Chapter 8 (Graphic Materials)

AACR2 RULE

8.7B9 Publication, Distribution, etc. [AACR2 Rev.]
Make notes on publication, distribution, etc., details that are not included in the publication, distribution, etc., area and are considered to be important.

RELATED AACR2 RULE

None.

LIBRARY OF CONGRESS POLICY

When a foreign firm, etc., is given in the source as emanator or originator, do not assume that the item was either made or released in that country if not so stated. . . .

Provide a note using the following construct:

A foreign [media type] ([Country])

For a U.S. emanator and foreign producer or a foreign emanator and a U.S. producer, do not make the note. [CSB 13]

For original items and historical collections, the Library of Congress supplements AACR2 Chapter 8 with the guidelines in *Graphic Materials* by Betz.

RELATED LIBRARY OF CONGRESS POLICY

7.4F2 Date of Publication, Distribution, etc.
Give a date of original production differing from the dates of publication/distribution or copyright, etc., in the note area (see 7.7B9 and 8.7B9). [emphasis added] Apply the provision if the difference is greater than two years. . . .
(When dealing with different media, see 7.7B7 and 8.7B7.) [CSB 33]

AACR2 TEXT EXAMPLES REVISED TO REFLECT LIBRARY OF CONGRESS POLICY

None required.

HISTORICAL BACKGROUND

AACR1 Rev. Rule 229.2G provided a note for motion pictures and filmstrips to record the country of release that was not implied in the description. AACR1 used this rule for only filmstrips and motion pictures, while AACR2 applies this note to all graphic materials covered by Chapter 8. In reality, the intent of the AACR1 Rev. rule is still applicable for filmstrips. In all other respects, this aspect of the two rules is the same.

For the remaining aspects of AACR2 Rule 8.7B9, AACR1 Rev. Ch. 12 had no equivalent rule. However, the imprint note provisions for separately published monographs could be used to record this information. (See *Historical Background* under Rule 2.7B9.)

NOTE EXAMPLES

Projection Graphic Materials
9.152   First released in England.
9.153   A foreign filmstrip (Canada).
9.154   A foreign slide set (England).
9.155   *Date on container: 1984.
9.156   *Cassette tape dated c1970; teacher's guide dated c1973.

Nonprojection Graphic Materials
9.157   *Place of publication suggested by Weitenkampf.
9.158   *No. 10 has variant name of publisher: James Ackermann & Co.
9.159   *Plates 34-44 have variant place of publication: St. Louis ; New York.
9.160   "The eighth publication of the Arion Press."
9.161   *Dated according to time period Schussele was in Philadelphia working for Duval.
9.162   *Distributor's name printed on adhesive label: Denoyer-Geppert Times Mirror.
9.163   *Printed in England.

Chapter 9 (Computer Files)

AACR2 RULE

9.7B9 Publication, Distribution, etc. [AACR2 Rev.]
   Make notes on publication, distribution, etc., details that are not included in the publication, distribution, etc., area and are considered to be important.

RELATED AACR2 RULE

9.4F3 Date of Publication, Distribution, etc. [AACR2 Rev.]
Give any other useful dates (e.g., dates of collection of data) in a note (see 9.7B7 and 9.7B9). [emphasis added]

LIBRARY OF CONGRESS POLICY

None issued for AACR2 Rev. Ch. 9.

RELATED LIBRARY OF CONGRESS POLICY

None issued for AACR2 Rev. Ch. 9.

AACR2 TEXT EXAMPLES REVISED TO REFLECT
LIBRARY OF CONGRESS POLICY

None required for AACR2 Rev. Ch. 9.

HISTORICAL BACKGROUND

Computer files were not covered by AACR1 or previous codes. The original AACR2 Chapter 9 specifically included production as part of the coverage of this note. While AACR2 Rev. Ch. 9 does not specifically indicate production, production is covered by the provisions of the revised rule.

NOTE EXAMPLES

9.164 *Distributed in the Netherlands by: Amsterdam : Sociological Institute, Tilburg University.
9.165 *Codebook produced by the Center for Human Resource Research, Ohio State University.
9.166 *User's manual distributed solely by: Washington, D.C. : American Political Science Association.
9.167 *Booklet and container cover have date: c1985.
9.168 *Date on disk label: c1983.
9.169 *Disk and manual, c1984; title page of manual, c1985.

Chapter 10 (Three-Dimensional Artefacts and Realia)

AACR2 RULE

10.7B9 Publication, Distribution, etc. [AACR2 Rev.]
Make notes on publication, distribution, etc., details that are not included in the publication, distribution, etc., area and are considered to be important.

RELATED AACR2 RULE

None.

LIBRARY OF CONGRESS POLICY

None issued.

RELATED LIBRARY OF CONGRESS POLICY

None issued.

AACR2 TEXT EXAMPLES REVISED TO REFLECT
LIBRARY OF CONGRESS POLICY

No examples were given in AACR2 or AACR2 Rev.

HISTORICAL BACKGROUND

Although AACR1 Rev. Ch. 12 and previous codes had no rule equivalent to AACR2 Rule 10.7B9, the imprint note provisions for separately published monographs in these earlier codes could be used for three-dimensional artifacts and realia. (See *Historical Background* under Rule 2.7B9.)

NOTE EXAMPLES

The broad scope of the prescribed sources of information from which data for Area 4 (Publication, Distribution, etc.) can be derived, i.e., the item itself, accompanying textual material, and the container "issued by the 'publisher' or manufacturer" of the object, results in relatively limited use of this note.

9.170   *Dates differ: Container c1982, Gameboard c1980.
9.171   *Place and name of probable producer derived from mailing label.

Chapter 12 (Serials)

AACR2 RULE

12.7B9 Publication, Distribution, etc. [AACR2 Rev.]
    Make notes on any variations, peculiarities, irregularities, etc., in the publication, distribution, etc., details of the serial. If these have been numerous, give a general statement.

RELATED AACR2 RULE

None.

LIBRARY OF CONGRESS POLICY

If the date of publication of the first issue (cf. 12.4F1) is later than the publication date of a subsequent issue, give the earliest date of publication in a note. [CSB 15]

RELATED LIBRARY OF CONGRESS POLICY

12.0B1 Sources of Information. Printed Serials.

Due to its length, this LC policy statement has been abridged to include only the parts related to the use of notes.

Serials

The basis for the description is the first issue of the serial. In determining which issue is first, disregard the date of publication, etc., and use the designation on the issues. For serials that carry numeric or alphabetic designations, the first issue is the one with the lowest or earliest (in the alphabet) designation. For serials that do not carry numeric or alphabetic designations, the first issue is the one with the earliest chronological designation. (If the actual first issue is not available, use these same guidelines to determine which issue should be used as the basis for the description.)

Since the title page (or title page substitute) of the first issue is the chief source of information for a printed serial, a title page that is published later to cover one or more issues cannot be used as the chief source. (However, data from such a title page may be put into the note area when necessary.) [emphasis added]

If the description has been formulated from the first issue of a serial, the body of the entry remains unchanged throughout the life of the serial. If issues after the first have data different from those recorded in the body of the entry, record the different data in the note area as necessary. [emphasis added] However, if the differences are in the title proper, create a separate record when appropriate (21.2C). (For changes in the main entry heading, see 21.3B.) . . .

Reprints of Serials

In order that the description of the reprint resemble and file with the description of the original, the earliest *issue* reprinted is used as the chief source for the first three areas of the description. Data for these areas may be taken from any place on the reprinted issue without the use of brackets. If it is known that the description of the original would include data that are not on the reprinted issue, the data may be supplied in brackets.

In area four the place of publication, publisher, and date of the reprint are recorded, using brackets if the data do not come from a prescribed source on the reprint.

The physical description area gives the physical description of the reprint, not the original.

A series is recorded if the reprint appears in a series.

Usually a single note (see 12.7B7g) gives important details about the original while other notes give necessary information about the reprint. Notes giving the source of the title or the issue on which the description is based are not given. [emphasis added] [CSB 38]

AACR2 TEXT EXAMPLES REVISED TO REFLECT LIBRARY OF CONGRESS POLICY

None required.

HISTORICAL BACKGROUND

AACR1 provided more detailed guidance in the use of notes related to the publication of a serial than does AACR2.

AACR1 Rule 167D was used to record the duration of a publication unless the statement of holdings had already given this information. AACR2, depending on the nature of the duration statement being recorded, uses either the Numeric and/or Alphabetic, Chronological, or Other Designated Area (AACR2 Rule 12.3), the Publication, Distribution, etc., Area (AACR2 Rule 12.5), the Numbering and Chronological Designation Note (AACR2 Rule 12.7B8); or the Publication, Distribution, etc., Note (AACR2 Rule 12.7B9).

AACR1 Rule 167P provided for a note to record variations in the place of publication, the name of the publisher, as well as publisher changes. This note included details on the use of an "Imprint varies" note. AACR2 provides for the use of all notes covered under the AACR1 rule, but lacks the detail of the earlier code.

AACR1 Rule 167R used a note "No more published?" when there was doubt about which issue of a serial was the last. This same note was placed directly before any contents note. This note can be made using AACR2, although no specific guidelines are provided for it in the current rule.

NOTE EXAMPLES

9.172   *No more published.
9.173   Published in: Homewood, Ill., 1976-fall 1979.

9.174 Published by: the Technology Promotions Division, Center for Non-conventional Energy Development.

9.175 Published: Falls Church, Va. : Woman Activist Fund, c1979-

9.176 Published by: Remote Sensing Committee of the National Council for Geographic Education, the Remote Sensing Committee of the Association of American Geographers, and the Dept. of Geography-Geology, the University of Nebraska at Omaha, July 1979-

9.177 First issue published by the University College of Botswana.

9.178 Published: Hyattsville, Md. 1956-1970; Belle Fourche, S.D. 1971-

9.179 Published: Arkansas, Dept. of Economic Development, Public Information Division, Mar./Apr. 1979 : Arkansas Dept. of Economic Development, Development Services Division, summer 1979-summer 1980 : Arkansas Dept. of Economic Development, fall 1980-<winter 1980>.

9.180 Published: New York : Traditional Acupuncture Foundation, summer 1978-<winter>1980 ; Columbia, Md.: Traditional Acupuncture Foundation, spring 1980-<summer 1980>.

9.181 Issues for Aug. 1973-<Apr.-Aug. 1980> published: New York, N.Y.: T. Belanger.

9.182 No. 2-<3> published by Gloucester Museum School.

9.183 Vols. for 1970-   published in Arlington, Va. by O.S. North.

9.184 Vol. for 1977 published by Dept. of Public Carriers.

9.185 Vol. 3 [1981]-   published: New York, N.Y. : American Showcase, in association with the One Club for Art and Copy, c1982-

9.186 Imprint varies.

9.187 Imprint varies: Division of the Budget, 1980/81.

9.188 1974 vol. not published.

9.189 Vols. for 1st and 2nd annual meeting never published. Cf. Union list of serials.

9.190 Information incorrect in document as to for sale by the Supt. of Docs.

1.7B10. Physical Description

EXTRAPOLATED GENERAL RULE

Make notes on important physical details that are not included in the physical description area.

RELATED AACR2 RULE
None.

GENERAL LIBRARY OF CONGRESS POLICY
None issued.

RELATED LIBRARY OF CONGRESS POLICY

1.5 Physical Description Area
The Library of Congress applies the following guidelines to the note area as well as the physical description area.

> In recording bibliographic details for items that have been, or will be, bound by someone other than the publisher, formulate volume and illustration statements in the physical description and note areas based on the item as issued by the publisher rather than as bound after publication. [emphasis added] For example, if LC binds a separately issued "volume 1" and "volume 2" of a monograph in one physical volume, "2 v." is the correct volume statement, not "2 v. in 1." (If, however, in another case the publisher issues a monograph as two bibliographic volumes in one physical volume, then "2 v. in 1" is appropriate; cf. 2.5B19.)
>
> In serials cataloging, avoid the use of a "v. in," etc., statement; instead, formulate the statement in terms of bibliographic units only (i.e., "v.").
>
> Illustrations should also reflect the characteristics of the item as issued, not what the cataloger can predict. For example, if maps are not physically attached to the item but are randomly inserted, record them as follows:
>
> 355 p. : 10 maps (3 col.) ; 23 cm.
> Three folded maps laid in.
> *not* Three folded maps in pocket.
>
> ("Three folded maps in pocket" is correct only when the item is issued with the maps in a pocket.)
>
> For loose-leaf works that are subsequently bound by LC after the works are completed, retain the loose-leaf statement. (Retain this statement also for items for which the publisher supplies bound vol-

umes or transfer binders for material of permanent value.) For example, if a loose-leaf service originally issued in 3 binders is bound by LC in 4 volumes, record the collation on the revised record as

3 v. (loose-leaf) ; 23 cm.

Exception: For ephemeral and "made up" sets lacking a collective title, base the volume and illustration statements on LC's copy and binding. [CSB 17]

The Library of Congress emphasizes that the item should be described *as issued* by the publisher. Although not stated in this rule interpretation, it would seem appropriate to provide an accurate description of the item in its current state in a local note (.7B20) if the description of the item as issued varies greatly from the item in hand creating the potential for a misleading description.

FORMAT

None prescribed. Due to the variety of information that can be included in this note, no formal structure is imposed or suggested. Chapters that have applications for this rule beyond the scope of the Extrapolated General Rule frequently call for a more formalized construct for those additions. See the individual chapter rules and examples for these formats.

CHAPTER APPLICATION

All eleven chapters for description include a form of the Extrapolated General Rule, modified to accommodate the specific document format being described. Chapter 5 (Music) changes the terminology of the rule heading slightly, adding the phrase "Duration of performance." Most chapters have applications for this rule that specifically provide notes on physical description beyond the scope of the Extrapolated General Rule. These additional applications are appropriate to the specific material format being described.

EXCEPTIONS AND ADDITIONS

Chapter 2 (Monographs) provides an additional instruction for notes on braille or other raised type books.

Chapter 3 (Cartographic Materials) provides an additional requirement to indicate whether an item is a photoreproduction and the method of reproduction used, if this is likely to affect use.

Chapter 4 (Manuscripts) includes the Extrapolated General Rule only. However, an additional AACR2 Rev. rule (Rule 4.7B23) provides for more detailed notes on the physical description of ancient, medieval, and Renaissance manuscripts. This additional rule includes notes on the style of writing, illustrative matter, collation, other physical details, and opening words.

Chapter 5 (Music) provides an additional requirement to state the duration of performance if stated on the item.

Chapter 6 (Sound Recordings) also provides an instruction for notes on the duration of performance. In addition, it prohibits giving physical details that are standard to the item.

Chapter 7 (Motion Pictures and Videorecordings) delineates the type of physical description notes that could be made if a greater level of detail is desired. These include sound characteristics, length of film or tape, color, form of print, film base, videorecording system, generation of copy, special projection requirements, and other physical details important to use or storage.

Chapter 8 (Graphic Materials) adds that important physical details should be given, especially if they affect the use of the item.

Chapter 9 (Computer Files, AACR2 Rev.) indicates that important physical details of files available by remote access should be recorded.

Chapter 10 (Three-Dimensional Artefacts and Realia) adds a qualifier to the Extrapolated General Rule that calls for giving important physical details if they affect use. In addition, this rule provides for notes describing the "various pieces" of an item if considered useful.

Chapter 12 (Serials) modifies the Extrapolated General Rule to provide notes for variations in the physical description of issues of a serial.

Chapter 2 (Books, Pamphlets, and Printed Sheets)

AACR2 RULE

2.7B10 Physical Description [AACR2 Rev.]
Make notes on important physical details that are not included in the physical description area.

Braille
Make notes on braille or other tactile books.

RELATED AACR2 RULE

2.5 Number of Volumes and/or Pagination [AACR2 Rev.]
2.5B13 If the paging is duplicated, as is sometimes the case with books having parallel texts, give both pagings and make an explanatory note (see 2.7B10). [emphasis added]

2.5B14 If a volume has a pagination of its own and also bears the pagination of a larger work of which it is a part, give the paging of the individual volume in this area and give the continuous paging in a note (see 2.7B10). [emphasis added]

2.5B22 If a publication was planned to be in more than one volume, but not all have been published and it appears that publication will not be continued, describe the incomplete set as appropriate (i.e., give paging for a single volume *or* number of volumes for multiple volumes). Make a note (see 2.7B10) to the effect that no more volumes have been published. [emphasis added]

2.5C Illustrative Matter

2.5C5 If some or all of the illustrations appear on the lining papers, make a note of this fact (see 2.7B10). [emphasis added]

2.5C7 [AACR2 Rev.] Describe illustrative matter issued in a pocket inside the cover of an item in the physical description. Specify the number of such items and their location in a note (see 2.7B10 and 2.7B11). [emphasis added]

2.5E2 Accompanying Material [AACR2 Rev.]

If the accompanying material is issued in a pocket inside the cover of the publication, give its location in a note (see 2.5C7, 2.7B10, and 2.7B11). [emphasis added]

These related rules delineate several types of notes that should be made under AACR2 Rule 2.7B10. They do not constitute an exhaustive list. They do, however, clarify why certain notes are used that otherwise may not seem appropriate as physical description notes, e.g., discontinued publications.

LIBRARY OF CONGRESS POLICY

None issued.

RELATED LIBRARY OF CONGRESS POLICY

2.5B17 Multipart Items

In recording multipart items consisting of numbered and unnumbered volumes (e.g., unnumbered *Constitution volume* and . . . *court rules volume* constituting part of numbered *Revised statutes* . . . set), record in the extent statement the numbered volumes only. Indicate the total of unnumbered volumes as part of the note accounting for the unnumbered volumes if this is not clear from the note itself. [emphasis added] [CSB 17]

2.5B22 Incomplete Multipart Items

This statement applies to cases in which the information is readily available that a multipart item, although not finished, has ceased publication.

If more than one volume was published, use "No more published." ...

If only one volume was published, combine in a single note a quotation of the part designation (as opposed to recording this designation in the title and statement of responsibility area) and the cataloger's statement "No more published." [emphasis added] [CSB 38]

AACR2 TEXT EXAMPLES REVISED TO REFLECT LIBRARY OF CONGRESS POLICY

None required.

HISTORICAL BACKGROUND

Under the rules for note order, AACR1 Rev. Rule 143D3f provided for notes related to the collation area and additional physical description. No further guidelines were offered.

AACR1 Rev. Rule 141B3c provided for a note on updating loose-leaf volumes. No equivalent instructions appear in AACR2, although nothing prohibits providing a note similar to notes created under AACR1 Rev.

AACR1 Rev. Rule 141B6 called for the use of a note to further explain duplicate paging in the Physical Description Area. This rule is equivalent to AACR2 Rule 2.5B13.

AACR1 Rev. Rule 141B7 called for a note to provide continuous paging information. This is equivalent to AACR2 Rule 2.5B14.

AACR1 Rev. Rule 141C4 provided for a "no more published" note equivalent to notes created under AACR2 Rule 2.5B22.

AACR1 Rev. Rule 141D5b provided for notes on illustrative matter in pockets. This rule is equivalent to AACR2 Rule 2.5C7.

These AACR1 Rev. Ch. 6 rules could be used for works that were not separately published monographs unless specific rules for the description of a format superseded or excluded their use.

NOTE EXAMPLES

Discontinued Publication
10.1 Earlier proceedings not published.
10.2 No more published.
10.3 "We expect to continue the publication ... annually"—Pref.

Physical Description
10.4 Issued with original leaf in a pocket.
10.5 Size of sheet unfolded: 56 x 77 cm.

10.6 Size of v. 2: 21 x 30 cm.

10.7 Interleaved.

10.8 Thumb indexed.

10.9 "Three volumes in one."

10.10 The samples are mounted.

10.11 The arrangements are printed in colors.

10.12 Page [1] is on leaf which serves as front paste-down.

10.13 The specimens are mounted on blank pages included in page count.

10.14 Vols 1-10 arranged according to the Dewey decimal classification system.

10.15 The leaves are joined end to end, with 4 blanks interspersed, and folded accordion style.

10.16 Twenty-one of the leaves are on a strip folded accordion style, with last leaf mounted on the portfolio-like cover; the three remaining leaves are mounted on the flaps of the cover.

10.17 Advertising matter included in paging.

10.18 The final 2 p. are advertisements.

10.19 Collection kept in a case (56 cm.) and a folder (79 cm.).

10.20 Issued in an envelope.

10.21 Issued in slipcase.

10.22 Issued in case (31 x 26 cm.).

10.23 Issued unbound in a case.

10.24 Vols. 2-5 issued in cases.

10.25 Issued in a portfolio (53 cm.).

10.26 Issued unsewn in a portfolio.

10.27 On 11 folded sheets, issued in portfolio.

10.28 On 10 folded sheets, issued in a solander case.

10.29 Issued within 2 printed covers. Full t.p. is on inner cover.

10.30 Eleven sections, unsewn, in paper wrappers; issued in a portfolio.

10.31 On 9 folded sheets and 1 half-sheet, issued in a solander case.

10.32 Three folded plans in pocket.

10.33 Six genealogical tables in pocket.

10.34 "Known casualties in battles and skirmishes of the Forty-ninth Virginia Infantry, C.S.A." (1 sheet) inserted.

10.35 The specimens are displayed on 16 album leaves.

10.36 Issued in loose 2-leaf sections in a printed paper cover in a case. The photos. are mounted.

10.37 Full-color facsim., issued in slipcase labeled: Werdener Psalter : Facsimile : Codices selecti LXIII.

Printing and Paper Details

10.38 Printed in raised letters.

10.39 Title page printed. Other leaves are mimeograph (partly photocopy).

10.40 Printed on double leaves.

10.41 Published in large print.

10.42 "One hundred and twenty copies have been printed, of which thirty are on Japan paper and ninety on Van Gelder paper"—p. i.

10.43 "Twenty of the edition of one hundred numbered copies are printed on paper made by hand from manila hemp . . . The remaining copies are printed on Mohawk Superfine Text"—Colophon.

10.44 Poem (p. [1]) and colophon (p. [4]) printed parallel to inner margin; p. [2]-[3] blank.

10.45 Printed on one side of the sheet (actually a strip of 5 connected sheets), which is folded accordian-style and removable from cover.

Pagination

10.46 Alternate pages blank (p. [5]-99).

10.47 Leaves 113-117 blank for "Notes and photographs."

10.48 Most alternate pages blank.

10.49 Page 464 blank.

10.50 Page 64 blank for notes.

10.51 Pages 522-528 blank.

10.52 Pages also numbered 77-86.

10.53 Pages 27-136 are numbered plates 1-112.

10.54 Plates numbered 1-25, with 6 unnumbered at end. All are mounted.

10.55 The individual plates here collected are numbered between 35 and 968 (the last published at Milan by "Gio. Ricordi" and at Florence by "Ricordi e C.").

10.56 Opposite pages bear duplicate numbering.

10.57 Pages 463-464 repeated in numbering.

10.58 Pp. 1-87e: opposite pages bear duplicate numbering.

10.59 Vols. 1-8 paged continuously (xcvi, 8974 p.).

10.60 Consists of [4] prelim. leaves and [128] illegibly printed pages.

10.61 Page number 130 misprinted 13.

10.62 Pages [1-4], repeated from v. 1 of the edition, contain Exodus XXXIX, 6-XL, 36; pages [158-160] include Deuteronomy I, 1-32.

10.63 Pagination as originally issued: xi, 333 p.

10.64 Pagination of work as originally issued: viii, 176 p., plus index beginning on p. 177.

10.65 Replacement page included, p. 31.

10.66 Vol. l: [44], 955, [1] p.; v. 2: [32], [961]-2258, [62] p.

10.67 Page [x] calls for one more leaf of plates than is known to exist.

10.68 Issued in loose-leaf binder.

10.69 Loose-leaf for updating.

10.70 Vol. 7: loose-leaf for updating.

Plates

10.71 Captions on verso of plates.

10.72 Fold. plate tipped in.

10.73 7 fold. leaves of plates in pocket.

10.74 One folded leaf of plates inserted.

10.75 Three folded col. leaves of plates inserted at end.

10.76 Seven of the plates are mounted photos.

10.77 The leaf of plates is a port. mounted as frontispiece.

10.78 The plates are mounted black and white photos, signed by the photographer.

10.79 The plates reproduce political posters.

10.80 Plates I-II accompanied by transparent folded guard sheets with outline drawings.

10.81 Thirteen plates, each, except for the port., marked "Proof." The plates are marked with volume and page numbers to indicate their positioning in the Cadell & Davies edition(s) of the Works of Robert Burns. Each plate is dated Jan. 1, 1814 (one: Jany. 1814).

Illustrations

10.82 The ill. is mounted.

10.83 The ill. is mounted on p. [5].

10.84 Ill. on 1 folded leaf in pocket.

10.85 Illustrative material and tables on 29 leaves in pocket of v. 2.

10.86 Figure 2 (on 1 folded sheet) in pocket.

10.87 Six folded p. of ill. inserted.

10.88 Part of ill. inserted.

10.89 Part of illustrative matter (folded) inserted.

10.90 Part of illustrative material (5 fold. sheets) inserted in pocket at end.

10.91 Some illustrations on 2 folded sheets in pocket.

10.92 Without illustrations despite the statement "Illustrated" on t.p.

10.93 The facsim. is a mounted photo.

10.94 The 6 ill. are mounted photos.

10.95 Exhibition poster (folded) inserted.

10.96 10 folded drawings in pocket.

10.97 The 7 col. ill. are samples of marbled paper.

10.98 One etching is mounted on t.p., the other is laid in at end.

10.99 Illustrations, in both black-and-white and in color, of 7 decorated bindings; with facsims. of 7 title pages.

10.100 The 13 (incl. illustrated t.p.) hand-colored prints, ca. 14 x 23 cm. each, are made from blocks averaging ca. 17.3 x 24 cm., perhaps those made by the artist for the original edition printed ca. 1792. Cf. Palau y Dulcet.

Maps

10.101 Map inside of back cover.

10.102 Col. maps inside folded covers.

10.103 Folded col. map on p. [3] of cover.

10.104 Three folded maps tipped in.

10.105 One col. map inserted.

10.106 One folded col. map inserted at end.

10.107 Fold. col. map inserted at end of v. 1.

10.108 Folded col. map inserted.

10.109 Map on folded leaf inserted.

10.110 Map on folded leaf in pocket.

10.111 Map 180 (3 plates) inserted.
10.112 Nine maps in pocket.
10.113 Three folded maps in pocket.
10.114 Six maps on 3 folded leaves in pocket.
10.115 Eight maps in pocket of v. 1.
10.116 Three folded leaves (1 map) in pocket.
10.117 Folded col. map in pocket; col. map on lining papers.

Engravings

10.118 Engraved throughout.
10.119 The t.p. is engraved.
10.120 Added engraved, col. t.p.
10.121 Engraved title pages.
10.122 Engraved t.p. and dedication leaf.
10.123 The engraved illustrations are hand-colored.
10.124 Prelim. p. [1] blank; p. [2] is added illustrated t.p., engraved.

Lining Papers

10.125 Map on lining papers.
10.126 Col. maps on lining papers.
10.127 Two maps on lining papers.
10.128 Col. ill. on lining papers.
10.129 Some ill. on lining papers.
10.130 Ports on lining papers.
10.131 Text on lining papers.
10.132 Lining papers have facsims. of the first and last pages of the author's teaching copy of Joyce's Ulysses.
10.133 Geneal. table and maps on lining papers.

Inserts

10.134 Annex containing abridged introd. and captions in English, French, German, Russian, and Spanish (61 p.) inserted.
10.135 Autographs on 3 leaves inserted.
10.136 "Forms package" inserted.
10.137 Four numbered pages inserted before p. 3.
10.138 "Kartenbeiheft zu Die deutsche Staatsangehörigkeit" (8 p.) inserted in pocket.
10.139 "Price list" (3 p.) inserted.
10.140 French and Greek text of Hebrews ([2] folded leaves) inserted.
10.141 "The text page planned for the Vulgate Bible (reduced)": 1 sheet, folded and pasted inside lower cover.
10.142 Publisher's slip describing cover art by Philip Warner laid in.

Inserts—Illustrations

10.143 Folded plan inserted.
10.144 Four charts on folded leaves in pocket.

10.145   Two folded charts inserted in v. 1.
10.146   Seven geneal. charts on folded leaves in front and back pockets.
10.147   "Time line" chart : 1 fold. leaf inserted.
10.148   Two diagrams inserted.
10.149   Four tables on folded leaves inserted at end.
10.150   One folded leaf of tables inserted.
10.151   Genealogical table (folded leaf) inserted in pocket.
10.152   Four folded geneal. tables inserted.
10.153   Pages [3]-[32] on folded leaves.

Chapter 3 (Cartographic Materials)

AACR2 RULE

3.7B10 Physical Description [AACR2 Rev.]

Make notes on important physical details that are not included in the physical description area, especially if these affect the use of the item.

Photoreproduction

If the item is a photoreproduction, give the method of reproduction if it is likely to affect the use of the item (e.g., when it is a blueline print).

RELATED AACR2 RULE

3.5B2 Extent of Item (Including Specific Material Designation) [AACR2 Rev.]

If there is more than one map, etc., on one or more sheets, specify the number of maps, etc., and the number of sheets. . . .

If the maps, etc., are printed in two or more segments designed to fit together to form one or more maps, etc., give the number of complete maps, etc., and:

a) the number of segments if all the segments are on a single sheet. . . .

b) the number of sheets if the segments are on separate sheets. . . .

Optionally, omit the specification of the number of sheets or segments from the specific material designation and, if desired, give such information in a note (see 3.7B10). . . .[emphasis added]

If an item consists of a number of sheets each of which is a complete map, etc., treat it as a collection and describe it as instructed in 3.5B1.

LIBRARY OF CONGRESS POLICY

None issued.

RELATED LIBRARY OF CONGRESS POLICY

None issued.

AACR2 TEXT EXAMPLES REVISED TO REFLECT LIBRARY OF CONGRESS POLICY

None required.

HISTORICAL BACKGROUND

AACR1 Rule 212E3 provided for notes dealing with the physical description. This rule was slightly more detailed than its AACR2 successor in that it called for notes on "imperfections and peculiarities" of the copy. It indicated these notes should be made "if they are likely to help in identification or in determining suitability for use." These "imperfections and peculiarities" would be recorded as a note under AACR2 Rule 3.7B20.

Unlike AACR2, AACR1 and previous codes did not provide note rules for cartographic reproductions.

NOTE EXAMPLES

10.154 Accompanied by a pin to hold the globe when opened.
10.155 Annotated with pencil and black ink.
10.156 Blue line print.
10.157 Braille with printed captions.
10.158 Composite remote sensing image of Michocán on lining papers.
10.159 Cut and mounted in 8 sections.
10.160 Each vol. has folded map in pocket.
10.161 Folded as pocket atlas 22 x 15 cm.
10.162 Geographic coverage complete in 8 sheets.
10.163 +Hand colored.
10.164 Ill. on verso.
10.165 Includes col. ill. of national flags in margins and ill.
10.166 Includes col. transparent overlays.
10.167 Includes 2 col. maps on 1 folded plate attached to p. 3 of covers: Majorca, scale 1:200,000 (48 x 61 cm.) and Palma, scale 1:10,000 (39 x 48 cm.).
10.168 Includes 3 graphs.
10.169 +Issued in clear plastic jacket with attached marker flap.
10.170 Issued in container.
10.171 Issued in folder.
10.172 +Issued in wooden box.
10.173 Map plates numbered 32 to 632.

10.174   +Mounted in a three-legged mahogany stand 46 cm. high with magnetic compass. Four wooden arms support a wooden zodiacal circle
and a brass meridian ring.

10.175   Pen-and-ink and watercolor.

10.176   +Printed on cloth, over an umbrella-like frame with ring at upper end
of axis for hanging.

10.177   Proof copy.

10.178   The regional cross sections are on 7 folded leaves in pocket.

10.179   Thirteen plates in portfolio bound into volume.

10.180   "Transparencies: 5 base maps, 19 overlays, 48 paper masters."

10.181   "Volume I will be followed by other volumes as time permits"—Verso
t.p.

Chapter 4 (Manuscripts)

AACR2 RULE

4.7B10 Physical Description [AACR2 Rev.]

Make notes on important physical details that are not given elsewhere in the description.

RELATED AACR2 RULE

**4.7B23 Ancient, Medieval, and Renaissance Manuscripts
[AACR2 Rev.; formerly AACR2 Rule 4.7B22]**

. . .

Style of Writing

Give the script used in a manuscript or the predominant script in
a collection. . . .

Illustrative Matter

Give ornamentation, rubrication, illumination, etc., and important
details of other illustrative matter. . . .

Collation

Give the number of gatherings with mention of blank, damaged, or
missing leaves, and any earlier foliation. . . .

Other Physical Details

Give details of owner's annotations, the binding, and any other
important physical details. . . .

LIBRARY OF CONGRESS POLICY

None issued. APPM, however, expands on the AACR2 text.

Physical Description/Condition

Give physical details not given elsewhere in the description that are considered important, including information on the physical condition of the material if it is damaged or fragile, and its legibility. [APPM 4.7B14]

RELATED LIBRARY OF CONGRESS POLICY

None issued.

AACR2 TEXT EXAMPLES REVISED TO REFLECT LIBRARY OF CONGRESS POLICY

None required.

HISTORICAL BACKGROUND

AACR1 did not have a general rule equivalent to AACR2 Rule 4.7B10 for notes dealing with the physical description of a manuscript, although several rules addressed the topic of physical description.

AACR1 Rule 207B5 provided for the use of a note to mention an item in a collection that required "particular" physical description. No further guidelines for the creation of this note were given.

AACR1 Rule 204C provided for a note to record any affixed, impressed, or pendant seals on legal papers.

AACR1 Rule 201B3 was the most comprehensive AACR1 rule for notes for the physical description of manuscripts. This rule is virtually identical to the related AACR2 Rev. Rule 4.7B23 (formerly AACR2 Rule 4.7B22) that deals with notes for ancient, medieval, and Renaissance manuscripts.

NOTE EXAMPLES

Although not stated in the rule, the following formalized constructs are implied by the text:

Signatures: [gathering information]
[Form of ms.] begins (on [location of incipit]): Incipit.

10.182 *Affixed by a blue seal from the Navy Department.
10.183 *Affixed by an official seal with a blue ribbon (in poor condition).
10.184 *Department of Justice seal affixed to the lower left side.
10.185 *Black and white portrait of Richard M. Nixon, 37th Pres. of U.S., on left side. Cancellation mark stating inauguration day. 6 cent postage stamp in upper right corner.

10.186   *Cloth yellowed and stained.
10.187   *Copies not exactly page by page duplicates.
10.188   *Embossed ship in upper left corner.
10.189   In right margin of p. [1]: 25825.
10.190   Ink, with annotations in red and blue pencil.
10.191   *Letter torn in middle fold.
10.192   *Letterhead: The White House, Washington.
10.193   *Letterhead in black type: Herbert Hoover.
10.194   *Letterhead on Wells' note: St. James's Court.
10.195   Measures 84-100 without music, numbered 1-17.
10.196   *Mounted on a mat (39 cm.); the ms. leaf itself measures 31 cm.
10.197   On blue-ruled paper; bound in front of several blank unruled leaves.
10.198   *On stationery of the New York Herald Tribune.
10.199   Pages [1] and [34] are blank.
10.200   *Paper watermarked: Charta Scriptorum Tho. S. & Co. London (?).
10.201   *Personalized letterhead.
10.202   *Printed form completed ms.
10.203   *Printed form with ms. inserts, signed.
10.204   Red and black guide letters at outer margins. Four leaves blank. In collective volume with spine label: Theatrical portraits — British portraits — M.S.S.
10.205   *Rubricated.
10.206   *Standard form for official letters. This was designated to the President of Paraguay.
10.207   *Water colors, pen and ink sketches, pencil and ink sketches bound in two loose leaf binders.

Chapter 5 (Music)

AACR2 RULE

5.7B10 Duration of Performance and Physical Description [AACR2 Rev.]

Duration

Give the duration of performance if it is stated in the item. Give the duration in English and in abbreviated form. . . .

General Physical Description

Make notes on important physical details that are not included in the physical description area.

RELATED AACR2 RULE

None.

LIBRARY OF CONGRESS POLICY

Duration

> In a statement of duration in the note area, separate the digits representing hours, minutes, and seconds by colons. If a duration is expressed in seconds only, precede it by a colon. Precede a statement of duration in the note area by "ca." only if the statement is given on the item in terms of an approximation. [MCB v. 13, no. 8]

The Library of Congress will continue to use the abbreviations "hr.," "min.," and "sec." to state the duration in the Physical Description Area rather than separate the time elements with colons.

RELATED LIBRARY OF CONGRESS POLICY

None issued.

AACR2 TEXT EXAMPLES REVISED TO REFLECT LIBRARY OF CONGRESS POLICY

1st Example

AACR2 TEXT
Duration: 18 min.

AACR2 TEXT REVISED
Duration: 18:00

2nd Example

AACR2 TEXT
Duration: about 1 hr., 10 min.

AACR2 TEXT REVISED
Duration: ca. 1:10:00

HISTORICAL BACKGROUND

AACR1 Rule 248E is essentially the same as AACR2 Rule 5.7B10 for duration of performance notes.

AACR1 and previous codes had no rule equivalent to AACR2 Rule 5.7B10 for recording information on the physical description of music. However, the physical description note provisions for separately published monographs in these earlier codes could be used for music. (See *Historical Background* under Rule 2.7B10.)

267

NOTE EXAMPLES

10.208 Duration: 6:00.

10.209 Duration: 1:00:00.

10.210 Duration: ca. 16:00.

10.211 Durations: ca. 6:00; ca. 6:00.

10.212 Duration: ca. 13:00-15:00.

10.213 Duration: ca. 29:00 (book 1); ca. 28:00 (book 2).

10.214 Duration: 10:00-19:00 (depending on performance method selected).

10.215 Duration: at least 10:00.

10.216 Duration of the 2nd excerpt: 1:20 without repeats.

10.217 Reproduced from ms.

10.218 Reproduced from arranger's ms.

10.219 Reproduced from holograph.

10.220 Reproduced from Davies holograph.

10.221 Part in score format.

10.222 Part for solo voices in score format.

10.223 Part for 2 violins in score format; includes part for violoncello.

10.224 Parts in score format; some orchestral cues included.

10.225 Part in score format; simple and embellished versions of violin part on two staves.

10.226 Violin parts in score format, violoncello/double bass/bassoon part in triplicate.

10.227 Bound at top, 5 pages in each group split into 4 parts of 2 measures each to allow for melodic permutations.

10.228 Continuo figures not printed in score.

10.229 Each page contains 6 p. of the full-sized vocal score.

10.230 Each symphony also paged separately.

10.231 Individual vocal parts can be inserted behind acc. to provide score format.

10.232 Issued in case.

10.233 Original version is superimposed in smaller notes below the piano orchestral score.

10.234 Part printed back-to-back for B♭ clarinet and A clarinet.

10.235 Parts for secondo and primo on facing pages.

10.236 Printed on double leaves.

10.237 The score, containing 4 miniature-score pages per page, is also numbered 3-81.

10.238 Summary in English and French tipped in at end.

Chapter 6 (Sound Recordings)

AACR2 RULE

6.7B10 Physical Description [AACR2 Rev.]

The new compact disc sound recording format necessitated a change to the bibliographic description rules in the original Chapter 6 as well as the addition of several examples.

Make notes on important physical details that are not included in the physical description area, especially if these affect the use of the item.

Standard Details

Do not give any physical details that are standard to the item being described (e.g., assume that all analog discs are electrically recorded, laterally cut, and designed for playing from the outside inward)....

Duration

Give the duration of each part contained in an item without a collective title and described as a unit (see 6.1G2 and 6.1G3; see also 6.7B18).

RELATED AACR2 RULE

None.

LIBRARY OF CONGRESS POLICY

Durations for Collections

If the individual works in a collection are identified in the title and statement of responsibility area, list the durations of the works in a note. If the individual works are listed in a contents note (6.7B18), give their durations there.

When recording individual durations in the note area, give them as they appear on the item (e.g., in minutes and seconds if so stated).

This refers only to the time elements. For proper formatting of durations notes see *Duration Format* below.

If only the durations of the parts of a work are stated (e.g., the movements of a sonata), if desired, add the stated durations together and record the total for the work in minutes, rounding up to the next minute.

Precede a statement of duration by "ca." only if the statement is given on the item in terms of an approximation. Do not add "ca." to a duration arrived at by adding partial durations or by rounding off seconds.

If the duration of a work is not stated on the item or if the durations of some but not all of the parts are stated, do not give a statement of duration for that work.

Do not approximate durations from the number of sides of a disc, type of cassette, etc. [CSB 13]

Duration Format

In a statement of duration in the note area, separate the digits representing hours, minutes, and seconds by colons. If a duration is expressed in seconds only, precede it by a colon. [MCB v. 13, no. 8]

Containers

Give a note on the presence of container(s) only when the number of containers is not clear from the rest of the description. [MCB v.12, no. 3]

RELATED LIBRARY OF CONGRESS POLICY

6.7B18 Contents

For the forms of durations recorded in a formal contents note, the Library of Congress will apply the same formatting decision as [indicated in the Library of Congress policy stated] above. [emphasis added] [MCB v. 13, no. 8]

6.5B1 Physical Description for Multipart Items

For multipart items, give only the number of physical units (e.g., discs) in the physical description area.

If the number of containers or discographic units (often called "volumes") differs from the number of physical units, give this information in notes. [emphasis added] [MCB v. 14, no. 12]

AACR2 TEXT EXAMPLES REVISED TO REFLECT LIBRARY OF CONGRESS POLICY

13th Example in AACR2 Rev. (10th example in AACR2)

AACR2 TEXT
Durations: 17 min. ; 23 min. ; 9 min.

AACR2 TEXT REV.
Durations: 17:00 ; 23:00 ; 9:00.

HISTORICAL BACKGROUND

AACR1 Rev. Rule 252F8 provided for notes on duration "if stated on the work or easily ascertainable." AACR2 does not require the duration to be stated on the item; however, the Library of Congress Rule Interpretation does. The AACR2 rule clearly delineates when a duration note should be made, while the AACR1 Rev. rule did not provide a similar explanation.

AACR1 Rev. Rules 252F10a-252F10d are essentially the same as the first paragraph of AACR2 Rule 6.7B10. AACR1 defined the term *container* to include "sleeves, slip cases, albums, boxes, etc." This definition is not provided in AACR2.

AACR1 Rev. Rule 252F10a stated that "any container holding only one disc was to be ignored." While not specifically stated in AACR2, this practice is still followed by the Library of Congress. This rule also provided for notes on groove characteristics. AACR2 has moved this information into the Physical Description Area (see AACR2 Rule 6.5C4).

AACR1 Rev. Rule 252F10b provided for notes on the physical characteristics of cylinders. AACR2 does not specifically provide for a note on this type of recording, although notes concerning this sound recording can still be made under the general instructions of the AACR2 rule.

AACR1 Rev. Rule 252F10c provided guidelines for notes on rolls including the type of mechanical instruments used for reproduction and their limitations. AACR2 does not provide similar guidelines, although these notes can be made under AACR2 and text examples in AACR2 illustrate their continued use.

AACR1 Rev. Rule 252F10d provided guidelines for the provision of physical description notes dealing with tapes. These notes included information on the material of the tape (if other than plastic), container information, and details that determine playback equipment. AACR2 does not provide similar guidelines, although these notes can still be made. Examples in the AACR2 text illustrate their use.

NOTE EXAMPLES

Durations

Note examples that do not use the 0:00:00 format are all spoken word sound recordings. Music sound recordings now all conform to the 0:00:00 format.

10.239   Duration: 1:49:00.
10.240   Durations: 23:15; 18:55.
10.241   Durations: 28:00; 6:24; 7:27; 7:42; 10:17.
10.242   Durations: ca. 19:00 each.
10.243   Duration: 23:00 (1st work).
10.244   Durations: 25:05 (1st-3rd works); 28:49 (4th-6th works).
10.245   Durations: 8 min., 30 sec. each segment.
10.246   Durations: 29 min. per program.
10.247   Durations: 15 min. each.
10.248   Durations on labels.
10.249   Durations on container.
10.250   Detailed contents and durations printed on container.

Reading Specifications

10.251   "Ambisonic UHJ stereo compatible."
10.252   *Analog recording.
10.253   "Artphone transcription system 2-channel re-recording from original monaural source."—Label.
10.254   Automatic sequence.

10.255 Compact disk.
10.256 Compact disks; in 2 containers.
10.257 Digital recording.
10.258 Digital recording; automatic sequence.
10.259 Digital recording (3rd work analog).
10.260 *Digitally processed.
10.261 "Direkt to Disk records, binaural."
10.262 "Disc-mastered at 1/2 speed."
10.263 Electronically reprocessed to simulate stereo.
10.264 "Encoded from surround sound master tapes and conforms to the BBC/ NRDC UHJ specifications"—Container.
10.265 Half speed mastered.
10.266 Half-speed remastering of the original recording.
10.267 In part mono.
10.268 In part stereo.
10.269 Manual sequence.
10.270 "Mastered from the original tape produced at the Center for Music Experiment, University of California at San Diego on March 28, 1975."
10.271 "Multiple microphone recording."
10.272 "Newly retransferred on 2 LPs"—Container.
10.273 Recordings in chronological order; re-processed for stereo effect.
10.274 "Side one: mono.; side two: stereo."—Container.
10.275 *"Reprocessed with high fidelity equipment."
10.276 "Sony systems digital recording."
10.277 "Stereo/quadraphonic."—Container.

Container

10.278 In container; manual sequence.
10.279 In container (19 cm.).
10.280 In 5 containers.
10.281 In loose-leaf binder (29 cm.).
10.282 Set in loose-leaf binder with script (29 cm.).

Chapter 7 (Motion Pictures and Videorecordings)

AACR2 RULE

7.7B10 Physical Description [AACR2 Rev.]

Make the following notes on the physical description when appropriate and if this level of detail is desired:

a) *Sound Characteristics*

Give any special characteristics of the sound component of a motion picture or videorecording (e.g., optical or magnetic, whether the sound track is physically integrated with the film or the sound is separate on a synchronized recording). . . .

b) *Length of Film or Tape*

Give the length in feet of a motion picture (from first frame to last) or videotape (from first programme signal to last). . . .

c) *Colour*

Give the process or colour recording system of a motion picture or videorecording, or any other details of the colour. . . .

d) *Form of Print*

Give the form of print of a film (e.g., *negative, positive, reversal, reversal internegative, internegative, interpositive, colour separation, duplicate, fine grain duplicating positive, fine grain duplicating negative*).

For master material held in checkerboard cutting form, state if A, B, C, etc., roll.

e) *Film Base*

Give the film base (i.e., *nitrate, acetate,* or *polyester*).

f) *Videorecording System*

Give the system(s) used for a videorecording. . . .

For videotape, give the number of lines and fields, followed by the modulation frequency (e.g., *high band, low band*) . . .

g) *Generation of Copy*

For videotapes, give the generation of the copy and either *master copy* or *show copy.* . . .

h) *Special Projection Requirements*

Give special projection requirements not given in the physical description area (see 7.5C2). . . .

j) *Videodiscs: Duration and Number of Frames*

Give the duration of the moving images and the number of frames of still images for videodiscs that contain both.

k) *Other [formerly AACR2 Rule 7.7B10j]*

Give any other physical details that are important to the use or storage of the motion picture or videorecording.

RELATED AACR2 RULE

7.5 Extent of Item (Including Specific Material Designation) [AACR2 Rev.]

7.5B1 Record the number of physical units of a motion picture or videorecording by giving the number of parts in arabic numerals and one of the following terms as appropriate:

> film cartridge
> film cassette
> film loop
> film reel
> videocartridge
> videocassette
> videodisc
> videoreel

... If none of these terms is appropriate, give the specific name of the item as concisely as possible.

Optionally, if general material designations are used (see 1.1C1), and the general material designation indicates that the item is a motion picture or videorecording, omit *film* or *video* from the specific material designation. ...

Give a trade name or other similar specification in a note (see 7.7B10). [emphasis added]

Videodiscs Consisting of Both Moving Images and Still Images
Due to its length this rule has been abridged to include only the part related to the use of notes.

7.5B2 [AACR2 Rev.] If the playing time is stated on the item, give it as stated. *Optionally,* whether the playing time is stated on the item or not, give in a note the number of frames of still images and the duration of the moving images (see 7.7B10j). [emphasis added]

LIBRARY OF CONGRESS POLICY

None issued. For archival moving image materials, the Library of Congress supplements AACR2 Chapter 7 with the guidelines in *Archival Moving Image Materials* by White-Hensen.

RELATED LIBRARY OF CONGRESS POLICY

None issued.

AACR2 TEXT EXAMPLES REVISED TO REFLECT LIBRARY OF CONGRESS POLICY

None required.

HISTORICAL BACKGROUND

AACR1 Rev. Rules 228A1 and 228O recommended the use of notes to record specifications that could not be stated succinctly in the physical description area.

AACR1 Rev. Rule 229.2D called for the use of a note to record necessary physical features not recorded previously in the description. This rule also provided for a note about special equipment required for projection. This latter provision is equivalent to AACR2 Rule 7.7B10h.

Overall, the various elements of the AACR2 rule greatly expand on the note provisions of AACR1 Rev. by more clearly delineating the types of physical characteristics to be noted. The AACR2 rule, however, lacks the general provisions of the previous rules.

NOTE EXAMPLES

10.283 U-matic.
10.284 *VHS.
10.285 *Sound in stereo.
10.286 *Technicolor.
10.287 *Uses sepia tones.
10.288 With captions.
10.289 Without narration.
10.290 *The first half of the film is b&w.

Chapter 8 (Graphic Materials)

AACR2 RULE

8.7B10 Physical Description [AACR2 Rev.]
Make notes on important physical details that are not included in the physical description area, especially if these affect the use of the item.

RELATED AACR2 RULE

8.5D4 Art Originals, Art Prints, Art Reproductions, and Transparencies [AACR2 Rev.]
Give the height × width of the item, excluding any frame or mount (see also 8.7B10).

Although not explicitly stated in the rule or the related rule, details about frames and mounts could be given in a note.

LIBRARY OF CONGRESS POLICY

None issued. For original items and historical collections, the Library of Congress supplements AACR2 Chapter 8 with the guidelines in *Graphic Materials* by Betz.

RELATED LIBRARY OF CONGRESS POLICY

None issued.

AACR2 TEXT EXAMPLES REVISED TO REFLECT LIBRARY OF CONGRESS POLICY

None required.

HISTORICAL BACKGROUND

AACR1 Rev. Rule 228A1 recommended the use of notes to record specifications that could not be stated succinctly in the physical description area. This is generally equivalent to the AACR2 rule.

AACR1 Rev. Rule 229.2D called for the use of a note to record necessary physical features not recorded previously in the description. This rule also provided for a note about special equipment required for projection. The first element of this rule is similar to the AACR2 rule, but the equipment provision is not stated in AACR2.

In AACR1 Chapter 15, AACR1 Rule 272C3a provided for the use of a note to show "peculiarities and irregularities." These were defined as:

imperfections
size of edition
copy number
artist's signature
remarque
state
restrike
paper, watermark, etc.
scale (for architectural drawing)

The AACR2 rule does not specifically itemize these cases, although such notes could be made under the more general provisions of this rule.

AACR1 Rule 272C3b provided for a note to record the base material if it was unusual for the medium, necessary to distinguish between two works, or a significant texture, color, or weight. Again, AACR2 does not specifically address any of these points.

In general, Chapter 15 of AACR1 provided much greater detail for the use of notes for pictures and other two-dimensional representations than is found in AACR2. The *Graphic Materials* manual amplifies AACR2 by including many of the elements provided in the earlier code.

NOTE EXAMPLES

Projection Graphic Materials
10.291   With captions.
10.292   Issued as 4 programs.

10.293   Issued in 2 parts.

10.294   Issued in loose-leaf notebook.

10.295   In container (26 x 26 x 7 cm.).

10.296   In 4 binders (18 cm.).

10.297   In 3 slidebooks.

10.298   In 2 pts.

10.299   Paper mounts.

Nonprojection Graphic Materials

10.300   *Frame: black and gold wood.

10.301   In portfolio (62 cm.).

10.302   The art prints are in mounts with mat openings; size of the mounts: 60 x 45 cm.

10.303   Issued in a case, with date: 1981.

10.304   *Issued in portfolio. The prints are mounted in 20 folders.

10.305   Issued unbound in folder.

10.306   Printed leaf and original prints issued loose in cover.

10.307   Portfolio contains 10 art prints and 2 sheets with text (t.p. and colophon).

10.308   Portfolio contains t.p. (pasted on inside back), [12] leaves of col. ill., and text booklet: Das Russische Ballett / von Pawel Barchan ([8] p. : ill. (some col.) ; 29 cm.).

10.309   Each plate accompanied by guard sheet with descriptive letterpress.

10.310   *Each set consists of 4 study cards, 16 activity cards, and a teacher notes manual.

10.311   2 prints : engraving ; on sheet 53 x 38 cm.

10.312   Vol. 1 is an untitled slipcase containing 48 leaves in 22 sections corresponding with the engraved t.p. and 21 numbered plates of Blake's publication. Each section contains reproductions of an uncolored proof of an individual engraving with other states of the engraving and related sketches.

Vol. 2 contains reproductions of the New Zealand set of watercolors (previously reproduced, with explanation, in: Illustrations of the Book of Job / William Blake. New York : Pierpont Morgan Library, 1935). Vol. 3 contains reproductions of colored proofs of the engravings.

10.313   Without visible plate mark.

10.314   *All numbered in the image.

10.315   *Bad tear in upper right corner.

10.316   *Blind stamp: Mushroom (artist's mark).

10.317   *Blind stamps: Artist's monogram; tamarind tree.

10.318   *Contemporary leather covered carte-de-visite album, heavily embossed; metal clasp missing.

10.319   *Extensive foxing on original mount.

10.320   *False biting detectable.

10.321   *Four photoprints evidently torn out of the album before acquisition.

10.322   *Full leather case, hinged.

10.323 *Hand coloring done in the 20th century.
10.324 *Image trimmed to or within plate mark at bottom.
10.325 *Images badly faded.
10.326 *Impression is untrimmed proof, with color registration marks in margins, and is cut to within color in upper margin. Label on verso states that the work is "painted [i.e. printed] in 19 [i.e. 9] colors."
10.327 *Ink stamp of publisher on recto.
10.328 *Modern photoprint from original photonegative made 1915.
10.329 *On each image there is a surface abrasion, lower right, on base of statue's pedestal, as though printing (?) had been obliterated on purpose.
10.330 *Photographer's hallmark embossed on separate piece of board mounted on lower right on mount.
10.331 *Photographer's stamp on verso.
10.332 *Plate mark indistinguishable.
10.333 *Print dismounted, tear repaired, and print remounted, 1979 May 13. S. Jones.
10.334 *Printed in black and brown.
10.335 *Printed in black, green, red, brown, gray, dark gray, ochre, dark brown, and yellow.
10.336 *Sheet trimmed at or within plate mark on right and left.
10.337 *Watermark: Fleur-de-lis.
10.338 *Signed on plate, lower right edge, and initialed in pencil, on right, below platemark.
10.339 *Signed on stone, and in pencil by the artist: signed in pencil by the printer with the note "last pull BB."
10.340 *Signed with the artist's pseudonym.
10.341 *Signed and dated in pencil. Inscription: to my friend Munakata.

Chapter 9 (Computer Files)

AACR2 RULE

9.7B10 Physical Description [AACR2 Rev.]

Make notes on important physical details that are not included in the physical description area, especially if these affect the use of the item.

Remote Access

If the file is available only by remote access, give physical details (e.g., colour, sound) if they are readily available and considered important.

RELATED AACR2 RULE

9.5 Footnote 3   Physical Description Area [AACR2 Rev.]

Do not give a physical description for a computer file that is available only by remote access. See 9.7B1c and 9.7B10.

LIBRARY OF CONGRESS POLICY

None issued for AACR2 Rev. Ch. 9.

RELATED LIBRARY OF CONGRESS POLICY

None issued for AACR2 Rev. Ch. 9.

AACR2 TEXT EXAMPLES REVISED TO REFLECT LIBRARY OF CONGRESS POLICY

None required for AACR2 Rev. Ch. 9.

HISTORICAL BACKGROUND

Computer files were not covered by AACR1 or previous codes. The original AACR2 Chapter 9 covered both the file description and the physical description of the computer file. This included information on the number of records or statements as well as the number of physical entities. This information is now recorded under AACR2 Rule 9.7B8 in AACR2 Rev. Ch. 9.

NOTE EXAMPLES

10.342 *Second disk is for data storage.
10.343 *Sound includes words and music.
10.344 *Color used to highlight spelling errors and grammatical errors.
10.345 *In binder.
10.346 *In container 19 x 19 x 4 cm.
10.347 *Housed in case: 27 x 22 cm.

Chapter 10 (Three-Dimensional Artefacts and Realia)

AACR2 RULE

10.7B10 Physical Description [AACR2 Rev.]

Make notes on important physical details that are not included in the physical description area, especially if these affect the use of the item.

Various Pieces

If the physical description includes *various pieces* and a description of the pieces is considered to be useful, give such a description.

279

RELATED AACR2 RULE

10.5B2 Extent of Item [AACR2 Rev.]
Add to the designation, when appropriate, the number and the name(s) of the component pieces. . . . If the pieces cannot be named concisely or if their number cannot be readily ascertained, add *(various pieces)* and *optionally* give the details of the pieces in a note (see 10.7B10). [emphasis added]

The Library of Congress will apply this rule option on a case-by-case basis.

LIBRARY OF CONGRESS POLICY

None issued.

RELATED LIBRARY OF CONGRESS POLICY

None issued.

AACR2 TEXT EXAMPLES REVISED TO REFLECT LIBRARY OF CONGRESS POLICY

None required.

HISTORICAL BACKGROUND

AACR1 Rev. Rule 229.2D provided for a note equivalent to the one called for in the first sentence of AACR2 Rule 10.7B10. The second part of the earlier rule, which provided for information about projection equipment, would not apply to materials covered by AACR2 Chapter 10.

The provision to describe "various pieces" in a note, covered by the second sentence of the AACR2 rule, was addressed by AACR1 Rev. Rule 228F only for games.

AACR1 Rev. Rule 228H provided for recording information on the type of stain on a microscope slide, as well as the type of microscope. AACR2 does not specifically call for recording this information, although it can be given.

AACR1 Rev. Rule 228J provided for recording any physical description information about models that could not be given succinctly in the Physical Description Area. It also called for container information and important additional specifications to be given in a note. AACR2 does not include these instructions.

AACR1 Rev. Rule 228L allowed for the alternative recording of all physical description information about realia in a note rather than in the Physical Description Area. AACR2 does not call for this.

These AACR1 Rev. rules, in general, provided better and more detailed guidelines on the types of notes that could be made than does the current AACR2 rule.

NOTE EXAMPLES

10.348   *Mounted in glass frame and surrounded with preserving fluids.

10.349   *Gold-tone base in open leaf design.

10.350   *Floral and bird-of-paradise design; fluted edge.

10.351   *Oval; decorated; heavily chased.

10.352   *Contains 1 set of rules, 1 teacher's guide, 4 player manuals, 4 shopping cards, 1 pad of play money, 1 deck of chance cards, 1 spinner, 4 crayons, 4 baby carriages.

10.353   *Vermeil wash inside cup.

10.354   *Elaborately tooled and engraved antique chalice.

10.355   *Scalloped edges with embossed decoration at corners.

10.356   *Floral design with beaded edge handles.

10.357   *Coupe shape with gold rim.

10.358   *Contains 1 basic rulebook (2014), 1 dungeon module B2 entitled The keep on the borderlands (9034), 1 4-sided die, 1 6-sided die, 1 8-sided die, 1 10-sided die, 1 12-sided die, 1 20-sided die, and 1 crayon.

10.359   *Exterior view in full color.

10.360   *Design: drawing of Francis Makemie based on a painting by Harry A. Ogden and showing the old Presbyterian Church in Ramelton, Co. Donegal.

10.361   *Format: first day cover cancelled: Ráth Mealtain Lá a Chéad Eisiúna, 2, IV, 1982.

10.362   *Format: Four 24p stamps mounted in gold-tooled green leather folder, inscribed: Francis Makemie, Bunaitheoir an Phreispitéireachais i Meiricéa, Rath Mealsain, 2 Aibréan 1982 = Francis Makemie, Father of American Presbyterianism, Ramelton, 2 April 1982.

10.363   *Contains a bear, a horse and a rabbit with holes for lacing and six laces.

Chapter 12 (Serials)

AACR2 RULE

12.7B10 Physical Description [AACR2 Rev.]

Make notes on important physical details that are not included in the physical description area. . . .

Make notes on variations in the physical details of issues of a serial.

RELATED AACR2 RULE

None.

LIBRARY OF CONGRESS POLICY

None issued.

RELATED LIBRARY OF CONGRESS POLICY

1.5 Physical Description Area

Due to its length, this LC policy statement has been abridged to include only the part related to the use of notes.

> In serials cataloging, avoid the use of a "v in," etc., statement; instead, formulate the statement in terms of bibliographic units only (i.e., "v.") [CSB 17]

AACR2 TEXT EXAMPLES REVISED TO REFLECT LIBRARY OF CONGRESS POLICY

None required.

HISTORICAL BACKGROUND

Although AACR1 and previous codes had no rule equivalent to AACR2 Rule 12.7B10, the physical description note provisions for separately published monographs in these earlier codes could be used for serials. (See *Historical Background* under Rule 2.7B10.)

NOTE EXAMPLES

10.364 Some combined issues.
10.365 Issued in combined form, 1978-79.
10.366 Some vols. issued in combined form.
10.367 Each issue published in 2 vols.
10.368 Each vol. issued in 2 pts.
10.369 Issued in two vols.
10.370 Issues for Dec. 1978 issued in 2 vols.
10.371 Report issued in several vols. a year.
10.372 Some issues published in 2 vols.
10.373 Vols. for <1979-1981> issued in 2 v.
10.374 Vols. for <1981> published in 2 or more tomes.
10.375 Vols. 1 (1967)-3 (1969) in v. 3; vols. 1 (1967)-6 (1972) in v. 6.
10.376 *Vols. covering 1790/91-1942 issued as two separate publications from the House and the Senate under title: Journal; Pennsylvania laws, 1943,

       no. 11 prohibited separate publication of the Journal; Laws, 1963, no.
       1, again permitted separate publication.

10.377   Tables published in 8 or more vols.

10.378   Includes a map.

1.7B11. Accompanying Material

EXTRAPOLATED GENERAL RULE

Location
Make notes on the location of accompanying material if appropriate.

Description
Give details of accompanying material neither mentioned in the physical description area nor given a separate description (see Rule 1.5E).

RELATED AACR2 RULE

1.5E1 Accompanying Material [AACR2 Rev.]

Give details of accompanying material (see Glossary, appendix D) in one of the following ways:

a) make a separate entry
or b) make a multilevel description (see 13.6)
or c) make a note (see 1.7B11) [emphasis added] . . .
or d) give the number of physical units in arabic numerals and the name of the accompanying material (using, when appropriate, a specific material designation) at the end of the physical description. . . .

Optional addition. If method d) is used and if more detail is desired, give the physical description of the accompanying material as instructed in the following chapters.

GENERAL LIBRARY OF CONGRESS POLICY

None issued.

RELATED LIBRARY OF CONGRESS POLICY

1.5E1 Accompanying Material

1) Usually make a separate entry for material that either is not issued at the same time as the main work or shows an important difference in titles or statements of responsibility from those appearing in the main work.
2) Do not apply multilevel description to any item.

Since the Library of Congress will not apply multilevel descriptions, this increases the use of the final portion of the Extrapolated General Rule that calls for making a note on accompanying material.

3) Generally record in a note material of the following types:

    a) The item is clearly of little bibliographic importance.

    b) Although the item might be eligible for method 4, it is best described by a less general terminology than that used under method 4.

    c) The item is best mentioned in a note because the title on the item is more a description than a true title. [emphasis added]

4) Generally record material at the end of the physical description when the item satisfies all the following conditions:

    a) It is issued at the same time and by the same publisher as the main work and essentially is of use only in conjunction with the main work.

    b) It is by the same author as the main work, or makes no mention of an author, or, if it is by a different author, the nature of the work makes unnecessary any note or added entry for this different author.

    c) The title is a general term (e.g., "teacher's manual") or is otherwise dependent on the title of the main work or lacks a title (e.g., "plates"). (When recording material at the end of the physical description, always use a generic term in English.)

Catalog separately all supplements, etc., to serials except for indexes that may be noted (according to 12.7B7; and 12.7B17;) or supplements, etc., that may be noted informally according to method c. *Exception*: Describe in a note supplements that are usable only in conjunction with the main work. [emphasis added]

Apply the optional provision of the rule on a case-by-case basis. [CSB 29]

In MCB v. 12, no. 6, p. 2, a Library of Congress cataloging decision was given that further clarifies AACR2 Rule 1.5E1. It states:

Normally consider options c & d [i.e., 3 & 4 of the Rule Interpretation] to be mutually exclusive with regard to a specific item of accompanying material. If the need is felt to give more information about accompanying material than can be given under option d (including the "optional addition"), describe the material in a note and omit it from the physical description area.] [emphasis added]

FORMAT

None prescribed. Due to the variety of information presented in this note, no one formalized structure is possible.

CHAPTER APPLICATION

This rule is present in all eleven chapters on description. Chapters 4 (Manuscripts), 9, and 12 (Serials) adapt the Extrapolated General Rule to better accommodate the specific material format being described.

EXCEPTIONS AND ADDITIONS

Chapter 4 (Manuscripts) calls for a note to record the details of accompanying material, especially for letters, legal documents, and collections. The rule does not include the instruction to cite the location of accompanying material or the instruction to give this information in a note unless a separate entry or description is provided.

Chapter 12 (Serials) calls for the use of this note to identify accompanying materials that are not a regular feature of a serial. In addition, for accompanying materials that are a regular feature of the serial, this note is used to record their frequency. The rule for citing the location of accompanying material is not present, nor is the directive to give this information in a note unless a separate entry or description is provided.

Chapter 2 (Books, Pamphlets, and Printed Sheets)

AACR2 RULE

2.7B11 Accompanying Material [AACR2 Rev.]

Location
Make notes on the location of accompanying material if appropriate.

Description
Give details of accompanying material neither mentioned in the physical description area nor given a separate description (see 1.5E).

RELATED AACR2 RULE

2.5C7 Illustrative Matter [AACR2 Rev.]
Describe illustrative matter issued in a pocket inside the cover of an item in the physical description. Specify the number of such items and their location in a note (see 2.7B10 and 2.7B11). [emphasis added]

2.5E2 Accompanying Material [AACR2 Rev.]
If the accompanying material is issued in a pocket inside the cover of the publication, give its location in a note (see 2.5C7, 2.7B10, and 2.7B11). [emphasis added]

LIBRARY OF CONGRESS POLICY

None issued.

RELATED LIBRARY OF CONGRESS POLICY

None issued.

AACR2 TEXT EXAMPLES REVISED TO REFLECT LIBRARY OF CONGRESS POLICY

None required.

HISTORICAL BACKGROUND

AACR1 Rev. Rule 155B1 called for the use of a brief informal note to describe minor supplements. Major supplements (AACR1 Rev. Rule 155A) were described using a "dashed-on" entry structure followed by a full description. The dashed-on structure used a long dash to represent the name of the author of the supplements unless that person was also the author of the main work. A second long dash was used to represent the title of the main work. These dashes were followed by the title of the supplement, an author statement when necessary, and the imprint and collation using prescribed punctuation. This note followed all the notes related to the main work but was placed before the tracings.

Notes for accompanying material that were not supplements were not provided in AACR1 Rev. AACR2 has expanded on the AACR1 Rev. rule to cover all types of accompanying material.

These AACR1 Rev. Ch. 6 rules could also be used for works that were not separately published monographs unless the specific rules for the description of the format superseded or excluded its use.

NOTE EXAMPLES

Accompanied By

11.1 Accompanied also by a portfolio (51 cm.) containing an original drawing for the illustrative headpiece to chapter 3, along with 15 original drawings for the 1922 ed. of La boule de gui and an extra suite of the plates to that work on Holland paper.

11.2 Accompanied by Appendix (22 p. : ill. ; 22 × 28 cm.) ; "Directory": p. 19-22.

11.3 Accompanied by "Appendix A — Options for the organization and delivery of services to older people in Alberta (16 p.), 1978."

11.4   Accompanied by "Errata sheet for NUREG/CR-1728, The Feasibility of epidemiologic investigations of the health effects of low-level ionizing radiation" (4 p. ; 28 cm.), separately issued Nov. 28, 1980.

11.5   Accompanied by "Executive summary and addendum" (iv, 26 leaves) by L.B. Hunter.

11.6   Accompanied by membership catalog (39 p.).

11.7   Accompanied by microfiches.

11.8   Accompanied by: "Notes from the editors" (22 p. : ill., ports. ; 19 cm.).

11.9   Accompanied by a sound cassette (60 min.).

11.10   Accompanied by study guide, instructor's manual, text bank, and 48 transparencies.

11.11   Accompanied by table of contents in English (5 leaves).

11.12   Vol. 1 accompanied by portfolio (12 col. maps on fold. leaves).

11.13   Fabric samples available to accompany this manual.

11.14   The print is in a separate wrapper.

Inserts

11.15   Addenda ([4] p.) inserted.

11.16   Annex containing abridged introd. and captions in English, French, German, Russian, and Spanish (60 p.) inserted.

11.17   "Estate plan questionnaire" (36 p.) tipped in.

11.18   "A footnote to the loves of M.A.": [2] p. laid in after p. 68.

11.19   "Forms package" inserted.

11.20   Sound recording (soundsheet) of the Inquisition song inserted.

11.21   Summary in French (19 p.) inserted.

Supplements and Indexes

11.22   Accompanied by Supplement, issued March 1981 (86 p.).

11.23   Kept up to date by annual supplements.

11.24   Kept up to date by cumulative supplements.

11.25   Kept up to date by annual pocket supplements and replacement volumes.

11.26   Kept up to date by cumulative pocket parts and new editions of individual volumes.

11.27   Kept up to date by pocket parts and cumulative supplements.

11.28   Supplement (8 p.) issued in 1964 and inserted.

11.29   Supplemental index(es), 1971-1976, included with each vol.

11.30   "Synopsis of Tyrol" in English, published as supplement (8 p.) and inserted at end.

11.31   "Will be updated annually with a cumulative pocket supplement corresponding to the April 1 revision date of 21 CFR Chapter I"—P. iii.

11.32   "The index will be prepared as a separate and bound section"—p. 883.

In Pocket/Portfolio

11.33   Accompanied by eight response cards (36 p. : ill. ; 21 cm.) in pocket.

11.34   Accompanied by "Guide for counseling employees" (20 p.) and "Employee workbook for choosing a supervisory position" (73 p.), in pocket.

11.35 Ten maps inserted in portfolio.
11.36 Atlas issued in portfolio.
11.37 Answer sheet in pocket.
11.38 Charts in pocket.
11.39 Cassette inserted in pocket.
11.40 The facsim. of the catalog ([4], 12 p. ; 22 cm.) is in a pocket inside lower cover.
11.41 Forty-one worksheets in pocket.
11.42 "Hummel art 11, current price list" (16 p.) in pocket.
11.43 Microfiche in pocket.
11.44 Microfiche inserted in pocket.
11.45 Minicatalog in pocket.
11.46 Plates in box.
11.47 Pocket contains a pamphlet, Far-out fun! (24 p.), a pair of 3-D glasses and a poster.
11.48 Protractors in pocket.
11.49 Sound disc in pocket of v. 1.

Chapter 3 (Cartographic Materials)

AACR2 RULE

3.7B11 Accompanying Material [AACR2 Rev.]

Location

Make notes on the location of accompanying material if appropriate.

Description

Give details of accompanying material neither mentioned in the physical description area nor given a separate description (see 1.5E).

RELATED AACR2 RULE

None.

LIBRARY OF CONGRESS POLICY

None issued.

RELATED LIBRARY OF CONGRESS POLICY

None issued.

AACR2 TEXT EXAMPLES REVISED TO REFLECT LIBRARY OF CONGRESS POLICY

None required.

HISTORICAL BACKGROUND

AACR1 Rule 212E9 provided for a note to record separately issued accompanying texts. Notes to record other types of accompanying material were not provided for in AACR1. AACR2 has expanded the rule to cover all types of accompanying material.

NOTE EXAMPLES

11.50 Index bound in.

11.51 Sound cassette title: Instructions, OSU main campus tactual maps.

11.52 Tape indicator, for use in locating streets, attached to p. [2] of cover.

Accompanied By

11.53 Accompanied by indexes: (55 p. ; 22 cm.).

11.54 Accompanied by: Index to Geographia plan of Bristol (14 p. ; 22 cm.).

11.55 Accompanied by street index (16 p. ; 22 cm.).

11.56 Accompanied by text. (72 p. : maps (some col.) ; 21 cm.).

11.57 Accompanied by text: Carte sismotectonique de la France / présentation et mode d'emploi par J. Vogt ; commentaire des cartouches par P. Godefroy (36 p. : maps ; 27 cm.); Accompanied by: Errata (1 leaf ; 11 x 15 cm.).

11.58 *Accompanied by wrapper entitled: Map of marked auto trails in Nebraska / Standard Oil Co. (Nebraska).

11.59 Accompanied by: Hendersonville, Tennessee map : a supplement to the 1978 Handy Map of metro Nashville and Davidson County, Tenn. 1978. ([16] p. : col. maps ; 19 x 23 cm.).

11.60 Accompanied by: Proposed congressional and legislative redistricting plan, April 1981. 1 folded col. map (44 x 56 cm. folded to 22 x 18 cm.).

Insert

11.61 Inserted: A general map of the roads of Scotland / Taylor and Skinner. 1 folded map (35 x 32 cm.).

11.62 Inserted: Madrid, plano del metro. Scale 1:23,000. 1 col. map (79 x 109 cm. folded to 19 x 14 cm.) On verso: Plano alrededores. Scale 1:75,000.

11.63 Text is inserted within the portfolio as "Tablica 1."

In Pocket

11.64 Course and bearing finder in pocket.

11.65 One folded col. map in jacket pocket (t. 1).

11.66 Three facsimiles of the 1685 maps in pocket of vol. 1.

Chapter 4 (Manuscripts)

AACR2 RULE

4.7B11 Accompanying Material

Give details of materials accompanying a manuscript or manuscript collection, especially (for letters) envelopes, enclosures, and endorsements; (for legal documents) accompanying papers and endorsements; and (for collections) unpublished guides.

This rule does not contain the provision of the Extrapolated General Rule for citing the location of accompanying material. Also, since there is no provision for accompanying material in the Physical Description Area of this chapter, that part of the Extrapolated General Rule calling for a note to record information on accompanying material if it is not present in the Physical Description Area does not apply.

RELATED AACR2 RULE

None.

LIBRARY OF CONGRESS POLICY

None issued. APPM also has no rule directly equivalent to AACR2 Rule 4.7B11.

RELATED LIBRARY OF CONGRESS POLICY

None issued.

AACR2 TEXT EXAMPLES REVISED TO REFLECT
LIBRARY OF CONGRESS POLICY

None required.

HISTORICAL BACKGROUND

AACR1 Chapter 10 (Manuscripts) provided for notes on accompanying material for letters, legal papers, and collections under three separate rules. AACR2 has combined these rules into one rule covering all three formats.

AACR1 Rule 202C (Letters) called for a note to record the presence of an envelope, endorsements, or enclosures, or the absence of an enclosure mentioned in the letter. The AACR2 rule is similar except that it does not specifically provide for mentioning the absence of an enclosure.

AACR1 Rule 204C (Legal Papers) called for the use of a note for accompanying papers and endorsements.

AACR1 Rule 207G (Collections) called for a note to record unpublished guides to a manuscript collection if it was owned by the repository. This information could be recorded in a separate note, or combined with a published descriptions note, if care was taken to distinguish between the two. AACR2, while calling for the note to be made, does not provide any further details.

NOTE EXAMPLES

11.67   Accompanied by a certificate of the authenticity of the ms. in the hand of the composer's grandson, Wilhelm Rust ([1] leaf).

11.68   Accompanied by a concert program of music in the collection given Jan. 14, 1940 at the Young Men's Hebrew Association, New York.

11.69   *Accompanied by a typewritten translation in English of the letter with notes in ink.

11.70   *Accompanied by an engraving of Washington Irving published for the Proprieters of the European Mag. by Sherwood, Jones & Co., London, April 1825. Signed.

11.71   *Accompanied by an envelope addressed to Miss Schneider, Champion Cottage, Champion Hill, London; and by a typewritten description of the contents of the letter.

11.72   *Accompanied by cadenza (1 l., holograph signed).

11.73   *Accompanied by envelope.

11.74   Accompanied by holograph sketch in pencil (62 p.).

11.75   *Accompanied by introduction (1 leaf, typescript) dated January 1980 and signed by A. Grove Day.

11.76   *Accompanied by the typewritten envelope. Postmarked Grand Cent. Annex, N.Y., Dec. 10, 7 a.m. 1937. Two .01 cent postage stamps in upper right corner. Stamped postage due .01 cent with a .01 cent cancelled postage stamp in lower left corner.

11.77   *Accompanied by translation (1 typewritten leaf).

11.78   *Accompanied by typewritten translation of the letters.

11.79   *Autograph, dated 1849, on slip of paper accompanies letter.

11.80   *Clipped signature accompanies letters.

11.81   *Cover letter, dated 19 August 1930, from Cape & Harrison to Faulkner, requesting certain changes to accommodate the printer, accompanies galleys.

11.82   *Includes envelope and calling card with ms. note to Sophie Menter.

11.83   *Letters accompanied by a portrait of Jules Massenet taken from a photograph.

11.84   Note in the composer's hand, extra copies of some lyrics ([6] leaves), and lyrics with changes for the English production ([10] leaves, 2 in the composer's hand, dated Jan. 31, 1951) inserted.

11.85 *Signed check accompanies letters.
11.86 *Transcription and translation by Gerhard Kirchhoff and Diane Kent of the Goethe Institute, Boston enclosed.

Finding Aids

11.87 Card catalog in the library.
11.88 Card index in the repository.
11.89 *Control file with collection.
11.90 *Finding aid in the library; selected items individually cataloged.
11.91 *Finding aid in the repository.
11.92 *Finding aid published by the library: J. Robert Oppenheimer; a register of his papers in the Library of Congress (Washington, 1974).
11.93 *Inventory at repository.
11.94 *Reel list in the library and finding aid and document checklist on reel 1.
11.95 *Register of names enclosed; card file of correspondence arranged alphabetically.
11.96 *Soundex index to families having children 10 years of age or younger available on 143 microfilm reels.
11.97 Unpublished calendar in the repository. Also described in: Catalog of the Manuscript and Archival Collections and Index to the Correspondence of John Torrey / compiled by Sara Lenley [et al.] Boston : G.K. Hall, 1973, p. 232-233.
11.98 Unpublished finding aid in the repository.
11.99 Unpublished finding aid and index in the repository.

Chapter 5 (Music)

AACR2 RULE

5.7B11 Accompanying Material [AACR2 Rev.]

Location

Make notes on the location of accompanying material if appropriate.

Description

Give details of accompanying material neither mentioned in the physical description area nor given a separate description (see 1.5E).

Although not stated in the rule, textual matter such as prefaces, performance instructions, historical notes, etc., are considered to be material accompanying the music and should be described under the provisions of this rule.

RELATED AACR2 RULE

None.

LIBRARY OF CONGRESS POLICY

None issued.

RELATED LIBRARY OF CONGRESS POLICY

None issued.

AACR2 TEXT EXAMPLES REVISED TO REFLECT LIBRARY OF CONGRESS POLICY

None required.

HISTORICAL BACKGROUND

Although AACR1 and previous codes had no rule equivalent to AACR2 Rule 5.7B11, the accompanying materials note provisions for separately published monographs in these earlier codes could be used for music. (See *Historical Background* under Rule 2.7B11.)

NOTE EXAMPLES

11.100 Foreword in Czech by Josef Ceremuga, with Russian translation by Z. Chergrintseva, German translation by Adolph Langer, and English translation by Jana Hanusova (p. [3-6]).

11.101 Pref. in English and German: p. [iii]-xvi.

11.102 Pref. in English, French, German, and Portuguese.

11.103 Prefatory matter also in Hungarian.

11.104 Includes prefatory notes on the quena and on Latin American music, in Spanish, English, French, and German.

11.105 Includes instructions for performance.

11.106 Includes instructions for performance in Dutch, French, and Italian.

11.107 Instructions for performance in German, English, and French (20 p.) laid in.

11.108 Composer's notes and performance suggestions and biographical note: p. [2].

11.109 Includes critical commentary.

11.110 Editorial notes in English and German ([6] p.).

11.111 Notes by Plotr Pozniak in Polish, English and German (p. 4-11); editorial notes in Polish and English (p. 71-77).

Inserts

11.112 Instructions for gong player (1 leaf) laid in.

11.113 "To facilitate turning over, a separate violin 1 part for no. 12 is inserted."

11.114 Map of Concord, Mass., portrait of Thoreau, profile, notes, and transparency laid in instruction book.
11.115 Lyric booklet (32 p. : ill. ; 26 cm.) laid in.
11.116 List of notation symbols and instrumentation (1 leaf ; 46 cm.) laid in.
11.117 Sound disc in pocket.
11.118 Transparencies.
11.119 Includes: Erklärung der Zeichen und symbole (1 leaf ; 30 × 43 cm.).
11.120 Accompanied by Top-kapi Quartett alla turca ; Tangents : für Schlaginstrumente [sound recording] / Siegfried Fink.
11.121 Song sung on the recording by Matthew Sakowsky in Ukrainian and English, with chorus and instrumental ensemble.
11.122 Instructions for dancing given in Ukrainian, with Russian translation, preceding the music arr. for piano.
11.123 Notes by Wendelin Świerczek in Polish, English, and German (p. 5-6); words printed as text with Polish translation by Jakuba Wujka (p. 20); editorial notes in Polish and English (p. 21-22).
11.124 General remarks and words printed as text in Polish with English translations (p. [3-4]).

Chapter 6 (Sound Recordings)

AACR2 RULE

6.7B11 Accompanying Material [AACR2 Rev.]

Location

Make notes on the location of accompanying material if appropriate.

Description

Give details of accompanying material neither mentioned in the physical description area nor given a separate description (see 1.5E).

RELATED AACR2 RULE

None.

LIBRARY OF CONGRESS POLICY

In the second sentence of 6.7B11, the phrase "not mentioned in the physical description area" modifies "accompanying material" not "details." [MCB v. 12, no. 6]

Make notes on accompanying program notes only if they are significant. [MCB v. 15, no. 7]

RELATED LIBRARY OF CONGRESS POLICY

None issued.

AACR2 TEXT EXAMPLES REVISED TO REFLECT LIBRARY OF CONGRESS POLICY

None required.

HISTORICAL BACKGROUND

AACR1 Rev. Rule 252F10e provided for a note to record supplementary visual materials. No additional details were given; however, examples for this rule in that text included program notes. AACR2 has expanded the note to include any type of accompanying material.

NOTE EXAMPLES

On Container

11.125	Program notes on container.
11.126	Identical program notes by Edward J. Smith on each container.
11.127	Program notes by Frederick Youens on container of v. 1.
11.128	Program notes by the composer on container.
11.129	Program notes in English, German, and French on container.
11.130	Program notes by Marcel Marnat in French and German on container.
11.131	Program notes by Joël-Marie Fauquet, translated by Charles Whitfield, on container.
11.132	Program notes by Thomas Kohlhase in German, French, and Italian, and by John Warrack in English on container.
11.133	Latin text with French and English translations and program notes in French and English on container.
11.134	Program notes and texts of the vocal works on container.
11.135	Program notes by Benjamin Folkman and words of the song A frog he went a courting on container.
11.136	Texts include English translations; program and biographical notes by Gerald Fitzgerald on container.
11.137	Texts include English translations for 1st and 3rd works; program and biographical notes on container.
11.138	Texts of the songs on container.
11.139	Texts, with English translations, on container.
11.140	On container: Notes on the composer / Peter Wolf. Notes on the music / Sonya Monosoff. Notes on the instruments / Lawrence Libin.
11.141	Program notes by Michael Steinberg on container with: Mahler's Tenth symphony, the conductor's view / Simon Rattle.
11.142	Program notes by Raymond Bantock (the composer's son) and notes on the conductor and orchestra on container.
11.143	Synopsis in Spanish on container.
11.144	Notes on the recording process and program notes on container.
11.145	Program notes and list of modern editions of works performed on container.

11.146　Personnel listed on container.

11.147　Personnel of the ensembles and program notes by Sy Johnson on container.

11.148　Notes on the organ by Walter Supper, with English and French translations, specifications, and registrations on container.

11.149　Program notes in German, specifications of the organ, and registrations of each work on container.

11.150　Biographical notes on the flutist on container.

11.151　"Furtwängler and Strauss" by Dennis Dobson on container.

11.152　Interview between the pianist and Rawle Dryson and biographical notes on container.

11.153　Notes on the composer's conducting career by Knut Franke in German and English on container.

11.154　Program notes and biographical notes on the performer on container.

11.155　Biographical notes by Eric Rees and original record numbers on container.

11.156　Program notes, principally on the performer, by Irving Kolodin on container.

11.157　Durations and program notes by Dee Baily on container.

Inserts

11.158　Descriptive leaflet in pocket of container.

11.159　Guide laid in container (30 cm.).

11.160　Notes with bibliography in container.

11.161　Booklet containing essays by Harry Halbreich in French, English and German, and libretto, with English and German translations (47 p. : ill.) laid in container.

11.162　Program notes, notes on the organ, and organ specifications (6 p. : ill.) bound in container.

11.163　In container with background essays by J.M. Llorens and others, texts with Spanish translations, melodies, and reproductions of miniatures from the mss. (123 p. : col. ill.) bound in.

11.164　With booklet (14 p.), verse ([7] leaves), and photographs ([7] leaves) inserted in container.

11.165　Transcription with English translation by Luana Pellegrineschi (12 p. ; 30 cm.) bound in container.

11.166　Program notes by Richard Mohr, synopsis, and libretto, with English translation ([15] p.) laid in.

11.167　Program notes in English and Italian, in part by Mario Messinis and Ellen Rosand and libretto in facsim. (Venetia : F. Nicolini, 1673) (32 p. : ill. ; 30 cm.) in container.

11.168　Biography of David Thomson and program notes by the editors of Time-Life Records (56 p. : ill. ; 23 cm.) laid in container.

11.169　Program notes and notes on Bohm's Dresden career, in part by him in German, English, and French laid in each container.

11.170　Personnel, durations, and original record numbers (4 p.) laid in container.

11.171 Program notes in Japanese and notes on the performers and recording process in Japanese and English (4 p. : ill.) inserted in container.
11.172 Program notes by C.E. Crumpacker including original recording dates, matrix and issue no., and durations ([12] p. : ill.) laid in container.
11.173 Program notes by Jack Diether on inner sleeve of container.
11.174 Program notes by Bursen and texts of the songs (8 p.) inserted in container.
11.175 Program notes by Doug Seroff and words of the quartets (10 p. : ill.) bound in container; program of the Jefferson County Quartet Reunion, Oct. 12, 1980 (20 p. : ill.) inserted.
11.176 Translations of the songs (2 p.) inserted in container.
11.177 Words of the songs on inner liner.
11.178 Words of the songs and poster inserted in container.

Chapter 7 (Motion Pictures and Videorecordings)

AACR2 RULE

7.7B11 Accompanying Material [AACR2 Rev.]

Location

Make notes on the location of accompanying material if appropriate.

Description

Give details of accompanying material neither mentioned in the physical description area nor given a separate description (see 1.5E).

RELATED AACR2 RULE

None.

LIBRARY OF CONGRESS POLICY

None issued. For archival moving image materials, the Library of Congress supplements AACR2 Chapter 7 with the guidelines in *Archival Moving Image Materials* by White-Hensen.

RELATED LIBRARY OF CONGRESS POLICY

None issued.

AACR2 TEXT EXAMPLES REVISED TO REFLECT LIBRARY OF CONGRESS POLICY

None required.

HISTORICAL BACKGROUND

AACR1 Rev. Rule 229.2E provided for a note to describe accompanying material not included in the Physical Description Area. It did not mention the use of this note to record the location of the accompanying material as does AACR2.

NOTE EXAMPLES

11.179   Course materials (drill book, reading book, and stop watch) also available.
11.180   Corresponding text available.
11.181   *Credits on container.
11.182   Includes bibliography in teacher's guide.
11.183   Intended to be used with lecture notes, study lessons, and text.
11.184   Intended to be used with study guide and text.
11.185   Intended to be used with workbook and text.
11.186   Teaching kit also available.
11.187   With printed material.

Chapter 8 (Graphic Materials)

AACR2 RULE

8.7B11 Accompanying Material [AACR2 Rev.]

Location
> Make notes on the location of accompanying material if appropriate.

Description
> Give details of accompanying material neither mentioned in the physical description area nor given a separate description (see 1.5E).

RELATED AACR2 RULE

None.

LIBRARY OF CONGRESS POLICY

None issued. For original items and historical collections, the Library of Congress supplements AACR2 Chapter 8 with the guidelines in *Graphic Materials* by Betz.

RELATED LIBRARY OF CONGRESS POLICY

None issued.

AACR2 TEXT EXAMPLES REVISED TO REFLECT LIBRARY OF CONGRESS POLICY

None required.

HISTORICAL BACKGROUND

AACR1 Rev. Rule 229.2E provided for a note to describe accompanying material not included in the Physical Description Area. It did not mention the use of this note to record the location of the accompanying material as does AACR2.

AACR1 Rule 272C4 provided for a note on textual materials accompanying a set of pictures. This rule was included under the heading "Related works" and also covered the provision of notes for related works and material published in a different form. These latter two provisions are covered under different rules in AACR2 (Rules 8.7B7 and 8.7B16, respectively).

NOTE EXAMPLES

Although not specifically mentioned in the rule, or shown as an example in the text, the most frequent use of this note for projected graphic materials is to record the characteristics of the sound accompaniment.

Projection Graphic Materials

11.188 Accompanied by a plexiglass display device.
11.189 Issued also with sound accompaniment on disc.
11.190 Issued also with sound accompaniment on disc, as 16 mm. filmstrip in cartridge, and as slide set.
11.191 Issued also with sound accompaniment on reel and with sound accompaniment in English.
11.192 Issued also with sound accompaniment on reel and in Spanish.
11.193 Sound accompaniment for automatic operation only.
11.194 Sound accompaniment for manual operation only.
11.195 Sound accompaniment compatible for manual and automatic operation.
11.196 Sound accompaniment for manual operation only; reverse side solely for listening.
11.197 Sound cassettes contain panel discussions.
11.198 *Supplementary booklet includes bibliography.
11.199 *Title on manual: Security training program.

Chapter 9 (Computer Files)

AACR2 RULE

9.7B11 Accompanying Material [AACR2 Rev.]
Make notes on the location of accompanying material if appropriate.

Description

Give details of accompanying material neither mentioned in the physical description area nor given a separate description (see 1.5E).

RELATED AACR2 RULE

9.5E2 Accompanying Material [AACR2 Rev.]

If no physical description is given (see footnote 3 at 9.5), give details of any accompanying material in a note (see 9.7B11). [emphasis added]

LIBRARY OF CONGRESS POLICY

None issued for AACR2 Rev. Ch. 9.

RELATED LIBRARY OF CONGRESS POLICY

None issued for AACR2 Rev. Ch. 9.

AACR2 TEXT EXAMPLES REVISED TO REFLECT LIBRARY OF CONGRESS POLICY

None required for AACR2 Rev. Ch. 9.

HISTORICAL BACKGROUND

Computer files were not covered by AACR1 or previous codes. The original AACR2 Chapter 9 indicated that accompanying material not mentioned in the file description area could be recorded in this note. This is similar to the revision of this rule except that the revised rule also indicates that the note would not be made if the accompanying material was described as a separate entry. The original rule also called for recording the ISBN of a codebook in this note.

NOTE EXAMPLES

11.200   *Accompanied by: 1 user's manual (1 v. (looseleaf) : ill. ; 23 cm.), 1 summary card, and 1 utility diskette.

11.201   *Accompanied by spelling checker disk with title: The Word Plus.

11.202   *Accompanying disk contains clip art.

11.203   *Accompanied by: Turbo database toolbox (1 disk, 1 manual); Turbo Gameworks (2 disks, 1 manual); Turbo tutor (1 disk, 1 manual); Turbo editor toolbox (2 disks, 1 manual); Turbo graphix toolbox (1 disk, 1 manual).

11.204   *Concordance documentation available: Chapel Hill : University of North Carolina Dept. of Romance Languages ; Ann Arbor, Mich. : Distributed by University Microfilms International, 1979.

11.205   *Documentation: 1970 Censuses of Population File (A, B, or C) Summary Tape (sample) Technical Document No. ST-4P. Arlington, Va. : Data Use and Access Laboratories (DUALabs), Aug. 1972.

11.206   *Manuals included: New Word user's guide, Getting started with New Word on your IBM personal computer, New Word supplementary notes for New Word version 2, New Word user area listing for IBM personal computers and compatible version 2, and The Word Plus (version 1.2) manual / by Wayne Holder.

11.207   *Primary publication: Two dictionary transcripts and programs for processing them, volume I: the encoding scheme, PARSENT and CO-NIX / by Richard Reichert, John Olney and James Paris. — Santa Monica, Calif. : System Development Corp., [1969?].

11.208   *Referenced publication: Canon of Greek text of works, from Homer to A.D. 200 / Luci Berkowitz. Irvine, Calif. : TLG Publications, 1977.

11.209   *Related reference: United States. Bureau of the Census. 1970 Census User's Guide, Part I and II. For sale by Superintendent of Documents, U.S. Government Printing Office, Washington, D.C. 20402.

11.210   *Text under same title also included.

11.211   *Three sheets of comments on the updated version included.

Chapter 10 (Three-Dimensional Artefacts and Realia)

AACR2 RULE

10.7B11 Accompanying Material [AACR2 Rev.]

Location

Make notes on the location of accompanying material if appropriate.

Description

Give details of accompanying material neither mentioned in the physical description area nor given a separate description (see 1.5E).

RELATED AACR2 RULE

None.

LIBRARY OF CONGRESS POLICY

None issued.

RELATED LIBRARY OF CONGRESS POLICY

None issued.

AACR2 TEXT EXAMPLES REVISED TO REFLECT LIBRARY OF CONGRESS POLICY

None required.

HISTORICAL BACKGROUND

AACR1 Rev. Rule 229.2E provided for a note to describe accompanying material not included in the Physical Description Area. It did not mention the use of this note to record the location of the accompanying material as does AACR2.

NOTE EXAMPLES

11.212   *With booklet entitled: The drug abuse lesson guide.
11.213   *Directions in lid.
11.214   *Directions in cover of box.

Chapter 12 (Serials)

AACR2 RULE

12.7B11 Accompanying Material [AACR2 Rev.]
Make notes on the location of accompanying material if appropriate. Give details of accompanying material neither mentioned in the physical description area nor given a separate description (see 1.5E).

Frequency
Give the frequency of accompanying materials that are a regular feature of the serial.

This rule is adapted to accommodate the continuing nature of serials. Any description of accompanying material, including its frequency of issue, should be given here.

RELATED AACR2 RULE

12.5E1 Accompanying Material [AACR2 Rev.]
Give, as instructed in 1.5E, the details of accompanying material that is intended to be issued regularly. If using 1.5E1d and if the serial is still in progress, give the name of the accompanying material preceded by three spaces. . . .

Make a note on the frequency of accompanying material (see 12.7B11). [emphasis added] If accompanying material is issued irregularly or is issued only once, describe it in a note or ignore it.

LIBRARY OF CONGRESS POLICY

None issued.

RELATED LIBRARY OF CONGRESS POLICY

None issued.

AACR2 TEXT EXAMPLES REVISED TO REFLECT LIBRARY OF CONGRESS POLICY

None required.

HISTORICAL BACKGROUND

Although AACR1 and previous codes had no rule equivalent to AACR2 Rule12.7B11, the accompanying materials note provisions for separately published monographs in these earlier codes could be used for serials. (See *Historical Background* under Rule 2.7B11.)

NOTE EXAMPLES
No examples were located.

1.7B12. Series

EXTRAPOLATED GENERAL RULE

Make notes on series data that cannot be given in the series area.

RELATED AACR2 RULE

1.6B2 Title Proper of Series [AACR2 Rev.]

If different forms of the title of the series (other than parallel titles) appear, choose the title given in the first of the prescribed sources for the series area as the title proper of the series. Give the other form(s) in the note area if of value in identifying the item. [emphasis added]

If the title of the series does not appear in the first of the prescribed sources of information and different forms appear elsewhere in the item, choose the title given in the other prescribed sources in the order of preference for the sources (e.g., if different forms appear in the second and third sources, choose the one appearing in the second source).

1.6J1 More Than One Series Statement [AACR2 Rev.]

The information relating to one series, or series and subseries, constitutes one series statement. If an item belongs to two or more series and/or two or more series and subseries, give separate series statements and enclose each statement in parentheses. Follow the instructions in 1.6A-1.6H in recording each series statement. . . .

If parts of an item belong to a different series and this relationship cannot be stated clearly in the series area, give details of the series in a note (see 1.7B12). [emphasis added]

LIBRARY OF CONGRESS POLICY

When an untraced nonroman script series is recorded in a series statement on a nonromanized bibliographic card, do not give a romanization of the series in a note. [CSB 22]

RELATED LIBRARY OF CONGRESS POLICY

1.6 Series Area

Due to its length, this LC policy statement has been abridged to include only the parts related to the use of notes. Additionally, in policy statements related to the creation of notes, statements referring to LC's series authority record or CIP practices have also been deleted.

Sources of Information
1) Basis for accepting or rejecting as a series. . . .
   a) *Information embedded in text*
      (1) *Preliminaries.*
         Generally, *accept* information embedded within text *in the preliminaries* as a source for the series. In such cases, however, select the series title proper carefully, insuring that extraneous words that the publisher did not intend to be part of the title proper are excluded. . . .
      (2) *Prefatory matter or text proper.*
         Generally, *do not* accept information embedded within *prefatory matter* or the text proper as a source for series. Instead transcribe the information as a quoted note. Follow the quotation by an indication of its source. [emphasis added] *Exception: titles already considered to constitute a series and classified as a collection in LC.* If such information was previously considered to constitute a series *and* that series is classified as a collection in LC, continue to transcribe the information as a series statement, without brackets. In addition, record in a general note the source of the series statement. [emphasis added] . . .
   b) *Series statement appears only on the jacket.*
      If the series has been established or reestablished, i.e., a series authority record exists in the name authority file, proceed under the general guidelines for already established series. Transcribe the series statement in brackets (cf. 1.6A2). In addition, record in a note the source of the series statement. [emphasis added] . . .
   c) *Series statement appears only in a bibliography.*
      Proceed in the same manner as stated above for series appearing only on jackets. [emphasis added] Do not undertake a special search of bibliographies for the sole purpose of discovering such series statements.
   d) *Series statement appears on a label or is stamped on the item.*
      Treat a series appearing on a label or that is stamped on the item in the same manner as if it were stated by printing. In addition, on the bibliographic record state in a note the fact that the series appears only on a label or is stamped on the item. [emphasis added] . . .
   f) *Lecture series.*
      The fact that a named lecture series bears an indication that it has been held more than once is not a sufficient reason to treat the name as a title that can be recorded in a series statement. Instead, treat the name as a series only
      (1) if it appears on the item as a series title, i.e., it is not extracted from another context (e.g., other title information, prefatory matter) *and*

(2) if it has (or is likely to have) data that remain constant from issue to issue (e.g., the same form of name and numbering, the same issuing body).

In case of doubt, do not treat the name as a series.

If rejected as a series, give the name and associated data that appear with the name in a note if it has not already been recorded in the body of the entry. [emphasis added] . . .

g) *Series statement appears only in cataloging data printed in book.*

Generally ignore a series statement that is found only in the cataloging data, foreign or domestic, printed in a book. *Exception*: if the series is classified as a collection in LC, transcribe the series, without brackets. In addition record in a note the source of the series statement: [emphasis added] Series statement from cataloging data on p. 2 of cover. . . .

i) *Selected issues of a periodical published also in hardcover editions.*

Several publishers (e.g., Haworth Press, Pergamon Press) published hardcover editions of *selected* issues of their (softcover) periodicals.

Do not consider such a hardcover edition to constitute an integral part of the periodical, i.e., do not consider it an analyzable issue *of* the periodical. Instead, when preparing the bibliographic record for the hardcover edition, add the pertinent information as a note, not as a series statement. [emphasis added] Do not make an added entry for the periodical. . . .

2) *Phrases that are not considered series titles*

a) *General.*

Distinguish between phrases that are true series and those that are not, with the latter sometimes ignored altogether and sometimes given as a quoted note. [emphasis added] Base the distinction and the consequent action primarily on judgment. If there is no clear judgment that can be made, however, apply the following guidelines:

(1) If the phrase is essentially a statement (or a re-statement) of the name of the body from which the item emanated, reject it as a series. Give the phrase as a note if the name of the emanating body is not given in the publication, etc., area. [emphasis added] (Ignore the phrase if the name of the emanating body is given in the publication, etc., area.) . . .

(2) If the phrase includes a sub-imprint name or the name of a subsidiary, a division, etc., of a publishing firm and is presumed to appear on all items from this arm of the firm, reject it as a series, but quote it as a note if the name is not given in the publication, etc., area. [emphasis added] . . .

(3) If the phrase includes the name of an in-house editor or the name or designation of some other official of the firm,

etc., reject it as a series, but quote it in a note. [emphasis added] . . .

Series Statements and Series Tracings

1) *General*

Although a series statement may include a parallel title (1.6C), other title information (1.6D), or a statement of responsibility (1.6E), the heading for the series will contain only a title proper or a uniform title heading or a name heading/title proper or a name heading/uniform title. . . .

2) *Series Titles Consisting Solely of a Corporate Body Name*

Treat a statement consisting solely of the name of a corporate body and a number as a series statement. Give the corporate name as the title proper. If the series is entered under title, assign a uniform title that consists of the title qualified by the term "(Series)" even if there is no conflict. (Apply these provisions even if the corporate body appears with the number solely as initials.) . . .

However, if such a corporate body is a commercial publisher, either give the statement as a quoted note if the corporate body is not recorded in the publication, etc., area, or give the number alone if the corporate body is recorded in the publication, etc., area. [emphasis added]

3) *Single series statement encompassing several series*

Depending upon the complexity of presentation in the item and grammatical integration of wording of series information encompassing several series, transcribe the information in one of the ways stated below.

a) *As a single series statement.*

If information is presented with no or minimal extraneous wording, transcribe it as a single series statement. If the series are traced, trace each explicitly. . . .

b) *As a quoted note.*

If the information includes extraneous wording grammatically linked or not readily omitted, transcribe it as a quoted note instead. [emphasis added] If the series are traced, trace each explicitly. [CSB 31]

1.6H Subseries

Due to its length, this LC policy statement has been abridged to include only the part related to the use of notes.

Applicability

These guidelines deal with the series area and related series tracings. Therefore, they apply whenever an item meets these conditions:

1) the item has an analyzable title (cf. 13.2);

2) the item also bears at least two titles that it shares with other items; the cataloger judges that the titles are related, one being a larger (usually more comprehensive in scope) title than the others; the other title(s) is (are) then a component of the larger one, i.e., subseries. (See below for separate, unrelated series that appear on an item.)

Note the following aspects:

1) If there is doubt whether one of the group titles is a subseries or a second series, treat it as a second series; this means that each series is recorded in its own series statement (cf. 1.6J1) and each series is established as a separate entity.
2) If one title is a multipart item and the other is a serial, treat each as a separate series.
3) If both titles are multipart items, apply LCRI 25.6A to determine if the two titles are to be treated as one entity or established separately.
4) Treat such phrases as "new series," "second series," "series 77" as part of the series numbering and not as a subseries if the phrase indicates a new designation system (cf. 12.3G); however, if the series is unnumbered, generally treat such a phrase as a subseries.
5) Treat an item with numbering following a designation such as "supplement to [title of a serial]" as a separate series.
6) Do not treat an unnumbered supplement as a series, but give the statement as a quoted note if it is not recorded in the title and statement of responsibility area and make an added entry for the serial itself on the bibliographic record for the analyzable title (cf. 21.28B). [emphasis added] [CSB 38]

FORMAT

None prescribed.

CHAPTER APPLICATION

This rule is present in all chapters for description except Chapter 4 (Manuscripts)

EXCEPTIONS AND ADDITIONS

The wording of this rule is identical in all the chapters in which it appears except for Chapter 12 (Serials). Chapter 12 uses this note to provide details about the numbering within a series when that numbering changes between issues.

Chapter 2 (Books, Pamphlets, and Printed Sheets)

AACR2 RULE

2.7B12 Series [AACR2 Rev.]
Make notes on series data that cannot be given in the series area.

AACR2 Rev. deleted the third example that appeared with the original AACR2 text of this rule. The deleted example provided an identification of the series in which a reprinted work was originally issued. This information would now be recorded under the combined notes relating to an original work rule (AACR2 Rev. Rule 1.7B22).

RELATED AACR2 RULE

None.

LIBRARY OF CONGRESS POLICY

None issued.

RELATED LIBRARY OF CONGRESS POLICY

None issued.

AACR2 TEXT EXAMPLES REVISED TO REFLECT LIBRARY OF CONGRESS POLICY

Although no LC Rule Interpretation has been issued to AACR2 Rule 2.7B12, the LC Rule Interpretation to AACR2 Rule 1.7B12 instructs that no romanization of a series is given in a note for an untraced nonroman script series that is recorded in a series statement on a nonromanized bibliographic record. Thus the first example in the AACR2 text would be incorrect according to LC policy.

HISTORICAL BACKGROUND

The ALA 1908 Rule 166 and the LC 1949 Rule 3.16E termed what is now called the series statement the "series note." This was considered the first note. AACR1 discontinued the use of this terminology and began the use of the term "series statement."

When a second series was associated with a work, the LC 1949 rule and AACR1 Rule 143F recorded the second series in the note area, rather than in what is now termed the Series Area. This note was not placed within parentheses but did use brackets when appropriate. This practice was discontinued with AACR1 Rev. Rule 142F, and the practice of multiple series statements began. This practice is continued in AACR2.

AACR1 Rev. Rule 142A1 and 143D4c provided for the use of a note to record the name of a series mentioned in an edition being reprinted. Although the continued use of such a note was implied in AACR2 by the third example to AACR2 Rule 2.7B12, the revision of the rule negated this.

A footnote to AACR1 Rev. Rule 142A1 addressed the situation of a phrase being used that was difficult to differentiate as a subtitle, a publisher's name, a series statement, or a "publisher's characterization of some or all of his books." The footnote recommended the use of a quoted note to record this information when "in doubt" as to whether the statement was a series statement. If the information was merely a variant of the publisher's name, the footnote indicated the statement could be ignored. AACR2 does not address these situations at all, but does not prohibit the use of the procedure given in AACR1 Rev. The Library of Congress Rule Interpretation to AACR2 Rule 1.6 indicates that it is continuing the use of the earlier practice.

These AACR1 Rev. Ch. 6 rules could be used for works that were not separately published monographs unless specific rules for the description of a format superseded or excluded their use.

NOTE EXAMPLES

Source of Series Statement
12.1   Series stamped on t.p.
12.2   Publisher and series stamped on t.p.
12.3   Series statement from label mounted on t.p.: Heft 19.
12.4   Series statement from accompanying booklet.
12.5   Series no. from label on verso t.p.

Series Statement Variation
12.6   Vols. 5-7 lack series statement.
12.7   Vol. 2 lacks series statement.
12.8   Vol. 2 lacks series.
12.9   Series statement in v. 8-   only.
12.10   Series title on t.p.: Trudy, vypusk 241 (301).
12.11   Series appears on half title page as: Encyclopédie-Roret.

Series Indication
12.12   "Abstract-Bibliography. Series 1: in seven parts."
12.13   "CPL bibliographies."

311

12.14 A Banker Research Unit survey.

12.15 "A Contemporary ob/gyn book."

12.16 "Continuing bibliographies in the indexed periodicals, 1950-1977": p. ix-x.

12.17 "Continuing education in ophthalmology."

12.18 "Early American collection."

12.19 "An Engineering news-record book."

12.20 "Goodhart-Willcox's build-a-course series."

12.21 "The Minnesota Symposia on Child Psychology, volume 15."

12.22 "Rate training manual and nonresident career course."

12.23 "A Twentieth Century Fund report."

12.24 *"West Key number system."

12.25 At head of title: West's California codes.

12.26 "A David C. Cook Foundation research project"—Cover.

12.27 *On cover: Topics in personnel.

12.28 Running title: Waverly novels. Woodstock.

12.29 Series on jacket: Blandford colour series.

12.30 Spine title: E.T.H. lectures, 1933-1934.

12.31 Stamped on cover: Working papers.

12.32 Hematologic complications of alcoholism, I published as: Seminars in hematology ; v. 17, no. 2.
Mild bleeding disorders, II, published as: Seminars in hematology ; v. 17, no. 4.

12.33 The Lyell lectures for 1957, issued without statement of authorship.

12.34 "Third volume in the series of biographical dictionaries of Princetonians"—Pref.

12.35 "Being volume 1 of a series concerning the ancestors and descendants of Arthur Parker Thomas and Clara Strong Phoenix, his wife."

12.36 R. Colas (Costume, 2719) lists this title as the 3rd part of a 6-part publication: Costumes des différens Etats de l'Italie.

12.37 Contains Education report series ER80-01, etc. of the Society of Manufacturing Engineers.

Publisher's Characterizations

12.38 "Amnesty International publication."

12.39 "An Atlantic Monthly Press book."

12.40 "A Commonwealth Fund book."

12.41 "A Dolphin book."

12.42 "An Elsevier professional publication."

12.43 "A Fireside book."

12.44 "A Halsted Press book."

12.45 "A Helen and Kurt Wolff book."

12.46 "A Laurence Urdang reference book."

12.47 "A Margaret K. McElderry book."

12.48 "New Directions paperbook 528."

12.49 "A Ronald Press publication."

12.50   "A Scientific American book."
12.51   "A Wiley-Interscience publication."

Numbering

12.52   Number in Russian series statement: no. 149 (1978).
12.53   "Number 7 in the series of historical reprints"—Cover, p. 2.
12.54   Vol. 4 of an unnamed series.
12.55   "Data series A."
12.56   "Series one"—p. [2] of cover.
12.57   "Second series."
12.58   "Series I, volume 2"—P. [33].
12.59   Vols. 3-5: Segunda serie.
12.60   Series also numbered BD. 6, continuing the original numbering.
12.61   No. 4 in list of children's "Reward books" printed on p. [4] of cover. On p. [1] of cover: Series IV. No. IV.

Chapter 3 (Cartographic Materials)

AACR2 RULE

3.7B12 Series [AACR2 Rev.]
   Make notes on series data that cannot be given in the series area.

AACR2 Rev. deleted the first example that appeared with the original AACR2 text of this rule. The deleted example suggested preliminary wording to identify the series in which a reprinted work was originally issued. This information would now be recorded under the combined notes relating to an original work rule (AACR2 Rev. Rule 1.7B22).

RELATED AACR2 RULE

None.

LIBRARY OF CONGRESS POLICY

None issued.

RELATED LIBRARY OF CONGRESS POLICY

None issued.

AACR2 TEST EXAMPLES REVISED TO REFLECT LIBRARY OF CONGRESS POLICY

None required.

HISTORICAL BACKGROUND

Although AACR1 and previous codes had no rule equivalent to AACR2 Rule 3.7B12, the series note provisions for separately published monographs in these earlier codes could be used for cartographic materials. (See *Historical Background* under Rule 2.7B12.)

NOTE EXAMPLES

12.62   "Oregon pathfinder maps."
12.63   "A Straub Publishing guide book."
12.64   "Texaco National Road Reports."
12.65   "A Signet Special, 451-XE2056"—Cover.
12.66   "Travel Aide India"—Cover.
12.67   "Texaco touring maps"—Table of contents.
12.68   At head of title: Picto-Map.
12.69   On each map: Noble Gems.
12.70   Title of each map: General highway map . . . County, Wyoming.
12.71   Regional format United States 1:100,000 scale series.
12.72   "Cartographic issue de la carte I.G.N.'Europe-Afrique' au 1:6 000 000."
12.73   "Chart: BLS H000, first edition, September 1977."
12.74   "WRA main report, part I, volume 2 of 25."

Chapter 5 (Music)

AACR2 RULE

5.7B12 Series
   Make notes on series data that cannot be given in the series area.

RELATED AACR2 RULE

None.

LIBRARY OF CONGRESS POLICY

None issued.

RELATED LIBRARY OF CONGRESS POLICY

None issued.

AACR2 TEXT EXAMPLES REVISED TO REFLECT LIBRARY OF CONGRESS POLICY

None required.

HISTORICAL BACKGROUND

In general, AACR1 Rule 247 defers to the provisions of AACR1 Rule 143 for monographs in providing series statements for music. (See *Historical Background* under Rule 2.7B12.) However, AACR1 Rule 247 does state that collective titles appearing on stock title pages are not considered series and should be ignored. AACR2 does not provide this guidance.

NOTE EXAMPLES

12.75 Added t.p.: The twelfth series.
12.76 At head of title: A Reader's digest family music book.
12.77 Each vol. also has consecutive series numbering (4, 8).
12.78 Page [2] of cover gives series numbering as 277.
12.79 Beginning with ser. D, v. 1, vols. also have consecutive numbering (beginning with 4).

Chapter 6 (Sound Recordings)

AACR2 RULE

6.7B12 Series
Make notes on series data that cannot be given in the series area.

RELATED AACR2 RULE

None.

LIBRARY OF CONGRESS POLICY

None issued.

RELATED LIBRARY OF CONGRESS POLICY

None issued.

AACR2 TEXT EXAMPLES REVISED TO REFLECT LIBRARY OF CONGRESS POLICY

None required.

315

HISTORICAL BACKGROUND

Although AACR1 Rev. Ch. 14 and previous codes had no rule equivalent to AACR2 Rule 6.7B12, the series note provisions for separately published monographs in these earlier codes could be used for processed sound recordings. (See *Historical Background* under Rule 2.7B12.)

NOTE EXAMPLES

12.80   At head of title: Musica de câmara do Brasil.
12.81   "Nostalgia-Repertoire Records"—Container.
12.82   "Limited edition collector's series"—Label on container of v. 1.

Chapter 7 (Motion Pictures and Videorecordings)

AACR2 RULE

7.7B12 Series
Make notes on series data that cannot be given in the series area.

RELATED AACR2 RULE

None.

LIBRARY OF CONGRESS POLICY

None issued. For archival moving image materials, the Library of Congress supplements AACR2 Chapter 7 with the guidelines in *Archival Moving Image Materials* by White-Hensen.

RELATED LIBRARY OF CONGRESS POLICY

None issued.

AACR2 TEXT EXAMPLES REVISED TO REFLECT LIBRARY OF CONGRESS POLICY

None required.

HISTORICAL BACKGROUND

Although AACR1 Rev. Ch. 12 and previous codes had no rule equivalent to AACR2 Rule 7.7B12, the series note provisions for separately published monographs in these earlier codes could be used for motion pictures and videorecordings. (See *Historical Background* under Rule 2.7B12.)

NOTE EXAMPLES

12.83   NBC white paper.
12.84   A National Geographic special.
12.85   A Project Head Start training videorecording.

Chapter 8 (Graphic Materials)

AACR2 RULE

8.7B12 Series [AACR2 Rev.]
Make notes on series data that cannot be given in the series area.

AACR2 Rev. added a second example to the original AACR2 text. This new example illustrates a way to record information about a varient form of the series name from that found on the label on the item.

RELATED AACR2 RULE

None.

LIBRARY OF CONGRESS POLICY

None issued. For original items and historical collections, the Library of Congress supplements AACR2 Chapter 8 with the guidelines in *Graphic Materials* by Betz.

RELATED LIBRARY OF CONGRESS POLICY

None issued.

AACR2 TEXT EXAMPLES REVISED TO REFLECT LIBRARY OF CONGRESS POLICY

None required.

HISTORICAL BACKGROUND

Although AACR1 Rev. Ch. 12, AACR1 Ch. 15, and previous codes had no rule equivalent to AACR2 Rule 8.7B12, the series note provisions for separately published monographs in these earlier codes could be

317

used for graphic materials. (See *Historical Background* under Rule 2.7B12.)

NOTE EXAMPLES

Projection Graphic Materials
12.86 Associated Press special report.
12.87 Current affairs case study.
         Newsweek educational program.
12.88 "A reading program"—Publisher's catalog.
12.89 Part 2 in a series. Part 1: To dream with open eyes. 1980.

Nonprojection Graphic Materials
12.90 *Series title from publisher's catalog.
12.91 "This portfolio is one of a series inspired by poet's text"—Leaf [5].
12.92 "This portfolio is the second in a series 'New approach in graphics' "—Printed leaf.
12.93 *Subseries title from printed label on verso. "No. 15" handwritten on verso.
12.94 *Ser. B-E are 2a ed., 1979.
12.95 *Photoprints are numbered 1-25; no. 4-9, 15, 18, 21, and 24 wanting.
12.96 *Evidently incomplete series titled "Gems of American Life," in which there are subseries (indicated by labels on verso), such as, "American Beauties" and "The Young Housekeeper." Handwritten numbers on verso: no. 14, 15, 20, 21, 31, 570-572, and 576.

Chapter 9 (Computer Files)

AACR2 RULE

9.7B12 Series [AACR2 Rev.]
Make notes on series data that cannot be given in the series area.

RELATED AACR2 RULE

None.

LIBRARY OF CONGRESS POLICY

None issued for AACR2 Rev. Ch. 9.

RELATED LIBRARY OF CONGRESS POLICY

None issued for AACR2 Rev. Ch. 9.

AACR2 TEXT EXAMPLES REVISED TO REFLECT LIBRARY OF CONGRESS POLICY

None required for AACR2 Rev. Ch. 9.

HISTORICAL BACKGROUND

Computer files were not covered by AACR1 or previous codes. The rule in the original AACR2 Chapter 9 is identical to the one in AACR2 Rev. Ch. 9.

NOTE EXAMPLES

12.97 *Title on manual: The Junior high school physical science programs.
12.98 *On container: Productivity family.
12.99 *Series title on some disks: Language arts series.

Chapter 10 (Three-Dimensional Artefacts and Realia)

AACR2 RULE

10.7B12 Series
Make notes on series data that cannot be given in the series area.

RELATED AACR2 RULE

None.

LIBRARY OF CONGRESS POLICY

None issued.

RELATED LIBRARY OF CONGRESS POLICY

None issued.

AACR2 TEXT EXAMPLES REVISED TO REFLECT LIBRARY OF CONGRESS POLICY

No examples were given in AACR2 or AACR2 Rev.

HISTORICAL BACKGROUND

Although AACR1 Rev. Ch. 12 and previous codes had no rule equivalent to AACR2 Rule 10.7B12, the series note provisions for separately published monographs in these earlier codes could be used for three-dimensional artifacts and realia. (See *Historical Background* under Rule 2.7B12.)

NOTE EXAMPLES

No examples were located.

Chapter 12 (Serials)

AACR2 RULE

12.7B12 Series [AACR2 Rev.]
> Give details of the numbering within a series when the numbering varies from issue to issue.

AACR2 Rev. deleted the first sentence and the first example from the original AACR2 text of this rule. The deleted sentence instructed the cataloger to record information about a series in which the original of a reproduction was issued. The deleted example illustrated one such note. This information would now be recorded under the rule for combined notes relating to an original work (AACR2 Rev. Rule 1.7B22).

RELATED AACR2 RULE

None.

LIBRARY OF CONGRESS POLICY

None issued.

RELATED LIBRARY OF CONGRESS POLICY

12.0B1 Sources of Information. Printed Serials.
Due to its length, this LC policy statement has been abridged to include only the parts related to the use of notes.

Serials
> The basis for the description is the first issue of the serial. In determining which issue is first, disregard the date of publication, etc., and use the designation on the issues. For serials that carry numeric

or alphabetic designations, the first issue is the one with the lowest or earliest (in the alphabet) designation. For serials that do not carry numeric or alphabetic designations, the first issue is the one with the earliest chronological designation. (If the actual first issue is not available, use these same guidelines to determine which issue should be used as the basis for the description.)

Since the title page (or title page substitute) of the first issue is the chief source of information for a printed serial, a title page that is published later to cover one or more issues cannot be used as the chief source. (However, data from such a title page may be put into the note area when necessary.) [emphasis added]

If the description has been formulated from the first issue of a serial, the body of the entry remains unchanged throughout the life of the serial. If issues after the first have data different from those recorded in the body of the entry, record the different data in the note area as necessary. [emphasis added] However, if the differences are in the title proper, create a separate record when appropriate (21.2C). (For changes in the main entry heading, see 21.3B.) . . .

Reprints of Serials

In order that the description of the reprint resemble and file with the description of the original, the earliest *issue* reprinted is used as the chief source for the first three areas of the description. Data for these areas may be taken from any place on the reprinted issue without the use of brackets. If it is known that the description of the original would include data that are not on the reprinted issue, the data may be supplied in brackets.

In area four the place of publication, publisher, and date of the reprint are recorded, using brackets if the data do not come from a prescribed source on the reprint.

The physical description area gives the physical description of the reprint, not the original.

A series is recorded if the reprint appears in a series.

Usually a single note (see 12.7B7g) gives important details about the original while other notes give necessary information about the reprint. Notes giving the source of the title or the issue on which the description is based are not given. [emphasis added] [CSB 38]

AACR2 TEXT EXAMPLES REVISED TO REFLECT LIBRARY OF CONGRESS POLICY

None required.

HISTORICAL BACKGROUND

AACR1 Rule 167F provided for the use of a note when there was "confusion in the use of series numbering" and when the "publication of preliminary editions not included in the regular series numbering" occurred. The AACR2 rule only addresses the first of these two situations.

NOTE EXAMPLES

12.100   Vols. 3-6 lack series statements.
12.101   *Each issue individually numbered in the series.
12.102   "A Wiley-Interscience Publication."

1.7B13. Dissertations

EXTRAPOLATED GENERAL RULE

Although most of the chapters for description have a provision for the use of a dissertation note, they all refer to Chapter 2 (Books, Pamphlets, and Printed Sheets) for specific instructions on the use and formatting of this note. Therefore, the specifics of AACR2 Rule 2.7B13 serve as general instructions for the development of dissertation notes for all appropriate chapters.

RELATED AACR2 RULE

None.

GENERAL LIBRARY OF CONGRESS POLICY

No interpretations have been issued by the Library of Congress to modify, or amplify on, AACR2 Rule 1.7B13. There have, however, been LC interpretations issued for AACR2 Rule 2.7B13, that serves as the general rule for this note.

RELATED LIBRARY OF CONGRESS POLICY

None issued.

FORMAT

See the specific formatting provisions given in Chapter 2.

CHAPTER APPLICATION

This note is not present in Chapter 10 (Three-Dimensional Artefacts and Realia) and Chapter 12 (Serials).

EXCEPTIONS AND ADDITIONS

None.

Chapter 2 (Books, Pamphlets, and Printed Sheets)

AACR2 RULE

2.7B13 Dissertations [AACR2 Rev.]

Thesis

If the item being described is a dissertation or thesis presented as part of the requirements for an academic degree, give[:]

Thesis

followed by a brief statement of the degree for which the author was a candidate (e.g., *(M.A.)* or *(Ph.D.)*, or, for theses to which conventional abbreviations do not apply, *(doctoral)* or *(master's)*),

the name of the institution or faculty to which the thesis was presented, and

the year in which the degree was granted. . . .

This results in the construct:

[Thesis] ([Degree])–[Institution], [date].

Revision or Abridgment

If the publication is a revision or abridgement of a thesis, state this. . . .

Edited Text

If the thesis is a text by someone else edited by the candidate, include the candidate's name in the note. . . .

No Formal Thesis Statement

If the publication lacks a formal thesis statement, give a bibliographic history note.

RELATED AACR2 RULE

None.

LIBRARY OF CONGRESS POLICY

If in cataloging a dissertation or thesis the academic degree is not equivalent to "doctoral" or "master's," qualify "thesis" by whatever statement is found on the item being cataloged.

In recording the name of the institution in a thesis note, give it in the form found on the item. Add the name of the place in which the body is located if it appears with the name of the institution. Use the well-established English form of the place name if there is one. (In case of doubt about the English form, consult *Webster's New Geographical Dictionary*.) [CSB 22]

RELATED LIBRARY OF CONGRESS POLICY

None issued.

AACR2 TEXT EXAMPLES REVISED TO REFLECT LIBRARY OF CONGRESS POLICY

5th Example:

AACR2 TEXT
Karl Schmidt's thesis (doctoral)—München, 1965.

AACR2 TEXT REVISED
Karl Schmidt's thesis (doctoral)—Ludwig-Maximilians-Universität, Munich, 1965.

6th Example:

AACR2 TEXT
Originally presented as the author's thesis (doctoral—Heidelberg) under the title: . . .

AACR2 TEXT REVISED
Originally presented as the author's thesis
(doctoral Ruprecht-Karl-Universität, Heidelberg, 1969) under title: . . .

HISTORICAL BACKGROUND

AACR1 Rev. Rule 146 addressed the treatment of both formal theses and other theses forms. A formal thesis note was created when cataloging the actual thesis or copies of it. For a doctoral thesis the note followed the construct:

Thesis—Institution

While a nondoctoral thesis had the construct:

Thesis (degree)—Institution

This note structure differs from that used in AACR2:

Thesis (degree)—Institution, date.

325

Unlike AACR1 Rev., AACR2 does not limit the inclusion of the statement of the degree to nondoctoral theses. Also AACR1 Rev. specified that the date of the degree was added only if it was present in the work and was different from the date of imprint. AACR2 requires the inclusion of the date of the degree whenever available.

AACR1 Rev. provided detailed guidelines for abbreviating degrees and naming different categories of institutions. These guidelines are not present in AACR2 and they differ from the guidelines given in the Library of Congress Rule Interpretation to AACR2 Rule 2.7B13.

AACR1 Rev. Rule 146G gave instructions for cataloging foreign theses that used the designation "praeses and respondent" while AACR1 Rev. Rule 146H; covered the use of Latin theses. Neither of these situations are specifically addressed by AACR2.

AACR1 Rev. Rule 146J gave detailed guidelines for noting the presence of the author's vita. AACR2 does not provide any guidelines under the dissertation note for mentioning a vita. A vita note could be developed, however, as a contents note.

AACR1 Rev. Rule 146K provided instructions for the use of notes with "non-thesis editions." Notes developed under this rule were informal thesis notes rather than the formal thesis notes mentioned above. AACR2 does not specifically address these situations, although notes identical to those constructed under AACR1 could be created using AACR2.

Works lacking formal thesis statements were given a note that indicated their relationship to the original theses (AACR1 Rev. Rule 146K1). This note incorporated many of the elements of the formal thesis note in a less rigid structure. AACR2 indicates that a bibliographic history note (AACR2 Rule 2.7B7) should be provided for this type of work.

Under AACR1 Rev., a work that had a thesis statement on a separate title page or on a mounted label was given both a formal thesis note and a note detailing the source of the thesis statement (AACR1 Rev. Rule 146K2). AACR2 does not specifically address this situation.

A work that was based on, or was a revision of, a thesis had a note provided that recorded its relationship to the original work (AACR1 Rev. Rule 146K3). This rule recommended a paraphrasing or quoting of the statement from the work itself. AACR2 merely specifies that a statement about the revision be made.

These AACR1 Rev. Ch. 6 rules could be used for works that were not separately published monographs unless specific rules for the description of a format superseded or excluded their use.

It might appear from this historical information that considerable differences exist between AACR2 and AACR1 Rev. in their treatment of theses. For formal thesis editions, a more consistent and complete structure has been developed over that used in AACR1 Rev. For non-thesis editions, these differences are, in fact, mainly present in terms of the details of the instructions given in the note rule rather than in the form and nature of the resulting note. Many of the examples used in both texts are the same or very similar. Likewise, many of the theses notes used by the Library of Congress under the provisions of AACR2 are often identical, or nearly identical, to notes previously developed under AACR1 Rev.

NOTE EXAMPLES

Formal Thesis

13.1   Thesis—University of Chicago.
13.2   Thesis—Pontificia Universidad Javeriana, Bogatá.
13.3   Thesis (M.A.)—University of North Carolina-Chapel Hill.
13.4   Thesis (M.L.S.)—University of California, Los Angeles, 1979.
13.5   Thesis (M.A.)—Pusan Taekakkyo, 1978.
13.6   Thesis (Ph.D.)—Harvard University, 1974.
13.7   Thesis (D.E.S.)—University of Yaounde, 1979.
13.8   Thesis (Dr. Ing.)—Technische Hochschule Berlin, 1980.
13.9   Thesis (doctoral)—Austin Presbyterian Theological Seminary, 1981.
13.10   Thesis (abogado)—Universidad Católica, 1962.
13.11   Thesis (final diploma)—University of Cape Town, 1982.
13.12   Thesis (licenciatura)—Universidad de Oviedo, 1977.
13.13   Thesis (tesis de grado)—Pontificia Universidad Javeriana, 1980.
13.14   "A dissertation submitted in partial fulfillment for the degree of Master of laws of the University of Delhi ... "
13.15   "Presented in partial fulfillment of the requirements for the Final Diploma in Library and Information Science, 1981"—T.p. verso.
13.16   "This thesis has been researched and prepared as one of the requirements for fellowship of the Library Association of Ireland."—p. vi.

Revision or Abridgement

13.17   Revision of thesis—University of Chicago.
13.18   Revision of thesis—Tulane University, 1975.
13.19   Revision of the author's thesis—Princeton University, 1981.
13.20   A revision of the author's thesis (Ph.D.).
13.21   Revision of thesis (M.A.)—University of Michigan, 1973.
13.22   Revision of thesis (Ph.D.)—Bryn Mawr, 1979.
13.23   Revision of thesis (doctoral)—Oxford University, 1961.
13.24   Revision of the author's thesis doctoral—École des hautes études en sciences sociales.
13.25   Revision of the author's thesis (M.A.—Monash University, 1977).
13.26   Revision of the author's thesis (doctoral—University of Dacca, 1979).
13.27   A revision of the author's thesis (doctoral)—Universität Hohenheim (Landwirtschaftliche Hochschule), 1980.

13.28 A slight revision of the author's thesis (doctoral—Bonn).

13.29 Revision of: Toward a prehistory of the San Francisco Bay area. Thesis (Ph.D.)—Harvard University, 1976.

13.30 "A revision of the author's thesis, The Ohio State University, 1980"— T.p. verso.

13.31 A revision of the author's thesis (Ph.D.—University of Chicago, 1974) with title: Variation and change in the Indus civilization.

13.32 Revision of the author's thesis (doctoral—University of Sussex) under the title: An analysis of the export performance and policies of Bangladesh since1950, with special reference to the income and employment implications of trade in manufactures.

13.33 A revision of the author's thesis (doctoral—Salzburg, 1972) under title: Der Begriff Ordnung im Werk von Hermann Broch.

13.34 A slight revision of the author's thesis (doctoral—Konstanz, 1979) under the title: Arbeiterbewegung, kommunale Selbstverwaltung und Weimarer Staat.

13.35 Revision of the 4th chapter of the author's thesis (D. Litt.—Bhāgalapura Viśvavidyālaya) with the title: Hindī vīrakāvya, 1600-1800.

13.36 Abridgement of the author's thesis (doctoral—Innsbruck, 1978).

13.37 Abridgement of the author's thesis (doctoral—Göttingen, 1976) originally presented under the title: Studien zum russischen Konstruktivismus.

13.38 Slightly abridged ed. of the author's thesis (doctoral)—Bremen, 1980.

13.39 Abstract of thesis (doctoral).

13.40 Abstract of thesis (Licenciatura)—Universidad de Extremadura.

13.41 An enlargement of the author's thesis (doctoral—Frankfort am Main, 1976).

No Formal Thesis Statement

13.42 Based on the author's thesis (Ph.D.).

13.43 Based on the author's thesis (M. Mus.)—Emporia State University.

13.44 Based on the author's thesis (Ph.D.—Massachusetts Institute of Technology).

13.45 Based on the author's thesis (doctoral—Australian National University, 1975).

13.46 Based on the author's thesis (doctoral—Boston University, 1979) with title: Intertemporal movements of real wages : a case study of Bangladesh, India & Indonesia.

13.47 "Based on parts of a doctoral thesis . . . accepted by the University of Nottingham, England, in 1971"—Preface.

13.48 Gómez Gasper's work based on thesis (Magister Scientiarum en Ciencias Marinas, Mención Biologia Marina)—Instituto Oceanográfico, Universidad de Oriente, Cumaná, Venezuela.

13.49 Originally presented as the author's thesis.

13.50 Originally presented as the author's thesis, Université René Descartes.

13.51 Originally presented as the author's thesis (University of Oxford, 1951).

13.52 Originally presented as the author's thesis (M.A.).

13.53 Originally presented as the author's thesis (Ph.D.).
13.54 Originally presented as the author's thesis (Ph.D.—Columbia University).
13.55 Originally presented as the author's thesis (Ph.D.—Vanderbilt University, 1980).
13.56 Originally published as the author's thesis (master's)—Pontificia Universidade Católica-RJ, 1979.
13.57 Originally presented as the author's thesis (doctoral)—Munich, 1976.
13.58 Originally presented as the author's thesis (graduate certificate—Westminster Theological Seminary, 1938).
13.59 Originally presented as the author's thesis (magistarski rad—Zagreb), 1976.
13.60 Originally presented as the author's thesis (mestre em filosofia da educação) Pontificia Universidade Católica de São Paulo.
13.61 "Originally a dissertation submitted to the faculty of the Graduate School of Music of The Catholic University of America."
13.62 Originally presented as the author's thesis (doctoral—Bombay University) under title: A social study of the cinema in Bombay.
13.63 Translation and abridgement of: Some psychological characteristics of Colombian priests, originally presented as the author's thesis (Ph.D.)—University of Chicago.

Non-Thesis Related Statements

13.64 Habilitationsschrift—Munich, 1980.
13.65 The author's Habilitationsschrift—Munich.
13.66 Revision of the author's Habilitationsschrift—Innsbruck, 1977.
13.67 Originally presented as the author's Habilitationsschrift, Munich, 1979.

Chapters 3-9

The dissertation rules in Chapters 3-9 refer the cataloger to the instructions given in Chapter 2. This is the only note rule in AACR2 for which this practice is followed, and it is due to the predominance of the monograph format for theses. Rather than repeat those detailed rules for each of the eight chapters, a practice similar to that used in AACR2 has been employed here. Refer to the guidelines and examples given in Chapter 2 for theses in formats covered by Chapters 3-9. The two examples below represent nonbook theses notes.

NOTE EXAMPLES

13.68 Thesis (M.F.A.)—New York University.
13.69 *Thesis (Ph.D.)—Harvard, 1977.

1.7B14. Audience

Make a brief note of the intended audience for, or intellectual level of, an item if this is supplied by the item.

RELATED AACR2 RULE

None.

GENERAL LIBRARY OF CONGRESS POLICY

None issued. See the Format section below for LC's formatting policy. See also the sections that follow for any LC policies or interpretations that apply to individual chapters for description.

RELATED LIBRARY OF CONGRESS POLICY

1.7A3 Forms of Notes
When nonroman data (including quotations) are being recorded in the note area, give them in romanized form in all cases, including those cards that contain nonromanized elements in the body of the entry.

When a note begins with a formal introductory term such as "contents," "credits," or "summary," do not use all caps in any case; instead, use upper and lower case as illustrated in AACR 2. [emphasis added] [CSB 22]

FORMAT

None prescribed. From its adoption of AACR2, however, the Library of Congress established by practice a policy of using the following construct for some formats:

Intended audience:

Due to a change in the print constant for this note in the MARC formats, since 1985 some LC catalog records with audience notes have utilized the construct:

Audience:

In order to provide examples that are as current as possible, the examples in this text that were originally created using the "Intended

330

audience:" construct have been modified to reflect the newer "Audience:" construct.

CHAPTER APPLICATION

This note is present in all chapters for description. Chapter 4 (Manuscripts) provides for expansion of the provisions of the Extrapolated General Rule. Although this note is composed by the cataloger, individual chapters prescribe the source from which catalogers may take the audience information.

EXCEPTIONS AND ADDITIONS

Chapter 4 (Manuscripts) utilizes this rule to identify limitations and restrictions on access to manuscripts, identify their availability, and indicate the status of literary rights.

Chapter 2 (Books, Pamphlets, and Printed Sheets)

AACR2 RULE

2.7B14 Audience
    Make a brief note of the intended audience for, or intellectual level of, an item if this information is stated in the item.

RELATED AACR2 RULE

None.

LIBRARY OF CONGRESS POLICY

    Give a note naming the intended audience for, or intellectual level of, a work only when the information can be quoted from the publication. (Ignore information given on CIP prepublication data sheets.) [CSB 18]

See *Note Examples* for an explanation of how the MARC format has affected the structure of this note on LC catalog records.

The Library of Congress sometimes adds an audience indication to a summary note when cataloging juvenile works. Two examples of this practice follow:

Summary: Nearly 30,000 entries are defined for the beginning reader through middle-grader. Includes a reference section with information about the solar system, weights and measures, flags, and other topics.

Summary: A law textbook designed to familiarize the high school student with Florida law, including criminal and juvenile justice, consumer law, family law, housing law, and individual rights and liberties.

RELATED LIBRARY OF CONGRESS POLICY

None issued.

AACR2 TEXT EXAMPLES REVISED TO REFLECT LIBRARY OF CONGRESS POLICY

None required.

HISTORICAL BACKGROUND

AACR1 and previous codes had no rule equivalent to AACR2 Rule 2.7B14 for books.

NOTE EXAMPLES

From its adoption of AACR2, the Library of Congress established by practice a policy of using the following construct for some audience notes:

Intended audience:

Due to a change in the print constant for this note in the MARC formats, since 1985 some LC catalog records with audience notes have utilized the construct:

Audience:

In order to provide examples that are as current as possible, the examples that follow have been modified to reflect the newer "Audience:" construct when appropriate.

14.1   For children.
14.2   For babies from the age of one year.
14.3   For 2-6 year olds.
14.4   For children aged 4-8.
14.5   For grades 1-3.

14.6   "For mental health, health, and human services professionals."
14.7   Audience: Renaissance specialists, linguistics, students of occultism, and historians of science.
14.8   Audience: Students of law and administration.
14.9   Authorized for instructional purposes.
14.10   At head of title: Confidential.
14.11   "Confidencial"—added t.p.
14.12   "Distribution limited to U.S. government agencies only."
14.13   For internal use.
14.14   "Prepared for distribution at the law office management programs, June-July 1981."
14.15   "Prepared for distribution at the Leveraged and single inventor leasing program. May-June 1981"—Page 5.
14.16   "For presentation at a creative manufacturing engineering program."
14.17   "Printed for the use of the Committee on the Judiciary, House of Representatives."
14.18   "(Top secret hearing held on September 16, 1980; sanitized and printed on February 18, 1981.)"

Chapter 3 (Cartographic Materials)

AACR2 RULE

3.7B14 Audience
Make a brief note of the intended audience for, or intellectual level of, an item if this information is stated in the item.

RELATED AACR2 RULE

None.

LIBRARY OF CONGRESS POLICY

None issued. See *Note Examples* for an explanation of how the MARC format has affected the structure of this note on LC catalog records.

RELATED LIBRARY OF CONGRESS POLICY

None issued.

AACR2 TEXT EXAMPLES REVISED TO REFLECT LIBRARY OF CONGRESS POLICY

None required.

HISTORICAL BACKGROUND

AACR1 and previous codes had no rule equivalent to AACR2 Rule 3.7B14 for cartographic materials.

NOTE EXAMPLES

From its adoption of AACR2, however, the Library of Congress established by practice a policy of using the following construct for some audience notes:

Intended audience:

Due to a change in the print constant for this note in the MARC formats, since 1985 some LC catalog records with audience notes have utilized the construct:

Audience:

No examples were located.

Chapter 4 (Manuscripts)

AACR2 RULE

4.7B14 Access and Literary Rights [AACR2 Rev.]

Access

Give, as specifically as possible, all restrictions on access to a manuscript or collection of manuscripts. . . .

Literary Rights

If the literary rights in a collection have been reserved for a specified period or are dedicated to the public and a document stating this is available, give[:]

Information on literary rights available.

RELATED AACR2 RULE

None.

LIBRARY OF CONGRESS POLICY

None issued. APPM, however, expands on the AACR2 text by providing for two different notes.

Restrictions and Access

If the item or material is not generally available to researchers, or if access is restricted, make a note either simply stating the fact of this restriction or specifying the details, including the date when the restriction will be lifted. [APPM 4.7B9]

Literary Rights and Copyright

If the literary rights in the material are unknown, no statement is necessary.

However, if the rights were dedicated or reserved under previous copyright law, include a descriptive note. If the collection was received after December 31, 1977, and if the copyright interests have been dedicated or reserved under new copyright law (Title 17, U.S.C.), include a descriptive note. [APPM 4.7B10]

RELATED LIBRARY OF CONGRESS POLICY

None issued.

AACR2 TEXT EXAMPLES REVISED TO REFLECT LIBRARY OF CONGRESS POLICY

None required.

HISTORICAL BACKGROUND

AACR1 Rule 207H (Restricted Access) was essentially the same as the restricted access section of AACR2 Rule 4.7B14.

AACR1 Rule 207J (Literary Rights) was also basically the same as the literary rights section of AACR2 Rule 4.7B14 except the prescribed statement varied slightly in its wording.

> AACR1—Information on literary rights available in the repository.
> AACR2—Information on literary rights available.

NOTE EXAMPLES

Restrictions and Access

14.19 *Use of collection restricted to library.
14.20 Access restricted.
14.21 In part, access restricted.
14.22 Access restricted, in part.
14.23 Access restricted in part until 1984.
14.24 Access restricted to those with written permission of Agnes de Mille.

335

14.25 Access restricted until 1988 except with written permission of Sara Roberta Church or Dr. Charles W. Crawford, Memphis State University. Miss Church may extend the term of restriction during her lifetime.

14.26 Access to patterns restricted until 1991.

14.27 *Access to some of the records is restricted under the provisions of Illinois Public Act 79-453 and the State Records Act of 1957, as amended.

14.28 *Open to investigators.

14.29 *Open to investigators with the permission of the Dean of Students.

14.30 *Open to qualified researchers.

14.31 *Open to researchers under library restrictions.

14.32 Open to researchers with permission of Miss Ruddel.

Literary Rights and Copyright

14.33 *Information on literary rights available in the Library.

14.34 *Literary rights of J. Robert Oppenheimer have been dedicated to the public.

Chapter 5 (Music)

AACR2 RULE

5.7B14 Audience [AACR2 Rev.]

Make a brief note of the intended audience for, or intellectual level of, an item if this information is stated in the item.

RELATED AACR2 RULE

None.

LIBRARY OF CONGRESS POLICY

None issued. See *Note Examples* for an explanation of how the MARC format has affected the structure of this note on LC catalog records.

RELATED LIBRARY OF CONGRESS POLICY

None issued.

AACR2 TEXT EXAMPLES REVISED TO REFLECT LIBRARY OF CONGRESS POLICY

None required.

HISTORICAL BACKGROUND

AACR1 and previous codes had no rule equivalent to AACR2 Rule 5.7B14 for music.

NOTE EXAMPLES

From its adoption of AACR2, the Library of Congress established by practice a policy of using the following construct for some audience notes:

Intended audience:

Due to a change in the print constant for this note in the MARC formats, since 1985 some LC catalog records with audience notes utilize the construct:

Audience:

In order to provide examples that are as current as possible, the examples that follow have been modified to reflect the newer "Audience:" construct.

14.35 "Easy."
14.36 "Audience level: intermediate/junior."
14.37 For juvenile violinist and cellist.
14.38 "Designed for performance by children of the 9 to 13 age range"—Pref.
14.39 For children.
14.40 Audience: Easy to intermediate grades.
14.41 "Written for performance by children of between nine and thirteen years of age."—P. [iii].

Chapter 6 (Sound Recordings)

AACR2 RULE

6.7B14 Audience [AACR2 Rev.]

Make a brief note of the intended audience for, or intellectual level of, a sound recording if this information is stated in the item, its container, or accompanying textual material.

This rule expands the source of the audience data beyond that of the item itself to include the container and accompanying textual material.

RELATED AACR2 RULE

None.

LIBRARY OF CONGRESS POLICY

None issued. See *Note Examples* for an explanation of how the MARC format has affected the structure of this note on LC catalog records.

RELATED LIBRARY OF CONGRESS POLICY

None issued.

AACR2 TEXT EXAMPLES REVISED TO REFLECT LIBRARY OF CONGRESS POLICY

None required.

HISTORICAL BACKGROUND

AACR1 Rev. and previous codes had no rule equivalent to AACR2 Rule 6.7B14 for sound recordings. However, AACR1 Rev. Rule 252F11 provided for a summary note for nonmusical recordings. This note could have been used to indicate an intended audience or intellectual level.

NOTE EXAMPLES

From its adoption of AACR2, the Library of Congress established by practice a policy of using the following construct for some audience notes:

Intended audience:

Due to a change in the print constant for this note in the MARC formats, since 1985 LC catalog records for audience notes have utilized the construct:

Audience:

In order to provide examples that are as current as possible, the examples that follow have been modified to reflect the newer "Audience:" construct.

14.42   Audience: Lawyers.
14.43   Audience: Ages 16 through adult.
14.44   Audience: Chemists and chemical engineers.
14.45   Audience: Religious audience.
14.46   Audience: Scientists who have not had formal training in the field.

Chapter 7 (Motion Pictures and Videorecordings)

AACR2 RULE

7.7B14 Audience [AACR2 Rev.]

Make a brief note of the intended audience for, or intellectual level of, an item if this information is stated in the item, its container, or accompanying textual material.

This rule expands the sources of the audience data beyond that of the item itself to include the container and accompanying textual material. Although the rule specifically addresses the use of this note for motion pictures, it also applies to videorecordings.

RELATED AACR2 RULE

None.

LIBRARY OF CONGRESS POLICY

None issued. See *Note Examples* for an explanation of how the MARC format has affected the structure of this note on LC catalog records.

For archival moving image materials, the Library of Congress supplements AACR2 Chapter 7 with the guidelines in *Archival Moving Image Materials* by White-Hensen.

RELATED LIBRARY OF CONGRESS POLICY

None issued.

AACR2 TEXT EXAMPLES REVISED TO REFLECT LIBRARY OF CONGRESS POLICY

None required.

HISTORICAL BACKGROUND

AACR1 Rev. Rule 229.2H provided a note to indicate "intended users" if the document was directed toward a specific group or a "narrowly defined" age group. This rule is essentially the same in its result as the current rule.

When a summary note (AACR1 Rev. Rule 229.2L) was provided for a document that also had an audience statement, the audience indication became a part of the summary note. There is no provision for this in AACR2, although the Library of Congress continues to use this technique. See examples under AACR2 Rule 7.7B17.

NOTE EXAMPLES

From its adoption of AACR2, the Library of Congress established by practice a policy of using the following construct for some audience notes:

Intended audience:

Due to a change in the print constant for this note in the MARC formats, since 1985 LC catalog records for audience notes have utilized the construct:

Audience:

In order to provide examples that are as current as possible, the examples that follow have been modified to reflect the newer "Audience:" construct.

14.47 Audience: General.
14.48 Audience: Ages 8 to 11.
14.49 Audience: Ages 13 through adult.
14.50 Audience: Children ages 3-12 and their parents.
14.51 Audience: Adults.
14.52 Audience: Adults and professionals.
14.53 Audience: Kindergarten through junior high school students.
14.54 Audience: Grades 5-6.
14.55 Audience: Intermediate grades through senior high school.
14.56 Audience: Junior high school through adult French language classes.
14.57 Audience: High school through adult.
14.58 Audience: Aircraft maintenance personnel.
14.59 Audience: Coca-Cola Co. sales personnel.
14.60 Audience: College students, adults, counselors, social workers, etc.
14.61 Audience: Dentists.
14.62 Audience: Highway engineers, technicians, and students.
14.63 Audience: Hospital and health care administrators and personnel.
14.64 Audience: Managers.
14.65 Audience: Medical and paramedical personnel.
14.66 Audience: Parents and prospective parents.
14.67 Audience: Teachers (kindergarten through senior high school) and college students.
14.68 Audience: Veterans Administration benefits counselors.

Chapter 8 (Graphic Materials)

AACR2 RULE

8.7B14 Audience [AACR2 Rev.]

Make a brief note of the intended audience for, or intellectual level of, a graphic item if this information is stated in the item, its container, or accompanying material.

This rule expands the sources of the audience data beyond that of the item itself to include the container and accompanying textual material.

RELATED AACR2 RULE

None.

LIBRARY OF CONGRESS POLICY

None issued. See *Note Examples* for an explanation of how the MARC format has affected the structure of this note on LC catalog records.

For original items and historical collections, the Library of Congress supplements AACR2 Chapter 8 with the guidelines in *Graphic Materials* by Betz.

RELATED LIBRARY OF CONGRESS POLICY

None issued.

AACR2 TEXT EXAMPLES REVISED TO REFLECT
LIBRARY OF CONGRESS POLICY

None required.

HISTORICAL BACKGROUND

AACR1 Rev. Rule 229.2H provided a note to indicate "intended users" if the document was directed toward a specific group or a "narrowly defined" age group. This rule is essentially the same in its result as the current rule.

When a summary note (AACR1 Rev. Rule 229.2L) was provided for a document that also had an audience statement, the audience indication became a part of the summary note. There is no provision for this in

AACR2, although the Library of Congress continues to use this technique.

NOTE EXAMPLES

From its adoption of AACR2, the Library of Congress established by practice a policy of using the following construct for some audience notes:

Intended audience:

Due to a change in the print constant for this note in the MARC formats, since 1985, LC catalog records for audience notes have utilized the construct:

Audience:

In order to provide examples that are as current as possible, the examples that follow have been modified to reflect the newer "Audience:" construct.

Projection Graphic Materials

14.69 Audience: Adults.
14.70 Audience: First filmstrip for adults; other three filmstrips for primary grades.
14.71 Audience: Grades 7-adult.
14.72 Audience: Junior high school through college.
14.73 Audience: Senior high school and vocational school.
14.74 Audience: Senior high school through college and industrial trainees.
14.75 Audience: Special education classes for junior and senior high school students and adults.
14.76 Audience: Medical personnel.
14.77 Audience: Professional fire fighters.
14.78 Audience: Religious groups and adults.

Nonprojection Graphic Materials

14.79 *Restricted: Information on reproduction rights available at Reference Desk.
14.80 *Restricted: Material extremely fragile; access by appointment only.
14.81 *Restricted: Permission for commercial use must be obtained in writing from Mrs. John Jones.
14.82 *Restricted: Unprocessed; access by appointment only.

Chapter 9 (Computer Files)

AACR2 RULE

9.7B14 Audience [AACR2 Rev.]

Make a brief note of the intended audience for, or intellectual level of, a file if this information is stated in or on the item, its container, or accompanying material.

This rule expands the source of the audience data beyond the item itself to include the accompanying material and container.

RELATED AACR2 RULE

None.

LIBRARY OF CONGRESS POLICY

None issued for AACR2 Rev. Ch. 9. See *Note Examples* for an explanation of how the MARC format has affected the structure of this note on LC catalog records.

RELATED LIBRARY OF CONGRESS POLICY

None issued for AACR2 Rev. Ch. 9.

AACR2 TEXT EXAMPLES REVISED TO REFLECT LIBRARY OF CONGRESS POLICY

None required for AACR2 Rev. Ch. 9.

HISTORICAL BACKGROUND

Computer files were not covered by AACR1 or previous codes. The original AACR2 Chapter 9 covered the elements present in this revised rule except that it did not include the container as one of the acceptable sources for the audience information. The original rule also called for indicating those files that were not available to all users of the catalog or list.

NOTE EXAMPLES

From its adoption of AACR2, the Library of Congress established by practice a policy of using the following construct for some audience notes:

Intended audience:

Due to a change in the print constant for this note in the MARC formats, since 1985 some LC catalog records with audience notes have utilized the construct:

Audience:

In order to provide examples that are as current as possible, the examples that follow have been modified to reflect the newer "Audience:" construct.

14.83   *For grades 5-7.
14.84   *Audience: Elementary grades.
14.85   *Audience: For journalists of all ages.
14.86   *Audience: For high school and college biology classes.
14.87   *Audience: Third-fifth grade reading level; 2-6 players.
14.88   *Audience: Textile and related industries.
14.89   *Audience: Cartographers; users are required to understand file content and structure of data to be run in conjunction with POLYVRT.
14.90   *Program designed for geographers, planners, geologists, meteorologists and others who have a professional interest in analyzing spatial data.
14.91   *Program may be used by persons unfamiliar with computer programming, but is tailored to those with expertise in cartography and/or spatial analysis.

Chapter 10 (Three-Dimensional Artefacts and Realia)

AACR2 RULE

10.7B14 Audience
Make a brief note of the intended audience for, or intellectual level of, an item if this information is stated in the item.

RELATED AACR2 RULE

None.

LIBRARY OF CONGRESS POLICY

None issued. See *Note Examples* for an explanation of how the MARC format has affected the structure of this note on LC catalog records.

RELATED LIBRARY OF CONGRESS POLICY

None issued.

AACR2 TEXT EXAMPLES REVISED TO REFLECT LIBRARY OF CONGRESS POLICY

None required.

HISTORICAL BACKGROUND

AACR1 Rev. Rule 229.2H provided a note to indicate "intended users" if the document was directed toward a specific group or a "narrowly defined" age group. This rule is essentially the same in its result as the current rule.

When a summary note (AACR1 Rev. Rule 229.2L) was also provided for a document that also had an audience statement, the audience indication became a part of the summary note. There is no provision for this in AACR2.

NOTE EXAMPLES

From its adoption of AACR2, however, the Library of Congress established by practice a policy of using the following construct for some formats:

Intended audience:

Due to a change in the print constant for this note in the MARC formats, since 1985 some LC catalog records with audience notes have utilized the construct:

Audience:

14.92 *Age: 9-30 months.
14.93 *For children 3 to 5 years old.
14.94 *For ages 10 to adult.
14.95 *Grades 4-6.
14.96 *Designed for teenagers.
14.97 *"The original fantasy role playing game for 3 or more adults, ages 10 and up."
14.98 *For two to six players.

Chapter 12 (Serials)

AACR2 RULE

12.7B14 Audience
Make a brief note of the intended audience for, or intellectual level of, a serial if this information is stated in the serial.

RELATED AACR2 RULE

None.

LIBRARY OF CONGRESS POLICY

Although there has been no interpretation issued by the Library of Congress for AACR2 Rule 12.7B14, LC's use of an "augmented Level One" serials description results in other title information being recorded in the Note Area rather than in the Title and Statement of Responsibility Area (see AACR2 Rule 1.0D1 for a description of the minimum elements required for a Level One description). LC's serial cataloging is termed "augmented" Level One because it contains more than the minimum required elements for Level One, but not all of the elements required for a Level Two description. Frequently, this other title information for serials identifies the users for whom a serial is intended.

RELATED LIBRARY OF CONGRESS POLICY

None issued.

AACR2 TEXT EXAMPLES REVISED TO REFLECT LIBRARY OF CONGRESS POLICY

No examples were given in AACR2 or AACR2 Rev.

HISTORICAL BACKGROUND

AACR1 and previous codes had no rule equivalent to AACR2 Rule 12.7B14 for serials.

NOTE EXAMPLES

14.99   The journal of dermatology & allergy for the practicing physician.

14.100   An anthem magazine for junior and teen choirs.

14.101   Journal for dental laboratory technicians.

14.102   Young people's magazine of astronomy and outer space.

14.103   A comprehensive source directory of products and services available to people who accommodate the physically disabled in a work, school, social or rehab environment.

14.104   Circulated to selected practicing dentists.

14.105   Designed for use with: The MacNeil/Lehrer report.

14.106   For physicians in family and internal medicine.

14.107   For the professional interior designer, architect, and contract specifier in the 17 western states.

14.108   Magazine for Atlantic and Gulf yachtsmen.

14.109   Provides information for legislators, boards of education and administrators.

14.110 Published for members of the International Association of Hospitality Accountants.

14.111 Serving the formulating, development and analytical chemist in all industries.

1.7B15. Reference to Published Descriptions

EXTRAPOLATED GENERAL RULE

Note the location of published descriptions of the item.

RELATED AACR2 RULE

None.

LIBRARY OF CONGRESS POLICY

No general rule interpretations have been issued by the Library of Congress to modify, or amplify on, AACR2 Rule 1.7B15. See the chapters below for any LC interpretations for specific material formats.

RELATED LIBRARY OF CONGRESS POLICY

None issued.

FORMAT

None prescribed in general or for the one chapter (4, Manuscripts) that specifically calls for the use of this note.

CHAPTER APPLICATION

This note is specified for use in only Chapter 4 (Manuscripts).

The use of references to published descriptions may occur for document formats other than manuscripts. Indeed, examples of this note in Chapter 1 of AACR2 are references to published descriptions of early printed monographs that are covered by the provisions of Chapter 2, Rules 2.12 to 2.18 (Early Printed Monographs).

Similarly, a cataloger could construct a note for other materials. The example below references a published description in a postage stamp catalog.

Stamp: Scott no. C 12.

EXCEPTIONS AND ADDITIONS

None.

Chapter 2 (Books, Pamphlets, and Printed Sheets)

AACR2 RULE

None.

RELATED AACR2 RULE

None.

LIBRARY OF CONGRESS POLICY

AACR2 Rule 2.12 limits the use of the rules for early printed monographs (Rules 2.12 to 2.18) to "books, pamphlets and broadsides published before 1821 in countries following European conventions in bookmaking." AACR2 Rule 2.18 (Bibliographic References) specifically addresses the use of bibliographic references for incunabula with an option to provide them for other early printed monographs. The Library of Congress has issued guidelines for the treatment of rare books in its publication *Bibliographic Description of Rare Books*. This document replaces AACR2 Rules 2.12 to 2.18, providing more detailed instructions than those in AACR2 (see CSB 16). Included in these guidelines is a rule for the use of notes to record references to published descriptions.

> Give references to published descriptions in a standard and abbreviated form, preceded by the word "References" and a colon. Generally give such references in the form: Surname, Forename Initial(s). Title Bibliography number (if appropriate), if no other briefer citation form is generally recognized. The title portion of the citation may be abridged to one or two key words if this adequately identifies the work. [BDRB 7C14]

These standard citation forms have been published by LC as *Standard Citation Forms for Rare Book Cataloging*.

The documents covered under these LC guidelines are broader than the 1821 criterion of AACR2. LC uses a pre-19th century printing date criterion for works following the European convention of bookmaking, but also applies these rules to post-1801 works that essentially continue the tradition of the hand-printed book. The use of these rules for other than pre-19th century rare books means that some LC cataloging for post-1801 materials will have a note identifying published descriptions.

RELATED LIBRARY OF CONGRESS POLICY

None issued.

AACR2 TEXT EXAMPLES REVISED TO REFLECT LIBRARY OF CONGRESS POLICY

None required.

HISTORICAL BACKGROUND

AACR1 Rule 184B for incunabula called for the use of a note to reference one or more descriptions of a work. It indicated that, if the best reference was to a "rare or inaccessible" source, a second reference should be made to one more accessible. The rule required always recording references published in the British Museum's *Catalogue of Books Printed in the XV Century* and in the *Gesamtkatalog der Wiegendrucke*. When a description was not available in these sources, but appeared in Hain, its supplement (Copinger), or appendices (Reichling), reference was made to them. The AACR1 rule also called for an indication of variations from the published descriptions. The AACR2 rule is not nearly as detailed as its AACR1 predecessor, but allows for the use of these references beyond incunabula at the cataloger's option. The LC guidelines extend coverage well beyond the incunabula period, but still do not provide the detailed instructions present in AACR1.

NOTE EXAMPLES

15.1   References: BAL 8845.
15.2   References: Book Club of Calif. Quarterly news letter, v. 13, no. 1 (1947), p. 7.
15.3   References: Russell 135 [dagger].
15.4   References: Sabin 11533.
15.5   References: Stewart, C.D. The Taylors of Ongar, A3i.
15.6   References: Taylor, W.T. Twenty-one years of Bird & Bull, 1980, A13.

Chapter 4 (Manuscripts)

AACR2 RULE

4.7B15 Reference to Published Descriptions [AACR2 Rev.]
Make notes on the best or fullest published descriptions of a manuscript or a collection of manuscripts and on published indexes or calendars.

RELATED AACR2 RULE

None.

LIBRARY OF CONGRESS POLICY

None issued. APPM, however, expands on the AACR2 text by providing instructions for recording references to descriptions under two different notes.

Finding Aids

Make a note on any finding aids the repository may have to the organization and contents of the material being described, including registers, inventories, calendars, series descriptions, card catalogs, indexes, institutional guides, etc.

If the finding aid has been published, make a bibliographic citation for it. [APPM 4.7B11]

Other Sources of Description

If the material has been reported to and is described in the *National Union Catalog of Manuscript Collections* (NUCMC), or other national guides, give the description number. . . .

Make citations to bibliographic references other than the finding aids relating to the materials being described. Include journal articles describing portions of the materials, guides describing the collection in terms of a particular subject focus, or other published descriptions, indexes, and calendars. [APPM 4.7B12]

RELATED LIBRARY OF CONGRESS POLICY

None issued.

AACR2 TEXT EXAMPLES REVISED TO REFLECT LIBRARY OF CONGRESS POLICY

None required.

HISTORICAL BACKGROUND

AACR1 Rule 207F is the same as the current rule except that the earlier rule also contained an instruction to note those works that have published a "substantial or significant portion" of the work. These notes were to be made when the information was "readily available." An "introductory note" to the general description of manuscripts (preceding AACR1 Rule 201) also stated this.

NOTE EXAMPLES

15.7 *Register enclosed with collection.
15.8 *Described in: Descriptive inventory of the Archives of the State of Illinois (Springfield, 1978).

15.9 *Described in: Milburn Books, Catalog 3, Lot No. 278.

15.10 *Described in: Naval Historical Foundation Manuscript Collection; a catalog (Washington, 1974).

15.11 *Described in: The Southern Historical Collection ; a guide to Manuscripts by Susan Sokol Blosser and Clyde Norman Wilson, Jr. (Chapel Hill, 1970).

15.12 *Described in sale catalog: The Richard Wagner collection . . . , p. 59.

15.13 More fully described in: South Carolina Historical Magazine, v. 82, no. 2 (April 1981), p. 187-190.

15.14 NUCMC MS 81-1145.

15.15 *References: Sonneck, O.G. Beethoven letters in America, p. 77-78 (includes facsim., transcription, and translation).

15.16 *For details on this exchange of letters see: An unpublished letter of Stendhal / by Bernard E. Wilson, in The Newberry Library Bulletin, v. 6, no. 6 (December 1965), p. 187-195.

15.17 *In Pinker correspondence, American publication of H.G. Wells' book, Love and Mr. Lewisham is discussed.

15.18 *See: "Anna B. Kuster Welty, No. 5601," by Dorothy M. Schullian, Journal of the History of Medicine and Allied Science, 2 (1947) : 262-265.

1.7B16. Other Formats

1.7B16 Other Formats [AACR2 Rev.]

> Give the details of other formats in which the content of the item
> has been issued. . . .
> For details of other formats available in the library, see 1.7B20.

RELATED AACR2 RULE

1.5A3 Physical Description Area
> If an item is available in different formats (e.g., as text and mi-
> crofilm; as sound disc and sound tape reel), give the physical descrip-
> tion of the format in hand.
> *Optionally,* make a note describing other formats in which it is
> available (see 1.7B16). [emphasis added]

GENERAL LIBRARY OF CONGRESS POLICY

> When formulating a note under this rule, introduce the note with
>
> "Issued also . . . " (e.g., "Issued also as . . . " , "Issued also in . . . " ,
> "Issued also on . . .") [CSB 12]

RELATED LIBRARY OF CONGRESS POLICY

None issued.

FORMAT

None prescribed.

CHAPTER APPLICATION

This note originally was present in only six of the twelve chapters
for description. It was used in Chapter 6 (Sound Recordings), Chapter
7 (Motion Pictures and Videorecordings), Chapter 8 (Graphic Materials), Chapter 9 (Computer Files), Chapter 11 (Microforms), and
Chapter 12 (Serials).

AACR2 Rev. added this rule to Chapter 2 (Books, Pamphlets, and
Printed Sheets), Chapter 3 (Cartographic Materials), and Chapter 5
(Music). Now only Chapter 4 (Manuscripts) and Chapter 10 (Three-
Dimensional Artefacts and Realia) do not include this rule.

EXCEPTIONS AND ADDITIONS

The use of this note in the ten chapters agrees with the provisions of the General Rule.

Chapter 2 (Books, Pamphlets, and Printed Sheets)

AACR2 RULE

2.7B16 Other Formats [AACR2 Rev.]
Give the details of other formats in which the content of the item has been issued.

RELATED AACR2 RULE

None.

LIBRARY OF CONGRESS POLICY

None issued.

RELATED LIBRARY OF CONGRESS POLICY

None issued.

AACR2 TEXT EXAMPLES REVISED TO REFLECT LIBRARY OF CONGRESS POLICY

None required.

HISTORICAL BACKGROUND

This rule was first introduced in AACR2 Rev. AACR2 and its predecessors had no rule equivalent to Rule 2.7B16.

NOTE EXAMPLES

16.1 Also issued without plates.
16.2 *Issued also in braille.
16.3 *Issued also on computer disk.
16.4 *Issued also as microfiche.
16.5 *Issued also as a sound cassette.

Chapter 3 (Cartographic Materials)

AACR2 RULE

3.7B16 Other Formats [AACR2 Rev.]
Give the details of other formats in which the content of the item has been issued.

RELATED AACR2 RULE

None.

LIBRARY OF CONGRESS POLICY

None issued.

RELATED LIBRARY OF CONGRESS POLICY

None issued.

AACR2 TEXT EXAMPLES REVISED TO REFLECT LIBRARY OF CONGRESS POLICY

None required.

HISTORICAL BACKGROUND

This rule was first introduced in AACR2 Rev. AACR2 and its predecessors had no rule equivalent to Rule 3.7B16.

NOTE EXAMPLES

16.6   Issued also in sheets.
16.7   Issued also on microfiche.

Chapter 5 (Music)

AACR2 RULE

5.7B16 Other Formats [AACR2 Rev.]
Give the details of other formats in which the content of the item has been issued.

RELATED AACR2 RULE

None.

LIBRARY OF CONGRESS POLICY

None issued.

RELATED LIBRARY OF CONGRESS POLICY

None issued.

AACR2 TEXT EXAMPLES REVISED TO REFLECT LIBRARY OF CONGRESS POLICY

None required.

HISTORICAL BACKGROUND

This rule was first introduced in AACR2 Rev. AACR2 and its predecessors had no rule equivalent to Rule 5.7B16.

NOTE EXAMPLES

No examples were located.

Chapter 6 (Sound Recordings)

AACR2 RULE

6.7B16 Other Formats [AACR2 Rev.]
Give the details of other formats in which the content of the item has been issued.

RELATED AACR2 RULE

None.

LIBRARY OF CONGRESS POLICY

Generally make a note on the availability of the item in another medium or other media, if this is known. Record these notes in the position of 6.7B16, 7.7B16, and use the term "issued." [CSB 13]

RELATED LIBRARY OF CONGRESS POLICY

None issued.

AACR2 TEXT EXAMPLES REVISED TO REFLECT LIBRARY OF CONGRESS POLICY

None required. The example in AACR2 would have required a revision. It was rewritten in AACR2 Rev. and no longer requires one.

HISTORICAL BACKGROUND

AACR1 Rev. Rule 252D allowed "collation" information to be supplemented by a note. It further stated that if the library owned the same recording in more than one physical medium, these could be cataloged on one entry with the variations in the collation specified in a "dash" entry (cf. Rev. Rule 152). With a dash entry, dashes were used to indicate that the main entry and title were the same as that of the work being cataloged. The dashes were followed by the phrase "Another issue" followed by any differing bibliographical details. If these differing details included data from the Physical Descriptions Area, they were recorded on a separate line. However, since this note was only permissible when the library owned the additional physical format described, the note served a different function from that of the AACR2 rule, and therefore is not equivalent. Moreover, AACR2 does not use the dash entry format.

NOTE EXAMPLES

16.8 Issued also as analog discs (410 500-1—410 501-1) and as cassettes (410 500-4—410 5010-4).
16.9 Issued also as a compact disc: ACC 48434D.
16.10 Issued also in cassette: 3301 294.
16.11 Issued also as cassettes (414 187-4) and compact discs (414 187-2).
16.12 Issued also on reel.
16.13 Issued also as transcripts no. 999 and 869.
16.14 Lecture issued also as videorecording.

Chapter 7 (Motion Pictures and Videorecordings)

AACR2 RULE

7.7B16 Other Formats [AACR2 Rev.]
Give the details of other formats in which the content of the item has been issued.

RELATED AACR2 RULE

None.

LIBRARY OF CONGRESS POLICY

> Generally make a note on the availability of the item in another medium or other media, if this is known. Record these notes in the position of 6.7B16, 7.7B16, and use the term "issued." [CSB 13]

For archival moving image materials, the Library of Congress supplements AACR2 Chapter 7 with the guidelines in *Archival Moving Image Materials* by White-Hensen.

RELATED LIBRARY OF CONGRESS POLICY

7.7B7 Edition and History

> When an item is known to have an original master in a different medium and the production or release date of the master is more than two years earlier than that of the item being cataloged, give an edition/history note. . . . Make a similar note when an item is known to have been previously produced or issued (more than two years earlier) if in a different medium, but the original medium is unknown. [emphasis added] . . .
>
> If the date of production or release of an original master or an earlier medium is unknown or if the difference between its production or release date and the production or release date of the item being cataloged is two years or less, indicate the availability of the other medium or media in a note according to 7.7B16 and 8.7B16. [emphasis added] . . .
>
> *Note:* The use of production versus release dates is left to the cataloger's judgment. Make the note that seems best to give information about either production or release of other formats on a case-by-case basis. [emphasis added] [CSB 15]

AACR2 TEXT EXAMPLES REVISED TO REFLECT LIBRARY OF CONGRESS POLICY

None required. This example in AACR2 would have required a revision. It was rewritten in AACR2 Rev. and no longer requires one.

HISTORICAL BACKGROUND

AACR1 Rev. Rule 228A3 allowed for the addition to the description of a work information about variant issues "added subsequently." The use of this note was limited to variations of motion pictures and filmstrips in the same medium that differed in their physical characteristics. AACR2 does not address the issue of subsequently added issues.

AACR1 Rev. Rule 229.2F allowed for a note to be made for the "existence of other versions" of a work. One example provided with the rule recorded the existence of another format. AACR2 uses the note to record variations in format rather than other versions. However, if one accepts a different version as a type of format, then the two rules are equivalent. Otherwise, other versions would be recorded as a note under AACR2 Rule 7.7B7.

NOTE EXAMPLES

Language Variation

16.15 Issued also in German.
16.16 Issued also in Bengali, Portuguese, and Spanish.
16.17 Issued also in English dubbed version.

Other Versions

16.18 Issued in 1978 in longer version.
16.19 Issued also in longer version (45 min.) and as videorecording.
16.20 Issued also in shorter version (24 min.).
16.21 Shorter version (15 min.) also issued.
16.22 Shorter version of the 1966 motion picture of the same name.
16.23 Longer version issued in 16 mm.
16.24 Longer version (51 min.) also issued.
16.25 Issued also with captions.
16.26 Issued also as videorecording and in junior version for viewers under age 12.
16.27 Issued also as documentary version and as musical version.

Other Format or Medium

16.28 Also issued in b&w and as videorecording.
16.29 Issued also as super 8 mm. and as videorecording.
16.30 Issued also in 35 mm.
16.31 Issued also as a filmstrip and as slide set.
16.32 Issued also as part of the filmstrip and slide set entitled: Stress in critical illness.
16.33 Issued also as motion picture.
16.34 *Issued as a motion picture in 1980 by Universal City Studios.
16.35 Issued also in other videorecording formats.
16.36 Issued also in other videorecording formats and as motion picture.
16.37 Issued also as 5 videocassettes and as motion picture.
16.38 Issued also in cassette with: Hug me and The Man who had no dream.
16.39 Also issued in two parts on separate cassettes and as motion picture.
16.40 Subsequently issued as videorecording in 1980.

Chapter 8 (Graphic Materials)

AACR2 RULE

8.7B16 Other Formats [AACR2 Rev.]

Give the details of other formats in which the content of the item has been issued.

RELATED AACR2 RULE

None.

LIBRARY OF CONGRESS POLICY

> Generally make a note on the availability of the item in another medium or other media, if this is known. Record these notes in the position of 6.7B16, 7.7B16, and use the term "issued." [CSB 13]

Although not stated in the policy, this note could also be applied to Rule 8.7B16.

For original items and historical collections, the Library of Congress supplements AACR2 Chapter 8 with the guidelines in *Graphic Materials* by Betz.

RELATED LIBRARY OF CONGRESS POLICY

7.7B7 Edition and History
> When an item is known to have an original master in a different medium and the production or release date of the master is more than two years earlier than that of the item being cataloged, give an edition/ history note. . . . Make a similar note when an item is known to have been previously produced or issued (more than two years earlier) if in a different medium, but the original medium is unknown. [emphasis added] . . .
>
> If the date of production or release of an original master or an earlier medium is unknown or if the difference between its production or release date and the production or release date of the item being cataloged is two years or less, indicate the availability of the other medium or media in a note according to 7.7B16 and 8.7B16. [emphasis added] . . .
>
> *Note*: The use of production versus release dates is left to the cataloger's judgment. Make the note that seems best to give information about either production or release of other formats on a case-by-case basis. [emphasis added] [CSB 15]

AACR2 TEXT EXAMPLES REVISED TO REFLECT
LIBRARY OF CONGRESS POLICY

None required. The two examples in AACR2 would have required revision. They were rewritten in AACR2 Rev. and no longer require any.

HISTORICAL BACKGROUND

AACR1 Rev. Rule 228A3 allowed for the addition to the description of a work information about variant issues "added subsequently." The use of this note was limited to variations of motion pictures and filmstrips in the same medium that differed in their physical characteristics. AACR2 does not address the issue of subsequently added issues.

AACR1 Rev. Rule 229.2F allowed for a note to be made for the "existence of other versions" of a work. One example provided with the rule recorded the existence of another format. AACR2 uses this note to record variations in format rather than other versions. However, if one accepts a different version as a type of format, then the two rules are equivalent. Otherwise, other versions would be recorded as a note under AACR2 Rule 8.7B7.

AACR1 Rule 272C4 provided for a note to record the existence of related works for pictures. These related works included the "publication of the material in a different form." AACR2 does not include this provision. Normally, this information for pictures would be covered under AACR2 Rule 8.7B7.

NOTE EXAMPLES

Projection Graphic Materials

16.41 Issued also in b&w.
16.42 Issued also as elementary version.
16.43 Issued also as secondary version.
16.44 Issued also as filmstrip.
16.45 Issued also as 16 mm. filmstrip in cartridge.
16.46 Issued also as microfiche set.
16.47 Issued also as motion picture.
16.48 Issued also as slide set.
16.49 Issued with 116 col. slides containing same content.
16.50 Issued also as individual slide sets under set title of the same name.
16.51 Issued also as 16 mm. filmstrip in cartridge and as slide set.
16.52 Issued also as slide set and videorecording.
16.53 Issued also as 16 mm. filmstrip in cartridge, as slide set, and as videorecording.
16.54 Issued also as slide set by: IBIS Media.
16.55 Issued also as slide sets under individual titles by: Center for Humanities.
16.56 Issued also with sound accompaniment on disc.
16.57 Issued also with sound accompaniment on disc and as slide set.
16.58 Issued also with sound accompaniment on disc, as 16 mm. filmstrip in cartridge, and as slide set.

Chapter 9 (Computer Files)

AACR2 RULE

9.7B16 Other Formats [AACR2 Rev.]

Give the details of other formats in which the content of the file has been issued.

RELATED AACR2 RULE

None.

LIBRARY OF CONGRESS POLICY

None issued for AACR2 Rev. Ch. 9.

RELATED LIBRARY OF CONGRESS POLICY

None issued for AACR2 Rev. Ch. 9.

AACR2 TEXT EXAMPLES REVISED TO REFLECT LIBRARY OF CONGRESS POLICY

None required for AACR2 Rev. Ch. 9.

HISTORICAL BACKGROUND

Computer files were not covered by AACR1 or previous codes. The original AACR2 Chapter 9 covered the elements present in the revised rule except that it required that information about the other formats had to be derived from the documentation. AACR2 Rev. does not have this requirement.

NOTE EXAMPLES

16.59   *Also available for the Apple Macintosh.
16.60   *Also available on single-sided, double density disks.
16.61   *Also available on 3 1/2 in. disks.
16.62   *Also available in microform and hard copy print.
16.63   *Also runs on IBM PCjr with DOS 2.1.

Chapter 12 (Serials)

AACR2 RULE

12.7B16 Other Formats [AACR2 Rev.]
    Give the details of other formats in which the content of the serial is, or has been, issued.

RELATED AACR2 RULE

None.

LIBRARY OF CONGRESS POLICY

None issued.

RELATED LIBRARY OF CONGRESS POLICY

None issued.

AACR2 TEXT EXAMPLES REVISED TO REFLECT
LIBRARY OF CONGRESS POLICY

No examples were given in AACR2. None are required for AACR2
Rev.

HISTORICAL BACKGROUND

AACR1 and previous codes had no rule equivalent to AACR2 Rule
12.7B16 for serials.

NOTE EXAMPLES

16.64   Also available in braille.
16.65   Available also in microform.
16.66   Also available in 16-millimeter microfilm.
16.67   Also available on microfiche from Pergamon Press.
16.68   Available on microfilm from University Microfilms International.
16.69   Available on microfilm from University Microfilms; on microfiche from
        Bell & Howell.
16.70   Introduction is not available in microform; it is available only in printed
        form.

1.7B17. Summary

EXTRAPOLATED GENERAL RULE

Give a brief objective summary of the item's content unless another part of the description provides enough information.

RELATED AACR2 RULE

None.

GENERAL LIBRARY OF CONGRESS POLICY

No general interpretations have been issued by the Library of Congress to modify, or amplify on, AACR2 Rule 1.7B17. See the sections that follow for any LC policies and interpretations that apply to individual AACR2 chapters for description.

RELATED LIBRARY OF CONGRESS POLICY

1.7A3 Forms of Notes
When nonroman data (including quotations) are being recorded in the note area, give them in romanized form in all cases, including those cards that contain nonromanized elements in the body of the entry.

When a note begins with a formal introductory term such as "contents," "credits," or "summary," do not use all caps in any case; instead, use upper and lower case as illustrated in AACR 2. [emphasis added] [CSB 22]

FORMAT

Although the rules themselves do not provide any particular format, this note traditionally begins with the word "Summary." Generally, a summary is less than fifty words in length and is often confined to one sentence.

CHAPTER APPLICATION

This note is not present in Chapter 3 (Cartographic Materials) and Chapter 5 (Music). Chapter 12 (Serials) does not use this note to record a summary statement.

EXCEPTIONS AND ADDITIONS

Chapter 6 (Sound Recordings) excludes the use of a summary for sound recordings that are primarily, or solely, musical.

Chapter 9 (Computer Files, AACR2 Rev.) adds the provision to indicate the purpose of the file.

Chapter 12 (Serials) uses this note to indicate the existence of cumulative or separately published indexes rather than to provide a summary.

Chapter 2 (Books, Pamphlets, and Printed Sheets)

AACR2 RULE

2.7B17 Summary [AACR2 Rev.]

Give a brief objective summary of the content of an item unless another part of the description provides enough information.

RELATED AACR2 RULE

None.

LIBRARY OF CONGRESS POLICY

For materials covered by this chapter, the Library of Congress generally uses a summary note only for juvenile materials.

Additionally, the Library of Congress has also issued the following Rule Interpretation:

> The Library of Congress overseas offices provide a subject note on records they create for their accessions lists. Those notes created by the New Delhi Office for books are now being included in Library of Congress bibliographic records. These notes which are tagged 520 in the machine-readable record, are introduced by "Summary: . . . "
>
> The overseas offices follow these guidelines when creating subject notes:
>
> 1) Make a concise statement, mentioning only major points of the contents. Phrases, rather than sentences, may be used when clarity and good taste permit.
> 2) Include objective statements only, avoiding any explicit or implicit evaluation of the contents from any point of view. If it is the contents of the work that show a bias, which it is important for the subject note to bring out, word the note carefully so that

it is clear the author's bias, not the cataloger's, is the one being related.

3) Depending on the particular contents of a work note that it is important to bring out such information as
   a) coverage of a time period or of a geographic area;
   b) educational level or slant of the material, e.g., " ... for home study ... " or " ... college-level instruction ... ";
   c) obvious purpose of the contents;
   d) genre of the contents, e.g., "handbook," "government report," "guidelines";
   e) any other major information considered important.

Descriptive catalogers at the Library of Congress have no responsibility for these notes, beyond the correction of specific errors. If the whole note needs recasting, however, the descriptive cataloger should delete it without formulating a replacement. [CSB 24]

RELATED LIBRARY OF CONGRESS POLICY

None issued.

AACR2 TEXT EXAMPLES REVISED TO REFLECT LIBRARY OF CONGRESS POLICY

None required.

HISTORICAL BACKGROUND

The provision of a summary note is basically new for the cataloging of books. No rule in AACR1 Rev. or its predecessors specially called for its use. A summary has been used in the past by the Library of Congress for juvenile books (see LC *Cataloging Service.* Bulletin No. 86, Jan., 1969). Although no policy statement has been issued to this effect for AACR2, LC is continuing this practice.

The capitalization of the introductory term for a summary note does differ between the two codes as have other introductory captions.

AACR1 — SUMMARY:
AACR2 — Summary:

NOTE EXAMPLES

Story Outline

17.1 Summary: The Hardy boys help out when a magician's tournament is threatened by mysterious happenings.

17.2 Summary: Judged guilty by the Inquisition, a condemned man is slowly tortured.

17.3 Summary: Kermit, Fozzie, and Gonzo set out for London where they and Miss Piggy search for the thief of Lady Holiday's jewels.

17.4 Summary: Ted, the son of a school administrator, rebels at having to live in Ethiopia when he dreams of returning home to Arizona. He becomes adroit at manipulating people around him in order to gain his ends, but then events get out of hand.

17.5 Summary: Toad trades Toad Hall for a fast red motorcar, only to later be jailed as a car thief.

17.6 Summary: Each car on the train has one more zoo animal than the one before, from the first car with an elephant to the last with ten birds.

Content Description

17.7 Summary: Famous American entertainers, authors, and political and sports figures recall their favorite childhood reading.

17.8 Summary: Handbook of simplified shadow puppet plays for use on the overhead projector. Included are puppet patterns, scripts, story boards and specific production details for seven plays.

17.9 Summary: A historical introduction to the guitar, with information on famous contemporary guitarists and suggestions for the aspiring musician.

17.10 Summary: The history of the growth of European power and influence in all parts of the world during the nineteenth century.

17.11 Summary: An introduction to karate techniques with exercises and drills designed to develop the necessary discipline.

17.12 Summary: An introduction to jazz, focusing on its historical development and famous performers.

17.13 Summary: The letters of the alphabet are introduced by words and pictures beginning with each letter.

17.14 Summary: Presents 120 of Aesop's classic tales rewritten for reading aloud.

17.15 Summary: A simple explanation of the basics of computer programming.

17.16 Summary: Traces the history of the typewriter from the invention of a writing machine in the 18th century to the sophisticated machines of the present day.

Nature

17.17 Summary: Activities, projects, and games for indoors and out when it snows.

17.18 Summary: An annotated bibliography of fiction and nonfiction titles, designed to focus on the history and character of the Upper Midwest, i.e., Michigan, Minnesota, and Wisconsin.

17.19 Summary: Brief text, written from a feline point-of-view, and photographs explore the world of cats and kittens.

17.20   Summary: A collection of poems written from the point of view of a child with a black mother and a white father.

17.21   Summary: A collection of seventy-nine prayers for girls, the majority asking for a particular good, virtue, or strength; others praying against weakness and evil, and the last twelve addressing themselves to a particular situation or condition.

17.22   Summary: A compilation of articles about television and its effect on politics, religion, education, and other aspects of American culture.

17.23   Summary: A complete, up-to-date listing of colleges and universities that offer scholarships to athletes, and of the sports for which scholarships are offered.

17.24   Summary: A dictionary describing over 200 signs, symbols, and liturgical items and their meaning in Catholic worship and practice.

17.25   Summary: Illustrations depict fairy folk among a variety of flowers described in the accompanying poems.

17.26   Summary: Instructions for making 11 different boats from common items. When finished, each boat will float.

17.27   Summary: More than 150 questions and answers dealing with such topics as science, sports, the entertainment field, games, literature, famous people, space, and medicine.

17.28   Summary: Photographs and text, including comments by the owners, portray the architecture and decor of 17 homes of people in the music industry.

17.29   Summary: Pictures of common objects and the parts of which they are composed, classed under general categories such as living things, transportation, and personal items, are identified by name.

17.30   Summary: Thirty-five one-act plays, most with fifteen or twenty minutes playing time, including fantasies, comedies, and several appropriate for different holidays.

17.31   Summary: Readings on various subjects, with Bible verses, questions for discussion, and prayers, for use in family devotions.

17.32   Summary: Recipes based on references to food in "The Wonderful Wizard of Oz."

17.33   Summary: A reproduction of an antique German toy book which folds out to show fourteen scenes in a nineteenth-century city park.

17.34   Summary: Text, illustrations, and suggested activities outline such basic concepts of geography as scale, maps, the globe, continental plates, and oceans.

17.35   Summary: A textbook of the theory and practical applications of electricity and electronics.

Chapter 4 (Manuscripts)

AACR2 RULE

4.7B17 Summary [AACR2 Rev.]
Give a brief objective summary of the content of an item unless another part of the description provides enough information.

Although there is a provision for the use of a summary note, it is not a note that is frequently provided. Instead, information about the nature of a manuscript is generally included under AACR2 Rule 4.7B1 (Nature, Scope, or Form of Manuscript(s)).

RELATED AACR2 RULE

None.

LIBRARY OF CONGRESS POLICY

None issued. The APPM manual does not provide for a summary note. Information about the nature of the manuscript is covered by APPM Rule 4.7B4 (Scope and Context/Abstract).

RELATED LIBRARY OF CONGRESS POLICY

None issued.

AACR2 TEXT EXAMPLES REVISED TO REFLECT LIBRARY OF CONGRESS POLICY

No examples were given in AACR2 or AACR2 Rev.

HISTORICAL BACKGROUND

AACR1 Rule 202C and Rule 202D made provision for a brief statement of the topic of a letter or collection of letters. This note could also be provided under AACR2, although it is not explicitly called for.

AACR1 Rule 203 provided for a statement of the subject of speeches, lectures, and sermons in a note or following the date of the manuscript. Again, the AACR2 rule could also provide a similar statement.

NOTE EXAMPLES

None provided due to the nature of the use of this note. See examples under AACR2 Rule 4.7B1.

Chapter 6 (Sound Recordings)

AACR2 RULE

6.7B17 Summary
Give a brief objective summary of the content of a sound recording (other than one that consists entirely or predominantly of music) unless another part of the description provides enough information.

RELATED AACR2 RULE

None.

LIBRARY OF CONGRESS POLICY

None issued.

RELATED LIBRARY OF CONGRESS POLICY

None issued.

AACR2 TEXT EXAMPLES REVISED TO REFLECT LIBRARY OF CONGRESS POLICY

None required.

HISTORICAL BACKGROUND

AACR1 Rev. Rule 252F11 provided for the use of a note to record the "summary of content of a nonmusical recording," in much the same way as AACR2 Rule 6.7B17. The capitalization of the introductory term differs between the two codes as it does with other captions.

AACR1 — SUMMARY:
AACR2 — Summary:

NOTE EXAMPLES

17.36 Summary: Actor, director, and dramatist Tyrone Guthrie discusses various phases of his career in the repertory theater, and philosophizes on the reasons for the theater's continuing growth and development. Includes excerpts of rehearsal sessions of plays he directed.

17.37 Summary: The author discusses the collecting of autographs, the language of autograph catalogs, and the features which make a particular autograph rare or desirable.

17.38 Summary: A basic review of secured transactions law under article 9 of the Uniform commercial code. Covers such topics as attachment, perfection, priorities, and foreclosure.

17.39 Summary: Documents the history of the musical box and its antecedents on side one, followed by music played on various musical boxes in the Victoria and Albert Museum on side two.

17.40 Summary: Dr. Auerbach discusses diseases that affect the skin, including acne, psoriasis, cancer, and allergies. He notes how these and other skin diseases can be treated, and comments on skin aging and wrinkling and the use of face lifts.

17.41 Summary: Elvis Presley discusses the start of his singing career, his experiences in the U.S. Army, and his career aspirations.

17.42 Summary: Illustrates the individual vowel and consonant sounds, both isolated and within words, of spoken English.

17.43 Summary: In the first sermon, Dr. Peale explains how the power of faith can help one live a better and healthier life. In the second sermon, Dr. Peale talks about belief in God and how it can work to make the impossible become possible.

17.44 Summary: Includes such selections as the duet "Wild & wooley West," Rogers' 1932 speech at the National Democratic Convention, his views on radio comedians, his plan to stop all wars, his plan to end all plans, his last broadcast of June 9, 1935, and others.

17.45 Summary: Monologues, comedy sketches, etc., featuring W.C. Fields in radio and motion picture appearances.

17.46 Summary: Mr. Landau and Mr. Rheingold discuss types of litigation currently going on involving environmental pollutants. They cover product liability causes of action, dealing with defenses, choice of forum, proof of causation, finding and use of experts, damage and fees, trial considerations, etc.

17.47 Summary: Offers instruction in the spelling and pronunciation of the Hawaiian language. Includes drills and supplementary exercises.

17.48 Summary: An oral history of the 76th Infantry Division from 1942 to 1945 and its operations in the Ardennes, the Rhineland, and Central Germany.

17.49 Summary: Part one discusses the language of Shakespeare's Hamlet and part two provides critical commentary on the play.

17.50 Summary: Poets reading their poetry include Gertrude Stein, Louis Untermeyer, Dorothy Parker, Lenore G. Marshall, Muriel Rukeyser, Ruth Stone, Anthony Hecht, Allen Ginsberg, Grace Schulman, and others.

17.51 Summary: Reproduces the songs and calls of fifty-nine species of birds commonly found in Florida.

17.52 Summary: Selected opinions of Justice Holmes both from the Massachusetts Supreme Judicial Court and the United States Supreme Court. Includes a speech delivered by Holmes on his 90th birthday.

17.53 Summary: Sketches Flaubert's fictional character, Emma Bovary, through the story of her rebellion against French provincial life in the nineteenth century.

17.54 Summary: Speakers deal with problems of representation, administrative agency proceedings prior to or concurrent with investigation, grand jury investigation, etc.

17.55 Summary: Taken from the science fiction story of the time machine that could be manipulated and that could take one into the remote future through the fourth dimension to a futuristic environment and people. The time traveler provides a commentary on the direction of our present society.

Chapter 7 (Motion Pictures and Videorecordings)

AACR2 RULE

7.7B17 Summary

Give a brief objective summary of the content of an item unless another part of the description provides enough information.

RELATED AACR2 RULE

None.

LIBRARY OF CONGRESS POLICY

None issued. For archival moving image materials, the Library of Congress supplements AACR2 Chapter 7 with the guidelines in *Archival Moving Image Materials* by White-Hensen.

RELATED LIBRARY OF CONGRESS POLICY

None issued.

AACR2 TEXT EXAMPLES REVISED TO REFLECT LIBRARY OF CONGRESS POLICY

None required.

HISTORICAL BACKGROUND

AACR1 Rev. Rule 229.2L provided for the use of a summary note in essentially the same situations as AACR2, but with more detailed guidelines as to its use. As with other captions, the capitalization of the introductory term differs between the two codes.

AACR1 — SUMMARY:
AACR2 — Summary:

AACR1 Rev. Rule 229.2M advised that, if the titles of parts of a work were not sufficiently descriptive to serve as a summary, a summary note was preferred over a contents note. AACR2 does not provide this guidance.

NOTE EXAMPLES

Story Outline

17.56   Summary: An animated film in which a friendly little hedgehog almost falls prey to an enchanting cat that plans to eat him. Without narration.

17.57   Summary: A comedy feature about a big city newspaper editor and his star reporter.

17.58   *Summary: An ex-convict and his friend raise money for an orphanage. Comedy.

17.59   Summary: Janiloo Hill, a former New York fashion model, and her eighty-year-old mother, Rita, once a Hollywood stunt woman, live without electricity or plumbing in Shakespeare, N.M., a one-time booming mining town which has become a ghost town. Shows how these women are restoring the town.

17.60   Summary: Features the Monty Python comedy troupe in a Gothic horror about a man who lives alone and is in constant fear of a hideous object which has set his life on a tragic and terrifying course.

Content Description

17.61   Summary: Explains the orientation of a military map. Tells how to find direction and location without the use of a compass.

17.62   Summary: Author Anthony Burgess takes the viewer on a tour of Rome, where he also lives and works. He shows the diversity of the city and its people, and tells of its superstitions, ruins, temples, theaters, and rich artistic and historical traditions.

17.63   Summary: An episode in the series hosted by actor Greg Morris which illustrates, through fictional characters and situations, how the child develops socially by learning about other people, relationships, rules, and role behaviors.

17.64   Summary: Examines the canine family, both domesticated and wild. Shows wolves, coyotes, jackals, and foxes in their natural habitats and discusses how their body configurations and behavior patterns help them survive in the wild. Also describes the various breeds of domesticated dogs and shows the numerous ways that they are used in human society.

17.65   Summary: Focuses on the Neonatal Intensive Care Unit of Children's Hospital, Los Angeles. Examines some of the life-and-death decisions made as well as the ethical dilemmas posed by new technologies available in the care of critically ill newborn babies.

17.66   Summary: Gathered in a park to picnic and swim, members of both sexes and representatives of a range of age groups dramatize the manifestation of sexuality at various stages of human development. Deals with touching, fantasies, communication, and values in the evolution of a healthy sexual identity and of a satisfying sexual relationship.

17.67   Summary: Shows how, through courage, determination, and persistence, Mary Louise Carson, Bernice Dombroski, and Marilyn McCusker won jobs in a man's world as coal miners in Pennsylvania.

17.68   Summary: Shows naval aircraft soaring to the beat of a modern jazz soundtrack.

17.69   Summary: Part I presents a review of solar energy systems and describes simplified design procedures and the economics of installing solar energy systems. Part 2 deals with automated design procedures, installation of solar components, and solar economics.

Nature

17.70   Summary: From the restless movement of the atoms in the universe, a hero is born who explores the depths of that universe, disappearing into its infinity. He returns, but is unnoticed. It is another time, and his time is past. An animated film.

17.71   Summary: An animated film which takes a humorous, yet serious look at the devastation of the earth caused by mankind's unrelenting search for progress. Without narration.

17.72   Summary: An animated satire about a father who tries, but fails, to tell his teenage son the facts of life.

17.73   Summary: Presents a documentary of Bill Moore, Chesapeake Bay waterman and boatbuilder, that shows how he constructs a deadrise workboat using traditional skills, tools, and techniques.

17.74   Summary: A dramatization, using actual members and locations of the American Armed Forces, of what could happen during the first minutes of a Soviet surprise attack. Explores the controversial issue of United States strategic vulnerability.

17.75   Summary: An experimental film which shows a dancer performing three movements that have been photographed in different ways, edited, and set to music. Without narration.

17.76   Summary: Using interviews, interspersed with dramatic sequences and the views of recognized authorities, teaches managers how to cope with stress, including how to pinpoint circumstances that trigger stress, recognize the signs of too much or too little stress, and modify certain behaviors and attitudes.

17.77   Summary: A parody of a Black James Bond movie, used to symbolize the theme of economic slavery. Set in Washington, D.C., shows the struggles a young Black faces when he tries to break out of his dependence on making a living through dealing with shady underworld characters.

Cast/Credits/Statements of Responsibility

17.78 Summary: An animated version of two famous nonsense rhymes, The owl and the pussy-cat by Edward Lear and Little birds by Lewis Carroll.

17.79 Summary: Actor Jack Klugman, in his TV role as Dr. Quincy, presents the message of lab safety by stressing the importance of constant awareness on the part of lab personnel. Uses dramatic vignettes to demonstrate the consequences of negligence, followed by corrective measures that lab personnel can take to avoid accidents.

17.80 Summary: Documents the importance of the space shuttle to America and the world. Shows shuttle tests, the training of astronauts, and space specialists at work. Includes brief comments on space exploration by novelists James Michener and Isaac Asimov.

17.81 Summary: As the septuagenarian chats with "60 minutes" interviewer Morley Safer, the camera cuts in and out of U.S. Congresswoman Millicent Fenwick's dawn-to-past-dusk day, documenting the energy and dedication with which she serves her New Jersey constituents. Also includes some family and archival photographs.

17.82 Summary: Dr. David W. Schteingart is interviewed by Dr. Irving H. Fox. Provides an overview of how a multidisciplinary approach can be used to effectively manage the obese patient. Discusses caloric restrictions, physical exercise and training, psychosocial support, and vocational rehabilitation.

17.83 Summary: Teaches basic writing skills for office workers, emphasizing the importance of preparing a first draft of a letter. Describes the three parts of a good business letter and presents examples. Hosted by Cicely Tyson.

17.84 Summary: Needlepoint authority Erica Wilson demonstrates the basic and fine points of embroidery used in creating graphics.

17.85 Summary: A futuristic visual presentation on working and living in the 21st century, shown at the Working in the 21st Century Conference, Richmond, Va., April 3-4, 1979.

Designated Objective or Audience

17.86 Summary: Designed for auto-tutorial use in conjunction with a beginning course in American sign language. Assuming no knowledge of any sign language, lessons 1-36 introduce new material (vocabulary, examples of usage, and dialogues or stories) and lessons 37-40 are review lessons. Incorporates the essential linguistic elements of ASL: vocabulary, morphology, syntax, mimetic/pantomimic devices, facial expressions, and fingerspelling.

17.87 Summary: Designed to alert boys to the possibility of sexual attack. Three vignettes show typical situations that lead to danger and how to avoid them.

17.88 Summary: Excerpts from interviews with various individuals concerning current attitudes about public schools in the United States. Includes comments and suggestions for improvements. Intended to stimulate discussions which will lead educators to develop a written plan of action.

17.89   Summary: Follows two young boys in their village at Don May, Thailand as they go about their daily routine, which includes taking an offering to the Buddhist monks, catching fish with their bare hands, and helping build a traditional Thai house. Intended to foster a better understanding and appreciation of varying life-styles and cultures in other parts of the world.

17.90   Summary: Sam the Safety Duck, an animated character, shows what can happen to children as the result of inconsiderate or wrongful behavior on the school bus and illustrates conduct rules to prevent injuries while riding the school bus.

17.91   Summary: Shows how a crew of stunt drivers created a three-car accident for the motion picture Ordeal by accident. Designed to create awareness of careless driving.

17.92   Summary: A training program on perception designed to help correct communication problems in management. Makes participants aware of their unconscious misperceptions about themselves, their coworkers, and their work environment.

17.93   Summary: Designed to acquaint new employees of the Mutual Benefit Life Insurance Company with the history and development of the company.

17.94   Summary: An overview of the Veterans Administration guidelines for a unified graphics communications system as developed by Malcolm Grear Designers. Designed for use in conjunction with the VA manual.

17.95   Summary: A short course in industrial energy conservation which has been designed for plant personnel and consultants who are responsible for energy cost reduction implementation.

17.96   Summary: Uses the format of a television game show to demonstrate the importance of proper fit and appropriate length of clothes. Designed to support and supplement ongoing socialization training of developmentally disabled adolescents and adults.

17.97   Summary: Demonstrates step-by-step procedures for giving a complete bed bath, and explains both the rationale and the nursing skill involved. Designed for classroom or individual use.

Technical Aspects

17.98   Summary: Presents a case study in management involving a conflict between an employee and a supervisor, and shows the attempts of their manager to deal with the situation. Designed with a freeze-frame ending to encourage viewers to develop their own strategies for managing conflicts.

Chapter 8 (Graphic Materials)

AACR2 RULE

8.7B17 Summary
   Give a brief objective summary of the content of an item unless another part of the description provides enough information.

RELATED AACR2 RULE

None.

LIBRARY OF CONGRESS POLICY

None issued. For original items and historical collections, the Library of Congress supplements AACR2 Chapter 8 with the guidelines in *Graphic Materials* by Betz.

RELATED LIBRARY OF CONGRESS POLICY

None issued.

AACR2 TEXT EXAMPLES REVISED TO REFLECT LIBRARY OF CONGRESS POLICY

None required.

HISTORICAL BACKGROUND

AACR1 Rev. Rule 229.2L provided for the use of a summary note in essentially the same situations as AACR2, but with more detailed guidance as to its use. As with other captions, the capitalization of the introductory term differs between the two codes.

   AACR1 — SUMMARY:
   AACR2 — Summary:

AACR1 Rev. Rule 229.2M advised that, if the titles of parts of a work were not sufficiently descriptive to serve as a summary, a summary note was preferred over a contents note. AACR2 does not provide this guideline.

NOTE EXAMPLES

Projection Graphic Materials
   17.99 Summary: Shows the daily activities of a forest ranger.
   17.100 Summary: Islam: its development, practices and beliefs, art, and culture.

377

17.101 Summary: Defines botany and discusses genetics, classification, and other major concerns in this field. Also shows botanists at work.

17.102 Summary: Part 1 explores the role of the respiratory muscles in ventilation. Explains pressure-volume changes, the role of pulmonary surfactant, and various types of airflow. Part 2 introduces lung volumes and capacities, and explores the various ways of determining alveolar ventilation. Also discusses pathological conditions causing hypoventilation and hyperventilation.

17.103 Summary: StoryStrip 1 tells the story of vampire Count Dracula, who stalks his victims through the fog of London. StoryStrip 2 tells about the scientist who was tormented by the creature he created.

17.104 Summary: A photographic enactment of Schuman's cantata of the same title, accompanied by a reading of the poem by Ernest Thayer.

17.105 Summary: Composer Nicolas Fagello discusses the creative process and prepares for the first performance of his work for symphonic band, Odyssey. Along with excerpts from the rehearsals, Mr. Fagello describes the motivations and concerns that guided him as he shaped the work.

17.106 Summary: An adaptation of the author's book about an elderly, Black schoolteacher who is taken into the lives and hearts of the Stone family.

17.107 Summary: A retelling of the Jewish legend of the golem created by Rabbi Lev to protect the Jews of Prague from the angry mob.

17.108 Summary: Uses archival and news photographs to explore the roots and tragic results of Senator Joseph McCarthy's allegations of Communist influence in the federal government.

17.109 Summary: Uses situational examples to describe various jobs in the building trades and industrial maintenance occupations, including the duties, working conditions, and habits and attitudes that employees are expected to demonstrate in these occupations. Includes some response frames.

17.110 Summary: Stories of youngsters' heroism, designed to promote the development of reading and listening skills.

17.111 Summary: Uses cartoon art and special graphic effects to teach young children a logical, orderly sequence of writing skills, from punctuation to paragraph development.

17.112 Summary: Uses paintings, dramatizations, and narration to create suspenseful scenes from classical novels. The outcome of the scene is left unfinished so that students will be encouraged to read the text.

17.113 Summary: Describes and demonstrates the abnormalities found in red blood cells and how they relate to anemias. Designed for individual or classroom use.

17.114 Summary: The first filmstrip examines the nature of the current energy crisis and explains why fossil fuel shortages cause higher energy costs. The second filmstrip discusses current energy sources and new alternatives.

Nonprojection Graphic Materials

17.115 *Summary: Demonstrates common anatomical terms and how to dissect the frog.

378

17.116 *Five horizontal rows show the braille and roman alphabets and numerals.

17.117 *Summary: Activity cards containing quizzes and informal games for programs in old age homes.

17.118 *Subject: Portraits of three Indians (half-length), separately titled.

17.119 *Subject: Two head-and-shoulders portraits in separate ornamental oval frames; one frame held by eagle.

17.120 *Subject: Studio portrait of New York Baseball team. Printed identifications on mount: manager McGunnigle, players Smith, Pinckney, Corkhill, Caruthers, Terry, Collings, Foutz, Hughes, O'Brien, Bushong, Clark, Visner, Lovett.

Chapter 9 (Computer Files)

AACR2 RULE

9.7B17 Summary [AACR2 Rev.]

Give a brief objective summary of the purpose and content of an item unless another part of the description provides enough information.

RELATED AACR2 RULE

None.

LIBRARY OF CONGRESS POLICY

None issued for AACR2 Rev. Ch. 9.

RELATED LIBRARY OF CONGRESS POLICY

None issued for AACR2 Rev. Ch. 9.

AACR2 TEXT EXAMPLES REVISED TO REFLECT LIBRARY OF CONGRESS POLICY

None required for AACR2 Rev. Ch. 9.

HISTORICAL BACKGROUND

Computer files were not covered by AACR1 or previous codes. The original AACR2 Chapter 9 was similar to the AACR2 Rev. rule except that the revised rule indicates that the summary note may be used to identify the purpose of a computer file as well as its content.

379

NOTE EXAMPLES

17.121 *Summary: Program performs univariate and multivariate analyses of variance, covariance, and regression.

17.122 *Summary: Helps develop an understanding of the relationships between energy, force and work. Also covers simple machines; the conservation of energy, potential and kinetic energy, and the various forms of energy.

17.123 *Summary: The objective of the survey was to ascertain the views of Federal employees about restrictions on their political activity, the effects of such regulations, and whether the employees' views and behavior would change if present regulations were altered.

17.124 *Summary: This study is composed of data on general economic and political attitudes, including attitudes toward the federal government, voting behavior, the employment history of the head of household and his/her expectations about financial change.

17.125 *Summary: Produced as part of the Phoenix program, file contains records of Vietnamese believed by U.S. to be aiding the Viet Cong. Information includes name, aliases, sex, age, birthplace, source of information, suspected role with Viet Cong, and official U.S. action taken against individual.

17.126 *Summary: Contains 2 sets of raw data: one containing information used to construct aggregate measures of fractionalization and concentration; the other containing data used to construct measures of inequality. The first set of data use these variables: city populations, language, ethnic group, export commodities, distribution of votes, etc. The second uses variables such as: distribution of farms, acreage, labor forces and gross domestic product.

17.127 *Summary: Provides information on the size, and composition of the housing inventory, the characteristics of its occupants, the changes in the inventory resulting from new construction and from losses, indicators of housing and neighborhood quality, characteristics of urban and rural housing units, for the United States and regions. Individual records for approximately 70,000 households are included in the yearly study.

17.128 *Summary: The General Social Surveys have been conducted during February, March, and April of 1972, 1973, 1974, 1975, 1976 and 1977. There are a total of 9,120 completed interviews (1,613 in 1972, 1,504 in 1973, 1,484 in 1974, 1,490 in 1975, 1,499 in 1976, and 1,530 in 1977). Each survey is an independently drawn sample of English-speaking persons of 18 years of age or over, living in non-institutional arrangements within the continental U.S. The cumulative data set merges all six surveys into a single file with each year of survey acting as a subfile. This arrangement of the data facilitates trend analysis on repeated questions of social concern over a six-year period.

17.129 *Summary: The survey gives basic county and state-level ecological or descriptive data for the years 1790-   . The majority of these ecological data sets were archived from the United States federal census reports of 1790-   , although selected bodies of data from other sources have been integrated into the collection as well. The data are organized in the form of forty-three data sets; the collection contains information on over 3400 counties and states. Most of the data are recorded at the county level, although thirteen of the data sets present data available only at the state level.

Chapter 10 (Three-Dimensional Artefacts and Realia)

AACR2 RULE

10.7B17 Summary [AACR2 Rev.]
Give a brief objective summary of the content of an item unless another part of the description provides enough information.

RELATED AACR2 RULE

None.

LIBRARY OF CONGRESS POLICY

None issued.

RELATED LIBRARY OF CONGRESS POLICY

None issued.

AACR2 TEXT EXAMPLES REVISED TO REFLECT LIBRARY OF CONGRESS POLICY

None required.

HISTORICAL BACKGROUND

AACR1 Rev. Rule 229.2L provided for the use of a summary note in essentially the same situations as AACR2, but with more detailed guidance for its use. As with other captions, the capitalization of the introductory term differs between the two codes.

AACR1 — SUMMARY:
AACR2 — Summary:

AACR1 Rev. Rule 229.2M advised that, if the titles of parts of a work were not sufficiently descriptive to serve as a summary, a summary note was preferred over a contents note. AACR2 does not provide this guideline.

NOTE EXAMPLES

17.130   *Summary: Citizens of outer space struggle to avoid civil war and learn about astronomy, map reading, spacecraft design, etc.
17.131   *Summary: Cross-sections and tissue samples of various flat worms.
17.132   *Summary: A slide system for the study of conditions of the rectum and colon.
17.133   *Summary: Eleven colorful pictures and an unbreakable mirror on two panels unfold and interlock in different patterns.
17.134   *Summary: Versatile combination of toy and puzzle. Two appealing figures, two different blocks, a base to hold them all. Figures fit into blocks, blocks fit into base, figures fit on top of each other. Turn base over and discover even more puzzle opportunities.
17.135   *Summary: Board game for two to five players. Designed to instruct players about the operation and development of a coal mine.
17.136   *Summary: Designed to encourage students to habitually produce the r sound correctly in isolation and in blends in conversational speech.
17.137   *Summary: Designed to help discover needs and attitudes regarding parenthood.
17.138   *Summary: Flannel board set designed to develop skills in classification, determination of relationships between objects and promote skills in using judgement and discrimination.
17.139   *Summary: Introduces the student to the value of each coin and how to count money.

Chapter 12 (Serials)

AACR2 RULE

12.7B17 Indexes
Make notes on the presence of cumulative indexes. When possible, give[:]

> the kind of index,
> the volumes, etc., of the serial indexed,
> the dates of the serial indexed, and
> the location of the index in the set or the numbering of the index
>   if it is issued separately.

Make a note also on separately published indexes.

RELATED AACR2 RULE

None.

LIBRARY OF CONGRESS POLICY

Do not account for an index to a single volume or single year on the bibliographic record for the serial being indexed unless the index is issued separately and is not intended to be bound with the volume it indexes. When indicating the presence of an index in a note, do not use the note "Includes index." Instead, specify volumes or parts of the serial that are indexed as well as the place where the index may be found or the information that the index is published separately. *Exception:* If an index is represented by its own bibliographic record (cf. 21.28B), do not note this index on the bibliographic record for the serial being indexed. [CSB 21]

RELATED LIBRARY OF CONGRESS POLICY

1.5E1 Accompanying Material

1) Usually make a separate entry for material that either is not issued at the same time as the main work or shows an important difference in titles or statements of responsibility from those appearing in the main work.
2) Do not apply multilevel description to any item.
3) Generally record in a note material of the following types:
   a) The item is clearly of little bibliographic importance.
   b) Although the item might be eligible for method 4, it is best described by a less general terminology than that used under method 4.
   c) The item is best mentioned in a note because the title on the item is more a description than a true title.
4) Generally record material at the end of the physical description when the item satisfies all the following conditions:
   a) It is issued at the same time and by the same publisher as the main work and essentially is of use only in conjunction with the main work.
   b) It is by the same author as the main work, or makes no mention of an author or, if it is by a different author, the nature of the work makes unnecessary any note or added entry for this different author.
   c) The title is a general term (e.g., "teacher's manual") or is otherwise dependent on the title of the main work or lacks a title (e.g., "plates"). (When recording material at the end of the physical description, always use a generic term in English.)
Catalog separately all supplements, etc., to serials except for indexes that may be noted (according to 12.7B7 and 12.7B17) or supplements

etc., that may be noted informally according to method c. [emphasis added] *Exception:* Describe in a note supplements that are useable only in conjunction with the main work.

Apply the optional provision of the rule on a case-by-case basis. [CSB 29]

AACR2 TEXT EXAMPLES REVISED TO REFLECT LIBRARY OF CONGRESS POLICY

None required.

HISTORICAL BACKGROUND

AACR1 Rule 170 called for a note to indicate the presence of cumulative or separately published indexes as does AACR2 Rule 12.7B17. The AACR1 rule, however, provided more detailed information about the index using a prescribed order. That rule also allowed for either a formal tabular form of note or an informal form. AACR2 does not mention these forms.

NOTE EXAMPLES

Indexes

17.140   Indexes: Vols. 2 and 3 (1974 & 1975)-vols. 4 & 5 (1976 & 1977).
17.141   Indexes: Vols. 33 (1976)-37(1980) in 1 vol. (Includes index to the bulletin under its earlier title).
17.142   Indexes: Vol. 1, no. 1 (Dec. 1956)-v. 23, no. 1 (Dec. 1978) issued as Vol. 23, no. 2 (Dec. 1978).
17.143   Indexes: Vols. 1-10, 1946-1955, in v. 11, no.1 (Includes index to journal under its earlier titles); vols. 11-20, 1956-1965, in v. 21, no.1; vols. 21-30, 1966-1975, in vol. 30, no. 3/4.
17.144   Indexes: An index is issued for each session which includes History of bills and resolutions.
17.145   Indexes: Index issued periodically during the year and cumulated annually.

Indexed by

17.146   Indexed selectively by: GeoRef.
17.147   Indexed selectively by: Index to dental literature.
17.148   Indexed by: Index to U.S. government periodicals,   -1987.
17.149   Indexed selectively by: Chemical abstracts.
          Indexed selectively by: Nuclear science abstracts.

1.7B18. Contents

EXTRAPOLATED GENERAL RULE

List the contents of an item, either selectively or fully, if it is considered necessary to show the presence of material not implied by the rest of the description; to stress items of particular importance; or to list the contents of a collection.

RELATED AACR2 RULE

1.1B10 Title Proper [AACR2 Rev.]

If the chief source of information bears both a collective title and the titles of individual works, give the collective title as the title proper and give the titles of the individual works in a contents note (see 1.7B18). [emphasis added]

1.1G Items without a Collective Title [AACR2 Rev.]

1.1G1. If, in an item lacking a collective title, one work is the predominant part, treat the title of that work as the title proper and name the other work in a contents note (see 1.7B18). [emphasis added]

1.1G4. If, in an item lacking a collective title, more than one (but not all) of the separately titled works predominate, treat the predominating works as instructed in 1.1G3, and name the other works in contents notes (see 1.7B18). [emphasis added]

GENERAL LIBRARY OF CONGRESS POLICY

No general interpretations have been issued by the Library of Congress to modify, or amplify on, AACR2 Rule 1.7B18. The Library of Congress has, however, issued interpretations to AACR2 Rule 2.7B18 (Books, Pamphlets, and Printed Sheets). These interpretations could be used in a broader sense as general guidance for the creation of contents notes for materials other than books. See *Library of Congress Policy* to Rule 2.7B18 for these interpretations. For policies and interpretations for other material formats, see the *Library of Congress Policy* in the appropriate chapter for that format.

RELATED LIBRARY OF CONGRESS POLICY

1.7A3 Forms of Notes

When nonroman data (including quotations) are being recorded in the note area, give them in romanized form in all cases, including those cards that contain nonromanized elements in the body of the entry.

> When a note begins with a formal introductory term such as "contents," "credits," or "summary," do not use all caps in any case; instead, use upper and lower case as illustrated in AACR 2. [emphasis added] [CSB 22]

FORMAT

No specific general instructions for formatting this note are provided. Traditionally, this note has been used with either a formal or informal structure. The AACR2 text examples in the individual chapters for description continue this traditional structure.

A formal contents note provides a listing of either the complete or partial contents of an item and follows this construct:

Contents: [Title] — [Title] — [Title].

Statements of responsibility for the individual works can be added to the note using the construct:

Contents: [Title] / [Statements of Responsibility] — [Title] / [Statements of Responsibility] — [Title] / [Statements of Responsibility].

For a partial contents note, the general construct remains the same except the term "Contents" is replaced by "Partial Contents."

CHAPTER APPLICATION

This note is present, in varying forms, in all the chapters for description. Chapter 12 (Serials) is the only chapter that does not include the provisions of the Extrapolated General Rule.

EXCEPTIONS AND ADDITIONS

Chapter 2 (Books, Pamphlets, and Printed Sheets) prescribes the use of titles in a contents note derived from the heads of parts rather than from titles appearing in the table of contents or similar lists.

Chapter 3 (Cartographic Materials) provides special instructions for the treatment of insets, including their scale. This note also is used to record the details of a collection of maps described as a unit.

Chapter 4 (Manuscripts) has the same provisions as Chapter 2.

Chapter 5 (Music) allows the addition of opus numbers necessary for identification of the work and also statements of responsibility not appearing in Area 1. In some instances, the musical form of the work is also provided.

Chapter 6 (Sound Recordings) allows for the use of statements of responsibility in the contents note if they have not been given in Area 1. The recording of the duration of the individual items, when available, is also provided for.

Chapter 7 (Motion Pictures and Videorecordings) allows for the addition of statements of responsibility not given in Area 1. The duration of individual items, when available, can also be recorded. The rule also has a provision for the description of unedited material, newsfilm, and stock shots.

Chapter 8 (Graphic Materials) allows for the use of statements of responsibility in the contents note if they have not been given in Area 1. The number of items (frames, slides, transparencies, etc.) can be added to the titles.

Chapter 12 (Serials) does not include the provisions of the Extrapolated General Rule. Instead this note is used to describe or identify inserts, other serials within a serial, and items with unique titles not cataloged separately. The use of a contents note for a monograph series is specifically prohibited.

Chapter 2 (Books, Pamphlets, and Printed Sheets)

AACR2 RULE

2.7B18 Contents [AACR2 Rev.]

List the contents of an item, either selectively or fully, if it is considered necessary to show the presence of material not implied by the rest of the description; to stress items of particular importance; or to list the contents of a collection or of a multi-part item.

When recording titles formally, take them from the head of the part to which they refer rather than from contents lists, etc.

RELATED AACR2 RULE

None.

LIBRARY OF CONGRESS POLICY

For books, give some type of contents note (unless there is a large number, generally more than 12) of items contained

1) when required by specific rules (e.g., 1.1G1, 2.1B2, 21.7B);
2) when necessary to justify an added entry for an item not mentioned in the body of the entry;

3) when the publication is in two or more volumes and each volume has a title of its own (apply a liberal interpretation to the word "title" in this context such that it includes a broader application rather than one confined solely to those statements on title pages that are one-for-one titles of distinct "works" within the item; ignore titles that consist only of letters or numbers unless the numbers represent time); *exception*: do not add the titles to bibliographic records for nonroman scripts that are represented by both nonromanized cards and machine-readable romanized records if the titles are analyzable;

4) when the cataloger has created a single bibliographic record that covers a number of ephemeral publications (note that the general limitation mentioned above on number of items to be cited does not apply here);

5) when a one volume publication is either a collection or a work produced under editorial direction (unless the title and statement of responsibility area adequately covers the contents of the item; in case of doubt, give a contents note); *exception*: do not apply the provisions of this paragraph to bibliographic records for nonroman scripts that are represented by both nonromanized cards and machine-readable romanized records;

6) when the publication contains items of particular importance that need stressing; some of the most typical cases encountered in the past that should be routinely considered as being important to this degree are

a) summaries in languages other than that of the text; . . .
   [Without this instruction, it might be expected that this type of note would come under AACR2 Rule 2.7B2 (Language of the Item and/or Translation or Adaptation).]

b) bibliographies and bibliographic references, discographies, filmographies, and indexes (except for those bibliographies, etc., that are obviously of little value);

c) appendices, provided they contain important matter;

d) volumes separating text from plates, text from maps, text from commentary, etc[.];

e) errata slips that are not printed as part of the publication[.]

(*Note:* Categories a)-d) above do not constitute a comprehensive list; they are merely illustrative of what is meant by category 6, representing the relatively clear-cut cases that appear with great regularity. More unusual situations, when they arise, should be evaluated without prejudice, particularly when it is a question of providing access to material not implied by the rest of the description.)

A contents note may be formal or informal. Use an informal contents note when specifying selected parts of an item (generally no more than three) and for summaries in languages other than that of the text, for bibliographies, discographies, filmographies, indexes, bibliographic references, appendices, and for errata slips. (If the information is already recorded in the body of the entry, do not make a separate note.) Use judgment in selecting a title, or inventing one, when transcribing an informal contents note[.]

(*Note:* On bibliographic records for nonroman scripts that are represented by both nonromanized cards and machine-readable romanized records, give the information in a statement composed in English by the cataloger whenever quoting romanized data would be meaningless.) When quoting title statements from the publication, *generally* include the statement of responsibility but not other title information and enclose the transcription within quotation marks. Give pagination or foliation unless the texts are scattered through the publication. (Record an unnumbered page or leaf within brackets.) . . .

For the types of contents notes shown in the following examples [i.e., discography, bibliography or filmography, summaries in other languages, errata slips and indexes] generally prefer a standardized construct rather than a quotation from the book. . . .

Generally, separate informal notes may be combined unless pagination needs to be expressed for each. . . . When specifying items not covered by the instructions on the informal contents note, use a formal contents note. Transcribe a formal contents note as follows:

1) begin the note with "Contents" or "Partial contents" (without quotation marks), followed by a colon-space;
2) generally, record the title proper that appears in the table of contents, unless another source gives a more authoritative account of the data; however, if the title appears on the title page, normally use the title page title; give other title information only when the title proper would be meaningless without it; [This differs from the AACR2 instruction not to use contents lists.]
3) include a first statement of responsibility (cf. 1.1F) if it differs in fact from the statement included in the body of the entry; omit names according to 1.1F5;
4) omit introductions already included in the body of the entry; generally omit prefatory and similar matter;
5) for publications in one volume
   a) omit chapter and section numbering;
   b) if the extent of the part being listed occupies a disproportionately large portion of the publication, include the extent within parentheses after the title (or after the title and statement of responsibility); record an unnumbered page or leaf within brackets;
   c) separate the items with a space-dash-space;
6) for publications in two or more volumes
   a) give the volume designation that is found on the item, except use Appendix B abbreviations for the terms and substitute

arabic numerals for roman; if there is no abbreviation for the term, give only the number if the term is long; if the roman numeral is required for clarity, retain it; separate the volume designation from the title by a period-space;

b) if the number of physical volumes differs from the number of bibliographic volumes, include the number of physical volumes within parentheses after the title (or after the title and statement of responsibility);

c) if the volumes are of different editions (cf. LCRI 2.2), include within parentheses edition statements and dates of publication, etc., after the title (or after the title and statement of responsibility);

d) separate each volume with a space-dash-space; if the set is incomplete, put the space-dash-space before each title (other than the first) that is being recorded and leave four spaces for the missing volume; if two or more titles are being transcribed for one volume, apply the punctuation conventions from 1.1G2 such that the titles by the same person, body, etc., are separated by a space-semicolon-space and titles by different persons, bodies, etc., are separated by a period-space.

When some of the volumes in a multipart publication have their own titles and some of the volumes do not, and it has been decided to make a formal contents note, use the statement "[without special title]" to represent the untitled volumes.

Bibliography Note[1]

Apply the following for noting the presence of bibliographies or bibliographical references in the note area:

1) If a publication contains a bibliography, that is, a list of citations or works grouped together in a single list, regardless of either the arrangement or the footnote-type numbering the citations might bear, use the term "Bibliography" (without quotation marks), followed by its pagination or foliation. The same applies to a bibliographical essay. (Record an unnumbered page or leaf within brackets.) However, quote the title as found on the publication if it is necessary to show the scope of the bibliography or if a statement of responsibility is needed. (*Exception*: On bibliographic records for nonroman scripts that are represented by both nonromanized cards and machine-readable romanized records, give the information in a statement composed in English by the cataloger whenever quoting romanized data would be meaningless). Make no distinction between a list of works consulted by the author in the preparation of the work and a list of works recommended for further reading. . . .

2) If the publication contains more than one bibliography, use the following note:

---

1. See italic paragraph on page xxxiii.

Includes bibliographies.

However, if there are bibliographies at the ends of chapters or sections in addition to a bibliography at the end of the publication (or elsewhere), ignore the scattered bibliographies.

3) If a publication contains bibliographic citations in the form of true footnotes, i.e., citations found at the bottom of pages and keyed by numbering to passages in the text, use the following note:

Includes bibliographical references.

(Bibliographic citations, notes, etc., assembled at the ends of chapters or sections, or at the end of the publication, are covered by paragraph 1 above.) However, if there are bibliographic citations in addition to a bibliography, ignore the bibliographic citations. (Under no circumstances attempt to discover if there are works mentioned in the bibliographic citations that are not mentioned in the bibliography.) [CSB 25]

RELATED LIBRARY OF CONGRESS POLICY

None issued.

AACR2 TEXT EXAMPLES REVISED TO REFLECT LIBRARY OF CONGRESS POLICY

None required.

HISTORICAL BACKGROUND

AACR1 Rev. Rule 148 provided general guidelines for the use of contents notes and detailed guidance for the creation of both formal (Rev. Rule 148B) and informal (Rev. Rule 148A) contents notes. These guidelines included specific instructions on the formatting of these notes. Informal contents were to precede formal contents notes in a description.

Formal contents notes employed a one-paragraph structure using caption or table of contents titles without quotation marks. Subtitles and qualifying statements, introductions and prefatory materials were generally excluded. The rule also provided guidance on the word order of elements in the note and the selection of names to record when multiple authorship was encountered. It further stipulated that terms such as "ed." and "comp." were not to be used. The use of volume numbers for multipart works was described in detail. Pagination (in parentheses) was allowed when a particular item was a "disproportionately large" part of the work. AACR2 prefers titles taken from the heads of parts rather than from either caption titles or tables of contents. AACR2 does not specifically provide for the structure of a formal contents note. The use of ISBD structure in these notes results in a somewhat different internal note structure from that created under AACR1:

AACR1
CONTENTS: [Author (inverted order with forenames represented by initials)]. [Title].—[Author]. [Title].—[Author]. [Title].

AACR2
Contents: [Title] / [Statement(s) of Responsibility] — [Title] / [Statements of Responsibility] — [Title] / [Statements of Responsibility].

AACR1 Rev. specifically provided for the use of the term "Partial Contents" while AACR2 does not mention its use.

AACR1 Rev. Rule 155B2 allowed for the inclusion of supplementary volumes in a formal contents note even in cases where the supplement was not numbered consecutively with the other volumes. Minor supplements were noted informally (AACR1 Rev. Rule 155B1). Although AACR2 does not specifically call for the inclusion of supplements in contents notes, no restrictions are placed on their inclusion there.

AACR1 Rev. allowed for the use of a multiple paragraph contents note. In these cases, each work had a separate paragraph and the term "CONTENTS" was a centered heading. A similar centered heading structure was used for collections of separately published pamphlets, except that imprint and series information was also added to the description of each element. AACR2 does not address this format structure.

Informal contents notes used quoted titles, with pagination specified, when the material was not scattered in the publication. Specific instructions were provided on the wording of bibliography and index notes. These two types of notes did not use quoted titles. AACR2 does not provide any specific guidelines for these situations.

These AACR1 Rev. Ch. 6 rules could be used for works that were not separately published monographs unless specific rules for the description of a format superceded or excluded their use.

It can be readily observed from this comparison of the two codes that AACR1 Rev. was more detailed and prescriptive in its instructions for use of the contents note than is AACR2. The same notes provided under AACR1 could, however, be constructed under the more general wording of AACR2 using a different construct for the formal contents note. The greater detail is simply missing in AACR2. This detail, in many instances, is provided by the Library of Congress Rule Interpretations to Rule 2.7B18. In many cases, these Rule Interpretations are virtually identical to the AACR1 Rev. provisions.

NOTE EXAMPLES

Formal Partial Contents

18.1 Partial Contents: Mysterium pansophicum — Sex puncta theosophica — Sex puncta mystica.

18.2 Partial Contents: v. 11. Fiction. Juvenile fiction — v. 12. Non-Dewey decimal classified titles — v. 13. Author index — v. 14. Title index — v. 15. Subject index.

Formal Contents—Unnumbered Units

18.3 Contents: The blue knight — The black marble — The new centurions — The choirboys.

18.4 Contents: Introduction — Literary criticism and the public sphere — The end of an institution? — The task of contemporary literary criticism — Promoters, consumers, and critics — Prolegomena to a history of literary criticism — Art evaluation and reportage — Critical theory, public sphere, and culture.

18.5 Contents: Who is Victor Hammer? / Rudolph Koch ; translated from the German by Ulrich Middeldorf — Mezzotints / Ulrich Middeldorf — Engravings & woodcuts — Inscriptions & symbols — Uncial typefaces. Foreword / R. Hunter Middleton. A master of punch-cutting / Hermann Zapf. Documentation of Hammer types / W. Gay Reading, Jr. — Four presses : a bibliography / Paul Holbrook ; with notes by Carolyn R. Hammer (p. [137]-195) — A Hammer bibliography / David Farrell (p. [197]-213).

Formal Contents—Numbered Units

18.6 Contents: I. Presidential message to the Congress — II. A White House report — III. President's budget reform plan — IV. President's proposals for tax reduction.

18.7 Contents: appendix A. Papers on U.S. immigration history — appendix B. Papers on international migration — appendix C. Papers on refugees — appendix D. Papers on legal immigration to the United States — appendix E. Papers on illegal migration to the United States — appendix F. Papers on temporary workers — appendix G. Papers on the administration of immigration law — recommendations and votes.

18.8 Contents: Bd. 1. A-Bt — Bd. 2. Bu-Fz.

18.9 Contents: bk. 1. Lesson plans, ideas, and activities for teaching the prereading skills. — bk. 2. Lesson plans, ideas, and activities for teaching recognition skills. — bk. 3. Lesson plans, ideas, and activities for teaching comprehension skills. — bk. 4. Lesson plans, ideas, and activities for teaching reading skills.

18.10 Contents: Canto 1. Creation (3 v) — Canto 2. The cosmic manifestation (2 v) — Canto 3. The status quo (4 v) — Canto 4. The creation of the Fourth Order (4 v) — Canto 5. The creative impetus (2 v) — Canto 6. Prescribed duties for Mankind (3 v) — Canto 7. The science of God (3 v) — Canto 8. Withdrawal of the cosmic creations (2 v) — Canto 9. Liberation (3 v) — Canto 10. The summum bonum (<1-5 >) — Canto 11. General history (<v. 1-5>) — Canto 12. The age of deterioration (<v. 1-2>).

18.11 Contents: Pt. 1. The fellowship of the ring — pt. 2. The two towers — pt. 3. The return of the king.

18.12 Contents: v. 1. Physical features of the characterization area — v. 2. Socioeconomic features of the characterization area — v. 3. Biological features of the characterization area.

18.13 Contents: v. 1, pt. 1. The basic principles of air traffic control. pt. 2. The co-ordination of civil and military air traffic.

18.14 Contents: v. 1-2. Author catalogue — v. 3-4. Systematic catalogue.

18.15 Contents: [1] Working manual — [2] Reference guide — [3] A glossary of EEO terminology.

18.16 Contents: 1. 1962-1970 — 2. 1971-1973 — 3. 1974 — 4. 1975 — 5. 1976-1977 — 6. 1978-1979 — [7] Current reporter.

18.17 Contents: v. A. Primary sources — [v. B] v. 1 BRB decisions, court decisions, table of cases — v. B., v. 2 BRB decisions, court decisions.

18.18 Contents: Bk. 1-2. 1858-1881 — Bk. 3. 1881-1889 — Bk. 4. 1890-1900.

18.19 Contents: [1] #106 — [2] #201 — [3] #203 — [4] #301 — [5] #303 — [6] #105 — [7] #109 — [8] #103 — [9] #104 — [10] #107 — [11] #108 — [12] #202 — [13] #302 — [14] #204 — [15] #401.

Formal Contents—Title Alterations

18.20 Contents: [v. 1. without special title] — v. 2. Jewish activities in the United States — v. 3. Jewish influence in American life — v. 4. Aspects of Jewish power in the United States.

18.21 Contents: pt. 1. Treasury, Postal Service, and general government . . . — pt. 3. Departments of Labor, Health and Human Services, Education, and related agencies — pt. 4. Department of Defense . . .

18.22 Contents: Rock Rodono : sketch third of "The Encantadas" — A Pisgah view from the rock : sketch fourth of "The Encantadas."

18.23 jil. 1. Laporan ringkasan = Summary report — v. 2. Water supply master plan and feasibility study for first stage improvements — v. 3. Wastewater and drainage master plan — v. 4. Program for handling solid wastes — v. 5. Supporting information.

Formal Contents—Statements of Responsibility

18.24 Contents: Historical setting / Richard P. Stevens — The society and its environment / Irving Kaplan — The economy / Donald P. Whitaker — Government and politics / Harold D. Nelson — National security / Robert Rinehart.

18.25 Contents: Organization & supervision / Sammye Lewis, Kathleen Becan-McBride — Personnel relations / Mary Beth Murphy — Monitoring quality control within the clinical laboratory / Frances Collins, Karen Lorimer — Budgetary considerations / Diann T. Duplantis — Education / Kathleen Becan-McBride — Communication / Kathleen Becan-McBride, Mary Beth Murphy — Appendix of additional cases / Kathleen Becan-McBride.

18.26 Contents: v. 1. Primary sources / edited by Ann Hughes — v. 2. Modern studies / edited by W.R. Owens.

18.27 Contents: Simulation as an evaluation tool / Ralph E. Cooper and William R. Huss — Cost analysis for program evaluation / Mark S. Thompson . . . [et al.] — Contextual evaluation, an ethnographic approach to program assessment / Gerald M. Britain — Measuring strength and integrity of treatments / William H. Yeaton and Robin Redner — Social indicators / William E. Bertrand, Nancy Beth Mock, and Robert R. Franklin — Combining time-series with interviews— evaluating the effects of a sexual assault / Jeanne C. Marsh — Combining process with impact evaluation—a long-term home care program for the elderly / Susan L. Hughes, Davis S. Cordray, and V. Alan Spiker.

18.28 Contents: Growth and development ; Oral pathology in the child adolescent / [edited by] Ray E. Stewart — The developing occlusion ; Guidance of the developing occlusion / [edited by] Thomas K. Barber — Pathogenesis and prevention of dental caries and peridontal disease ; Fluorides and dental health / [edited by] Stephen H. Wei — Patient management ; Restorative and surgical management / [edited by] Kenneth C. Troutman.

18.29 Contents: Bird of paradise / by Franklin Rosemont — Porcupines / by Franklin Rosemont — To begin then, not now / by Philip Lamantia — Hero among the signs / [Hal Rammel]

18.30 Contents: A day in the life of All things considered / Susan Stamberg — Listening for America — Telling the news — Commemorating giants — Celebrating the seasons — Speaking of writing — Finding things out — After all.

18.31 Contents: v. 1. Text — v. 2. Introduction — v. 3. Studies on the sources / with an introductory essay by Andrew Lang.

Formal Contents—Open Entries

18.32 Contents: — Section 3. Safe operation of auxiliaries.

18.33 Contents: — v. 3. Asia / by D.A. Canedo, D. Waltisperger.

18.34 Contents: pt. 2. Child support enforcement — pt. 3. Financial circumstances — pt. 4. Social services.

18.35 Contents: — v. 4. Wholesale and retail trade, restaurants, and hotels — v. 7. (Small industrial) Mining and quarrying. Electricity, gas, and water. Construction. Manufacturing.

Informal Contents—Addenda, Corrigenda, Errata, etc.

18.36 Addenda ([4] p.) inserted.
18.37 Additions and corrections inserted.
18.38 Corrigenda slip inserted.
18.39 Errata slip inserted.
18.40 Errata to be inserted.
18.41 Erratum slip laid in.
18.42 Errata slip and table (2 p.) inserted.
18.43 Errata slip inserted in v. 1.
18.44 Erratum slip with copyright statement inserted.
18.45 Vol. 1 had errata slip inserted.
18.46 Errata slip inserted in Adams County vol.
18.47 Errata slip inserted at prelim. p. [5].
18.48 With errata leaves (v. 2, p. [60]-[62], 3rd group).

Informal Contents—Advertisements

18.49 The final 2 p. are advertisements.
18.50 Pages i-iii contain advertisements.
18.51 Advertisements on p. [1]-15 at end.
18.52 Publisher's advertisements on p. [379]-[396] at end.
18.53 Pages 1-3 at end advertise other works by the author.
18.54 Advertisements on p. [1]-4 at front and p. [1]-8 at end, the latter including testimonials dated Oct. 13, 1835-May 16, 1836.
18.55 Publisher's (Henry's) advertisements on p. [297]-[304] at end.
18.56 Publisher's catalog, dated Oct. 1906, on p. [1]-40 at end.

Informal Contents—Appendices

18.57 Vol. 2: Appendix.
18.58 Appendices: p. 387-512.
18.59 Three appendices inserted.
18.60 Includes nine appendix volumes.
18.61 Appendix contains the texts of the relevant treaties.
18.62 Appendix includes documents.
18.63 Appendices list current monographs and periodicals published by universities in the Dominican Republic.
18.64 "Apéndice" (Legislative and documental): p. 215-245.
18.65 Appendix (p. 103-114) contains interview of author Christina Guzman.
18.66 "Appéndice" (p. 411-490) contains legislation for the autonomous regions.
18.67 Appendix (p. [113]-173) includes related documents.
18.68 Appendix includes an excerpt in English from section 7-8 of the Clayton act and an excerpt in German of Merger guidelines of the U.S. Dept. of Justice.
18.69 Appendices: A. House file 2536, City housing codes — B. Nationally recognized codes — C. Uniform Residential Landlord and Tenant Law, chapter 562A, Iowa Code, 1979 — D. Fire escapes and other means of

escape from fire, chapter 103, Iowa Code, 1979 — E. Sample job descriptions — F. State agencies concerned with code enforcement.

18.70 "Appendix: Chronology of Weber's principal writings in translation": p. [174]-[179]

18.71 "Appendix" contains: Of the Scythian rites (p. 89-95); A dissertation upon the Athenian Skirophoria . . . (p. [97]-122); A second dissertation upon the mystical signification of the bough and the umbrella . . . (p. [123]-169, including "Postscript": Of the religion of the Pelasgi).

Informal Contents—Bibliography, Discography, etc.[2]

18.72 Bibliography: last printed page.
18.73 Bibliography included on cover.
18.74 Vol. 2 includes bibliography.
18.75 Includes bibliography.
18.76 Bibliography: columns 346-351.
18.77 Bibliography: leaf 48.
18.78 Bibliography: leaves 18-19.
18.79 Bibliography: p. xxiii.
18.80 Bibliografia: p. 173.
18.81 Bibliography: p. [96].
18.82 Bibliography: p. 494-502.
18.83 Bibliography: p. [xxv]-xxxi.
18.84 Bibliography: p. [285]-[286].
18.85 Bibliography: 5th prelim. page.
18.86 Bibliography: 7th-12th prelim. page.
18.87 Bibliography: leaf [3] of the introductory part.
18.88 Bibliography: p. [9] (1st group).
18.89 Bibliography: p. 47-60 (2nd group).
18.90 Bibliography: p. F/112-F/116.
18.91 Bibliography: pt. 1, leaves v-ix.
18.92 Bibliography: 1st pt., p. xxiii-xxviii.
18.93 Bibliography: v. 1, 6th prelim. page.
18.94 Bibliography: v. 1, leaves [1]-9.
18.95 Bibliography: v. 1, p. 467; v. 3, p. 14.
18.96 Bibliography: v. 1, pt. 1, p. 15.
18.97 Cartography: p. 100-101.
18.98 Discography: p. 146-163.
18.99 Filmography: p. 303-305.
18.100 Bibliography: p. 3-19.
　　　　Discography: p. 203-210.
18.101 Discography: p. 167-176.
　　　　Filmography: p. 177-178.
　　　　Bibliography: p. 179.
18.102 Includes bibliography and discography.
18.103 Bibliography and glossary slip inserted.

---

2. See italic paragraph on page xxxiii.

Informal Contents—Bibliography, Discography, etc.— Quoted Title[3]

18.104   "Basic musical composition" [of Plotnichenko]: p. 123-[131].
18.105   "Bibliographical note: John Adams": p. 219-221. "Bibliographical note: John Quincy Adams": p. 411-413.
18.106   "Bibliography of M.I. Finley": p. [312]-318.
18.107   "A bibliography of the works of Phillips Barry": leaves xv-xix.
18.108   "Bibliography of sources used by Irving": v. 1, p. xxxix-xlvi.
18.109   "Books and pamphlets banned by the War Department": p. 109-113. "Chrono-discographie": p. 104-[127].
18.110   "A chronological listing of Peter Finley Dunne's Mr. Dooley essays": p. 143-298.
18.111   "Essay bibliography": p. 12-19 (1st group).
18.112   "Further reading": p. 121.
18.113   "List of works": p. [211]-213.
18.114   "John Coltrane recordings": p. A-C.
18.115   "LSD bibliography": leaves [3]-[53], 1-19; "Mescaline bibliography": leaves 1-31 at end.
18.116   "Motion pictures and filmstrips": p. 137-146.
18.117   "Nota bibliografica": v. 1, p. 53-64.
18.118   "Selected readings": p. 159-293.
18.119   "Suggestions for further reading": p. 259-260.
18.120   "The works of Arthur Annesley Ronald Firbank" (bibliography): p. [151].

Informal Contents—Bibliography, Discography, etc.— Non-Quoted Title[3]

18.121   Bibliography of E. Krenek's works: musical (p. 318-323), written (p. 325-347).
18.122   Bibliography of works by and about Flaubert: p. 384-400.
18.123   Bibliography of the author's works: p. 18-21.
18.124   Catalog of works by Walter Piston: p. [187]-193.
18.125   List of author's major publications: p. [4] of cover.
18.126   List of the author's works: p. 349-359.
18.127   List of works of Marx and Engels cited: p. 225-238.

Informal Contents—Bibliographies, Discographies, etc.[1]

18.128   Includes discographies.
18.129   Includes filmographies.
18.130   Includes bibliographies and discography.
18.131   Includes bibliographies and index.
18.132   Includes bibliographies, discographies, and indexes.
18.133   Vol. ‹2- › includes bibliographies.
18.134   Vols. 1-   include bibliographies and indexes.

Informal Contents—Bibliographical References[1]

18.135   Includes bibliographical references and index.
18.136   Includes bibliographical and discographical references and index.

---

3. See italic paragraph on page xxxiii.

18.137 Includes music, bibliographical references, and indexes.

18.138 Commentary vol. includes bibliographical references.

Informal Contents—"Contains," "Includes," etc.— [Generic Statements]

18.139 Includes autobiography by the honoree.

18.140 Includes chronological table of important historical events.

18.141 Includes commentary and analysis of the work.

18.142 Includes corrected reprint (1969) of vol. 2.

18.143 Includes numerous documents, chiefly in English and German.

18.144 Includes glossary of technical terms.

18.145 Includes legal citations and index.

18.146 Includes legislation (p. 122-157) in Dutch with German translation.

18.147 Includes excerpts from legislation.

18.148 Libretto; includes the music (vocal score): p. 53-63.

18.149 Includes lists of artists, managers, music publishers, producers, and record companies.

18.150 Includes music (melodies with chord symbols): p. 39-43.

18.151 Includes 9 poems not in the 1st ed.

18.152 Includes unacc. melodies.

18.153 Vita.

18.154 Vol. 9 contains court rules and v. 10, tables and index.

Informal Contents—"Contains," "Includes," etc. . . . [Specific Work(s)]

18.155 Also included are a section of ms. annotations by an 18th-cent. English owner of the codex and minor non-germane fragments.

18.156 The codex contains major fragments of the Georgics, books 3-4, and of the Aeneid (on leaves 11-76).

18.157 Consists of: Walden, selections from The Maine woods, Cape Cod and Miscellanies, and Excursions and Poems.

18.158 Contains 14 original etchings, and text, both original and from the I ching.

18.159 Contains Technical papers FC80-610-618, 620-629 of the Society of Manufacturing Engineers.

18.160 Includes: The dissidents, individualism, and the historic role of the worker.

18.161 Includes all the stories previously published in her Cast a cold eye, and two others.

18.162 Includes "Ascension Day 1964", which was separately published in London magazine, Aug. 1964.

18.163 Includes (p. 1-2) an extract from John Galsworthy's An appeal to all horse lovers, published earlier the same year in: The Army Veterinary Corps : its works and its needs, and how it is helped by the R.S.P.C.A.

18.164 Includes official bilingual text of the Territorial Land Use Regulations of Mar. 3, 1977.

399

18.165 Includes poem for the occasion by Oliver Wendell Holmes, to be sung to Luther's Judgment hymn.

18.166 Includes reproductions of Blake's engraving of the Laocoön group and of his relief etchings, On Homers' poetry and On Virgil, and The ghost of Abel.

18.167 Includes text of the Uniform Law on Cheques.

18.168 Includes the author's translation of the Book of Jonah.

18.169 Includes the text of the Registered Clubs Act 1976 and the Registered Club Regulations 1978.

18.170 Includes the text of the SALT I and II agreements and related documents.

18.171 "Including a list of narrow gauge railways in America, 1871-1949, compiled by Brian Thompson; new updated list through 1980 of narrow gauge railways in Canada, Alaska, Montana, Hawaii, and Washington compiled by James Eakin."

18.172 Includes Tables of statutes, rules, etc. cited, words and phrases, general index to forms, 1 v. and General index, 2 v., published separately in 1969.

18.173 Missouri Lodge of Research officers, Secretary-Treasurer combined report, 1978-1979: p. 201-204.

18.174 Vol. 2 includes the memorandum and exhibits in support of Alger Hiss's petition, prepared by Victor Rabinowitz for the National Emergency Civil Liberties Foundation, Inc.

Informal Contents—Quoted Titles—Non-Bibliographies

18.175 "Archaeological Resources Protection Act of 1979": p. 187-197.

18.176 "Catalogue of the exhibition": p. 313-342.

18.177 *"Chronological list of Soviet space flights": p. 202-[204].

18.178 "Collector's price guide" ([4] p.) inserted in v. 2.

18.179 "Executive summary": p. ix-xx.

18.180 "Exhibition catalogue" by R.E. Ahlborn: p. 47-92.

18.181 "The Foreign Agents Registration Act of 1938, as amended and the rules and regulations prescribed by the Attorney General": p. 355-394.

18.182 "List of contracting states" inserted.

18.183 "Philadelphia Phillies statistics: individual and team statistics, from the 1981 Media guide": p. [1]-[54] (2nd group).

18.184 "The Roskilde passion": p. 83-133.

18.185 "Table of cases": p. xiii-xvii.

18.186 "Text of laws affecting Jews (translation)"—p. 123-177.

18.187 "Text of the Occupational Safety and Health Act": p. 263-293.

18.188 "Tirocinium, or, A review of schools": p. [187]-220.

18.189 "Twelve bindings" (illustrated catalog): p. [2]-[14] at end.

18.190 "Type specimens": p. [21]-[29].

18.191 "Updated director-head librarian addenda" ([8] p.) inserted.

Informal Contents—Titles with Statements of Responsibility

18.192 "A bibliography of writings by Paul Radin, compiled by Richard Werner": p. [1001]-1010.

18.193 "The literature of the Custer fight, by Dr. Edgar I. Stewart."—p. 247.

18.194 "Bibliography of the dalmation, submitted by Alfred E. Treen."

18.195 "A prospectus of, and list of subscribers to, the works on ornithology, etc. by John Gould, F.R.S.": p. 1-26.

18.196 "Afterword" (by William Everson): p. [11]-[13].

18.197 "Advance to bold mission thrust, 1970-1980 / Frank K. Means": p. [310]-457.

18.198 Includes: Uniform rules of contract guarantees / International Chamber of Commerce in English, French, and Bulgarian.

18.199 Program notes and synopsis by C. Rizzuto: p. 1-4.

Informal Contents—Indexes[4]

18.200 Includes index.

18.201 Includes indexes.

18.202 Includes cumulative indexes.

18.203 Includes unnumbered index volume.

18.204 Vol. 1- includes index.

18.205 Includes index in v. 1.

18.206 Includes indexes (v. 2).

18.207 Index of names and places in v. 2 (addenda in v. 3).

18.208 Vol. 2: Film index.

18.209 Includes index to both the works of Lemière and Vachon.

18.210 Includes index, prepared by B.N. Muzelius.

18.211 Vol. 3- includes bibliographical references and index.

Informal Contents—Summaries in Languages Other Than That of the Title Page

18.212 Summaries in English, French, German, and Russian.

18.213 Summaries in English, French and Russian; table of contents also in English, French and Russian.

18.214 Summary also in English.

18.215 Summary and abstract in English ([7] leaves) inserted in v. 1.

18.216 Summary and legends also in English, German and Russian.

18.217 Summary and list of reproductions in English and Russian.

18.218 Summary in French; list of illustrations and table of contents also in French.

Chapter 3 (Cartographic Materials)

AACR2 RULE

3.7B18 Contents [AACR2 Rev.]

Map Collections Described as a Unit

If a collection of maps is described as a unit (see 3.0J), make notes on the state of the collection at the time of description and indicate the composition of the complete collection if possible. Give variations

---

4. See italic paragraph on page xxxiii.

between sheets in the collection. Complete this note when the collection is complete. . . .

Individual Cartographic Items
   List the contents of an item, either selectively or fully, including: insets; maps, etc., printed on the verso of a map, etc., sheet; illustrations, etc. Make notes on maps, insets, etc., on the recto before those on the verso of a sheet. Give the scale of insets, etc., if it is consistent. If the insets, etc., are numerous and/or minor, make a note in general terms.

RELATED AACR2 RULE

None.

LIBRARY OF CONGRESS POLICY

None issued.

RELATED LIBRARY OF CONGRESS POLICY

None issued.

AACR2 TEXT EXAMPLES REVISED TO REFLECT LIBRARY OF CONGRESS POLICY

None required.

HISTORICAL BACKGROUND

AACR1 Rule 212E1 addressed the use of a note to record the "holdings of composite sets." This note essentially corresponds to the first paragraph of AACR2 Rule 3.7B18. These two codes vary only in their wording and the greater level of detail specified in AACR1. The notes that result from the use of the two codes are the same.

Partial contents notes were covered by AACR1 Rule 212E10a. When a collective title was used for several insets, the number of items was recorded in parentheses following the title. When insets surrounded the map, they were recorded in a clockwise sequence. AACR2 Rule 3.7B18 does not specifically provide instructions for the recording of the number of insets when a collective title is encountered nor does it prescribe the clockwise sequence. Both codes allow for the use of a general note for minor insets.

AACR1 Rule 212E10b provided for a note to record items on the verso of the map. This information was recorded in a separate note following any note for insets. The rule prescribed the use of the phrase "On verso" in the note. AACR2 requires that information about the contents on the recto of a map be recorded before information dealing with details on the verso of the map. No separate notes for the recto or verso of the map are called for nor is the phrasing "On verso" required. AACR2 also calls for recording the scale of an inset. AACR1 does not specifically mention scale data in regard to insets, although an example to AACR1 Rule 212E10b gives the scale of an inset.

NOTE EXAMPLES

Formal Contents

18.219 Contents: Western section — Eastern section.

18.220 Contents: World history atlas — United States history atlas — Hammond headline world atlas.

18.221 Contents: General — Population — Agriculture — Industry — Transportation — Communication — Bank — Education — Health — Regional development.

18.222 Contents: Nevada — Utah — Salt Lake City and vicinity — Las Vegas area — Reno area — Ogden area.

18.223 Contents: Helena, Georgia : McRae, Georgia : welcome to McRae, the hub of south Georgia, an excellent climate, and a wonderful location for industry — Telfair County, Georgia.

18.224 Contents: Newberry — [Newberry County].

18.225 Contents: [Map of Mountain Lake showing points of interest and borough-owned lands] — Election districts — Zoning map.

18.226 Contents: Tavernier, Key Largo — Islamorada — [Upper Keys].

18.227 Contents: [Colorado] — Denver and vicinity — Grand Junction area — Boulder area — Fort Collins area — Colorado Springs area — Pueblo area.

18.228 Contents: [Central Portland] — [Portland region].

18.229 Contents: A map of the British colonies in North America . . . / J. Mitchell, 1755 — A map of the most inhabited part of Virginia . . . / J. Fry and P. Jefferson, 1775 — A topographical map of Hudson River . . . / C.J. Sauthier, 1776 — The provinces of New York and New Jersey . . . / Capt. Holland, 1776 — A map of the most inhabited part of New England . . . / T. Jeffreys, 1774.

18.230 Contents: Sheet 1 — Sheet 2 — Sheet 3 — Sheet 4 — [Sheet] 5.

18.231 Contents: Easy locator index with instructions (35 p.) — Base 1-Jerusalem — Base 2-Holy Land — Base 3-Old Testament lands — Base 4-New Testament lands — Base 5-Bible world.

18.232 Contents: [1] Vaal triangle: updated June 1970 — [2] Light industries: updated June 1970.

18.233   Contents: Fasc. 1. Geografía de la población — Fasc. 2. Geografía económica.
18.234   Contents: v. 1. Report — v. 2, pts. 1-3. Structural, stratigraphic analysis and hydrocarbon distribution maps and cross-sections — v. 3. Regional synthesis maps and stratigraphic charts.

Informal Contents—Insets
18.235   Some maps include inset.
18.236   Sheet of Harburg includes inset.
18.237   Includes 6 insets.
18.238   Includes 6 insets and list of branch lines not shown on map.
18.239   Includes city center inset and advertisements.
18.240   Includes island inset.
18.241   Includes inset showing "Main tectonic units" and reliability diagram.
18.242   Includes insets of Bornholm and central Copenhagen.
18.243   Includes insets of Corsica and Paris metropolitan area, distance table, expressway list, list of members of the "Comité national du jour du soleil," and advertisement.
18.244   Includes insets of "The map of Korea," Je ju-do, and 3 other insets.
18.245   Includes inset of New Zealand and political map of Australasia.
18.246   Includes inset of Radnor [town] and coats of arms.
18.247   Includes inset of Whigham and advertisements.
18.248   Insets: [Viking Graben region, North Sea] — Structural framework. Scale1:5,000,000.
18.249   Insets: Mécanismes au foyer en France et dans les régions voisines : échelle 1/7 500 000 — Tectonique active et sismicité de la partie occidentale del'Europe moyenne [ca. 1:6,250,000 — Corse].

Informal Contents—Other Maps
18.250   Ancillary maps: Little Mountain — Whitmire — Prosperity — Peak — Pomaria — Silverstreet — Chappells.
18.251   Ancillary maps on verso: Roma, pianta monumentale, grande raccordo anulare e attraversamenti : scala 1:30.000 — Dintorni di Roma : scala 1:150.000.
18.252   Includes ancillary map of city center.
18.253   Includes ancillary maps of "Earthquake catastrophes," "Windstorm catastrophes," "Flood catastrophes," and "Other natural catastrophes."
18.254   Map of central city in cover.
18.255   "With Univ. of Va. centerfold."
18.256   "With Williamsburg center fold."
18.257   "With downtown center fold."
18.258   Includes 16 detachable outline maps.
18.259   Includes transcript overlay of district lot boundaries to be used with map index.
18.260   Thirty two descriptive route maps on verso.
18.261   On verso with index: Ionia County map.

18.262 "Access Map of District" on cover.

18.263 Charts of "Public recreational areas," indexed map of "Birmingham and vicinity" with inset of "Downtown Birmingham," map of "Western Florida," and 4 insets on verso.

18.264 Indexed maps of "Centro de Lima" and "Lima metropolitana y alrededores," chart of road signs, and 23 local maps on verso.

18.265 Map of "La Salle Parish, Louisiana" with text, ill., and advertisements on verso.

18.266 Maps of annual events in Hungary, castles and nature preserves in Hungary, Budapest, and Lake Balaton, and ill. (some col.) on verso.

18.267 Maps on verso: Generalized business district design concept — Existing zoning — Existing land use 1964 — Physical characteristics influencing development.

18.268 Maps on verso: Shenandoah Nat'l Park, Virginia — Wilmington, Delaware — Annapolis, Maryland — Richmond, Virginia — Washington and vicinity — Central Washington — Baltimore and vicinity — Colonial Williamsburg — Norfolk and vicinity.

18.269 On verso: Wide screen project — Regional tour — Regional tour planning map.

18.270 On verso: 1:750,000: Weltraumbild : [Hessen] — Wirtschaft : [Hessen].

Informal Contents—Bibliographies

18.271 Bibliography: leaf [2].

18.272 Bibliography: p. 159.

18.273 Bibliography: [9] 1st group-[1].

18.274 Bibliography in accompanying text.

18.275 Includes bibliographical references.

18.276 Includes source note and reliability diagram.

18.277 Encomiums and references: leaf [7] (1st group).

Informal Contents—Indexes

18.278 Index map: leaf [3].

18.279 Index maps on lining papers.

18.280 *Each sheet includes an index map.

18.281 Most volumes include separate folded index map.

18.282 Indexed.

18.283 Indexed for points of interest.

18.284 Indexed for streets.

18.285 Index bound in.

18.286 Includes indexes.

18.287 Includes index and advertisement.

18.288 Includes indexes and "McHenry Shores inset."

18.289 Includes indexes, area map, and advertisements.

18.290 Includes index, col. ill., location map, administrative map, and indexed map of "Bangui."

18.291 Includes indexes, indexed set of "University of Arizona," inset of "Downtown Tucson," "Area map," and 6 insets.

18.292 Includes index, list of counties, and col. ill.

18.293 Includes index to adjoining sheets, glossary, ill., and list of abbreviations.

18.294 Includes index to datums.

18.295 Includes index to Landsat images.

18.296 Includes park index, school directory, inset of Atlanta Airport, location map, and advertisements.

18.297 Includes road index, statistical table, location map, and col. ill.

18.298 Recreation indexes and distance list on verso.

18.299 Includes shopping center index and advertisements.

18.300 Includes street index.

18.301 Index, indexed map of "Morgan County, Alabama," text, ill., and advertisements on verso.

18.302 Indexes, directories, schedules of ferry and train services, and text on verso.

18.303 Indexes, maps of "Fort Worth-Dallas and vicinity" and "Houston and vicinity," and 6 urban maps on verso.

Informal Contents—Titled Non-Cartographic Resources

18.304 "Portugal guide-book (maps, all about hotels, pensions, auberges, camping, complete roll of hospitals, pharmacies, police stations)"—Cover p. 4.

18.305 Information about forests and parks and activities of the Jewish National Fund on verso.

18.306 Schedule of Frontier Days activities May 11-14 on verso.

18.307 "The soils of each mapping unit" on verso.

18.308 Table of "Interpretations for the general soil map of Pennsylvania for selected uses" on verso.

18.309 "The Virginia Peninsula & vicinity in history"—P. ii-iii.

18.310 Includes "Mineral production value," "Mineral production," and "Workers involved" tables and "Uses of principal minerals."

18.311 Includes "Transmission network—single line diagram," "power transmission lines," and "System at a Glance."

18.312 "Includes water resource projects . . . expected to be in existence by 1980"—Legend.

Informal Contents—General Non-Cartographic Resources

18.313 Includes: address, products, number of employees, SIC, phone number, and executive's name.

18.314 Includes advertisements.

18.315 Advertisements on verso.

18.316 Includes advertisements and inset of "Downtown Holland, one way streets."

18.317 Includes coats of arms.

18.318   Includes county boundary diagram.
18.319   Includes rural directories.
18.320   Includes Kenning service station directory, 3 island insets, and 19 urban insets.
18.321   Includes distance chart.
18.322   Includes glossary and index.
18.323   Includes 4 graphs.
18.324   Includes guide to using Pin code, "Pin map of India," and "Route map of Indian airlines."
18.325   Includes key to abbreviations.
18.326   Includes list of "Zip codes of cities and communities in Nevada and Utah."
18.327   Location maps on cover.
18.328   Location map and col. ill. on cover.
18.329   Includes location map, distance chart, and diagram showing roads.
18.330   Includes notes.
18.331   Includes notes and indexed table of administrative divisions.
18.332   Includes notes, table of "License terms and history," and index map.
18.333   Includes 2 tables and map of "Southern Africa."
18.334   Includes population table and insets of Reunion-Mauritius, Seychelles, Johannesburg region, and Ogbomosho-Ilorin region.
18.335   Includes tables of radio beacons and "Chart numbering system" and "Conversion table."
18.336   *Descriptive text on verso.
18.337   Text and gazetteer on verso.
18.338   Text, advertisements, and maps of Muskegon County and Montague/Whitehall on verso.
18.339   Text, civic information, distance list, and advertisements on verso.
18.340   Text, indexed Chamber of Commerce member list, and list of Board of Realtors members on verso.
18.341   Text, indexed table of cheese data, and col. ill. on verso.
18.342   Includes text.
18.343   Includes text of instruction.
18.344   Includes text and table of hydrologic unit data.
18.345   Includes text and "Time comparison table."
18.346   Includes text, indexes, inset of Central America, 2 island insets, ancillary map of "Extent of the Aztec world," and col. ill.
18.347   Includes text, street index, lists of map sponsors and city officers, location map, inset of Cumming region, and advertisements.

Chapter 4 (Manuscripts)

AACR2 RULE

4.7B18 Contents [AACR2 Rev.]

List the contents of an item, either selectively or fully, if it is considered necessary to show the presence of material not implied by the rest of the description; to stress items of particular importance; or to list the contents of a collection.

> When recording titles formally, take them from the head of the part to which they refer rather than from contents lists, etc.

RELATED AACR2 RULE

4.7B1 Nature, Scope, or Form [Note] [AACR2 Rev.]
Due to its length, this rule has been abridged to include only the part related to the use of notes.

> In describing a collection of manuscripts, name the types of papers, etc., constituting the collection and mention any other features that characterize it. If the collection is of personal papers, give enough data to identify the person, either as a brief initial statement or as part of the summary of the nature of the collection. If necessary, give the contents (see 4.7B18) as part of that summary. [emphasis added]

Although there is a provision for a contents note in AACR2, it is not a note that is frequently provided. Instead, information about the contents is covered by AACR2 Rule 4.7B1 (Nature, Scope, or Form of Manuscript(s)).

LIBRARY OF CONGRESS POLICY

None issued. Information about the content of a manuscript is covered by APPM Rule 4.7B4 (Scope and Context/Abstracts).

RELATED LIBRARY OF CONGRESS POLICY

None issued.

AACR2 TEXT EXAMPLES REVISED TO REFLECT LIBRARY OF CONGRESS POLICY

None required.

HISTORICAL BACKGROUND

AACR1 Rule 201B3 provided a contents note for ancient, medieval, and Renaissance manuscripts containing works by various authors and for "composite" manuscripts. AACR2 does not specifically address the use of a contents note for ancient, medieval, and Renaissance works, but a note, similar to notes developed under AACR1, could be made under the general provisions for a contents note.

Although AACR1 and previous codes had no rule that specifically covered the remaining contents note provisions of AACR2 Rule 4.7B18, the contents note provisions for separately published monographs in these earlier codes could be applied to manuscripts. (See *Historical Background* under Rule 2.7B18.)

NOTE EXAMPLES

18.348 *No. 1. Letter February 8, Admiralty — No. 2. [Letter 18]23? October 25, Adm'y [to] Dr. Hooker?

18.349 *Letter no. 1. 1903 Nov. 16, New York [to] My dear Senator — Letter no. 2. 1907, Feb. 22, Fernandina, Fla. [to] Homer [i.e. David Homer Bates].

18.350 The 75th anniversary year of the Eistophos Science Club of Washington, D.C. / Mary Waterman — Seventy-five years of physics / Langhorne Brickwedde — Some changes in American archeology / Marion Sterling — The changing role in government and science / Virginia Abbot — Science writing / Charlotte Colton — Space exploration / Mary Libbie Dryden — Women in science : the changing picture / Charlotte Sitterly.

18.351 The pamphlets are: Catalogue of an exhibition of paintings, pastels, drawings and woodcuts illustrating Col. T.E. Lawrence's book "Seven pillars of wisdom". [London, 1927] — Proceedings at the unveiling of the memorial to Lawrence of Arabia, 3 October 1936. Oxford, 1937.

18.352 *Includes manuscript music, 1 leader part and 11 parts.

Chapter 5 (Music)

AACR2 RULE

5.7B18 Contents [AACR2 Rev.]

Titles

　　List the separately titled works contained in an item.

Additions to Titles

　　Add to the titles opus numbers (if they are necessary to identify the works named) and statements of responsibility not already included in the title and statement of responsibility area.

Musical Form

　　If the works in a collection are all in the same musical form and that form is named in the title proper of the item, do not repeat the musical form in the titles in the contents note. . . .

Other Contents

　　Make notes on additional or partial contents when appropriate.

　　When deciding on the title proper for music scores, one should follow AACR2 Rev. Rule 5.1B1. Accordingly, additional elements such as medium of performance, key, date of composition, and number (opus, thematic index, dramatic division, etc.) become part of the title proper, rather than other title information, and are, therefore, included in the titles of works given in the contents note.

The restriction on not repeating musical form in the contents note does not apply if the form is named only in the uniform title.

RELATED AACR2 RULE

None.

LIBRARY OF CONGRESS POLICY

None issued. However, some practices by LC have been observed from cataloging examples.

Additions to Titles

Information pertaining to dramatic divisions (i.e., Act number and/ or Scene number) is added to the title, when appropriate.

Information such as number, key, date of composition, or medium of performance, when added to the contents note in addition to the title proper, follow these patterns:

> numbers (opus, thematic, dramatic division, etc.), key, and date of composition are frequently enclosed in parentheses and placed immediately after the title proper.
>
> medium of performance information (especially for voices) is frequently enclosed in parentheses and placed after the statement of responsibility (if one is included).

Parallel Titles

AACR2 does not specifically provide for the inclusion of parallel titles in the contents note. If, however, the parallel title is parallel to part of the title proper, LC includes this information in the contents note. Parallel titles are formatted in accordance with AACR2 Rule 1.1D with each parallel title preceded by space, equals (=) sign, space.

Statements of Responsibility

Although AACR2 does not specifically provide for including poets' names for song collections, this does fall into the statement of responsibility area within the contents note and, as such, is included. LC has not limited this use to only poets' names, but also includes the textual source, even when a specific author is not known.

Duration

AACR2 does not specifically provide for the addition of a duration statement in a contents note for music. However, when available, the Library of Congress has been including these statements formatted according to its policy. Duration statements are enclosed in parentheses and generally given as the last element for each title (or title and statement of responsibility) listed in the contents note.

RELATED LIBRARY OF CONGRESS POLICY

None issued.

AACR2 TEXT EXAMPLES REVISED TO REFLECT LIBRARY OF CONGRESS POLICY

None required.

HISTORICAL BACKGROUND

AACR1 Rule 248F and previous codes contained essentially the same provisions as AACR2 Rule 5.7B18. In addition, these earlier codes also provided for the following information not specifically mentioned in AACR2:

Poets' names for song collections with texts by various poets.
A second title in parentheses if a song collection contained titles in two languages.

NOTE EXAMPLES

18.353   Errata slip inserted.

Formal Contents—Distinctive Titles

18.354   Contents: Soliloquy — Serenade — Swallowtail — Rainbow — Midnight spell.
18.355   Contents: Separation (ship-burial) — Marginal state — Reunion.
18.356   Contents: Lauds — The return — The hills — The may tree — The dream — Cressida — Departure — Prime.
18.357   Contents: Wachet auf, ruft uns die Stimme (3 verses) — Komm, Heiliger Geist, Herre Gott — In allen meinen Taten — Gott, der Vater, wohn' uns bei.
18.358   Contents: Tunings (2:40) — Fanfarades (3:00) — Acclamations (2:40).
18.359   Contents: Drei Märsche — Maskeraden — Fünf Arien — Fünf Menuette — Anhang ("Transpositionen für Instrumente bis a").

18.360   Contents: Alleluia, all praise be to God : from Cantata 142 — O quench us with thy goodness : from Cantata 22 — O Lord, we sing thy praise : from Cantata 129 — What God ordains is just and right : from Cantata 24 — If it should seem against His will : from Cantata 186 — Lord, grant that I may honour : from Cantata 107 — Now thank we all our God : from Cantata 79.

18.361   Contents: The angel Gabriel : English carol — Saint Luke — A child this day : English carol — A child's present to his child saviour / text by Robert Herrick — A babe in the cradle : Austrian carol — King Herod and the cock : English carol — Saint Matthew — A New Year's carol / text by Martin Luther.

18.362   Contents: Variazioni frugali : (Siebenmal Birchermüesli) — Fantasia opulenta : (Bei Tisch im Hause Rossini).

18.363   Contents: Full anthems: He that hath my commandments ; O give thanks unto the Lord ; Out of the deep (I) — Verse anthems: Everlasting God ; Except the Lord had helped us ; God, which as on this day ; I will magnify thee, O Lord ; O hear my prayer, Lord ; O how happy a thing it is ; O Lord, my God, in all distress ; O Lord, turn not away thy face ; Out of the deep (II) ; What child was he — Sacred songs: Almighty Lord and God of love ; Out of the deep (III).

18.364   Contents: I ne'er saw true beauty till this night (I, 5) — Queen Mab hath been with you (I, 4) — How silver-sweet sound lovers' tongues by night (II, 2) — O serpent heart . . . (III, 2) — . . . sad hours seem long (I, 1) — . . . it was the nightingale (III, 5) — Come weep with me (IV, 1) — . . . empty tigers (V, 3) — . . . never was a story of more woe (V, 3).

18.365   Contents: Confirma hoc Deus ; Justorum animae ; Terra tremuit / William Byrd — Ave Virgo gloriosa / Richard Dering — Tibi laus / Peter Philips — O nata lux ; O sacrum convivium / Thomas Tallis — Omnes gentes plaudite ; Psallite Deo : part 2 / Christopher Tye — Precamur sancte Domine : (Christe qui lux es) / Robert White.

18.366   Contents: El cóndor pasa / Daniel Alomía Robles — Estrella hermosa / Ignacia Arbulú Pineda — Muliza y Chimayche / [Anon.] — La huanuqueña / Mariano Ignacio Prado — Selva selva / [Anon.].

18.367   Contents: Two settings from Ahab / Jeffrey Hall ; H. Melville's Moby Dick — A busy man speaks : Portrait no. 3 / R. Bruce Hobson ; Robert Bly — Trois Poêmes de Georges Bataille : op. 73 / René Leibowitz ; English version by Maurice Wright — Vier Lieder nach Gedichten von Paul Celan : op. 86 / René Liebowitz ; English versions by Maurice Wright.

18.368   Contents: Walsingham / anon. — Three pieces. Prelude ; Coranto ; Almain / William Corkine — Alman / Alfonso Ferrabosco II — Five pieces. Hark, Hark ; Touch me lightly ; Life ; Death ; Pavan / Tobias Hume — Woodycock / anon. — If my complaints / John Dowland ; set by William Corkine.

18.369 Contents: The original song (Unacc. ; Flemish words) — Tandernaken / Tyting (3 parts) — Tander naken / Jacob Obrecht (3 parts) — Tanndernac / Antoine Brumel (3 parts) — Taunder naken / Henry VIII (3 parts) — Tandernaken / Erasmus Lapicida (3 parts) — Tandernaken / Alexander Agricola (3 parts) — Tandernack / Pierre Alamire (4 parts) — Tandernack quatuor / Ludwig Senfl — Tandernack quinque / Senfl — Tandernack vf dem rin lag / Paulus Hofhaimer.

18.370 Contents: Aspice Domine : SSAATB / William Byrd — O lux beata trinitas : SSAATB / William Byrd — Jubilate Deo : SSAATB / Richard Dering — Laboravi in Gemitu : SSAATB / Thomas Morley — Adolescentulus sum ego : SAATBB / William Mundy — Ad te levavi : SSAATB / Robert White — Four rounds from Pammelia. Benedic, Domine ; Domine fili ; Laudate nomen Domini, laudate ; Laudate nomen Domini super omnes / Thomas Ravenscroft.

18.371 Contents: The ragwort : for soprano, clarinet (or viola) & piano — The dandelion : for soprano & clarinet (or viola).

18.372 Contents: Geburtstagmusik = Birthday music (ca. 5:30) — Hochzeitsmusik = Wedding music (ca. 3:00) — Trauermusik = Funeral music (ca. 3:00).

18.373 Contents: Brausen des Waldes = Softly the forest / Bjørnstjerne Bjørnson — Ich hatt' eine Flöte aus Weidenholz = I once had a newly cut willow pipe / Vilhelm Krag — Im Glück wir lachend gingen = In bliss we walked with laughter / Holger Drachmann — Ich hör' in der nacht = I heard in the night / Holger Drachmann.

18.374 Contents: In the merry month of May : from Canzonets to three voyces (1608) / Henry Youll (1:20) — Ah! lovely infant = La bella pargoletta / Vincenzo Bell'Haver (1:45) — Your shining eyes : from the First set of English madrigals (1604) / Thomas Bateson (1:50) — Now am I free once more = Nun bin ich einmal frei / Jacob Regnart (2:30) — We see that men do ever = Nous voyons que les hommes / Jacques Arcadelt (3:00) — Good man, you are complaining = Gut G'sell, du machst dein Klagen / Gregor Lange (2:50) — This season now delights me = Herzlich tut mich erfreuen / Melchior Schaerer (2:15) — Sure there is no God of love / Thomas Thomkins (2:30) — Beauty from the world may vanish = Le beau du monde s'efface / Pascal l'Estocart (1:30) — This is the time = Dies ist die Zeit / Jacob Regnart (1:25) — Now is the summer springing : from Ayres or fa la's for three voyces (1627) / John Hilton the younger (ca 2:00).

18.375 Contents: The earth goeth on the earth (Melrose Abbey, 18th century) — Hymnus circa exsequias defuncti / Prudentius, 4th century — Two epitaphs from Arbroath Abbey (1822-1847) — Colours of rain and iron / Salvatore Quasimodo ; translated by Jack Bevan.

18.376 Contents: Upon Julia's clothes / text by Robert Herrick — The turtle / text by Ogden Nash — Une allee du Luxembourg / text by Aloysius Bertrand — The ancient Mariner (Verse 10) / text by Samuel Taylor Coleridge.

18.377 Contents: Prologue / poem, Anne Bradstreet — Know the world / poem, Archibald MacLeish — The two trees / poem, Archibald MacLeish — The linden branch / poem, Archibald MacLeish — Black boy / poem, Norman Rosten — Caliban / poem, Norman Rosten — Interlude — The snow fall / poem, Archibald MacLeish.

18.378 Contents: Sound of the flute / Blake — Lord, make me to know my end / from Psalm 39 — One day I wrote her name upon the strand / Spenser — To everything there is a season / Ecclesiastes — Seafarer / Old English — Roll on, thou deep and dark blue ocean / Byron.

18.379 Contents: Eternitie / words by Robert Herrick (SSAATTBB) — Vain wits and eyes / words by Henry Vaughan (SATB, SATB) — A hymn to God the father / words by John Donne (SSAATB) — The search / words by Henry Vaughan (SATB) — A song / words by Richard Crashaw (SAB).

18.380 Contents: Cahier 1. Très facile à facile — Cahier 2. Facile à moyenne force.

18.381 Contents: Instructions — v.1. Solos for voice, 3-58 — v. 2. Solos for voice, 59-92 — [v. 3] Instructions.

18.382 Contents: v.1. Pièces à une et à deux violes (1686-89).

18.383 Contents: [1]. Preces and responses ; First preces and psalms ; Second preces and psalms ; Five-part litany ; The short service ; The second service ; The third service ; Doubtful and fragmentary works — 2. The great service.

18.384 Contents: Waltz, op. 96, no. 1 — Contredanse, op. 96, no. 2 — Zhuluska's variation : op. 102, no. 2 — Quarrel : op. 102, no. 3 — National dance, op. 64/2, no. 1 — Scene, op. 64/2, no. 2 — Minuet, op. 64/2, no. 4 — Dance, op. 64/3, no. 4 — Romeo and Juliet : op. 64/2, no. 6.

18.385 Contents: Lament 1 — History 1 — Lament 2 — Arioso — Recitative — Salutation — Aria con obbligato — Intermezzo — Dramatic quartet : History 2 — Trio and close.

18.386 Contents: Soneto VIII ; Soneto IX ; Soneto XI ; Soneto XIV ; Soneto XVI ; Soneto XXII / Eríquez de Valderrábano — Tiento II ; Romanesca II ; O guárdame las vacas : romanesca ; Fantasia II ; Fantasia IV / Alonso Mudarra — Tiento / Miguel de Fuenllana — Fantasia XIV ; Fantasia XIII / Luis Milan.

Formal Contents—Generic Titles

18.387 Contents: v.1. Madrigali a cinque voci, libro primo — v. 2. Il secondo libra de madrigali a cinque voci.

18.388 Contents: ser. A. Motets (v.) — ser. B. Masses (v.) — ser. D. Madrigals (v.).

18.389 Contents: No. 1, op. 17, B♭ major — No. 2, op. 34, no. 1, A major — No. 3, op. 34, no. 2, F major — No. 4, op. 47, no. 1, E minor — No. 5, op. 47, no. 2, C major.

18.390 Contents: In A major (3) 1833-1834 — In G minor (4) 1835 — In G minor (5) 1867.

18.391   Contents: The complete sonatas and partitas for unaccompanied violin — The six sonatas for violin and clavier.

18.392   Contents: Set a5 in g — Set a5 in a — Set a5 in c — Set a5 in F — Set a5 in C — Set a6 in G — Set a6 in C — Set a6 in F — Set a6 in B flat — Set a6 in c.

18.393   Contents: No. 4 in G — No. 5 in C minor — No. 6 in E minor.

18.394   Contents: bd. 1. No. 1-9 — bd. 2. No. 10-16.

18.395   Contents: Quintet in E-flat major, op. 44, for two violins, viola, cello, and pianoforte — Quartet in E-flat major, op. 47, for violin, viola, cello, and pianoforte — Trio no. 1 in D minor, op. 63, for violin, cello and pianoforte — Trio no. 2 in F major, op. 80, for violin, cello and pianoforte —Trio no. 3 in G minor, op. 110, for violin, cello and pianoforte — String quartet no. 1 in A minor, op. 41, no. 1 — String quartet no. 2 in F major, op. 41, no. 2 — String quartet no. 3 in A major, op. 41, no. 3.

Formal Contents—Incomplete

18.396   Contents: — v. 2. First position pieces for viola and piano : grades I and II.

18.397   Contents: v. 2. The division flute (volume 2, 1708) and pieces from other sources.

Informal Contents

18.398   Contains works by Francesco da Firenze and others.

18.399   Includes instructions for performance in Italian and English.

18.400   Includes pref. and notes in English, German, and Italian.

18.401   Contains works by Beethoven, Clementi, Haydn, W.A. Mozart, F.X. Mozart, Schubert, and Wagenseil.

18.402   "An antiphon Ecce Dominus veniet and eight settings of the Deo gratias which bear no indications concerning their authorship, are given in the present volume as an appendix"—P. 27-29.

18.403   Appendix contains the libretto of the 1st ed., notes on the opera, and summary of the publication in English (p. [429]-[510]).

18.404   Biography of John Paul II with reprints of newspaper articles and photos of his travels: p. 6-23.

18.405   Contains no. 3-5 of the composer's Six duo concertants pour flute et alto, published ca. 1780 by Le Duc, Paris.

18.406   Contains studies and exercises, music arr. for flute, complete 1st flute parts from orchestral works, and flute parts from solos for flute and piano.

18.407   Bibliography: p. 137-139.

18.408   Includes bibliographical references.

18.409   "Discografia de Raymond Thevenot": p. 2.
         Discography: p. 135-137.

18.410   Includes chord symbols and indexes.

18.411   Includes 5 alternative sections for soprano or alto with string orchestra (p. 33-56), the work resulting from the inclusion of these substitutions comprising RV 611.

18.412 Includes lists of works and discographies for each composer represented.
18.413 "Includes masterpieces by Bach, Diabelli, Glinka, Handel, Haydn, Mendelssohn, Mozart, Offenbach, and others."—Cover.
18.414 Includes only the 39 Psalms for which tunes were provided in the original edition in facsimile and modern transcription.
18.415 Includes paraphrases of poems from Prayers from the ark by Carmen Bernos de Gasztold before each movement.
18.416 Includes Psalms and sacramental rites.
18.417 Includes synopsis by the composer.
18.418 Libretto: p. xiii-xxi.
18.419 "Revisionsbericht": [37]-38.
18.420 "Textkritischer Kommentar" in German: p. 115-133.
18.421 Vol. 4 includes "Chord dictionary in all the scales" and v. 5 includes "Scales and arpeg[g]ios."

Chapter 6 (Sound Recordings)

AACR2 RULE

6.7B18 Contents [AACR2 Rev.]

Titles

List the titles of individual works contained on a sound recording.

Additions to the Title

Add to each title statements of responsibility not included in the title and statement of responsibility area and the duration of the piece (see 1.5B4). . . .

Other Contents

Make notes on additional or partial contents when appropriate.

RELATED AACR2 RULE

6.7B6 Statements of Responsibility [Note] [AACR2 Rev.]

Make notes on variant names of persons or bodies named in statements of responsibility if these are considered to be important for identification. Give the names of performers and the medium in which they perform if they have not been named in the statements of responsibility and if they are judged necessary. Make notes relating to any other persons or bodies connected with a work that are not named in the statements of responsibility. . . .

Incorporate the names of performers into the contents note if appropriate (see 6.7B18). [emphasis added]

LIBRARY OF CONGRESS POLICY

When durations are recorded in a formal contents note, the Library of Congress is applying its own interpretation to AACR2 Rule 6.7B10, regarding when such a duration note should be included, how it should be derived, and how it should be formatted. (MCB v. 12, no. 10 and MCB v. 13, no. 8. See the discussion under Rule 6.7B10 in this text (p. 265) and the *Related Library of Congress Policy* that follows for further details.)

RELATED LIBRARY OF CONGRESS POLICY

6.7B10 Physical Description [Notes]

If the individual works in a collection are identified in the title and statement of responsibility area, list the durations of the works in a note. If the individual works are listed in a contents note (6.7B18), give their durations there. [emphasis added]

When recording individual durations in the note area, give them as they appear on the item (e.g., in minutes and seconds if so stated). If only the durations of the parts of a work are stated (e.g., the movements of a sonata), if desired, add the stated durations together and record the total for the work in minutes, rounding off to the next minute.

Precede a statement of duration by "ca." only if the statement is given on the item in terms of an approximation. Do not add "ca." to a duration arrived at by adding partial durations or by rounding off seconds.

If the duration of a work is not stated on the item or if the durations of some but not all the parts are stated, do not give a statement of duration for that work. Do not approximate durations from the number of sides of a disc, type of cassette, etc. [CSB 13]

AACR2 TEXT EXAMPLES REVISED TO REFLECT LIBRARY OF CONGRESS POLICY

2nd Example

AACR2 TEXT
Contents: The fourth millennium / Henry Brant (9 min.) — Music for brass quintet (14 min.)

AACR2 TEXT REVISED
Contents: The fourth millennium / Henry Brant (9:00) — Music for brass quintet (14:00)

HISTORICAL BACKGROUND

AACR1 Rev. Rule 252F12 stated that the scope and form of the contents note established for monographs (AACR1 Rev. Rule 148) and music (AACR1 Rule 248F) also apply to sound recordings. An additional provision was made, however, to include a performer's name, when necessary, in a contents note. In AACR2, this latter provision is mentioned under AACR2 Rule 6.7B6 but results in similar contents note statements. As is the case with contents notes in other chapters, the location of the statement of responsibility in a contents note developed under AACR1 differs from that developed under AACR2. Unlike AACR2, AACR1 had no specific provision for the inclusion of a duration statement in a contents note.

NOTE EXAMPLES

Formal Contents—Distinctive Titles

18.422 Contents: v. 1. Country gardens — v. 2. To a Nordic Princess — v. 3. [without special title] — v. 4. [without special title].

18.423 Contents: From the Bavarian highlands — O happy eyes : op. 18, no. 1 — Love : op. 18, no. 2. My love dwelt in a northern land : op. 18, no. 3 — Spanish serenade : op. 23 — The snow : op. 26, no. 1 — Fly, singing bird, fly : op. 26, no. 2 — The prince of sleep.

18.424 Contents: Judicial notice I-II (2 cassettes) — Testimony, viva voce evidence I-II (2 cassettes) — Expert witnesses I-II (2 cassettes) — Rule against hearsay I-II (2 cassettes) — Exceptions to hearsay I-V (5 cassettes) — Materiality and privileges I-II (2 cassettes) — Burdens, presumptions, & the relationship between the two.

18.425 Contents: Tape 1. Psychoanalysis and psychoanalytically-oriented psychotherapy / Merton M. Gill, Jerome D. Oremland — Tape 2. Discussion of Dr. Gill's address / Paul A. Dewald & Merton M. Gill. The process of change in psychoanalytic psychotherapy / Paul A. Dewald.

18.426 Contents: Tape 1. From schizophrenia to creativity / by Silvano Arieti. Working with the office patient / by Larke Huang.

18.427 Contents: 16 different songs on several older coin-operated disc music boxes — 2 selections of tunes played on the Wheelbarrow Piano of Ghent, Belgium — 4 selections of tunes scored in the late 1800 for a concert player piano — Itona crank organ (parlor model) — 3 selections of the sound of the Photo Player, a suction activated calliope.

18.428 Contents: 1ère ptie.: Le désert. Les orioles. Ce qui est écrit sur les étoiles. Le cossyphe d'heuglin. Cedar Breaks et le don de crainte — 2e ptie.: Appel interstellaire. Bryce Canyon et les rochers rouge-orange — 3e ptie.: Les ressuscités et le chant de l'étoile Aldébaran. Le moqueur polyglotte. La grive des bois. Oma, leiothrix, elepaio, shama. Zion Park et la cité céleste.

18.429   Contents: Overture medley (Boswell Sisters, Cab Calloway, Mills Bros., Burns & Allen) — Dinah (Bing Crosby) — Take a letter : (skit) (Burns & Allen) — Where's Bing Crosby (The Major & the Minors, Burns & Allen) — Here lies love (Crosby, with Eddie Lang, guitar) — Tiger rag (Mills Brothers) — I'm the drummer (Vincent Lopez Orchestra) — Trees (Donald Novis) — Crazy people (Boswell Sisters) — And you were mine (Kate Smith) — Minnie the Moocher (Calloway & chorus) — Please : (finale) (Crosby).

18.430   Contents: Overture — When my dreams come true (vocal) — Groucho's love scene (with Margaret Dumont) — When my dreams come true (Harpo, harp) — Groucho & Chico pun around — Monkey doodle do (vocal) — Groucho & Chico play auction — Dance number — I want my shirt : (Toreador song) — Gypsy love song (Chico, piano) — Finale.

18.431   Contents: 1-2. Products liability overview — 3. Punitive damages. Damages — 4. Legal innovation and imagination — 5. Psychic injuries — 6-7. A tort law update — 8. Whither the civil jury?

18.432   Contents: No. 6, part 1 — Spannerisms — Circle — Making friends — Miss slap botty trio — No. 6, part 2.

18.433   Contents: Hamilton County breakdown / Green — Salty dog blues / Zeke Morris — Teardrops in my eyes / Sutton — Ocean of diamonds / Carnahan — Byron's barn / Berline — Rolling in my sweet baby's arms / trad. — I'll just stay around / Flatt — Jackrabbit / Berline — Last old shovel / Scott — Hickory Hollow / D. Dilliard.

18.434   Contents: Derby Day : overture / William Alwyn (London Philharmonic Orchestra ; the composer conducting) — Helter Skelter : a comedy / Francis Chagrin (London Philharmonic Orchestra ; John Pritchard, conductor) — Beckus the dandipratt : comedy overture / Malcolm Arnold (London Symphony Orchestra ; Nicholas Braithwaite, conductor) — Street corner : overture / Alan Rawstorne (London Philharmonic Orchestra ; John Pritchard, conductor) — Yorick : overture / Geoffrey Bush (New Philharmonia Orchestra ; Vernon Handley, conductor) — Agincourt : an overture / Walter Leigh (New Philharmonia Orchestra ; Nicholas Braithwaite, conductor).

18.435   Contents: La bataille : pavana / anon. French, mid-16th c. — L'homme armé / anon. French, early 15th c. — Il sera pour vous conbatu/L'ome armé / Robert Morton — O rosa bella / John Dunstable — Galliard after Lavecha / anon. English, late 16th c. — Blame not my lute / anon. English, mid-16th c. — Patrie pacis / anon. English, 14th c. — Amor potest/ad amorem / anon. French, 13th c. — Aime sospiri / anon. Italian, mid-15th c. — Chi passa per sta strada / Filippo Azzaiolo — Hoftanz und Hupfauff / anon. German, 16th c. — Es taget vor dem Walde / Ludwig Senfl — Es taget vor dem Walde / anon. German, 16th c. — J'ai le rebours / Pierre Certon — Tastar de corde ; Recercar / Joan Ambrosio Dalza — Belle qui tiens ma vie / anon. French, 16th c. — Kalenda maya / Raimbault de Vaqueiras — Danse royale / anon. French, 13th c. — Don vient cela / Claudin de Sermisy — Me lykyth ever / anon. English, early 15th c. — Mir ist schönst brauns Maidelein / Caspar Othmayr — Amors, amors / anon., late 15th or early 16th c. — Tant apart / anon., 15th c. — Tout a par moy / Walter Frye — Saltarello / anon. Italian, 13th or 14th c.

18.436 Contents: Bidin' my time (5:02) — How long has this been going on (3:22) — Soon (3:47) — Lady be good (4:23) — But not for me (3:13) — A foggy day (2:43) — It ain't necessarily so (5:57) — Love is here to stay (5:05) — 'S wonderful (3:22) — Nice work if you can get it (3:40) — Embraceable you (3:05).

18.437 Contents: Aïda. Pur ti riveggo / Verdi (with Montserrat Caballé, soprano) (13:13) — Don Carlo. Ascolta!/Dio che nell'alma infondere / Verdi (with Sherrill Milnes, baritone) (5:52) — Don Carlo. Io vengo a domandar / Verdi (with Sherrill Milnes, baritone) (10:45) — Faust. Il se fait tard / Gounod (with Mirella Freni, soprano) (9:27) — Mefistofele. Rivolgi a me lo sguardo/Lontano, lotano / Boïto (with Montserrat Caballé, soprano) (3:07) — Mefistofele. Forma ideal purissima / Boïto (with Josella Ligi, soprano) (9:21).

18.438 Contents: Ariettes oubliées / texts by Paul Verlaine (16:00) — Fete galantes II / texts by Paul Verlaine (9:00) — cinq poèmes de Baudelaire (25:41).

18.439 Contents: Excalibur: Siegfried's funeral march ; Tristan und Isolde. Prelude to act 1; Parsifal. Prelude to act 1 (abridged) / Wagner (8:12 ; 10:38 ; 8:58). Carmina burana. O fortuna / Orff (2:44) — Ordinary people: Canon / Pachelbel (4:55) — Kramer vs. Kramer: Mandolin concerto. 1st movement / Vivaldi (2:56) — "10": Bolero (abridged) / Ravel (14:55) — Apocalypse now: Ride of the Valkyries / Wagner (5:19).

18.440 Contents: Hopak / Modest Moussorgsky ; arr. by James Mattern (1:18) — Miller's dance from Three cornered hat (3:13) ; Suite from El amor brujo (6:09) / Manuel de Falla ; arr. by James Mattern — Folk song suite / Béla Bartók ; arr. by James Mattern (6:23) — Toccata / Edmund Haines (1:29) — Brass quintet no. 1 / James Hopkins (8:53) — Sonata breve / James Mattern (7:15).

18.441 Contents: M. Thomas Collier his galiard (recorders, lute) (1:18) — Sir Henry Umptons funerall (recorders, lute) (5:27) — Sir John Smith his almain (lute) (2:04) — I saw my lady weep (countertenor, lute) (5:10) — M. Henry Noel his galiard (recorders, lute) (1:51) — M. Giles Hobies galiard (recorders, lute) (1:31) — Go, crystal tears (countertenor, lute) (3:23) — Semper Dowland, semper dolens (recorder, lute) (5:57) — M. Nicholas Gryffith his galiard (recorders, lute) (2:16) — Sorrow stay (countertenor, lute) (3:25) — The earle of Essex galiard (recorders, lute) (1:43) — Whitehead his almand (recorders, lute) (1:31) — In darkness let me dwell (countertenor, lute) (4:32).

18.442 Contents: La sacre du printemps / Igor Stravinsky (35:00 ; Cleveland Orchestra) — Music for strings, percussion and celesta / Béla Bártok (30:00 ; BBC Symphony Orchestra) — La mer / Claude Debussy (24:00 ; New Philharmonia Orchestra) — Pierrot Lunaire : op. 21 / Arnold Schoenberg (34:00 ; Yvonne Minton, Sprechstimme ; Pinchas Zukerman, violin, viola ; Lynn Harrell, violoncello ; Michel Debost, flute, piccolo ; Antony [sic] Pay, clarinet, bass clarinet ; Daniel Barenboim, piano) — Lulu-suite / Alban Berg (30:00 ; Judith Blegen, soprano ; New York Philharmonic) — Sechs Stücke für Orchester, op. 6 (12:20) ; Funf Stücke für Orchester, op. 10 (4:17) / Anton Webern (London Symphony Orchestra).

18.443   Contents: Rosetta blues / Rosetta Howard, J. Mayo Williams (Rosetta Howard) (2:55) — My daddy rocks me / J. Bernie Barbour (Trixie Smith) (2:56) — Jazzin' babies' blues / Richard M. Jones (Georgia White) (2:59) — Georgia grind / Spencer Williams (Blue Lu Barker) (3:00) — Blue deep sea blues / Armstrong (Blue Lu Barker) (2:51) — Jaybird blues / Jordan (Peetie Wheatstraw) (3:05) — My pony / Johnny Temple (Johnny Temple) (3:05) — Doggin' the dog / Joe Turner, J. Mayo Williams (Joe Turner) (2:48) — Box car shorty / Pleasant Joseph, Sam Price (Cousin Joe) (2:46) — Box car shorty's confession / Pleasant Joseph, Sam Price (Cousin Joe) (2:46).

18.444   Contents: Body and soul / Edward Heyman ... [et al.] (3:30) — Embraceable you / Ira & George Gershwin (4:42) — In the still of the night / Cole Porter (2:47) — The man I love / Ira & George Gershwin (5:17) — Les feuilles mortes / Jacques Prevert, Joseph Kosma (5:35) — My cousin in Milwaukee / Ira & George Gershwin (2:25) — Someone to watch over me / Ira & George Gershwin (5:15) — When day is done / B.G. de Sylva, Robert Katscher (3:11) — With a song in my heart / Lorenz Hart, Richard Rodgers (3:12) — I'm just wild about Harry / Noble Sissle, Eubie Blake (1:52) — Autumn in New York / Vernon Duke (5:37) — I got rhythm / Ira & George Gershwin (1:54).

Formal Contents—Generic Titles

18.445   Contents: No. 1 in C (8:51) — No. 2 in B♭ (13:16) — No. 3 in C (9:10) — No. 4 in D (5:59) — No. 5 in A (9:20).

18.446   Contents: A major, op. 1, no. 3 (9:00) — G minor, op. 1, no. 10 (10:00) — F major, op. 1, no. 12 (10:00) — D major, op. 1, no. 13 (12:00) — A major, op. 1, no. 14 (7:00) — E major, op. 1, no. 15 (8:00).

18.447   Contents: Deuxième suite (11:12) — Cinquième suite (6:54) — Première suite (10:16) — Troisième suite (11:52) — Quartrième suite (8:20) — Sixième suite (8:38).

18.448   Contents: For flute, violin, harpsichord, strings, and basso continuo in A minor, S. 1044 (21:00) — For flute, oboe, violin, strings, and basso continuo in D major, S. 1064 (16:00) — For two recorders, harpsichord, strings, and basso continuo in F major, S. 1057 (16:00).

18.449   Contents: Sonata for flute and piano in B flat major (22:00) — Serenade for flute and piano, opus 41 (23:00) — Six variations for flute and piano, opus 105 (19:00) — Allegro and minuet for two flutes (with Alain Marion, flute) (6:00) — Trio concertante in G major for flute, bassoon, and piano (with: Paul Hongne, bassoon) (22:00) — Ten variations for flute and piano, opus 107 (42:00) — Trio for three flutes in G major (with: Alain Marion, Christian Lardé, flutes) (10:00).

18.450   Contents: Toccata I (4:07) ; Canzona I (3:48) ; Ciacona in C (2:58) ;
Toccata III (5:30) / Johann Kaspar Kerli — Ciacona in C / Johann
Pachelbel (1:55) — Parthie in G / Johann Joseph Fux (20:09) — Div-
ertimento in F / Georg Christoph Wagenseil (12:10).

Formal Contents—Mixed (Distinctive and Generic)

18.451   Contents: L'arlésienne suite. Suite no. 1 (16:00) ; Suite no. 2 (11:00)
— Carmen suite. Suite no. 1 (13:00) ; Suite no. 2 (16:00).

18.452   Contents: Etudes, op. 10 — Etudes, op. 25 — Preludes, op. 28 — The
place of the etudes and preludes in Chopin's life : narration — Methods
of practicing the etudes and preludes.

18.453   Contents: Introduction : trio sonata for flute, violin, and continuo —
The art of canon. Ricercare a 3 ; Fuga canonica ; Four canons on the
royal theme ; Four canons on variants of the theme ; Canon a 4 ;
Ricercare a 6.

18.454   Contents: Prelude and fugue in C minor (1924) (8:27) — Double fugue
in E flat major (1924) (15:34) — March from Turandot : (1950-51) /
arr. MacDonald & Stevenson (5:45) — Prelude : John Dowland's
fancy : (1934) (3:12) — Four miniatures : (1918-20) (9:50) — Prelude
and fugue in D minor/major (1924) (9:20) — Three illuminations
(1916) (with Christopher Kay, speaker) (5:51).

18.455   Contents: Six etudes, op. 16 ; Sonatina no. 3 ; Chorale prelude, Meine
Seele bangt und hofft zu Dir / Ferruccio Busoni — Eleven children's
pieces ; Six studies for piano, op. 70 ; Two ricercari on the name
B.A.C.H. / Alfredo Casella.

18.456   Contents: Variations on a theme by Paganini : op. 35 (23:06) — Two
rhapsodies, op. 79 (15:00) — Three intermezzi and rhapsody, op. 119
(15:00).

Formal Contents—Incomplete

18.457   Contents: v. 1 Konzerte —   — v. 3. Orchesterwerke — v. 4. Oper —

Formal Contents—Partial Contents

18.458   Partial Contents: Ballades, op. 10, No. 1 in D minor : after the Scottish
ballad Edward : Andante ; No. 2 in D major : Andante.

18.459   Partial Contents: Four songs: Liebeshymnus : op. 32, no. 3 ; Ver-
führung : op. 33, no. 1 ; Winterliebe : op. 48, no. 5 ; Waldseligkeit :
op. 49, no. 1.

18.460   Partial Contents: La licorne, ou, The triumph of chastity. Introduction/
Danse de la licorne/Marche ; Danse des chasseurs ; Danse de la jeune
fille ; Danse de chasseresses ; Valse ; Rumba ; Andante nobile et
Postlude.

18.461   Partial Contents: Suite from the opera Le coq d'or. King Dodon in his
palace ; King Dodon on the battlefield ; King Dodon with Queen
Chimaka ; Marriage feast and lamentable end of King Dodon.

Informal Contents

18.462   Contains also Fortuna desperata / Antoine Busnoys (7 min.).

18.463   Contains dance pieces, principally of the 17th century, from Germany, Bohemia, France, England, the Netherlands, Italy, and Spain.

18.464   Contains duets from op. 29, 33, 34, 37, 43, 74, 78, 79, 101, and 138, as well as Sommerruh.

18.465   Contains performances by the Golden Leaf Quartette, Birmingham Jubilee Singers, Four Great Wonders, Famous Blue Jay Singers, Dunham Jubilee Singers, Ravizee Singers, Bessemer Sunset Four, Heavenly Gospel Singers, Kings of Harmony, and the C.I.O. Singers.

18.466   Contains reminiscences and discussions of various musical topics by the conductor Sir Thomas Beecham, commentaries on him by various of his musical associates, and brief excerpts from his commercial recordings, including rehearsals.

18.467   Contains replacement arias written by Rossini for later performances of the opera: Sulla stil de' viaggiatori ; Cimentando i venti e l'onde ; Concedi amor pietoso ; Per lui che adoro.

18.468   Includes a 55 min. biography of the comedian entitled: Magnificent rogue : the adventures of W.C. Fields. From the radio program: Biography in sound. Narrated by Fred Allen and featuring the reminiscences of Field's friends and colleagues.

18.469   Includes a fragment of a rehearsal of Don Juan.

18.470   Includes between the 2 scenes of the 2nd act of the composer's Leonora overture no. 3 (not no. 2 as stated on item).

18.471   Includes the plainsong sequence Benedicta es.

18.472   Includes 2 additional cassettes: 1980 updates of titles 2 and 3.

Chapter 7 (Motion Pictures and Videorecordings)

AACR2 RULE

7.7B18 Contents [AACR2 Rev.]

Individual Works or Parts

List the titles of individual works contained in, or the parts of, a motion picture or videorecording.

Additions to the Titles

Add to each title any statements of responsibility not included in the title and statement of responsibility area, and the duration if known. . . .

Other Contents

Make notes on additional or partial contents when appropriate. . . .

Unedited Material and Newsfilm
> Give a description, using standard abbreviations, of the action and length of each shot on unedited material, newsfilm, or stock shots.

RELATED AACR2 RULE

7.1B2 Title Proper
Due to its length, this rule has been abridged to include only the part related to the use of a contents note.

Unedited Material and Newsfilm
> Include in a supplied title for unedited material, stock shots, and newsfilm all the major elements present in the picture in order of their occurrence (e.g., place, date of event, date of shooting (if different), personalities, and subjects). . . .
> *Optionally,* give a description of the action and length of each shot in a note (see 7.7B18). [emphasis added]

7.7B6 Statements of Responsibility [Note] [AACR2 Rev.]
Due to its length, this rule has been abridged to include only the part related to the use of a contents note.

Cast
> List featured players, performers, narrators, and/or presenters. . . .
> Incorporate names of the cast into the contents note if appropriate (see 7.7B18). [emphasis added]

LIBRARY OF CONGRESS POLICY

None issued. When recording a durations statement for motion pictures and videorecordings, the Library of Congress uses the "min., sec." style, e.g., 9 min. 52 sec., rather than the style it uses for AACR2 Rule 6.7B10 (MCB v. 12, no. 10 and MCB v. 13, no. 8), e.g., 9:56.

For archival moving image materials, the Library of Congress supplements AACR2 Chapter 7 with the guidelines in *Archival Moving Image Materials* by White-Hensen.

RELATED LIBRARY OF CONGRESS POLICY

None issued.

AACR2 TEXT EXAMPLES REVISED TO REFLECT LIBRARY OF CONGRESS POLICY

None required.

HISTORICAL BACKGROUND

AACR1 Rev. Rule 229.2M provided for essentially the same notes covered by the basic part of AACR2 Rule 7.7B18. The AACR1 Rev. rule, however, did not provide any special instructions for unedited material and newsfilm.

NOTE EXAMPLES

18.473 Contents: Augustus — The Special Olympics — Picnic — Outward Bound.

18.474 Contents: module 1. Accountability in nursing practice — module 2. Patient advocacy in nursing practice — module 3. Human rights in nursing practice — module 4. Who lives, who dies, who decides — module 5. The moral value of health care.

18.475 Contents: no. 1. Kindergarten puppy training — no. 2. Novice dog obedience — no. 3. Open dog obedience — no. 4. Utility dog obedience — no. 5. Training for tracking.

18.476 Contents: pt. 1. Play it cool with hot. Airmail, hardhats and barricades — pt. 2. Edges, openings and warning guards. Hoists, forklifts and conveyors. Tearoff and disposal — pt. 3. Ladders. Lifting. Housekeeping — pt. 4. Steep roof work. Shake jobs. Tile jobs.

18.477 Contents: module 1. Fundamentals of cancer (13 min.) — module 2. The immortal cell (19 min.) — module 3. Surgery and radiation (24 min.) — module 4. Chemotherapy and immunotherapy (21 min.) — module 5. A very special kind of care (18 min.).

Chapter 8 (Graphic Materials)

AACR2 RULE

8.7B18 Contents [AACR2 Rev.]

Individual Works or Parts
List the titles of individually named parts of a graphic item.

Additions to the Titles
Add to each title any statements of responsibility not included in the title and statement of responsibility area, and the number of cards, frames, slides, etc., when appropriate. . . . Make notes on additional or partial contents when appropriate.

RELATED AACR2 RULE

None.

425

LIBRARY OF CONGRESS POLICY

> In listing individually named parts of a graphic item, add the duration of the accompanying sound (cassette, disc, etc.) after the number of frames, slides, etc., if given. . . .
>
> In the absence of the number of frames, slides, etc., add to the titles/statements of responsibility the duration of the accompanying sound, if given. [CSB 13]

When recording a duration statement for graphic materials, the Library of Congress uses the "min., sec." style, e.g., 9 min. 52 sec., rather than the style it uses for AACR2 Rule 6.7B10 (MCB v. 12, no. 10 and MCB v. 13, no. 8), e.g., 9:56.

For original items and historical collections, the Library of Congress supplements AACR2 Chapter 8 with the guidelines in *Graphic Materials* by Betz.

RELATED LIBRARY OF CONGRESS POLICY

None issued.

AACR2 TEXT EXAMPLES REVISED TO REFLECT LIBRARY OF CONGRESS POLICY

None required.

HISTORICAL BACKGROUND

AACR1 Rev. Rule 229.2M is essentially the same as AACR2 Rule 8.7B18. The AACR1 Rev. rule, however, indicated that a contents note was "particularly appropriate" if the titles of parts were descriptive enough to substitute for a summary. Otherwise a summary note was preferred over a contents note. Although AACR2 does not provide this guidance, both notes are seldom used on the same catalog record.

For pictures, AACR1 Rule 272C7 allowed for the use of a contents note for pictures cataloged as a set. AACR2 does not specifically address pictures although AACR2 Rule 8.7B18 would allow for a continuation of the previous AACR1 practice.

NOTE EXAMPLES

Projection Graphic Materials

FORMAL CONTENTS—TITLES ONLY
18.478   Contents: The booming twenties — The crash of '29 — Industrial strife — The New Deal — The dust bowl — Politics and mass media.

18.479   Contents: International airport — Children's hospital, pts. 1-2 — Hotel — City within a city.

18.480   Contents: 1. Electrical test equipment — 2. Testing for leaks — 3. Evacuating a refrigeration system — 4. Charging the system — 5. Adding compressor oil — 6. Troubleshooting a hermetically sealed compressor motor.

18.481   Contents: 1-2. Filing skills — 3-4. Filing systems — 5-6. Telephone communications — 7-10. Daily business communications.

18.482   Contents: module 1. The M.A.P.S. method — module 2. The M.A.P.S. method : principles underlying the M.A.P.S. method — module 3. Making M.A.P.S. work for you.

18.483   Contents: pt. A. Planning, design, costs — pt. B. Bedding, safety, environment.

18.484   Contents: Pt. 1. Slime molds, protozoa, sponges, coelenterates, flatworms, nematodes, rotifers, moss animals, lamp shells, molluscs, and segmented worms — pt. 2. Arthropods (insects, crustaceans, spiders, and allics) and echinoderms (starfish, sea urchin, sea cucumber) — pt. 3. Chordates (tunicates) and vertebrates (fish, amphibians, reptiles, birds, mammals).

18.485   Contents: Storystrip 1. First glimpse of the subconscious — Storystrip 2. Psychoanalysis — Storystrip 3. Oedipus complex.

FORMAL CONTENTS—TITLES (LENGTH OF ITEM)

18.486   Contents: The CB detectives (59 fr.) — The curious boy (65 fr.) — Seasoned sailors (72 fr.) — The clue in the typewriter (64 fr.).

18.487   Contents: Design and manufacturing (80 fr., 84 fr.) — Merchandising and promotion (79 fr., 72 fr.).

18.488   Contents: General office terminology, pts. 1-2 (109 fr.) — Billing and customer service terminology, pts. 1-2 (104 fr.) — Accounting and bookkeeping terminology, pts. 1-2 (112 fr.) — Data processing terminology, pts. 1-2 (131 fr.) — Purchasing terminology (54 fr.).

18.489   Contents: 1. Organizing the composition (59 fr.) — 2. Constructing the composition (56 fr.) — Revising the composition (47 fr.) — Using composition skills (46 fr.).

18.490   Contents: 1. General concepts (45 slides) — 2. Clinical considerations (62 slides).

18.491   Contents: 1-2. History of typesetting technology (66 fr., 69 fr.) — 3-4. History of type (48 fr., 64 fr.) — 5-6. The language of type (62 fr., 64 fr.) — 7. Anatomy of a typeface (50 fr.) — 8. Building a typeface library (60 fr.).

18.492   Contents: A. Knowledge and skills (63 fr.) — B. Material culture (71 fr.) — C. Economic development (63 fr.) — D.-E. Socio-political systems (109 fr.) — F. Religion and philosophical thought (57 fr.) — G. Language, aesthetics (62 fr.) — H. Seeing relationships (41 fr.).

FORMAL CONTENTS—TITLES (LENGTH OF ITEM AND DURATION)

18.493   Contents: What is a computer? (66 fr., 13 min., 45 sec.) — Do you need a computer? (79 fr., 18 min., 40 sec.) — How to use a computer

(65 fr., 15 min., 30 sec.) — How do computers work? (71 fr., 14 min., 50 sec.) — How to program a computer (57 fr., 17 min., 20 sec.) — What do computers mean? (45 fr., 7 min., 20 sec.).

18.494   Contents: Basic one-step problems, pts. 1-2 (47 fr., 13 min., 54 sec.; 50 fr., 12 min., 6 sec.) — Intermediate one-step problems, pts. 1-2 (51 fr., 14 min., 16 sec.; 56 fr., 11 min., 22 sec.) — Advanced one-step problems, pts. 1-2 (54 fr., 14 min.; 60 fr., 12 min.) — Introduction to two-step problems, pts. 1-2 (59 fr., 17 min., 38 sec.; 67 fr., 13 min., 24 sec.).

18.495   Contents: 1. Analyzing transactions, journalizing, and posting (83 fr., 24 min., 15 sec.) — 2. Providing the ledger (76 fr., 27 min., 45 sec.) — 3. Preparing the worksheet (57 fr., 21 min., 45 sec.) — 4. Preparing the income statement & statement of owner's equity (73 fr., 29 min., 15 sec.) — 5. Preparing the balance sheet & closing entries (80 fr., 29 min., 30 sec.) — 6. Closing, balancing & ruling the ledger post-closing trial balance (66 fr., 29 min.).

18.496   Contents: lesson 1. First blood (64 fr., 10 min.) — lesson 2. A soldier's lot (68 fr., 10 min.) — lesson 3. Winning the West (49 fr., 7 min.) — lesson 4. The war afloat (59 fr., 8 min.) — lesson 5. On to Richmond (51 fr., 7 min.) — lesson 6. Nations at war (66 fr., 10 min.) — lesson 7. An endless slaughter (51 fr., 7 min.) — lesson 8. The drive to victory (65 fr., 10 min.).

FORMAL CONTENTS—TITLES/STATEMENTS OF RESPONSIBILITY

18.497   Contents: The glorious whitewasher / Mark Twain (83 fr.) — Two Thanksgiving gentlemen / O. Henry (69 fr.) — The sister years / Nathaniel Hawthorne (77 fr.) — Tom Sawyer loves Aunt Polly / Mark Twain (64 fr.).

18.498   Contents: 150 million years ago : the terrible lizards / illustrator, David Nicholson (73 fr., 15 min.) — The stone-age cave men / illustrator, Mimi Florance (70 fr., 12 min.) — Building the pyramids / illustrator, Nancy Keresty (65 fr., 12 min.) — The Olympics of ancient Greece / illustrator, Basil Ossetian (66 fr., 12 min.).

INFORMAL CONTENTS

18.499   Includes bibliography in instructor's guide.

Nonprojection Graphic Materials

FORMAL CONTENTS

18.500   *Partial Contents: No. 1. The landing Japanese army, welcomed by every nation, at Vladivostok — No. 4. The Japanese army defeated the German-Austrian army near Usri, Siberia — No. 5. The first battle near Manturia. The Japanese soldiers defeated the enemys cavarly [sic] — No. 7. The Japanese cavalry taking possession of Khobarovski, pursueing and attacking the enemies [sic] — No. 14. Our cavalrys occupied Khabarovsk, and march-past took place in front at the enemys gan-boats [sic] — No. 17. Our army attacks from sky, water, and shore, and requlsed [sic] enemy of Siberia.

18.501 *Contents: Agriculture, 1909-1917 — Canneries, 1909-1916 — Coal mines, 1908-1910 — Glass factories, 1908-1924 — Street trades, 1908-1924 — Tenement homework, 1910-1924 — Children in W.Va., Oct. 1924 — Miscellaneous child labor, 1908-1924.

18.502 *Contents: [no. 1] Estimating and measuring — [no. 2] Water — [no. 3] Sorting — [no. 4] Colour — [no. 5] Out of doors — [no. 6] Movement — [no. 7] Structures — [no. 8] Senses — [no. 9] Clothes — [no. 10] Air — [no. 11] Plastics — [no. 12] Flowers.

18.503 *Contents: ser. A. Osservazioni, riflessioni, sentimenti — ser. B. Dalla campagna al mare — ser. C. Città, lavora, scuola, vita religiosa — ser. D. Attravaverso i secoli — ser. E. Nel mondo.

18.504 Contents: Lake shore / Robert Burkert — Your day in court / Warrington Colescott — Driving wheel / Jack Damer — Big biker / Raymond Gloeckler — Negev / Victor Kord — Maschera rotto / Dean Meeker — Borzoi watching / Frances Myers — Cubes separated III / Marko Spalatin — Oval 10 / Arthur Thrall — Slings and arrows of outrageous fortune / William Weege.

INFORMAL CONTENTS

18.505 Contains 4 pages of text and 17 art prints in mounts with mat openings.

18.506 Leaf [1] has mounted portrait of Cooper (engr. by Wm. E. Marshall after C.L. Elliott) and "D. Appleton & Co." printed beneath it.

18.507 The poems are Ars poetica (Arte poetica) and summing up (Sumario).

18.508 Portfolio contains 24 loose plates and an 8 page booklet (31 cm.) consisting of t.p. and a table of contents which includes the captions in French and in English translation.

18.509 Suite includes "Un coup de dés" by S. Mallarmé ([20] p. on a "circular accordion fold").

Chapter 9 (Computer Files)

AACR2 RULE

9.7B18 Contents [AACR2 Rev.]

Individually Named Parts
List the parts of a file. . . .

Other Contents
Make notes on additional or partial contents when appropriate.

RELATED AACR2 RULE

None.

LIBRARY OF CONGRESS POLICY

None issued for AACR2 Rev. Ch. 9.

RELATED LIBRARY OF CONGRESS POLICY

None issued for AACR2 Rev. Ch. 9.

AACR2 TEXT EXAMPLES REVISED TO REFLECT LIBRARY OF CONGRESS POLICY

None required for AACR2 Rev. Ch. 9.

HISTORICAL BACKGROUND

Computer files were not covered by AACR1 or previous codes. The original AACR2 Chapter 9 is identical to the rule in AACR2 Rev. Ch. 9.

NOTE EXAMPLES

18.510   *Contents: Arithmetic practice — Odell woods — Odell lake — Change — Wrote note.

18.511   *Contents: Dr. Oz's cavern / by John Cunningham III — Inchworm / by Helen Adams and John Russ — Spell-off / by Ennio Murroni.

18.512   *Contents: disk 1. MasterType — disk 2. MasterType training ground.

18.513   *Contents: 1. Graph — 2. Function limits — 3. Polyroot — 4-5. Newton 1-2 — 6. Interaction — 7. Multi-integrals — 8. Least squares — 9. Line graph — 10. Row reduction — 11. Matrix — 12-13. Linear program 1.2.

18.514   *Contents: Cohort file 1. Mature men (45-49 yrs.) — Cohort file 2. Mature women (45-49 yrs.) — Cohort file 3. Young boys (14-24 yrs.) — Cohort file 4. Young girls (14-24 yrs.).

18.515   *Contents: 1. General sample (1954 logical records) — 2. Poverty sample (422 logical records) — 3. Black sample (145 logical records) — 4. Appalachian sample (140 logical records) — 5. Spanish-speaking sample (137 logical records).

18.516   *Contents: 1. Aggregate data (7,300 logical records) — 2. Annual events data (800 logical records) — 3. Daily events data (30,000 logical records) — 4. Intervention events data (12,000 logical records) — 5. Raw data (168,000 logical records).

18.517   *Includes demo programs, song maker/editor, song-part linker, module maker, module playback, and kaleidoscopic maestro. There are 3 different module interfaces: Applesoft, Integer BASIC, and Machine Language.

18.518   *Disk includes Tutorial and Utility programs. Back up disk also included.

18.519   *Program includes: a calculator, notepad, appointment book, auto-dialer, and ASCII table.
18.520   *Includes dBase II on-disk tutorial.

Chapter 10 (Three-Dimensional Artefacts and Realia)

AACR2 RULE

10.7B18 Contents [AACR2 Rev.]

Individual Works or Parts
   List the individually named parts of an object.

Other Contents
   Make notes on additional or partial contents when appropriate.

RELATED AACR2 RULE

None.

LIBRARY OF CONGRESS POLICY

None issued.

RELATED LIBRARY OF CONGRESS POLICY

None issued.

AACR2 TEXT EXAMPLES REVISED TO REFLECT LIBRARY OF CONGRESS POLICY

None required.

HISTORICAL BACKGROUND

AACR1 Rev. Rule 229.2M is essentially the same as AACR2 Rule 10.7B18. The AACR1 Rev. rule, however, indicated that a contents note was "particularly appropriate" if the titles of parts were descriptive enough to substitute for a summary. Otherwise a summary note was preferred. Although AACR2 does not provide this guidance, both notes are seldom used on the same catalog record.

431

NOTE EXAMPLES

18.521   *Contents: Breakout — Double — Cavity — Progressive.

18.522   *Contents: The gobbler — Getting together — Busy bee — Sea search — Pop-o — Play around the rainbow.

18.523   *Contents: no. 1. La cenicienta = Cinderella. Caperucita roja = Little Red Riding Hood. Pinocho = Pinocchio — no. 2. Los tres cochinitos = Three little pigs. El patito feo = The ugly duckling. Los tres ositos = Goldilocks — no. 3. El circo = The circus. Animales salvajes = Forest animals. La granja = The farm — no. 4. Servidores públicos = Public servants. La familia = The family. Abecedario = Alphabet.

18.524   *Inset portrait of Rev. Herbert McDermott, pastor from 1901-1917.

18.525   *Exterior view, including churchyard.

Chapter 12 (Serials)

AACR2 RULE

12.7B18 Contents

Give details of inserts, other serials included in the serial, and important special items with specific titles, unless they are catalogued separately. Do not give contents notes for monographic series.

RELATED AACR2 RULE

None.

LIBRARY OF CONGRESS POLICY

None issued.

RELATED LIBRARY OF CONGRESS POLICY

None issued.

AACR2 TEXT EXAMPLES REVISED TO REFLECT LIBRARY OF CONGRESS POLICY

None required.

HISTORICAL BACKGROUND

Although the basic intent of this note in both AACR1 and AACR2 is similar, there are minor differences between them. AACR1 Rule 167S1 instructed that contents notes were not to be made for monographs in a series if the monographs were analyzed, might be analyzed, or were considered "relatively unimportant." AACR2 simply instructs that monograph series are not given contents notes.

AACR1 Rule 167S2 prescribed the use of a note to identify other serials included in the serial being cataloged. These other serial notes identified "special items" warranting added entries, characterized the serial, or named parts needed for completeness. AACR2 adds the element of "inserts," but does not provide the rationale for the use of the note as did AACR1. AACR2 also does not mention the added entry aspect for "special items." AACR2 specifically precludes the use of this note if the "special items" are cataloged separately. AACR1 does not mention this.

NOTE EXAMPLES

18.526 Contains reports from divisions of the Service, and related bodies that pertain to job service in North Dakota.

18.527 Includes bibliographies.

18.528 Includes bibliographical references and book reviews.

18.529 Includes membership directories of Westchester Library Association and Health Information Libraries of Westchester.

18.530 Includes the proceedings of the meetings of the Société de médecine légale et de criminologie de France.

18.531 Includes occasional special issues called: Jamaica intercom annual.

18.532 Includes reports by Jamaica Bauxite Mining Limited . . . [et al.].

18.533 Includes some articles from: Indian journal of public administration.

18.534 Vols. include supplementary data for the next succeeding years.

18.535 Annual summary included with 1st quarterly report.

18.536 Beginning with the 80th Congress, Mar. 1947, a section, Daily digest, is included.

18.537 Vols. 1, 6, 8-9, 11, 13- consist of Proceedings of the International School of Nuclear Physics.

18.538 Includes the annual report of the Water Resources Division, <1979/ 80>.

18.539 Includes the proceedings of the 1st-<3rd> International Congress on Child Abuse and Neglect, 1976-<1981>.

18.540 Issues for 1977-   include the proceedings of the Informatics Conferences, previously published as single volumes by Aslib, entitled: Informatics 1-3.

18.541 Vols. for <1980-> include semi-annually: Designers west resource directory.

18.542 Issues for fall 1978/spring 1979-fall 1979/spring 1980 constitute the proceedings of the ninth annual meeting of the North East Linguistic Society.

.7B18. Contents

18.543   Issues for Sept./Oct. 1980-<Jan./Feb. 1981> include section: The public
         journal of the National Council on Alcoholism.
18.544   Vols. for 1981-   issued with its accountability report for fiscal year
         1979-

1.7B19. Numbers Borne by the Item (Other Than Those Covered in 1.8)

EXTRAPOLATED GENERAL RULE

Note important numbers, other than ISBNs (or ISSNs), borne by the item.

In some cases, notes made under this rule will give important alphabetic or alphanumeric combinations rather than only numbers.

RELATED AACR2 RULE

1.8B3 Standard Number [AACR2 Rev.]
> Give any number of an item other than an International Standard Number in a note (see 1.7B19). [emphasis added]

GENERAL LIBRARY OF CONGRESS POLICY

None issued. See the sections that follow for any LC policies or interpretations that apply to individual AACR2 chapters for descriptions.

RELATED LIBRARY OF CONGRESS POLICY

1.6 Series Area
Due to its length, this LC policy statement has been abridged to include only the parts related to the use of notes.

Source of Information
> 2) *Phrases that are not considered series titles*
> b) *Letters or numbers not associated with a series title.*
> Do not treat as a series statement a number that cannot be associated with a series title. Give the information as a quoted note instead. [emphasis added] (Ignore the number altogether on a bibliographic record for a serial.)
>
> Do not treat as a series statement a combination of letters and numbers (or letters alone) that cannot be associated with a series title if there is evidence that the combination is assigned either to every item the entity issues for internal control purposes or to certain groups of items for internal control or identification. Give such a combination as a quoted note. [emphasis added] (Ignore the combination

altogether on a bibliographic record for a serial.) In any case of doubt, reject the combination as a series statement.

Series Statements and Series Tracings

1) *General*

Although a series statement may include a parallel title (1.6C), other title information (1.6D), or a statement of responsibility (1.6E), the heading for the series will contain only a title proper or a uniform title heading or a name heading/title proper or a name heading/uniform title. . . .

2) *Series Titles Consisting Solely of a Corporate Body Name*

Treat a statement consisting solely of the name of a corporate body and a number as a series statement. Give the corporate name as the title proper. If the series is entered under title, assign a uniform title that consists of the title qualified by the term "(Series)" even if there is no conflict. (Apply these provisions even if the corporate body appears with the number solely as initials.) [CSB 31]

1.6G Numbering within Series

Due to its length, this LC policy statement has been abridged to include only the part related to the use of notes.

3) *More Than One System of Numbering*

Consider to have more than one numeric *system* of designation only if there is a one-to-one relationship between each numeric system and the item itself. Generally, record all separate systems of numeric designations in the series statement,[1] separating each designation by space-equals sign-space. . . .

[1]Omit the additional numeric designation(s) if given in overly complicated or lengthy statement(s) and give the information in a note instead. [emphasis added] [CSB 31]

FORMAT

Two chapters, 5 (Music) and 6 (Sound Recordings), provide instructions for the construction of a formal note (see the discussion under these chapters below).

In the other chapters an informal note is used although numerous examples in the AACR2 text use the following construct:

Nature of the number (or name of the body associated with the number): ##.

A separate note is made for each number group as shown in the example below:

Publisher's no.: 1175
"Y201."

CHAPTER APPLICATION

This note applies to all chapters for description other than Chapter 4 (Manuscripts).

EXCEPTIONS AND ADDITIONS

Chapter 5 (Music) uses this note to record plate or publisher's numbers.

Chapter 6 (Sound Recordings) uses this note to record the publisher's alphabetic/numeric serial number.

Chapter 2 (Books, Pamphlets, and Printed Sheets)

AACR2 RULE

2.7B19 Numbers [AACR2 Rev.]
Give important numbers borne by the item other than ISBNs (see 2.8B).

RELATED AACR2 RULE

2.8B2 International Standard Book Number (ISBN)
Give any other number in a note (see 2.7B19). [emphasis added]

LIBRARY OF CONGRESS POLICY

None issued.

RELATED LIBRARY OF CONGRESS POLICY

None issued.

AACR2 TEXT EXAMPLES REVISED TO REFLECT LIBRARY OF CONGRESS POLICY

None required.

HISTORICAL BACKGROUND

AACR1 Rev. and previous codes had no rule for monographs exactly equivalent to AACR2 Rule 2.7B19. AACR1 Rev. Rule 142A1 did have a footnote that addressed the issue of numbers/letters given with a monograph that were not related to a series. This footnote provided for the inclusion of these numbers/letters in a quoted note unless the work was issued by a commercial publisher. In this latter case the number/letter was not included in the bibliographic description.

This AACR1 Rev. Ch. 6 rule could be used for works that were not separately published monographs unless specific rules for the description of a format superseded or excluded its use.

In 1971, the Library of Congress began to provide the Superintendent of Documents classification number, when it was available at the time of cataloging, as the last note (see *Cataloging Service Bulletin* no. 104). In these notes, LC used the construct:

Supt. of Docs. No. : [class number].

This note can still be made using the AACR2 rule although no specific mention is made about it.

NOTE EXAMPLES

Alpha/Numeric

19.1 "3444."
19.2 "97-4."
19.3 "97-1A."
"97-1B."
"97-1D."
19.4 "ANSI Z39.30-1982."
19.5 "DOD-D-1000/DOD-STD-100/includes metric"
19.6 "FWS/NFC-L/82-1."
19.7 "FWS/OBS-79/40."
"FWS/OBS-79/41."
"FWS/OBS-79/42."
19.8 "NAVEDTRA 10078."
19.9 "ST/LIB/13/Rev. 4."
19.10 S/N 027-000-01065-2
19.11 S/N 052-070-05549-9 (v. 1)
S/N 052-070-05541-3 (v. 2)
S/N 052-070-04883-2 (v. 3)
S/N 052-070-05543-0 (v. 4)
19.12 "NRC FIN no. B1090-9"—Cover.
"NUREG/CR-1728."
S/N 052-010-02681-0
Item 1051-H-11
19.13 "ACM order no. 5334790."
19.14 "IEEE catalog no. 81CH1654-3."
19.15 "Clearinghouse no. SP 017 375."
19.16 "Code number: D-12."

19.17 "Contract 4-16-0004-80-010."
19.18 "U.S.D.L. contract no. 20-36-79-46."
19.19 "Prepared under U.S. Government contract no. 53-319R-8-93."
19.20 "Issue 39."
19.21 Item 1045-A, 1045-B (microfiche)
19.22 Item Y 4.Ap6/1:T68/4/982/pt. 1-
19.23 "Serial no. 48."
19.24 "Data series A."
19.25 Supt. of Docs. no.: 1 19.2:M 32/13
19.26 Vol. 1: No. 827; v. 2: No. 828.
19.27 Vol. 3: Index no. 40063.
19.28 Vol. 1: N4-4369/N6-4364. Vol. 2: N4-4370/N6-4364.
19.29 "Energy Committee serial no. 96-160."
"Commerce Committee publication no. 96-126."

Source Statements

19.30 On t.p.: 5850.
19.31 "3563"—V.2.
"C707"—V.3.
19.32 "III"—Spine.
19.33 "B-200100"—Prelim. p.
19.34 "OTA-TM-O ; v. 8."—P. 4 of cover.
19.35 "wr21"—Colophon.
19.36 On spine: VAT 3225; Vat lat. 3225.
19.37 "ANS order no.—650012"—Verso t.p.
19.38 "Grant no. 78-SS-AX-0048"—P. [2].
19.39 "NPS 1749"—P. [92].
19.40 Stamped on t.p.: Project #CPA-WA-10-19-1081.
19.41 "Project WS 1.41"—Added t.p.
19.42 "Publication number 554 (formerly PN-2022)"—Cover.

Corrections

19.43 "Library of Congress card number in publication is incorrect."
19.44 "Serial no. 96-78" incorrect in publication.

Chapter 3 (Cartographic Materials)

AACR2 RULE

3.7B19 Numbers

Give important numbers borne by the item other than ISBNs or ISSNs (see 3.8B).

RELATED AACR2 RULE

3.8B2 Standard Number

Give any other number in a note (see 3.7B19). [emphasis added]

LIBRARY OF CONGRESS POLICY

None issued.

RELATED LIBRARY OF CONGRESS POLICY

None issued.

AACR2 TEXT EXAMPLES REVISED TO REFLECT LIBRARY OF CONGRESS POLICY

None required.

HISTORICAL BACKGROUND

Although AACR1 and previous codes had no rule equivalent to AACR2 Rule 3.7B19, the number note provisions for separately published monographs in these earlier codes could be used for cartographic materials. (See *Historical Background* under Rule 2.7B19.)

NOTE EXAMPLES

Alpha/Numeric

19.45	"76."
19.46	"29 — 859 — 81."
19.47	"14,513."
19.48	"4.500/267/5-77."
19.49	"2000/137/4-76."
	"5000/8-77."
19.50	"064005A101."
19.51	"A102-1-R1080."
19.52	"Best.-Nr. 10 0415."
19.53	"C b."
19.54	"Carte no. 3280 V."
19.55	"Cat. no. 313/1."
19.56	"CART-M-77-17."
	"077-414."
19.57	"D."
19.58	"DMA Stock No. NVPUB107."
19.59	"Dep. Legal: M-43. 495-1980."
19.60	"ISP — WCM — 78."
19.61	"L.LN A. LN."
19.62	"Map 2386."
19.63	"March 1980 4-R-37393. March 1980 base 4-R-34039-1."
19.64	"NMP /77/109."

19.65 "Plate A-2."
19.66 "Project No. 32046—2-80."
19.67 Publisher's no.: 1136.
19.68 "R76/404 Cat. No. 77-2223 8."
19.69 "Réf. 22734/5/69."
19.70 "UNZA/GEOG./AYM."

Source Statements
19.71 "Ref. No. M6/6"—Cover, p. 4.
19.72 In lower right corner: JFK/79-81.
19.73 In upper margin: Figure IV-13.
19.74 On spine: 272.
19.75 Stamped on t.p.: 860.

Chapter 5 (Music)

AACR2 RULE

5.7B19 Publishers' Numbers and Plate Numbers [AACR2 Rev.]
Give publishers' numbers and/or plate numbers that appear on the item. Precede the numbers by *Publisher's no.:* or *Pl. no.:*, as appropriate. If a number is preceded by an abbreviation, word, or phrase designating a publisher, give that abbreviation, word, or phrase as part of the number.

Multi-Volume Items
In describing an item in several volumes, give inclusive numbers if the numbering is consecutive; otherwise give individual numbers or, if there are more than three of these, the first number and the last number separated by a diagonal slash.

Give letters preceding a number before the first number, letters following a number after the last number, but letters preceding and following numbers in conjunction with each number. . . .

Reprints
In describing a reprint, give the plate or publisher's number(s) together with the statement that the item is a reprint (see 5.7B7).

RELATED AACR2 RULE

5.4D3 Publishers' Numbers and Plate Numbers [AACR2 Rev.; formerly AACR2 Rule 5.4D2]
Give publishers' numbers and plate numbers in the note area (see 5.7B19). [emphasis added]

5.8B2 Standard Number
Give any other number in a note (see 5.7B19). [emphasis added]

LIBRARY OF CONGRESS POLICY

> Transcribe a publisher's number even if a plate number is also transcribed. Transcribe the statement as it appears, even if this mean[s] giving again a publisher's name already transcribed in the publication, distribution, etc., area. . . .
>
> When transcribing two or more distinct numbers, give each in a separate note. (Follow the rule as written for the transcription of numbers for an item in multiple volumes.) Transcribe a publisher's number before a plate number. [CSB 33]

The Library of Congress has decided that this note will be given in the last note position, regardless of whether notes are required by succeeding note rules.

RELATED LIBRARY OF CONGRESS POLICY

None issued.

AACR2 TEXT EXAMPLES REVISED TO REFLECT LIBRARY OF CONGRESS POLICY

None required.

HISTORICAL BACKGROUND

AACR1 Rule 245D provided for recording plate or publishers' numbers in the imprint area rather than as a note. These numbers served as a means of identification, and were added only if an imprint date was lacking. Brief definitions of the two numbers were given (similar to those given in the LC Rule Interpretation to AACR2 Rule 5.7B19). Except for the location of the information on the catalog record, the AACR1 rule is essentially the same as AACR2 Rule 5.7B19.

NOTE EXAMPLES

Plate Numbers
19.76   Pl. no.: 20228.
19.77   Pl. no.: AV 363.
19.78   Pl. no.: BH.BK.805.
19.79   Pl. no.: B.M.Co. 13941.
19.80   Pl. no.: CTW C-062219.
19.81   Pl. no.: E. & Co. 786.
19.82   Pl. no.: WW-42.
19.83   Pl. no.: A.L. 25697-A.L. 25698.

19.84   Pl. no.: LPM DM2-LPM DM3.
19.85   Pl. no.: D. 15.663-
19.86   Pl. no.:   /1397.
19.87   Pl. no.: VLA-104-30 (score); VL-104-11 (parts).

Publisher's Number

19.88   Publisher's no.: 8072.
19.89   Publisher's no.: 40.186/01.
19.90   Publisher's no.: XXXV.
19.91   Publisher's no.: H1021.
19.92   Publisher's no.: M 10.463.
19.93   Publisher's no.: dvfm 1436.
19.94   Publisher's no.: 12 0514 05 (v.2).
19.95   Publisher's no.: B & B 22813 (1374).
19.96   Publisher's no.: 6806-
19.97   Publisher's no.: 7188a-
19.98   Publisher's no.: 6860-6862.
19.99   Publisher's no.: Edition Eulenburg no. 4708.
19.100 Publisher's no.: Wilhelm Hansen edition no. 4347 A.

Chapter 6 (Sound Recordings)

AACR2 RULE

6.7B19 Publishers' Numbers [AACR2 Rev.]

Publishers' Numbers

Give the publisher's stock number (usually an alphabetic and/or numeric symbol) as found on the item. Precede each number by the brand or trade name associated with it on the label or container (see 6.4D2) and a colon. . . .

Multi-Numbered Items

If the item has two or more numbers, give the principal number if one can be ascertained, otherwise give both or all. If one of the numbers applies to the set as a whole, give it first and designate it as such.

Separately Numbered Units

If the item consists of separately numbered units, give inclusive numbers if the numbering is consecutive; otherwise give individual numbers or, if there are more than three of these, the first number and the last number separated by a diagonal slash.

RELATED AACR2 RULE

6.8B2 Standard Number

Give any other number in a note (see 6.7B19). [emphasis added]

LIBRARY OF CONGRESS POLICY

When applying rule 6.7B19 to include the label name and number in a note, make this note the first one.

Transcribe spaces and hyphens in publisher's numbers on sound recordings as they appear. Separate the first and last numbers of a sequence by a dash. . . .

When the item bears both a set number and numbers for the individual items (e.g., discs), give only the set number unless it does not appear on the individual items; in that case give the set number first, followed by the numbers of the individual items in parentheses. . . .

Give matrix numbers only if they are the only numbers shown on the item. Follow each matrix number by the word *matrix* in parentheses. [CSB 14]

RELATED LIBRARY OF CONGRESS POLICY

None issued.

AACR2 TEXT EXAMPLES REVISED TO REFLECT LIBRARY OF CONGRESS POLICY

None required.

HISTORICAL BACKGROUND

AACR1 Rev. Rule 252C provided for "serial identification" (set or individual item numbers) in the imprint area, rather than as a note. The format varied depending on whether the publisher was known primarily as a publisher of recordings or not. The LC Rule Interpretation to AACR2 Rule 6.7B19, which delineates procedures for multi-numbered items in a set, is essentially a restatement of AACR1 Rev. Rule 252C3 except for the location in which the number information is to be recorded, i.e., LC records this information as the first note while AACR1 Rev. called for it to be recorded in the imprint area.

NOTE EXAMPLES

19.101 Bead: 9.
19.102 Center for Cassette Studies: 36128.
19.103 Colonial Williamsburg Foundation: WS-110.
19.104 Columbia Special Products: ASL 163.
19.105 Foundation for Christian Living: FCL no. 241.
19.106 Gothic: 68005.
19.107 Harmonia mundi: 999.

19.108   Kicking Mule Records: KM 216.
19.109   Motivational Programming Corp.: 020 12198.
19.110   Musical Heritage Society: MHS 4253.
19.111   Rare Recorded Editions: SRRE 162.
19.112   RCA Red Seal: ARL-3727.
19.113   Time-Life Records: STL-J15.
19.114   University of Michigan Records: SM0009.
19.115   Westminster Choir: WC 3.

Multi-Numbered Items

19.116   Zafiro: AFL 801-808.
19.117   American Chemical Society: 469, 371.
19.118   Dischi Ricordi: RCL 27010–RCL 27011, RCL 27015–RCL 27016.
19.119   H. and L. Record Co.: HL 7241, 8451-8452, 62961-62962, 80171, 80779, 80881.
19.120   Deutsche Grammophon: 2740 231 (2562 205-2562-208).
19.121   Erato: STU 71292 (STU 71293-STU 71295).
19.122   Musical Heritage Society: MHS 824293 (MHS 4293-MHS 4294).
19.123   Aulos: RV 53 523 AUL (on container: FSM 53 523 AUL).
19.124   Pape: 6621516 (label on container: FSM 53 709).

Matrix Numbers

19.125   Melodiĭa: S10-10699 (matrix)–S10-10700 (matrix).
19.126   Serbien [sic] Orthodox Church, Belgrade: 3A/3366 A-2 (matrix)-3A/3366 B-1 (matrix).
19.127   Sonic Arts: TX 2 (matrix)–TX 3 (matrix).

Chapter 7 (Motion Pictures and Videorecordings)

AACR2 RULE

7.7B19 Numbers [AACR2 Rev.]

Give important numbers borne by the item other than ISBNs or ISSNs (see 7.8B).

RELATED AACR2 RULE

7.8B2 Standard Number

Give any other number in a note (see 7.7B19). [emphasis added]

LIBRARY OF CONGRESS POLICY

None issued. For archival moving image materials, the Library of Congress supplements AACR2 Chapter 7 with the guidelines in *Archival Moving Image Materials* by White-Hensen.

RELATED LIBRARY OF CONGRESS POLICY

None issued.

AACR2 TEXT EXAMPLES REVISED TO REFLECT LIBRARY OF CONGRESS POLICY

No examples were given in AACR2 or AACR2 Rev.

HISTORICAL BACKGROUND

Although AACR1 Rev. Ch. 12 and previous codes had no rule equivalent to AACR2 Rule 7.7B19, the numbering note provisions for separately published monographs in these earlier codes could be used for motion pictures and videorecordings. (See *Historical Background* under Rule 2.7B19.)

NOTE EXAMPLES

19.128 *#16-020.
19.129 Program no. 1155.
19.130 "Program no. 1608"—Guide.
19.131 "Program no. 1402"—Publisher's catalog.

Chapter 8 (Graphic Materials)

AACR2 RULE

8.7B19 Numbers
Give important numbers borne by the item other than ISBNs or ISSNs (see 8.8B).

RELATED AACR2 RULE

8.8B2 Standard Number
Give any other number in a note (see 8.7B19). [emphasis added]

LIBRARY OF CONGRESS POLICY

None issued. For original items and historical collections, the Library of Congress supplements AACR2 Chapter 8 with the guidelines in *Graphic Materials* by Betz.

RELATED LIBRARY OF CONGRESS POLICY

None issued.

AACR2 TEXT EXAMPLES REVISED TO REFLECT LIBRARY OF CONGRESS POLICY

No examples were given in AACR2 or AACR2 Rev.

HISTORICAL BACKGROUND

Although AACR1 Rev. Ch. 12 Rev., AACR1 Ch. 15, and previous codes had no rule equivalent to AACR2 Rule 8.7B19, the numbering note provisions for separately published monographs in these earlier codes could be used for graphic materials. (See *Historical Background* under Rule 2.7B19.)

NOTE EXAMPLES

Projection Graphic Materials
19.132   "Program no. 79"—Guide.
19.133   "Program no. 210"—Script.

Nonprojection Graphic Materials
19.134   *Reorder no.: 41555.

Chapter 9 (Computer Files)

AACR2 RULE

9.7B19 Numbers [AACR2 Rev.]
Give important numbers borne by the item other than ISBNs and ISSNs (see 9.8B).

RELATED AACR2 RULE

9.8B2 Standard Number [AACR2 Rev.]
Give any other number assigned to a file in a note (see 9.7B19).
[emphasis added]

LIBRARY OF CONGRESS POLICY

None issued for AACR2 Rev. Ch. 9.

RELATED LIBRARY OF CONGRESS POLICY

None issued for AACR2 Rev. Ch. 9.

447

AACR2 TEXT EXAMPLES REVISED TO REFLECT LIBRARY OF CONGRESS POLICY

None required for AACR2 Rev. Ch. 9.

HISTORICAL BACKGROUND

Computer files were not covered by AACR1 or previous codes. The original AACR2 Chapter 9 was the same as the rule in AACR2 Rev. Ch. 9.

NOTE EXAMPLES

19.135   *Part No. 014-096-003.
19.136   *Disk A702.
19.137   *"PHY145A."
19.138   *"C3300."
19.139   *20034.
19.140   *On disks: 031005680.
19.141   *On manual: 6137856.
19.142   *Future corporation data disk (6936716). Maintenance disk (6936685).
19.143   *System disk, serial no. 2055186; system disk (backup copy), serial no. 2055186.

Chapter 10 (Three-Dimensional Artefacts and Realia)

AACR2 RULE

10.7B19 Numbers
Give important numbers borne by the item other than ISBNs or ISSNs (see 10.8B).

RELATED AACR2 RULE

10.8B2 Standard Number
Give any other number in a note (see 10.7B19). [emphasis added]

LIBRARY OF CONGRESS POLICY

None issued.

RELATED LIBRARY OF CONGRESS POLICY

None issued.

AACR2 TEXT EXAMPLES REVISED TO REFLECT LIBRARY OF CONGRESS POLICY

No examples were given in AACR2 or AACR2 Rev.

HISTORICAL BACKGROUND

Although AACR1 Rev. Ch. 12 and previous codes had no rule equivalent to AACR2 Rule 10.7B19, the numbering note provisions for separately published monographs in these earlier codes could be used for three-dimensional artifacts and realia. (See *Historical Background* under Rule 2.7B19.)

NOTE EXAMPLES

19.144 *No. 3255.
19.145 *"AG 011."
19.146 *POM 1745.
19.147 *On box: "1011."
19.148 *Gamco. #152GA01.
19.149 *Trend Enterprises: T-095.
19.150 *Whitman: 4678.

Chapter 12 (Serials)

AACR2 RULE

12.7B19 Numbers [AACR2 Rev.]
Give important numbers borne by the item other than ISSNs (see 12.8B).

RELATED AACR2 RULE

12.8B2 International Standard Serial Number (ISSN)
Give any other number in a note (see 12.7B19). [emphasis added]

LIBRARY OF CONGRESS POLICY

None issued.

RELATED LIBRARY OF CONGRESS POLICY

1.6 Series Area
While the Library of Congress has not issued an interpretation to AACR2 Rule 12.7B19, it has issued an interpretation to AACR2 Rule 1.6 which has a bearing on the use of this note with serials. Due to its

length, this LC policy statement has been abridged to include only the part related to the use of notes.

Source of Information

2) *Phrases that are not considered series titles*

b) *Letters or numbers not associated with a series title.*

Do not treat as a series statement a number that cannot be associated with a series title. <u>Give the information as a quoted note instead.</u> [emphasis added] (Ignore the number altogether on a bibliographic record for a serial.)

Do not treat as a series statement a combination of letters and numbers (or letters alone) that cannot be associated with a series title if there is evidence that the combination is assigned either to every item the entity issues for internal control purposes or to certain groups of items for internal control or identification. <u>Give such a combination as a quoted note.</u> [emphasis added] (Ignore the combination altogether on a bibliographic record for a serial.) In any case of doubt, reject the combination as a series statement. [CSB 31]

1.6G Numbering within Series

Due to its length, this LC policy statement has been abridged to include only the part related to the use of notes.

5) *Numbering Grammatically Integrated*

If the numbering is grammatically integrated with the title proper of the series, record it as it appears in the source. Record series numbering in the access point in its prescribed position. <u>(If the analytic record is for a serial, precede the title by a mark of omission and add an appropriate note.)</u> [emphasis added] [CSB 31]

AACR2 TEXT EXAMPLES REVISED TO REFLECT LIBRARY OF CONGRESS POLICY

No examples were given in AACR2 or AACR2 Rev.

HISTORICAL BACKGROUND

Although AACR1 and previous codes had no rule equivalent to AACR2 Rule 12.7B19, the numbering note provisions for separately published monographs in these earlier codes could be used for serials. (See *Historical Background* under Rule 2.7B19.)

NOTE EXAMPLES

19.151   Catalogue no. 5426.0.
19.152   "NUREG-0750."
19.153   "MtAn 1-2-1."

1.7B20. Copy Being Described, Library's Holdings, and Restrictions on Use

GENERAL RULE

1.7B20 Copy Being Described, Library's Holdings, and Restrictions on Use [AACR2 Rev.]

Copy Being Described
　　Give important descriptive details of the particular copy being described. . . .

Library's Holdings
　　Give details of the library's holdings of a multipart item if those holdings are incomplete. . . .

Restrictions on Use
　　Indicate any restrictions on the use of the item.

RELATED AACR2 RULE

None.

GENERAL LIBRARY OF CONGRESS POLICY

The Library of Congress has issued an interpretation to AACR2 Rule 1.7B20. The wording of the interpretation, however, specifically addresses its use for monographs. See *Library of Congress Policy* under Rule 2.7B20 for this interpretation.

RELATED LIBRARY OF CONGRESS POLICY

None issued.

FORMAT

No formatting instructions were provided in AACR2. The Library of Congress has issued formatting instructions for monographs in its rule interpretation to AACR2 Rule 2.7B20. See *Library of Congress Policy* under Rule 2.7B20 for these instructions.

CHAPTER APPLICATION

This note is not present in Chapter 4 (Manuscripts).

EXCEPTIONS AND ADDITIONS

Chapter 9 (Computer Files — AACR2 Rev.) adds to the General Rule the provision to record a locally assigned file or data set name as well as the date the file was transferred or copied to another source.

Chapter 2 (Books, Pamphlets, and Printed Sheets)

AACR2 RULE

2.7B20 Copy Being Described, Library's Holdings, and Restrictions on Use [AACR2 Rev.]

Make these notes as instructed in 1.7B20.

RELATED AACR2 RULE

2.5B16 Number of Volumes and/or Pagination [AACR2 Rev.]

If the last part of a publication is missing and the paging of a complete copy cannot be ascertained, give the number of the last numbered page followed by + *p*. Make a note of the imperfection (see 2.7B20). [emphasis added]

LIBRARY OF CONGRESS POLICY

[To 1.7B20] Copy Being Described and Library's Holdings

For monographs, routinely make notes on any special features or imperfections of the copy being described. Carefully distinguish such copy-specific notes from other kinds of notes that record information valid for all copies of an edition, introducing the copy-specific note with the phrase

"LC copy . . . ,"
"LC set . . . ,"
or
"LC has . . ."

as appropriate. [CSB 12]

RELATED LIBRARY OF CONGRESS POLICY

2.7B7 Edition and History [Note]

Due to its length, this LC policy statement has been abridged to include only the part related to the use of copy-specific notes.

Limited Editions

Give limited edition statements, preferably in quoted form, for editions of 500 copies or less. If the statement cannot be quoted, phrase it so that the number does not come first (to avoid spelling out the number; cf. Appendix C.3). . . .

When the statement of limitation includes the unique number of the copy being cataloged, give only the statement of limitation here. Give the copy number (introduced by the phrase "LC has copy") as a copy-specific note (cf. LCRI 1.7B20). [emphasis added] [CSB 34]

2.7B4 Variations in Title

Due to its length, this LC policy statement has been abridged to include only the part related to the use of notes.

Binder['s] Titles

If a binder's title varies significantly from the title proper of the item (cf. 21.2A), record it in a note and make an added entry for it.

If a monograph has been bound only for LC's collections (i.e., it was not bound by the publisher or it was one of the multiple copies that were bound subsequent to publication as part of a cooperative acquisitions program), give only the note and not the added entry. In such a case, make the note a copy-specific one (LCRI 1.7B20), e.g.,

LC copy has binders title . . .

In case of doubt, do not assume that the item was bound only for LC. [CSB 27]

AACR2 TEXT EXAMPLES REVISED TO REFLECT LIBRARY OF CONGRESS POLICY

None required.

HISTORICAL BACKGROUND

AACR1 contained no rule directly equivalent to AACR2 Rule 2.7B20. Some of the examples provided with AACR1 Rev. Rule 143D3f did, however, use copy-specific notes. A footnote to that rule detailed the wording the Library of Congress would have used for one of the examples.

This AACR1 Rev. Ch. 6 rule could be used for works that were not separately published monographs unless specific rules for the description of a format superseded or excluded its use.

NOTE EXAMPLES

Copy Held

20.1 LC holdings recorded in shelflist only as of 2/5/82.
20.2 LC has no. 38.

20.3 "Copy #1 of 100"—Verso of t.p.
20.4 LC has no. III of the presentation copies.
20.5 LC has no. 5, with ms. notes pertaining to the specimens in this copy on p. [7].
20.6 LC has no. 27, signed by author.
20.7 LC copy unnumbered.
20.8 LC copy is not numbered but has all 59 samples. It has 2 copies of the catalog, one attached to the portfolio, the other laid in.
20.9 On cover, in pencil in the composer's hand: Return to Cole Porter, Waldorf Towers 41-C, New York.
20.10 LC copy designated "A.P. XX."
20.11 LC copy bound in cloth.
20.12 "Of this book 50 copies have been bound in cloth"—Colophon. LC has cloth-bound copy.
20.13 LC has hardbound, unsigned copy.
20.14 LC copy is paperbound.
20.15 LC copy has fore-edge painting (view of Gloucester) on marbled edge.
20.16 LC copies designated "Printer's copy."
20.17 LC copy designated "out of series."
20.18 LC has copy on Japan paper.
20.19 LC copy not the first impression. Cf. Papers of the Bibl. Society of Amer. v. 64 (1970), p. 49.
20.20 Four folded leaves of plates (Placed by LC in a pocket).
20.21 LC copy on microfilm only.
20.22 LC copy replaced by microfilm.

Peculiarities and Imperfections

20.23 LC copy imperfect: p. 91-94 bound upside down.
20.24 Foreword wanting.
20.25 LC has no. 394, with 2 duplicate leaves, one a blank between the two facing pages form the title page.
20.26 Plates i and ii reversed in LC copy and plate vii positioned as frontispiece.
20.27 Plates xix and xx reversed in LC copy.
20.28 Plates no. 13, 15-16, 18, and 21 are omitted.
20.29 Without the price list mentioned in pref.
20.30 LC Copy: Bound for Lessing Rosenwald by the Lakeside Press. Includes 8 col. aquatints, 6 of them with a black-and-white aquatint of the same subject. The bound vol. lacks p. 51-54 and 73-74. Two folded sheets laid in the vol. comprise: a t.p. dated 1939, p. 51-54 (51 and 53 numbered in ms.), and a blank leaf.

Incomplete Multipart Set

20.31 *Library has: v. 2 only.
20.32 *Library has: v. 1-3.
20.33 *Library lacks v. 4.

Chapter 3 (Cartographic Materials)

AACR2 RULE

3.7B20 Copy Being Described, Library's Holdings, and Restrictions on Use [AACR2 Rev.]
Make these notes as instructed in 1.7B20.

RELATED AACR2 RULE

None.

LIBRARY OF CONGRESS POLICY

None issued.

RELATED LIBRARY OF CONGRESS POLICY

None issued.

AACR2 TEXT EXAMPLES REVISED TO REFLECT
LIBRARY OF CONGRESS POLICY

None required.

HISTORICAL BACKGROUND

AACR1 Rule 212E3 provided for a note to record the physical characteristics of a map. These characteristics included "imperfections and peculiarities of the copy."

AACR1 Rule 212E11 provided for a note to record "significant peculiarities, irregularities," etc., of the copy.

The use of either of these rules would result in the creation of notes similar to those created under AACR2 Rule 3.7B20. AACR1, however, had no rule equivalent to the "incomplete multipart set" aspect of the AACR2 rule.

NOTE EXAMPLES

20.34 LC copy has "Map Studio" pasted over "Instructa" at head of title.
20.35 Stamped on LC copy: Produced under contract printing.
20.36 Transferred from the collection of the Canal Zone Library-Museum, 1980.
20.37 *Library's copy lacking sheet 3.

Chapter 5 (Music)

AACR2 RULE

5.7B20 Copy Being Described, Library's Holdings, and Restrictions on Use [AACR2 Rev.]
Make these notes as instructed in 1.7B20.

RELATED AACR2 RULE

None.

LIBRARY OF CONGRESS POLICY

The Library of Congress considers this local information. Therefore, it will not appear on printed cards or be displayed in automated records. [MCB v. 12, no. 3]

RELATED LIBRARY OF CONGRESS POLICY

None issued.

AACR2 TEXT EXAMPLES REVISED TO REFLECT LIBRARY OF CONGRESS POLICY

None required.

HISTORICAL BACKGROUND

AACR1 Rule 246C provided for the use of a "dash" entry to indicate that the library held a second copy necessary for performance. No other rules in AACR1 or previous codes provided for the creation of copy-specific notes for music, although the provisions for separately published monographs in these earlier codes could be used for music. (See *Historical Background* under Rule 2.7B20.) A portion of this note in AACR2 that was unique to Chapter 5 was deleted in AACR2 Rev. It called for recording the number of copies held. This note was mandatory if it affected the use of the item in performance.

NOTE EXAMPLES

20.38   LC set incomplete: v. 3 (Arabesque no. 4) wanting.
20.39   LC copy: Folded and bound in case (18 cm.). A few words of 3rd stanza text torn away at lower margin.

20.40   LC copy has 6 parts ; lacks the Klavierauszug.

Chapter 6 (Sound Recordings)

AACR2 RULE

6.7B20 Copy Being Described, Library's Holdings, and Restrictions on Use [AACR2 Rev.]
Make these notes as instructed in 1.7B20.

RELATED AACR2 RULE

None.

LIBRARY OF CONGRESS POLICY

None issued.

RELATED LIBRARY OF CONGRESS POLICY

None issued.

AACR2 TEXT EXAMPLES REVISED TO REFLECT LIBRARY OF CONGRESS POLICY

None required.

HISTORICAL BACKGROUND

Although AACR1 Rev. and previous codes had no rule equivalent to AACR2 Rule 6.7B20, the copy-specific note provisions for separately published monographs in these earlier codes could be used for sound recordings. (See *Historical Background* under Rule 2.7B20.)

NOTE EXAMPLES

20.41   LC lacks program note insert.
20.42   LC lacks v. 1: GV 64.
20.43   LC copy imperfect: text insert wanting.
20.44   LC set incomplete: MHS 3825 lacking.

Chapter 7 (Motion Pictures and Videorecordings)

AACR2 RULE

7.7B20 Copy Being Described, Library's Holdings, and Restrictions on Use [AACR2 Rev.]
Make these notes as instructed in 1.7B20

RELATED AACR2 RULE

None.

LIBRARY OF CONGRESS POLICY

None issued. For archival moving image materials, the Library of Congress supplements AACR2 Chapter 7 with the guidelines in *Archival Moving Image Materials* by White-Hensen.

RELATED LIBRARY OF CONGRESS POLICY

None issued.

AACR2 TEXT EXAMPLES REVISED TO REFLECT LIBRARY OF CONGRESS POLICY

None required for AACR2 Rev. No examples were given in AACR2.

HISTORICAL BACKGROUND

Although AACR1 Rev. and previous codes had no rule equivalent to AACR2 Rule 7.7B20, the copy-specific provisions for separately published monographs in these earlier codes could be used for motion pictures and videorecordings. (See *Historical Background* under Rule 2.7B20.)

NOTE EXAMPLES

No examples were located.

Chapter 8 (Graphic Materials)

AACR2 RULE

8.7B20 Copy Being Described, Library's Holdings, and Restrictions on Use [AACR2 Rev.]
Make these notes as instructed in 1.7B20.

RELATED AACR2 RULE

None.

LIBRARY OF CONGRESS POLICY

None issued. For original items and historical collections, the Library of Congress supplements AACR2 Chapter 8 with the guidelines in *Graphic Materials* by Betz.

RELATED LIBRARY OF CONGRESS POLICY

None issued.

AACR2 TEXT EXAMPLES REVISED TO REFLECT LIBRARY OF CONGRESS POLICY

None required for AACR2 Rev. No examples were given in AACR2.

HISTORICAL BACKGROUND

AACR1 Rule 272C3a provided for a note to record "peculiarities and irregularities" of pictures providing they were "of sufficient interest." The note included copy numbers, signature of the artist, etc. This same note could be provided under the guidelines of AACR2, although the sufficient interest aspect is required.

No rules were present in AACR1 Rev. that covered recording copy-specific information for graphic material formats, although the provisions of the AACR1 Rev. rules for separately published monographs could be applied to these graphic materials. (See *Historical Background* under Rule 2.7B20.)

NOTE EXAMPLES

Projection Graphic Materials
20.45   *Library's copy lacks teacher's guide.

Nonprojection Graphic Materials
20.46   In LC collections.
20.47   Signed in medium, lower left corner. Signed in ink with full name on right and numbered V on left, below plate mark.
20.48   Gift of Prof. Wright.

Chapter 9 (Computer Files)

AACR2 RULE

9.7B20 Copy Being Described, Library's Holdings, and Restrictions on Use [AACR2 Rev.]

Copy Being Described
Make these notes as instructed in 1.7B20.

File Name
If desired, give a locally assigned file or data set name.

Date
If desired, give the date when the content of the file was copied from, or transferred to, another source.

RELATED AACR2 RULE

9.7B4 Variations in Title [Note] [AACR2 Rev.]
Make notes on titles borne by the item other than the title proper. *Optionally*, give a romanization of the title proper. . . .
Optionally, transcribe a file name or data set name if it differs from the title proper. For a locally assigned file name or data set name, see 9.7B20. [emphasis added]

LIBRARY OF CONGRESS POLICY

None issued for AACR2 Rev. Ch. 9.

RELATED LIBRARY OF CONGRESS POLICY

None issued for AACR2 Rev. Ch. 9.

AACR2 TEXT EXAMPLES REVISED TO REFLECT LIBRARY OF CONGRESS POLICY

None required for AACR2 Rev. Ch. 9.

HISTORICAL BACKGROUND

Computer files were not covered by AACR1 or previous codes. The original AACR2 Chapter 9 covered most of the elements present in this revised rule, although the provision to record a data set name was added with AACR2 Rev. 1983. The original rule did not include the provision for recording the date the content of the file was copied or transferred to another source. It did call for providing a "temporary" note for incomplete sets of multipart items if the library hoped to complete the set. AACR2 Rev. Ch. 9 does not include this specific instruction.

NOTE EXAMPLES

No examples were located.

Chapter 10 (Three-Dimensional Artefacts and Realia)

AACR2 RULE

10.7B20 Copy Being Described, Library's Holdings, and Restrictions on Use [AACR2 Rev.]
Make these notes as instructed in 1.7B20.

RELATED AACR2 RULE

None.

LIBRARY OF CONGRESS POLICY

None issued.

RELATED LIBRARY OF CONGRESS POLICY

None issued.

AACR2 TEXT EXAMPLES REVISED TO REFLECT LIBRARY OF CONGRESS POLICY

None required for AACR2 Rev. No examples were given in AACR2.

HISTORICAL BACKGROUND

Although AACR1 Rev. and previous codes had no rule equivalent to AACR2 Rule10.7B20, the copy-specific note provisions for separately published monographs in these earlier codes could be used for three-dimensional artifacts and realia. (See *Historical Background* under Rule 2.7B20.)

461

NOTE EXAMPLES

20.49   *Container autographed by the game's creator.
20.50   *Library's copy lacks maps.

Chapter 12 (Serials)

AACR2 RULE

**12.7B20 Copy Being Described, Library's Holdings, and
Restrictions on Use [AACR2 Rev.]**
Make these notes as instructed in 1.7B20.

RELATED AACR2 RULE

None.

LIBRARY OF CONGRESS POLICY

None issued.

RELATED LIBRARY OF CONGRESS POLICY

None issued.

AACR2 TEXT EXAMPLES REVISED TO REFLECT
LIBRARY OF CONGRESS POLICY

None required for AACR2 Rev. No examples were given in AACR2.

HISTORICAL BACKGROUND

AACR1 Rule 160F provided for a note to record the library's holdings
of a serial or to refer a patron to another library record (i.e., Kardex,
Union list, etc.) that contained serial holdings information. AACR2 is
essentially the same except that no specific mention is made of referring
users to other library catalogs.

NOTE EXAMPLES

20.51   Issues for Feb. 1981-May 1981 were classed: A 105.28: (nos.)
20.52   *Library has: 1968 to date.
20.53   *Library lacks 1956.

1.7B21. "With" Notes

GENERAL RULE

1.7B21 "With" Notes [AACR2 Rev.]

If the title and statement of responsibility area contains a title that applies to only a part of an item lacking a collective title and, therefore, more than one description is made (see 1.1G2), make a note beginning *With:* and listing the other separately titled works in the item in the order in which they appear.

RELATED AACR2 RULE

1.1G2 Items without a Collective Title [AACR2 Rev.]

If, in an item lacking a collective title, no one work predominates, *either* describe the item as a unit (see 1.1G3) *or, optionally,* in the case of cartographic materials (see 3.1G1), sound recordings (see 6.1G1), motion pictures and videorecordings (see 7.1G1), computer files (see 9.1G1), and microforms (see 11.1G1), make a separate description for each separately titled work, linking the separate descriptions with notes (see 1.7B21). [emphasis added]

GENERAL LIBRARY OF CONGRESS POLICY

The "with" note is appropriate only in the following case: two or more works issued independently have been subsequently placed together under one cover or comparable packaging. For two or more works that have been issued together in one cover or other packaging, create one bibliographic record, applying either 1.1G or 1.10. (For an exception, see LCRI 7.1G1.)

Since the Library of Congress is only applying this rule to items issued separately and later placed together, very few "with" notes are actually being made by LC catalogers for material other than rare books. Although the rule provides for this note regardless of whether the items were issued independently or together, the Library of Congress will catalog all items issued together as a unit, thus eliminating the use of this note in most instances.

For each item listed in a "with" note, give the title proper (or uniform title if one has been assigned), the statement of responsibility, and the entire publication, distribution, etc., area. If there are more than two works, cite all the other works in the record for the first work; in the records for succeeding works, cite only the first work. Use ISBD punctuation, except omit the period-space-dash-space between areas. . . .

If the works are too numerous to be listed in the "with" note, make an informal note such as the following:

No. 3 in a vol. with binder's title: Brownist tracts, 1599-1644.

[CSB 38]

The instructions in this Rule Interpretation restate information given in AACR1 Rev. Rule 145E for separately published monographs. The form of the note has been revised to conform to ISBD punctuation requirements.

Since the "with" note is used as a linking device between the bibliographic records, a uniform title (if one is assigned) is used when formulating the note to ensure proper access to the record (cf. LCRI 1.7A4). In addition to the uniform title, the cataloger may also include the title proper if it is deemed necessary to accurately describe the item in hand.

RELATED LIBRARY OF CONGRESS POLICY

None issued.

FORMAT

In those chapters for description in which this note is used, a formal structure is prescribed except in Chapter 3 (Cartographic Materials). The formal note begins with the term *"With:"*. Chapter 3, while following the same basic structure for this note, does not prescribe an introductory phrase.

CHAPTER APPLICATION

This note was not present in Chapter 4 (Manuscripts), Chapter 8 (Graphic Materials), and Chapter 10 (Three-Dimensional Artefacts and Realia). AACR2 Rev. added coverage to Chapter 8 and Chapter 10.

EXCEPTIONS AND ADDITIONS

Chapter 3 (Cartographic Materials) does not specifically call for the use of the introductory phrase "With:". In so doing, the formal structure of the note is abolished, allowing for the use of expanded introductory phrases that can be combined with other information to accommodate better the material being described. Other than this omission, the wording of the rule is identical to the General Rule.

Chapter 6 (Sound Recordings) contains the General Rule. In addition, the rule calls for the use of a devised title if the individual items are not titled.

Chapter 2 (Books, Pamphlets, and Printed Sheets)

AACR2 RULE

2.7B21 "With" Notes [AACR2 Rev.]

If the title and statement of responsibility area contains a title that applies to only a part of an item lacking a collective title and, therefore, more than one entry is made, make a note beginning *With:* and listing the other separately titled works in the item in the order in which they appear there.

RELATED AACR2 RULE

None.

LIBRARY OF CONGRESS POLICY

None issued.

RELATED LIBRARY OF CONGRESS POLICY

None issued.

AACR2 TEXT EXAMPLES REVISED TO REFLECT LIBRARY OF CONGRESS POLICY

None required.

HISTORICAL BACKGROUND

AACR1 Rev. Rule 145 provided a great deal of detail for the use of notes for works bound together. Many of these instructions now appear in the LC Rule Interpretation to Extrapolated General Rule 1.7B21.

AACR1 Rev. Rule 145A addressed works issued together in one cover and works issued separately and subsequently bound together. AACR2 does not differentiate between the two, although the LC Rule Interpretation does restate this difference. AACR1 Rev. Rule 145A also addressed note order, stating that, for the first work in the volume, the

465

"with" note should be placed last, but for succeeding works in the volume, the note should be given "prominence." AACR2 note order places "with" notes last in most chapters, regardless of the position of the work within a volume.

AACR1 Rev. Rule 145B and Rev. Rule 145C provided notes for works issued together under one cover, or in a case. These notes began with the phrase "issued with." AACR2 specifically calls for the use of only the word "With."

AACR1 Rev. Rule 145D provided a note for works issued separately and subsequently bound together. This note began with the phrase "bound with." AACR2 has changed the wording to "With."

AACR1 Rev. Rule 145E presented the form in which other works were to be cited. This form generally followed standard bibliographic citation order, giving the author's name first in inverted order. AACR2 uses the order of elements in the bibliographic description and ISBD punctuation when citing other works. (See also AACR2 Rule 1.7A and the LC Rule Interpretation to it, LCRI 1.7A).

AACR1 Rev. Rule 145F addressed items bound together that were numerous or were classified as a collection. When these items were also cataloged separately, a note was used to record their location in the collection. AACR2 does not address this issue.

These AACR1 Rev. Ch. 6 rules could be used for works that were not separately published monographs unless specific rules for the description of a format superseded or excluded their use.

NOTE EXAMPLES

Due to the infrequent use of this note by the Library of Congress, many of the examples that follow are for "early printed monographs." Notes for these works were probably developed under the provisions in *Bibliographic Description for Rare Books.*

21.1 With: Feeding chases in the Adbelie penguin / David H. Thompson.
21.2 With: Arcturidae from the Antarctic and Southern Seas (Isopoda, Valvifera) / George A. Schultz. Washington, D.C. : American Geophysical Union, 1981.
21.3 With: An enquiry into the evidence of Archbishop Cranmer's recantation . . . / by William Whiston . . . London : Printer for John Whiston . . . , 1736.
21.4 With: The mummified seals of southern Victoria Land, Antarctica / Wakefield Dort, Jr. — Atmospheric ammonia nitrogen / Edmund B. Wodehouse and Bruce C. Parker — A taxonomic study of a dominant coryneform bacterial type found in Antarctic soils / Roy M. Johnson and Robert D. Bellinoff.

21.5 With: The Paths of virtue delineated . . . London : Printed for and sold by the booksellers, 1768.

21.6 With: Polish partition. French / Gotlieb Pansmouser. A Londres : De l'imprimerie de P. Elms[l]y . . . [i.e. Berlin : s.n., ca. 1775]. Bound together subsequent to publication.

21.7 With: Reflections on courtship and marriage. Whitehaven : Printed for John Dunn, bookseller . . . , 1775 — Letters of advice from a lady of distinction to her niece the Duchess of **********, shortly after her marriage. London : Printed for Henry Colburn . . . , 1819. Bound together subsequent to publication.

21.8 With: Sketch of a residence among the Aboriginals of northern Queensland for seventeen years / by James Morrill ; [written and edited by Edmund Gregory]. Boston : Printed at Newcomb's Steam Print. Offices, 1864.

21.9 With: Supplement to The origin of printing. [London : J. Nichols], 1781 — Biographical memoirs of William Ged. London : Printed by and for J. Nichols, 1781 — An address to the public on the Polygraphic Art . . . London : Printed at the Logographic Press, for the proprietors, and sold by T. Cadell . . . Robson and Clarke . . . and J. Sewell . . . [1788].

21.10 Formerly bound with: [Concordia de la Reyna dona Elianor ab lo cardenal de Commenge. S.l. : s.n., 150-?] (Goff F-72).

21.11 Formerly bound with: [Sentencia arbitral de Guadalupe. S.l. : s.n., 150-?] (Goff F-93).

21.12 Issued in case, with: Delilah / Marcus Goodrich.

21.13 Issued in a case, with: The immense journey / by Loren Eiseley.

21.14 In a case with: La loule de gui / Ronald Dorgelès. [Paris] : Editions de la Banderole, [1922].

21.15 Issued in a case, with: The Screwtape letters & Screwtape proposes a toast / C.S. Lewis.

Chapter 3 (Cartographic Materials)

AACR2 RULE

3.7B21 "With" Notes [AACR2 Rev.]

If the title and statement of responsibility area contains a title that applies to only a part of an item lacking a collective title and, therefore, more than one entry is made, make a note beginning *With:* and listing the other separately titled works in the item in the order in which they appear there.

RELATED AACR2 RULE

3.1G4 Items without a Collective Title [AACR2 Rev.]

Optionally, make a separate description for each separately titled part of an item lacking a collective title. For the statement of the extent in each of these descriptions, see 3.5B4. Link the separate descriptions with notes (see 3.7B21).

LIBRARY OF CONGRESS POLICY

None issued.

RELATED LIBRARY OF CONGRESS POLICY

None issued.

AACR2 TEXT EXAMPLES REVISED TO REFLECT
LIBRARY OF CONGRESS POLICY

None required.

HISTORICAL BACKGROUND

AACR1 did not provide a rule for "with" notes for cartographic
materials. However, AACR1 Rules 212F2-212F4 provided several cataloging possibilities for multiple maps printed on a single sheet without
a collective title. One of the methods offered was to create a record for
one title and mention the others in a note. This has the same result as
AACR2 "with" notes.

NOTE EXAMPLES

Due to the limited use of this note by the Library of Congress, examples of "with" notes are given under AACR2 Rule 2.7B21.

Chapter 5 (Music)

AACR2 RULE

5.7B21 "With" Notes [AACR2 Rev.]

If the title and statement of responsibility area contains a title that
applies to only a part of an item lacking a collective title and, therefore,
more than one entry is made, make a note beginning *With:* and listing
the other separately titled works in the item in the order in which they
appear there.

RELATED AACR2 RULE

None.

LIBRARY OF CONGRESS POLICY

None issued.

RELATED LIBRARY OF CONGRESS POLICY

None issued.

AACR2 TEXT EXAMPLES REVISED TO REFLECT LIBRARY OF CONGRESS POLICY

AACR2 TEXT
With: Die Mittagshexe ; and, Das goldene Spinnrad / Antonín Dvořák.

AACR2 TEXT REVISED
With: [Polednice]. Die Mittagshexe ; and [Zlaty kolovrat]. Das goldene Spinnrad / Antonín Dvořák.

HISTORICAL BACKGROUND

Although AACR1 and previous codes had no rule equivalent to AACR2 Rule 5.7B21, the "with" note provisions for separately published monographs in these earlier codes could be used for music. (See *Historical Background* under Rule 2.7B21.)

NOTE EXAMPLES

Due to the limited use of this note by the Library of Congress, examples of "with" notes are given under AACR2 Rule 2.7B21.

Chapter 6 (Sound Recordings)

AACR2 RULE

6.7B21 "With" Notes [AACR2 Rev.]
If the title and statement of responsibility area contains a title that applies to only a part of an item lacking a collective title and, therefore, more than one entry is made, make a note beginning *With:* and listing the other separately titled works in the item in the order in which they appear there.

Supplied Title
If the individual works are not titled, supply titles as instructed in 6.1B1.

This is the only chapter that adds the directive to supply titles if the individual items are not titled. The Library of Congress Rule Interpretation for the General Rule instructs the cataloger to use uniform titles in all cases if one has been assigned to the work. Since this note provides a linking device between separate bibliographic records, the uniform title should be given in this note even if the individual items are titled.

RELATED AACR2 RULE

6.1G4 Items without a Collective Title [AACR2 Rev.]
Optionally, make a separate description for each separately titled work on a sound recording. For the statement of the extent in each of these descriptions, see 6.5B3. Link the separate descriptions with a note (see 6.7B21). [emphasis added] For instructions on sources of information, see 6.0B.

LIBRARY OF CONGRESS POLICY

None issued.

RELATED LIBRARY OF CONGRESS POLICY

None issued.

AACR2 TEXT EXAMPLES REVISED TO REFLECT LIBRARY OF CONGRESS POLICY

None required.

HISTORICAL BACKGROUND

AACR1 Rev. Rule 252F1 was essentially the same as the AACR2 rule except for note order. There appears to have been some indecision over the best position for this note. AACR1 placed this note in the last note position while AACR1 Rev. moved it to the first note position. AACR2 has returned it to the last position.

AACR1 Rev. Rule 252F1 also provided for the use of uniform titles in this note, but applied this directive only to cases of "musical performance." AACR2 does not qualify the use of uniform titles for only musical performances.

Although the earlier rules did not state a specific form for citing other works, the text examples illustrated the use of a standard bibliographic citation form, giving the author's name in inverted order first, followed by title and publication information. AACR2 uses the order of the bibliographic description and ISBD punctuation when citing other works. (See also AACR2 Rule 1.7A4.)

NOTE EXAMPLES

Due to the limited use of this note by the Library of Congress, examples of "with" notes are given under AACR2 Rule 2.7B21.

Chapter 7 (Motion Pictures and Videorecordings)

AACR2 RULE

7.7B21 "With" Notes [AACR2 Rev.]
If the title and statement of responsibility area contains a title that applies to only a part of an item lacking a collective title and, therefore, more than one entry is made, make a note beginning *With:* and listing the other separately titled works in the item in the order in which they appear there.

RELATED AACR2 RULE

7.1G4 Items without a Collective Title [AACR2 Rev.]
Optionally, make a separate description for each separately titled work on a motion picture or videorecording. For the statement of the extent in each of these descriptions, see 7.5B3. Link the separate descriptions with notes (see 7.7B21). [emphasis added]

LIBRARY OF CONGRESS POLICY

None issued. For archival moving image materials, the Library of Congress supplements AACR2 Chapter 7 with the guidelines in *Archival Moving Image Materials* by White-Hensen.

RELATED LIBRARY OF CONGRESS POLICY

None issued.

AACR2 TEXT EXAMPLES REVISED TO REFLECT LIBRARY OF CONGRESS POLICY

None required.

HISTORICAL BACKGROUND

Although AACR1 Rev. Ch. 12 and previous codes had no rule equivalent to AACR2 Rule 7.7B21, the "with" note provisions for separately published monographs in these codes could be used for motion pictures and videorecordings. (See *Historical Background* under Rule 2.7B21.)

471

NOTE EXAMPLES

Due to the limited use of this note by the Library of Congress, examples of "with" notes are given under AACR2 Rule 2.7B21.

Chapter 8 (Graphic Materials)

AACR2 RULE

8.7B21 "With" Notes [AACR2 Rev.]
> If the title and statement of responsibility area contains a title that applies to only a part of an item lacking a collective title and, therefore, more than one entry is made, make a note beginning *With:* and listing the other separately titled works in the item in the order in which they appear there.

RELATED AACR2 RULE

None.

LIBRARY OF CONGRESS POLICY

None issued. For original items and historical collections, the Library of Congress supplements AACR2, Chapter 8, with the guidelines in *Graphic Materials* by Betz.

RELATED LIBRARY OF CONGRESS POLICY

None issued.

AACR2 TEXT EXAMPLES REVISED TO REFLECT LIBRARY OF CONGRESS POLICY

None required.

HISTORICAL BACKGROUND

This rule was first introduced in AACR2 Rev. There was no equivalent rule in the original AACR2. Although AACR1 Rev. Ch. 12 and previous codes had no rule equivalent to AACR2 Rev. Rule 8.7B21, the "with" note provisions for separately published monographs in these codes could be used for graphic materials. (See *Historical Background* under Rule 2.7B21.)

472

NOTE EXAMPLES

Due to the limited use of this note by the Library of Congress, examples of "with" notes are given under AACR2 Rule 2.7B21.

Chapter 9 (Computer Files)

AACR2 RULE

9.7B21 "With" Notes [AACR2 Rev.]

If the title and statement of responsibility area contains a title that applies to only a part of an item lacking a collective title and, therefore, more than one entry is made, make a note beginning *With:* and listing the other separately titled works in the item in the order in which they appear there.

RELATED AACR2 RULE

9.1G4 Items without a Collective Title [AACR2 Rev.]

Optionally, make a separate description for each separately titled part of an item lacking a collective title. For the statement of the extent in each of these descriptions, see 9.5B2. Link the separate descriptions with notes (see 9.7B21). For instructions on sources of information, see 9.0B.

LIBRARY OF CONGRESS POLICY

None issued for AACR2 Rev. Ch. 9.

RELATED LIBRARY OF CONGRESS POLICY

None issued for AACR2 Rev. Ch. 9.

AACR2 TEXT EXAMPLES REVISED TO REFLECT LIBRARY OF CONGRESS POLICY

This rule did not appear in the AACR2 text. None required for AACR2 Rev. Ch. 9.

HISTORICAL BACKGROUND

Computer files were not covered by AACR1 or previous codes. The original AACR2 Chapter 9 had no provision for the use of a "with" note.

473

NOTE EXAMPLES

21.16   *With: PCTalk.
21.17   *With: MacPaint / Bill Atkinson.
21.18   *With: Sudden death / Curtis P. Clogston.

Chapter 10 (Three-Dimensional Artefacts and Realia)

AACR2 RULE

10.7B21 "With" Notes [AACR2 Rev.]

If the title and statement of responsibility area contains a title that applies to only a part of an item lacking a collective title and, therefore, more than one entry is made, make a note beginning *With:* and listing the other separately titled works in the item in the order in which they appear there.

RELATED AACR2 RULE

None.

LIBRARY OF CONGRESS POLICY

None issued.

RELATED LIBRARY OF CONGRESS POLICY

None issued.

AACR2 TEXT EXAMPLES REVISED TO REFLECT
LIBRARY OF CONGRESS POLICY

None required.

HISTORICAL BACKGROUND

This rule was first introduced in AACR2 Rev. There was no equivalent rule in the original AACR2. Although AACR1 Rev. Ch. 12 and previous codes had no rule equivalent to AACR2 Rev. Rule 10.7B21, the "with" note provisions for separately published monographs in these codes could be used for three-dimensional artifacts and realia. (See *Historical Background* under Rule 2.7B21.)

474

NOTE EXAMPLES

Due to the limited use of this note by the Library of Congress, examples of "with" notes are given under AACR2 Rule 2.7B21.

Chapter 12 (Serials)

AACR2 RULE

12.7B21 "Issued with" Notes [AACR2 Rev.]

If the description is of a serial issued with one or more others, make a note beginning *Issued with:* and listing the other serial(s).

RELATED AACR2 RULE

None.

LIBRARY OF CONGRESS POLICY

None issued.

RELATED LIBRARY OF CONGRESS POLICY

None issued.

AACR2 TEXT EXAMPLES REVISED TO REFLECT LIBRARY OF CONGRESS POLICY

None required.

HISTORICAL BACKGROUND

AACR1 Rule 171A provided for the use of a "bound with" note for serials. AACR2 has changed the heading terminology, dropping the word "Bound" in order to make the term applicable to all serial formats. The AACR1 rule also stated that this note for serials bound together or a serial bound with a monograph(s) would vary from a "bound with" note for monographs, since it would require information on the exact location of the second work, as well as the location of the issues if the second work was a serial.

AACR1 Rule 171B provided specific rules for formatting a "bound with" note, including the type and order of information to be given. AACR2 does not provide these detailed guidelines for "with" notes for serials.

NOTE EXAMPLES

21.19 *With: National poultry improvement plan. Directory of participants handling waterfowl, exhibition poultry, and game birds, ISSN 0271-7948.

21.20 Issued with: Escola de Medicina da Fundagão Técnico-Educacional Souza Marques.

1.7B22. Combined Notes Relating to the Original

GENERAL RULE

1.7B22 Combined Notes Relating to the Original [AACR2 Rev.]

In making a note relating to an original, combine the data into a single note (see 1.7A4, 1.11F, and 11.7B22).

RELATED AACR2 RULE

1.7A4 Notes Citing Other Editions and Works [AACR2 Rev.]

Notes Relating to Items Reproduced

In describing an item that is a reproduction of another (e.g., a text reproduced in microform; a manuscript reproduced in book form; a set of maps reproduced as slides), give the notes relating to the reproduction and then the notes relating to the original.

Combine the notes relating to the original in one note, giving the details in the order of the areas to which they relate. [emphasis added]

GENERAL LIBRARY OF CONGRESS POLICY

None issued.

RELATED LIBRARY OF CONGRESS POLICY

None issued.

FORMAT

None prescribed, except for the statement regarding the order of the elements, i.e., area of description order, given in AACR2 Rev. Rule 1.7A4.

CHAPTER APPLICATION

This note was originally present only in Chapter 4 and Chapter 12. The 1982 Revisions to AACR2 extended its use to Chapter 8 and Chapter 11. AACR2 Rev. gave Rules 4.7B22 and 12.7B22 new numbers, 4.7B23 and 12.7B23. These rules are treated in this text in Chapter 23.

EXCEPTIONS AND ADDITIONS

Chapter 8 (Graphic Materials) limits the application of this rule to art works.

Chapter 8 (Graphic Materials)

AACR2 RULE

8.7B22 Note Relating to the Original [AACR2 Rev.]
Make a note relating to the original of a reproduced art work as instructed in 1.7B22.

RELATED AACR2 RULE

AACR2 Rev. Rule 8.7B22 replaced AACR2 Rule 8.7B8 (Characteristics of Original of Art Reproduction, Poster, Postcard, etc.) cancelled by the same revision (AACR2 Rev. 1982).

LIBRARY OF CONGRESS POLICY

None issued. For original items and historical collections, the Library of Congress supplements AACR2 Chapter 8 with the guidelines in *Graphic Materials* by Betz.

RELATED LIBRARY OF CONGRESS POLICY

None issued.

AACR2 TEXT EXAMPLES REVISED TO REFLECT LIBRARY OF CONGRESS POLICY

None required.

HISTORICAL BACKGROUND

AACR1 Rule 272C6 called for a note to record the location of the original of a picture when the work being cataloged was a reproduction. AACR2 agrees with the AACR1 rule, but is not limited in its application only to pictures.

478

NOTE EXAMPLES

Nonprojection Graphic Materials

22.1 *Original: Painting in the Phillips Collection, Washington, D.C.
22.2 *Original: Watercolor in the Picture Division, Public Archives of Canada, Ottawa, measures 29.3 × 32.5 cm. (sheet).
22.3 *Original: Sixth plate daguerreotype measures 9 × 7 cm.

1.7B23 Miscellaneous

EXTRAPOLATED GENERAL RULE

Due to the miscellaneous nature of this note, no extrapolated general rule could be developed.

RELATED AACR2 RULE

None.

GENERAL LIBRARY OF CONGRESS POLICY

None issued.

RELATED LIBRARY OF CONGRESS POLICY

None issued.

FORMAT

None prescribed or possible due to the miscellaneous nature of this rule.

CHAPTER APPLICATION

This note was first introduced in AACR2 Rev. and is present only in Chapter 4 and Chapter 12. These two rules were covered under Rules 4.7B22 and 12.7B22.

EXCEPTIONS AND ADDITIONS

Chapter 4 (Manuscripts) uses this note to record information about ancient, medieval, and Renaissance manuscripts and collections of these manuscripts. This note records details regarding style of writing, illustrative matter, collation, other physical details, and opening words.

Chapter 12 (Serials) uses this note to indicate that the issue on which the description is based is not the first issue of the serial.

Chapter 4 (Manuscripts)

AACR2 RULE

4.7B23 Ancient, Medieval, and Renaissance Manuscripts [AACR2 Rev.; formerly AACR2 Rule 4.7B22]

In addition to the notes specified above, give the following notes for ancient, medieval, and Renaissance manuscripts and collections of such manuscripts.

Style of Writing

Give the script used in a manuscript or the predominant script in a collection. . . .

Illustrative Matter

Give ornamentation, rubrication, illumination, etc., and important details of other illustrative matter. . . .

Collation

Give the number of gatherings with mention of blank, damaged, or missing leaves, and any earlier foliation. . . .

Other Physical Details

Give details of owner's annotations, the binding, and any other important physical details. . . .

Opening Words

If the manuscript is given a supplied title, quote as many of the opening words of the main part of the text as will enable the item to be identified.

RELATED AACR2 RULE

None.

LIBRARY OF CONGRESS POLICY

None issued. APPM has no rule directly equivalent to AACR2 Rule 4.7B23.

RELATED LIBRARY OF CONGRESS POLICY

None issued.

AACR2 TEXT EXAMPLES REVISED TO REFLECT LIBRARY OF CONGRESS POLICY

None required.

HISTORICAL BACKGROUND

AACR1 Rule 201B3 identified the notes that should be made for ancient, medieval, and Renaissance manuscripts. It provided for the same notes as the AACR2 rule, although it called for notes identifying the country or place of writing and on scribes and annotations. AACR2 covers this information by providing separate notes for the place of writing (AACR2 Rule 4.7B8) and statements of responsibility (AACR2 Rule 4.7B6).

AACR1 Rule 201B3 also provided for a note on the location of the original when the manuscript in hand was a photoreproduction or facsimile. AACR2 and AACR2 Rev. treat reproductions of manuscripts in multiple copies under Chapter 2 (Books, Pamphlets, and Printed Sheets), Chapter 3 (Cartographic Materials), Chapter 5 (Music), and Chapter 11 (Microforms), depending upon the format of the material reproduced.

NOTE EXAMPLES

No examples were located.

Chapter 12 (Serials)

AACR2 RULE

12.7B23 Item Described [AACR2 Rev.; formerly AACR2 Rule 12.7B22]

If the description is not based on the first issue, identify the issue used as the basis for the description.

RELATED AACR2 RULE

None.

LIBRARY OF CONGRESS POLICY

This LC policy statement was issued for AACR2 Rule 12.7B22. It now applies to AACR2 Rev. Rule 12.7B23.

> In the "Description based on" note give the numeric and/or chronological designation of the issue cited in the form that is [i.e., it] would

be given if the piece were the first issue of the serial and the numeric and/or chronological designation were being recorded in area 3. However, if there is more than one numeric designation, give only the one that would have appeared first in area 3. Do not use brackets in this note to indicate either that the designation was supplied or that it came from other than a prescribed source for area 3. [CSB 18]

RELATED LIBRARY OF CONGRESS POLICY

None issued.

AACR2 TEXT EXAMPLES REVISED TO REFLECT LIBRARY OF CONGRESS POLICY

None required.

HISTORICAL BACKGROUND

AACR1 and previous codes had no rule directly equivalent to AACR2 Rev. Rule 12.7B23 for serials. AACR1 Rule 161B stated that the "title page or title page substitute" of the latest volume formed the basis for the catalog record except when the serial had ceased publication and an earlier title had continued longer than the later title. No specific requirement was given to indicate when information from another source was used. In AACR2 this rule is numbered 12.7B22.

NOTE EXAMPLES

23.1   Description based on: 5th (Nov. 24, 1970).
23.2   Description based on: 9th (Calendar year 1978).
23.3   Description based on: 8'me (1975-1976).
23.4   Description based on: Aug. 31, 1979; title from cover.
23.5   Description based on: Oct. 1, 1979-Sept. 30, 1980; title from cover.
23.6   Description based on: Oct., Nov., and Dec. 1978; title from cover.
23.7   Description based on: ER EEI 81-002 (29 Jan. 1981).
23.8   Description based on: FY79; title from cover.
23.9   Description based on: Fiscal year 1982; title from cover.
23.10 Description based on: Issue 22 (Jan. 4-10, 1981).
23.11 Description based on: No. 5 and 6 (fall 1978/spring 1979).
23.12 Description based on: No. 698 (Mar. 29th, 1977); title from cover.
23.13 Description based on: Second quarterly report, 1960; title from cover.
23.14 Description based on surrogate.
23.15 Description based on surrogate of: Feb. 1981.
23.16 Description based on: Vol. 1, no. 4 (June 1980); title from masthead.

Bibliographic Description of Previously Published Materials in Microform

The bibliographic description of microforms that reproduce previously pub lished materials has developed into an irreconcilable controversy between those who believe that the original publication should be emphasized in the description, with data relating to the microform given in a note, and those who believe that the microform should be given emphasis instead, with data relating to the original publication given in a note. The Library of Congress holds to the first position, i.e., describing the original, which is essentially the AACR1 principle. The second position, describing the document format in hand, is the general AACR2 position as presented in AACR2 Rule 0.24, which states that

> the starting point for description is the physical form of the item in hand, not the original or any previous form in which the work has been published.

An example given earlier in this rule states that

> a printed monograph in microform should be described as a microform (using the rules for chapter 11).

Since most cataloging agencies follow Library of Congress policy, the note examples presented in this appendix illustrate the combined note relating to the microform used as a result of the LC policy. Chapter 11 of the AACR2 text is used by the Library of Congress only for the cataloging of original microform editions. In order to present both approaches to cataloging of microforms, this appendix includes the AACR2 Chapter 11 rules for notes, including the latest AACR2 rule revisions, followed by the Library of Congress policy statement and the AACR1 historical background on which the LC policy is based.

Chapter 11. Microforms

11.7B NOTES [AACR2 Rev.]

Make notes as set out in the following subrules and in the order given there. However, give a particular note first when it has been decided that note is of primary importance. If the item being described is a reproduction of an original in another form, make one note on the original, giving the details in the order of the areas to which they relate (see 11.7B22).

11.7B1 Nature, Scope, or Artistic or Other Form of an Item [AACR2 Rev.]

Make notes on these matters unless they are apparent from the rest of the description.

11.7B2 Language

Make notes on the language(s) of the item, unless this is apparent from the rest of the description.

11.7B3 Source of Title Proper [AACR2 Rev.]

Make notes on the source of the title proper if it is other than the chief source of information, or when the chief source of information is a container or eye-readable matter (see 11.0B1).

11.7B4 Variations in Title [AACR2 Rev.]

Make notes on titles borne by the item other than the title proper. *Optionally,* give a romanization of the title proper.

11.7B5 Parallel Titles and Other Title Information [AACR2 Rev.]

Give the title in another language and other title information not recorded in the title and statement of responsibility area if they are considered to be important.

11.7B6 Statements of Responsibility [AACR2 Rev.]

Make notes on variant names of persons or bodies named in statements of responsibility if these are considered to be important for identification.

Give statements of responsibility not recorded in the title and statement of responsibility area.

Make notes on persons or bodies connected with a work, or significant persons or bodies connected with previous editions and not already named in the description.

11.7B7 Edition and History [AACR2 Rev.]

Make notes on other microform editions of the item being described.

11.7B9 Publication, Distribution, etc. [AACR2 Rev.]

Make notes on publication, distribution, etc., details that are not included in the publication, distribution, etc., area and are considered to be important.

11.7B10 Physical Description [AACR2 Rev.]

Make the following physical description notes.

Reduction ratio

Give the reduction ratio if it is outside the 16×-30× range. Use one of the following terms:

low reduction   (for less than 16×)
high reduction   (for 31×-60×)
very high reduction (for 61×-90×)
ultra high reduction (for over 90×; for ultra high reduction give also the specific ratio, e.g., *(Ultra high reduction, 150×)*)
reduction rate varies

Reader

Give the name of the reader on which a cassette or cartridge microfilm is to be used if it affects the use of the item. . . .

Film

Give details of the nature of the film. . . .

Other Physical Details

Make notes on other important physical details that are not included in the physical description area.

11.7B11 Accompanying Material [AACR2 Rev.]

Make notes on the location of accompanying material if appropriate. Give details of accompanying material neither mentioned in the physical description area nor given a separate description (see 1.5E).

11.7B12 Series [AACR2 Rev.]

Make notes on any microform series in which the microform has also been issued.

11.7B13 Dissertations

If the item being described is a dissertation, make a note as instructed in 2.7B13.

11.7B14 Audience [AACR2 Rev.]

Make a brief note of the intended audience for, or intellectual level of, a microform if this information is stated on the item, its container, or accompanying eye-readable material.

11.7B16 Other Formats [AACR2 Rev.]

Give the details of other formats in which the content of the item has also been issued. For a reproduction of previously existing material, see 11.7B22.

11.7B17 Summary [AACR2 Rev.]

Give a brief objective summary of the content of an item unless another part of the description provides enough information.

11.7B18 Contents [AACR2 Rev.]

List the contents of an item, either selectively or fully, if it is considered necessary to show the presence of material not implied by the rest of the description;

> to stress items of particular importance; or
> to list the contents of a collection.

When recording titles formally, take them from the head of the part to which they refer rather than from contents lists, etc.

11.7B19 Numbers

Give important numbers borne by the item other than ISBNs or ISSNs (see 11.8B).

11.7B20 Copy Being Described, Library's Holdings, and Restrictions on Use [AACR2 Rev.]

Make these notes as instructed in 1.7B20.

11.7B21 "With" Notes [AACR2 Rev.]

If the title and statement of responsibility area contains a title that applies to only a part of an item lacking a collective title and, therefore, more than one entry is made, make a note beginning *With:* and listing the other separately titled works in the item in the order in which they appear there.

11.7B22 Note Relating to the Original [AACR2 Rev.]

Make a note relating to an original as instructed in 1.7A4 and 1.11F.

RELATED RULE

1.7A4 Notes Citing Other Editions and Works [AACR2 Rev.]

Due to its length, this rule has been abridged to include only the part related to the use of notes related to the original.

Notes Relating to Items Reproduced

In describing an item that is a reproduction of another (e.g., a text reproduced in microform; a manuscript reproduced in book form; a set of maps reproduced as slides), give the notes relating to the reproduction and then the notes relating to the original. Combine the notes relating to the original in one note, giving the details in the order of the areas to which they relate.

LIBRARY OF CONGRESS POLICY FOR CATALOGING MICROREPRODUCTIONS

The statement below is the final Library of Congress policy for the cataloging of microreproductions. The policy will be applied and recommended by the Library as "rule interpretation" rather than rule revision.

1) *Materials covered.* This policy applies to reproductions in micro- and macroform of previously existing materials. Specifically the policy applies to micro- and macroreproductions* of

> books, pamphlets, and printed sheets
> cartographic materials
> manuscripts
> music
> graphic materials in macroform
> serials

It applies to reproductions of dissertations issued by University Microfilms International and "on demand" reproductions of books by the same company.

It is the intent of this policy to apply AACR 2 in determining the choice and form of access points but to emphasize in the bibliographic description data relating to the original item, giving data relating to the reproduction in a secondary position. As a result, rule 1.11 and chapter 11 of AACR 2 will not be applied to these materials except to provide directions for the formulation of the note describing the micro- or macroform characteristics of the reproduction. (Items that are microreproductions of material prepared or assembled specifically for bringing out an original edition in microform will be cataloged as instructed in chapter 11 of AACR 2.)

2) *Bibliographic description*

a) *General.* Apply chapter 2 to books (including dissertations cataloged as books), pamphlets, and sheets; chapter 3 to cartographic materials; chapter 4 to manuscripts (including dissertations not cataloged as books); chapter 5 to music; relevant portions of chapter 8 to graphic materials in macroform; and chapter 12 to serials. Transcribe the bibliographic data appropriate to the work being reproduced in the following areas:

> title and statement of responsibility
> edition
> material (or type of publication) specific details for cartographic materials and serials
> publication, distribution, etc.
> physical description
> series

Record in the note area all details relating to the reproduction and its publication/availability. Introduce the note with the word that is the specific material designation appropriate to the item.

*For the purpose of this statement the term "macroreproduction" refers only to macroreproductions produced "on demand."

    b) *Microreproductions.* Add the general material designation "[microform]" in the title and statement of responsibility area according to 1.1C2. Record in the note area the bibliographic details relating to the reproduction required by 11.4, in the order and form provided by this rule, followed by the details required by 11.5-7. If a note of the 11.7B10 type is necessary, transcribe it before any series statement required by 11.6. . . .

    c) *Macroreproductions.* Do not use a general material designation in the title and statement of responsibility area. Use the word "Photocopy" to introduce the note giving the details of the macroreproduction. . . .

University Microfilms International

This statement applies to that part of the output of University Microfilms International (UMI) consisting of 1) regular university dissertations that are made available through either micro- or macroform (xerography) processes and 2) previously published books that are subsequently made available "on demand" in either micro- or macroform. It does not apply to dissertations issued in print runs or to books issued as regular* publications or republications.

For UMI output in categories 1) and 2) above, the Library of Congress will apply the policy stated above whether the UMI item is in micro- or macroform. This treatment of UMI micro- and macroforms is necessary because items may be available in both forms. One library may acquire a work that has been reproduced xerographically while another library may acquire the same work reproduced in microform. Thus, both items need to be cataloged in a manner that emphasizes the bibliographic details of the original, regardless of the medium used to present the particular reproduction of the intellectual content contained therein.

    *By "regular" is meant full publication, not just availability "on demand."

HISTORICAL BACKGROUND

AACR1 Rule 191 called for describing primarily the original if it could be determined "from the reproduction or from a reliable source."

AACR1 Rule 191A stated that the original was to be "described in the body of the entry, in the collation, and in the first group of notes" by applying the general rules for cataloging the format of the original.

AACR1 Rule 191B stated that the reproduction was "described in a note following any notes that pertain to the original." Further instructions were given that this note should incorporate three elements including: type of reproduction, production details, and physical description. Rules 191, 191A, and 191B essentially correspond to the current LC interpretation providing for the description of the reproduction in a note.

AACR1 Rule 191C called for describing the photoreproduction in the bibliographic description when it was "prepared or assembled specifically for the purpose of bringing out an original edition in microfilm." This rule corresponds to the circumstances under which the Library of Congress will currently use Chapter 11 to describe a microform original.

NOTE EXAMPLES

A.1　*Microfiche. Buffalo, N.Y. : Hein, 1975? 5 microfiches ; 10.5 × 15 cm.

A.2　*Microfiche : negative. Springfield, Va. : N.T.I.S., 1981. 1 microfiche ; 11 × 15 cm.

A.3　*Microfiche : negative. Eugene : Microform Publications, College of Health, Physical Education and Recreation, Univ. of Oregon, 1982. 1 microfiche ; 11 × 15 cm.

A.4　*Microfilm. Ann Arbor, Mich. : University Microfilms International, 1978. 1 microfilm reel ; 35 cm.

A.5　*Microfilm. New Haven, Conn. : Yale University Library, 1980? 1 microfilm reel ; 35 mm.

A.6　*Microfilm. [Los Angeles] : Photoduplication Service, Univ. of Southern California Library, [1982]. 1 microfilm reel ; 4 in., 35 mm.

A.7　*Microfilm. Superior, Wis. : Research Microfilm Publishers, 1952. 4 microfilm reels ; 35 mm. (Periodicals in musicology. Series A. German periodicals (1869-1943)).

A.8　*Microfilm. Woodbridge, Conn. : Research publications, inc., 1979. 1 reel ; 35 mm. (Fowler collection of early architectural books ; Reel 26, No. 141).

A.9　*Ultrafiche reproduction. Commerce Clearing House. 14 sheets ; 10.5 × 15 cm.

Library of Congress
Rule Interpretations to AACR2
Revised Rule 1.7A

1.7 NOTE AREA

There is no mention of an "at head of title" note apart from an example under 2.7B6. According to 1.1A2, 1.1F3, etc., other title information and statements of responsibility appearing at head of title are transposed to their proper position. Occasionally, however, a phrase or name that is clearly not other title information or a statement of responsibility appears at head of title. Use an "at head of title" note for these and any other indeterminate cases. [CSB 11]

1.7A1 Punctuation

Start a new paragraph for each note; end each paragraph with a period or other mark of final punctuation; if the mark of final punctuation is a closing bracket or parenthesis, however, add a period. [CSB 24]

1.7A3 Forms of Notes

When nonroman data (including quotations) are being recorded in the note area, give them in romanized form in all cases, including those cards that contain nonromanized elements in the body of the entry.

When a note begins with a formal introductory term such as "contents," "credits," or "summary," do not use all caps in any case; instead, use upper and lower case as illustrated in AACR2. [CSB 22]

1.7A4 Notes Citing Other Editions and Works

Form of Citation

In citing a serial in a note on a bibliographic record for a serial, apply LCRI 12.7B. In other situations, when citing another work or another manifestation of the same work, in general give the uniform title for the work if one has been assigned to it. Otherwise, give its title proper.

If the work being cited is entered under a name heading that differs from the main entry heading on the work being cataloged, and the difference is not apparent from information given in the body of the entry, add the name after the title (uniform title or title proper). Use the name in the form that appears in whatever source is at hand. (For personal names, approximate the form required by 22.1-22.3 if there is no source at hand or if the form in the source at hand is unsatisfactory for any reason.) Separate the name from the title by a space-slash-space. . . .

Notes Citing Other Editions and Works

When a revised edition (other than a revised translation, cf. 25.2B) of a work is being cataloged and

1) it has a different title from that of the previous edition, or
2) it has a different choice of entry from that of the previous edition (for reasons other than the change to AACR2), e.g., 21.12B,

link the new edition with the immediately preceding edition[1] by using AACR2 style for connecting notes on both AACR 2 and non-AACR 2 records.

1) *Title change only.* If the title has changed since the previous edition but the choice of main entry remains the same, make a note on the record for the later edition to link it to the previous edition. Also make a related work added entry on the record for the later edition to link it to the earlier edition. Add neither the note nor the added entry or the record for the earlier edition. Always make the added entry on the record for the later edition according to the AACR2 choice and form of entry, as well as the AACR2 form of the title proper or uniform title (cf. LCRI 21.30G). (Note that the phrase "choice of main entry remains the same" means that both editions, if cataloged according to AACR2, would have the same choice of main entry.)

The following pattern is suggested for the note:

Rev. [enl., updated, etc.] ed. of: [Title proper. Edition statement. Date].

Do not include the place or name of the publisher in such notes unless needed for identification (e.g., to distinguish between two versions published in the same year). . . .

Note that the wording of the introductory phrase may vary depending on the situation and the presentation of the information in the text.

2) *Choice of entry change.* If the choice of entry has changed since the previous edition, make a note on the record for the later edition to link it to the previous edition. Also, make a related work added entry in the record for the later edition to link it to the earlier edition. Do not make either a note or an added entry on the record for the earlier edition. Always make the added entry in the record for the later edition according to the correct AACR 2 choice of entry and form of heading, as well as form of title proper or uniform title (cf. LCRI 21.30G).

[1]If the immediately preceding edition is not in LC's collections, make the connection to the most recent edition in the collection. If no previous edition is in LC, use any information available in the item being cataloged to construct a note or added entry, but do not ordinarily do further research to establish details about the earlier edition.

Use the form of note suggested under 1) above, where the title changes or remains the same, and add the first statement of responsibility. . . .

Note that if the new edition has a different choice of entry solely because of the change in cataloging rules (i.e., the earlier edition, if recataloged, would also have the same choice of entry), do *not* make a note or an added entry in the record for the new edition. . . . [CSB 22]

Bibliography

A.L.A. Cataloging Rules for Author and Title Entries. 2nd ed. Chicago: American Library Association, 1949.

American Library Association. Committee on Cataloging: Description and Access. *Guidelines for Using AACR2 Chapter 9 for Cataloging Microcomputer Software.* Chicago: American Library Association, 1984.

American Library Association. Government Documents Round Table. Documents Cataloging Manual Committee. *Cataloging Government Documents: A Manual of Interpretation for AACR2.* Chicago: American Library Association, 1984.

Anglo-American Cataloging Rules. North American Text. Chicago: American Library Association, 1967.

Anglo-American Cataloging Rules: Chapter 6, Separately Published Monographs; incorporating Chapter 9, "Photographic and Other Reproductions," and Revised to Accord with the International Standard Bibliographic Description (Monographs). North American Text. Chicago: American Library Association, 1974.

Anglo-American Cataloging Rules: Chapter 12, Revised, Audiovisual Media and Special Instructional Materials. North American Text. Chicago: American Library Association, 1975.

Anglo-American Cataloging Rules: Chapter 14, Revised, Sound Recordings. North American Text. Chicago: American Library Association, 1976.

Anglo-American Cataloguing Committee for Cartographic Materials. *Cartographic Materials: A Manual of Interpretation for AACR2.* Chicago: American Library Association, 1982.

Anglo-American Cataloguing Rules. 2nd ed. Chicago: American Library Association, 1978.

Anglo-American Cataloguing Rules. 2nd ed., 1988 revision. Chicago: American Library Association, 1988.

Anglo-American Cataloguing Rules. 2nd ed. Revisions. Chicago: American Library Association, 1982.

Anglo-American Cataloguing Rules. 2nd ed. Revisions 1983. Chicago: American Library Association, 1984.

Anglo-American Cataloguing Rules. 2nd ed. Revisions 1985. Chicago: American Library Association, 1986.

Anglo-American Cataloguing Rules. 2nd ed. Chapter 9, Computer Files. Draft Revision. Chicago: American Library Association, 1987.

Betz, Elisabeth W. *Graphic Materials: Rules for Describing Original Items and Historical Collections.* Washington, D.C.: Library of Congress, 1982.

Catalog Rules: Author and Title Entries. American ed. Chicago: American Library Association, 1908.

Cutter, Charles A. *Rules for a Dictionary Catalog.* 4th ed., rewritten. Washington, D.C.: Government Printing Office, 1904.

Dodd, Sue A. *Cataloging Machine-Readable Data Files: An Interpretive Manual.* Chicago: American Library Association, 1982.

Dodd, Sue A. and Sandberg-Fox, Ann M. *Cataloging Microcomputer Files: A Manual of Interpretation for AACR2.* Chicago: American Library Association, 1985.

Hensen, Steven L. *Archives, Personal Papers, and Manuscripts: A Cataloging Manual for Archival Repositories, Historical Societies and Manuscript Libraries.* Washington, D.C.: Library of Congress, 1983.

International Conference on Cataloging Principles. *Statement of Principles Adopted at the International Conference on Cataloging Principles, Paris, October, 1961.* Annotated ed. London: IFLA Committee on Cataloging, 1971.

International Federation of Library Associations and Institutions. *ISBD(M), International Standard Bibliographic Description for Monographic Publications.* 1st Standard ed. London: IFLA Committee on Cataloging, 1974.

International Federation of Library Associations and Institutions. Working Group on the General International Standard Bibliographic Description. *ISBD(G), General International Standard Bibliographic Description.* Annotated text. London: IFLA International Office for UBC, 1977.

Library of Congress. *Bibliographic Description of Rare Books: Rules Formulated under AACR2 and ISBD(A) for the Descriptive Cataloging of Rare Books and Other Special Printed Materials.* Washington, D.C.: Library of Congress, 1981.

Library of Congress. *Cataloging Service Bulletin.* No. 1- . Washington, D.C.: Library of Congress, 1978-

Library of Congress. *National Union Catalog.* Washington, D.C.: Library of Congress, 1956-

Library of Congress. *Rules for Descriptive Cataloging in the Library of Congress.* Washington, D.C.: Government Printing Office, 1949.

Library of Congress. *Standard Citation Forms for Rare Book Cataloging.* Washington, D.C.: Library of Congress, 1982.

Music Library Association. *Music Cataloging Bulletin.* Vol. 1- . Ann Arbor, Mich.: Music Library Association, 1970-

Smiraglia, Richard P. *Cataloging Music: A Manual for Use with AACR2.* Lake Crystal, Minn.: Soldier Creek Press, 1983.

Swain, Olive. *Notes Used on Catalog Cards: A List of Examples.* 2nd ed. Chicago: American Library Association, 1963.

White-Hensen, Wendy. *Archival Moving Image Materials: A Cataloging Manual.* Washington, D.C.: Library of Congress, 1984.

Index to Pre-AACR2 Rules Cited

This index provides access to those locations in the text where references are made to cataloging rules that pre-date AACR2. Primarily, this information is located in the *Historical Background* sections of each chapter but they may also occur in other parts of the text. The structure for the entries in this index follows this pattern:

Pre-AACR2 rule cited   AACR2 rule or text under consideration   Page

A separate index section has been provided for rules issued in the revision to Chapter 6 (Separately Publishing Monographs) to differentiate them from referenced Chapter 6 rules from the original AACR1 text. The numbering of the rules in the revision was not consistent with the numbering in the original AACR1 text. This rule numbering difference is also true for the revisions to Chapter 12 (Audiovisual Media and Other Instructional Materials) and Chapter 14 (Sound Recordings), however no references have been made in this text to other than the revised rules from these chapters.

To aid in the use of this index, the basic note types as indicated by the breakdown of .7B in AACR2 Rev. are:

.7B1	Nature, Scope, or Artistic Form	.7B13	Dissertations
.7B2	Language and/or Translation or Adaptation	.7B14	Audience
		.7B15	Reference to Published Descriptions
.7B3	Source of Title Proper	.7B16	Other Formats
.7B4	Variations in Title	.7B17	Summary
.7B5	Parallel Titles and Other Title Information	.7B18	Contents
		.7B19	Numbers Borne by the Item
.7B6	Statements of Responsibility	.7B20	Copy Being Described, Library's Holdings, and Restrictions on Use
.7B7	Edition and History		
.7B8	Material Specific Details		
.7B9	Publication, Distribution, etc.	.7B21	"With" Notes
		.7B22	Combined Notes Relating to the Original
.7B10	Physical Description		
.7B11	Accompanying Material	.7B23	Miscellaneous
.7B12	Series		

Cutter

284	iii

ALA 1908

166	2.7B12	310

LC 1949

3.16E	2.7B12	310

AACR1

Chapter 6 (Separately Published Monographs)

131	Notes in General	xliii
143	5.7B12	315
143F	2.7B12	310
144B	Notes in General	xl
144D	Notes in General	xliii, xliv, xlv
144E	Notes in General	xlviii

Chapter 6 Revised (Separately Published Monographs)

132A Rev.	Notes in General	xliii
134B4a Rev.	2.7B1	4
136D Rev.	2.7B7	175
141B3c Rev.	2.7B10	257
141B6 Rev.	2.7B10	257
141B7 Rev.	2.7B10	257
141C4 Rev.	2.7B10	257
141D5b Rev.	2.7B10	257
142A1 Rev.	2.7B12	311
	2.7B19	437
142F Rev.	2.7B12	311
143 Rev.	Notes in General	xl
143B1a Rev.	2.7B4	94
143B2c Rev.	2.7B1	3
143C Rev.	Notes in General	xl, xli, xliv, xlv
143C3 Rev.	Notes in General	xlv
143C4 Rev.	Notes in General	xliv
143D Rev.	Notes in General	xlviii
143D2 Rev.	2.7B4	94
	2.7B5	116

148 Rev.	2.7B18	391
	6.7B18	418
	Notes in General	xlii
148A Rev.	2.7B18	391
148B Rev.	2.7B18	391
150 Rev.	2.7B4	94
152 Rev.	6.7B16	357
155 Rev.	12.7B7	216
155A Rev.	2.7B11	287
155B1 Rev.	2.7B11	287
	2.7B18	392
155B2 Rev.	2.7B18	392

Chapter 7 (Serials)

160C	12.7B5	129
160D	12.7B6	167
160E	12.7B6	168
160F	12.7B20	462
160H	12.7B8	229
160J	12.7B6	168
160K	12.7B7	216
161B	12.7B23	483
162A	12.7B5	129
167A2	12.7B4	111
167B	12.7B1	47
167C	12.7B8	229
167D	12.7B9	251
167E	12.7B8	230
167F	12.7B8	230
	12.7B12	321
167G	12.7B7	215
167H	12.7B7	215
167J	12.7B6	168
167K	12.7B4	111, 112
	12.7B5	129
167L	12.7B4	112
167M	12.7B6	168
167N	12.7B6	168
167P	12.7B9	251
167Q	12.7B7	215
167R	12.7B9	251
167S1	12.7B18	432
167S2	12.7B18	433
168	12.7B7	216
168A	12.7B7	216
168B	12.7B7	216

207G	4.7B11	292
207H	4.7B14	335
207J	4.7B14	335
207K	4.7B7	191

Chapter 11 (Maps, Atlases, etc.)

212E1	3.7B1	11
	3.7B18	402
212E2	3.7B3	76
	3.7B4	98
212E3	3.7B10	263
	3.7B20	455
212E5	3.7B8	222
212E6	3.7B1	11
	3.7B2	58
212E7	3.7B6	141
212E8	3.7B7	187
212E8a	3.7B7	187
212E8b	3.7B7	187
212E9	3.7B11	290
212E10a	3.7B18	402
212E10b	3.7B18	403
212E11	3.7B20	455
212F2	3.7B21	468
212F3	3.7B21	468
212F4	3.7B21	468

Chapter 12 Revised (Audiovisual Media and Special Instructional Materials)

227D Rev.	7.7B9	245
228A1 Rev.	7.7B10	274
	8.7B10	276
228A3 Rev.	7.7B16	358
	8.7B16	360
228F Rev.	10.7B10	280
228H Rev.	10.7B10	280
228J Rev.	10.7B10	280
228L Rev.	10.7B10	281
228O Rev.	7.7B10	274
229.2A Rev.	7.7B5	123
	7.7B7	202
	8.7B5	124
	8.7B7	205
	10.7B5	127

Chapter 13 (Music)

248 *cont.*	5.7B4	101
	5.7B5	121
248A	5.7B1	25
	5.7B2	62
248B1	5.7B1	26
248B2	5.7B1	26
248B3	5.7B1	26
248B4	5.7B1	26
248B5	5.7B1	26
248C	5.7B2	61
248C1	5.7B2	61
248C2	5.7B2	61
248C3	5.7B2	62
248C4	5.7B2	62
	5.7B6	144
248D	5.7B8	224
248E	5.7B10	267
248F	5.7B18	411
	6.7B18	418
248F4	5.7B5	121

Chapter 14 Revised (Sound Recordings)

252C Rev.	6.7B19	444
252C3 Rev.	6.7B19	444
252D Rev.	6.7B16	357
252F1 Rev.	6.7B21	470
252F2 Rev.	6.7B2	64
	6.7B3	80
252F3 Rev.	6.7B1	35
252F4a Rev.	6.7B1	35
	6.7B6	149
252F4b Rev.	6.7B1	35
252F5 Rev.	6.7B2	64
	6.7B6	149
252F6 Rev.	6.7B7	197
252F7 Rev.	6.7B7	197
252F8 Rev.	6.7B10	270
252F9 Rev.	6.7B7	197
252F10a Rev.	6.7B10	270
252F10b Rev.	6.7B10	271
252F10c Rev.	6.7B10	271
252F10d Rev.	6.7B10	271
252F10e Rev.	6.7B11	296
252F11 Rev.	6.7B6	149
	6.7B14	338
	6.7B17	370

Chapter 15 (Pictures, Designs, and Other Two-Dimensional Reproductions)

Index to AACR2 Rules Cited

This index provides access to those locations in the text where AACR2 rules are cited that have a relationship to the provision of notes in a catalog record. The structure for the entries in this index follows this pattern:

AACR2 rule cited   AACR2 rule or text under consideration   Page

To aid in the use of this index, the basic note types as indicated by the breakdown of .7B in AACR2 Rev. are:

.7B1 Nature, Scope, or Artistic Form
.7B2 Language and/or Translation or Adaptation
.7B3 Source of Title Proper
.7B4 Variations in Title
.7B5 Parallel Titles and Other Title Information
.7B6 Statements of Responsibility
.7B7 Edition and History
.7B8 Material Specific Details
.7B9 Publication, Distribution, etc.
.7B10 Physical Description
.7B11 Accompanying Material
.7B12 Series

.7B13 Dissertations
.7B14 Audience
.7B15 Reference to Published Descriptions
.7B16 Other Formats
.7B17 Summary
.7B18 Contents
.7B19 Numbers Borne by the Item
.7B20 Copy Being Described, Library's Holdings, and Restrictions on Use
.7B21 "With" Notes
.7B22 Combined Notes Relating to the Original
.7B23 Miscellaneous

Chapter 2 (Books, Pamphlets, and Printed Sheets)

Chapter 3 (Cartographic Materials)

Chapter 4 (Manuscripts)

Chapter 5 (Music)

Chapter 8 (Graphic Materials)

Chapter 9 (Computer Files)

9.5C1 Rev.	9.7B1	43
9.5E2 Rev.	9.7B11	301
9.7B1 Rev.		41
	9.7B2	68
9.7B2 Rev.		68
	9.7B1	43
9.7B3 Rev.		83
9.7B4 Rev.		107
	9.7B20	460
9.7B5 Rev.		125
9.7B6 Rev.		163
9.7B7 Rev.		208
	9.7B8	226
9.7B8 Rev.		225
	9.7B10	279
9.7B9 Rev.		247
9.7B10 Rev.		278
	9.7B8	226
9.7B11 Rev.		300
9.7B12 Rev.		318
9.7B13 Rev.		329
9.7B14 Rev.		342
9.7B15	9.7B1	43
9.7B16 Rev.		361
9.7B17 Rev.		379
9.7B18 Rev.		429
9.7B19 Rev.		447
9.7B20 Rev.		460
	9.7B4	107
9.7B21 Rev.		473
9.8B	9.7B19	447
9.8B2 Rev.	9.7B19	447

Chapter 10 (Three-Dimensional Artefacts and Realia)

10.1B1 Rev.	10.7B3	85
10.5B2 Rev.	10.7B10	280
10.7B1		45
10.7B3		84
10.7B4 Rev.		108
10.7B5 Rev.		126
10.7B6 Rev.		164
10.7B7		210
10.7B9 Rev.		248
10.7B10 Rev.		279
10.7B11 Rev.		302
10.7B12		319

Index to Library of Congress Rule Interpretations Cited

This index to Library of Congress Rule Interpretations provides access to those locations in the text where references are made to LCRIs and MCB published LC decisions. It also contains entries for references made to LC's APPM and BDRB manuals. LCRI references include LCRIs issued for a specific rule as well as those which have a bearing on a cataloging rule other than the rule for which they were specifically issued. That is, the LCRI for AACR2 Rule 1.6 may address more than just LC's policy for the Series Area, it may have something to say about notes also. LCRIs issued for specific note rules are found in the chapter for that note rule under the heading *Library of Congress Policy*. The structure for LCRI and MCB entries in this index follows this pattern:

AACR2 rule cited   AACR2 rule or text under consideration   Page

MCB references are differentiated from LCRI statement by (MCB) following the AACR2 rule number.

APPM and BDRB do not follow AACR2 rule numbering. Because of that, references to policy statement in these two works are given in separate sections at the end of this index. The pattern of entries there is:

APPM or BDRB policy   AACR2 rule or text under   Page
cited   consideration

To aid in the use of this index, the basic note types as indicated by the breakdown of .7B in AACR2 Rev. are:

.7B1	Nature, Scope, or Artistic Form	.7B6	Statements of Responsibility
.7B2	Language and/or Translation or Adaptation	.7B7	Edition and History
		.7B8	Material Specific Details
.7B3	Source of Title Proper	.7B9	Publication, Distribution, etc.
.7B4	Variations in Title		
.7B5	Parallel Titles and Other Title Information	.7B10	Physical Description
		.7B11	Accompanying Material

Chapter 1 (General Rules for Description)

Chapter 21 (Choice of Access Points)

APPM

BDRB

Topical Index

Catalog Source Record Index

This index gives identifying information for the catalog source from which a note example was derived. These sources include the Library of Congress (indicated by LC card order numbers and LC manuscript control numbers (preceded by MS)); records from the OCLC database contributed by participating libraries (indicated by OCLC control numbers preceded by #); examples from APPM, Betz, and Dodd with page numbers indicated; and local catalog records. It should be noted that some of the source catalog records have been changed by LC and other libraries since they were first selected. Thus, there may be instances where a note example from an indicated source may differ somewhat from the way it appears in this text. This is particularly true of music and serial records which were obtained from the *National Union Catalog*. In some cases these records, retrievable in OCLC by LC card order number, represent LC catalog records which have been modified by the library entering the OCLC record.

.7B1 Nature, Scope or Artistic Form of the Item

1.1	81-40079	1.20	81-119525	1.39	82-466914
1.2	81-68305	1.21	81-9811	1.40	81-470473
1.3	81-51886	1.22	80-67670	1.41	81-111025
1.4	81-121045	1.23	81-2269	1.42	82-465773
1.5	81-106360	1.24	81-15390	1.43	82-466269
1.6	81-101668	1.25	81-116518	1.44	83-460136
1.7	81-13562	1.26	81-480425	1.45	81-900586
1.8	80-8675	1.27	81-479565	1.46	79-941805
1.9	81-1297	1.28	82-460255	1.47	80-908679
1.10	81-161209	1.29	81-483395	1.48	81-152518
1.11	81-165425	1.30	81-14783	1.49	82-460930
1.12	81-130736	1.31	81-11937	1.50	81-128816
1.13	81-15244	1.32	81-109778	1.51	82-466197
1.14	81-7453	1.33	82-462694	1.52	82-466273
1.15	81-2537	1.34	82-465379	1.53	81-156899
1.16	81-9402	1.35	81-900218	1.54	81-670044
1.17	80-622961	1.36	81-483292	1.55	81-6789
1.18	81-1989	1.37	82-670205	1.56	81-145360
1.19	81-13935	1.38	83-460338	1.57	81-13349

1.58	81-16176	1.110	81-901370	1.162	82-693301
1.59	81-168387	1.111	81-50269	1.163	82-693309
1.60	81-479638	1.112	81-14468	1.164	#8425588
1.61	81-468811	1.113	81-463454	1.165	81-690293
1.62	81-66362	1.114	73-87156	1.166	82-675305
1.63	81-67173	1.115	82-465143	1.167	Local Record
1.64	81-4006	1.116	82-466596	1.168	82-692568
1.65	81-80640	1.117	81-483287	1.169	82-692656
1.66	81-170379	1.118	83-460055	1.170	82-691298
1.67	81-14703	1.119	81-113500	1.171	81-691277
1.68	81-13330	1.120	81-467053	1.172	82-693368
1.69	81-156409	1.121	81-11299	1.173	81-692036
1.70	82-466195	1.122	82-466914	1.174	82-693105
1.71	82-227561	1.123	81-147050	1.175	82-675369
1.72	80-70802	1.124	81-620646	1.176	82-675258
1.73	81-65528	1.125	82-463492	1.177	82-675093
1.74	81-13331	1.126	81-147843	1.178	81-694356
1.75	81-9576	1.127	81-165774	1.179	81-693484
1.76	81-133465	1.128	80-128731.	1.180	82-691936
1.77	81-4626	1.129	81-10156	1.181	82-692615
1.78	81-900139	1.130	82-210105	1.182	82-675087
1.79	81-18538	1.131	82-25504	1.183	82-692000
1.80	81-162784	1.132	81-10036	1.184	82-675104
1.81	81-184667	1.133	81-481885	1.185	82-675284
1.82	82-24387	1.134	81-470246	1.186	81-693636
1.83	81-139897	1.135	81-160069	1.187	81-693950
1.84	81-187864	1.136	81-155514	1.188	82-692218
1.85	83-124552	1.137	81-17384	1.189	82-675265
1.86	83-3257	1.138	82-463244	1.190	82-691605
1.87	81-12077	1.139	81-3606	1.191	81-694400
1.88	81-8037	1.140	82-462417	1.192	82-690388
1.89	81-125679	1.141	81-169831	1.193	82-691609
1.90	82-197757	1.142	81-622056	1.194	81-690159
1.91	81-16789	1.143	80-624196	1.195	82-692303
1.92	81-2562	1.144	81-181091	1.196	82-693480
1.93	81-2268	1.145	81-117452	1.197	82-692663
1.94	81-140497	1.146	80-69436	1.198	82-690371
1.95	81-4952	1.147	83-460589	1.199	82-690375
1.96	81-4735	1.148	81-481306	1.200	81-692699
1.97	81-12726	1.149	82-466595	1.201	82-691617
1.98	81-139430	1.150	82-466925	1.202	82-675030
1.99	81-66131	1.151	81-148137	1.203	82-675374
1.100	81-19088	1.152	81-902054	1.204	81-694356
1.101	82-466815	1.153	81-111563	1.205	82-693351
1.102	81-13463	1.154	81-222418	1.206	82-693475
1.103	81-2565	1.155	81-18861	1.207	82-675217
1.104	81-120	1.156	82-465153	1.208	#8366061
1.105	81-13527	1.157	82-693492	1.209	83-675053
1.106	81-133695	1.158	82-693493	1.210	#7458394
1.107	81-601468	1.159	82-690388	1.211	82-691936
1.108	81-4571	1.160	82-693507	1.212	82-675369
1.109	81-13119	1.161	82-693410	1.213	82-675218

1.370	82-771042	1.422	81-770845	1.474	82-771044
1.371	81-770967	1.423	81-770615	1.475	82-771084
1.372	82-770709	1.424	81-770730	1.476	81-770855
1.373	82-771104	1.425	81-771031	1.477	81-770678
1.374	82-770143	1.426	81-770706	1.478	82-771087
1.375	82-770403	1.427	81-770709	1.479	82-770174
1.376	82-770229	1.428	81-770373	1.480	81-770272
1.377	81-770215	1.429	81-770446	1.481	81-770318
1.378	82-771032	1.430	81-770377	1.482	81-770725
1.379	82-770320	1.431	81-770403	1.483	81-80368
1.380	81-770744	1.432	82-770251	1.484	82-770048
1.381	81-770710	1.433	81-770534	1.485	82-771050
1.382	81-770428	1.434	81-770455	1.486	83-750345
1.383	81-770697	1.435	81-770499	1.487	81-770496
1.384	81-770525	1.436	81-770729	1.488	81-770668
1.385	81-770893	1.437	81-770382	1.489	81-770432
1.386	81-770889	1.438	81-770688	1.490	81-770521
1.387	82-771098	1.439	83-750576	1.491	88-770378
1.388	81-901538	1.440	81-770430	1.492	81-771169
1.389	81-770538	1.441	81-474849	1.493	81-770628
1.390	81-771094	1.442	82-770193	1.494	81-770368
1.391	80-904998	1.443	81-770225	1.495	81-770675
1.392	81-770829	1.444	81-770371	1.496	81-770524
1.393	82-770606	1.445	81-770333	1.497	82-771005
1.394	81-770530	1.446	81-770410	1.498	81-770109
1.395	81-770309	1.447	81-770787	1.499	81-770467
1.396	82-770330	1.448	82-464281	1.500	81-770336
1.397	82-770203	1.449	81-770342	1.501	82-770210
1.398	82-770857	1.450	81-770616	1.502	82-770495
1.399	82-770145	1.451	81-771030	1.503	81-770679
1.400	81-770481	1.452	81-770857	1.504	81-770977
1.401	81-770251	1.453	81-770348	1.505	81-770611
1.402	82-772443	1.454	81-770280	1.506	81-770288
1.403	81-770826	1.455	81-770315	1.507	81-770089
1.404	81-770741	1.456	81-770568	1.508	81-771153
1.405	82-770200	1.457	81-770743	1.509	81-770253
1.406	81-770360	1.458	82-770032	1.510	81-770609
1.407	81-770817	1.459	81-770292	1.511	81-770574
1.408	81-472384	1.460	81-770222	1.512	81-770402
1.409	81-770295	1.461	81-770440	1.513	81-771130
1.410	82-770414	1.462	82-770033	1.514	81-770526
1.411	82-770542	1.463	82-770811	1.515	82-770408
1.412	81-771213	1.464	81-770451	1.516	81-770350
1.413	81-770310	1.465	81-770806	1.517	81-770284
1.414	81-770577	1.466	82-770959	1.518	81-770330
1.415	81-770393	1.467	81-770439	1.519	81-770558
1.416	81-770352	1.468	81-770220	1.520	81-770427
1.417	81-770708	1.469	82-770677	1.521	81-770441
1.418	82-771079	1.470	82-771069	1.522	81-770503
1.419	81-770301	1.471	81-770338	1.523	81-771136
1.420	82-772236	1.472	81-770172	1.524	88-770378
1.421	81-770828	1.473	81-770448	1.525	81-770968
				1.526	81-771027
				1.527	81-770631
				1.528	82-770592
				1.529	82-770103

1.684	Dodd, p. 130	1.700	#8064571	1.716	81-641101
1.685	Dodd, p. 221	1.701	#8053896	1.717	81-641275
1.686	Dodd, p. 222	1.702	Local Record	1.718	81-643604
1.687	Dodd, p. 126	1.703	81-640377	1.719	81-1176
1.688	Local Record	1.704	81-641485	1.720	79-55785
1.689	Local Record	1.705	81-641178	1.721	81-641633
1.690	Local Record	1.706	81-2948	1.722	81-4559
1.691	Local Record	1.707	81-641844	1.723	81-642353
1.692	Local Record	1.708	82-645647	1.724	81-643447
1.693	Local Record	1.709	81-643060	1.725	81-642556
1.694	Local Record	1.710	81-640201	1.726	81-642815
1.695	Local Record	1.711	81-641982	1.727	81-642977
1.696	Local Record	1.712	81-2559	1.728	81-641230
1.697	#7352130	1.713	81-641616	1.729	81-641960
1.698	#8743821	1.714	81-1966	1.730	81-641148
1.699	#9040825	1.715	81-646174	1.731	82-642651

.7B2 Language of the Item and/or Translation or Adaptation

2.1	83-460729	2.33	81-152046	2.65	80-54543
2.2	83-460083	2.34	81-163741	2.66	81-131057
2.3	81-900254	2.35	81-483903	2.67	81-484376
2.4	80-905512	2.36	81-115537	2.68	81-111618
2.5	81-479024	2.37	81-480114	2.69	81-137508
2.6	81-197807	2.38	81-902995	2.70	81-482778
2.7	81-465612	2.39	81-110370	2.71	81-481295
2.8	81-127451	2.40	81-483185	2.72	81-154442
2.9	81-143572	2.41	80-154351	2.73	81-107704
2.10	81-155248	2.42	81-134250	2.74	83-460713
2.11	81-130020	2.43	81-81753	2.75	81-116920
2.12	81-135470	2.44	81-106452	2.76	80-901680
2.13	81-138796	2.45	82-464997	2.77	81-466258
2.14	81-153950	2.46	81-166574	2.78	81-102666
2.15	81-107487	2.47	81-108926	2.79	82-221428
2.16	81-85054	2.48	81-118829	2.80	81-133443
2.17	81-13481	2.49	81-15113	2.81	81-16789
2.18	81-479897	2.50	81-143870	2.82	82-139757
2.19	81-117368	2.51	81-143895	2.83	81-161963
2.20	81-111068	2.52	81-471137	2.84	80-153457
2.21	81-185586	2.53	81-106890	2.85	81-10769
2.22	81-122588	2.54	81-130928	2.86	81-471578
2.23	81-103232	2.55	81-116513	2.87	80-145679
2.24	81-119128	2.56	81-115189	2.88	81-980356
2.25	81-122910	2.57	81-101921	2.89	78-991
2.26	82-465684	2.58	81-145643	2.90	81-141313
2.27	81-470625	2.59	80-151345	2.91	81-903419
2.28	81-102852	2.60	81-105823	2.92	81-129190
2.29	81-474407	2.61	81-474071	2.93	83-460673
2.30	81-105641	2.62	81-481526	2.94	81-80387
2.31	82-191400	2.63	80-146467	2.95	81-900137
2.32	82-466906	2.64	81-145643	2.96	81-124818

2.253	81-643780	2.258	81-641737	2.263	81-643173
2.254	75-646453	2.259	81-642480	2.264	81-640651
2.255	81-640772	2.260	81-640526	2.265	81-641413
2.256	81-641633	2.261	81-642207		
2.257	81-643245	2.262	81-4061		

.7B3 Source of Title Proper

3.1	83-461287	3.35	82-675028	3.69	Betz, p. 114
3.2	82-466925	3.36	#7394731	3.70	Betz, p. 91
3.3	81-473186	3.37	82-770789	3.71	83-460342
3.4	82-466847	3.38	82-770790	3.72	Dodd, p. 136
3.5	81-471137	3.39	APPM, p. 33	3.73	Local Record
3.6	81-163805	3.40	APPM, p. 38	3.74	Local Record
3.7	82-465684	3.41	#7823089	3.75	Local Record
3.8	81-171330	3.42	82-465397	3.76	Local Record
3.9	81-130628	3.43	82-772500	3.77	Local Record
3.10	81-474106	3.44	81-770611	3.78	Local Record
3.11	82-466906	3.45	81-770705	3.79	Local Record
3.12	81-481871	3.46	81-770306	3.80	Local Record
3.13	81-159480	3.47	81-770221	3.81	Dodd, p. 218
3.14	82-465683	3.48	81-770445	3.82	Local Record
3.15	82-466598	3.49	81-770783	3.83	Dodd, p. 213
3.16	81-483194	3.50	81-80368	3.84	Dodd, p. 222
3.17	82-465516	3.51	81-771074	3.85	Local Record
3.18	83-460083	3.52	80-750681	3.86	Dodd, p. 126
3.19	63-3989	3.53	81-760304	3.87	Dodd, p. 194
3.20	83-460396	3.54	81-760606	3.88	Local Record.
3.21	82-693113	3.55	81-760284	3.89	Dodd, p. 77
3.22	82-675375	3.56	81-740115	3.90	Local Record
3.23	82-675085	3.57	81-707068	3.91	Local Record
3.24	82-693369	3.58	81-720068	3.92	Local Record
3.25	82-675033	3.59	Local Record	3.93	Local Record
3.26	82-675248	3.60	80-720211	3.94	81-641787
3.27	82-675272	3.61	#7821531	3.95	81-640717
3.28	82-675266	3.62	83-460526	3.96	81-640249
3.29	82-690738	3.63	Betz, p. 61	3.97	81-642442
3.30	82-675251	3.64	Betz, p. 108	3.98	81-640053
3.31	#9227883	3.65	82-466944	3.99	81-642506
3.32	82-690353	3.66	81-483336	3.100	81-641923
3.33	82-675297	3.67	Betz, p. 61	3.101	81-642346
3.34	82-675265	3.68	82-463459	3.102	81-641565

.7B4 Variations in Title

4.1	81-123379	4.6	81-141755	4.11	81-467052
4.2	81-1956	4.7	83-460832	4.12	81-126555
4.3	81-3892	4.8	80-624235	4.13	82-100377
4.4	81-607136	4.9	81-105003	4.14	81-178039
4.5	81-164247	4.10	81-467053	4.15	81-163072

4.172	#13000432	4.186	81-641190	4.200	#2449537
4.173	#13320962	4.187	81-644057	4.201	81-640874
4.174	#13405463	4.188	81-641152	4.202	81-640215
4.175	#7855864	4.189	81-640784	4.203	81-640868
4.176	#8842846	4.190	81-645011	4.204	81-640345
4.177	81-644090	4.191	81-641869	4.205	81-643060
4.178	81-641764	4.192	81-641245	4.206	81-641052
4.179	81-641983	4.193	81-642111	4.207	81-643081
4.180	81-640612	4.194	81-642772	4.208	81-1176
4.181	81-641482	4.195	81-641541	4.209	81-641615
4.182	81-649516	4.196	81-641149	4.210	81-642508
4.183	81-1176	4.197	81-642615	4.211	81-642617
4.184	81-642032	4.198	81-642188	4.212	81-642953
4.185	81-642006	4.199	81-2559	4.213	81-644835

.7B5 Parallel Titles and Other Title Information

5.1	82-134324	5.25	81-468517	5.49	83-75251
5.2	81-471131	5.26	81-81410	5.50	81-770396
5.3	82-466947	5.27	81-177651	5.51	81-770770
5.4	81-483305	5.28	81-179	5.52	81-771187
5.5	81-155731	5.29	81-461	5.53	81-760319
5.6	81-163741	5.30	81-2022	5.54	82-760195
5.7	81-478915	5.31	81-14820	5.55	82-762161
5.8	81-602103	5.32	81-17158	5.56	81-760226
5.9	81-602390	5.33	81-104292	5.57	80-750207
5.10	82-11446	5.34	81-101339	5.58	81-760496
5.11	81-601422	5.35	81-136838	5.59	81-760359
5.12	82-465156	5.36	81-110210	5.60	81-700229
5.13	80-83273	5.37	81-984040	5.61	80-707848
5.14	81-65587	5.38	81-152301	5.62	80-730300
5.15	81-150025	5.39	83-121264	5.63	Betz, p. 106
5.16	81-600517	5.40	81-85054	5.64	Betz, p. 108
5.17	81-600537	5.41	81-132988	5.65	Betz, p. 101
5.18	81-601704	5.42	81-185721	5.66	81-483336
5.19	81-600537	5.43	81-123042	5.67	Local Record
5.20	81-602063	5.44	81-670010	5.68	Local Record
5.21	81-139947	5.45	82-692641	5.69	81-640918
5.22	81-165615	5.46	83-684884	5.70	81-1143
5.23	81-191676	5.47	82-675034	5.71	81-641147
5.24	81-602103	5.48	81-675405	5.72	81-641475

.7B6 Statements of Responsibility

6.1	81-114671	6.7	81-10979	6.13	81-12585
6.2	81-135501	6.8	82-466848	6.14	81-101504
6.3	81-137395	6.9	82-460257	6.15	81-120975
6.4	81-607116	6.10	81-601468	6.16	82-465497
6.5	81-111618	6.11	81-108116	6.17	81-132142
6.6	80-153489	6.12	81-18705	6.18	81-47855

6.175	#3536315	6.227	82-772613	6.279	81-760226
6.176	81-771178	6.228	82-770796	6.280	81-760361
6.177	81-770281	6.229	81-770255	6.281	81-760658
6.178	81-770387	6.230	81-771202	6.282	81-760421
6.179	81-770260	6.231	81-770352	6.283	80-750636
6.180	82-770298	6.232	81-760250	6.284	81-760191
6.181	82-770111	6.233	81-760189	6.285	81-760238
6.182	81-770310	6.234	81-760269	6.286	80-750173
6.183	82-770541	6.235	80-750790	6.287	81-760197
6.184	81-18827	6.236	81-760203	6.288	81-760274
6.185	79-92121	6.237	81-760228	6.289	81-760346
6.186	81-770458	6.238	81-760095	6.290	80-750702
6.187	81-770459	6.239	81-760296	6.291	81-760136
6.188	81-770278	6.240	81-760243	6.292	81-760233
6.189	81-770536	6.241	80-750460	6.293	79-750921
6.190	81-770325	6.242	81-760322	6.294	81-760404
6.191	82-770606	6.243	81-760042	6.295	81-760043
6.192	81-770805	6.244	81-760231	6.296	82-760029
6.193	82-771091	6.245	80-750428	6.297	80-750724
6.194	81-771237	6.246	81-760386	6.298	81-760352
6.195	83-752021	6.247	81-760336	6.299	79-740836
6.196	81-770419	6.248	81-760299	6.300	81-760283
6.197	82-772541	6.249	81-760267	6.301	81-750265
6.198	82-770795	6.250	81-760260	6.302	79-740901
6.199	82-772038	6.251	81-760240	6.303	81-760274
6.200	82-770510	6.252	80-750523	6.304	80-740299
6.201	81-770378	6.253	82-760298	6.305	81-740050
6.202	82-770069	6.254	80-750686	6.306	81-760281
6.203	81-770253	6.255	81-760246	6.307	81-760616
6.204	81-770626	6.256	81-760354	6.308	81-760319
6.205	81-770697	6.257	81-760049	6.309	82-760219
6.206	82-770865	6.258	81-760380	6.310	82-760149
6.207	82-770891	6.259	81-760339	6.311	82-760153
6.208	83-750345	6.260	81-760039	6.312	81-760317
6.209	81-771079	6.261	82-761757	6.313	81-760353
6.210	82-770414	6.262	81-760245	6.314	78-741358
6.211	81-770481	6.263	81-760496	6.315	79-740856
6.212	82-770148	6.264	80-750125	6.316	81-740140
6.213	81-771109	6.265	81-760372	6.317	81-740014
6.214	81-770391	6.266	80-750724	6.318	80-740301
6.215	81-770418	6.267	80-750779	6.319	81-740100
6.216	81-770251	6.268	79-750481	6.320	80-701168
6.217	82-770172	6.269	81-760294	6.321	80-706889
6.218	81-770526	6.270	82-760015	6.322	81-700061
6.219	82-770003	6.271	81-760435	6.323	80-706891
6.220	81-770306	6.272	82-760315	6.324	81-700954
6.221	82-770509	6.273	82-760556	6.325	Local Record
6.222	81-771077	6.274	81-750317	6.326	81-700546
6.223	81-770971	6.275	80-750605	6.327	81-700612
6.224	81-770513	6.276	81-760247	6.328	81-706584
6.225	82-770098	6.277	81-760201	6.329	81-706893
6.226	82-770433	6.278	81-760333	6.330	80-707067

6.331	81-706924	6.377	82-466899	6.423	81-644203
6.332	80-701717	6.378	Betz, p. 64	6.424	81-640890
6.333	81-706157	6.379	83-460682	6.425	81-640303
6.334	81-706161	6.380	Betz, p. 73	6.426	81-640868
6.335	81-700097	6.381	Betz, p. 73	6.427	81-642288
6.336	81-700969	6.382	Betz, p. 72	6.428	81-644082
6.337	80-701699	6.383	82-466948	6.429	81-641051
6.338	81-700273	6.384	Betz, p. 70	6.430	81-642057
6.339	81-700213	6.385	Betz, p. 73	6.431	81-644196
6.340	80-701722	6.386	Betz, p. 73	6.432	79-645897
6.341	80-701013	6.387	83-460682	6.433	81-621262
6.342	82-706034	6.388	#7050422	6.434	81-641047
6.343	81-700020	6.389	Betz, p. 72	6.435	81-645961
6.344	81-706058	6.390	Betz, p. 72	6.436	81-640103
6.345	82-706406	6.391	82-463459	6.437	81-644194
6.346	81-700689	6.392	Betz, p. 73	6.438	81-642035
6.347	81-700441	6.393	Dodd, p. 126	6.439	81-642335
6.348	81-700756	6.394	#13405463	6.440	81-642428
6.349	81-730709	6.395	#13766979	6.441	81-644057
6.350	81-730529	6.396	Local Record	6.442	81-640419
6.351	81-730683	6.397	Dodd, p. 77	6.443	81-642126
6.352	82-730230	6.398	Local Record	6.444	82-642479
6.353	81-730631	6.399	#13074050	6.445	81-642042
6.354	81-730752	6.400	Local Record	6.446	81-641415
6.355	80-730775	6.401	Local Record	6.447	81-642618
6.356	81-730244	6.402	Local Record	6.448	81-645006
6.357	81-730150	6.403	#13321341	6.449	81-641528
6.358	82-730242	6.404	#11904020	6.450	81-644050
6.359	80-720469	6.405	#12656268	6.451	81-642887
6.360	82-720078	6.406	Local Record	6.452	81-642005
6.361	81-720043	6.407	Local Record	6.453	81-640514
6.362	81-730003	6.408	#11706354	6.454	81-641275
6.363	80-730772	6.409	Local Record	6.455	81-641232
6.364	Betz, p. 64	6.410	Local Record	6.456	81-641053
6.365	Betz, p. 64	6.411	#7855864	6.457	81-645781
6.366	83-460682	6.412	#7352130	6.458	81-642528
6.367	82-466573	6.413	#8167706	6.459	80-648186
6.368	82-464356	6.414	#7820511	6.460	77-912257
6.369	82-466573	6.415	#8881458	6.461	81-643873
6.370	Betz, p. 63	6.416	#8842846	6.462	81-640841
6.371	Betz, p. 123	6.417	#9040825	6.463	81-3003
6.372	Betz, p. 64	6.418	81-202376	6.464	81-642991
6.373	83-460392	6.419	81-642255	6.465	81-641049
6.374	82-466900	6.420	81-640290	6.466	81-640846
6.375	Betz, p. 63	6.421	81-644074		
6.376	83-460342	6.422	81-641117		

.7B7 Edition and History

7.1	81-80862	7.3	81-107310	7.5	81-68931
7.2	81-4284	7.4	81-166182	7.6	81-135209

Catalog Source Record

7.7	81-17218	7.59	81-106477	7.111	80-6185
7.8	81-68642	7.60	81-101997	7.112	81-183598
7.9	81-122728	7.61	81-123189	7.113	81-40937
7.10	81-102668	7.62	82-465386	7.114	81-17745
7.11	81-16366	7.63	81-13122	7.115	81-18207
7.12	81-18518	7.64	81-16413	7.116	81-19271
7.13	81-2900	7.65	81-124988	7.117	81-607118
7.14	81-14971	7.66	81-213456	7.118	81-2948
7.15	81-16632	7.67	81-14505	7.119	81-12625
7.16	81-12878	7.68	81-670032	7.120	81-15941
7.17	81-190309	7.69	81-1363	7.121	81-15100
7.18	80-28592	7.70	82-466262	7.122	81-66242
7.19	82-466679	7.71	81-2930	7.123	81-17865
7.20	81-21466	7.72	80-155675	7.124	81-4918
7.21	81-16611	7.73	81-484861	7.125	81-7260
7.22	81-4660	7.74	81-247	7.126	81-13982
7.23	81-137064	7.75	81-484864	7.127	81-47784
7.24	81-197903	7.76	81-484869	7.128	81-13443
7.25	81-622214	7.77	81-780	7.129	81-13207
7.26	81-50011	7.78	83-460588	7.130	81-482182
7.27	80-54170	7.79	83-460173	7.131	81-7242
7.28	81-7928	7.80	81-506	7.132	81-6295
7.29	81-67669	7.81	81-6256	7.133	81-4550
7.30	81-4895	7.82	81-481305	7.134	81-4635
7.31	81-469022	7.83	81-14506	7.135	81-18259
7.32	81-981	7.84	81-480235	7.136	81-9146
7.33	81-980552	7.85	81-601484	7.137	81-15937
7.34	81-8297	7.86	83-460160	7.138	81-19344
7.35	81-5219	7.87	81-174808	7.139	81-17320
7.36	81-123224	7.88	81-13718	7.140	81-19097
7.37	81-18773	7.89	81-2903	7.141	81-43598
7.38	81-21807	7.90	81-4652	7.142	82-45164
7.39	81-16043	7.91	81-4061	7.143	81-13361
7.40	81-460381	7.92	81-2126	7.144	81-4573
7.41	82-621212	7.93	82-463261	7.145	81-6481
7.42	81-18036	7.94	82-142932	7.146	81-4277
7.43	82-21173	7.95	81-145570	7.147	81-17346
7.44	81-601005	7.96	83-460833	7.148	81-14829
7.45	81-621840	7.97	81-67412	7.149	81-158560
7.46	81-172211	7.98	81-10113	7.150	81-15374
7.47	80-624356	7.99	81-126612	7.151	81-12190
7.48	79-107947	7.100	81-15349	7.152	82-3180
7.49	81-15963	7.101	81-158642	7.153	81-80950
7.50	81-177292	7.102	81-4775	7.154	81-12549
7.51	82-463975	7.103	81-17963	7.155	79-40702
7.52	82-465335	7.104	81-19204	7.156	81-8972
7.53	2-466594	7.105	81-482879	7.157	80-14701
7.54	78-55368	7.106	81-16724	7.158	81-4234
7.55	81-128646	7.107	81-14894	7.159	81-134324
7.56	81-47504	7.108	81-6925	7.160	81-43179
7.57	81-110858	7.109	81-80681	7.161	83-162404
7.58	81-68572	7.110	81-18214	7.162	83-460079

7.319	APPM, p. 37	7.371	82-770889	7.423	81-760136
7.320	MS82-108	7.372	81-770352	7.424	81-760211
7.321	#8521633	7.373	81-771170	7.425	80-750416
7.322	MS82-24	7.374	82-770042	7.426	81-760308
7.323	MS82-314	7.375	83-752362	7.427	80-750382
7.324	81-771092	7.376	82-770137	7.428	81-760272
7.325	#8643562	7.377	81-770281	7.429	81-760187
7.326	#7407317	7.378	81-66302	7.431	82-760021
7.327	82-770824	7.379	81-770874	7.432	82-760485
7.328	#7557618	7.380	81-770465	7.433	81-760271
7.329	#8541824	7.381	81-770317	7.434	81-760207
7.330	#9246702	7.382	81-790351	7.435	81-760300
7.331	MS82-27	7.383	81-67183	7.436	80-750125
7.332	MS82-2	7.384	81-770741	7.437	82-760825
7.333	82-462257	7.385	82-771112	7.438	81-740034
7.334	82-465148	7.386	82-770795	7.439	81-760208
7.335	MS82-172	7.387	80-22799	7.440	81-760458
7.336	MS82-101	7.388	81-771077	7.441	81-760045
7.337	MS82-111	7.389	80-69744	7.442	82-760291
7.338	MS81-1145	7.390	81-80368	7.443	81-740044
7.339	MS82-195	7.391	82-770143	7.444	80-740124
7.340	#8041219	7.392	81-65530	7.445	81-740043
7.341	MS82-137	7.393	82-770871	7.446	81-760201
7.342	MS82-129	7.394	81-770759	7.447	81-760377
7.343	#8635171	7.395	81-770479	7.448	79-740856
7.344	#7608843	7.396	81-77064	7.449	81-760039
7.345	MS82-141	7.397	82-770846	7.450	80-750207
7.346	#7608855	7.398	81-770634	7.451	82-760047
7.347	82-466494	7.399	83-752498	7.452	81-760320
7.348	83-460053	7.400	81-740014	7.453	80-750307
7.349	#7769200	7.401	80-740303	7.454	81-760190
7.350	82-770829	7.402	81-751129	7.455	80-740307
7.351	MS82-169	7.403	81-740045	7.456	81-760248
7.352	#8204489	7.404	81-740171	7.457	81-760103
7.353	82-770592	7.405	81-760268	7.458	80-750427
7.354	81-770495	7.406	82-760488	7.459	81-760231
7.355	81-770986	7.407	80-750551	7.460	81-760260
7.356	81-770985	7.408	80-750515	7.461	80-750510
7.357	81-770461	7.409	81-740282	7.462	81-760436
7.358	81-771025	7.410	81-760626	7.463	81-760343
7.359	82-770846	7.411	79-750921	7.464	81-760365
7.360	82-771003	7.412	81-760102	7.465	81-760354
7.361	81-770410	7.413	81-760262	7.466	82-760342
7.362	81-770494	7.414	81-760362	7.467	82-760242
7.363	81-770407	7.415	81-760290	7.468	81-760657
7.364	81-770168	7.416	81-760264	7.469	80-750523
7.365	82-770137	7.417	81-760197	7.470	82-760612
7.366	81-770412	7.418	81-760298	7.471	81-760253
7.367	81-771027	7.419	81-760212	7.472	82-760391
7.368	82-770464	7.420	81-760340	7.473	80-750608
7.369	81-770411	7.421	82-760015	7.474	82-760298
7.370	81-770459	7.422	81-760137	7.475	81-760340

7.633	81-1480	7.648	81-642266	7.663	81-642073
7.634	81-7088	7.649	81-642080	7.664	81-642811
7.635	81-642188	7.650	81-642507	7.665	81-641632
7.636	81-642350	7.651	81-641488	7.666	75-646453
7.637	81-642204	7.652	81-640704	7.667	75-646453
7.638	81-642783	7.653	81-642695	7.668	81-640904
7.639	81-642080	7.654	81-641916	7.669	81-642303
7.640	81-3833	7.655	81-643736	7.670	81-643215
7.641	81-643012	7.656	81-642527	7.671	81-641690
7.642	81-642563	7.657	80-649258	7.672	81-640989
7.643	81-642773	7.658	81-2450	7.673	81-641407
7.644	81-641175	7.659	81-640904	7.674	81-642783
7.645	80-645485	7.660	12-3648	7.675	81-645165
7.646	81-641413	7.661	Local Record	7.676	81-640894
7.647	81-642772	7.662	81-644203		

.7B8 Material Specific Details

8.1	82-693340	8.36	Local Record	8.71	81-642760
8.2	82-693465	8.37	Local Record	8.72	81-640952
8.3	82-692568	8.38	Local Record	8.73	81-641186
8.4	81-692611	8.39	81-640348	8.74	81-645072
8.5	81-692512	8.40	81-642507	8.75	81-640969
8.6	81-693636	8.41	81-642423	8.76	75-644696
8.7	81-690598	8.42	81-640910	8.77	81-642506
8.8	82-693524	8.43	81-640436	8.78	81-640950
8.9	82-693062	8.44	81-640053	8.79	81-640290
8.10	81-692285	8.45	81-640974	8.80	81-641583
8.11	81-675604	8.46	81-2247	8.81	81-641365
8.12	82-693448	8.47	81-641661	8.82	81-642347
8.13	81-675748	8.48	81-641633	8.83	82-647932
8.14	82-675088	8.49	82-23435	8.84	81-642467
8.15	82-675110	8.50	81-642352	8.85	82-20533
8.16	82-770786	8.51	81-642352	8.86	81-641960
8.17	82-770825	8.52	81-642431	8.87	81-641178
8.18	82-770827	8.53	81-642126	8.88	81-640761
8.19	#7861055	8.54	81-641982	8.89	81-640216
8.20	82-465397	8.55	81-643080	8.90	82-642651
8.21	82-771040	8.56	81-644241	8.91	81-640319
8.22	81-771148	8.57	80-910381	8.92	81-640345
8.23	83-752853	8.58	77-640518	8.93	81-640530
8.24	81-770902	8.59	81-643060	8.94	81-642861
8.25	81-770520	8.60	Local Record	8.95	81-642332
8.26	82-792438	8.61	81-643447	8.96	81-641634
8.27	81-771005	8.62	81-642541	8.97	81-642300
8.28	82-770297	8.63	81-643310	8.98	81-641788
8.29	82-13943	8.64	81-642135	8.99	81-644241
8.30	80-51659	8.65	81-643336	8.100	81-646469
8.31	80-915857	8.66	81-643341	8.101	81-642352
8.32	Local Record	8.67	81-642901	8.102	81-641031
8.33	Local Record	8.68	81-642305		
8.34	Local Record	8.69	80-645485		
8.35	Local Record	8.70	81-642351		

.7B9 Publication, Distribution, Etc.

9.151	81-707638	9.165	Dodd, p. 217	9.179	81-641763
9.152	81-720280	9.166	Dodd, p. 78	9.180	81-641549
9.153	81-730447	9.167	Local Record	9.181	81-641577
9.154	82-720000	9.168	#11217079	9.182	81-640348
9.155	Local Record	9.169	#12273036	9.183	81-640320
9.156	Local Record	9.170	Local Record	9.184	81-640276
9.157	Betz, p. 64	9.171	Local Record	9.185	81-643341
9.158	Betz, p. 64	9.172	Local Record	9.186	81-642632
9.159	Betz, p. 64	9.173	81-641031	9.187	81-643739
9.160	82-466840	9.174	81-641387	9.188	81-643509
9.161	Betz, p. 96	9.175	81-644203	9.189	81-640786
9.162	#7821531	9.176	81-643243	9.190	81-641374
9.163	#7821531	9.177	81-640692		
9.164	Dodd, p. 79	9.178	81-640864		

.7B10 Physical Description

10.1	81-6661	10.35	81-482882	10.69	81-3833
10.2	81-984040	10.36	81-464954	10.70	81-136739
10.3	82-465668	10.37	81-471137	10.71	81-116795
10.4	82-466909	10.38	82-466596	10.72	81-110370
10.5	81-462616	10.39	82-466567	10.73	81-3004
10.6	81-100935	10.40	81-153938	10.74	82-462430
10.7	83-460155	10.41	81-17523	10.75	81-140220
10.8	81-140447	10.42	02-27712	10.76	82-460020
10.9	81-14894	10.43	81-153938	10.77	82-466951
10.10	82-465328	10.44	81-464956	10.78	81-484867
10.11	81-482880	10.45	82-462226	10.79	83-460087
10.12	82-466064	10.46	81-109245	10.80	37-2071
10.13	81-481878	10.47	81-155847	10.81	83-460651
10.14	81-111604	10.48	81-136777	10.82	82-466564
10.15	82-463966	10.49	81-174057	10.83	81-481869
10.16	82-466842	10.50	81-51507	10.84	81-166464
10.17	81-107838	10.51	81-82552	10.85	81-127582
10.18	81-478315	10.52	81-479974	10.86	80-151745
10.19	83-460056	10.53	81-470246	10.87	82-466341
10.20	82-622467	10.54	83-460588	10.88	81-191415
10.21	82-466848	10.55	81-466802	10.89	81-153519
10.22	81-601476	10.56	81-119371	10.90	81-160431
10.23	81-481878	10.57	82-466196	10.91	81-600699
10.24	81-135886	10.58	81-482152	10.92	82-466179
10.25	81-484867	10.59	81-620746	10.93	82-463247
10.26	82-466274	10.60	82-460930	10.94	82-462533
10.27	82-465391	10.61	82-466850	10.95	81-112548
10.28	82-466182	10.62	83-460083	10.96	81-208258
10.29	82-463249	10.63	82-466952	10.97	82-466684
10.30	82-466264	10.64	82-466953	10.98	82-462766
10.31	83-460067	10.65	81-112272	10.99	81-481237
10.32	80-108358	10.66	83-460341	10.100	82-466846
10.33	81-483593	10.67	07-22832	10.101	81-468606
10.34	81-80829	10.68	81-172211	10.102	81-161409

10.259	83-750188	10.299	82-720083	10.339	Betz, p. 63
10.260	#11404080	10.300	#7050422	10.340	Betz, p. 63
10.261	81-760597	10.301	81-483336	10.341	Betz, p. 63
10.262	82-760413	10.302	81-483336	10.342	Local Record
10.263	82-761781	10.303	83-460526	10.343	Local Record
10.264	82-760079	10.304	#85-39900	10.344	Local Record
10.265	83-750168	10.305	83-460050	10.345	#11789074
10.266	81-760630	10.306	82-466591	10.346	#11459420
10.267	82-760056	10.307	82-466573	10.347	#12771215
10.268	82-760298	10.308	83-460154	10.348	#8064571
10.269	81-760037	10.309	83-460392	10.349	#9040947
10.270	80-750529	10.310	#8279908	10.350	#9040856
10.271	82-760128	10.311	83-460682	10.351	#9040826
10.272	82-762017	10.312	83-460049	10.352	#7855864
10.273	82-760172	10.313	82-466946	10.353	#8881153
10.274	82-760350	10.314	Betz, p. 115	10.354	#8881153
10.275	#9345958	10.315	Betz, p. 65	10.355	#8635872
10.276	81-760042	10.316	Betz, p. 67	10.356	#9040825
10.277	81-760195	10.317	Betz, p. 67	10.357	#7432782
10.278	81-760360	10.318	Betz, p. 66	10.358	#8864642
10.279	81-740030	10.319	Betz, p. 65	10.359	#7432782
10.280	82-760023	10.320	Betz, p. 66	10.360	#8842659
10.281	81-740282	10.321	Betz, p. 123	10.361	#8842846
10.282	81-740063	10.322	Betz, p. 91	10.362	#8842659
10.283	81-706599	10.323	Betz, p. 66	10.363	#8901516
10.284	Local Record	10.324	Betz, p. 95	10.364	81-641316
10.285	Local Record	10.325	Betz, p. 66	10.365	81-642268
10.286	Local Record	10.326	Betz, p. 66	10.366	81-641186
10.287	Local Record	10.327	Betz, p. 67	10.367	81-641051
10.288	81-706476	10.328	Betz, p. 66	10.368	81-645064
10.289	80-701346	10.329	Betz, p. 109	10.369	81-640460
10.290	Local Record	10.330	Betz, p. 67	10.370	81-640226
10.291	81-730684	10.331	Betz, p. 67	10.371	81-640612
10.292	80-730940	10.332	Betz, p. 66	10.372	81-644164
10.293	81-720064	10.333	Betz, p. 66	10.373	81-644191
10.294	80-725044	10.334	Betz, p. 66	10.374	81-641543
10.295	82-720078	10.335	Betz, p. 66	10.375	81-641752
10.296	81-720068	10.336	Betz, p. 98	10.376	#2449537
10.297	82-720000	10.337	Betz, p. 67	10.377	81-641198
10.298	81-720155	10.338	Betz, p. 63	10.378	77-640400

.7B11 Accompanying Materials

11.1	56-4003	11.9	81-479463	11.17	81-154893
11.2	82-462418	11.10	81-15572	11.18	82-241649
11.3	81-483575	11.11	81-483859	11.19	81-112562
11.4	81-600796	11.12	75-527623	11.20	81-16818
11.5	82-158499	11.13	81-124702	11.21	81-480330
11.6	82-463044	11.14	83-460713	11.22	81-157378
11.7	81-10334	11.15	80-52837	11.23	82-15974
11.8	82-462519	11.16	81-101402	11.24	81-161424

11.180	81-700766	11.192	81-730459	11.204	Local Record
11.181	Local Record	11.193	81-730743	11.205	Dodd, p. 194
11.182	80-701699	11.194	81-730509	11.206	#13639956
11.183	81-706194	11.195	79-731048	11.207	Dodd, p. 140
11.184	81-706197	11.196	80-730772	11.208	Dodd, p. 136
11.185	81-706196	11.197	81-725003	11.209	Dodd, p. 194
11.186	81-707302	11.198	Local Record	11.210	#11501585
11.187	81-706536	11.199	Local Record	11.211	#11652326
11.188	82-466840	11.200	#12096731	11.212	#8064571
11.189	80-730871	11.201	Local Record	11.213	#8129327
11.190	80-730458	11.202	#13400852	11.214	#8079951
11.191	81-730108	11.203	#13820025		

.7B12 Series

12.1	81-107391	12.35	81-111005	12.69	82-675262
12.2	82-242722	12.36	82-466569	12.70	82-675267
12.3	81-104248	12.37	81-139043	12.71	82-692256
12.4	83-460160	12.38	81-164699	12.72	82-692641
12.5	81-105698	12.39	81-4346	12.73	81-693668
12.6	72-88417	12.40	81-6780	12.74	81-67540
12.7	78-991	12.41	81-43292	12.75	81-771134
12.8	42-47272	12.42	81-4321	12.76	79-53751
12.9	68-31485	12.43	81-16724	12.77	82-772364
12.10	83-460316	12.44	81-2301	12.78	82-451384
12.11	82-464862	12.45	81-47900	12.79	77-771012
12.12	82-207781	12.46	81-18206	12.80	81-760310
12.13	81-7674	12.47	81-10779	12.81	81-760600
12.14	81-215247	12.48	81-18698	12.82	82-760122
12.15	81-16814	12.49	81-14746	12.83	81-700894
12.16	81-4010	12.50	81-15244	12.84	81-700304
12.17	81-153257	12.51	81-4356	12.85	80-707411
12.18	81-154459	12.52	81-14992	12.86	81-730165
12.19	81-8298	12.53	81-168963	12.87	80-730763
12.20	81-20004	12.54	81-101251	12.88	81-730469
12.21	81-17326	12.55	81-150133	12.89	82-720002
12.22	82-601028	12.56	81-483188	12.90	#7821531
12.23	81-67971	12.57	81-904951	12.91	83-460393
12.24	#8248913	12.58	81-65729	12.92	82-466591
12.25	81-155449	12.59	79-100694	12.93	Betz, p. 110
12.26	83-71023	12.60	81-128675	12.94	#8775176
12.27	#8642185	12.61	82-465158	12.95	Betz, p. 67
12.28	82-463987	12.62	82-675172	12.96	Betz, p. 68
12.29	81-670221	12.63	82-675168	12.97	#12676731
12.30	83-460174	12.64	82-675259	12.98	#13872072
12.31	81-623620	12.65	82-675086	12.99	#11903901
12.32	81-150816	12.66	82-675090	12.100	81-644242
12.33	82-466679	12.67	82-675259	12.101	Local Record
12.34	81-47074	12.68	82-691936	12.102	81-641271

.7B13 Dissertations

13.1	81-462048	13.24	80-143788	13.47	81-139068
13.2	81-127990	13.25	82-940649	13.48	81-106452
13.3	82-243899	13.26	81-902008	13.49	81-174635
13.4	81-108422	13.27	81-166738	13.50	81-191083
13.5	81-133716	13.28	80-153749	13.51	82-466817
13.6	81-172110	13.29	82-620548	13.52	81-467967
13.7	80-126688	13.30	81-14825	13.53	81-13523
13.8	81-112471	13.31	81-900569	13.54	81-1600
13.9	81-81174	13.32	81-905286	13.55	81-18336
13.10	80-120605	13.33	81-116441	13.56	81-171080
13.11	83-159211	13.34	83-460124	13.57	81-178175
13.12	80-152383	13.35	81-900283	13.58	81-129561
13.13	81-126376	13.36	81-153378	13.59	83-460039
13.14	81-902704	13.37	81-128675	13.60	81-112880
13.15	83-169213	13.38	81-102348	13.61	81-11967
13.16	82-226046	13.39	81-100465	13.62	81-6268
13.17	81-19876	13.40	81-107482	13.63	81-204058
13.18	81-7541	13.41	81-107378	13.64	81-138116
13.19	83-3624	13.42	81-47013	13.65	81-482268
13.20	79-900989	13.43	82-621925	13.66	81-158302
13.21	81-7437	13.44	81-13751	13.67	81-160035
13.22	81-15991	13.45	81-18465	13.68	80-701344
13.23	81-18674	13.46	81-903583	13.69	Local Record

.7B14 Audience

14.1	81-153818	14.24	MS82-190	14.47	80-701621
14.2	81-68773	14.25	MS82-128	14.48	81-700103
14.3	81-6072	14.26	MS82-125	14.49	81-700041
14.4	81-6391	14.27	APPM, p. 43	14.50	81-707086
14.5	81-6193	14.28	#8039052	14.51	81-700379
14.6	81-603297	14.29	APPM, p. 40	14.52	81-701048
14.7	81-14177	14.30	#8204489	14.53	81-701128
14.8	81-157744	14.31	#8000542	14.54	81-706098
14.9	81-118722	14.32	MS82-184	14.55	81-706152
14.10	81-108354	14.33	#8417999	14.56	81-700693
14.11	81-141099	14.34	APPM, p. 39	14.57	79-701330
14.12	81-149233	14.35	81-472381	14.58	81-700652
14.13	81-483749	14.36	82-772195	14.59	80-701326
14.14	81-81929	14.37	83-750555	14.60	82-706484
14.15	81-81032	14.38	82-770525	14.61	80-707487
14.16	81-139043	14.39	81-147500	14.62	81-706786
14.17	81-601890	14.40	81-770429	14.63	81-706787
14.18	81-601145	14.41	82-770400	14.64	82-706501
14.19	#8973942.	14.42	81-740072	14.65	81-700548
14.20	MS82-55	14.43	79-740316	14.66	80-707205
14.21	MS82-155	14.44	81-740195	14.67	82-706442
14.22	MS82-27	14.45	80-740163	14.68	81-706292
14.23	MS82-274	14.46	81-740198	14.69	81-720249

14.70	81-730683	14.84	#13072744	14.98	Local Record
14.71	81-730272	14.85	#13400852	14.99	81-641471
14.72	80-730507	14.86	#12085906	14.100	81-640266
14.73	81-730523	14.87	#13000432	14.101	81-641306
14.74	81-730244	14.88	Dodd, p. 80	14.102	81-640070
14.75	80-730573	14.89	Dodd, p. 80	14.103	81-642552
14.76	80-720211	14.90	Dodd, p. 118	14.104	81-640103
14.77	80-731001	14.91	Dodd, p. 223	14.105	81-641111
14.78	81-730509	14.92	#8779939	14.106	81-644094
14.79	Betz, p. 71	14.93	#8901516	14.107	81-641142
14.80	Betz, p. 71	14.94	#8270818	14.108	81-640952
14.81	Betz, p. 71	14.95	#7820511	14.109	81-621262
14.82	Betz, p. 72	14.96	#7855864	14.110	81-1600
14.83	Local Record	14.97	#8864642	14.111	81-640044

.7B15 Reference to Published Descriptions

15.1	82-463244	15.7	#8819317	15.13	MS82-1566
15.2	82-465166	15.8	APPM, p. 42	15.14	MS81-1145
15.3	81-481877	15.9	#7608868	15.15	#8580521
15.4	82-465344	15.10	APPM, p. 30	15.16	#9541123
15.5	81-484865	15.11	APPM, p. 36	15.17	#8643562
15.6	82-462224	15.12	#7608843	15.18	APPM, p. 41

.7B16 Other Formats Available

16.1	81-483288	16.25	81-706276	16.49	81-730361
16.2	Local Record	16.26	80-701759	16.50	81-730777
16.3	Local Record	16.27	81-707191	16.51	80-731001
16.4	Local Record	16.28	80-701664	16.52	81-730475
16.5	Local Record	16.29	81-700981	16.53	80-730881
16.6	81-675562	16.30	81-700498	16.54	81-730699
16.7	Local Record	16.31	81-706152	16.55	81-730782
16.8	85-753226	16.32	80-707622	16.56	81-730416
16.9	85-754630	16.33	81-706117	16.57	81-730422
16.10	81-760359	16.34	Local Record	16.58	80-730658
16.11	85-752315	16.35	82-706482	16.59	Local Record
16.12	81-740226	16.36	81-706053	16.60	Local Record
16.13	81-740140	16.37	81-706031	16.61	Local Record
16.14	79-740767	16.38	81-707559	16.62	Dodd, p. 80
16.15	81-707230	16.39	80-707483	16.63	Local Record
16.16	81-701367	16.40	81-701551	16.64	80-648689
16.17	82-700440	16.41	80-730788	16.65	81-640658
16.18	80-701285	16.42	81-730273	16.66	79-641066
16.19	81-700668	16.43	81-730253	16.67	81-642609
16.20	81-700479	16.44	80-720424	16.68	81-641752
16.21	80-700006	16.45	79-731275	16.69	81-642442
16.22	81-701023	16.46	80-720482	16.70	79-641066
16.23	80-701300	16.47	81-730385		
16.24	80-701972	16.48	81-730142		

.7B17 Summary

17.1	81-16112	17.51	81-740101	17.101	80-730615
17.2	81-l6432	17.52	80-740301	17.102	80-730826
17.3	81-4583	17.53	80-740303	17.103	81-730144
17.4	81-9528	17.54	81-740282	17.104	80-730300
17.5	81-2783	17.55	81-740014	17.105	81-730631
17.6	81-8609	17.56	81-700808	17.106	81-730611
17.7	80-68575	17.57	81-701030	17.107	79-731209
17.8	81-8424	17.58	Local Record	17.108	81-730491
17.9	81-670039	17.59	81-700551	17.109	79-730964
17.10	81-13719	17.60	80-706934	17.110	79-730077
17.11	81-2753	17.61	81-707206	17.111	81-730324
17.12	81-21807	17.62	80-701161	17.112	81-730121
17.13	81-19950	17.63	81-706917	17.113	81-720088
17.14	81-40447	17.64	80-701802	17.114	80-730569
17.15	81-20027	17.65	81-701482	17.115	#8161355
17.16	80-26648	17.66	81-700041	17.116	#7601375
17.17	81-795	17.67	82-700362	17.117	#7957432
17.18	81-10771	17.68	81-706642	17.118	Betz, p. 87
17.19	81-14373	17.69	81-706416	17.119	Betz, p. 88
17.20	81-11777	17.70	81-700613	17.120	Betz, p. 91
17.21	81-14064	17.71	81-700229	17.121	Dodd, p. 81
17.22	81-7557	17.72	81-701023	17.122	#12676731
17.23	81-4498	17.73	81-701293	17.123	Local Record
17.24	81-43459	17.74	81-700520	17.124	Local Record
17.25	81-1727	17.75	81-700512	17.125	Dodd, p. 81
17.26	81-711	17.76	82-706501	17.126	Local Record
17.27	81-10523	17.77	80-707631	17.127	Local Record
17.28	80-22152	17.78	81-700261	17.128	Local Record
17.29	81-7149	17.79	81-707344	17.129	Local Record
17.30	81-19180	17.80	81-701186	17.130	#8420774
17.31	81-14116	17.81	82-706395	17.131	#7633619
17.32	81-3708	17.82	81-707080	17.132	Local Record
17.33	81-10299	17.83	81-706739	17.133	#8758177
17.34	81-19315	17.84	80-706137	17.134	#8779939
17.35	81-2450	17.85	79-701312	17.135	Local Record
17.36	79-749715	17.86	81-707292	17.136	#8567730
17.37	81-740166	17.87	81-706581	17.137	#7855864
17.38	79-741071	17.88	82-706447	17.138	#7253205
17.39	82-740002	17.89	81-700257	17.139	#8519502
17.40	79-740316	17.90	82-700352	17.140	81-641577
17.41	80-740126	17.91	80-701276	17.141	81-642222
17.42	81-740030	17.92	81-706599	17.142	81-640864
17.43	81-740283	17.93	81-700555	17.143	81-640940
17.44	81-740034	17.94	80-707597	17.144	12-36438
17.45	81-740033	17.95	81-706196	17.145	81-641813
17.46	79-741059	17.96	81-700268	17.146	81-641788
17.47	79-741082	17.97	81-706453	17.147	81-640935
17.48	81-740099	17.98	82-706009	17.148	77-640518
17.49	79-740885	17.99	80-730874	17.149	81-643014
17.50	79-740836	17.100	82-730081		

.7B18 Contents

18.1	81-158842	18.53	81-483631	18.105	81-13186
18.2	81-111604	18.54	83-460650	18.106	81-51886
18.3	81-19092	18.55	83-460147	18.107	79-102032
18.4	81-15188.	18.56	81-484856	18.108	81-4506
18.5	82-465370	18.57	81-621371	18.109	81-142947
18.6	81-601113	18.58	81-126555	18.110	71-8282
18.7	81-602159	18.59	81-182737	18.111	81-184505
18.8	81-167509	18.60	81-602159	18.112	81-165748
18.9	81-16589	18.61	81-121509	18.113	81-11624
18.10	73-169353	18.62	81-158690	18.114	81-148528
18.11	81-139600	18.63	79-104316	18.115	82-466567
18.12	81-601825	18.64	81-133534	18.116	81-1152
18.13	82-670256	18.65	81-109245	18.117	81-110210
18.14	81-102888	18.66	81-104523	18.118	81-81520
18.15	81-112562	18.67	81-118936	18.119	81-150983
18.16	81-136739	18.68	81-166738	18.120	82-462234
18.17	81-136171	18.69	81-621295	18.121	81-110810
18.18	81-130532	18.70	81-18053	18.122	81-103956
18.19	81-481733	18.71	82-465497	18.123	81-114431
18.20	81-13207	18.72	81-120602	18.124	81-16364
18.21	81-601881	18.73	81-139732	18.125	82-164592
18.22	82-462767	18.74	81-481764	18.126	81-163095
18.23	81-940838	18.75	81468811	18.127	81-114328
18.24	81-7928	18.76	81-140478	18.128	81-120727
18.25	81-10827	18.77	81-138018	18.129	81-109880
18.26	81-113501	18.78	81-138075	18.130	81-7217
18.27	81-14333	18.79	81-130516	18.131	81-65128
18.28	81-11276	18.80	81-141179	18.132	81-483901
18.29	81-149024	18.81	81-670108	18.133	82-462809
18.30	81-109459	18.82	81-122192	18.134	81-464177
18.31	82-464355	18.83	81-116790	18.135	81-149751
18.32	81-138803	18.84	81-136433	18.136	81-67213
18.33	81-180033	18.85	81-114005	18.137	80-66188
18.34	81-601474	18.86	81-120916	18.138	81-484848
18.35	82-119619	18.87	81-483289	18.139	81-484473
18.36	80-52837	18.88	81-483001	18.140	81-483662
18.37	78-911233	18.89	81-102883	18.141	83-460033
18.38	83-159211	18.90	81-154877	18.142	60-60198
18.39	81-107771	18.91	82-100335	18.143	81-102418
18.40	82-600182	18.92	81-470466	18.144	81-126036
18.41	82-462231	18.93	81-182911	18.145	81-116137
18.42	81-152393	18.94	81-110068	18.146	81-167767
18.43	81-157828	18.95	81-980338	18.147	81-144459
18.44	81-82397	18.96	81-166316	18.148	82-466811
18.45	82-464345	18.97	81-171042	18.149	81-112774
18.46	80-624189	18.98	81-8867	18.150	82-465949
18.47	82-463992	18.99	81-8198	18.151	82-464851
18.48	83-460341	18.100	81-4130	18.152	81-105095
18.49	81-478315	18.101	81-902815	18.153	81-178439
18.50	81-465754	18.102	81-1168	18.154	81-620746
18.51	82-461090	18.103	81-143777	18.155	82-465683
18.52	83-460145	18.104	81-464032	18.156	81-481871

18.319	81-675572	18.373	81-750016	18.427	81-760600
18.320	82-693368	18.374	82-772393	18.428	81-760038
18.321	82-691620	18.375	83-750037	18.429	82-760387
18.322	81-675361	18.376	82-772172	18.430	82-760080
18.323	82-693420	18.377	82-772528	18.431	81-740072
18.324	81-692699	18.378	83-750586	18.432	81-760206
18.325	82-693300	18.379	82-770182	18.433	81-760300
18.326	82-692275	18.380	81-771067	18.434	80-740350
18.327	82-693113	18.381	81-770295	18.435	81-760221
18.328	82-692912	18.382	81-770619	18.436	82-761712
18.329	82-695430	18.383	83-750353	18.437	82-743229
18.330	82-690535	18.384	81-770271	18.438	82-743164
18.331	82-693422	18.385	81-770382	18.439	81-750209
18.332	81-692976	18.386	81-770369	18.440	81-750434
18.333	82-691610	18.387	82-772364	18.441	82-761967
18.334	82-691609	18.388	77-771012	18.442	82-762050
18.335	81-693668	18.389	83-750563	18.443	82-762137
18.336	#9061541	18.390	82-772357	18.444	83-750777
18.337	82-693456	18.391	78-54301	18.445	83-750634
18.338	82-691288	18.392	81-770342	18.446	81-750465
18.339	82-690982	18.393	81-770630	18.447	82-761847
18.340	82-690848	18.394	81-770167	18.448	81-750501
18.341	82-693321	18.395	80-69744	18.449	82-761901
18.342	82-693404	18.396	81-770277	18.450	83-750380
18.343	82-690350	18.397	81-750694	18.451	83-750691
18.344	81-693484	18.398	83-750331	18.452	82-750111
18.345	81-693645	18.399	82-772484	18.453	81-760227
18.346	81-690559	18.400	83-750563	18.454	83-750369
18.347	82-690652	18.401	83-750271	18.455	78-750209
18.348	#8368839	18.402	82-770200	18.456	81-750531
18.349	#8374701	18.403	81-771202	18.457	81-760604
18.350	82-465148	18.404	81-770530	18.458	81-750258
18.351	82-463493	18.405	81-770701	18.459	81-750150
18.352	#9236257	18.406	81-770890	18.460	81-760288
18.353	81-770620	18.407	81-770311	18.461	80-750459
18.354	81-770325	18.408	82-770143	18.462	81-760129
18.355	81-770365	18.409	81-770661	18.463	81-750101
18.356	81-770360	18.410	79-53751	18.464	81-760222
18.357	81-770432	18.411	82-770042	18.465	82-760315
18.358	83-750249	18.412	82-770491	18.466	80-750551
18.359	81-77041	18.413	81-770429	18.467	81-760446
18.360	81-770278	18.414	82-770064	18.468	81-740033
18.361	81-770207	18.415	82-770340	18.469	82-760140
18.362	81-770255	18.416	81-770894	18.470	83-750640
18.363	81-770534	18.417	82-770534	18.471	81-760670
18.364	81-770343	18.418	81-771077	18.472	81-740185
18.365	81-770330	18.419	81-770653	18.473	81-701586
18.366	81-770543	18.420	81-770412	18.474	81-707063
18.367	81-770368	18.421	81-770467	18.475	80-701007
18.368	81-770368	18.422	83-750717	18.476	81-700863
18.369	82-772612	18.423	83-750404	18.477	81-707090
18.370	82-772621	18.424	70-740767	18.478	80-730768
18.371	82-772260	18.425	79-740843	18.479	81-730447
18.372	83-750284	18.426	79-741009	18.480	81-730029

18.481	81-730020	18.503	#8775176	18.525	#8635872
18.482	80-720457	18.504	82-466899	18.526	81-642947
18.483	80-720389	18.505	83-460064	18.527	81-643218
18.484	80-720175	18.506	82-464356	18.528	81-641004
18.485	81-730162	18.507	83-460393	18.529	81-640094
18.486	79-730077	18.508	45-2064	18.530	81-643402
18.487	80-730654	18.509	82-466840	18.531	81-642814
18.488	81-730414	18.510	#11892239	18.532	81-643947
18.489	82-730227	18.511	#13072744	18.533	76-913025
18.490	80-720127	18.512	#11847575	18.534	81-643276
18.491	80-730817	18.513	#13166342	18.535	81-641374
18.492	81-730106	18.514	Dodd, p. 215	18.536	12-364381
18.493	81-730748	18.515	Dodd, p. 216	18.537	81-642953
18.494	80-730814	18.516	Dodd, p. 81	18.538	81-643045
18.495	81-730030	18.517	#11380229	18.539	81-642299
18.496	80-730820	18.518	#11642942	18.540	81-640877
18.497	80-730804	18.519	#11870216	18.541	81-641142
18.498	80-730784	18.520	#11936995	18.542	81-641581
18.499	81-720057	18.521	#8340183	18.543	81-640891
18.500	Betz, p. 112.	18.522	#8560044	18.544	81-641971
18.501	Betz, p. 116.	18.523	#7751827		
18.502	#8279908	18.524	#8635872		

.7B19 Numbers Borne by the Item
(Other Than Those Covered in 1.8)

19.1	81-166585	19.28	81-81030	19.55	82-692620
19.2	81-601765	19.29	81-601152	19.56	82-691612
19.3	81-601797	19.30	81-107818	19.57	82-69331
19.4	82-8739	19.31	83-115490	19.58	81-675403
19.5	81-132842	19.32	81-177438	19.59	82-693098
19.6	82-603781	19.33	81-600795	19.60	81-690929
19.7	81-601825	19.34	81-600050	19.61	82-693349
19.8	81-600517	19.35	82-241649	19.62	81-691654
19.9	82-101067	19.36	81-481871	19.63	81-692250
19.10	81-601018	19.37	81-127929	19.64	81-692587
19.11	81-601845	19.38	81-601018	19.65	81-692250
19.12	81-600976	19.39	81-602102	19.66	82-690548
19.13	81-162006	19.40	81-621840	19.67	82-693369
19.14	81-80770	19.41	81-161532	19.68	81-675113
19.15	81-65917	19.42	81-156748	19.69	82-675292
19.16	81-106081	19.43	81-602699	19.70	82-691648
19.17	81-601979	19.44	81-600928	19.71	82-675081
19.18	81-1434	19.45	81-693645	19.72	82-693399
19.19	81-601202	19.46	82-693487	19.73	81-690205
19.20	82-466514	19.47	81-690207	19.74	82-675007
19.21	81-601349	19.48	82-691619	19.75	82-675238
19.22	81-601415	19.49	82-6916212	19.76	81-770360
19.23	81-601390	19.50	82-690929	19.77	81-770300
19.24	81-481597	19.51	82-691954	19.78	81-770316
19.25	81-601552	19.52	82-690377	19.79	79-92121
19.26	81-621371	19.53	82-693465	19.80	81-770434
19.27	81-147825	19.54	82-693407	19.81	81-770338

19.82	81-770275	19.106	81-760364	19.130	81-707081
19.83	81-771067	19.107	81-760135	19.131	81-707086
19.84	82-771003	19.108	81-760305	19.132	81-720166
19.85	81-770168	19.109	79-749715	19.133	81-720165
19.86	81-770617	19.110	80-750388	19.134	#7821531
19.87	81-770623	19.111	81-760191	19.135	Local Record
19.88	81-770462	19.112	81-760260	19.136	#11804680
19.89	81-770352	19.113	80-750125	19.137	#13800648
19.90	82-772558	19.114	81-760444	19.138	#12102215
19.91	81-770287	19.115	79-750481	19.139	Local Record
19.92	81-7705	19.116	81-760050	19.140	#13714775
19.93	81-770297	19.117	79-740489	19.141	#12986098
19.94	81-770277	19.118	81-760613	19.142	#13116911
19.95	81-770463	19.119	81-760564	19.143	#11700023
19.96	81-770295	19.120	81-760372	19.144	#7633619
19.97	81-770736	19.121	81-760037	19.145	#8167706
19.98	81-770276	19.122	80-750590	19.146	#8413576
19.99	82-770889	19.123	82-760558	19.147	#8864642
19.100	83-750055	19.124	82-760147	19.148	#8560044
19.101	81-760207	19.125	82-760351	19.149	#8129327
19.102	80-740026	19.126	81-760185	19.150	#8499038
19.103	81-760226	19.127	81-760598	19.151	81-640726
19.104	81-760246	19.128	Local Record	19.152	77-647602
19.105	81-740283	19.129	81-707064	19.153	81-641149

.7B20 Copy Being Described and Library's Holdings

20.1	62-40922	20.19	82-463995	20.37	Local Record
20.2	81-174392	20.20	81-623720	20.38	82-770511
20.3	81-11970	20.21	81-140883	20.39	82-770033
20.4	82-466274	20.22	81-140883	20.40	83-750347
20.5	81-482882	20.23	81-160141	20.41	82-762127
20.6	81-125199	20.24	82-90098	20.42	82-761875
20.7	81-480343	20.25	81-481343	20.43	82-760366
20.8	83-461287	20.26	81-483288	20.44	82-750209
20.9	82-463211	20.27	07-22832	20.45	Local Record
20.10	82-466264	20.28	82-466568	20.46	81-720068
20.11	81-470473	20.29	81-483288	20.47	83-460048
20.12	81-83786	20.30	82-466498	20.48	83-460057
20.13	81-470468	20.31	Local Record	20.49	Local Record
20.14	82-465164	20.32	Local Record	20.50	Local Record
20.15	82-463987	20.33	Local Record	20.51	81-642255
20.16	81-83224	20.34	81-690159	20.52	Local Record
20.17	82-465672	20.35	81-693484	20.53	Local Record
20.18	02-27712	20.36	82-690477		

.7B21 "With" Notes

21.1	81-16517	21.8	82-463628	21.15	81-9404
21.2	81-14981	21.9	82-464867	21.16	Local Record
21.3	82-465528	21.10	82-465667	21.17	Local Record
21.4	81-14621	21.11	82-465666	21.18	Local Record
21.5	82-464583	21.12	81-9401	21.19	80-645049
21.6	83-460528	21.13	81-9426	21.20	81-640916
21.7	82-464586	21.14	56-4003		

.7B22 Combined Notes Relating to the Original

22.1	Betz, p. 68	22.8	81-643022	22.15	81-641916
22.2	Betz, p. 68	22.9	81-641374	22.16	81-641852
22.3	Betz, p. 68	22.10	81-641982	22.17	81-4010
22.4	81-640075	22.11	81-640784	22.18	81-4234
22.5	81-641948	22.12	81-642197	22.19	81-640287
22.6	81-641475	22.13	81-795		
22.7	81-642470	22.14	81-641581		

.7B23 Miscellaneous

23.1	81-640075	23.7	81-641982	23.13	81-641852
23.2	81-641948	23.8	81-640784	23.14	81-4010
23.3	81-641475	23.9	81-642197	23.15	81-4234
23.4	81-642470	23.10	81-795	23.16	81-640287
23.5	81-643022	23.11	81-641581		
23.6	81-641374	23.12	81-641916		

Appendix A

A.1	#9266512	A.4	Local Record	A.7	#9634160
A.2	#8335132	A.5	#8750180	A.8	Local Record
A.3	#8384774	A.6	#8965944	A.9	#7625555

Jerry Saye is associate professor in the School of Information and Library Science at the University of North Carolina at Chapel Hill, where he teaches courses on organization of materials and abstracting and indexing. He has taught also at Drexel University and worked as head cataloger at Fairmont State College. He has published articles on cataloging and database management in several professional journals, including the *Journal of the American Society for Information Science, Cataloging and Classification Quarterly,* and the *Journal of Education for Librarianship.*

Sherry Vellucci is director of library and media services at Westminster Choir College; she was previously choral librarian at Westminster and LC cataloger at Princeton University. As a member of the Music Library Association, Vellucci served as chair of the Working Group on the *National Union Catalog* from 1985 to 1987 and currently serves on the board of directors.